THE POLICE
AND THE PEOPLE

French Popular Protest
1789–1820

THE POLICE
AND THE PEOPLE

French Popular Protest

1789-1820

━━

R. C. COBB

OXFORD
AT THE CLARENDON PRESS
1970

Oxford University Press, Ely House, London W. 1

GLASGOW NEW YORK TORONTO MELBOURNE WELLINGTON
CAPE TOWN SALISBURY IBADAN NAIROBI DAR ES SALAAM LUSAKA ADDIS ABABA
BOMBAY CALCUTTA MADRAS KARACHI LAHORE DACCA
KUALA LUMPUR SINGAPORE HONG KONG TOKYO

PRINTED IN GREAT BRITAIN

A MON AMI

MAURICE CHAUVIREY

provincial de Paris

en souvenir de la rue d'Obligado
et du quartier des Ternes,
et du bon temps passé ensemble
dans les années 30 et 40

CONTENTS

ABBREVIATIONS   xi

INTRODUCTION   xiii

I. THE SOURCES OF FRENCH POPULAR HISTORY AND THEIR INTERPRETATION 1789-1818

PART ONE: THE POLICE, PUBLIC AUTHORITY, AND THEIR
AUXILIARIES: ASSUMPTIONS AND HABITS

  1. Introduction   3
  2. The informer and his trade   5
  3. *Moutons de prisons* and 'prison plots'   8
  4. The *gendarme* as witness   13
  5. The *commissaire de police* and his clientele   14
  6. Police assumptions on the habits of violence and disorder   17
  7. Men to look for   26
  8. The police and credibility   37
  9. The Thermidorians as historians   45

PART TWO: *L'ESPRIT PUBLIC* AND THE LANGUAGE
OF ORTHODOXY

  10. *L'Esprit public* and the changing language of orthodoxy   49
  11. The winning side   58
  12. The *sans-culotte*, by himself   61
  13. Lebois and Babeuf   71
  14. '*Le mal français*'   72
  15. Conclusion   76

II. 'POPULAR MOVEMENTS', POPULAR PROTEST, AND REPRESSION IN FRANCE 1793-1818

PART ONE: THE PATTERN OF POPULAR PROTEST 1795-1815

  1. Popular violence   85
  2. Urban and rural riot   92
  3. Desertion and *insoumission* 1793—year VII   93

4. The regional incidence of desertion   97
5. Beggars and vagrants: the *bandes* of 1811–12   104
6. The barometer of popular protest and disaster 1795–1812   109

PART TWO: THE POPULAR MOVEMENT IN DECLINE AND THE
NATURE OF *SANS-CULOTTE* MILITANCY (1795–1815)

7. *A la recherche du sans-culotte*   118
8. The role of militant minorities   121
9. The *sans-culotte* and the outside world   129
10. Causes and consequences of the failure of the popular
    movement from 1795 to 1815   131
    (i) The White Terror   131
    (ii) Moral and economic boycott   150
    (iii) The cost of militancy   154
    (iv) Pauperization   156
    (v) The diseases of the poor   158
    (vi) Suicide   158
    (vii) The year IV   160
    (viii) Exile   161
    (ix) Repression   165
    (x) *Résidence surveillée*   167
    (xi) The age of militancy   168
    (xii) The second generation   169

PART THREE: THE POPULAR MOVEMENT IN ITS PRIME: THE
SANS-CULOTTES OF THE YEAR II

11. Thermidorian language and assumptions   172
12. War and Terror (1793–4)   176
13. 'Communalism' and the popular movement (autumn
    and winter of 1793)   181
14. '*Hébertisme*'   183
15. *Sans-culottes* and Jacobins   184
16. Conclusion   195

III. DEARTH, FAMINE, AND THE COMMON PEOPLE

PART ONE: TOWN AND COUNTRY

1. Introduction   215
2. The hierarchy of need   218
3. The country in the town   223
4. Divided families   224

CONTENTS ix

5. Provincial monopolies 228
6. Dearth and the *retour au pays* 230
7. Prostitution 234
8. Rural migrations 240
9. Dearth and social disunity 243

PART TWO: POPULAR ATTITUDES AND THE POLITICS
OF DEARTH

10. Dearth and verbal exaggeration 246
11. Popular attitudes to food 249
12. *Sans-culotte* institutions and the *'problème des subsistances'* 252
13. Dearth as a technical problem: productivity and shortage 257
14. The calendar of dearth 263
15. Government and the problem of dearth: 'Physiocrates' and 'Traditionalists' 269
16. Dearth and popular credulity 278
17. Dearth and inequality 283
18. Regional antagonisms 284
19. 'Food plots' for popular consumption 288
20. The *sans-culotte* view of the countryman 290
21. The countryman's view of the townsman 293
22. Dearth and Terror 302
23. Popular food morality 308
24. 'Communalism' and the food problem 312
25. Conclusion 317

NOTES
Section I 325
Section II 331
Section III 360

NAME INDEX 381

INDEX OF PLACE NAMES 388

ABBREVIATIONS

A.A.G.   Archives administratives de la Guerre (Vincennes)
A.H.G.   Archives historiques de la Guerre (Vincennes)
A.H.R.F.   Annales historiques de la Révolution française
A.N.   Archives nationales
A.P.P.   Archives de la Préfecture de Police (Quai des Orfèvres)
Arch. Seine Maritime   Archives départementales de la Seine-Maritime
    (the same applies for other Departments)
Arch. Dieppe   Archives communales de Dieppe (the same applies for
    other towns)
B.M.   British Museum
B.N.   Bibliothèque Nationale

INTRODUCTION

IN March 1967 Mr. Keith Thomas, Fellow of St. John's College, and I were invited by Dr. S. Gopal and the University Grants Commission of India to take part in a seminar on 'Modern Techniques in Historical Studies', held at the University of Delhi, and attended by forty Indian historians. Mr. Thomas spoke on topics relating to sixteenth- and seventeenth-century English social history, while I did the same for eighteenth- and early nineteenth-century France. The subjects that I was asked to discuss were food problems, dearth, and famine, town and country, interpretations of popular protest movements, and religion and irreligion. Each topic was then discussed in the context of modern Indian history, with one or two talks followed by a general discussion, at each session. Finally, at the University of Calcutta, I was asked to lecture on 'Enforced food procurement for the urban markets in Revolutionary France'. In May I was invited by M. Pierre Guiral, Professor of Contemporary History at the University of Aix-en-Provence, to give a lecture to his graduate students and research pupils on the subject of the revolutionary police, within the framework of a general course on the police and police records in modern France being given in the course of the year at that University. My talk, entitled *Aspects de la police révolutionnaire*, dealt primarily with the interpretation of police evidence as historical material for the study of popular history during the French Revolution, and with the changing language of orthodoxy. There was also much discussion from the Indian side during the April seminar on the value of police records and information supplied by informers as a source for the history of Indian nationalism and protest.

The present book is a product of this hybrid parentage, and is an accident of my stay in India and my visit to Aix. It would not have been written without the stimulus afforded by discussions with my Indian and French colleagues and friends. It certainly has many of the disadvantages of an accidental and mixed birth, for it has grown out of lectures and discussion on subjects which are not evidently related, and it does not possess any clear central theme, other than 'popular history'. The three sections into which it is divided do have, however, a relationship, both in their order of appearance and in their actual topics.

The first section deals entirely with evidence: it is an attempt to discuss the value of certain source material for the history of popular movements and popular protest during the revolutionary era in France. The main purpose has been to explore the assumptions and the presuppositions shared by the police and by other repressive authorities on the subject of popular habits, frequentations, riot, and proneness to violence and to sedition, and to examine the changing language of orthodoxy. It is not about people and events, and so it is more concerned with the meaning of words than with the presentation of a narrative. I have suggested that such evidence needs to be subjected to a certain amount of questioning and that things are not always what they seem to be made to say they are. After examining the relative value of the different sources—police, informers, *commissaires*, *gendarmerie*, Government officials, *commissaires observateurs*, Thermidorian lists, *sans-culotte* apologia, and the Army—I have suggested various directions for future research, particularly the exhaustive exploitation of provincial and municipal records, which are those which are likely to throw the most light on a series of movements and of forms of protest which were themselves all narrowly 'communalist' or regionalist in character.

In the second section, I have attempted to give a general account of the various stages of the 'popular movement', emphasizing in particular the accidental character of its emergence and temporary achievements, but concentrating more on its decline and rapid collapse and on the various forms of protest that, *faute de mieux*, took the place of effective popular militancy at the political level, and the fact that all had in common failure and hopelessness. The approach has been throughout to replace the question commonly asked: 'Why did the popular movement fail in the course of the French Revolution?', a question largely irrelevant since the 'movement' never had any chance at all of success, at least under its own momentum and without outside help, by the question: 'How did a popular movement in its own right ever emerge at all?': for this is perhaps the most astonishing fact about the history of the French Revolution. Approached from this angle, the built-in weaknesses and fragility of the *sans-culotte* movement can more easily be perceived, even in the context of the autumn of 1793.

By choosing a period of a little over twenty years for the study of both movement and protest, I have had three aims in view: firstly, further to illustrate the transient nature of the popular movement of the year II, less apparent when studied solely in the context of the relations between *sans-culottes* and Jacobins; secondly, to illustrate the constant strength of the various anti-*sans-culotte* forces—popular royalism, White terrorism, improved techniques of repression, and so on; thirdly, by following militants over a period of years and into a new generation, to bring out more clearly the role of exceptional individuals and the importance of militant minorities in movements none of which could accurately be described, at any time (even during the *sans-culotte* period) as *mouvements de masse*, embracing as they did only a small percentage of the population as a whole.

So much for the positive side. I have also suggested various negative factors that, taken together, along with an increasingly effective political repression, may have acted as deterrents to popular political commitment, for, inevitably, any study of popular movements must also take into account the fact that long-term militancy is a luxury few can afford, and that a popular movement may be defeated as much by disease, apathy, and economic ruin, by moral and material boycott, by the sense of isolation, as by direct repressive action.

One of the most persistent themes in this section is popular violence, in word and in deed, and popular insistence on and attachment to violent solutions. The emphasis is less on political aims and organization—subjects already admirably explored by Albert Soboul, George Rudé, and Kåre Tønnesson—than on mentalities and attitudes. I have attempted to do for individual militants what Jacqueline Chaumié has done, with such skill and imagination, for the archetypal Counter-Revolutionary, the Comte d'Antraigues; and though I am too much of a *frondeur* to wish to belong to any 'school', it is towards Robert Mandrou's collection, *Histoire des mentalités*, that I would feel the strongest pull.[1] But I

---

[1] I owe much also to the inspiration of Louis Chevalier. His admirable book *Les Parisiens* (Paris, 1967) appeared too late for me to be able to use it extensively in the present study. I would be proud if my *esquisse* could in any way be compared to a work displaying so much imagination, compassion, literary awareness, and personal experience. Our books at least have in common a love of Paris and a total rejection of sociology and quantification. Louis Chevalier's book will be a model to all human—as opposed to economic—historians concerned to write about the common people in an urban setting.

have also given a brief narrative account of popular protest in the years that follow the short period of militancy.

This section might be described as an interim report on a period of French popular history, somewhere between research already carried out fairly exhaustively (primarily on the *Armées révolutionnaires*), and research at present in progress on the years III and IV in certain Departments—for I am a local historian, not a national one—rather than a detailed work of scholarship based on the exhaustive exploitation of the material available. I have rather attempted to indicate certain *points de repère* than to write a complete history of popular protest. I have, however, whenever possible, used illustrative material from widely scattered sources. It will perhaps be objected that these are, in fact, so scattered, so fragmentary, as to deny the present study any value as an over-all account of the varying fortunes of the *petit peuple* between 1793 and 1818 on the national level. And this is an objection that I would readily accept, for I have not attempted to legislate for the whole of France: a great many of my examples have been drawn from two Departments (the Seine-Maritime and the Bouches-du-Rhône) widely different from each other in every respect; from the municipal records of a dozen or so towns; my notes for the *Armées révolutionnaires* on militants and revolutionary wild men everywhere; from personal case histories, mostly from Paris; and from fairly abundant material for Lyon, the Bourbonnais, the Forez, parts of Burgundy, the Comtat; finally from Prefects' reports relating to the 1812 crisis. At best, by spreading my illustrations over a very wide area, I can at least hope to emphasize the essentially fragmentary character of movements and protests that never had much hope of impinging on national events (the White Terror, for instance, might, for a time, capture the south-east, but France could, for a time, do without the south-east), as well as to bring out the enormous diversity of popular militancy and violence from one place to another. If I have proved that it is impossible to write a national history of French popular protest, that one can only write that of Norman, or Lyonnais, popular protest, I shall have achieved one of the things that I set out to do.

So my account is impressionistic, rather than exhaustive. What I am attempting to suggest is that, in this place, things were like this, in that place, like that; that the verb *terroriser* conjugates quite differently from one Department to another; that Terror and

Counter-Terror are infinitely varied, that the map of violence is as fragmented as that of France's 'electoral geography'; and that, between all these things, there is hardly a common factor, other than the same words, with different meanings. *Assassiner*, in Normandy, means what it seems to mean; but over most of the Midi it may as often express the intention as the achievement, and a great many people there live to use the anguished phrase: 'Au secours, je suis assassiné'—and in popular history language is all-important, as well as exceedingly deceptive.

If, again, it is objected that this section lacks any attempt at a synthesis, it can only be replied that to seek a synthesis between a series of movements that are utterly apart and particular, or on the subject of people as elusive as the slippery *sans-culottes*, may be a useful intellectual exercise, but it will produce bad history, at least in this intractable context. Something at least will have been achieved if I have succeeded in convincing my readers that popular history, in France as in India, can be studied with profit only in very limited, regional terms. The greatest compliment that could be paid me would be that someone should take up some of my very tentative hypotheses, test them out against a municipal background, and find them quite wrong. Nothing could be further from my intentions than to drill the *petit peuple* into tight formation, march them up the hill, and march them down again. My subject is chaotic, and I may well have written about it chaotically!

The third, and most important, section is about popular attitudes to dearth and famine and to the problems of food supply. It is the most important, because, with its depth and variety in terms of material, it offers an ideal opportunity to test out the assumptions of the first section, and to give body and illustration to the general account of the popular movement. One could have chosen some other topic—for instance, religion—in order to conduct a similar exercise. But dearth appeared a subject more suitable than any other, for a number of reasons. It was the problem to which the common people, at all times, devoted the most attention; no other topic took up so much time in popular debate, no other could inspire fiercer passions, greater fears, more hysteria, more envy, more violence, and more unreason. One can find no better illustration of the processes of myth and rumour; and attitudes to dearth conditioned popular attitudes to everything else: government, the countryside, life and death, inequality, deprivation, morality, pride, humiliation, self-esteem. It is the central theme in all forms of popular political expression. Nor were the common people living solely in a world of myth and panic fear; for dearth and famine were in fact the greatest single threat to their existence, as the crisis of 1795 was amply and hideously to demonstrate. Nor indeed were the common people ill advised to pay so much attention to food and drink. It was all very well for Robespierre to sneer about a popular concern for 'vulgar groceries', but Robespierre sat down to a comfortable and neat table every day: the young Duplay girls saw to it that the Friend of the Poor had only the best. For the *petit peuple* these were matters of life and death. Also I have chosen the topic because I too am much concerned with food and drink and have done a lot of work on dearth.

I have envisaged the problem then primarily from the angle of the popular mentality. But as it is also, to some extent, a technical problem, I have attempted to consider it as one of relative regional productivity or shortage in terms of *pays fromenteux* and *pays disetteux*, a diversity that greatly contributed, in the first place to the difficulties of distribution in times of shortage, real or feared, and in the second place to what one region thought of another. It is also a problem that strongly conditioned the relationship between town and country. Since the frontiers between the two are at the best of times extremely fluid, and since, in time of dearth with more people on the roads, they become even more difficult to define, before describing the various aspects—material, technical, political, mental—of dearth I have given a brief description of a population still torn between town and country, and have produced fragmentary evidence, both from literary sources and from the minutes of the *commissaires de police* of various Sections, for both the rural orientations and the provincial origins of the Paris population. The conditions of the years II, III, and IV made the conflict into a reality, raising urban France against rural France. I have therefore devoted some time to describing what the *sans-culotte* thought of the peasant, and what the peasant thought of the *sans-culotte*.

However tenuous, there is then a connection between my three sections and a logic in their sequence, though owing to the nature of my material, to the extreme individualism of popular movement, and to my own unsystematic mind, there is a danger that this will not be apparent to some readers. I have done my best

to put out a few guiding lights as to where I am going, on what dark
journey I am next taking my readers; I have also endeavoured to
put out a few warning ones, to mark the pitfalls, ravines, and
swamps of popular history, particularly in its comparative study:
'So-and-so, who attempted to write an Anatomy of Revolution,
disappeared here without a trace.' At least no one is likely to accuse
me of writing history that is either comparative or 'scientific', or
of seeking to establish general laws.

My main concern throughout has been to allow people to speak
for themselves and to give as much licence as possible to individual
behaviour and to popular habit. I am writing about people, not
about movements; about attitudes, prejudices, and mentalities, not
about thought. Thus my first section is devoted to what the repressive authorities said and thought about the people and about what
the people said about themselves; my second is about movement
and protest, over a long period; and my third is about what the
people thought, feared, and did about dearth over much the same
period. Throughout, I have tried to make a distinction between the
individual voice of protest and the collective voice of orthodoxy.
The basis of my documentation is language; and so I have drawn
almost as much on literary sources—particularly Restif, Mercier,
Vidocq, and Duval—as on historical evidence, in order to give
movement to names, warmth and animation to professional or
provincial groups. When these have not been sufficient, I have not
been afraid to fall back on my own imagination and do some of the
thinking of the *petit peuple* for them. A certain amount of guess-
work and imaginative reconstruction is indispensable, especially
in a field so under-represented as popular history. I may be being
unhistorical, but I do not think I am being arrogant, for I have
lived with the *sans-culottes* of our day, even more with the *habitants
de garnis*, for a number of years, so that I do not think of them as
strangers; this was not as a result of a desire to go slumming, in
order to work off guilt about my education, but by choice, out of a
taste for what some would call low company, and for the sense of
fraternity derived from the *gros rouge*. Since 1935 I have walked
French popular history, drunk it, seen it, heard it, participated in
it, walking hand in hand with fraternity and liberty, both first discovered by me in Paris, I have been deeply involved in every event
affecting the French people during the last thirty-two years. I make
no claim to impartiality, for I am inside, not outside, my subject;

I have acquired a new nationality—a fact which, I fear, may be apparent to the reader, as this is my first book in English—and I do not merely believe, I know that the *sans-culottes* are still with us, though they are fast disappearing in the France of the *Plan* and of the super-technocrats. This short book, like my *Armées*, has been written with love. Perhaps I have taken too many liberties. Certainly I have some fears for this half-way house of a study; I hope, at least, that it is not boring, for the people about whom I am writing were and are not.

If there is any merit in this book, its presence is due primarily to the Indian historians, who, in the discussions that we had together over a period of three weeks, gave me both a new stimulus and a quite fresh approach to such subjects as town and country, dearth and rumour, violence and riot, credulity, provincial monopolies of urban trades, grain transport, popular justice. One member of the seminar, my old friend Professor Barun De, of the Indian Institute of Management, Calcutta, after hearing my paper on dearth, commented on chaos with a French clarity, reducing the gist of my arguments to eight points, all of which, he said, had their exact parallel in the Indian context: (1) regionalization of shortage; (2) fear of scarcity leading to scarcity (*de la crainte de manquer naît la disette*); (3) panic and propaganda on both sides of the food barrier, resulting in violence against producers and merchants and millers; (4) the connection between dearth and disease; (5) over-government, resulting in the *disette factice* and so on; (6) popular justice, 'communalism', and the call for a closed economy; (7) hatred and suspicion of cash crop substitutes; (8) Robespierre and Plenty (myth aided by hindsight). The clarity was, in fact, in Professor De's head, not in my paper. I would also like to thank Professor Nurul Hasan and the late Mrs. K. N. Hasan, Professor Topanray Choudhari, Dr. Satish Chandra, Dr. Ranajit Guha, Professor B. H. Bhatia, Professor Sharma, Dr. S. Gupta, Dr. S. Bhattacharya, Dr. Suresh Singh (Deputy Civil Commissioner, Palamau, Daltongaj, Bihar), Dr. Ashish Bhose, Dr. K. K. Das Gupta, for the many and fruitful ideas that I derived from their papers and interventions in the discussion. Without them, this book would not have been written (perhaps rather a poisoned compliment to such kind and stimulating people). I also wish to thank Dr. S. Gopal, Reader in South Asian History in the University of Oxford, and the Indian

University Grants Commission for having invited my wife and myself to India, Dr. Gopal for having given us dinner in Lady Hardinge's bedroom, in his father's official residence, my former pupil Mrs. Narayani Gupta, Dr. Romila Thapar, and Mrs. Mazundar, for having made our stay in Delhi so pleasant, and Professor N. K. Sinha for having invited me to the University of Calcutta. My debt to Professor De is treble; for, having taken a double dose of dearth, he also guided us through parts of popular Calcutta; and, on many occasions in this book, while writing of Paris, I have also had Calcutta in mind. My warmest thanks are also due to my old friend Pierre Guiral for his unfailing kindness and friendliness. The discussion that followed my talk at Aix was particularly valuable to me, especially on the subject of the *gendarme* as a witness.

As on a previous occasion, my greatest debt is to Professor Norman Hampson, to whom I submitted the first draft of this book. As a result of his suggestions and criticism, the first section has been largely rewritten and greatly reduced, and much of the illustrative material in the other two sections has been removed from the text and demoted to footnotes. In one respect only, in what he describes as 'my inordinate love of detail', have I remained deaf to his warnings, believing, as I do, that twenty-five examples to illustrate a point are better than fifteen, and that fifty are better still. The reader, who has been warned of this idiosyncrasy, has only to steer clear of the footnotes if he does not share my appetite. Professor Hampson has been the most perceptive and constructive critic of my previous work; on this occasion, his advice has been all the more valuable in that it was sought at a stage when it could still be effective.

I am grateful to the Master and Fellows of Balliol College for leave of absence for the Hilary and Trinity Terms of 1967. I was able to use this period of leisure to continue research in Paris, Dijon, Besançon, Marseille, and Dieppe, and to collect much of the new material included in this book.

Nyon, September 1967

I

THE SOURCES OF
FRENCH POPULAR HISTORY
AND THEIR
INTERPRETATION
1789-1818

PART ONE

THE POLICE, PUBLIC AUTHORITY, AND THEIR AUXILIARIES: ASSUMPTIONS AND HABITS

'Constater aussi s'il porte à son habit quelque ruban, ou
autre marque, pouvant être reputée signe de ralliement.'
Traité de Police

I. INTRODUCTION

POPULAR movements have, in the last ten years, become so fashionable as a subject of historical research and of historical discussion that they have recently been incorporated as a Special Subject in the comparative study of such movements in France and England, in the Honours syllabus of a new university. Historians have been for so long concerned either with government and thus with protest as viewed from the government end and as a problem of repression, or with the historical origins of political creeds and of various forms of socialist thought, to the exclusion, therefore, of any form of protest that did not appear 'seminal' and forward-looking; such an exclusion in fact engulfs most traditional forms of popular agitation. At last they have turned to protest and defiance, particularly in their crudest and most hopeless forms, as subjects in their own right. Current fashion too, with its insistence on any form of protest that is extravagant, spectacular, and, in its ultimate aims, futile and irrelevant, has also something to do with this change of focus. And with some historians at least, failure in protest has become a virtue in itself. Thus a subject which, from the research point of view, is still in its infancy, has achieved almost alarming respectability as a matter for largely intellectual debate, and the deserter, the mutineer, the primitive rebel, the rural bandit, the market rioter, the urban criminal, the pickpocket, and the village prophet have been taken in as honoured, pampered members of Senior Common Rooms. A promotion so rapid may well be premature, for the subject itself is far more intractable than it would appear at first sight, poses problems of investigation that are almost unique, and demands a degree of imagination, awareness, and experience that is not easily attained by the researcher, unless, as a result of long residence and wide reading, particularly into literary sources, he has become steeped in the culture and in the assumptions of the society that he is studying. If it is that of a foreign people, he has to make the further effort of acquiring, at least in mental terms, a second nationality.

An initial difficulty is that popular movements can seldom be allowed to witness for themselves; many of them have been so primitive, so unsophisticated, so incoherent, and so secretive, as to leave no written records at all and scarcely any indications of motivations, leadership, or programme, other than in the crudest of slogans—and slogans are, by intent, themselves misleading—often superimposed on a movement from outside. Few popular movements have been, even momentarily, successful, have attained their objectives, achieved a part of their programme, or seen their own institutions given a semi-permanent, recognized, status: hence the unique interest of the *mouvement sans-culotte*, able to witness for itself, for a time, in its own language, through its own organs, in defence of its own programme. For most of those that have been unsuccessful, the evidence has necessarily come from outside, and the most prolific and zealous historians of popular protest have been the police, spies, and informers in the government's service, magistrates and army commanders, themselves often the most regular recipients, along with men of wealth and local influence, of the literature of protest, in the form of ill-spelt threats and anonymous letters signed with a vengeful pseudonym: *the Avenger, le Justicier, Rebecca*. Certainly, at all levels, repressive authorities were likely to do their best to be well documented on movements that cultivated mystery and that affected the apocalyptic language of revenge. Every anonymous call to arms—*Peuple, lève-toi, il est tems, fais battre le tocsin*—torn down from a wall in the markets, after going the rounds of the various subordinate authorities would eventually come under the scrutiny of the Public Prosecutor, of the Committee of General Security, or of the Minister of Police. At this high level at least, the desire to understand would be genuine. But the zeal of subordinate officials might be less inspired by the search for truth, than by the desire to prove their own vigilance and perspicacity before the event, especially if, on previous occasions, their warnings had gone unheeded.

2. THE INFORMER AND HIS TRADE

Of all these contemporary historians of popular movements, the informer is undoubtedly the least reliable. He has to convey the inestimable and unique value of his information, for, to be successful, he needs to prove that he has access to secrets that would otherwise be unknown to the authorities, and, in order to make money, he needs to provide a great deal of information, whatever its worth, information generally being paid for by bulk. There is never any lack of information from this source; nor are informers afraid of saying the same thing twice or three times, because there is just the chance that they may obtain double or triple payment for the same item. There is also, in their reports, a great deal of padding (with a view to volume) and a great deal of special pleading (with a view to illustrating the trouble that the informer has taken and the cunning demonstrated in penetrating the code words and security checks of those who are the object of his scrutiny). In the early stages at least of his activities, the informer may even be self-appointed, doggedly subjecting authority at every level with information it has not sought, about people in whom it is not particularly interested; and so he may have to plug away for months or years, churning out, with increasing desperation, a mass of information before he even attracts attention or, by accident, luck, or perseverance, puts his finger on a person or a group that subsequently proves a gold mine. It follows that once he has obtained the ear of authority, probably through some subordinate official anxious for promotion, the informer will persevere on the same track, repetitively denouncing the same people, the same categories, in the hope that they will last him out for as many months or as many years as possible. Nor will he denounce them all in one go, for then he will have used up his subjects: he will inform on them in driblets, by twos or threes, multiply the accomplices, and keep a few picture cards up his sleeve to the last. To make a clean sweep of a 'faction' in one go would be a form of professional suicide. It would also seem over-simple, almost too good to be true; for, just as there cannot be the 'perfect plot', there cannot be the 'perfect repression'. Even the repressive authorities would not like it: from their point of view too, a 'plot' must be made to last as long as possible, in order to bring in certain groups of people, one group after another, over a matter of months or of years. Both for Fouquier-Tinville, and for the many—and generally rival (and there is no profession in which rivalry can be more damaging and dangerous)—*moutons* and *dénonciateurs* who worked so assiduously for him, there could not be just one *hébertiste* faction—nineteen men, eighteen of them condemned together—just one *dantoniste* faction—fifteen men, condemned together—there had to be *la queue de Danton, les sequelles de Vincent et de Ronsin*—to be rounded up later, in order to keep the Committees interested and opinion alarmed. Always some men would have to be kept over, for use later, because convincing death labels and useful categories of suspects could not be allowed to fall into abeyance (new ones, it is true, could be invented). A good 'faction' was like a good trade mark, to be allowed to circulate for as long as it drew an audience and provoked a ready response. In a revolutionary regime, there was, of course, some danger in this; for, if some people were left over too long, they might not only survive, but actually replace those who had been saving up their destruction for an appropriate day. It was a matter of very fine calculation, both on the part of the repressive authorities, and of the informer, who was always in danger of 'jumping the gun' by denouncing those whom the government intended to keep in reserve or even to promote, and who might then denounce the informer. In 1794, the Jacobin dictatorship tried to keep both *hébertisme* and *dantonisme*—for there must always exist a threat from both sides, an elementary rule known to any informer and to any repressive government—on the boil too long, with a result that it finally succumbed under a double assault of *la queue* and *les sequelles*. This is one of the risks of revolutionary government. Even so, in this desire to draw matters out, the professional interests of the informer would correspond with the tactics usually adopted by a repressive regime which would prefer not to take on too many people at once and to make the 'purge' a permanent form of government. The 'purge', like any good medicine, needs to be used in limited quantities, and at regular intervals, if it is to have the proper effect on the health of the body politic.

In this at least, the interests of the informer and of his eventual customer are generally in unison. But it follows too that an informer will often construct an elaborate 'plot' where there is an

open and probably harmless association, that he will make machia-
vellian conspirators of simple and angry men, and that he will scent
daggers—or pretend to scent daggers—where there are kitchen
knives and spoons. For the informer, nothing can be quite what it
seems and if men come together, at regular intervals—perhaps on
a Saturday afternoon, at a fixed rendezvous, and in an attire that
will induce immediate mutual recognition—it cannot be merely to
play bowls or practise archery or jump over hurdles: these are
merely covers for activities far less innocent. Of course this *déformation professionnelle* should not be immediately written off as self-
interested: some informers, indeed those that do the most damage
to those that they inform, really have their heart in their work or
are merely silly. (There are always a great many sillies and a great
many cranks in the profession.) In any country where a government is sufficiently unpopular and sufficiently repressive—and this
is much more the case with rulers who are dealing with a people of
a different nationality, or even with specific classes of their own
people—any coming together of any locals, for any purpose, may
be potentially seditious. Even within a national framework, both
the police and their informers will keep a wary eye on public baths,
Turkish baths (places where it is sometimes possible to pass the
night without having to declare one's identity or fill up a form),
sports clubs and dining clubs, fencing establishments, and literary
societies, as well as on theatres, cockpits, opera-houses, music-
halls, beerhouses, cafés, restaurants, and fairs. There have, after
all, been any number of conspiracies in *hammans* and *Bains Chinois*,
and shooting clubs often have a double purpose. Even a tennis
court can be dangerous, and in Dublin the players in a football
match were shot down by an enraged military. International sport
can sometimes offer the shortest and safest route to political freedom, and cricket has been known to result in riot. In most early
nineteenth-century *Dictionnaires de la Police*, the word 'association'
(so close in place as well as in meaning to the even more dangerous
word '*attroupement*') will be picked out for special reference, as a
coming together of anything more than a dozen or, at most, twenty
people, for any purpose whatever. If they meet regularly and in
the same place this is a cause for further suspicion, for their
activities will then come under the familiar heading of '*réunions
habituelles*', easier no doubt to control, but suggesting too a purpose
determined and so probably seditious. And for any revolutionary

regime, especially, it is not desirable that small groups of people should meet one another regularly and under the same roof: such a thing can only be a *conciliabule*, even if it is not *nocturne*. Even funerals—in some instances, *especially* funerals—can be considered not so much as due to concern for the dead as a pretext for the seditious enterprises of the living. As a character in *Bas les cœurs!*— not an informer, but one who had suffered much from informers and from their even more unpleasant amateur rivals, middle-class *dénonciatrices*—observed, on such an occasion, *ce fut un enterrement comme les autres, beaucoup plus de vivants que de morts.*[1] It can, of course, equally be the case that the most dangerous person at a funeral is the one in the coffin. Only a pauper's funeral can be guaranteed absolutely safe.

3. MOUTONS DE PRISON AND 'PRISON PLOTS'

There was one group of persons, ranging at different times from three or four hundred to over a thousand, which was the object of very special surveillance by the revolutionary police in 1793, during the year II and the Thermidorian Reaction. This group, far from being self-elected, had had companionship, of a very mixed kind thrust upon it by the authorities. This was the population of the Paris prisons, a population which attained, in Paris, as well as in such provincial towns as Versailles and Orléans, its most monstrous proportions in the summer of 1794.

In one sense at least, the Revolutionary Government contributed to its own panic fears; for the more people there were in prison, the more potential suspects were thus created, and the more likely a 'prison plot' would become (and a 'prison plot' is more credible in a large urban prison than in a tiny rural *maison d'arrêt*). No coming together could have greater possibilities for potential sedition, especially as prisoners moved about, from one *chambrée* to another, in conditions of remarkable freedom. In order to obtain information about what these dangerous people were saying and doing, the terrorist authorities had recourse to a specialized type of informer, *le mouton des prisons*. Unlike their counterparts outside, these people worked, not for money, but for their freedom. But, like their *confrères*, they were thus kept constantly on the treadmill, revealing one prison plot after another, with each new

---

[1] Georges Darien, *Bas les cœurs!* (Paris, Pauvert, 1954).

revelation' hoping to obtain their release. The hope was naïve, for it was clearly in the interests of a suspicious government to keep these people in prison as long as possible, so as to be in contact with a maximum number of political suspects. If necessary, once they had been 'exploded', they could be moved from one prison to another. Fouquier-Tinville was particularly susceptible to this type of informant, and the 'prison plot' is an essential element in any of his indictments. His most celebrated *mouton*, Charles Jaubert, was held for over fourteen months—indeed, his zeal was probably the cause of such a prolonged detention—repetitiously denouncing plots in Sainte-Pélagie, the Luxembourg, Saint-Lazare, the Abbaye (he almost completed the Grand Tour). No such 'plot' was complete without his contribution. Eventually, in the year III, he was released, returning to his native Hainaut, where he proceeded to denounce the local authorities; but he was never again to flourish as he had in the golden summer of 1794. Jaubert was the best known of a large group of *moutons*, and he had many, and dangerous, competitors, including his rival in repetitive zeal and in long-winded sneaking, Saiffert, a doctor of German origin.[1]

'Prison plots' certainly suited the Revolutionary Government. They offered a convenient and expeditious way of getting rid of people against whom no convincing charge could be made; and they could be used again and again, unlike the 'food plot', for food might become more plentiful. There is no rigged trial of the year II without its *complot des prisons*; each of the 'factions' apparently, at one time or another, sent its emissaries around the larger prisons, drawing up lists of those who were to be freed and of those for the guillotine, when the great day came. At least, this is the activity with which they are credited in government indictments, for it is difficult to believe that 'conspirators', even as imprudent as Mazuel and Ronsin, would ever have made promises quite so rash and quite so premature.

The *moutons* themselves appear to have believed in the information which they so sedulously plied—theirs was, after all, a vocation of a kind, but what is much more alarming is that the leading terrorists seem to have believed in it too. There were two possible solutions; one was to diminish the peril by no longer sending any-one to prison for political offences, the other was to kill off the prison population (the *moutons* being kept to the last). The

[1] R. C. Cobb, 'Jaubert et le procès des hébertistes', A.H.R.F., no. 147.

Revolutionary Government took the second course, and was about halfway through its programme when it was overthrown on 9 Thermidor. The Thermidorian Government at first decided on the former course: it had been able to kill off most of the members of the Commune without sending them to prison at all, and Robespierre and his colleagues were only in prison for a few hours. But, before the winter was out, it began once more to increase the prison population. By the spring of 1795 some of the old *moutons* and a number of new ones are reporting on a new spate of 'prison plots', and, in a dozen or more towns, these are followed, in the summer by prison massacres. The 'plots' were probably as imaginary as those of the year II, but the massacres were real enough.

Being a *mouton des prisons* might not be a job with a great future, but both the Jacobin and the Thermidorian authorities and popular opinion, with their common belief in 'prison plots', could offer him at least temporary employment. At worst, it might save his head, and, at best, it might enable him to be promoted into the more comfortable ranks of those who informed from outside. There was a certain crude logic both in government thinking and in popular fears. The *robespierristes* would argue that, since everyone who was in prison in the summer of 1794 must be an enemy of the people (his mere presence there proved that), then any hope of salvation would be a movement from inside that would enable the prison population to topple the government; and popular fears still favoured a solution *à la Septembre*. The historian is likely to remain unconvinced; even so, the vast amount of material (as much as one-third of the papers of the Revolutionary Tribunal and of those of Fouquier-Tinville consist of denunciations and counter-denunciations of competing *moutons* concerning plots, most of them of extraordinary complexity) relating to the discovery and the description of these various plots, is important in itself as revealing the particular *climat* of the year II, a *climat* that has been confirmed, from a very different angle, in the prison memoirs of 1795 and of subsequent years.

The 'prison plot' had, then, much to recommend it, both to Jacobins and to Thermidorians (it was only a matter of changing one's prisoners). It commended itself also to popular opinion, always prepared to believe that people literally banged on the outer doors of prisons, in order to gain admittance to these privileged places—and the prisoners, it was known, lived like fighting cocks,

supplied by the best *traiteurs* in town and surrounded by a
numerous and devoted *valetaille—afin mieux de comploter contre
la chose publique*. But, from the government point of view, there
was a danger in this reliance on *moutons*; for a prison plot could
be credible only if it were shown to benefit from complicities both
inside and outside, and this put members of the prison service
under suspicion. Each *mouton* denounced one or two *porte-clefs*,
some were even so bold as to denounce a *directeur*, an *économe*, or
a *concierge*. A number from each category were brought into each
purge trial, and a few were guillotined. Yet it is dangerous for a
repressive government thus to attack its own gaolers.

Finally, informers, in their zeal to convince, not only blew up a
plot out of bubbles, but even went one stage better and provided
it with its characteristic paraphernalia of 'infernal machines',
bombs, and similar contraptions familiar to artisans. These would
be placed, to be dramatically discovered, under iron bedsteads in
attic rooms, in cellars, or pointing out of blinded windows facing
on to the course of a procession. This is perhaps the height of the
profession, a level at which its members are indistinguishable from
the *agents provocateurs*. And what better one than a well-tried
informer? Certainly the contraptions have survived, to be seen
still, abandoned in seldom-used lavatories of the *Archives nationales*.
And so have their records, stacked in boxes, in the *Archives de la
Police*.

It is at this specialized level that the line—always a tenuous one
—dividing the informer from the police (for an experienced informer may eventually earn his place in the police, and this carrot
will be held most persistently before him to keep him at work with
little or no pay)—becomes the most difficult to trace. The temptation here for the historian, and one that he must resist, is to fall
into the same trap as did so many continental radicals and
exaspérés of the last century and of the early years of this and to
write off all bomb plots and acts of individual terrorism as *les accessoires de la maison Vidocq*.[1] For there were genuine bomb plots that
took the police by surprise, and the fact that the police knew about
a great many others did not necessarily imply that they had invented them for their own nefarious purposes. It is perhaps a banal

---

[1] Georges Darien, in his condemnation of the French anarchists, in *La Belle
France*, is a very good example of a *déformation* that is common to Vallès and to
L'Assiette au beurre, and, more recently, to *Le Canard enchaîné*.

thing to say, but most eighteenth- and nineteenth-century police were probably more concerned with preventing bombs from going off than with lighting their fuses, and with knocking the revolver out of the raised hand, than with pressing on the trigger. (Many Frenchmen would argue that the raised hand had itself been recruited by the police, but this is being silly or deliberately perverse; for, on any public occasion, the position of the police is to face inwards, to turn their backs on the cortège of the great, and watch the crowd of spectators, where the danger is likely to come from; and even the quite amazingly inefficient police at Sarajevo saw the bomb lobbed from the pavement and the revolver being pointed at the archducal pair. No one would suggest, from the fact that the Austrian security officials had warned Vienna of a possible *attentat* during the Archduke's visit, that they were actually conniving at such an attempt.)[1] We are here in one of the most confusing jungles of historical evidence and interpretation, partly because there has seldom been a bomb plot anywhere in Europe without at least one police spy being involved in it at one stage or another; even so, the wisest course is no doubt to accept the most probable interpretation, rather than to go out of one's way to seek out the most complicated one. For even in this murky zone, the simple explanation is often the right one. The greatest victory of generations of informers, *dénonciateurs*, and common or garden *mythomanes* has been to convince not only their employers, but also historians, that the simple explanation cannot be the right one.

The informer is dependent, for his employment, on the police; and the latter are dependent on the informer for much information that would otherwise be unobtainable. It is the job of the police to assess the information and to pass it on to higher authority; both the informer and the police trade in the same type of material and there generally exists between them a clear understanding of what sort of material each is after and how it should be interpreted. The police are, however, likely to be bamboozled by the informer: often their only protection against him is to check his evidence with that provided by another of his kind; and since, as we have said, the greatest danger to an informer is another informer, the police have always encouraged the rivalries within this most unfraternal and unco-operative profession, having a clear vested interest in the extreme isolation in which each individual informer must live.

[1] Vladimir Dedijer, *The Road to Sarajevo* (London, 1967).

Ultimately, in this peculiar, but very necessary, relationship, it would be hard to say just who would be fooling whom, it being very much of a case of *intoxication mutuelle*.

4. THE *GENDARME* AS A WITNESS

With regard to the police, it is necessary to distinguish between the ordinary police—urban and rural, judicial and frontier—and the various political, and often semi-secret organizations which existed in most European countries in the late eighteenth century and which, in conditions of revolutionary disturbance, multiplied, fanning out into rival groups, addressing their reports to their different masters, and spying on and denouncing one another. As far as France is concerned, it is reasonable to assume that the *gendarme* will attempt to tell the truth, in his own, unadorned, rustic, inimitable way. His weakness is likely to be sheer ignorance and lack of imagination, and he will not be a good witness when dealing with cultivated and intelligent people. The *gendarme* is not a politician,[1] but a soldier, his master is not a police official, but the Minister of War, and his normal beat is the countryside, not the city. He is more likely to be concerned with the poacher, the smuggler, the *chauffeur*, than with the politically seditious, and it is only in periods of extensive rural disorder that the *rapports de gendarmerie* are liable to take on a political content, though they are at all times excellent sources for the study of rural crime: murder, poisoning, arson, turbulence at festivities, family feuds.

Even on these occasions, the *gendarme* will probably report accurately what he saw; he is both too unimaginative and too honourable to invent, and owing to his political candour, he will be unlikely to know what type of information would please his superiors. When it is a matter of reconstructing the narrative of events, the flash-point, the development, and the end of a riot, the *gendarme* represents the most reliable source available while the officers of the *gendarmerie*, being particularly concerned with recruitment, have a lot of very valuable information to offer on

---

[1] A number of *gendarmes* attached to the Revolutionary Tribunal were, however, condemned to death, in the spring of 1794 as 'accomplices of Hébert and Ronsin', about whose 'guilt' they are said to have expressed doubts (A.N. W 130, Tribunaux révolutionnaires, affaire du gendarme Lebrasse et autres). Their execution coincided with a similar holocaust among the Paris police organizations.

such subjects as peasant health and life expectancy, the drinking and eating habits of the countryside, popular violence, rural church-going. One should not, however, ask too much of the *gendarme*; he will have little light to throw on motivations, and, unlike the police, he is not a social historian. We can rely on him for facts, but there is probably little to be learnt from him about the assumptions of the repressive authorities.

5. THE *COMMISSAIRE DE POLICE* AND HIS CLIENTELE

Rather more may be gathered, both about the assumptions of the repressive authorities, and, especially, about the language and attitudes of the urban *petit peuple*, from the *commissaire de police* of a Paris Section, particularly during the Revolutionary Government, when he was an elected official, and dismissable as such, dependent on the Section and, socially, very close to the *sans-culotte*.[1] In Paris, and in other large cities, many of these officials were to be dismissed, disarmed, and arrested, as former terrorists, in the course of the Thermidorian Reaction; in the South, a number fell victims to the White Terror. The *commissaire* was too close to the people to witness against them; and, himself an *homme de quartier*, he seldom looked outside it. His angle of vision was also that of the *sans-culotte*.

The reports of the *commissaires* for the revolutionary period are abundant in *faits divers* and *chiens écrasés*, but contain only the rarest information of political interest; and even this takes a great deal of finding. The *commissaire* was out for a quiet life, and asked only to be left alone with his pregnant girls, his drunks, his dead horses and run-over errand boys, his *filles de joie*, his runaway children, and his everlasting *plaques*. Anything else was out of the ordinary run and would involve extra work, and the possibility of eventual reprimand. It is a tribute to his position that, at times of riot, or when a regime was overthrown, while suspected informers were attacked, the *commissaires* were left alone.

The *commissaire* was not, however, a free agent, and he enjoyed much less independence than most of the Sectionary officials.

---

[1] Comminges, the *commissaire* of the Section de la Montagne, was a printer by trade; one of the Lille *commissaires* had been a shoemaker, a trade that he took up again in the year III. Many had been employed in the luxury trades, and had sought paid employment under the Revolution, in 1793 or in the year II, as a result of the imposition of the *maximum*.

Both before, during, and after the Revolution, he was subjected to very detailed instructions as to what he was to look for and even how he was to report it when he had found it. After the Revolution, he was even given model *procès-verbaux* that would cover almost any predictable situation and that he was expected to copy word for word, as if Revolution and Anarchy were to be let loose if a single comma were omitted. It is not therefore much use taking the reports of the *commissaire* at their face value and as an example of his own literary merits. One must compare them with the various *Traités de Police* drawn up to guide him minutely in his job and to instruct him how to face up to any predictable situation.

Much may be learnt from these *Traités*, both about the repressive authorities and about the *petit peuple*. In one *Traité*, for instance, under VOL, the *commissaire* is instructed, among other things, 'constater si le prévenu est dans la classe des domestiques ou des vagabonds'.[1] No wonder, then, that in the reports of the years II, III, and IV, so many servants and *filles de confiance* are identified as petty thieves. Perhaps they were, but the *commissaire* would clearly be looking out for them from the start. Equally, on the related subjects of rumour, riotous assembly, and tumult, the *commissaire* is told, with regard to a person suspected of spreading false information: 'constater s'il porte à son habit quelque ruban, ou autre marque, pouvant être reputée signe de ralliement'. When so clearly told what to find, it was hardly surprising that, in most city disturbances between 1793 and the 1820s, the local *commissaire* could generally recollect that, well to the fore of the riot, there was a man or woman with a sprig of oak, a flower, a piece of paper bearing a slogan, a ribbon or a cockade in his hat or her hair, that a man, who stood out from the rest of the crowd because he was so tall, was bearded, had a black moustache, was wearing a *bonnet de police*; that a woman, with her long hair streaming down her back, was brandishing a broom or a piece of bread on the end of a pike.

The same preoccupation and presuppositions with regard to popular behaviour emerge in the instructions under ATTROUPEMENT. The *commissaire* is to draw up his report in the following manner: '. . . Avons trouvé un rassemblement d'environ **** personnes sans armes, et formant plusieurs groupes, au milieu de chacun desquels était un individu qui parlait aux autres. . . .' The police,

---

[1] Alletz, *Traité de la police moderne* (Paris, 1823). I have drawn heavily on this standard work for my examples of police instructions.

thus duly forewarned, would have little difficulty, after a disturbance, in producing one or two *meneurs*. The *commissaire* may not even trust to his own imagination or experience, or even to the evidence of his own eyes, when dealing with rumour, such a constant preoccupation with revolutionary and post-revolutionary authority. Under ALARME, the subjects are suggested to him, significantly, as *la crainte de la disette, l'enlèvement des enfants*. And if the *commissaire*, under MORT VIOLENTE, is instructed to remove the body as quickly as possible to a covered place out of the public gaze, this insistence does not reveal so much a consideration for popular susceptibilities, as a fear of popular violence, habituated to the sight of violent death.

Finally, he is given a clear indication of the priorities that should guide his surveillance, when he is told to keep a special look out for *les marchands forains, colporteurs,*[1] *revendeurs, portefaix, commissionnaires,* . . . *les établissements sur la rivière pour les blanchisseuses* . . . *les coches, galiotes, bacs, batelets, passages d'eau* . . . *les bains publics, les écoles de natation, les mariniers et toute espèce d'ouvriers sur les ports, les pêcheurs et les blanchisseurs* (the French police, any time between 1760 and 1830, were obsessed by rivers and convinced that disaster preferred to walk on the water. Their fears were not entirely ungrounded; many riots, especially those provoked by hunger, started at the waterside and were confined to the great river or seaports),[2] . . . *les porteurs d'eau* . . . *les porte-falots* . . . *les fripiers* . . . *les brocanteurs.* . . . The *commissaires* were thus provided with a series of ready-made *classes dangereuses*, along with domestic servants, vagrants, and the idle. So, once more, it is not surprising that these establishments, these places, and these trades figure so repetitively in their reports of popular turbulence. The *commissaires* of the Sections on the banks of the Seine, along with all this extra work, had also the drowned and the half-drowned to contend with; characteristically, they were instructed first of all to attempt to revive them, then to find out who they were and why they had

---

[1] Restif, *Les Nuits de Paris* (Paris, 1790), viii. 1817: '. . . J'ai toujours abhorré les Chanteurs-des-rues, et en général tous les Colporteurs; ce sont des Misérables sans moeurs, des Fainéans, des Inutiles. . . .'

[2] For riverside and seaport riots, see Section III, pp. 218–23. Once the war had begun, coastal and deep-sea fishermen, particularly those on the Channel coast, were added to the *commissaire*'s lists as the object of special *surveillance*. They were suspected, not without reason, of trading with the English fleet and of exchanging information with the enemy.

committed this ultimate crime. With their path so minutely laid out, it is not surprising that so many of their reports should make monotonous reading. It is then most important to have in mind these and similar instructions when attempting to assess the information supplied by the *commissaires* on the subject of popular disturbances, protest, and behaviour.

6. POLICE ASSUMPTIONS ON THE HABIT OF VIOLENCE AND DISORDER

So much for the *commissaire*, not such a bad historian, in the context of the year II, of popular behaviour, if not of the popular movement, and an excellent historian, in the context of the years III and IV, of popular misery, hopelessness, and death (the pages devoted to MORT VIOLENTE and to SUICIDE, in the current *Traité*, must have been much thumbed by the end of 1795–6). Now for the police proper, political and criminal; and of these there were many. Indeed they continued to multiply throughout the Revolution, much to the advantage of the criminally inclined, who must have found safety in such an administrative jungle; and, if the collapse of Government in Paris in June–July 1789 can be attributed in part both to the insufficiency and the unreliability of the police, there would never be another occasion in French history when it could be said that Paris was under-policed. It was very much the contrary. Reliability was another matter. So at no time during the Revolution was there any lack of material from this source; indeed, it increased in volume daily, with the creation of each new police organization. Of these, by the summer of 1794, there were at least half a dozen, reporting variously to the Committee of General Security, to the Committee of Public Safety, to the Minister of the Interior, to the Minister of War, to the *mairie*, to the Commune, to Fouquier-Tinville, to the Administration de Police (a body that grouped under its orders the fifteen sections of *la police criminelle*), to the Department and to the *Commission des Subsistances*. After Thermidor, under a regime that lived in fear of the common people —and had good cause to do so—there was a further spate of information, as new organizations grew up, while others went down —*corps et âme*—in a series of subterranean purges. But if the Jacobin dictatorship and Thermidor were *régimes policés*, in which a multitude of *polices* fought it out among themselves (always a happy situation for the ordinary citizen), the Directory and, above all, the Empire were *régimes policiers*, in which a multitude of *polices*, now in harmony, not only continued to inform, even more voluminously, but also ruled. A police that informs will slant its information to the authorities to be informed, it has to be careful about the choice of its information, and will generally seek to please; a police that rules can create its own information, it can even create events. This is a distinction that it is important to keep in mind when considering the relative value of police material, as a source for the history of the popular movement, during the revolutionary period, the Directory, and the Empire.

The police—these *polices*—are then always committed historians; unfortunately, they are very often the only ones. And they should never be dismissed lightly; for, in certain conditions, their own safety and survival, as well as that of their masters, would depend on their ability to understand their habitual customers—political or criminal—to reconstruct their assumptions, to penetrate their mentality, to become familiar with their habits, in work or at leisure, and so to predict their actions. A good policeman, at least in eighteenth-century conditions and in a city like Paris, could always expect to be a couple of steps ahead of a riot, a sedition, a turbulence, and so to be forearmed. He could pride himself on being able to distinguish between habitual, almost permissible, disorder, and a commotion that overstepped the boundaries tacitly agreed upon between the repressive authorities and those who were most liable to be repressed. For in any urban community there would always be a certain degree of complicity between the police and those the police considered potentially dangerous. There was always a great deal of give and take, a carefully measured mutual toleration (combined with wariness), while informers commonly worked their ticket both ways; if the police knew about the 'dangerous', even displaying towards them a sort of loving fascination, the 'dangerous' knew the police and enjoyed exchanging with them pleasantries that drew both corporations together, for a time, in common contempt for the law-abiding citizen and the law-maker. The police left the *faubouriens* very much to themselves, so long as they stayed in their *faubourgs*; that of Saint-Marceau was a semi-recognized *zone franche*, into which the police rarely penetrated. They stood aside, too, on Sunday and on Monday evenings, when the drunken *faubouriens* returned from the *guinguettes* of Issy and Clamart, so long as they stuck to their usual routes of return. It was only if they went off course that there might be trouble.[1] Again, a great deal of violence was tolerated, even expected, during Carnival—for that was one of its purposes—and the police would not intervene when the bourgeois took a drubbing from a group of disguised apprentices, so long as these did not carry arms as well as masks.[2] In this sense, the police of the old regime were much more permissive than the far severer, more bureaucratic police of the Directory and the Empire. The experience of the Revolution had come between the two.

The police had what no historian can acquire unless he is working on a near-contemporary movement: experience.[3] They know what has happened before, and have a very good idea where and when it is likely to happen again. They know that some trades— and people from some provinces and some villages—are more violence-prone, more brutal, more anarchic, more explosive, more easily provoked, than those from another trade or another province or village. They know too, or think they know—and we are here more concerned with the assumptions of the police than with what was or was not so, for we can at least identify the former, even if we cannot distinguish between degrees and types of violence, proneness to violence, giving them provincial or professional labels— what particular form of violence from such and such a trade, or such and such a province may affect.[4]

It is the duty of the police to be two steps ahead of potential violence, wherever it might spring up in its swift obscenity, and to

---

[1] This, according to Restif, *Les Nuits*, i. 50, is what happened on the night of 13 July 1789. 'Dans la journée, les Bandits du faubourg Saintmarcel étaient passés devant ma porte, pour aler se réunir aux Bandits du faubourg Saintantoine. Ces Bandits étaient Mendians-de-Race, avec les horribles Tireurs-de-bois-flotté. . . .'

[2] Restif, as usual, is less liberal than the police. He tells the Marquise of a hold-up that he has just witnessed: '. . . Le trait des Filous la fit gémir sur les folies du carnaval; elle désirait qu'il fût sévèrement défendu de se masquer ailleurs que dans les maisons particulières, à moins qu'on ne sortît en voiture: la Mascarade particulière est innocente, pour divertir une assemblée d'amis: mais la publique est dangereuse dans une grande ville, comme la Capitale. . . .'

[3] The experience of contemporary Paris may, however, be put to admirable use for the exploration of the past. Louis Chevalier, in his *Les Parisiens*, illustrates the survival of family dynasties in the food and drink trades, especially in the Quartier des Halles, and of the *sans-culotte* mentality among the independent artisans, *ajusteurs*, *bricoleurs*, and backyard engineers of Belleville and Aubervilliers.

[4] See note A, p. 325.

recognize a prevalence to violent solutions among certain trades
and people from certain regions. They therefore also need to be
well acquainted with the calendar of violence and riot, almost as
fixed as that of the saints. To the general eighteenth-century
pattern of May to September, Sundays and Mondays, feast days,[1]
hot days, the Revolution adds the anniversaries of revolutionary
journées, or of counter-revolutionary atrocities. The recent dead,
or the not so recent (so long as there are sons and daughters,
nephews and nieces alive, since revenge will hardly extend to the
third generation), call out for vengeance, and a revolutionary
period multiplies, in each town, the occasions for a collective incitement to murder, and thus gives force to dates, both national and,
more often, local: 9 Thermidor, Christmas (in the south only),
21 January (again in the south), 31 May, 15 August, and so on.[2]
The police had to be as historically orientated as vindictive crowds;
and, in the south-east, the old killing days were still being celebrated in 1798 and even in 1815. They were there so numerous as
to be of little use as pointers to massacre, killing in this part of the
world going on pretty well throughout the year.

Powerless, until after the event, in the face of individual outbreaks of crime—murder, suicide—the police are on the contrary
well primed in the patterns of collective violence. They can predict
the habitual point of departure of riot: the wine shop (which under
all our regimes had to close down by ten in the winter and eleven
in summer), the *bal public*, and the even more dangerous *bal musette*,
the habitual rendezvous of all manner of urban riff-raff (where
inspectors and soldiers had always to be present during perform-
ances), the fair, those watching jugglers and wrestlers (allowed
only to operate at fixed points in the city and up to four in the

---

[1] Restif, *Les Nuits*, iv. 809: (*LXXII Nuit: le feu de la Saint-Jean*) '. . . C'était
le soir de la veille de Saintjean. Tout le monde alait à la Grève voir tirer un feu
mesquin; du moins tel était le but du grand nombre. Mais certains Gens en
avaient un différent. Les Filous regardaient cette fête comme un bénéfice annuel;
d'Autres, comme une facilité pour se livrer à un libertinage brutal. Toutes les
occasions d'attroupement, quelles qu'elles soient, devraient être supprimées à
cause de leurs inconvénients. . . .' In the course of the White Terror, the eve of
the Saint-Jean was to prove a favourite murder night. See below, p. 144.

[2] Also, in the course of the White Terror, Whitsun, Ascension Day, Palm
Sunday, Saint Peter, Saint John, Saint Bartholomew's Day. Nights, were, of
course, more dangerous than days being more conducive to the activities both
of thieves and of murder gangs, to prison massacres and to *farandoules* leading
to massacres. The night favoured violence as well as love. See below, on the
White Terror, pp. 131–149.

afternoon),[1] the river-port, the laundry boats, the carters' inns on the fringes of the city, and anywhere else where the wandering sort were likely to be found in large numbers, the horse market, the teeming lodging-houses behind the Grève, the Cité,[2] the rue Saint-Denis and the rue Saint-Martin, the rues des Gravilliers, au Maire, Transnonain, Beaubourg, des Ménétriers, du Poirier,[3] the Pont-Neuf,[4] the Palais-Royal,[5] the Faubourg Saint-Marceau,[6] and, nearby, the old parish of Saint-Médard,[7] the slaughter-houses and the schools of anatomy, the Gros Caillou.[8]

The police also keep an extraordinarily strict check on travellers;[9] the most wretched pedlar has to have a valid passport and a *livret* that is up to date. They are constantly harrying lodging-house keepers, who are frequently vetted, the police favouring night searches, so as to catch suspects defenceless in their night attire, to check on their papers, in the fight against desertion and crime. *Logeurs* could be threatened with the removal of their *patentes*, a penalty which would deprive them furthermore of the right to sell food and drink. They had to be able to produce a clean record from the police and to prove that they were able to read and write, before

[1] Alletz, op. cit., s.v. BATELEURS.

[2] In Sue's Paris, the Cité is still the principal centre of the *tapis franc* (*Les Mystères de Paris*, Paris, Pauvert, 1958).

[3] Georges Duval, *Souvenirs thermidoriens* (Paris, 1843).

[4] An additional proof of ill intent, in the reports of the *commissaire* of the Section du Muséum, is contained in the much-repeated phrase: '. . . inculpé d'avoir parlé avec véhémence sur le Pont-Neuf', where a ready-made audience could be collected in a matter of seconds. It was also the stamping-ground of street singers of *complaintes* (A.P.P. A/A 187 and Mercier).

[5] 'Quel antre, quel gouffre, que ce Palais Royal, on y rencontre des visages d'assassins, des mines sales et brutales . . .' (*Le Nouveau Paris*, 1797).

[6] The Faubourg, writes Mercier, 'dans tous les tems, a été le refuge des ouvriers, de toutes les classes, confondus avec le chiffonier, le vidangeur, le cureur de puits, le débardeur, le tondeur de chiens, le marchand de tisane, le symphoniste ambulant, la marchande de châtaignes, le mendiant . . .' (ibid.).

[7] 'C'est de ce redoutable faubourg que se sont élancés les forcenés qui ont bu avec délectation le sang humain . . .' (ibid.). By the year IX, however, he has changed his tune, depicting the *faubouriens* as the pliable victims of wicked men from the centre of the city: '. . . Dans la cité étaient les mains directrices de tous les mouvements des Suburbains . . . Vous, dieux invisibles de la révolution, qui commandiez arbitrairement les catastrophes . . . tous, vous avez trompé la simplicité, la bonne foi, le patriotisme des vertueux Suburbains . . .' (*Néologie ou Vocabulaire de Mots Nouveaux*, Paris, an IX, s.v. SUBURBAINS).

[8] 'Invalides et blanchisseuses. Il y règne un mauvais esprit. On le fait surveiller' (Police report for August 1815, A.N. F7 2038).

[9] See note B, p. 327.

being allowed to exercise their trade at all. Nor did the *sage méfiance* stop there; even ordinary householders who put up a relative from the country were supposed to declare their guests to the *commissaire*, though, judging from the frequent reminders, it is likely that they seldom did.

The police of all successive regimes, from 1789 to 1820, kept an equally careful check on prostitutes, themselves an indispensable source of information:[1] how they were recruited, by whom, how long girls had been in the trade, whether they had been to hospital for treatment, what other trades they might practise, how much they paid for their rooms, why they had become prostitutes, how long they had been in Paris, what was their place of origin, what was the profession of their parents, whether they had a lover, who were their most frequent customers, what they learnt from them, whether they had been previously convicted[2].

The police kept a particularly watchful eye on the old-clothes trade (disguise was an obsession with all French law-enforcement authorities); *fripiers* were specifically forbidden to purchase or sell military uniforms or equipment, their books were frequently inspected, and they were allowed to practise only in specified quarters. Like the *logeurs*, they had to show a clean record before obtaining a *patente*. Similar attention was paid to *brocanteurs* and all manner of *revendeurs* and *revendeuses*, the most important single category among the regular clientele of the *commissaires* of the years II, III, and IV.[3] *Brocanteurs* were suspected, rightly, of trading in stolen goods. Theirs was a trade that could be taken up at short notice, as a stop-gap, in order to tide a person over a period of distress; its unauthorized exercise was probably the principal means of existence of part of the floating population that had only recently arrived in the city. For similar reasons, *chiffonniers*, possibly one stage further down the social scale, were an object both of suspicion, mockery, and contempt; society has never been kind to these useful people.[4]

[1] Restif is doubtful as to their value as informers. One tells him: 'Mon principal emploi est de découvrir les Filous et de les vendre; et comme je ne mets à contribution que les Libertins, on s'en moque . . .' (*Les Nuits*, v. 1152).

[2] For examples see the reports of Comminges, *commissaire* of the Section de la Montagne, A.P.P. A/A 95–8.

[3] A.P.P. A/A 61–2, 95–8, 187–8.

[4] He was also a traditional bogy-figure. Evoking the *Cris de Paris*, the long-drawn-out falling yell of the *vitrier*, Chevalier comments: '. . . C'est à qui chantera sa marchandise sur un mode haut et déchirant. Le déchirement n'est pas que

They had their eye, too, on ironmongers and locksmiths, who were frequently reminded that it was forbidden to display keys of any dimension, on open stalls, or at the annual junk market (*marché aux fers*); and their premises were regularly inspected, in search of *rossignols* and other articles of the housebreaker's kit.[1] The police were also much concerned with preventing arms from falling into the wrong hands; *marchands de cannes* were forbidden to manufacture or sell sword-sticks, and gunsmiths had a long list of prohibited goods, most of them arms small enough to be hidden in clothing.[2]

Even organ-grinders and street singers were regarded as potential sources of sedition. The former were only to play tunes that had previously been performed at one of the official opera-houses. The latter were to show their sheets of music to the police before they were given a licence; any departure from the text, any improvisation, would be punished with the withdrawal of their *patentes*.[3] *Afficheurs* had to be able to read and write and were obliged to wear at all times, like anyone else who followed an outdoor trade, a large metal badge, AFFICHEUR, with their name and number.[4] The sale of patent medicines was forbidden on the open market, at fairs, or on stalls, and advertisements vaunting their merits were at once to be removed.[5]

The police can trace to their respective quarters the people of provincial or foreign origin who, once in the city, still huddle together, often in lodging-houses that advertise the fact—*Hôtel des Lyonnais*, *Hôtel des Avignonnais*, *Hôtel des Limousins*—and who are easy to find too because they tend to specialize in certain trades. They are well aware of the flux and the reflux of seasonal employment; they know, for instance, that chimney-sweeps, who are likely to come either from Savoy or from the Puy-de-Dôme, cannot leave the city, to seek other work in their home areas, before April

---

des oreilles. Les enfants s'enfuient et les chiens hurlent quand retentit le cri du chiffonnier, voleur d'enfants, tueur de chiens . . .' (*Les Parisiens*, p. 199).

[1] '. . . Il existe un abus qui menace toutes les propriétés particulières. . . . Des Férailleurs et Revendeurs établis sur les Quais, dans les Rues et sur les Ports, exposent journellement en vente des trousseaux de clefs, sans leurs serrures, en sorte que le Voleur n'a plus d'autre difficulté que celle de les adapter aux serrures . . . et cette facilité est la source de quantité de vols . . .' (Commission administrative de police, aux commissaires, Thermidor an III, A.P.P. A/A 96).

[2] See note C, p. 328.

[3] Alletz, ORGUES DE BARBARIE, CHANTEURS AMBULANS.

[4] AFFICHEUR.

[5] APOTHICAIRES.

(*leur état ne leur permet pas de quitter Paris avant floréal*).[1] They
are well aware that chimney-sweeps are likely to lodge in the
Section du Panthéon; that the Sections of Montreuil, Bondy, and
the Temple have a large rural population, who habitually work
outside the city; that the Section des Invalides is potentially dangerous because it contains the extremes of wealth and poverty,
side by side—*gagne-deniers, blanchisseuses*, and *ci-devants*. They can
allow for the habits of people from the rural *communes* around
Paris who, in periods of dearth, will crowd into the city, in search
of employment, particularly at the end of the summer; for they
will not move very far—a *journalier* from la Chapelle will head for
the Faubourg Saint-Denis, artisans from Saint-Denis, Clichy,
Belleville, Bagnolet, Montmorency will move in no further than the
Faubourg du Nord, the Faubourg Montmartre, or Bondy. Those
who come to Paris, in the hope of obtaining a more adequate bread
ration, from Passy, Boulogne, and Saint-Germain, will choose the
Section des Champs-Élysées, and a market gardener or a *journalier*
from the very poor commune of Vincennes will set up in one of
the Sections of the Faubourg. Those who have come in from
Fontenay-aux-Roses, Auffargis, Longjumeau, Sceaux, Antony,
and, above all, Versailles (whence there is a veritable *sauve-qui-peut*
during the revolutionary years) are easily traced to the Sections of
the Left Bank, and are not likely to cross the river. Every countryman or every Parisian who, having settled in the country, is driven
back, by hard times, into the capital, will look for a roof in the
quarter nearest to his route of access, just as, in the nineteenth
century, the rue des Flandres was to become the stopping-off point
of populations from the Nord, the Ardennes, the Pas-de-Calais,
and the Aisne.

Backing their experience, guiding their vigilance, indicating
their fears and assumptions, are half a dozen *Traités de Police*,
Dictionnaires de la Police, and hundreds of ordinances and instructions, some of them dating back to François Ier. Everything has

---

[1] Restif too was well aware both of seasonal migrations and of the habitual
time-table of various sections of the working population: '. . . On joue au Billard
pendant la journée; il est tant d'inutiles à Paris! Cependant ce ne sont pas les
inutiles proprement dits qui font le grand nombre au Billard; ce sont les
Souteneurs-de-Filles, et les Domestiques. . . . Les longues soirées d'hiver . . .
sont le tems des parties intéressantes. La raison en est que tous les Domestiques,
alors revenus de la campagne ou de la Province, ont achevé leur service journalier
à 5 heures; que les Semestres sont à Paris, et que les Filles-perdues gagnent
davantage . . .' (*Les Nuits*, viii. 1823).

been thought of, everything has been taken care of, everyone can be accounted for, every *métier* carries its easily recognizable metal badge: AFFICHEUR, ALLUMEUR, PORTEUR DE LA HALLE, PORTEFAIX, BROCANTEUR, COCHER, BOUQUETIÈRE, MARCHANDE DE FALOURDES, PORTEUR D'EAU, RAMONEUR, COMMISSIONNAIRE, CROCHETEUR, FRI-PIER, CRIEUSE DE FRUITS, BROCHEUSE, delivered by the police, together with name and number in large letters, that anyone employed in these outdoor trades had to wear all the time, even on Sundays and feast days; and many *métiers* wore, in addition, a costume that set them apart from a mile off, as distinctive as those, generally very accurate, of the various series of *les Cris de Paris*. There was no mistaking a Breton or a Bretonne, a Norman horse-dealer, a Picard *fort*, a Limousin plasterer or carpenter, an Auvergnat water-carrier, a Savoyard *commissionnaire*, a Flemish pedlar. There are many references too, in police reports, to women *qui ont l'air d'être de la campagne*; a corpse recovered from the Seine and brought before the *commissaire* of the Section du Muséum *nous a paru être mari-nier*.[1] There was a lot to be said for regionalism and folklore from the point of view of repression.[2]

If ever a regime could have claimed to have thought of everything, that of late eighteenth-century France could surely have done so. For the police had not only traced, and so circumscribed, every possible source of violence, tumult, and crime; they had also worked out model case histories for the commonest forms of sexual misbehaviour. In the case of abortion, the *commissaire* was told to ask the girl if her lover had given her a potion that he stated he had obtained from a doctor, or, alternatively, whether he had knocked her down several times and kicked her in the stomach. In that of castration, he is to look first of all for a female suspect as the most likely to have committed such a crime, after having been raped. There is a small pocket novel on the subject of kidnapping: a man, apparently respectable, has ingratiated himself into the confidence of a father, capturing the affections of his teen-age son; they go out together, visit the Jardin des Plantes and the promenades, wax-works and fairs, picture galleries, watch jugglers and listen to street singers, walk in the Palais Royal; and then, after a few weeks, the father returns home to find that his son has left the house. He

---

[1] See below, Section III, p. 362 and A.P.P. A/A 61–2, 95–8, 187–8 (commis-saires de police des Sections des Arcis, de la Montagne et du Muséum, ans II, III, et IV). [2] See note D, p. 328.

reports to the police; the *commissaire* sets about his task; he is to ask the portress if she has seen them going out with a parcel (presumably containing clothing) under each arm; when the boy is finally traced to the home of the kidnapper, he is to be questioned gently by his father. He tells of his fortnight of freedom: out late at night, gambling, women, drink, though, strangely enough, there is no suggestion of sexual assault (perhaps the boy has been saved just in time?). His father forgives him and tells him to beware of strangers. Children who have been the object of sexual assault are to be questioned about the colour of the wallpaper and the furnishings of the rooms to which they have been taken. It is assumed in cases of assault in which children have been the victims that the culprit should have attempted to calm down the little girl and stop her crying, by giving her sweets, telling her not to say anything to her papa and mamma. And in cases of murder, the *commissaire* is strongly recommended to confront the suspect with the body, particularly if it has been horribly mutilated, as a likely means of producing an admission of guilt. In the case of infanticide, he is to question neighbours whether they have heard screams and is to search for bloody linen. No wonder Jews were not allowed to take their names from the Old Testament or from those of towns. No wonder the crime of crimes should have been to refuse to reply to an official inquiry or to give inaccurate information about one's identity.[1]

7. MEN TO LOOK FOR

Evidence from police sources reveals much more about the attitudes and assumptions of the repressive authorities than it does about popular attitudes and motivations and popular movements as such. In the present section, we are once more dealing with evidence, and its interpretation, rather than with facts. What sort of people were the police after? What were their favourite categories of suspects, for riot or sedition or violence? What caused the police

[1] For the location of the provincial or rural population in Paris, see Section III, pp. 228–9. For similar examples in the Paris of today, see *Les Parisiens, Troisième Partie: Les Lieux*, with particular reference to the changing location of prostitution and pleasure, to the rag-and-bone men and tramps of Maubert-Mouffetard, principal quarter of the native-born Parisian, to the brief North African destiny of the Goutte-d'Or, to the influence of *berrichon* on the Paris dialect, etc. For 'case histories', see Alletz, S.V. AVORTEMENT, RAPT, VIOL, INFANTICIDE, ASSASSINAT, JUIFS, IDENTITÉ.

to go after certain groups of people, from a particular trade or from a certain province, rather than others? What credit can one accord to their evidence, especially when, on their lists, the same sort of people, often too the same people, turn up again and again? Does this indicate that they are habitually violent, that they are professionals of sedition, or rather that, for reasons of their own, the police wish to suggest that they are? These are the sort of questions that one is likely to raise, when confronted with police material on the subject of the composition of a riotous assembly, of a club, of a conspiracy.

In the matter of riot and crowd composition, for instance, perhaps the principal concern of the police, once order has been restored, is to produce culprits, and credible culprits, and the more the better, rather than to identify the actual rioters—a much more difficult undertaking in the case of a spontaneous and accidental riot; and in eighteenth-century terms, most riots were accidental; the use of violence for political ends was rarely premeditated, until organized violence became one of the great weapons of revolutionary minorities. The police's second chief concern would be to establish the existence of organized leadership. A further object would be to prove the existence of a hidden *bailleur de fonds*, who had 'contrived' a riot by hiring his rioters. What better way of proving such a thesis than to provide each rioter with a certain sum of money—the same sum—after his arrest, and then to find it in his pocket? For this, one suspects, is what often happened. The rioter might well protest that the compromising *louis* had found its way into his clothing while he was in the hands of the police, but it was only his word against that of the authorities. And the superiors of the police were often as anxious as the police themselves to suggest that a riot had thus been 'bought'. This lessened their own responsibility, by giving popular protest an artificial and purely seditious character.

In all probability, in eighteenth-century conditions, and in a rabbit-warren like pre-Haussmann Paris, many of the actual rioters got away—and in Lyon, thanks to the *traboules*, more still. But anyone, or almost anyone—for he has to be believable as a rioter— will do; the important thing for the police is to be able to produce rapidly—preferably the same day—a certain number of bodies; and as, in the eyes of magistrates, the zeal and effectiveness of the police are likely to be measured by the number of arrests, it will

always be better to produce a hundred, rather than ten, 'rioters';
these are never very difficult to find; ordinary bystanders will do
at a pinch, especially after the police have suitably disarranged their
clothing and disordered their hair, after throwing away their hats;
and then there are always any number of lamplighters or errand
boys or porters who are found not to be wearing their brass badges
or whose papers are not completely in order, and these too will do.
Indeed, the multiplication of these brass and paper checks seems to
have fulfilled a twofold purpose; not only did it permit the police
rapidly to identify any person and see that he was about his own
business and lawfully employed, it was also a means of rounding up
suitable victims when they were needed, and of gaining promotion
for a proper display of zeal. This is not to suggest that the police
deliberately set out to mislead the magistrates and the higher
authorities; but to come back empty-handed would be to admit
impotence. If rioters could not be found, they had to be invented.
Unfortunately, when attempting to gauge the size and extent of any
given riot, we generally have only the word of the police to go on.

Secondly, the police will endeavour to prove their own thesis
about the origins, motivations, and leadership of a riot by the type
of people they arrest. They have this advantage too over historians,
in that they can both create and write their own history. If there is
among the arrested a predominance of carters or of coal-heavers, it
does not necessarily follow that the riot was sparked off by grievances specific to those two occupations. It does follow, however,
that the police, for reasons of their own, want to accredit that thesis
with the magistrates. One reason, in the eighteenth century, would
be the desire to see their powers extended to include the anarchical
communes on the fringe of Paris, le Havre, Rouen, Lyon, and so on
(Montrouge and Gentilly, Charenton and Ivry, Ingouville, Sotteville, La Guillotière, and la Croix-Rousse) where those of the
travelling sort were likely to roost during their regular visits to the
cities. Carters, pedlars, horse-dealers, bargees, *flotteurs*, *tireurs à
la corde*, in fact transport workers in general, will do nicely in any
riot arising from the circulation of grain in time of shortage (*arrêt*,
unloading, *taxation populaire*, enforced sale, etc.), for they are the
people most likely to be at the scene of such a disturbance (a bridge,
a lock, a river port, the entry to a town), and they are also the first
hit in time of dearth, being far from home, from the sources of
family supply. They are almost professional 'strangers', with no

one to stand up for them (which is why they had such a strong
tradition of co-operation and were so violent against all who were
not of their following). Of course, it was dangerous to push them too
far; they were well organized and well placed to hit back, especially
in time of war, with the threat of a transport strike, or simply by
tying up their barges or leading away their horses. Again, if, in the
course of the Revolution, it suited certain authorities to suggest
that a given riot had counter-revolutionary origins and aims, the
most convincing evidence was to produce, among the arrested, a
striking proportion of domestics, barbers, hairdressers, and prostitutes. And if it were intended to demonstrate that a disturbance
was the work of criminal elements, it would be important to show
the presence of horse-dealers, old-clothes merchants (excellent
material, in any case, as the profiteers of hard times and the vultures
of the poor), and similar traditional allies of crime. *Marchands de
vin*, too, are good for almost any occasion: under the *ancien régime*
they were rightly seen as the most effective protagonists of anti-
clericalism, especially in small town and countryside; they are
known to influence opinion, and their opportunities in this respect
increase in time of war or civil disturbance, with more people on
the road; they harbour suspects, they water their wine, they keep
open after hours (ten in winter, eleven in summer); their establishments are the ideal point of departure of riot; because of the hybrid
nature of their trade they span the usual divisions between town
and country, with a mixed clientele of urban artisans, rural or
semi-rural *vignerons, faubouriens*, travellers, carters, pedlars, horse-
dealers, and soldiers. Under the old regime, no rural riot was
complete without its complement of poachers, smugglers, *faux-
sauniers*; but the Revolution forcibly drove these people into
respectability, though it is likely that they soon found other fields
in which to exercise their talents for law-breaking. It is hard to
imagine a *faux-saunier* settling down to regular employment. A
great revolution will change the pattern and composition of riot,
old favourites are discarded, enemies of the King and of the Faith
are replaced by enemies of the people.

Others remain: vagabonds and beggars, *habitants de garnis, sai-
sonniers*, water-carriers, 'strangers' unassimilated or recently assimi-
lated, provincials. These are at all times convincing candidates;
they are easy to find; they live in lodging-houses or under bridges
and arcades; they huddle together, *entre pays*, in identifiable

quarters; they eat together in cheap restaurants run by people from their own part of the world, and recommended to them before their departure from home; the city has no claim on them; they can be given a passport and forcibly sent back to their place of origin. They are arrested at, or near, the place of riot, the examining magistrate is given the tip: 'depuis combien de tems es-tu à Paris, citoyen?' And if the unfortunate man replies, as he will reply, for the police have already ascertained this: 'depuis deux mois seulement', then the point has been made, the riot is the work of *gens sans aveu*. Equally revealing is the question so constantly put by the *commissaires* to those brought before them on charges of riotous behaviour, insulting language, petty theft, trading without a *patente*, and so on: 'à lui demandé s'il a été incarcéré'. The same applies to certain categories of provincial origin: in Paris, Limousins, Savoyards, Auvergnats, in particular, stand out, they are physically recognizable, are credited with extreme brutality, and, when not the object of fear, are the butt of the sharp humour of the Parisian. One should not be surprised to see these unfortunates turning up again and again; it was an admirable way of dissociating the mass of the population from the minority of riot.

The Revolution, which put a premium on every type of violence —verbal, political, collective, and family—and which enormously extended hate-categories, naturally added considerably to the list of expendables, whether provincial or professional. Domestics, in particular, fell under suspicion, and Government informers and agents will usually attribute a role to former servants, in any movement, club, or *journée* that they seek to discredit; the word *larbin*, better still, *larbin en mal de place*, is freely used, as a term of abuse, by all sides, about one another.[1]

After May 1793, Lyonnais became a top priority with repressive authorities all over France, first of all as 'federalists', and, from the year III onwards, as refugees from the White Terror, or, just the opposite, as ultra-royalists and members of the murder gangs. It would seem that the inhabitants of the capital of the south had found it prudent, for one reason or another, to leave their homes and seek work and refuge in Paris or in the towns of the Midi. So, if we are to believe the reports of the police and of the other repressive authorities, there is scarcely any act of violence or gesture of revolt without at least one Lyonnais being present, generally in a leading role, and holding up, for all to see, like a priest giving the benediction, the indispensable *signe de ralliement*. They are said to be at the head of the Faubourg, in the hunger riots of Germinal and Prairial year III,[1] while the Avignon authorities, faced with a recrudescence of popular discontent, in the former month, attributed this neo-terrorism to the presence in the city of doubtful elements that had fled from Lyon.[2] In Pluviôse of the following year, a witness of the massacres of the Fort Saint-Jean in Marseille has no hesitation in identifying the leader of the *sabreurs* as a 'dénommé Bon, Lyonnais'; and after mentioning several other *égorgeurs* by name, he concludes that there were many others 'qu'il n'a pu connoître, entr'autres, beaucoup de Lyonnois'.[3] (As he did not know them, he had presumably recognized them by their accent.) A particularly frightful murder, when seven people were stabbed to death in a *bastide* near Tavel, is attributed by the Avignon authorities this time to a group of Dauphinois or Piémontais— it did not apparently make much difference.[4] After Prairial, the Paris police are given special instructions to round up Lyonnais for disarmament and arrest. In the following year, at the time of the Babeuf scare, they once more qualify for attention, as leading *exclusifs*;[5] and, in every anti-terrorist 'purge' between 1796 and 1815, the Lyonnais are not forgotten.[6] There are specific references to them in police reports of May, June, and September 1816 and April 1817.[7] No plot or conspiracy could do without them and, for a list of suspects to look convincing, the presence of at least a few seems to have been a matter of form; the police are men of habit,

[1] Cobb and Rudé, 'Le Dernier Mouvement populaire de la Révolution à Paris. Les journées de germinal et de prairial an III' (*Revue Historique*, October–December 1955).

[2] '. . . Il nous revient de tous côtés . . . que tous les jours des gens sans aveu, chassés des villes voisines, affluent dans celle-ci de toutes parts et principalement par le Rhône . . . il seroit même important d'établir un corps de garde au port du Rhône, pour vérifier les passeports de ceux qui débarquent, car la ville de Lyon, où les malveillans sont poursuivis, vomit dans celle-ci toutes ses immondices . . .' (Arch. Vaucluse 3/L/34*, agent national à la municipalité, 22 germinal an III).

[3] Arch. Bouches-du-Rhône L 3072 (assassinats politiques, an III).

[4] Arch. Vaucluse 3 L 28* (agent national du district d'Avignon, au juge de paix du canton de Pujant, 29 nivôse an III).

[5] A.N. F7 3054 (rapports de police, an IV).

[6] R. C. Cobb, 'Note sur la répression contre le personnel sans-culotte, de 1795 à 1801', in *Terreur et subsistances*, pp. 179–210.

[7] A.N. F7 3028–9 9 (rapports de police 1815–1818).

perhaps they merely became used to a mixture that had done such yeoman service in the past. In the year V, Mâconnais republicans credit the murders committed in their town to killers sent from Lyon. Many of the murders committed in the south-east between 1796 and 1799 are likewise attributed to gangs led by *compagnons* or ex-soldiers who sport the tell-tale nickname of *le Lyonnois*.

Lyon then clearly had a bad name with all the police authorities (save, of course, with those of Lyon itself, who were quick to indicate other whipping boys)[1] and with repressive institutions of entirely opposite political affiliations. It was a great disadvantage to have been born anywhere near the place, or to have lived there any length of time; the unfortunate Contamin, although he was in fact from the small town of Crémieu, in the Isère, figures on every police list drawn up, in the various purges of 1796, 1798, 1800, 1807, 1808, 1813, 1815, as *Contamin, lyonnois*; the last reference to him in a Paris police list is in 1818. Possibly he then succeeded in shaking off his pursuers by dying.[2]

Other favourites with the Marseille police are the Nîmois. People from Nîmes, we are told, came down to the great port to carry out political murders, that were presumably directed from a secret headquarters in the former city. Second-class favourites with the Marseille authorities under the Directory are Catalans, Genoese, Piedmontese, Corsicans, and negroes, while Parisian authorities, perplexed and horrified by the persistence of violence and the flowering of vengeance in the city, attribute both to the presence in the port of foreigners, the scrapings of every Mediterranean shore.[3]

What is one to make of this concentration on Lyonnais, on Dauphinois, on Nîmois? On the part of the police and of the other local authorities, it may merely arise out of the natural tendency to exculpate one's own people by incriminating the 'stranger'. Lyon dominates the whole valley of the Rhône, from the Genevan border to the Mediterranean; and if most of the grain that travelled on the

---

[1] See note F, p. 329.

[2] R. C. Cobb, 'Note sur la répression', loc. cit., and A.N. F7 3029.

[3] '. . . Depuis longtems les départements des Bouches-du-Rhône et du Var avoient éprouvé des fluctuations de bien et de mal et avoient été le théâtre de toutes les passions exaltées par la châleur du climat et par le mélange de tous les mauvais sujets du midi de l'Europe. . . . Des scélérats de toutes les parties du monde s'étoient agglomérés à Marseille et par les crimes les plus révoltans avoient donné à la France une idée horrible de ses habitans . . .' (Rapport . . . par les représentants . . . Auguis et Serres sur leur mission . . ., ventôse an III).

river to the Second City went against the current, most of the people who did went with it; it was a normal reaction on the part of the Avignon authorities, on the report of 'strangers', to look northwards for trouble. Lyonnais were much more likely to head for the sea than to move up to Paris.

Yet, according to the police of Lyon, acts of violence committed in that city were generally the work of people from outside. 'Ce sont les gens de la Guille', echoes *Gnafron* when informed of a particularly sanguinary murder; and la Guillotière has the advantage, at least at the time of the Revolution, of being out of the Department altogether. Its inhabitants, although they are only on the other side of the Rhône from the old centre of the city, can be described as Dauphinois; it is also a *commune* with a long-established reputation for crime.[1] The local police point too to the inhabitants of the Monts du Lyonnois and of the Forez, as well as to the Stéphanois —men from the hills—who crowd into the inns of Saint-Jean, as prone to settle accounts in blood; the mountaineer is as much a murderer designate as a true-born *sans-culotte*.[2] The sanguinary heroes of Henri Béraud's historical novels concerning Lyon in the early industrial period are not natives of that city, though they can see it from their cottages and can walk to it, once the black flag of revolt is perceived; they are peasants and weavers from the neighbouring Ain.[3] There is a similar emphasis, in reports on the Marseille massacres of the year III, on the participation of sailors, easily distinguishable, of course, by their clothing and hair style. Sailors, too, are convenient murderers designate, for they belong to the family of the homeless and the rootless; one expects to see them *in* Marseille, but they are no more *of* Marseille than a Forézien shepherd, who comes regularly to Lyon to sell goat cheese, is of Lyon.

Maybe the police were at least right in this: massacres, murders, acts of violence are more likely to be the work of men living away from their homes, away from their usual places of employment, cut off from the ties of property, family, and neighbourhood, than 'locals'. That is why sailors, soldiers, pedlars, and horse-dealers are such good candidates. Yet there is much evidence the other way; most of the murders committed in Lyon were the work of

[1] One of Vidocq's criminal heroes, an Avignonnais, negotiates the disposal of a haul of stolen jewellery with an inhabitant of la Guillotière (*Les Chauffeurs du Nord*, Paris, 1845). See also R. C. Cobb, *L'Armée révolutionnaire à Lyon*.

[2] See note G, p. 329.

[3] Henri Béraud, *Les Lurons de Sabolas* (Paris, 1934).

local people, who could recognize their victims; those who took part in the prison massacres there had read the *Liste des Dénonciateurs*;[1] and a thoughtful *comité* had made the work of massacre easier by making it obligatory to display the names of all lodgers, in large letters and at eye level (*à une hauteur commode*),[2] at the entry to each house in the city. In Arles, suspected murderers are reported to have told their victims that they were avenging a parent. Even more in the rural lynchings of the White Terror, everyone knew everyone else, murderers and victims often had the same surnames; people knew whom they were killing and why they were killing them.[3]

However it may be, in such instances, the police are likely to get their way in the end and to establish, by sheer persistence, truths for one reason or another convenient to them. 'A force de persécution, on devient conspirateur.' A man like Contamin was almost driven into militancy and clandestinity, by continuous proscription. The police themselves may have believed in their evidence; it certainly had the advantage of corresponding closely with popular local prejudices. For, if the Lyonnais were everywhere suspect, so were the *faubouriens*. The Parisians eyed with alarm the Versaillais, the inhabitants of the Section du Finistère lived in fear of the people of Ivry; when there was a riot in Rouen, both the police and local opinion were quick to proclaim: 'ce sont les Sottevillois'; when there was trouble in le Havre, the Havrais looked to the heights of Ingouville, Graville, and Sanvic—it was from there, they said, that danger came, had always come. The police were locals too; and no doubt most of them had been brought up in the prejudices and assumptions of the common people.

In the course of time, while the old favourites never entirely disappear—each successive police organization inherits the documents, the *fiches*, and the *Listes* of its predecessors; there is too a remarkable continuity in the actual personnel of the various political *polices*, once the holocausts of the spring of 1794 had taken their

---

[1] Renée Fuoc, *La Réaction thermidorienne à Lyon* (Lyon, 1955).

[2] '. . . un écriteau, placé à une hauteur commode, en indiquant en caractères très lisibles les personnes qui habitent sa maison désignera à tous les citoyens qui l'on doit conserver et qui l'on doit écarter . . .' (Arch. Rhône L 164*, comité de Lyon, séance du 21 brumaire an III). The *comité* was thinking in terms of public office; but a few months later, its suggestion would be taken much more literally, in terms of human life.

[3] See, on the White Terror, note 3C, p. 359.

toll—new categories come into police awareness. To the categories already mentioned, after the Babeuf Conspiracy, the police of the Directory add Toulousains; and there can be no republican conspiracy from 1796 to 1799 without the presence of one of these. Again, as a result of the two Malet Conspiracies, Jurassiens qualify for police attention; and they too are not forgotten in a series of later purges. As France expands into *la Grande Nation*, conspiracy and riot, in police evidence, become more cosmopolitan. In their daily reports to their Minister, the Paris police now take in a variety of Italians. And we hear of *l'affaire de Fenestrelle*, *l'affaire de Turin*, *l'affaire Arena*. Belgians too, for the first time, come to the front, especially after 1814, when they are suspected either of being emissaries of the exiled regicides, or of having served in the armies of the Empire.

After 1814, too, the police have to contend with Polish surnames, and as their spelling worsens, their surveillance extends to those lodging-houses and cafés known to be the favourite rendezvous of the easterners (foreigners, like provincials, are easy to find, and the police would have had no difficulty in tracking down Heine's Three Polish Heroes). The English have never been off the list; at each successive dearth crisis, the emissaries of the English Government are seen, in various parts of France, making massive purchases of grain, in order to drive up prices and aggravate shortage; in the year III, in 1801, in 1812, they are reported as spreading dangerous rumours about impending famine in the northern Departments.[1] Most of those of 1815 and 1816 are either soldiers or tourists— some of the former are suspected of Bonapartist sentiments; others are stated to be interfering Protestants, come to collect evidence about the sufferings of the Cevenols. And so, to the many other categories of suspicion, are added those who read, or write for, the *Morning Chronicle*,[2] those who merely take in foreign papers[3] (this is where the *portier* comes in), those who are in touch with Brussels and who receive *Le Nain jaune* from there, those who have recently returned from Antwerp, while the habitual *blanchisseuses* of the Gros Caillou are now joined by *Invalides*, newcomers

---

[1] See below, note Z, p. 370.

[2] 'Le général Fornier-d'Albe. On annonce qu'une société qui se réunit chez lui paraît envoyer au *Morning Chronicle* les fausses nouvelles qu'il rapporte sur ce se passe en France' (report for 4 February 1816, A.N. F7 3028).

[3] 'Lamory, rue des Rosiers, indiqué comme recevant souvent des journaux étrangers . . .' (report for 16 February 1816, ibid.).

in the police spectrum. On 30 May 1816, the Minister is informed of 'rassemblements de *Protestants* et de *Juifs*, rue Saint-Louis, signalés comme fort suspects';[1] the next day, it is the turn of 'francs-maçons, se mêlant de discussions politiques'. There are frequent references too to those returning from *la Grande Nation*.[2] Among those arrested in connection with the distribution of *Le Nain jaune* are an *étudiant en droit* and an ex-officer with a Corsican name.

But the police have not forgotten their old friends: a few broken-down survivors of *comités révolutionnaires*, terrorist refugees from Lyon, the Nièvre—for so long a neo-terrorist stronghold—the Yonne, the Nord, Toulouse, the Jura, the floating population,[3] those who had been banished from Paris in 1813, and who had returned without the permission of the Sub-Prefects of their places of confinement, in the common, but mistaken, belief that, as victims of the Imperial police, they could expect to be well received by the repressive authorities of the new regime. We even come across the old eighteenth-century, and revolutionary, favourite, *Moustache*, most often a bandit or highwayman, then the arche-typal *septembriseur*, and, in the context of the year II, the com-mander of a people's army, in that of the year III a terrorist bandit; this time he has been brought up to date, to suit nineteenth-century conditions: he is an 'ouvrier en coton, tenant des propos séditieux'. The police have not yet quite shed the eighteenth century and the Revolution, they are very reluctant to part with anyone who is an old customer; but already there are signs of a nineteenth-century type of suspect. In the *affaire des Patriotes* of 1816, there is, per-haps for the last time, a mixture of both old and new elements that spans two generations of protest; among the accused later confined to the dungeons of the Mont Saint-Michel is an aged ultra-revolu-tionary, one of three survivors of the deportations of 1800.[4] In a

---

[1] A.N. F7 3028.

[2] 'Dassonville, maître de danse, venant de Galicie'; 'Trumpf, marchand, tanneur, venant de Saint-Pétersbourg'; 'Ravendino, Georges, ex-employé au ministère de la justice, dans le duché de Varsovie, venant de Londres'; 'Louis Letort, graveur, venant de Gratz'; 'Vignes, ex-secrétaire, vice-consul chancelier du consulat de Barcelone'; 'Leroy (Charles), ex-employé dans la maison de l'ambassadeur de France à Saint Pétersbourg'; 'Jumelle, domestique, venant de Pressbourg en Hongrie' (A.N. F7 3028-9).

[3] 'Ouvriers cordonniers de la Haute et Basse Normandie, venant, dit-on, dans des intentions criminelles' (report for October 1816, A.N. F7 3029).

[4] *Les Armées révolutionnaires*, ii. 891. Poor Lefranc had welcomed the Restor-ation as an end of tyranny and oppression.

very few more years, the police would have to cut down on the veterans, death having at last removed them from effective surveillance even though their names might outlive them for a few more years on the police lists. It was, however, still possible to keep an eye on their children.[1] But even the police had eventually to move with the times, however reluctantly they might lag behind and stick to the old, faithful bogies that had stood them in good stead time and time again. With students and *mécaniciens* admitted to the lists, we are moving out of the vastly prolonged Middle Age of the *sans-culotte*, and are at last leaving behind the proverbial *forcené révolutionnaire*. Even the assumptions of a police that faces resolutely backwards, feeding on the experience of the previous twenty years, which, by the Restoration, it was beginning fully to absorb, are likely finally to change, in accordance with the new sources of danger, new categories of the dangerous, and new habits of violence and sedition.

8. THE POLICE AND CREDIBILITY

However interested many of their assumptions, however unreliable much of their evidence, one should not underestimate the French police of the revolutionary period and of the early nineteenth century. They were conservative observers, with a wealth of experience to guide them; their merit, which is also that of the magistrate and, ideally, of the popular historian, is to know what was generally known at the time, and, to simple questions, find simple answers; they were, in fact, going on a mixture of common sense, experience, and feasibility. It is, in particular, with this last aspect of police methods of observation and reporting that I shall deal in the present section, with special reference to the habits of the criminal classes and to the norms of popular sociability and frequentations. It may be objected that almost everything stated under this heading is so self-evident as hardly to be worth including in an examination of evidence; but what was self-evident to the eighteenth-century police was not always self-evident to the man engaged in some form of crime, and while the police had very strong ideas about what they considered to be the norms of social behaviour—what sort of people would consort with what sort of

[1] 'Paganel, fils de régicide . . . se rendant dans la Belgique. On vérifie ce départ' (report for 15 May 1816, A.N. F7 3028).

people—there was little place in their system for those who did not conform to those norms; and there were always people who did not habitually keep the sort of company that the police expected them to keep. In short, police experience was well adjusted to the habitual, the self-evident, and the normal, but it was unable to cope with anything out of the ordinary run of social behaviour, with eccentricity or extreme forms of individualism. For the 'picaresque', too, the police were completely outstripped by novelists like Le Sage and Diderot.

One should not underestimate the French police—a mistake many of their habitual customers made, ending up with the *chaîne* as a result—for they were, on most occasions, a few steps ahead of professional crime. *Les filous, les voleurs, les assassins*—categories that recur like a trinity, in the correspondence between the *commissaires* and the Commission—were seldom a match for the police. They had the fatal weakness of boastfulness, conceit, and sociability; they could not go about their business quietly, could not resist bragging of their *coups* in public, and, like homing birds, both before and after a big operation they headed for their habitual inns and *tabagies* with a conservatism similar to that displayed by Sue's villainous habitués of the *tapis francs*. The *filou* was not a contemplative. He needed the company and the admiration of his own kind. He had many of the conceits and many of the virtues of the French soldier—quick on the draw, generous, gay, amorous—'du pain, du *chnick* d'abord, puis des femmes et l'ennemi, voilà le programme du militaire français', as one of Vidocq's heroes puts it gustily.[1] His pleasure would be incomplete if, after some murderous foray, he could not share it with the sort of girls that could be found in the carters' inns on the fringes of cities. The task of the police was enormously facilitated by the regular habits of the criminal;[2] and in revolutionary or early nineteenth-century Paris or Lille it was as easy to find a professional criminal as it was a *savetier* or a street singer on his usual beat on the Pont-Neuf. It was a matter of knowing *where*, also of knowing *when*. The *chauffeurs*, after one of their operations on the French side of the border, walk through the night, crossing over into the Hainaut at dawn; 'ils atteignirent les faubourgs de Tournay. Leur premier soin fut de chercher une auberge; heureusement que dans les faubourgs les gîtes, destinés aux rouliers et aux cultivateurs, sont

---

[1] Vidocq, *Les Chauffeurs du Nord*.   [2] See note H, p. 330.

ouverts dès le point du jour. . . .'[1] This is the sort of thing that Vidocq, with his long experience both sides of the fence, would know, the police would know, and the popular historian can learn from them. In a similar situation, within a city, a man anxious to avoid the attentions of the police, rather than risk a *garni*—the quickest way to discovery—might head for a Turkish bath; but the police would have sensed his reasoning and gone there ahead of him. The location of crime was never difficult to establish, often it was a matter of common knowledge, the criminal elements living openly in those places where they were the most likely to be left alone, that is, in the *faubourgs* and in the semi-rural *communes* on the edge of cities.[2]

Equally indicative of the presuppositions of the police and their reasoning as observers of popular behaviour is Vidocq's admirable description of the chain of complicities available, both in Lille and in small towns both sides of the frontier, to the *chauffeurs*, and his identification of the various accessories, each in his chosen role.[3] This, though written over forty years after the events described, is first-rate popular history and a good example of how the police, from a knowledge both of the habits of crime and of the relations between crime and certain trades—the criminal cannot operate in a vacuum, the days of Robin Hood, and even of *Cartouche*, are over, he needs information, and, after the event, he needs a safe hide-out, he has too to dispose of what he has stolen—can reconstruct the complicated interrelations of a *bande* with other sections of the population. Everything falls into place, and it becomes at once apparent why the French police, of all regimes, should have paid such particular concern to itinerants, to people who always had a legitimate excuse to go from one place to another and to be anywhere at almost any time, without attracting attention, the small tray of articles that they carried from a strap that hung round their necks being for them the most effective of passports. They were ideal spies, sent to map out the lay of the land and to observe the habits and time-tables of farmers. Like the little *bouquetières*, who

---

[1] Vidocq, *Les Chauffeurs du Nord.*

[2] In Messidor year III, Isabel, the *agent national* of the tribunal of the District de Montivilliers, referring to the activities of a *bande* led by a former barber, turned horse-dealer, comments: 'il paroît indubitable qu'il existe une association de scélérats dont le refuge est dans ce qu'on appelloit autrefois la *plaine* de la commune d'Ingouville, asile de mauvais sujets . . .' (*Terreur et subsistances*, p. 249).

[3] See note I, p. 330.

figure so prominently in eighteenth-century novels of libertinage, their bouquets being the receptacles of love notes,[1] the *colporteurs* are also the *agents de liaison*. One can appreciate, too, the utility of the old-clothes merchants and inn-keepers, after the *coup*, as well as that of *brocanteurs*, without whose help there would be no easy profit to be made. And one can appreciate why all these trades should have been so high on the lists of police assumptions, in connection with violence, sedition, and crime. The blacksmith is the obvious source of information about rural wealth, the size of a family, the number of labourers living in, for he is in touch with half the countryside.

Vidocq's individual bandits and their accomplices are as credible, too, in their various social mutations, as the celebrated *Poulailler*, a very ordinary thief, 'tour à tour domestique, cordonnier, marchand de chevaux':[2] just the sort of progression so often encountered in police reports. For the police, the man who frequently changes his occupation, or who claims to several occupations, is potentially as dangerous as the man who physically is constantly on the move and who has no visible ties. The police, like the economic historians, prefer their society to be fossilized; Vidocq is writing history on the move. This is what popular history should be; for people do not stand still and wait while Professor Labrousse and his pupils fit them into a 'social structure' from which they will no longer be allowed to move up or down.

Of course, most of Vidocq's deductions are obvious. They are none the less valuable, for criminals, too, despite a reputation for guile, greatly inflated by popular credulity, are, in the period in which we are concerned, also obvious. Little mystery and no romance attach to their persons; they are merely brutal, often bestial, generally pathetic and pitiable, and certainly no match for a police well experienced in their ways. It was rather to redress the balance that Vidocq felt the need to put at the head of his *bande* a Criminal Avenger of superhuman intelligence. In this respect, he served both his second profession and his bourgeois public, because police will like to nurture the belief that criminals are full of cunning—it adds to the merits of their captors—and the bourgeois public will expect to shudder with fright on reading of the misdeeds of men both desperate and devious. Yet one is constantly

---

[1] See, for instance, Laclos, *Les Liaisons dangereuses.*
[2] *Le Tableau de Paris*, x. 7.

struck, on reading the cross-examination of suspected *sabreurs*, during the White Terror in the south-east of France, by the cussed stupidity of people who contradict themselves over and over again. Nearly all of them collapse in the face of persistent questioning, or take refuge in some hopeless litany: 'je n'y étais pas, je n'en savois rien', when they have been identified by the victims' relatives and by some of their accomplices.[1] One or two of them were so stupid that they even killed the wrong people.

There was no mystery about the habits of political crime in a place like Marseille; any inhabitant of the port, between 1795 and 1799, would know that fights and stabbings would take place on the *Cours*, at dusk; the Aixois did not need to be told, when informed of a political murder, that it too had been committed on the *Cours*, while the Nîmois, with an even more persistent tradition of political violence, could run to at least four murder stations: the *Cours*, the *Esplanade*, the *Calquières*, and in front of the *Citadelle*. It was common knowledge—and a matter of common sense—in Avignon, that when a murder had been committed there, the body of the victim would be tipped over the celebrated bridge into the Rhône. In Lyon, with its two rivers, and a dozen or so bridges, the choice was much wider. Political murders had to be public murders; otherwise they would lose half their point. The police and the magistrates, in each town, quickly arrived at their own rules of feasibility.[2]

This applies as much to a chain of complicity and of accessories, to the location of violence, as to the likelihood of frequentations. *Dis-moi qui tu fréquentes, et je te dirai qui tu es*, at least within the limits of accepted experience and contemporary credibility (for the police did not make allowance for *Cinderella*). When this was not so, the police would conclude that something altogether out of the ordinary was afoot. It was, for instance, in the normal course of things that a water-carrier, from the Section de Montreuil, should

[1] See Section III, pp. 360 ff.

[2] There is a good example of this type of reasoning in the cross-examination of a suspected *sabreur* by the presiding judge of the Aix tribunal in the winter of the year VII; the judge asks the man: 'D. Connaissez-vous la rue Saint-Martin à Marseille?' 'R. J'y passais tous les jours, c'était mon quartier.' 'D. Ne vous y êtes-vous trouvé armé d'un bâton?' 'R. Jamais je n'ai porté de bâton.' 'D. Je vous observe que c'est trop fort, qu'il n'y a pas d'homme [à Marseille] qui n'aît porté de bâton une fois dans la vie.' 'R. J'en ai porté en faisant mon Tour de France . . .' (Arch. Bouches-du-Rhône L 3094, assassinats politiques, an VII).

have been observed, in Ventôse year III, having a meal in an inn in the company of a *chiffonnier*, a *chaudronnier*, a *brocanteur*, a *crocheteur*, and a *menuisier*. Nothing could have been more reassuring, and this was the sort of company that he would be expected to keep. And what did they talk about? Their respective trades, hard times, and the *tête de veau* that they were eating.[1] The police had rather fixed ideas about what was the proper company to keep. They could tell a *petit-maître* from a gentleman, and spot the valet, by his mien, when dressed up like his master.

It was when frequentations did not conform to pattern and precedent, and when new faces were suddenly seen in large numbers occupying the tables of the regular clientele, that the attention of the police and of the other repressive authorities would be aroused. In the vocabulary of the police and of their masters, *mine patibulaire* often simply meant *mine inconnue*; and even in the reports of popular repressive institutions during the *sans-culotte* period, *les gens de mauvaise mine* are generally people unknown in the place, about whom one has no information. A *bourgeois de Paris* had no business drinking in a carters' inn in Montrouge, and people who had got as high in society as *Edmond* should not normally take a plunge into the *bas-fonds* and live it up with *brocheuses* and *blanchisseuses* in an attic in the Faubourg Saint-Marceau.[2] It could only be concluded that people who went in for this sort of 'slumming' were up to no good. If a well-dressed gentleman was seen in earnest conversation with a group of building labourers, the immediate assumption of the police, or of an inn-keeper who kept his eyes open, was that he had come to stir up trouble; here, at last, it would seem, the police were face to face with the elusive *bailleur de fonds*. A visible zeal for charitable works was equally likely to be ill construed. It was not so bad for a gentleman to frequent *une vile catin*; what was unforgivable, however, was to frequent *une vile catin de la plus basse classe*. People were not to be allowed to opt out, and attempts to cross class barriers, especially downwards, would at once be interpreted as revealing seditious intentions. The police were not romantics, they could not appreciate why Restif's *Démophile*, the *Gentilhomme-Populaire*, should seek to escape from an estate that was cramping, and marry the daughter of a shop-

[1] See note J, p. 331.
[2] Restif de la Bretonne, *Le Paysan perverti ou les dangers de la ville* (Paris, 1776).

keeper.[1] They had never felt the allure of the small room over the sweet-shop or the desire to adopt, at least for a time, as long as there was a way back still open, a totally unfamiliar mode of existence.

Or perhaps they would not allow themselves such fantasies; for, in a well-ordered society, such examples would in themselves be subversive of an accepted hierarchy. A *déclassé* was a living insult to the police and to everything that the police stood for; he was also an inconvenient witness of the relations, best kept private, between police and common people, for that was a dialogue that required no eavesdroppers. The police would be the last people to discover fraternity—and, indeed, one can hardly blame them, for fraternity would mean at least temporary unemployment for many of their number, as a police can only subsist on the mutual suspicions that different classes, different professional and provincial groups, entertain about each other. They took such a static view of society that they could not possibly have foreseen an occasion when a bourgeois and his family could be seen lending a hand, with pick and shovel, alongside *Démophile* and labourers and shop-keepers, in the Champ de Mars. They were as much victims of their own conservatism as of a habit of suspicion that read into any frequentation that was in the least out of line with what they considered to be normal, the manifestation of all manner of evil intent or planned sedition. These are weaknesses common to most police witnesses of people and of events; but certainly the police of eighteenth-century France pushed their suspiciousness to a degree that would have led them to mark down such picaresque characters as *Gil Blas* or *Jacques le Fataliste*, in their pleasure in varying company, as *hommes aptes à surveiller*.

But, within their own limits, which were those of their previous experience, they were sharp, if not entirely disinterested, observers of the usual norms of frequentations, though when these norms began to change, as they must have done in the spring of 1789 (when any man with his eyes about him might have seen, for instance, a *Garde Française* in the unlikely company of an *homme de lettres*), they seem to have been caught unawares. Perhaps they were victims of their own accumulated lore and attached too much confidence in their ability to predict the likely behaviour of the *petit peuple*. Mercier too, writing in the 1780s on the subject of

---

[1] Restif de la Bretonne, *Le Palais-Royal*, IIIme partie, ii, *Seigneur-Populaire*, p. 69.

the Gordon Riots, would make a similar mistake. But it is not in the
nature of a police to predict what has never happened before; their
function and their habit are rather to suggest that because something has happened in a certain way over and over again, then it is
likely to happen in much the same way on many more occasions in
the future. The police, in other words, are good historians of habit
and routine, of the *déjà vu*; and if one is often impressed by their
perspicacity, by their ability to take a situation to pieces and then
to recreate it, it is because one has the impression of having been
that way before. The best compliment that one can make the
French police as historians of popular behaviour is the comment,
made in all sincerity: *Oui, c'est tout-à-fait ça.* Nor should one be
surprised at this ability to render popular attitudes and habits to
the life, for who, more than a *commissaire*, would have heard so much
of the spoken thoughts and insults of the common people? Finally,
they had at their disposal a considerable amount of specialized
information, of the kind that makes Simenon such an acute observer of the habits and assumptions of the *petits bourgeois* of
provincial France and Belgium. Just as the police know their
Parisian in work and in leisure and can predict the normal calendar
of riot and drunkenness, Maigret knows that some trades—shopkeepers, employees of chain stores—take their day off on Mondays;
others—those who work in Musées—on Tuesdays. Maigret, too,
one feels, could deal with any situation within the margin of
predictability: he would draw on his own experience; some impression, long lost, would suddenly recur to him; no situation was
entirely novel. One cannot imagine what he would make of a
revolutionary situation; probably, he would be deeply disturbed.
Perhaps he refuses to be shaken out of cherished habits. Perhaps
Maigret is attached to the old ways, like the professional criminal
of eighteenth-century France, who hated the Revolution because
it had destroyed the old criminal code—and criminals are flattered
by a ferocious one—and deprived them of *ces vieilles perruques*, the
old judges of the Tournelles, for whom they had felt a mixture of
fear, respect, and even affection based on familiarity—for they had
met often enough, even if only in contrasting positions. Maigret's
world is predictable, and therefore reassuring.

So apparently was that of Mercier and of Restif. We have, however, over both, the advantage of hindsight; *Le Nouveau Paris* does
not tell quite the same story as *Le Tableau*; Mercier has had a

serious fright and his once amiable Parisian has become *la houaille*, an object of fear. Restif, on the other hand, came through rather better than any of the other observers, including the police, because he was an individualist and an eccentric; he had long seen the danger signs ahead, had long seen the blood in the sky, and, having kept low company, had perceived the savage vindictiveness and brutal envy marked in the faces of the *faubouriens*. The police lived on the past, merely adding to their repertoire, without subtracting from it any of their old favourites. They were good historians of habit, of the stable, of routine, and could catch up with the professional criminal, almost as conservative as they were. But they were weak on movement and, during the Revolution, were often panting a few months behind events, using the old labels about new people, and relying on their past experience to face up to new situations which had no precedent. This is why they were better observers of behaviour than of Revolution; for they could think of politics only in terms of a certain, limited, number of adjectives, that they deal out, again and again, in a language as stilted as that of the Thermidorians.

9. THE THERMIDORIANS AS HISTORIANS

If the police are often the only contemporary observers of the *petit peuple*, and, later, of the *sans-culottes*, whose accounts have survived, the first historians of the 'popular movement' of the year II are the Thermidorians of the year III. They were still sufficiently close to events to possess a wealth of detail about the composition of popular institutions, militancy, and revolutionary language, sufficiently close also to allow their own prejudices and assumptions a full range, in the picture that they set out to give of the popular militant. We shall return in more detail to Thermidorian history when dealing with the fate of the *sans-culottes* in the course of the year III; at this stage, we shall attempt to draw attention to certain predominant traits in the Thermidorian portrait of the former *dominateurs*. The Thermidorians did not think of themselves as historians, nor were they intending to write history. They had a much more immediate purpose in mind: their reports, their lists, their *Actes d'Accusation*, sought to convince; they were extremely effective forms of propaganda. During the Thermidorian Reaction, when lists of terrorists are drawn up, and often printed, in each

Section, in each town, it is not unusual to find included the names of a few poor Bretons, *commissionnaires*, porters, people employed in those trades where sheer physical strength is the only necessary qualification—with the comment that they are quite illiterate and can scarcely speak a word of French.[1] The point here is to emphasize the depths to which the former terrorists had been prepared to stoop in order to recruit their henchmen; in most such cases, the man could be released after questioning—one of the Bretons was freed after only a few days in prison, on 21 Thermidor;[2] he had been misled, 'il ne connoissoit rien aux affaires publiques'.[3] But the point had been made. The Bretons were as good material as the Auvergnats, or the water-carriers from the Aveyron, or Jewish *fripiers* from Bohemia. These, then, had been the jumped-up masters of Sectionary domination. Just as the police tended to prove a certain thesis about the origins and aims of a riot by the sort of people they arrested, so inclusion in the Thermidorian *Listes* had been carefully considered; those who drew up the *listes de désarmement* knew what they were about.

It was not just a matter of dealing with the *meneurs*, putting them out of harm's way; the lists are meant to speak for themselves. And as well as poor Bretons, and a *porteur de meubles*, of whom it is stated: 'c'est un ouvrier, et lorsqu'il manquoit souvent de pain, il trouva tout injuste',[4] they will contain their due proportions of *ex-galériens*, *ex-notaires* (a very accident-prone profession), young men of good family gone to the dogs,[5] *anciens employés des Loteries* (implying that *sans-culottisme* had been self-interested, offering employment to those who had been put out of work by the Revolution), *anciens commis des Fermes* (similar implications).

Much, too, is made of mobility, in order to suggest chronic fecklessness and insecurity. The entry would then run something like this: 'Natif de Bohême, à Paris depuis 1770, marchand bon-

---

[1] 'Il ne sait ni lire ni écrire, ne parle pas même françois, bégayant à peine un jargon breton . . .' (A.N. F7 4734 d 4 Guégon).

[2] Ibid.

[3] 'Il a pu être mené, jamais meneur', it is said of an *ouvrier vannier*, a former member of the comité of the Section Poissonnière. He too is stated to be illiterate and is likewise released in Thermidor year III (A.N. F7 4653 d 3 Cordier).

[4] A.N. F7 4347 d 4 (Guénard). He is released in Fructidor year III.

[5] This of Rouyer, a terrorist of Moulins: 'ex-avocat sans cause . . . homme sans principes et sans mœurs, frondant partout l'harmonie de l'ordre social, jaloux de toutes les réputations, . . . a profité de la révolution pour se venger du mépris que son immoralité lui avoit valu . . .' (A.N. F1b II Allier I).

netier, puis agent de change, puis marchand de chanvre',[1] or, even better: 'avant la Révolution, joueur de gobelets et escamoteur sur les quais, où il disoit aussi les bonnes aventures . . . soumissionnaire pour les troupes . . . mathématicien . . . auteur d'un ouvrage intitulé *Le petit magicien républicain . . .*',[2] or: 'au début de la Révolution, peintre et restaurateur de tableaux, puis ouvrier aux carrières . . .'.[3]

And then there are the adjectives in vogue at this time: a man cannot be allowed just to have been a *cordonnier*, he is a *cordonnier-toujours-ivre, un tailleur-qui-bat-sa-femme, un savetier-ignorant-et-stupide, marchand-de-vin-violent-et-emporté, perruquier-insolent-et-joueur*; if it is a monk, then it will come out as *ex-moine-paillard-et-débauché*; a clerk, *ex-commis-renvoyé-pour-indélicatesse*. The jackpot would no doubt go to: *ex-valet de bordel, ne sachant ni lire ni écrire*.[4] If the fellow is in trade on his own account, then he will emerge as *un courtaud de boutique*. If he has been on the stage—and how this will suit Thermidorian requirements!—then it will come out as *mauvais comédien sifflé aux Célestins*, or *membre d'une troupe ambulante de saltimbanques*—and the Thermidorians are especially keen to draw a parallel between terrorist militancy and experience in the circus or on the fairground: for are not both occupations concerned with quackery? Of such, as a further condemnation, it will sometimes be added: 'a eu une suite importante parmi les femmes ignorantes de la Section.'[5] If the poor wretch has a large family, he is *accablé d'enfants en bas âge*[6]—offering a suggestion of plebeian *néo-lapinisme*. If, on the other hand, he is unmarried, then it is likely that he is 'un jeune débauché livré à la société et fréquentant les filles publiques de la plus basse classe'. A common Thermidorian accusation against the ex-terrorist is 'd'avoir mis en réquisition pour son usage personnel les filles de la campagne'. The *Listes* are so formalized as to write themselves, from one end of the Republic to another.[7] Some of the combinations are so repetitive

---

[1] F7 4753 d 5 (Kruber, member of the comité de l'Homme-Armé).

[2] A.N. F7 4775 3 d 3 (Rouy, member of the comité des Lombards).

[3] A.N. F7 4775 42 d 4 (Ventujol, member of the comité de l'Observatoire).

[4] A.N. F7 4775 46 d 5 (Tabourin, member of the comité de Guillaume-Tell).

[5] A.N. F7 4775 3 d 3 (Rouy).

[6] A.N. F7 4775 26 d 2 (Tamponnet, member of the comité de la Section des Droits de l'Homme).

[7] Regional variations were, however, allowed for; in the Avignonnais literature of Thermidor, the ex-terrorist *sable le tavel à longueur de journée*, but in Nantes it is *muscadet*, the Norman prototype *ne vit que d'eau-de-vie et de jurons*, the

as to appear to designate new trades, or double trades; a Thermidorian *logeur* cannot be separated from his siamese twin of *souteneur*, he has, it would appear, taken out, like History with Honours, a double *patente* as *logeur-et-souteneur*. The *Listes* make such repetitive reading that it is often possible to predict, well in advance, what adjective will accompany which trade. The Thermidorians made every effort to get their message across to their middle-class readers, and nothing was left to their imagination.

This is not to dismiss out of hand, as historical evidence capable of having a bearing on popular militancy, the Thermidorian 'case history' as presented in the *Listes*, or in hundreds of pamphlets printed during the vast *enquête* on terrorism of the spring and summer of 1795—a literature which was to do so much to condition the emergence of the White Terror. We cannot, in fact, do without the Thermidorians, for, like the police, they are often the only historians that we possess at this level. The reports were no doubt accurate in their factual details; there is no reason to disbelieve them when they state that a juggler was a member of a Paris *comité*, or that a Bohemian Jew, who had had a variety of professions, ranging from *agent de change* to *fripier*, had been a leading militant. Generally—and in this we can distinguish them from the evidence produced by Duval—they can be trusted on the subject of trade and occupation. What is revealing of their intentions is both the choice of their *dossiers*—there was clearly a good deal of selectiveness before the *Listes* saw the light of day—and the comments that accompany them. The Thermidorians are seeking to accredit a moral judgement on the popular movement that suits their own class view of society. As long as we are aware of this, there is no reason why we should not use the abundant, and unique, evidence presented in their reports.

This section has been concerned to recreate the assumptions both of police and of Thermidorian witnesses and to ask, above all, the question: What are they out to prove? The next task is to examine the changing language of orthodoxy, whether it comes from official sources, or from the people themselves, or from those who view the people with indifference or with marked distaste.

Lillois *aboyeur ne sort guère de l'estaminet que pour se rendre au club*, the Lyonnais *mathevon* can never be seen without *le pot à la main*, breaking, with his free hand, the seals placed on confiscated property.

PART TWO

L'ESPRIT PUBLIC
AND THE
LANGUAGE OF ORTHODOXY

'. . . Ce n'est qu'un cri unanime à remercier le
Gouvernement. . . .'
(Any address of the year II or the year III)

10. *L'ESPRIT PUBLIC* AND THE CHANGING LANGUAGE OF ORTHODOXY

RIOT, conspiracy, turbulence, sedition, and crime are not the only
concerns of a police that, during and much more after the revolutionary period, became more and more invasive, more and more
numerous, and more and more long-winded. Every regime will
get the police that it deserves. All French authorities, from the old
regime to the Restoration, were avid for information on an
enormous variety of subjects. They were obsessed, in particular,
with something called *esprit public*—not just 'public opinion', not
just what could be picked up and pieced together from snatches of
open conversation, café talk, table talk, *Terrasse des Tuileries* talk,
quai-side talk, market gossip and rumour, Pont-Neuf *complainte* or
sedition, but also what people thought, or were supposed to be
thinking. They believed that, with sufficient information, they could
penetrate people's minds, and they would have liked to have had
the powers of *le Passe-Muraille*,[1] an oppressed clerk in an insurance
office who accidentally discovered that he could move painlessly
through walls, penetrate the intimacy of locked rooms, and
receive, in purple-walled bedrooms, *les secrets de l'oreiller*. (The
French police, it is true, could generally obtain these from the more
co-operative *filles de joie*.) But as they did not have this enviable gift,
they had to make do with what could be heard in public or to pick
out what could be made of a family quarrel from the listening post
of a staircase lavatory, one of Restif's favourite crouching vantage

[1] Marcel Aymé, *Le Passe-Muraille* (Paris, 1951).

points. The more they were informed, the more they were pleased; what could be written in three lines would take on more authority spun out to three pages, and a denunciation, to be effective and to attract attention, needed to be long-winded.

Fouquier-Tinville always wrote voluminous indictments, and the official reports by Barère, Billaud-Varenne, Saint-Just, and Courtois on plots and conspiracies are small theses, immensely boring and endlessly repetitive. The elementary rule of those who supplied the authorities with reports on *l'Esprit public* might have been: 'If you have nothing to say, say it at length.' It was a rule well appreciated by every *commissaire observateur* when he sent in his daily report and by every *agent national* under the Revolutionary Government, when he filled in his *rapports décadaires*. If to be well informed was to be voluminously informed, the royal, Jacobin, Thermidorian, Directorial, and, Imperial, and, once more, royal, authorities got what they wanted. To the endless questionnaires sent from Paris downwards there came in reply an even more considerable stream of paper upwards. An *agent national* who filled in his answers briefly or to the point, a Prefect who replied in a few lines, was likely to be reprimanded for laziness and lack of zeal. But the worst offence of all was to write, in the appropriate column, *rien à signaler, il ne s'est rien passé, point de suspects, point de détenus, aucun désordre, point de déserteurs, aucune condamnation, aucun retardataire, l'esprit public est partout bon,* or, even worse, *Oui* or *Non*, without further elaboration—clear proof of utter incompetence or of deliberate covering-up. We find the Committees writing to an *agent national* or to a *comité de surveillance* to suggest that something of importance must have happened, while a Prefect of 1812 receives a terrible ticking-off from the Minister of the Interior for having reported: 'la situation de mon Département est satisfaisante de tout point de vue.' What was the use of that? And if really nothing at all had happened, then something had to be invented. *Agents nationaux, commissaires,* Prefects, and so on were unlikely to make the same mistake twice, and they could be trusted, after one such slip, always to find something to report, and at length.

They had, too, the example of the Intendants to guide them. In the winter of 1793, there are reports by two *commissaires observateurs* on a conversation eavesdropped on the terrace of the Café Chrétien. The one who knew what he was about stated that he had heard

un particulier habillé . . . [a detailed description of appearance] tenir des propos obscènes et indignes d'un républicain, il a avili la représentation nationale, il a mal parlé de la Convention, il a insulté à la souveraineté nationale, il s'est moqué des Sauveurs du Peuple, il a attenté au Gouvernement Révolutionnaire, il a exprimé des vœux nettement contre-révolutionnaires, il a souhaité la destruction du régime républicain, il s'est montré l'agent stipendié de Pitécobourg,

and so on. From the other, either a novice or a man of singular candour, we merely learn that all the fellow had said was 'Merde à la Convention'. Top marks to No. 1, a reprimand for No. 2.

One might, at this stage, mention *Rule Two*, which applies to the revolutionary and, more particularly, the Jacobin period: 'Never call anything what it is, always use a euphemism; never use plain speech, always use the language of riddles'. (One could find no more eloquent example of the dangers of a classical education, when even quite humble police officials begin using the language of the Sphinx.) For one thing, it was longer; for another, the revolutionary authorities—particularly at the top—showed a prissy reluctance to call a spade a spade. The result is that even market porters and fishwives declaim in the language of *la rhétorique*. So a soldier is *un défenseur de la Patrie*; the guillotine, *le glaive de la justice*; *Pitt et Cobourg, les tigres muselés*; a man of law, *un chien courant de la féodalité*; a priest, *un vieux druide*; a grain merchant, *la sang-sue du peuple*; and a large farmer could only be *un cultivateur avide et égoïste*. (*Rule Three*: 'Use two adjectives rather than one.') So rigid are the rules of the game that the reports could almost write themselves; and one can go from one end of France to the other to hear the same long-winded information expressed in the same ponderous prose. Here indeed one is far removed from the voluble anger and the volcanic joy of the b*****g and f*****g *Père Duchesne*, and from the picturesque and expressive language of the common people. To move from one of these reports to the minutes of a *société populaire* or of an *assemblée sectionnaire* is like moving from a London club to a sergeants' mess on a Saturday night. *Vox populi*, filtered through these reports, becomes un-recognizable.

Yet, in revolutionary France, everywhere people talked there would be listeners; and, even at the height of the Terror and of the Thermidorian Reaction, people talked loud and clear. One is con-stantly amazed at their impudence and their imprudence. It took a Robespierre to induce the French—temporarily—to watch what they said. So the *commissaires* were great walkers: they listened in a hundred cafés, in every club and *assemblée*, on the *quais*, on the terrace of the Tuileries, in public baths, in swimming-baths, in laundry boats, in billiard rooms, at the hairdresser's (an excellent listening post), among the spectators at the guillotine or at its provider, the revolutionary tribunal, in queues, in *guinguettes* in the villages on the slopes above the Seine, in the markets, at the fairs, and in public lavatories. They talked to *portières* and *logeurs*, and in the evening they sat down in the back rooms in *cabarets* and wrote their copious reports, which often bear the round red stains of glasses, on everything that they had heard. The habit, once acquired, went on: there were too many vested interests at stake, and a police, once created, is not easily dismissed. *L'Esprit public* is the daily breakfast reading of the Thermidorian Committees, of a series of Ministers of Police, of the Prefects and Sub-Prefects. Sometimes the handwriting of the *observateurs* is the same—they are the lucky ones, also the long-winded ones—but the language changes, the revolutionary euphemisms are dropped, to be replaced by other, equally dangerous, *exercices de style*. What does not change is the volume.

Another golden rule (*Rule Four*), sedulously followed under successive regimes, is always to tell one's superiors the sort of information that they would like to hear. The *commissaires* sent out into the Departments around Paris in September 1792 by Roland are constantly meeting local authorities or ordinary members of the public who cannot contain their enthusiasm and their gratitude: 'Tout va changer pour le mieux depuis l'installation du Ministre patriote.' Many are incapable of speaking of 'le vertueux Roland' without the tears welling up in their eyes. The general consensus of the reports sent to the elderly bore was that Roland was the Saviour of France. Some of these early *commissaires du Pouvoir Exécutif*, militants on the fringes of the so-called *hébertiste* group, were to describe him, only one year later, as *le traître Roland*, in reports addressed to other masters. The *observateurs* who work first for Garat, then for Paré, never hear a good word spoken of Hébert, Ronsin, Vincent; people are fed up with the fractiousness and violence of *ces ambitieux*, and look to the Committees and to the Convention for leadership. But there is much support, too, for Danton, the *sans-culottes* want an end to Terror and repression, there is a general revulsion against the Cordeliers, Hébert has no popular support, opinion is eternally grateful to the Revolutionary Government for having unmasked the *factions* and saved the Republic (*une fois de plus*—for the Republic is always being saved *in extremis*).

It is hardly surprising that the Committees should so easily have convinced themselves—and they wanted to be convinced—that the *hébertistes* were a small, embittered group of have-nots, men with frustrated ambitions, with no popular support and no appeal to the general mass of *sans-culottes* (despite the fact that the *Père Duchesne* sometimes ran to 200,000 readers) and that, consequently, there would be no public commotion if they were tried and duly executed. Only two *observateurs* out of thirty had the courage to report that popular opinion was worried by the spectacle of what was clearly a rigged trial and that many *sans-culottes* were not wholly convinced of the guilt of the *conjurés*. Hébert and his friends did then enjoy some popular support, but, they hastened to add, only among the lowest orders, the ignorant, and the credulous. The Committees could thus convince themselves that the *sans-culottes* were entirely behind them and that there was no connection between *hébertisme* and an autonomous popular movement; indeed that such a movement did not even exist. Fortunately they did possess other, more authentic, sources of information; and the minutes of *assemblées* and *sociétés sectionnaires* gave out a very different sound, if the Revolutionary Government had cared to listen to it. Fouquier-Tinville was in receipt of anonymous placards stuck up in the markets and at street corners which claimed that Hébert and his friends were martyrs and had suffered the same fate as Marat (and Marat, it was suggested, would soon come under posthumous disgrace). Fouquier put this kind of thing away in his files, to use in future indictments.

Once the 'factions' had been dispatched, the higher authorities began to show less concern for *l'esprit public*. Popular institutions had, in the meantime, been safely muzzled when they were not pushed into self-destruction. The popular press had been destroyed and little enough remained for opinion to be public about, food problems, religion, wages, high prices, the subjects about which people most liked to talk, having come under the Government ban on 'dangerous topics'. There is then a sharp decline in the number of reports, for there is little to report on during Robespierre's

Red Summer. With unanimity at last achieved, or at least officially proclaimed, the *observateurs* reflect the general happiness. 'Ce n'est qu'un cri unanime, entend-on dire dans les lieux publics, le Gouvernement révolutionnaire a sauvé UNE FOIS DE PLUS la chose publique, les factions sont détruites, les complots de l'étranger sont déjoués, ce n'est qu'un cri universel: Vive la République! Vive la Convention! Vive Robespierre!' Another variant would be: 'Ce n'est qu'un cri unanime à condamner l'athéisme et l'immoralité', and another 'Ce n'est qu'un cri unanime à remercier les Comités d'avoir déjoué les calculs de Pitécobourg', and, after the Admirat affair: 'Ce n'est qu'un cri unanime à féliciter les défenseurs du peuple d'avoir échappé aux couteaux' ('MILLE couteaux' of course), 'des vils assassins stipendiés de Pitécobourg', and so on. One is very unanimous that summer. There are, it is true, occasional references to *les restes des factions*, to *la queue de Danton*, and to *les sequelles de Ronsin et de Vincent*, timid hints that all is not entirely well in the best, the most virtuous, the most unanimous of Republics, in response to the veiled threats that emanated, at regular intervals, and in unusually sphinx-like language, from the Pope of the Supreme Being, but they are scarcely perceptible in the harmony of unanimity. Indeed, during this period the reports of *observateurs* are almost indistinguishable from the stunted, fake enthusiasm of congratulatory addresses and collective expressions of gratitude— no people, it would appear, could be more grateful to its rulers than the French; it is grateful again and again—to a government both vigilant and wise. The reports might all have been copied from a set text, with just the date to fill in; it is possible that the *observateurs* worked on them together. They had certainly captured the style of the day. The Revolutionary Government wanted unanimity, and unanimity is what it got, even from its police, its spies, and its subordinate agents. This is what Georges Lefebvre has described, in an article on the Law of 22 Prairial, as 'the spontaneous expression of public opinion'.[1]

It is very different after Thermidor. The volume of reports on popular opinion and on popular disturbance is the measure of a regime's fear of the common people, and the Thermidorians had every reason to be afraid of the general mass of a population that was soon starving, cold, and desperate. But during the first few

---

[1] Georges Lefebvre, *Études révolutionnaires* (Paris, 1955), 'Sur la loi du 22 prairial'.

weeks at least unanimity is once more the keynote; Robespierre is unanimously execrated, 'ce n'est qu'un cri unanime à remercier le Gouvernement d'avoir sauvé la chose publique de mille périls, le règne de la justice est enfin rétabli', and so on. Unanimity, however, has been overdone and the *observateurs* are soon well aware that the new masters fear above all the just anger of a hungry people. Popular complaints are 'interpreted'; if the *faubourgs* murmur, it is because opinion there is being worked up against the Committees and the Convention, and the just grievances of the wage-earner and the craftsman are being exploited to political purpose by evil-intentioned persons. When popular discontent breaks out in the form of riot, this too is explained in political terms. The *observateurs* have little to say about hunger and a lot to say about sedition. Hunger is an embarrassing topic for a regime the rulers of which eat unusually well, and the police would be ill advised to report literally what they can see and to draw too lurid a distinction between the fat and the thin—the two principal classes of Thermidorian France. It is much more acceptable to report that people are basically good and loyal, even grateful (goodness knows for what); that they are patient in adversity; that they know that the government is concerned with their ills and is actively seeking to alleviate their suffering; but that politicians, ex-terrorists, *buveurs de sang*, adventurers, and so on, by fishing in troubled waters, are seeking to undermine their loyalty to the Convention (what is left of it) and to the Republic in order to canalize their anger and despair into political channels, so as either to re-establish *le règne de la Terreur* or to bring the Princes back.

The crisis, then, is not the fault of the government; and, for a property-holders' regime like Thermidor, it is easier to organize repression—tempered by a little charity, especially in Paris, where it shows—than to alienate the countryside by the reimposition of price controls and by a further recourse to billeting and garrisoning. The Thermidorian police and *agents nationaux* gave the government the sort of information that it needed to justify, at least in its own eyes, a massive use of force against a people misled. But this complicity between a police that seeks to please and occasionally to frighten higher authority, and a higher authority that seeks to be reassured and to have its own prejudices and assumptions confirmed and its priorities reinforced, is ultimately a dangerous one for the government. (It is significant that the

Thermidorians got much better information from the army, but would not listen to it; indeed, some *commandants de place*, who had merely reported honestly and with sympathy on the distress of the common people, and had expressed fears for the future, were simply dismissed for having expressed 'Jacobin' notions.)[1]

As, under the Directory, and still more under the Empire, the police became better organized, more numerous, and, above all, more centralized—there is a safeguard for any regime in a multiplicity of different, and preferably rival, police organizations, for the information supplied will be more varied and the police themselves, engaged in obscure civil wars, will not become all-powerful—and with the Minister of Police holding a monopoly of information, this danger greatly increased. During the Empire, police reports are clumsy, sycophantic, and often completely asinine; there are endless references to the love and reverence inspired by the person of the Emperor, to popular gratitude for his generous concern for the needy, to the pride of a people enjoying the benefits of his dynasty, and so on. The police are no longer reporting on the people, they are thinking for them, and thinking right.

Of course, if the Imperial Government really wanted to know what people were saying and doing, there were always the far more accurate reports of the *gendarmerie* and of garrison commanders to fall back on. Neither of these attempted to disguise unpleasant truths and they reported, with a military bluntness, on the alarming spread of desertion in many Departments; on the marauding raids of rural bands of beggars, especially during the crisis of 1812; on attacks on posts of the *Droits Réunis*; on the increasing warweariness of the population from 1809 onwards; on the attachment of the wage-earner to the memory of the *maximum*; on rowdiness, generally provoked by neo-terrorist elements in the army, at the *comédie* (soldiers, more quarrelsome than the police, were much more inclined thus to report on each other, and so every officer's *dossier* is a mine of information about opposition within the army,

---

[1] For instance, Taillefer, the brother of the *Conventionnel*, who was acting *commandant de place* at Amiens, at the time of the Germinal Days there, is arrested, on 20 Germinal, and interrogated by the Committee of General Security, at the request of Blaux, *représentant en mission*, for having predicted the rising, for having shown too much sympathy to the rioters, and because he is suspected of being in touch with the neo-terrorists of the Lot, the Department of origin of himself and his brother the doctor. (See *Terreur et subsistances*, pp. 281, 284, 285, 'La journée du 14 germinal à Amiens'.) The 'crime' of Taillefer is to have suggested that people who are hungry are likely to take the law into their own hands.

and about popular disorders, often said to have been encouraged, or winked at, by neo-Jacobin *commandants de place*). They even reported on the disgraceful scenes in such republican strongholds as Chambéry, Grenoble, or Geneva, on the celebration of the Emperor's Feast Day, when anti-clerical officers took the opportunity to denounce 'fanaticism' and to evoke the year II.[1]

Such is the pressure for promotion that officers of high or middling rank can always be relied upon to report on those in the rank just above them, whether for political or personal failings— rarely for military ones—and the study of the *Archives administratives de la Guerre* is the best possible antidote to a romantic view of the comradeship of arms and of regimental solidarity. The worst offenders, it is true, were staff officers (when reporting on other staff officers) and a number of commanders of high rank had clearly missed their vocation as high-class informers and police agents. The military were not afraid to report unwelcome news; and they generally had a more accurate and more compassionate appreciation of popular grievances and motivations than the police or the Prefects. The regime would have done well to have paid more attention to its soldiers. They were seldom fools, and some of them were surprisingly literate and *au fait* with local conditions where they did garrison duties, both in the French and in the foreign Departments. The military also had the advantage over the police of being able to go to bed with the local females, one of the surest means of sounding out the feelings of a local population. For the most part, they had a strong vested interest in the survival of the regime and regarded the Bourbons with abhorrence. The police, on the other hand, were often rogues primarily concerned with their own survival and not to be depended upon when conditions worsened; and the Prefects and Sub-Prefects were mostly arch-flatterers and totally servile. But an autocratic regime, which has destroyed all possible means of the free expression of opinion at any level, and has become increasingly obsessed with an *esprit public* that it has driven underground and has no means of gauging, is forced to rely more and more on its police.

The imperial government, in its last years, had succeeded in cutting itself off from all disinterested advice. Of the military, only

[1] On the use of personal dossiers of officers in the A.A.G. as a source for the history of neo-Jacobinism in garrison towns, see *Les Armées révolutionnaires*, ii, *Épilogue*, with reference to the *chefs de bataillon* Chastel and Gourgonnier (p. 889).

the courtiers were listened to, and they, like the police and the
Prefects, gave the sort of information that they knew would be
welcome. The more a regime is a police regime, the poorer its
information is likely to be. This is a problem as much for the
historian as for the regime, and if the internal history of Imperial
France, especially at the local level, has been so much neglected,
it is due principally to the standardized quality of the information
available. There is something sickening about the servility of the
language used by Napoleonic Prefects, the constant theme of which
is the generosity of the Emperor, the gratitude of the ignorant
masses, the charitable efforts of the Emperor's public officials and
of certain private persons (decorated for what they had done for
the poor). The France that emerges is featureless and static. The
reports of the secret police contain a mass of worthless gossip and
are even less informative than those of the old revolutionary
commissaires observateurs. The Prefects no doubt read the reports
of the *gendarmerie*, but they seldom passed them on. The Minister
of War, who must have received a great deal of very disturbing information, sat on it; he was not a policeman.

II. THE WINNING SIDE

The value of the informer, of the police, of the *gendarmerie*, and
of the army as interpreters of popular opinion and as witnesses
of popular violence and unsuccessful riot has now been discussed
at some length. But when a riot is successful, it is no longer
a riot, it becomes a *journée* or even a Revolution, to be suitably
commemorated in papier-mâché triumphal arch and column, to
be replaced, if the regime lasts long enough, by something more
solid in stone or marble. Here the police records will be of little
help. There are no arrests, at least among the rioters; the police,
in the face of success, will discreetly disappear, leaving the terrain
to the victors. And, just as no one is likely to claim participation in
an unsuccessful riot, but will produce witnesses to declare that
they have never left their place of work, everyone wants to be in on
an event that has acquired immediate historical respectability. The
numbers of the *Vainqueurs de la Bastille* began increasing from
15 July—a phenomenon comparable to that of the multiplication,
in more recent times, of the *Résistants de Septembre*. The municipal
authorities, concerned to keep the club fairly exclusive (recognized

Vainqueurs enjoyed a pension and were given a uniform), had the
greatest difficulty in checking the credentials of the many claimants to a part in the final assault. Some may have been genuine,
and merely unlucky in not attracting the notice of Hulin or Parein,
the principal authorities in the matter. Others, having possibly seen
the whole thing out in a wineshop in the faubourg or near the
Grève, were later able to persuade themselves, and their neighbours,
that they could not have missed such an occasion to distinguish themselves. It was hard to have been within yards of a great Revolution.

By all accounts, the *10 août* was a truly national achievement,
with *fédérés* from every Department present in the forecourt of the
Tuileries; but it is impossible to know any more about the assailants: the only record is that of the killed and the seriously wounded.
One is constantly surprised by the distances that people covered in
order to be present at the crucial stage of the night of 9–10 Thermidor, within touching distance of the celebrated Merda. There
were claimants for the front seats who had come to Paris from
Gisors, Montgeron, Sens, Joigny, Auxerre, and even further afield.
It is quite likely that they actually were in the capital at the time—
most of them had perfectly good reasons for being there: the man
from Montgeron had come up with a congratulatory address in his
pocket (as it mentioned Robespierre, it remained in his pocket);
the woman from Gisors had come, as she did once a fortnight, to
sell butter and eggs on the Paris markets; the official from Sens had
an arrest warrant to deliver; the *notaire* from Joigny had some legal
business to transact with a Parisian colleague; and the *commissaire*
from Auxerre had come to see his brother. But it is difficult to see
what such a mixed bag of people were doing inside the Maison
Commune in the course of that long drawn-out night: the man
from Sens might conceivably have become closely involved in
events as a result of having to contact a *comité révolutionnaire*; the
petitioner from Montgeron could likewise have witnessed what was
happening in and around the Convention; but the others can
hardly have been drawn to the scene of the most decisive of all
revolutionary *journées*. Probably, having returned to their homes,
they could not resist saying that they had seen what they had heard;
they had been so near the scene of events in any case for it not to
make much difference.

Similarly a whole regiment of officers claim to have been in the
saddle—on this occasion, the right position was to have been on

horseback, the wrong to have been on foot, an unusual situation in every way—defending the Convention and putting down royalism in Vendémiaire year IV, repeating the claim, with tireless persistence, in one *curriculum vitae* after another addressed to their superiors, to support their demands for promotion, from 1796 to 1814 (after that date, this particular *fait d'armes* is dropped from the list of their campaigns). For an ambitious officer, the worthwhile laurels were to be gathered in Paris, and it was more important to have 'saved the Republic' in the rue Saint-Roch than to have taken part in a great victory on the frontier.

During the White Terror, in the south-east, where opinion was strongly behind the murder gangs, especially in rural areas, at each village lynching there will be one or two strident women—*La Mère Fabre, la femme Barbasse*—pushing to the fore and boasting: 'C'est moi qui lui ai foutu le grand coup, c'est moi qui lui ai arraché les yeux, c'est moi qui lui ai coupé la b***, c'est moi qui lui ai sectionné la tête du col, c'est moi qui lui ai foutu la hache sur le crâne, c'est moi qui ai "pété" le beau Gérard, c'est moi qui lui ai piqué au ventre, j'en ai les mains pleines de sang.'[1] And these boasts seem in character with the frightful savagery of these peasant women when given an opportunity to express their hatred of the rural terrorists who had made life uncomfortable for them during the previous year. In any case there are witnesses to all these remarks, though the women concerned, when cross-questioned, not without approval, by the very understanding judges of the Aix or Nîmes courts, claim that they could not remember ever having said anything of the sort; in any case, 'elles n'avaient rien vu, rien entendu'. Obviously there was a time and a place for everything. The judges themselves attached little importance to such remarks, acquitting those who were accused of having made them; perhaps, with their experience of the area, they viewed them as typical examples of rural boastfulness. Equally, they may have approved of the gentle sentiments so vigorously expressed. Certainly they were not at all severe to those who not only said, but did, such things.

Similar boasts were made on the evenings of the September Massacres in Paris by self-proclaimed *massacreurs* who, on returning to their Sections, proudly displayed sabres still stained with

---

[1] See below, Section II, pp. 131–49, on the White Terror, and Section III on the ferocity of feminine vocabulary and the violence of feminine incitement, particularly in periods of extreme dearth.

fresh blood, axes, knives, and daggers, similarly coloured: 'j'en ai le bras rompu', while the weapons of killing went the round of the usual customers of the local wine-shop. Some of these braggarts, brought to trial in the year IV as *septembriseurs* (a once-proud designation that had, in changed circumstances, become one of horror and opprobrium), were to explain that they had coloured their sabres in butchers' buckets before returning to their Sections, in an effort to impress their neighbours and to win the admiration of patriotic girls. Others continued to assert, even after Thermidor, that they had been present at the Carmes or the Abbaye, still luxuriating in their title of *septembriseurs* and enjoying the look of fear, the lowered voice, or the sudden silence that followed them in the street, in the areas where they were known.

12. THE *SANS-CULOTTE*, BY HIMSELF

The political inquisitions of the year II put a further premium on claims of this type, jogging many faulty memories into action, with such questions as: 'Où étois-tu au 14 juillet?', 'As-tu signé la pétition du Champ-de-Mars?', 'As-tu pris les armes le 10 août?' 'Qu'as-tu fait le 31 mai et le 2 juin?', and so on. The questions were so clearly awaiting the right answer that there must have been a very strong temptation to give it; and there was little danger in doing so if, in the meantime, one had moved to a new quarter. The world of the Section was both closed and self-sufficient; it was often sufficient to move half a mile—or a few yards—to acquire a new political identity and a more attractive, fuller, more orthodox *curriculum vitae*. The Sectionary institutions, however, soon became aware of this danger of letting through the impure with the pure, and during the 'purges' of July and August 1793 they established various methods for mutual consultation in order to ensure that a man's past would follow him from the Gardes Françaises to the Muséum, from the Bondy to l'Homme Armé. The Paris Sections corresponded, with a similar purpose in mind, with those of other towns; and these *scrutins épuratoires* accounted for much of the vast amount of Sectionary correspondence that has survived, even inducing these exceedingly jealous bodies to set up semi-permanent institutions to guarantee a minimum of co-operation. Despite these checks, a person might survive for many months—or altogether— on false credentials.

It is well to remember, too, that most of the documents from which such information is derived, in the personal case histories of individual *sans-culottes*, are either in the form of petitions from prisoners or in that of public professions of political orthodoxy on the part of those undergoing a *scrutin épuratoire* in an *assemblée générale*. Our knowledge of the revolutionary militant is based entirely on the public image that he seeks to present, not on the private record.[1] If individual *sans-culottes* ever kept diaries or a journal, none has survived; this is a source which exists only for the other side—for the sort of people who were denounced by the *sans-culottes* and who later wrote up their prison recollections, for provincial *notaires* who lived through the Terror behind closed shutters, working off their feelings in a diary kept well out of sight of the servants.[2] So the petitioner of the year II, whether to recover his freedom or to demonstrate his suitability for public employment under the Terror, is likely to present a somewhat doctored version of his life since 1789: yes, he had taken up arms on all the correct occasions; yes, he had never missed a *journée*, he had been to the Champ-de-Mars and only escaped death by throwing himself on the ground at the first salvo; he had lost a finger in the forecourt of the Tuileries; he never missed his guard duties; he attended his *assemblée générale* every night that it met; his five or six sons were all serving the Republic, in the army or the navy; his three or four daughters were either married to *défenseurs de la patrie* and raising *vengeurs*, or were busily engaged in making uniforms or bandages or in other activities befitting *mères des Gracchi*; he had paid all his taxes punctually; he had succoured the aged and the needy; had adopted an orphan; had taken in an aged patriotic pauper; had married *une brave ouvrière*; had been to all the great *Fêtes* (and enjoyed them); had denounced three royalists and five *fanatiques* and seven hoarders; had reported the hiding-place of an *émigré rentré*; had secured the arrest of a *prêtre réfractaire* living in a wardrobe; had witnessed against a counter-revolutionary before the revolutionary tribunal; had always publicly upheld the respect due to the Convention and to the Committees, to the Revolutionary

---

[1] 'Quelques aspects de la mentalité révolutionnaire', in *Terreur et subsistances*, p. 3.

[2] See, for instance, *Le Mémorial du Citoyen d'Auxerre*, the diary of a *notaire* from that town during the Terror period, preserved in manuscript in the Archives de l'Yonne, from which we have quoted on the subject of *déchristianisation* (*Les Armées révolutionnaires*, ii. 661).

Government, to Paris, to *la loi sainte du maximum*, to the Revolution; had preached against immorality; had drawn the attention of the *commissaire de police* to a 'shop' in which prostitutes exercised *leur vil métier*; had never over-charged; had eschewed all luxuries and idle pursuits, gambling and billiards; drank in moderation, as befitted a *brave sans-culotte*; 'n'avait jamais mis en doute les nouvelles officielles'; had made the *Bulletin des Lois* his table reading at meal-time, and the *Déclaration des Droits de l'Homme et du Citoyen* the bedtime recitation of his small children; wore his own hair and dressed modestly and without ostentation. No wonder an exhaustive research into a few hundred of these model lives, into a thousand or so *dossiers* from these calendars of revolutionary saints becomes nauseatingly monotonous. Like certain police reports, these potted patriotic biographies write themselves. Their authors seek not only perfection and a political purity as white as snow, they also tend to demote themselves socially, in order to meet the prevailing mode. (Of the operation—*parachutage* would be the modern expression—by which a stranger with a past suddenly turns up in a new Section, or in a new town, where he is unknown, cynical *sans-culottes*—for such people do exist—say 'il est venu chez nous se refaire une virginité républicaine'—and political virginity, unlike the real thing, can be lost and regained any number of times.) In the year II a man who describes himself as a *menuisier* is revealed, on further inspection, as an *entrepreneur en bâtiment*; a *traiteur* will sometimes become a *gargotier*, and a man with a large furniture store masquerades as a *brocanteur*. In so many of these model *sans-culottes*, all married to *braves ouvrières*, it is hard to recognize the well-to-do patrician couples, the *notables* of 1789 . . . and of 1795. One would never guess that many of these 'artisans'—Daniel Guérin calles them *bras nus*—had servants.

In Paris, it is true, there were too many checks to allow for the emergence of large numbers of pseudo-*sans-culottes*, but even there one must always allow for a certain degree of 'plebeianization' when *sectionnaires* are invited to report on themselves. But in provincial towns, where, if memories were better, there also existed a certain solidarity in keeping up an appearance of orthodoxy in the face of the outer world, often to acquire *sans-culotte* status it was sufficient to call oneself a *sans-culotte*. Who, for instance, other than the Roannais themselves, was to know that the members of the *comité* and of the other revolutionary institutions of this small town in the

Forez, in the year II, were, for the most part, the local bigwigs who had been in control of affairs ever since 1789 ?[1] Certainly a number of people would never have got into the club at all if Valframbert's detailed series of conditions for entry had been seriously applied.[2] A great many of these *sans-culottes* did *not* work with their hands, could *not* tile a roof, did *not* know how to make a pair of shoes, were *not* useful. The trouble was that there was a vast range of disagreement about what constituted a *sans-culotte*, and as in the year II it was a good thing to be, if one could not get in under one count —social origin, economic status, category of employment—one could go round to the back and get in under quite another—moral worth, revolutionary enthusiasm, simplicity of dress or of manner, way of life, services rendered to the Revolution (including *dons patriotiques*, for these would help), past sufferings at the hands of various 'oppressors' (Musquinet Lapagne hit the jackpot with a *lettre de cachet*, but few could produce so good a card, and even having that card did not make Sade into a *sans-culotte*), from the old regime to the *Commission des Douze*.

So much for the value of the *dossier individuel* of the year II as source material for the historian of popular movements. It is by no means useless; for the same man will not always be consistent and in a series of petitions he will probably give himself away with some contradiction, and some of these case histories are patently sincere, those who write them being too simple and too ignorant to dress themselves up as something else. But they need to be carefully scrutinized and should never stand alone without being checked against other sources, if these exist; and they often do, as the Sectionary movement had much of its time taken up with personal recrimination. One should always have in mind what those who write them are seeking to prove. Each year has its exigencies, its good words and its bad words, revolutionary years are much longer than most, and nothing could be more unlike the year II than the year III.

In 1795, the model biography even of the same man reads very

---

[1] This information was supplied to the author by Mr. Colin Lucas, lecturer at the University of Sheffield, who is preparing a study of the mission of Javogues in the Département de la Loire. I am further indebted to Mr. Lucas for his many and perceptive comments relating to the course of the Terror in the Loire and in Lyon and for having drawn my attention to the box BB 18 690, an invaluable source for the history of the White Terror in the Loire.

[2] See 'The Revolutionary Mentality in France', *History*, October 1957.

differently. Let us first of all allow him to describe himself, in his own terms, in an effort to convince his Thermidorian critics of his innocence or to obtain his release, this time from a Thermidorian prison. The vocabulary *en vogue* has changed, the word *sans-culotte* has been consigned to oblivion (the current word for it is *buveur de sang*), and those who, in the previous year, have suffered self-inflicted social demotion walk once more in their own clothes. The erstwhile *menuisier* now makes no bones about being a building contractor; the *brocanteur* is a *marchand de meubles*; the *ouvrier tapissier* of the year II is the *marchand de tapis* of the year III; the *commis* is revealed as *un homme de loi* (a profession no longer decried); the *herboriste* calls himself an *apothicaire* and the ex-*gargotier* is now putting out an appetizing sign as a *traiteur*; all sorts of subtle changes have been going on within the *corps social* of provincial France. *Le règne des honnêtes gens* is that of the big, not of the little; of the fat, not of the thin (which, in Thermidorian vocabulary, becomes *famélique*);[1] and this time there are instances of social inflation, with the *sans-culotte* artisan attempting to blow himself into more Thermidorian proportions.

This is one tendency. Another—especially when it is obviously no use masquerading, and the Thermidorians are quick to recognize *ceux qui sont habillés en ouvrier*—is to insist, on the contrary, on the humbleness of one's condition in order to diminish one's political responsibility, and plead 'je n'ai pas voulu de mal', 'j'ai cru bien faire', 'je n'entendais rien à la chose publique', 'on m'a dit de faire une pétition . . ., une motion', 'j'ai voté comme on m'a dit de le faire', 'j'ai fait comme les autres citoyens', and so on. A great many former *meneurs* are now trying to move down to the subordinate rank of *menés*. Now it goes to the tune of: 'Je n'étois qu'un pauvre artiste, sans talens et sans lumières. Comment aurois-je entendu quelque-chose aux affaires publiques?',[2] now to the tune

[1] Mercier (*Néologie*, ii. 112) offers an unconsciously apt description of the France of the year III; under MANGEURS, we read: '. . . Un paysan de Montrouge, plein de bon sens, appelait la révolution française le combat des Mangeurs et des Mangés. . . .' There would be no doubt in which category one should place the Thermidorians, their feet well under the groaning table.

[2] '. . . Ces hommes . . . firent un crime à Bonnijoly de les avoir méprisés. Aussi fut-il incarcéré sous le nom odieux du complice de Robespierre. Un revendeur de tabac le complice de Robespierre! . . . Il est bon de vous faire observer . . . que, né dans les Montagnes des Cevennes, l'idiome de son pays ne s'accorde point avec celui de Nîmes, et qu'à peine peut-il se faire entendre en françois pour faire son petit négoce; semblable à un Allemand ignorant qu'on accuseroit d'avoir

of: 'Je ne m'occupois que de mon petit commerce pour faire vivre ma femme et mes enfans en bas âge' (and children, this year, are always *en bas âge*, some of them even appear to be younger than in the year II). A *compagnon maçon*, accused of previous *menées hébertistes*, writes in his defence, in the year III: 'ils disent qu'ils pensoient que je pouvois avoir des liaisons avec les ennemis [de la chose publique]; un malheureux maçon peut-il être soupçonné? J'avois assez à faire pour travailler à l'existence de trois petits individus et à celle de ma femme. . . .'[1] Children are likewise frequently invoked as witnesses to a recently discovered political innocence. The once-proud *sans-culotte* has now become the ignorant, deferential, almost whining, poor wretch, asking to be let off ('Have pity on my wife and children, Sir'), throwing himself on Thermidorian mercy. This was just what the *honnêtes gens* wanted him to do; for, in the language of the day, there were, too, accepted images of the former *sans-culottes*: the *meneurs*, the *dominateurs*, the *aboyeurs*, noisy, impudent, tyrannical rascals, out for themselves and their gang (people who, in normal times, would have been shouting for the *commissaires priseurs*, to drive up the bids, at the *Hôtel des Ventes*, their proper habitat); and, on the other hand, their henchmen, the *menés*, ignorant and brutish creatures who could not have been expected to know any better. It is the distinction made by a Lyon merchant, on the subject of the *mathevons*: 'd'une part des gens sans mœurs, gens sans moral, enfin des fripons, d'une autre part, des brutes manouvriers absolument ignorans . . .'.[2] The more the *brutes manouvriers* rolled in the mud, their hands outstretched, the more it pleased the Thermidorians. This, they would say, was the material out of which the Terror forged its instruments, these were the people who presumed to lord it over their betters (a favourite expression of the time is *s'être présumé de se mêler de la Révolution*). Such people could safely be forgiven, and by thus emphasizing the varying degree of responsibility between a minority of militants (*dominateurs*) and an amorphous mass of *pauvres hères* (another year III word), Thermidorian

voulu renverser la liberté par des discours françois . . .' (Bonnijoly au comité de législation, 26 fructidor an III, A.N. D III 86 d 1 17, comité de législation, Gard, Nîmes).

[1] A.N. F7 4678 d 2 (Doinelle, compagnon maçon, Section du Contrat Social).

[2] A.N. F1b II Rhône I (Barde, de Lyon, au Ministre, 27 vendémiaire an III).

clemency and charity—and the official trade mark of the new regime had been forgiveness and harmony—could increase the isolation of the former and complete the divisions within the popular movement. The Thermidorian authorities were specialists at what might be described as *la clémence injurieuse*.

A few former *sans-culotte* activists, however, refused either to get back into the ranks of the *honnêtes gens*, by admitting to what they had always been, or to go down on their knees and beg for Thermidorian forgiveness and the few crumbs of bourgeois charity. The year 1795 was the real test of militancy. Attacked, denounced, disarmed, these stalwarts fought back in the *assemblées*; arrested, they stuck to their guns, in their petitions from prison; and, as the reactionary character of the new regime became more and more apparent, very early on, in the course of the months of Brumaire and Frimaire year III, they felt less and less inclined to have any truck with the *nouveaux modérantistes*. They were both courageous and tremendously imprudent; convinced of their own righteousness, convinced too, so accustomed had they become to leadership, that it would be only a matter of time before they were back in the saddle, with a Terror fiercer than ever *à l'ordre du jour*, they took openly to threatening those who were the new masters, singing, in their favourite inns, the old songs, and outlining a programme that would make the Terror of the year II seem a very tame affair indeed. From their prisons emerged a stream of righteous indignation and of threats. Why were they being victimized, *eux, les sauveurs de la République*, while *émigrés* and other enemies of the Revolution were emerging and openly boasting of vengeance soon to be enjoyed? Yes, certainly, they were still *sans-culottes*, and proud of having been so long *sur la brèche*; they regretted nothing, had nothing to be ashamed of, having sacrificed their time and their families in the interests of public safety. And they recalled the perils and emergencies of the previous year, of which the Thermidorians, whose main purpose was to ensure what they described as *le retour au règne des lois*, did not at all wish to be reminded, more especially as many of their leaders had spent the emergency in prison. Already, in Nivôse year III, months before the massacres, a terrorist from Villefranche-sur-Saône is stated not to have 'discontinué depuis la révolution du 9 thermidor de corrompre l'esprit public en disant hautement dans des assemblées de commune que Robespierre étoit mort victime de la Révolution et de son patriotisme, que le parti qui dominoit actuellement étoit celui de l'aristocratie, que dans peu de tems le martyr Robespierre seroit panthéonisé . . .'.[1]

We find people using the same impetuous language all over the country, during the winter months. If the Thermidorians wanted to convince public opinion—and not only the *honnêtes gens*—that the terrorists were still dangerous, that, indeed, they were making active preparations to return to power, they had only to quote the militants themselves, who, from their habitual headquarters—inns or cafés known to all—sang and shouted their intentions through the winter night. Of course, what they said or sang, when in convivial company, and among themselves, may have been greatly exaggerated, or completely misreported, by hostile witnesses, out to ingratiate themselves with the new authorities; but many of the remarks attributed to them are altogether in accordance with what they themselves write in their petitions and addresses, as well as with an over-confidence that made them convinced that Thermidor was only a passing phase and that their time would soon come round again. A few were, in any case, too much compromised for any recantation to be worth while or acceptable.

This was particularly the case with those who, as employers, had used their position to build up a party among poor labourers and artisans. Of one such, a building contractor, it is stated in Brumaire year III: '. . . je dois ajouter qu'il a de fortes entreprises comme charpentier et que le besoin que les ouvriers ont de lui lui donne la faculté de [les faire] devenir des garçons charpentiers, des serruriers, des menuisiers, &ca.'[2] For such, there could be no for-

---

[1] Arch. Rhône 33 L 78* (comité de surveillance de Villefranche, séances des 17 et 22 nivôse an III). For similar examples of neo-terrorist boastfulness and threats, in Dijon, and, above all, in Salon, Saint-Chamas, and Martigues, where the former *sans-culotte* leaders appear to have been suicidally imprudent, to the extent of organizing nightly *farandoules*, to the tune of *vive les sans-culottes, vive la Terreur, la guillotine en permanence*, see Section II, p. 348.

[2] A.N. F7 4675 d 4 (Devèze, charpentier, section de la République, Marc-Antoine Bourdon au Comité de sûreté générale, 23 brumaire an III). See also F7 4659 d 5 (Damilot). Damilot, *marchand de vin*, former *commissaire aux accaparements*, former member of the *comité* of the Section des Gardes-Françaises, is described as 'moteur et conseil des pauvres ouvriers qui logent en grand nombre dans cette rue' [rue de l'Égoût]. His profession would make him a natural leader of the poor in his community. A similar case is that of Pierre-Jean Blette, member of the former *comité* of Bonne-Nouvelle, described as enjoying *une honnête aisance*, and 'employant 25 à 30 ouvriers'. He is a *fabricant de rubans* (A.N. F7 4603 d 5 Blette).

giveness; militants of this calibre, 'jouissant d'une armée si dangereuse', had little to hope for, as they stood out so far from among
the general mass of *sectionnaires*; but at least such spirited efforts
at self-justification, among so much breast-beating and so many
expressions of regret, are all the more refreshing for being rather
rare. Not that the historian should show any preference for those
who thus chose the stony path, rather than conform; for nothing
could be more natural than to seek to be Thermidorian in
Thermidorian times, and *sans-culotte* in *sans-culotte* ones. And
many of these irreconcilables were more misguided than
courageous. It would, in any case, be impudent for historians,
who risk nothing, to set up as moral judges and to make a great
virtue of fidelity.

This being said, the great advantage of the personal *dossier* of the
year III, as opposed to that of the year II, is that it enables the
historian to distinguish between the time-server, the eternally
orthodox, the cannon fodder of the revolutionary movement, and
the much rarer men of outstanding conviction, of signal bravery or
temerity, of chronic over-optimism, of obstinate conceit, who
emerge in the bitter conditions of defeat—though they will seldom
admit to defeat—and proscription (which they will accept as an
honour, as well as a testimony to their own importance). These
are the people who will turn up again and again in successive anti-
terrorist purges and in the daily reports addressed to the Minister
of Police. Some themselves chose the most rapid path to exile or
martyrdom; no other solution ever occurred to them. Others,
probably more numerous, because in the year II they had belonged
to certain institutions and had occupied certain posts, had exile or
martyrdom thrust upon them. It did not make much difference in
the end. Few of them would be allowed to survive; and, reading
their own apologia, one can appreciate why.

A popular movement needs to be studied over a period of time,
as well as in statistical depth through the various layers of social
composition. And its study should draw on all sources available:
first, those of collective interest, the minutes of popular institutions;
secondly, the reports of the police and of the other repressive
authorities; thirdly, the personal case histories, drawn up, in
particular circumstances, and to meet immediate needs, in the year
II or the year III, by people who were themselves actors in the
popular movement. Beyond 1795, the popular movement enters

into the night of history, occasionally to be glimpsed, in the brief, flickering light of the report of a police spy or of an official. It is doubtful whether, as far as France is concerned, there are other sources available. Most of the *sans-culottes* are too low in the social hierarchy to figure in the papers of the *notariat* (these might, however, be explored to reveal the reality which a certain number of provincial so-called *sans-culottes* attempted to hide), though the individual tragedies that overtook many of them might be further illustrated in the records of bankruptcy suits. Individuals can be pursued into the army or through the courts. But after 1795 the subject itself almost entirely disappears, at least in the form of a recognizable, even national, movement. It is possible, for instance, to study *sans-culotterie* nationally; for, over a few months, it existed nationally. But such a study would have to be undertaken with extreme caution: there is a great divergence between Parisian and provincial *sans-culottes*, not only in terms of origin, but even in those of political aims (the Lyon revolt of May 1793 was *sans-culotte*-inspired and very much *sans-culotte*—far more so than the movements in the Paris Sections—in content). But, at least at that time, there were institutions common to the movement all over France. From 1795 onwards, however, there is no movement, there are no popular institutions, only tiny groups of harassed militants, while popular protest takes on forms too sporadic, too localized, too intermittent, for it to be possible to study it on any other than a regional level. Both Thermidor and the Directory were very much 'regional' regimes, there was no single centre of power in the year III, each *députation* acting like a sovereign state, in the interests of its own Department, each municipality looking to itself, to purchase grain on the Baltic market, and to outbid its neighbours in the home areas of provisioning.

If this was so on the government side, how much more was it true of the opposition, or oppositions, so many, so varied, so intolerant of one another, with which the Thermidorians and the Directorials had to contend! France from 1795 to 1798 is a jungle of provincial egoisms, and the popular movement cannot be perceived except in the setting of a commune or of a District. For instance popular royalism took on an 'ultra' complexion in the south-east and in the valley of the Rhône, but elsewhere it tended to constitutionalism, under the leadership of moderates.

13. LEBOIS AND BABEUF

The only time it is possible to assess what has survived of *sans-culotte* and Jacobin militancy, on a national scale, is with the repression that followed the Babeuf Plot. Babeuf had kept detailed lists of subscribers to his journal, he and Germain had also drawn up *listes des hommes aptes à commander*, for each Department, while the police completed the set with a third list of *hommes aptes à surveiller*. By comparing all three one can at least discover what has become of the militants in the conditions of the year IV. The list of subscribers is the most valuable because the most genuine: people subscribed because they wanted to. Babeuf made the mistake of believing that people who subscribed to his paper would be pre-pared to risk themselves in his plot, when most of them were merely malcontents who liked to read an opposition point of view, not conspirators. The other lists are of more doubtful value as signposts to the fate of militancy. Babeuf and his companions were ridiculously over-optimistic, thinking that almost everyone who had been arrested for terrorism in the year III could be counted on. In consequence, they reckoned on the potential support of as many as five thousand former *sans-culottes* for Paris alone (some-thing like the number of those who had been arrested after Ger-minal and Prairial, in the year III) and at least fifty thousand for the Departments—a possible estimate for those singled out as former militants at the same period. Indeed, there are indications that, when counting up their likely adherents, the *babouvistes* simply had recourse to the printed lists of *désarmement* drawn up by the Thermidorian *comités civils*. It was reasonable enough to suppose that people who had suffered anything up to six or nine months' imprisonment would not have any particular love for the bourgeois Republic; but it was unreasonable to think that, after so many hard-ships, most of them would be prepared to go through the whole process again, at much greater risk, and in a completely different form of militancy. Basically, Babeuf confused former militants, who had always been loyal to the Convention and who had acted in open assembly, with present conspirators who were being asked to take part in a secret sedition. His calculations, in any case, were never put to the test; and the principal interest of the second list is to indicate what were the hopes of the conspirators. Those who had the misfortune to be named on it had not been consulted.

Militancy this time was thrust surreptitiously upon them, a poor service to men who had already paid heavily for what they had undertaken voluntarily and *en connaissance de cause*. Inclusion on Babeuf's list would later earn some of them deportation to the Isles or to Cayenne, in the year IX.

As for the third list, that drawn up by the police, it was copied almost entirely from the second; the police were prepared to take Babeuf's word for it and to treat these people as if they really had been potential conspirators. Both Babeuf and the police were looking backwards to the year II. Babeuf copied the police of the year III, and the police of the year IV copied Babeuf. Ultimately all we can learn from all three lists is where certain militants were living at the beginning of the Directory, how many were still refugees in Paris, how many had returned to their homes, and how many had escaped massacre in the year III (quite a useful directory of militancy, in rather a negative sense), and what they liked to read—information of more positive interest. These people were not necessarily the hard core of the irreconcilables; more probably they were fairly well-educated men who liked to read something that did not play to the tune of the *honnêtes gens*; Lebois having been suppressed, Babeuf would do. Most of the names are familiar to the historian of the year II; which is not surprising, because they had been gathered on the basis of their owners' activities in Sectionary politics or in repressive institutions during that year.

14. *LE MAL FRANÇAIS*

Various possible approaches have now been suggested to the study of the popular movement in a given country, over a given, limited period (long enough, however, to allow for the inclusion of an emerging new generation of militants and protesters). The historian has been put on guard against the language and assumptions of the authorities, against the habitual priorities of police action and the value and the limitations of the individual *dossier*, of the personal apologia, as well as of the military *curriculum vitae*, as material for more detailed research. It may be objected that this approach is over-suspicious and too mechanical: that we have, in fact, caught the French disease, which is to read into every assumption and every interpretation of the French police and of the French authorities a depth of calculation and guile that may never have existed; that, in short, we have acquired, from over-frequentation of police and judicial sources, the habit of intellectualizing about straightforward matters and of writing our history in the knowing, nudging way (*On sait, hein! On est au courant, hein! On ne nous fait pas marcher, hein!*) in which *Le Canard enchaîné* writes of the *coulisses* of contemporary politics. Could it not be, after all, that the police should be taken at their word, that they were simply trying to do their job properly, that there were in fact *meneurs, signes de ralliement*, and distributions of money on the occasion of each riot, that infernal machines really were found under the beds where the police claimed to have found them? Might it not be the case that the Lyonnais were especially given to political violence, that some of them played a leading part in the White Terror, travelling south to take part in massacre? Or that certain murders actually were committed by Nîmois, that it is a reasonable assumption that political crimes are more likely to be committed by strangers than by natives, and that domestics, itinerant workers, and *gens sans aveu* were particularly dangerous? Or that the police knew better than we do, as they were there and we were not, that, far from trying to pull the wool over the eyes of the magistrates in order to secure the conviction of those they considered ought to be guilty, far from vindictively persecuting unfortunates because they came from a certain trade, a certain province, or a certain part of a city, they were merely trying to bring in people whom they had every reason to believe guilty? Are we not being over-sensitive in drawing attention to the differences in the meaning of words—and, consequently, in assumptions, as used in the year II and in the following year? Could it not be that most people who described themselves as carpenters, in either year, were carpenters?

Other objections spring to mind. Of course, as witnesses of popular behaviour, the Thermidorians are suspect; they had experienced, during the previous year, the effects of popular government, and had undergone what has been aptly described as *la grande peur de la bourgeoisie française*. Their attitude to the common people was similar to that of Duval, the memorialist of the *jeunesse dorée*: the revolutionary rank-and-file was recruited from the poorest streets of the Gravilliers, while the militants who were to lead the *comités révolutionnaires* were hairdressers, discharged servants, corrupt lawyers, tanners, and rag-and-bone merchants.[1] Other witnesses—or persons who describe themselves as such—have elaborated on similar themes, adding, to Duval's selection, *portiers*, a great favourite with Mercier and to be recommended to any police, the much-quoted *savetiers*, whom Mercier respects as men of sound sense, but who were constantly picked upon by middle-class contemporaries, no doubt on account of their habitual working position—what right had these squatting creatures to loll in a requisitioned armchair in green silk? There were the usual accompaniment of *décrotteurs* and *tondeurs de chiens*, who likewise spent their working lives on their haunches. One expects too—and finds —a percentage of *brocanteurs*, *fripiers*, barrow-boys, pedlars, *commissionnaires*, street singers, jugglers, magicians, alchemists, readers in cards, patent-medicine vendors, and other, similar, noisy and ridiculous people. The mixture will not be complete without a sprinkling of ex-monks and crooked lawyers.

This, then, is the Thermidorian picture of *sans-culotte* rule. Or rather it is the picture which the Thermidorians sought to accredit with contemporaries and which so many others, in their wake and using the material they assembled, have attempted to accredit with historians. Yet there is little reality to the Thermidorian show-case. Of a hundred and forty members of revolutionary committees of the year II, we have found only two *savetiers*. There are, however, eleven *cordonniers* (much grander people); only four *perruquiers*; seven former servants (five from a single Section in the *noble Faubourg*); only two *fripiers*; only two *brocanteurs*; only one tanner; no *décrotteur*; no *tondeur de chien*; no street singer. We do find, however, thirteen people engaged in the drink trade (*marchands de vin, limonadiers, aubergistes*); fifteen people in building, several of them contractors; ten *peintres* of various sorts; nine watch-makers, jewellers, or goldsmiths; eight bakers or pastrycooks; seven grocers; seven tailors; three doctors; three *officiers de santé*; four dentists; a few *tonneliers, vanniers, chaudronniers, poëliers*; five *commis*; and the occasional printer, compositor, miniaturist,

---

[1] Georges Duval, op. cit., on the subject of the *comités révolutionnaires*, ii. 33: '... Ce ramas de misérables était, à Paris, et à peu près dans toutes les grandes villes, presque toujours présidé par un perruquier, ou par un huissier, un recors, ou bien encore par un ancien valet de chambre de bonne maison qui avait dénoncé et fait guillotiner son maître. ... On vit aussi à Paris quelques savetiers élevés à la présidence.... Le tanneur Guibon présidoit le comité ... de la section des Sans-culottes, composé presque en entier de chiffonniers....'

schoolmaster, doll manufacturer, fan-maker.[1] In short, a general picture that bears very little resemblance to the *petit monde* described, with such an air of authority, by Duval and others. But the fact that both the *honnêtes gens* and young *fils de famille*, *clercs de procureur*, and other *embusqués* had often been the victims of *sans-culotte* rule does not automatically eliminate them as witnesses of the popular movement of the year II. No doubt these people really had been as intolerable, as interfering, as brutal, and as ugly as this type of literature sought to suggest; certainly they had managed to make themselves exceedingly offensive to a vast number of their fellow citizens. It was probably no great concern to their Thermidorian chroniclers whether they had been up against cooks or watch-makers, *vidangeurs* or fan-makers; what they had mainly recalled was that their persecutors were insolent and brutal, had no manners, and behaved in a grotesque manner. It was natural enough to compensate for the humiliations of the year II by ridiculing their former persecutors, *les maîtres d'hier*, from the safety of the year III. The Thermidorians were not setting themselves up as historians of social composition; but they can be relied upon to convey the ambience of popular government and the fear and indignation of its victims. Triumphantly to catch the Thermidorians out with their fabricated armies of rag-and-bone men, tanners, hairdressers, and servants is a pursuit so easy as to be scarcely worth undertaking.

What is worth doing, however, is to attempt to recapture their assumptions about an experiment in popular government that had been principally directed against people of their own kind; there can have been few leading Thermidorians, few members of the *jeunesse dorée*, who did not have a relative who, at one time or another, had encountered *sans-culotte* justice and been faced by half a dozen rough men with drooping moustaches, sitting under the bust of Marat, behind a table covered with a green baize cloth and laden with scattered papers. The experience in itself, whatever the outcome, was not something one would be likely easily to forget.

[1] These figures are based on an exhaustive examination of the personal *dossiers* in the *Série alphabétique F*7 (Papers of the Committee of General Security, in the A.N.).

15. CONCLUSION

Many of these objections then are quite valid. There is a danger in crediting too much to the guile and to the subtlety of the police, people often as stupid as the *gendarmes*. And there is no reason why the Thermidorians should not have been able to describe their former persecutors accurately; they had, after all, seen a great many of them from the wrong side of the table. But our principal purpose has been to identify and to explain the presuppositions of the police, the assumptions of the *honnêtes gens*, and the standardized language of the subordinate agents of the Revolutionary Government, rather than to decide whether these assumptions were or were not correct. The important fact is the sheer repetition of certain affirmations. It can hardly be likely that so many Lyonnais really were the sort of people the police assumed they were, and one does know, for instance, that Duval was talking nonsense—very few domestics, *savetiers*, hairdressers, and *chiffonniers* exercised revolutionary functions in 1793–4. One also knows, from the literature of the year III, that these were just the people best suited to the Thermidorian image of the terrorist.

This is of interest in itself, for we are not concerned here with the actual history of the popular movement but rather with its first historians. The aim, at this stage, is to underline what witnesses thought about the popular movement and to suggest why they should attribute militancy to some trades rather than to others. Of course the police were not always wrong, wilfully misguided, or deliberately deceitful; they would not have been much good if they had been. But it is as well to know what they were after. Certainly the Thermidorians could sometimes be accurate; but it is important to recall that they were not disinterested observers, that they had a horror of the common people, and that, for them, anyone who was not of their own class would look very like the proverbial ungrateful servant, the wretched *savetier*, or the rag-and-bone man. They were taking both a moral and a physical view of the *petit peuple*; the domestic-who-denounced-his-Master fits the book, just as the ugly, villainous-looking inhabitant of the rue au Maire fits the book; the *chiffonnier* has the advantage of being, and looking, filthy; the tanner works in a smelly trade, and himself smells; domestic servants are cunning rascals, *perruquiers* are proverbially impudent, and vastly conceited. (And is not the *sans-*

culotte movement a piece of colossal impudence?) As long as we realize all this, there is no reason why we should reject their evidence out of hand.

Furthermore, army officers are not always liars; many who claimed to have participated in such-and-such a *journée* no doubt did so, but they cannot all have done so. Finally, we have attempted to read between the lines of a language that, both in 1793–4 and in 1795, and again during the Empire, has become so formalized as to be almost meaningless; yet behind this verbal façade there are various reticences, various insinuations, that are often easy to discover. This is not an attempt to lay down hard and fast rules about a problem that is both elusive and constantly altering. The intention has been rather to suggest certain lines of approach, to put out a few warning signs when things might not be quite what they seem to be, and to emphasize, from a considerable body of evidence, drawn from widely scattered areas of France, that when, up and down the country, a great many people are saying the same thing, in the same words, it is not necessarily true, but it is significant. For we have nowhere quoted from isolated instances; and we have been sufficiently subjected to the monotonous, insistent language of the year II and to the almost equally formalized vocabulary of the Thermidorians to be able to distinguish between the voice of collective orthodoxy, and that of anguished, individual indignation. The letters that Vincent wrote to his wife on the eve of his execution, those that the unfortunate Ducroquet addressed to his mistress in similar conditions, the anonymous appeals to insurrection that appeared at night on walls in the *quartier des Halles*, do not need any interpreting; they are self-explicit.

Nor is this the place to discuss the conventions of popular language, save in so far as they apply to the *sans-culottes* when describing themselves, or to the *sabreurs* and their female accomplices when boasting of their exploits. The always exaggerated language of the common people belongs by right to the realms of rumour, panic, fear, violence, and revenge; it reaches its fullest, most catastrophic expression in conditions of dearth and near-famine and disease, or in the terrible 'pay-off' of the White Terror in the south-east. The Revolutionary Government knew what it was doing, knew how dangerous words could be, when it forbade the *sans-culottes* to talk about food shortage, rationing, repression, and religion, and when it decreed that women should not have a voice in the discussions of the *assemblées générales* and of the *sociétés populaires*. Popular language can then be reserved for the analysis of popular reactions to dearth, for the role of women in popular protest, and for the mentality of the White Terrorist.

The police authorities, in insisting on the role of leadership and on the search for the *signes de ralliement*, are in fact subscribing to an interpretation of riot and of all forms of popular protest long a favourite with historians—both of extreme Right and of various socialist and Marxist tendencies—and most commonly described as that of the 'role of associations': freemasonry, secret societies, trade unions, the clergy, national or provincial pressure groups, political organizations, and so on. Such an interpretation assumes that a popular movement cannot be self-led and that the common people are too stupid to look after things for themselves.[1] It is a thesis that, for obvious reasons, has always had a strong appeal to the right-wing mind and to the intellectual, two studies in arrogance. But, apart from drawing attention to it *en passant* when referring to the assumptions of the police, it is not intended in this study to analyse popular movements from this angle. For France and the period under discussion it is hardly relevant; for unless we are prepared to consider temporary, accidental institutions like the Sections, which were put to a political use far removed from what had originally been intended for them, or the collective strike action of transport workers, as 'associations', it is clear that the thesis has no application to our subject. The police, as we have seen, used the word in the widest possible sense, for any coming together of more than a dozen persons for any purpose whatsoever, so that a funeral or a wedding could be so described. But this is not what anti-popular or intellectual historians have in mind. In the history of the French Revolution, the role of 'associations' can be discerned only in the organization of the *Compagnies* that directed the murder gangs of the White Terror, or of the *chauffeurs*, neither of them particularly secret, nor intellectual. It is, in short, the sort of false

---

[1] Not unexpectedly, Mercier takes a similar view. Under the word AGITATEUR (*Néologie*, i. 17) he writes: 'Le peuple ne peut jamais être que trompé sur son intérêt et sur sa volonté, dans les associations particulières où l'on parle en son nom, sans mission et sans caractère. Qui composera ces associations? des oisifs, des mécontens, des ambitieux, des Agitateurs, des ennemis de la chose publique ayant pour mandat de tout bouleverser. . . . Tel Agitateur d'un peuple est un grand homme; tel autre n'est qu'un misérable stipendié. Les époques, les intentions, le succès, imprimeront à ce mot les acceptations les plus opposées. . . .'

problem that might make a good examination question, but that is not likely to illuminate our understanding of a late eighteenth-century or an early nineteenth-century popular movement. It can be rejected out of hand.

As 'popular movement' implies an element of organized protest, we have been more concerned with the sources for the exploration of riot, disorder, violence, and popular political organization than with those that bear more directly on the everyday life of the common people, on pauperization, disease, and death, those negative factors that may explain the disappearance of a popular movement and that will be explored with reference to dearth and the fear of shortage. The problems of interpretation that have been tentatively suggested apply to the French police, to French informers, to the French army, the French popular movement, and to existing French records. It would be unlikely that the principal problems facing the police of another country would be the same as those that exercised the police of revolutionary France. The police in France are an important—even a principal—source of information. Elsewhere this may not be so. And France, having experienced a Revolution that was unique, formed revolutionary institutions that were unique, possesses sources that are also unique. It is very unlikely that a *fonds* on the scale of that of the Committee of General Security or one like those of so many *Archives départementales*, as far as the Revolution is concerned, could be discovered in any other country. The historian of popular protest in France is a privileged person. But no two Terrors are alike, methods of *surveillance* and repression vary from country to country, and so do the degree and the forms of popular militancy and the flashpoints of riot. (One could not imagine an animal provoking a terrible riot in France, at any period, yet, in India, many disturbances have been inadvertently so caused.) Each national or provincial society will secrete its own characteristic sources of violence and produce its own traditional form of protest; by failing to understand this one of the Neapolitan ministers of Charles III brought on the Mutiny of Esquilache. A comparative history of popular protest, over a given period, is certainly possible; but it is unlikely to reveal anything other than differences, or similarities too self-evident to be worth discovering. (Grain riots, as Professor Rudé has suggested, will everywhere tend to take place on market days, near or on the market, will tend to be directed against mills and millers, cornfactors and State granaries, and so on.) The present study is about France and French difficulties.

Certain problems of interpretation, however, may be generalized. Every police is likely to have its pre-ordained victims, its favourite customers, its habitual sources of information, and its own standards for interpreting them. These must be discovered, if that is possible; and if it is not there will usually be enough indications for the historian to be able to hazard a reasonable guess. Informers, too, have everywhere their own problems, and in most places they can be relied upon to make a little go a long way and to produce a great deal of information, however worthless. The military, again, have their own way of looking at things. They will rarely, though it has occurred in recent times, adopt either the perspectives or the attitudes or the methods of the police. *Dénonciateurs* and *dénonciatrices* are, unfortunately, an international phenomenon; any period of war or civil disturbance or acute shortage is likely to stimulate that vocation, while portresses, wherever they exist, are sure to be the most zealous auxiliaries of the police. The habit of planting informers in prisons is ancient and universal. Finally, as the history of popular protest is generally also that of failure, disenchantment, and ultimate hopelessness, so also popular protest is more often backward-looking than heading towards *les lendemains qui chantent* (and these too have been a long time in coming).

One should not ask too much of such history, one should not apply to it intellectual standards, or approach it in a spirit of patronizing arrogance, but rather in one of compassion. The historian who goes slumming is bound to have the door slammed in his face; he will never be able to emulate *le Passe-Muraille*. To analyse something called *l'esprit public* is not an exercise in public opinion polls; and it is impudent to believe that it is possible to remove the popular brain, take it to pieces, look at the pieces, then put it together again. Popular history, as Restif knew, and Louis Chevalier knows, has to be walked as well as read; nor is it the sort of history that can be speedily written. It took Albert Soboul well over ten years to complete his research on the Paris *sans-culottes* and to produce the definitive work on their movement. It is a subject that requires an intimate knowledge of both ends of society—popular habits and motivations, the fears and assumptions of Authority—and an intimate understanding of what each side thinks of the other, how much each knows of the other; for this is always a *pas de deux*, and sometimes, as Soboul reminds us, a *pas de trois*.[1] It is, therefore, a doubtful subject for the Anglo-Saxon type of doctoral thesis, and lends itself more to the massive requirements of the French *doctorat-ès-lettres*, which, along with Soboul, has produced Pierre Caron on the September Massacres and Louis Chevalier on the population of Paris in the nineteenth century. It would, then, be a pity if the fact that 'popular movements' have now become respectable were to produce a spate of half-hearted assaults on problems that are more in need of a loving care and of a great deal of imagination. At least we can congratulate ourselves on the fact that it is no longer bad company to keep and that the historian who keeps it is less likely to be upbraided by another Sir Lewis Namier: 'Why do you bother with these *bandits*?'[2]

[1] See Section II, pp. 120–1.
[2] Quoted by R. B. Rose, whose thesis on the *Enragés* was examined by Namier at the University of Manchester.

II

'POPULAR MOVEMENTS', POPULAR PROTEST, AND REPRESSION IN FRANCE 1793–1818

'Qui assemble le peuple, l'émeut.'
(The Prefect of the Bas-Rhin, in a letter to the
Minister of the Interior, 27 July 1812)

II

POPULAR MOVEMENTS, POPULAR PROTEST, AND REPRESSION IN FRANCE 1793-1815

PART ONE
THE PATTERN OF POPULAR PROTEST
1795-1815

'A la Révolution il faut du sang.'
(*Attributed to a terrorist from Salon*)

I. POPULAR VIOLENCE

To some extent at least, any revolution is likely to be a popular revolution; for it is impossible to overthrow an existing order—and most orders destroyed by revolutions have been repressive—by force, without at least the physical participation of a section of the common people, whether as a rebellious crowd or as a group of mutinous soldiers. Revolutions are opened—and closed—by violence. The violence is mostly provided, at least to begin with, by the common people of the towns, or by the rural poor; later, as new repressive organizations are formed to replace those swept away or dissolved, the violence may become more controlled, and may be put into the service of government and even used against those who provided the initial force to topple the previous order of things. But, as long as the exercise of government remains a matter of dispute between various groups, the opportunity and the temptation for recourse to popular violence will remain. It is likely always to take some time to push or ease the people out of a revolutionary situation once they are no longer needed. They may, it is true, be temporarily dismissed, but if the revolution is prolonged and runs into such emergencies as war, defeat, invasion, and rebellion, they are likely to come back, angrier, more vengeful, and in larger numbers. For their bodies are needed, either on the frontiers and in the armies to defend the regime and push back the forces of counter-revolution, or at home to protect the capital and the other cities against hidden and open enemies. As the tempo of violence and terror increases, the role of the people will increase correspondingly. But, if the pace of the revolution can be slackened and the new regime stabilized at home and abroad, the people can

be disbanded and sent back home, the need for violence will decrease, and what violence is retained can be exercised by specialists.

The principal weapon of the people, then, is collective violence,
or the threat of it—more often the threat than the thing itself. But
violence, though popular-operated, may not necessarily be used
in the interest of the people, though they will always provide the
physical force. A riot, once started, can be canalized by politicians
into directions that suit their own purposes and that may have little
relation to popular grievances. The people are indispensable, but
they can be deceived: violence can be mobilized, enlisted, by the
government, or by factions; through the medium of the press,
journalists can designate to popular violence specific enemies who
are not especially dangerous to the popular cause, while leaving
unchanged general conditions that weigh most heavily on the
urban poor. Violence can so often be the alibi for the absence of any
coherent policy. It will always have a popular appeal which will
become more insistent the longer the revolutionary crisis lasts and
the more enemies of the people the crisis raises up, month by
month: a number of skilful journalists and ambitious demagogues
raised themselves up on the shoulders of violence and made their
careers out of it; some of them—many thought rather suitably—
were later destroyed by it.

Of course, violence was not the only weapon of the common
people. But the threat of it was always present, not only in the
crudest form of popular discontent, the riot or the demonstration,
when the people surrounded the Convention, as they did confus-
ingly often—so many *journées*, so many quasi-*journées*, that did not
quite come off, or only half occurred, though they still get a date—
pointing their guns on the building, even if they did not actually
light their fuses. Perhaps they never intended to; but this is not
the kind of question that the sane legislator is ever likely to put to
the test. For the eye-witness, as for the historian after him, the
prudent course was to suppose that people who were pointing guns
were likely to fire them if they did not get what they wanted; the
best thing was to keep them waiting as long as possible, so that they
went home to dinner, taking their guns with them.

Even in the most sophisticated forms of popular political
activism—*le mouvement sans-culotte, le mouvement sectionnaire*—
violence was always just under the surface. There were frequent
hints at *la juste colère du peuple*; orthodoxy was enforced by fear,

thanks to the system of voting by show of hand; the 48 Paris Sections, if sufficiently pushed, might combine, on some specific issue—they were always talking about it—to force the hand of the Revolutionary Government; the *sectionnaires* were constantly asking for more terror and more repression, believing that violence held the cure for most evils. The Sections themselves were powerful, even dangerous, because they controlled the artillery companies and could give the orders to trundle out the cannon *pour sauver encore une fois la République* (there was a lot of this) as a final argument when all else failed. They could do so, but at the height of their political effectiveness they very seldom did; for the *sectionnaires* ultimately showed considerable reluctance to use force against the *représentation nationale*—to do so seemed an act of political cannibalism—as long as anything was expected of it. They still preferred persuasion, though the persuading might be brutally worded. Even in the year III, they hesitated when the balance of force was still wholly on their side. We cannot then speak of crude violence, at least when dealing with the more organized political manifestations of the popular movement. It was violence tempered with unstated conventions and with a considerable respect for revolutionary legality; for such a thing existed and the *sans-culottes* really believed in it.[1]

Both contemporaries and several generations of liberal or reactionary historians were shocked by the spectacle of popular violence during the French Revolution. Contemporaries feared that these new, unexpected, and unpredictable forms of violence might be used against property-holders and respectable people, rather than against poachers and lawbreakers. In fact, what seems to have shocked contemporaries and historians alike is that the violence should have been popular (and, by implication, lawless, brutish, chaotic, undirected). Mercier, in 1797, frequently refers to the violent language of the common people, rich in incitation to murder, varied too in cannibalistic metaphor—'j'aimerais te manger le foie', 'j'aimerais t'ouvrir le ventre et te manger les tripes', 'je voudrais manger la tête d'un bourgeois', 'mangeons une bonne fressure d'aristocrate',[2] and so on—and he describes the evolution

---

[1] See the very pertinent remarks of M. Sydenham (*The French Revolution*, 1965) on the subject of the popular respect for the Convention and for the recognized rules of 'revolutionary legality'.

[2] See note A, p. 331.

of this popular violence in its verbal expressions: 'Les mots *car-nage, sang, mort, vengeance*, cet ABC de l'idiome jacobite [*vengeance*, in fact, belongs by right to the Thermidorian period, even on the admission of the Thermidorian local authorities] est répété, crié, hurlé . . . par la *Huaille*. La *Huaille* a régné pendant près de quinze mois, a despotisé la ville. . . .' Referring to the verb *lanterner*, he observes: 'Ce mot signifioit autrefois perdre son tems à ne rien faire . . . au commencement de la révolution, il signifioit pendre un homme à une lanterne. *Guillotiner* et *guillotine* ont pris un tel ascendant que ces mots ont totalement effacé ceux de *lanterne* et de *lanterner*. . . .'[1]

J'ai entendu [he claims to recollect] crier à mon oreille: 'Que les Français périssent, pourvu que la liberté triomphe!' J'en ai entendu un autre s'écrier dans une section: 'Oui, je prendrois ma tête par les cheveux, je la couperois, et l'offrant au despote, je lui dirois: Tyran, voici l'action d'un homme libre.' Ce sublime de l'extravagance étoit composé pour les classes populacières, il a été entendu, il a réussi. . . .

We may recall the women of the people, as depicted by *la Lanterne Magique*, eating the 'corps nuds et palpitans de leurs victimes'; and this was the language which, in the year III, changed sides, to be used by former terrorists when describing the horrors of the White Terror; in Pluviôse of that year, the survivors of the first wave of massacres in Nîmes—and the future victims of the next—describe the scene: 'Chacun de ces infortunés a souffert mille morts avant d'expirer, on les mutila, et les assassins couverts de sang portoient et élevoient en trophées les membres encore palpitans qu'ils venoient de couper. . . .' There is by then a standard vocabulary of massacre. A jeweller from the Section des Lombards is accused, in a Thermidorian report, 'de s'être flatté d'avoir coupé dix-huit têtes' in September 1792, and, whatever we make of this popular boastfulness, there is no doubt as to the intentions of the man who made the report. They are as clear as those of Mercier and the lantern slide lecturer. All conveniently forgot the violence of others—of the old royal government, of the old royal army, and of *la Royale*, with its barbarous punishments; of the old penal system and the *bagne*, with its ball and chain and similar refinements; of the old police ordinances and the language of the old administration, which, when addressed to the common people, could express itself only in threats and in the promise of retribution; of the treat-

[1] See note B, p. 332.

ment of Protestant children, especially in the Généralité de Rouen; of the old ruling class, and of their servants; of the Parlements, and of the *basoche*; of the cavalier of the *maréchaussée*; of the *Garde française*, so proud of his proficiency in killing quickly and hardly admissible into the inner sanctum of regimental solidarity until he had a corpse or two to his credit; of the hussar and the dragoon; of the sailor, and of the *guet*—just as everyone often tends to ignore the violence of 1795 and the years following and to forget that Terror could be White as well as Blue. Nor do they ask themselves how else the people could exercise their will and get their grievances seen to.

Certainly an enraged crowd, a group of rioters in full cry, the repeated invitation of *A mort!* screamed like a litany, the bestiality of massacre and lynching, the near-cannibalism of some women and a very few male rioters, are repellent, dreadful, hideous, and above all depressing, just as the corpses that are strewn so copiously in every print, patriotic or counter-revolutionary, of the great revolutionary *journées* or of the great massacres are absolutely inadmissible, whatever their clothing, whichever their uniform, just as severed heads and headless bodies cry out endlessly against the Revolution and all its works.

Certainly, too, what is so often clothed over and 'historicized' as something called the 'popular movement' (how much is the historian's terminology dominated by thought of syllabus or by the search for a chapter heading?) was frequently cruel and cowardly, base and vengeful, barbaric and not at all pretty to watch.[1] Professor Rudé's Crowd is somehow altogether too respectable; one hesitates to credit all these worthy shopkeepers and all these honest apprentices, family men too, with such horrors, and, in identifying the assailants, one is in danger of leaving the assailed out of the picture. Any honest historian of popular movements—and especially those of the French Revolution—must at times be seized with doubts. Is he not attempting to steer away from a violence that, on close inspection, becomes unbearable? Is he not trying to find excuses for brutality and murder? Is he not taking refuge in the convenient jargon of collective behaviourism to explain, to rationalize, massacre? Is there not something indecent, obscene, on his part, thus to pause, for so long, among yellowed sheets that describe, in the stilted language of French law, the

[1] See note C, p. 332.

details of a village lynching, or of a Christmas Day brawl ending in bloodshed? Is he not trying to get it both ways—the exhilaration of riot, experienced in the safety of a record office? Is he not making his *homme révolutionnaire* gentler, kinder, more tolerant, more whimsical, than he really was? Is he not trying to take the sting out of the *massacreur* by emphasizing the conceit, the *naïveté*, and the credulity of the *sans-culotte*, even if the one is not, in a particular instance, the other? Should not he, who, in fact, would never march behind the banner, would always stay at home, or who would be the first to run at the sound of firing, keep away from popular protest altogether and take refuge in the History of Parliament? Most historians of the French Revolution must have asked some of these questions, at one time or another, and especially in moments when they have been glutted with horror. And it would of course be both dishonest and misleading to represent the 'popular movement' as a study in rumbustious good fellowship, enthusiasm, generosity, fraternity, and hope, or as an early groping towards various forms of socialism, while leaving out of account the violence.

Yet this violence is not so odious and inadmissible as that of war or of diplomacy; it was never gratuitous, nor was it ever exclusive to any one class—or any one party: all classes, all parties were enthusiastic advocates of violence when there was a good chance of using it against their immediate enemies, though they tended to discover the advantages of mercy when they looked like being on the losing side. Just as riot is never an exclusive occupation (at least in Europe), just as the crowd is an evanescent, fleeting thing, so violence, in its physical form, is only incidental in a revolutionary movement rich in every possible element. The *septembriseur* was active for, at most, three days; but he had a lifetime as a shoemaker, a butcher, a shopkeeper. The blacksmith's hammer, which beat away so insistently and with such clangour that smithies had to be in backyards, from 5 a.m. to 8 p.m. in summer, from 7 a.m. to 6 p.m. in winter (no wonder the *sans-culotte* movement had the best run for its money in the autumn and winter months!), might be used once in a century on a human skull; and the butchers' apprentices, who so constantly wielded the axe, the chopper, and the knife, and whose appearance was so fearful, are said to have been the gentlest of souls, save when, rarely, roused. Violence is never excusable; but it is the job of the revolutionary historian to make it understandable—and this is perhaps already half-way to an excuse—to understand it himself, watch it rise and fall, and to keep it in its proper place, which is not on the dust-cover of a book concerned with the common people.

A much greater problem than these personal and moral ones is to estimate which types of violence were considered permissible, and which were not, in popular and in revolutionary terms. For violence was not born fully armed *tous crocs dehors* in 1789; nor did it go out of revolutionary France in 1794 or in 1799. It is always there, it always, unfortunately, has to be lived with, and it is always changing its forms. In the period under consideration, it ranged from the drunken and verbal, from fear and panic, from calculated incitement to murder, from clueless mad rumour, from carefully phrased threats, to the bloodless violence of most *journées*, to the bloody holocaust of the Tuileries, to prison blood-baths, to rural lynchings, rigged trials, and judicial murders, the death labels so generously enlarged upon by Saint-Just and Robespierre, the language of Thermidorian class vengeance, individual murders that had nothing at all to do with the Revolution (though they tended rather to be put out of business by the collective violence of the period), to private suicides (that had a lot to do with the Revolution), to religious savagery and anti-religious atrocity. Its victims were, at least by modern standards, limited in number, and, as far as the violence of the common people was concerned, were more often wood and stone, glass and china, than flesh and blood.

We must not make too much of violence, at least in its crudest form: like the Terror, like meat, it was a rare luxury, a week-end affair, or the accident of Feast Days and anniversaries. (The Revolution attempted, vainly, to cut down on the former, but multiplied the latter, the anniversary of past violence becoming the pretext for new violence.) It was much more talked about than done, and it is its comparative rarity, not its frequency, that makes it so mysterious. And the common people were not altogether to blame: they had been brought up in a bad school by the old rural police; and they were taught in a worse one by the Revolutionary Government of the year II. Later, in 1795, they had violence forced upon them; there was no other weapon left. And once the faubourg—all the faubourgs—had been disarmed, the only hope was the Infernal Machine, though this was a form of violence favoured by individual enthusiasts. It was not in the popular tradition, and came from abroad, probably from Italy. Violence and riot are one aspect—the most hopeless—of the popular movement. But as the popular movement was itself largely hopeless, they must figure large in the history of this period.

2. URBAN AND RURAL RIOT

The history of the popular movement, in its most elemental, crudest, and most visible form, is that of the crowd, or riot, both urban and rural, though it may well be objected that a series of disconnected riots, spread over a period of six or seven years and in response to immediate and generally unrelated stimuli, can hardly be described as a 'movement'. The difficulty here is that without riot there is very little left to write about. Save for a brief period of effective political activism in 1793–4, the 'popular movement' could only express itself either through the food riot or through attempted 'coalitions'. As these were illegal, they were considered by the authorities as 'riotous assemblies' and so also eventually took the form of riot, or else of monster petitions that, since they brought many petitioners together in one place, would again be considered as 'assemblies' and would end, if not in riot, then in massacre. The history of the crowd, at least for Paris, has been so well covered by George Rudé that it would be both superfluous and impudent to embark on a further analysis of the various riots and *journées* which marked the history of the capital—and, in many cases, of France—between April 1789 and Vendémiaire year IV. It would in any case be difficult to pursue this particular subject beyond that date; for the types of urban riot that Rudé deals with disappear entirely, at least from the Paris scene—though there are urban riots of a similar nature elsewhere in 1810–12—for reasons that will become apparent. Rural disorders, on the other hand, scarcely ever cease; they are endemic in the period 1790–2,[1] during most of the Directory, and they were extensive at least in the north-east in 1801–2, and again in 1812–14.

The difficulty here is to distinguish between agrarian disturbances arising out of attempts to preserve seigneurial rights and so on, traditional law-breaking like smuggling and poaching, and, espe-

---

[1] Michel Vovelle, 'De la mendicité au brigandage: les errants en Beauce sous la Révolution française' (Actes du 86ᵐᵉ Congrès national des Sociétés savantes, Montpellier, 1961).

cially after 1795, sheer banditry. For during the Directory banditry was never purely criminal; it always took on political undertones, even in the north of France; and in the south-east it is inextricably bound up with the activities of the various murder gangs in the movements of the White Terror, so that it is impossible, in this instance, to draw a clear line between criminal violence and gang operations that are politically orientated. The operations of the *chauffeurs* may be doubtful; but they do surely represent one form at least of popular commitment and in many areas the only form, for the *chauffeurs* do not emerge on a large scale till 1795, when banditry might be the one opening left to the popular protester. The activities of the various *Compagnies*, however, quite clearly qualify for inclusion in any study of popular movements. For the White Terror was a movement which, if not led by those of popular origin, drew for its rank and file on much the same elements as Rudé's Crowd and the Paris *sans-culotterie*. It is important to remember that, on a regional basis, one of the most effective and persistent 'popular movements' during the revolutionary period was counter-revolutionary, ultra-royalist, and, to some extent, anti-urban.

3. DESERTION AND *INSOUMISSION* 1793–YEAR VII

Apart from riot, early attempts at 'coalitions' (where the transport workers proved particularly effective), banditry, and White terrorism, popular protest would eventually be likely to take the form of desertion, or of *insoumission*, since a man can hardly desert from a corps he has never joined. Both are of double interest to the historian of popular protest: first of all, in their own right, as an example of increasing war-weariness and of the alienation of important sections of the common people from a regime in which they no longer felt any stake and with whose declared aims they had become increasingly out of sympathy. For, save in certain particular rural areas, desertion was not a popular phenomenon in the year II; *la resquille* was, on the contrary, one of the favourite themes of Sectionary denunciation during the period of popular militancy, and in the minutes of *sociétés populaires* and *comités de surveillance* there are frequent hints that the sons, nephews, and relatives of the well-to-do and the well-connected were less likely to end up on the frontiers or in the Vendée than those of poor artisans and shopkeepers. There are repeated popular complaints too about the readiness with which the army transport and supply services—*charrois militaires, habillement,* and so on—welcomed in suitably recommended *fils de famille.* We hear of the *gentilshommes charretiers*[1] and of a mass of *garçons perruquiers* safely employed in the *charrois* or in the hospital services, of a *fils de Conventionnel* who managed to get himself attached to the headquarters of the Revolutionary Cavalry in Versailles,[2] and of a banker's son who, though he had never set his hand to a printer's block in his life, succeeded in being taken on as a compositor at the *imprimerie des lois.*[3]

Many of these complaints, like those concerning meals in restaurants or prisons or the distribution of meat, may no doubt be attributed to jealousy, the *sans-culottes* wanting those fairly safe jobs to be reserved for their own children or even for themselves, or arguing that, if they were not to have them, then no one should, a dog-in-the-manger attitude characteristic of the popular movement throughout the French Revolution. And *sans-culotte* militants were better placed than *fils de Conventionnels* to be noisily virtuous on the subject of the patriotic 'blood tax', because most of them would not be called upon to pay it, being either over twenty-five or mobilized in skilled crafts for war production. Even so, the sense of indignation, however noisy, appears genuine; it accounts for *sans-culotte* suspicions of people like Mazuel, who, as a captain in the *fédérés* after the *10 août*, had taken such a very long time to leave Paris for Nancy (there was so much *chose publique* to be saved in Paris before he could safely deprive the capital of his vigilance), and who, as one of the leaders of the *cavalerie révolutionnaire* in the year II, managed to find excuse after excuse not to leave Versailles for Lyon, or elsewhere (a reluctance that was to cost him his head).[4] Of his staff, rather gaudy young men, mostly actors, it was likewise felt that they spent too much time consorting with courtesans and attending plays when they had no business to be in Paris at all. *Insoumission* and *la resquille* were viewed then in class terms, while desertion was, quite rightly, taken as characteristic of counter-

---

[1] Arnaud de Lestapis, 'Gentilshommes charretiers', *Revue des deux mondes,* September 1953.
[2] *Les Armées révolutionnaires,* pp. 175–6, 819.
[3] Ibid., p. 198.
[4] Ibid., pp. 131–9, and *L'Armée révolutionnaire parisienne à Lyon et dans la région lyonnaise,* p. 26.

revolutionary commitment. It could hardly have been otherwise; for deserters, being outside the law, would, like the *prêtres réfractaires*, and often with their encouragement, be driven into banditry and armed resistance. Much of the time and effort of *comités de surveillance* was taken up in 1793-4 with tracking down deserters to their village, forest, or mountain hide-outs; and much of the hostility felt by the *sans-culottes* to the farmers drew its strength from the belief that they were harbouring deserters and were even encouraging their children and their farm hands to evade military service, out of selfishness as well as out of hatred for the townsman's Republic. Even though most deserters at this stage of the Revolution were probably men of the people—the *fils de famille* did not have to desert, because they were able to find themselves safe jobs in the cities or in the rear areas—those who encouraged them to take to the woods were not. In the year II, desertion is definitely not a form of popular protest.

The position changes already in the year III. The *sans-culottes*—or their sons—were prepared to fight for their own regime, even for that of the Jacobins; they were less enthusiastic about fighting for the Thermidorians, especially when they began to realize from letters received from their wives that, while they were revolutionizing Europe, their families were being allowed to starve at home. No doubt the main offenders were the *jeunesse dorée*, but they were *embusqués* rather than deserters, while the neo-terrorists still counted on army support. But the first *bandes* date from this period (we hear of them already, in the woods of Monville, behind Dieppe, in Brumaire year III). In the years that follow, desertion takes on the magnitude of a 'popular movement'. In the year IV volunteers and conscripts no longer desert in driblets but in large groups, *avec armes et bagages*, avoiding the bridges and commandeering boats to cross the rivers in their path westwards. In the course of that year we hear of a whole company of soldiers, in uniform, with their regimental numbers on their collars, walking from Sarrelouis, the length of half a dozen Departments, to reach the outskirts of Melun (they were from the Seine-et-Marne), without at any stage being challenged.[1] In Frimaire year IV, the Dieppe authorities hear reports of bodies of deserters, supplied with artillery and a baggage train, robbing and killing in the forests of the cantons of Envermeu

---

[1] A.N. F9 316 (Ministre de la Guerre au Ministre de l'Intérieur, 23 nivôse an IV).

and Longueville.[1] The enormous extension of desertion in the year IV and the year V—probably the peak—is the most striking testimony to the powerlessness of the Directory almost anywhere outside Paris.[2] From the year V to the year VII there are increasingly frequent reports, from a variety of Departments: Somme, Oise, Seine-et-Marne, Seine-Inférieure, Calvados, Tarn,[3] Basses-Alpes, Allier, Aisne, Gard, Vaucluse, Bouches-du-Rhône, Ardèche, Lozère—of every conscript from a given canton having returned home and living there unmolested. Better still, many of them did not return home: they had never left it in the first place. There is something splendid about defiance of government on such an impudent scale. In the year VII too the severed fingers of right hands—the commonest form of self-mutilation—begin to witness statistically to the strength of what might be described as a vast movement of collective complicity, involving the family, the parish, the local authorities, whole *cantons*. The man who was out of step by then was the unfortunate *commissaire du directoire* who found himself, in small town or village, attempting to resist the general trend. They did their best—one of them came out with the suggestion that the young men who had cut off their fingers should be made to parade, in women's bonnets, on the *fêtes décadaires*. It might, he argued, revive popular interest in these ill-attended occasions, as the common people could always be drawn by the spectacle of someone's public humiliation or discomfort (particularly someone known by name), and it would also shame the offenders in the eyes of the younger female population.[4] The

[1] Arch. Seine-Maritime L 5240 (administration municipale d'Envermeu, à celle de Dieppe, s.d. frimaire an IV).

[2] A *commissaire* from Lautrec was convinced that desertion had a political origin. 'Il est persuadé que l'Angleterre, qui épie tous nos mouvements et à qui les crimes ne coûtent rien, entretient des agens dans chaque département pour rembourser aux parens les frais des garnisaires . . .' (A.N. F9 316, administration du Tarn au Ministre, 11 messidor an VII).

[3] '. . . Des émissaires du royalisme placés sur la route qui conduit à l'armée d'Italie depuis Saint-Pons jusqu'à Nîmes . . . s'emparent de nos réquisitionnaires et conscrits et après leur avoir dépeint le dénuement vrai ou faux où se trouvent nos armées et les dangers inévitables qu'ils courent en s'y rendant, les font rétrograder sur leurs foyers ou leur procurent des contrefeuilles . . . au moyen desquelles, côtoyant les montagnes qui entourent le levant bordant le septentrion de notre département, ils se rendent . . . dans quelques lieux de la ci-devant Gascogne . . .' (A.N. F9 386).

[4] A.N. F9 316 (Désertion, Tarn) (juge de paix du canton de Lautrec, au Ministre, 9 brumaire an VII): '. . . Si l'on ne croit pas pouvoir les rendre utiles dans les armées . . . ils pourroient être condamnés à marcher le décadi à la suite

government also employed such desperate remedies as the *colonnes mobiles*, garrisoning, collective fines, the arrest of relatives, the repetition of which suggests that they were hardly effective. Even the Empire, with a vastly more numerous and more reliable rural police, did not succeed in more than temporarily slowing down the speed of the haemorrhage which, from 1810, and above all from 1812, once more reached catastrophic proportions. There could have been no more eloquent referendum on the universal unpopularity of an oppressive regime; and there is no more encouraging spectacle for a historian than a people that has decided it will no longer fight and that, without fuss, returns home. Prefects and Sub-Prefects did what they could to keep desertion figures secret; but no one, not even a Napoleonic official, could make deserters invisible. They tried at least to prevent them from crossing back into the French part of the Empire. The common people, at least in this respect, had their fair share in bringing down France's most appalling regime.

4. THE REGIONAL INCIDENCE OF DESERTION

But the study of desertion and *insoumission* has another, less direct interest in retrospective regional terms. Just as lists of subscribers to Lebois and to Babeuf enable the historian to take a general count of surviving militancy two years after the collapse of *la sans-culotterie*, the study of the regional incidence of desertion offers a valuable indication of the strength or weakness of surviving Jacobinism and, for that matter, of popular militancy (by that time, largely indistinguishable) from one region to another, three or four years after the experiment in popular government. For the *sans-culotte* movement was patriotic, and long after the *sans-culottes* had disappeared as an effective, collective political force, the indignation inspired by desertion would represent one of the more characteristic attitudes of the *exclusifs* and of other surviving elements of popular militancy. By the same token, the scale of desertion, in the year V or the year VII, would offer at least a good indication of the lack of revolutionary enthusiasm of a locality, a

de la municipalité, au milieu de quatre femmes et portant comme elles une quenouille et une coiffe. . . . En punissant ainsi la lâcheté par la honte . . . on auroit l'avantage certain d'attirer aux fêtes décadaires ce public encore si indifférent pour les institutions républicaines mais toujours si avide de ce plaisir malin qu'on trouve dans l'embarras d'autrui. . . .'

canton, or an *arrondissement*, in the year II. In other words, the study of the relative incidence of desertion, like that of the reopening of churches to public worship, offers not only a crude means of measuring republican commitment at the time of the inquiry, but also an indication of the degree of revolutionary fervour of the same area three or four years previously. It would be reasonable to assume, for instance, that a *commune* which had been constantly behind on its *réquisitions*, that had given proof of stubborn ill will towards Paris or another neighbouring city, and in which the *maximum* had been evaded and the urban food commissioners and *apôtres* had been molested, would be likely to have a particularly high rate of desertion in the year VII. It could also be assumed that the rural authorities that had displayed a marked hostility to the urban consumer in the year II would be likely to give shelter to deserters in the year V.

Desertion would in any case be more widespread in the countryside than in the towns, not only because the countryside was less patriotic, less revolutionary, but also because it was easier to hide and to obtain food there. Thus the scale of desertion will further illustrate one of the central themes of the year II: the conflict between town and country. Ideally, a complete map of desertion and *insoumission*, Department by Department, *canton* by *canton*, would present a retrospective guide to local and regional attitudes to terror and repression and to the whole system of the year II. One would possess in such a map a pointer as valuable as the *carte de la déchristianisation* that is being drawn up by Michel Vovelle (as part of his doctoral thesis) for the whole area of the Rhône Valley, from Lyon to the delta, an area which is of special significance both for the history of the Terror and for that of the *Compagnies* of 1795 onwards.

Unfortunately, there is not sufficient material to make such a map possible on a national scale. The best we can do is a sketch map drawn from scattered areas. Even if the material existed, the figures would need to be interpreted with caution. A Department that has a very high desertion rate is not necessarily very unpatriotic and strongly opposed to the Republic. It may merely be very wild and easy to hide in. One must expect more deserters to be noted in the Nord, the Ardennes, the Moselle, the Bas-Rhin, the Somme, the Meuse, the Marne, or the Seine-Inférieure, all within easy walking distances of the various army zones, than in the Haute-Vienne or the Creuse. And the same could be said of the different regions within a Department; the authorities of the Tarn, in the year VII, complain that the northern part of the Department lends itself to desertion, owing to its inaccessibility, and we have similar complaints from the Cantal in the year IV.[1] For the deserters stated to be present in a given Department are not necessarily from that Department; on the contrary, they are almost certainly from somewhere else, for deserters, like other outlaws, are likely to be frequently on the move. In Floréal year VII, the authorities of the Oise complain of the stream of deserters passing through the Department towards the neighbouring Somme;[2] a month later, those of the Somme make similar complaints, except that the stream is now said to be towards the Oise.[3]

There are also a number of accidental factors the importance of which it is hard to calculate: the presence, in a given town, of a doctor who is known to be obliging, of a *conseil de santé* that has the reputation of being easy-going, will attract recruits from a wide area beyond the Department or the *canton*. Again, to quote the authorities of the Oise, this was why Amiens became something of a Mecca to the potential *embusqué* of the year VII. Yet at all periods the Somme had been an intensely revolutionary bastion. Much, too, will depend on the degree of zeal displayed by the local *gendarmerie*, a zeal which, the *gendarmes* being *du pays*, will be related to the general attitudes of the local population. The same could be said of rural *maires* and of local municipal authorities. It was with desertion as it had been with the *maximum*, the *recensements*, and the *réquisitions* of the year II: local officials followed the general consensus of opinion of their *administrés*, they seldom attempted to lead it; they were much more concerned first of all in gauging it, then with not colliding with it head-on, than with attempting to change it. Local officials were not heroes; and a *maire* who went out of his way to track down deserters would soon have the whole

---

[1] A.N. F9 316 (commissaire du Directoire dans le Tarn au Ministre, 11 prairial an VII): '... Il est d'autres cantons très, ——? très populeux, qui n'en fournissent pas un seul (tant l'influence des prêtres réfractaires y est grande) et où les fuyards de tout le département sont sûrs de trouver un asile.... Les colonnes mobiles ne peuvent rien dans un pays de montagnes et de forêts . . .', and *Les Armées révolutionnaires*, ii. 590.

[2] A.N. F9 316 (Désertion, Commissaire du Directoire dans l'Oise au Ministre, 27 floréal an VII).

[3] Ibid. (Commissaire du Directoire dans la Somme au Ministre, 13 prairial an VII).

rural community on his back—to arrest a deserter was to aggress against a whole family—one had to make one's choice, it would be unwise thus to antagonize the family of a well-to-do farmer, and if one deserter was to be tolerated, then all had to be, all, at least, from the circle of wealthy property-holders. A *maire* could display his zeal on the cheap at the expense of the family of some poor woodcutter or day labourer. There was not much point in earning the congratulations of a distant *commissaire du Directoire*, of an *agent de recrutement* with an office in the *chef-lieu*, if, before they arrived, one was to be shot in the back from behind a hedge. So the attitudes of local authorities—there were some exceptions, a few officials prepared to risk their lives for the rather shabby Republic of the year IV, even in the countryside—would reflect those of the areas in which they had to live.

It was, for instance, characteristic that, ordered by the *agent national* of Avignon to arrest a deserter in his own home, in Thermidor year III, a *lieutenant de gendarmerie* should have reported 'que ses gendarmes avoient été insultés et que cela les décourageoit beaucoup . . . le lendemain ledit lieutenant est venu me prévenir qu'il étoit impossible de saisir l'homme en question dans sa maison à cause de son immensité et la grande quantité d'avenues dans des jardins immenses, (qu')au surplus ses gendarmes ne vouloient plus lui obéir . . . qu'il étoit plus prudent d'attendre de le voir passer dans les rues que d'aller dans sa maison . . .'. The young man had little to fear, for he belonged to one of the wealthiest families of the city.[1] The same official had reported, a month earlier, 28 Messidor year III:

. . . Dans le département de Vaucluse il s'y trouve à présent environ 5 à 6,000 déserteurs ou de la première réquisition . . . ils ne craignent pas de dire publiquement qu'ils ne veulent pas partir, et si on employoit contre eux une force médiocre, il est à présumer qu'il arriveroit les plus grands malheurs. Les muncipalités ne veulent ou n'osent pas faire la moindre démarche. . . .[2]

In the papal city, deserters from the bourgeoisie lived openly at home throughout the Thermidorian Reaction; and in Prairial

---

[1] Arch. Vaucluse 3 L 26* (agent national du district d'Avignon au représentant Boursault, 15 thermidor an III). The young man, Carrière *cadet*, is denounced by the local neo-terrorists as one of the leaders of the White Terror murder gangs in the year IV.

[2] Ibid. (agent national du district d'Avignon au représentant Réaz, 28 messidor an III).

year III, they flocked to arms, when called to put down the neo-
terrorist rising in Toulon. Fortunately, they did not have to leave,
as the rising collapsed before they had been enrolled. It was only
in the *Carreterie* that it was possible to find women whose husbands
were serving in the armies.[1]

Avignon is typical both of a region notoriously hostile to the
Revolution, and of a class which, after Thermidor, preferred to
fight its own battles at home, in the streets of Paris and of other
towns, against its class enemies, in the ranks of the *jeunesse dorée*,
to revolutionizing the rest of Europe in a threadbare uniform.
Duval makes no bones about having been an *embusqué*. In the
northern cities, desertion was primarily a class affair, at least until
the year IV, and many of the women who are stated to have taken
a leading part in the *journées* of Germinal and Prairial had husbands
in the armies; the fishermen's wives who led the Dieppe riots of
Floréal and Prairial complained that it was particularly heartless to
allow their children and themselves to starve standing up while
their husbands served the Republic in the navy.[2] But the husbands
were not slow to draw their own conclusions; and, as we have seen,
by the year IV desertion was no longer confined to one class.

It flourished most, however, in the areas that had been the worst
disposed towards the urban revolution of 1793–4. It is without
surprise that one reads, in a report dated 14 Ventôse year V from
the *commissaire du Directoire* at Villeneuve-la-Guyard in the Yonne,
that 'nulle part la désertion n'a fait plus de progrès que dans ce
canton; il y a plus de 120 déserteurs qui se refusent au départ, il y
en a 16 à Villeblevin, commune qu'habite le commissaire [Lorillon],
dont deux portent son nom . . .'.[3] For this Lorillon had, in the
year II, been *agent national* of the District de Sens, as well as a
fervent enemy both of Paris and of the *sans-culotte* municipality
of Villeblevin, which he had eventually succeeded in having removed.[4] One is not surprised to hear what a *commissaire* in the
Tarn has to say in a letter of 11 Prairial year VI: '. . . Je ne dois

[1] Ibid. 3 L 34* (agent national d'Avignon, au représentant Goupilleau de
Montaigu, 6 prairial an III) and *Les Républicains avignonnais traduits devant le
tribunal criminel de la Drôme, au peuple français* (Valence, 24 floréal an V).

[2] Arch. Dieppe D 1 6 (séances de la municipalité des 14 et 16 prairial et du
19 messidor an III).

[3] A.N. F1b II Yonne I (commissaire du Directoire près l'administration
cantonale de Villeneuve-la-Guyard, au Ministre, 14 ventôse an V).

[4] *Les Armées révolutionnaires*, ii. 517, 521, 523–6.

pas vous dissimuler . . . que les quatre détachements que nous avons fournis ne proviennent que des cantons qui ont constamment marché dans la ligne de la Révolution. . . .'[1] In the Allier, the centre of trouble the same year is in the canton of Bourbon-l'Archambault; in the village of Ygrande 'de 23 conscrits qui sont partis, 22 sont revenus et restent tranquillement dans leurs foyers . . .'.[2] In the year II, this *canton* had been denounced by the energetic revolutionary authorities of Moulins, Montluçon, and Gannat as a *foyer de fanatisme*, and had been subjected to the noisy attention of revolutionary battalions.[3] One is not surprised to hear the complaints of a former *commissaire* in the *canton* of Cœuvres in the Aisne, in a letter dated 20 Nivôse year V:

> . . . Tout à coup, dès le moment que l'on a su ma destitution, on sonne les cloches avec affectation. . . . Plus de deux tiers peut-être des volontaires partis dans le tems pour l'armée sont de retour dans leurs foyers où ils restent paisiblement. On a, par de fausses attestations complaisamment apostillées par les anti-républicains en place, fait obtenir depuis plusieurs mois des congés ou exemptions de service à plus de 20 fuyards les plus sains et les plus vigoureux de ce canton. . . . Maintenant ils se montrent avec insolence . . . ils narguent impunément les parens de ceux qui sont à leurs postes. . . .[4]

For both this Department and this District (Soissons) had shown exceptional hostility to the food commissioners of the year II, and, apart from the District de Provins and that of Sens, no place in the Paris provisioning zone had been more unpopular with the *sansculottes* of the capital.

When, in Fructidor year VII, the administration of the Department of the Basses-Alpes sighs: 'Depuis longtems l'esprit public est nul dans ce Département',[5] it might have been echoing the denunciations of the *apôtres* from Valence and from Marseille who had been sent to evangelize the place in the autumn of 1793. In Thermidor year VII, recruiting riots break out in the canton of

---

[1] A.N. F9 316 (Administration du Tarn, au Directoire, 7 thermidor an VI).

[2] A.N. F9 301 (l'agent national forestier de Cérilly, au Directoire, 7 messidor an VII).

[3] *Les Armées révolutionnaires*, ii. 630.

[4] A.N. F9 301 (Louis Baudet, ex-commissaire dans le canton de Cœuvres, au Ministre, 20 nivôse an V) and R. C. Cobb, 'L'Armée révolutionnaire dans l'Aisne' (*Revue du Nord*, pp. 132, 133, 134).

[5] A.N. F9 301 (administration des Basses-Alpes, au Ministre, 9 fructidor an VII) and *Les Armées révolutionnaires*, ii. 561, 570.

Goderville which, five years previously, had been repeatedly denounced for its unwillingness to carry out the requisitions in
favour of the Rouen, le Havre, and Dieppe markets;[1] while, already
in Messidor year II, the Dieppe authorities draw attention to the
collusion between the municipality of Biville-la-Rivière and the
deserters living openly in the village;[2] only a few weeks previously
a group of farmers from this village had been called to Dieppe to
explain why they had not supplied an eighth of the grain required
of them for the market of the port. The map of desertion, at least
seen through these few fragments, coincides again and again with
la carte de la mauvaise volonté with reference to the provisioning
policies of the year II. It would probably coincide also with that of
open resistance to *déchristianisation*. But, in the present state of
research, it is impossible to do more than suggest that such parallels
may exist elsewhere between revolutionary ill will and apathy in
the year II and the extent and acceptance of desertion in the year V,
the year VI, and the year VII.

It is a parallel that would be well worth pursuing more thoroughly in a number of similar areas, previously ill noted by the
Paris or other city authorities of the *sans-culotte* period : the District
de Provins, the District de Beauvais, the District de Pontoise, the
District de Compiègne, to quote some of the more notorious
examples. In local and regional terms, the polarizations of the year
II are likely to be those of the year VI or VII and, in many instances, those who, in the year II, had discharged their functions
to the maximum interest of their *sans-culotte* brothers back in Paris
or Toulouse were those who, when they had survived—for many
were murdered in between—were denouncing the tacit acceptance
of desertion from the year V onwards.

Desertion not only reflects regional and class attitudes; when it is
very widely accepted it represents an important, if negative, attitude on the part of the common people. It is then what might be
described as a 'popular movement by default', like the non-
participation of so many *sans-culottes* in the *journée du 9 thermidor*.

---

[1] Arch. Seine-Maritime L 5340 (comité de Dieppe à l'agent national du
district, s.d. messidor an II).

[2] A.N. F9 316 (Désertion, Seine-Inférieure, arrêté de l'administration
centrale du département du 21 thermidor an VII) and R. C. Cobb, 'La Mission
de Siblot au Havre-Marat' and 'L'Armée révolutionnaire parisienne au Havre-
Marat et dans le district de Montivilliers', *Annales de Normandie*, May and
October–December 1953.

Popular militancy should not be defined only in its positive forms; people must be allowed to opt out of a system or of a commitment if they feel so inclined. This is why desertion is an integral part of our subject, especially in a period when the common people had few other means of openly expressing their hostility to a regime which had repressed and impoverished them in a heartless and systematic manner.

5. BEGGARS AND VAGRANTS: THE *BANDES* OF 1811–12

The police, as the previous section shows, had their own ideas about the 'popular movement' and their own priorities with regard to potential sedition. They were above all obsessed by the dangers of all sorts presented by large groups of people on the move; and their principal concern was to control, when they could not prevent, the movement of population. Highest on their list came *oisifs*, 'sturdy beggars', urban and rural vagrants who, in time of dearth, during the winter months and even more in the spring, at the opening of the *période de la soudure*, roamed the countryside, sometimes, in periods of extreme hardship, in armed bands, ranging from farm to farm and demanding food and shelter as a right (one such band insisted on supper, a bed, and a good breakfast, for twenty or thirty companions), using threatening language, hinting at a return visit in even greater force, with the reminder that barns, thatched roofs, crops, and fodder burn easily even in winter when suitably helped.

The imperial police in particular harried vagrants. A series of ferocious *arrêtés* of 1806–12 virtually made the genuine vagrant who absented himself from the workhouse an outlaw. Any such association of even two vagrants on the move, unless they were husband and wife, father and son, or mother and daughter, was treated as a seditious turbulence, instantly punishable before a summary court by deportation. Any movement of vagrants in the countryside after dusk was subject to similar punishment.

The imperial authorities were likewise concerned to make vagrants the responsibility of the *communes* from which they came— this was another way of keeping them off the roads. And, in times of distress, rather than give them material relief in money or in food—which, it was felt, they would then sell to obtain drink— the favourite solution was to organize public works that would keep them occupied in one place and under the local authorities. The

Napoleonic police went on the assumption that a beggar was not dangerous as long as he was in his own community; it was when he ganged up with others—especially with other townsmen—and then, under the anonymity of a mask, proceeded to comb a wide neighbourhood, that he became a potential outlaw and a danger to order and property. So the first concern of the authorities, once such *attroupements* were stated to be on the march, was to have them rounded up by the *gendarmerie* or the army, and sent back to their towns of origin. (They were not particularly afraid of the rural vagrant; for, they argued, he was known, had a name, and, being identifiable, would stop short of such extreme acts as arson or begging while armed.)

The danger was real enough. During the winter of 1811 and the first three months of 1812, the Prefects speak of enormous armies of beggars on the move in the countryside. Most of them, they suggest, are 'foreigners', who have come from the neighbouring Department—a characteristic reflex both of police and of public authorities when faced with violence or disorder on an unaccustomed scale. As usual, the Seine-Inférieure appears to have been the most disturbed Department; the Prefect, in a letter dated 8 April 1812, when the crisis was at its height, notes: 'le désœuvrement est toujours à craindre surtout parmi le peuple. . . . Les mendians se multiplient chaque jour. . . .'[1] In July, referring to the previous spring, he writes: 'Des troupes de plus de 500 mendians assiégeoient les portes des propriétaires, des cultivateurs, des marchands . . .',[2] and, in September, in his general report on the dearth, he produces much more alarming figures, for two other traditional centres of extreme hardship in time of dearth: the regions of le Havre and Dieppe:

> Dans l'arrondissement du Havre, la mendicité s'étoit accrue à un tel point dès l'hiver de 1811 que des troupes de plus de 1.200 individus se répandoient à certains jours de la semaine [Mondays and Tuesdays] dans les communes et demandoient des aumônes qu'il eût été souvent dangereux de leur refuser. . . . Dans l'arrondissement de Dieppe il s'en formoit des attroupemens de 1,800 à 2,000 . . .[3]

The Prefect of the neighbouring Department of the Somme was to report on 24 June that 'les indigens . . . sans exagérer . . . alloient

---

[1] A.N. F 11 718 (Préfet de la Seine-Inférieure au Ministre, 8 avril 1812).
[2] Ibid. (Préfet de la Seine-Inférieure au Ministre, 31 juillet 1812).
[3] Ibid. (Préfet de la Seine-Inférieure au Ministre, 8 septembre 1812).

mendier au nombre de plus de 60.000 . . .'.[1] The authorities of
Amiens, in 1795, give a similar figure for vagrants combing the
district in March–April of that terrible year;[2] in view of the over-
population of the Somme, his estimate does not appear to have been
exaggerated. The Prefects of the Finistère and the Cher refer, more
modestly, to groups of from twenty to forty as operating in the
countryside;[3] despite their small numbers, their methods seem to
have been equally alarming. The Prefect of the Cher, in a letter
dated 19 March, at the height of popular panic and alarm, explains:

Voici comment s'exerce cette mendicité. Pendant le cours de la
journée les mendians (dont le nombre excède toute croyance) marchent
isolément et vont de porte en porte; l'usage est de donner à chacun un
morceau de pain, et l'on n'oseroit les refuser, crainte du feu dont ils
menacent; à l'entrée de la nuit, et au nombre de 20, quelquefois 30, ils
se présentent dans une ferme isolée (comme elles le sont pour la plupart
dans ce département), alors, ils ne mendient plus, il faut leur donner à
souper, à coucher, puis à déjeuner . . . les forces manquent pour les
arrêter, les prisons manquent pour les enfermer. . . .[4]

The Prefect of the Finistère has a similar story to tell: 'La mendicité faisoit des progrès effrayans,' he writes, in August, of the
previous winter, 'les mendians se réunissoient par bandes de trente
à quarante pour aller au loin lever l'impôt de leur subsistance sur
le travail d'autrui; et leur audace croissante étoit déjà parvenue au
point qu'ils n'étoient point fâchés d'être redoutés. . . .'[5] The
Prefect of the Oise believes that the groups of beggars passing
through certain areas of the Department, in the spring of 1812,
have come from the neighbouring *communes* of the Somme and
the Eure. 'Dans le canton de Chaumont', he states, in a letter dated
24 March to the Minister of the Interior, 'qui avoisine le Département de l'Eure, les pauvres vont la nuit, en assez grand nombre, et
quelquefois masqués, frapper chez les fermiers et les sommer de
leur livrer en dehors de leur habitation du pain et de se retirer afin
qu'ils ne puissent pas les reconnoître . . .',[6] but, a fortnight later,

---

[1] A.N. F 11 718 (Préfet de la Somme au Ministre, 24 juin 1812).
[2] Arch. Somme Lc 1433 (district d'Amiens, prairial an III) and A.N. D §1 9
mission de Duport dans le district d'Abbeville, messidor an III).
[3] A.N. F 11 708 (Préfet du Cher au Ministre, 19 mars 1812) and A.N. F 11 710
(Préfet du Finistère au Ministre, 26 août 1812).
[4] A.N. F 11 708 (as above).
[5] A.N. F 11 710 (as above).
[6] A.N. F 11 715 (Préfet de l'Oise au Ministre, 24 mars).

he expresses the opinion that many of them are in fact locals:
'. . . Les sous-préfets et les maires . . . sont persuadés que plusieurs
des gens qui vont quêter avec le visage masqué sont de leurs voisins
qui ont du bled chez eux. . . .'[1]
Several Prefects attribute the insurrectionary character of some
of these *attroupements* to the presence in the ranks of beggars of
large numbers of townsmen. 'Si, dans le fort de la disette, il a été
commis quelques excès, dans les campagnes,' said the Prefect of
the Orne, 'les habitans des villes qui s'y répandoient en troupe
nombreuse en ont été presque les seuls auteurs. . . .'[2] The Prefect
of Rennes complains that the weavers of the *chef-lieu* have left their
workshops, to scour the countryside in large groups.[3] In March
1812 the Prefect of the Loir-et-Cher is told of the presence of
armed bands of beggars in the communes of Moisy, Semerville,
and Ouzouer-le-Doyen, in the neighbourhood of Blois.[4] In the
Eure-et-Loir, 'au 1ᵉʳ janvier 1812, les campagnes étoient couvertes
de mendians, qui, voyageant en troupes, visitoient les fermes & les
moulins, demandoient insolemment du pain . . .'.[5] But elsewhere
rural vagrants invaded the towns: Parthenay, in the Deux-Sèvres,
'à été infesté de mendians . . .'. The Prefect adds the comment:

On a remarqué . . . la maladresse du curé; prêchant sur l'aumône, il
lança des reproches violens contre les riches qui ne donnoient pas assez,
et sembla les désigner à la haine du peuple. Les habitans aisés accusèrent
le curé d'avoir prêché la loi agraire; j'eus occasion de lui faire quelques
remontrances, et pour prouver qu'il avoit mal interprété ses intentions,
il prêcha le jour suivant sur les devoirs des pauvres, avec si peu de
mesure que les riches durent à leur tour le protéger contre l'animadversion
des indigens. . . .[6]

In the Sarthe, the pattern is more familiar: 'La misère étoit
extrême [in the spring of 1812]. Des mendians, rassemblés par
troupes plus ou moins nombreuses, parcouroient les campagnes,
jetoient l'alarme. . . .'[7]

[1] Ibid. (7 avril).
[2] Ibid. (29 avril).
[3] A.N. F 11 711 (Préfet de l'Ille-et-Vilaine, 14 juin).
[4] A.N. F 11 712 (Préfet du Loir-et-Cher, 24 mars).
[5] A.N. F 11 709 (Préfet de l'Eure-et-Loir, 4 juin). Referring to the small town
of Nogent-le-Rotrou, the Prefect writes in November 1812: '. . . Sur une population de 7,000 âmes, il en est 2,400 qui se livrent à la mendicité et qui se répandent dans les campagnes environnantes. . . .'
[6] A.N. F 11 718 (Préfet des Deux-Sèvres, 10 août).
[7] A.N. F 11 716 (Préfet de la Sarthe, 12 août).

As always, when it is a matter of extensive vagrancy and rural disorder on a semi-insurrectionary scale, the Norman Departments, the Somme, and the Eure-et-Loir—in the year IV, the area of the notorious *bande d'Orgères*, and, thanks to the immense forest of Orléans, with the Loiret, a traditional centre of rural banditry—top the list. Girardin, the Prefect of Rouen, refers to vagrancy as entrenched in the Seine-Inférieure 'from time immemorial'.[1] But some of the Breton and western Departments were also affected. There are no reports of vagrancy in the south; and the Aube, which the Prefect describes, with some exaggeration, as 'the poorest Department in the Empire' (there would have been plenty of other candidates for that much-disputed title, from the Ardennes to the Lozère, the Ardèche, the Aveyron, or the Cantal), while undergoing extreme hardship—the mortality was exceptionally heavy in the winter of 1811 and the spring of 1812—seems to have been preserved from the operations of large-scale vagrancy, despite an enormous forested region round Ervy; the Department was, however, like that of the Marne, heavily garrisoned. It is possibly for the same reason that there are no reports of beggar groups in the Nord, the traditional terrain of the *chauffeur* and the smuggler; the Nord was also particularly well placed, at least in this particular crisis, to receive early relief, with the massive import of grain from the Dutch and Rhenish Departments. There is nothing surprising, then, either about the location of the beggars' armies or about their methods, reflecting as they do the old hostility of the townsman for the well-to-do farmer and for the country population as a whole that one encounters, especially in the Norman Departments and the Somme, in the course of the year III and the year IV.

What is surprising, given the repressive conditions of the Empire, as far as the common people were concerned, is the relative permissiveness both of local authorities—naturally prudent, as they were, in the immediate path of these 'invasions'—and of the Prefects and Sub-Prefects, who, when faced with disorder on this scale, preferred to use persuasion rather than the *gendarmerie*, enticing the vagrants back to their towns with the promise of the free distribution of food (*les soupes à la Rumfort*) and with the organization of relief in the form of public works. It was a measure of their success that outbreaks of actual rioting were few,

[1] A.N. F 11 718 (Préfet de la Seine-Inférieure, 11 septembre).

despite the gravity of a situation where dearth and disease were accompanied by explosive political undertones and, in many places, the most alarming rumours. Certainly, it would be wrong to suggest that the common people had been schooled, since 1795, in the habit of obedience—there is nothing deferential about the behaviour of the beggars as described in these reports, and there is no doubt about their extreme hostility to the urban and rural well-to-do; rather it would seem that, as a result of the May Decrees, the urban consumer was readily convinced of the good intentions of the Imperial Government.

6. THE BAROMETER OF POPULAR PROTEST AND DISASTER 1795–1812

Let us briefly consider the fortunes and misfortunes of the common people between the Thermidorian Reaction and the end of the Empire. White terrorism, one of the most effective weapons against the former *sans-culotte* militants and their masters, was already on the decline by 1803, after eight anarchical and sanguinary years in the south-east and the Rhône Valley. The great murder year was 1795; but there appear to have been almost as many murders in the year IV, and in the following year the activities of the *compagnies* became even bolder. Political assassinations were frequent throughout the year VII (there is little evidence for the year VI), with a cluster of murders in the Vaucluse in September 1799. There was a further spate of murders in and around Lyon in the year VIII and the year IX. But by 1802, the movement had exhausted itself, though there are eleven political murders recorded for the Rhône in 1803 and 1804. Lyon was no doubt exceptional in this respect, even in the south east. This was not, however, the end of the story; for the movement was to revive, often under the same leadership and with the same *sabreurs*, in the favourable circumstances of the summer of 1815, when it re-emerged in much the same areas, even in the same villages, as in 1795 onwards, and sought out much the same sort of victims, now doubly suspect. Indeed, a number of people were murdered in the Gard, the Bouches-du-Rhône, the Vaucluse, and the Lozère in 1815 mainly because their near-relatives had been murdered in the previous White Terror. A number of the murderers, too, on both occasions, had lost parents to one or another of the Revolutionary Terrors.

For any assessment of the two White Terrors, it is essential to keep in view this succession of events.[1]

There was a general flare-up of the traditional hunger riot in 1795, when there were spring and summer riots in all the principal towns of the north (Paris, Saint-Germain-en-Laye, Versailles, Mantes, Rouen, Sotteville, Darnétal, le Havre, Dieppe, Fécamp, Saint-Valéry-en-Caux, Saint-Valéry-sur-Somme, Honfleur, Caen, Lisieux, Pont-l'Évêque, Alençon, Amiens, Abbeville, Calais, Arras, Lille, Dunkirk, Péronne, Troyes, to mention some of the more serious outbreaks), and even in such places as Bordeaux. Popular violence rose to two peaks, first in Ventôse–Germinal, then in Floréal–Prairial—there is a remarkable concordance between the dates of riots in the whole area of the Lower Seine, a concordance that led some of the higher authorities to refer to the spread of disorder as 'an electrical shock'.

But this kind of riot disappeared in the year IV; the situation was by then so fearful that the potential rioter was either dead or dying, busy pawning his remaining possessions, including his bedding, queuing for bourgeois charity, roaming the countryside in search of food, or enlisting in the *bandes* of *chauffeurs*.[2] A great many potential rioters took the extreme remedy of committing suicide—in Paris, the suicide figures had never been so high, even in the year III. The only urban disturbances in the year IV were led by women. On previous less desperate occasions they had always managed to bring out the men, but this time they failed to do so. There followed a series of good harvests in 1796, 1797, and 1798, and this for the time being delivered the Directory from this traditional danger. The regime was fortunate in this respect at least, if in no other—for no other French government has had to contend with open defiance and disobedience and an administrative strike on quite such a scale. Regional disturbances occurred once more in the Nord, the Pas-de-Calais, and the Somme in the crisis of 1801–2; the former Prefect of the Pas-de-Calais was to attribute them to the machinations of 'English agents', who had come over to drive up the price of grain by massive secret purchases, and thus provoke an artificial crisis and arouse popular fears. These were followed by nearly ten years of peace on the markets—one

[1] 'The White Terror', in *The Times Literary Supplement*, 10 August 1967. For the White Terror in the south see below, pp. 131–49.

[2] See note D, p. 333.

of the longest breaks ever allowed to a French government in eighteenth- or early nineteenth-century conditions.

But if dearth, and its usual accompaniments of grain riots, *arrêts*, and panic, receded for a decade, the diseases of the poor knew no remission throughout these years, but increased in virulence with each added year of war in the first fifteen years of the century.[1] Dysentery and typhus were particularly prevalent in a series of villages in the Seine-et-Marne, along the military high roads to the east, almost without interruption from 1806 to 1815, as well as in the *communes* on the eastern periphery of Paris, again the point of entry of troops from the Rhine. In the former region the epidemics reached their height in two waves, from the winter of 1811 to the end of the summer of 1812, and from the winter of 1814 to the end of the summer of 1815. Both waves coincided with massive French or allied troop movements.

The principal sources of infection were the villages of Vaudoy-en-Brie, an important centre on the high road from Paris to Bar-le-Duc; Champdeuil, on the road from Melun to Meaux; and a cluster of localities on the edge of the Forêt de Fontainebleau, south of Melun and on or near the road from Gien and the Gâtinais: Guercheville, Amponville, Jacqueville, Achères-la-Forêt, Ury, Dormelles, and Noisy-sur-École; in all, there was heavy mortality between 1810 and 1812.

The second outbreak occurred in the small towns of Château-Landon, Moret, and Montigny-sur-Loing, and in the neighbouring village of Écuelles, again all localities situated on or near the military high roads from the south-east and from the centre to the capital, from 1814 to 1815. The epidemics also lapped the eastern fringes of Paris; Pantin was the centre of a series of disasters—cholera, dysentery, typhus—that were endemic from 1808 to 1812 and were attributed by the medical authorities to the extreme poverty of the inhabitants of the *commune*.[2] In 1812 the area of

---

[1] Asked to explain the causes of these diseases—mostly typhus and various forms of dysentery—medical officers from Melun and Nemours were to report: 'C'est . . . dans la continuité de la guerre qu'il faut chercher la cause de cette dépopulation.' 'L'état continuel des guerres dans lequel la France a été plongée depuis vingt-quatre ans en est la cause principale . . .' (A.N. F8 79, Épidémies, Seine-et-Marne, 1806–1815). See also below, pp. 219–22.

[2] '. . . C'est la classe indigente qui est particulièrement attaquée . . . tous les ans, dans les mois d'été les habitans . . . sont attaqués . . . de fièvres bileuses . . . de choléra, de dyssenterie . . . les gens riches n'ont aucune communication avec les pauvres . . .' (A.N. F8 77, Épidémies, Seine).

infection spread to Bondy, Bobigny, Noisy-le-Sec, La Villette, and Fontenay-sous-Bois. '. . . C'est la misère profonde de la plupart des habitans . . .', says a report of this last *commune*,[1] while in Saint-Denis there were annual bouts of typhus, during the summer months, from 1805 to 1812.[2] In 1806 and 1807 there were two recurrent outbreaks of typhus, this time south of Paris, in the vicinity of Sceaux: Créteil, Bonneuil, and Maisons.[3] Thus, by 1810 to 1812, the capital was lapped by diseases of the poor to the north, east, and south, while the disasters in the east of Europe were further aggravated by extremely destructive outbreaks in localities in which troops had been garrisoned, during the three successive years, along the roads of the Seine-et-Marne. By some miracle, Paris itself remained free from infection.

The year 1812 not only saw a massive deployment of vagrants and heavy mortality among the poor to the east of Paris, but also witnessed a resumption of the traditional market riot. The worst occurred in Caen, on 2 March 1812, a Monday:

le lundi est toujours un jour difficile [observed the Prefect of the Cal-vados, in his report for 7 April], malgré l'extrême misère, les ouvriers le passent dans l'oisiveté et [dans] toute la débauche à laquelle ils peuvent se livrer. . . . La halle étoit fort agitée, des femmes furieuses vouloient acheter les grains à un prix arbitraire et réclamoient la taxe. . . . Dès que je fus sur la place, une foule considérable me suivit en criant *Du pain et l'ouvrage*. . . .

A mill and a grain store were attacked and pillaged, the house of a grain merchant was sacked and set on fire, the grain barges in the port were unloaded by a crowd of several thousand, among which women from the *faubourg* of Vaucelles—textile workers and laun-dresses—appear to have been the leading spirits and the most vociferous in incitement. The rioters were soon joined by a group of conscripts, who were due to leave the town on the following day; the Prefect, the magistrates, and the police were insulted.

The riot also had serious political undercurrents; for it was rumoured among the crowd that the Emperor had died in Moscow and that a Council of Regency had been proclaimed; and the rumours persisted for the next month, coinciding with the worst period of the dearth crisis, which, as always, was almost as severe in this Department as in the Seine-Inférieure. On 14 April the

---

[1] A.N. F8 77 (Épidémies, Seine).   [2] Ibid.   [3] Ibid.

Prefect was to inform the Minister of the Interior: 'On répand ici la nouvelle de séditions très graves à Amiens [there had been a minor disturbance there a week before, on the 7th] et à Lyon; dans cette dernière ville, le peuple auroit désarmé la troupe et tiré le canon sur elle'—a further tribute to the reputation enjoyed by the Second City even among the common people, as well as among the repressive authorities, for, in fact, the rumour was completely unfounded, and Lyon and the Rhône were one of the quietest areas throughout the crisis; on 19 April, the Prefect reports further: 'on vint me rapporter qu'à l'instant même . . . une femme, épuisée de faim, avait lancé ses deux enfans du pont de Vaucelles dans l'Orne, & s'y étoit précipitée après eux. . . . Ce bruit avoit causé une vive et dangereuse impression; il étoit le sujet de l'entretien des groupes qui environnoient la halle; je ne savois moi-même qu'en penser, lorsque les recherches les plus exactes me donnèrent la conviction que ce récit étoit faux, & conséquemment l'œuvre de la malveillance. . . . Hier un homme atteint de la démence s'est avisé de traverser une partie du faubourg de Vaucelles, & de se jeter dans la rivière; il a été de suite transformé en un homme que la faim avoit réduit aux derniers excès du désespoir. Il a été sauvé & est maintenant à Beaulieu dans une loge de fou. . . .' Two days later, the wretched man informed the Minister: 'On fait circuler sur les bords de la mer les bruits les plus absurdes et les plus fâcheux. Des étrangers bien vêtus ont été remarqués parcourant la côte et se plaisant à donner les nouvelles les plus alarmantes. La révolte de Lyon est toujours mise en avant; on ajoute que . . . l'Ambassadeur de Russie a pris la fuite, que l'Impératrice elle-même s'est retirée en Allemagne. . . .' On 26 April, he writes: 'Il faut que je dise à V. E. encore que la publicité donnée aux désordres qui affligent l'Angleterre à raison de la cherté des grains, loin de prouver que ce fléau est commun à toute l'Europe, qu'il est le résultat nécessaire d'une mauvaise récolte, et d'encourager à la patience, provoque les séditieux; le peuple cite ces détails dans tous ses entretiens et s'en autorise dans ses projects de troubles. Les briseurs de métiers de Manchester et de Nottingham sont à la veille de trouver des imitateurs dans l'arrondissement de Vire. Déjà un fabricant (M. Triel), qui emploie un grand nombre d'ouvriers, a reçu une lettre anonyme çmenaante. . . .' No wonder the Napoleonic Prefects feared food riots more than any other form of public protest, for it would be hard to discover a more characteristic example of the relationship between dearth, rumour, and panic than these reports from Caen.

The Imperial authorities had been seriously disturbed by the extent of a riot that they thought no longer possible under the repressive conditions of 1812 ('disorders of this kind,' states another Prefect in the course of the same crisis, 'which were possible under the previous regime, can no longer be seriously feared, thanks to the reverence and fear inspired by the person of His Majesty'). Like most of their predecessors in the year III, they attributed it to the intervention of contrived sedition. The Prefect was blamed for his lack of foresight, and, within a week of the riot, after the garrison had been strongly reinforced, a court martial was set up to try the ringleaders. Its verdict was exceptionally severe; on 14 March eight persons were condemned to death: Lhonneur, *maître d'écriture*, Samson, *excoriateur*, Barbanche, *marin*, fille Goujeon, *fileuse*, femme Prévost, *dentellière*, Vesdy, *blanchisseur*, fille Tilly, *rentière*, femme Retour, *filassière*; nine more were sentenced to eight years' hard labour, and a further nine to five years' imprisonment. Most of those convicted were women textile workers from Vaucelles, as well as day labourers, porters, and *badestamiers*.[1]

Much of the severity of the military judges can be attributed to what they regarded as the many and dangerous parallels between the March 1812 riot and events in Caen in 1789 and during the Revolution. On the day of the riot, women had been heard evoking the fate of M. de Belsunce, a young army officer lynched in July 1789 when he had attempted to disperse a riotous crowd; and there had been ugly reminders of the attachment of the *petit peuple* to the *maximum*. A little later, in April, when the news of the March Decrees reached Caen, it was at once rumoured that the government, following the example of the Prefect of the Seine-et-Marne, had decided to establish a *maximum* 'et de taxer le bled à f. 33 l'hectolitre. Des blanchisseuses ont quitté leurs bateaux et se sont mises à danser en rond presque sous les fenêtres de la Préfecture. . . .' This was the sort of thing that the Imperial authorities most wanted to avoid. The Prefects, a number of whom had served

[1] A few days later the local wits placarded up in the town: 'Le Préfet a perdu l'appétit, le Maire a perdu l'honneur, et ils ont mis la France aux fers.' Samson's *nom de guerre* was *L'Appétit*, and one of the women condemned to a heavy prison sentence was named Lafrance. Even the Empire had not entirely destroyed the irreverence of popular humour.

under the old regime, in positions of repressive authority, were well aware of the strength of rumour and of the remarkable persistence of popular memory. Throughout the 1812 crisis there are constant evocations of the *maximum*, although authorities at all levels are extremely careful never to use the word in public (they use it often enough, and with horror, in their reports to the Minister) and to point out that the March and May Decrees did not constitute anything of the sort. In such circumstances the *petit peuple* was its own best historian.

Caen was the most serious outbreak of popular disorder in 1812, owing to its political implications. There were market disturbances, as there had been in the spring and summer of 1795, in the Pays d'Auge, at Honfleur, Pont-l'Évêque, and Lisieux, all places extremely sensitive to shortage or to the threat of it. Apart from in the Calvados, the most serious threat to public order occurred at Issoudun on 25, 26, 27, 28, and 29 April; it was, in fact, mostly talk, various inhabitants of the Faubourg Saint-Paterne threatening to set fire to the houses of the rich, two women being accused of having said 'qu'elles mettroient le feu aux quatre coins de la ville', and the *maire* being in receipt of anonymous threats of arson; there was also an attack on the office of the *droits réunis*. On the last day, 29 April, however, a huge granary belonging to Heurlant-Dumez, the richest landowner in the area, went up in flames. Again repression was vigorous; and again most of those sentenced were women. There were disorders at the end of January in Rennes and in Fougères; on 10 March the Prefect of the Indre-et-Loire refers to a crime wave that he attributes to poverty: 'les voleurs et les assassins ont attaqué particulièrement des porteurs de bleds. . . .' On 16 March in the course of a market riot in Beaune, the *maire* was knocked down. There was a riot in Elbeuf in the same month; and, after a series of arrests in the Eure, ninety offenders were sent to Rouen for trial. On 7 April, a group of women attempted to prevent a grain convoy from leaving Amiens for Abbeville.

On the whole the regime got off lightly. The Napoleonic order did not intend to place itself at the mercy of a grain riot; the Prefects, a vastly improved police, the regulations concerning 'associations' and 'assemblies', saw to that. A few poor *dentellières* were no match for such a concentration of bureaucratic repression, especially when they had no programme other than *Nous ne voulons pas mourir de faim debout,* no organization to fall back on, and little to encourage them other than the memory of the realities of the year II and the slogans of the year III. In all the riots of 1812, they seem to have enjoyed only a minimum of masculine support. The Empire also had a much wider provisioning area to draw on than had been available either to the old royal government or to revolutionary France, when, in times of shortage, Paris food commissioners would poach on the provisioning areas of Rouen, Amiens, Lille, Metz, Troyes, Dijon, and even Lyon, thus driving up the price of grain. In 1812 Paris, the stricken Norman Departments, the Somme, and the Nord received massive supplies fairly rapidly—the situation in Rouen was beginning to improve in the second half of July—over land or by waterway from the Ruhr and other Rhineland Departments, as well as from Holland. Lyon and the Rhône were similarly saved from the full effects of the dearth by imports from Swabia and the Palatinate.

At home, in the meantime, the sting was taken out of riot and the people were eventually kept quiet—there were no riots after the end of April—by a massive mobilization of private charity on the part of the Prefects and Sub-Prefects to finance the soup kitchens in the cities. At the end of the year those that had contributed most to the organization of the *soupes à la Rumfort* received a shower of decorations—the *Ordre de la Réunion* was the great stand-by—graded in gold and silver medals; they had earned them; for they had soon reduced the potential rioter to the humble recipient of *notables'* charity. In some Departments, Rolls of Honour were drawn up, with the amounts contributed by each person, for display at the *mairie* or the *sous-préfecture* (in le Havre, the Hombergs and the other inhabitants of the Grand Quai top the list, with the masonic lodge of *L'Aménité* a close second; in the Norman countryside, Protestant landowners, by their generosity, were to earn the rather grudging thanks of the Prefect, Girardin). The pulpit was likewise mobilized—the *curés* cannot all have been as stupid as the over-zealous incumbent of Parthenay—to preach submission, patience, and gratitude. Napoleon's regime was thus made safe from the grain riot, not only by repressive legislation and the use of troops, but also by a combination of the charity bazaar, the pillage economy of conquest, and by the existence of a European market in grain that stretched without barriers from the Atlantic to the Ems, from the Channel to the Adriatic. Belgian

and Swiss intermediaries, Dutch and Rhenish corn-factors, and
the suppliers of the armies in Spain (largely grain-merchants from
the Lauragais) did very well indeed out of a crisis that had been
solved by the spring of 1813 (though with a considerable increase
in mortality in Rouen,[1] in the Eure,[2] in the Gers,[3] in the Ille-et-
Vilaine,[4] and in the Indre-et-Loire[5]) when the restrictive decrees
and regulations were withdrawn.

There was even as a result of the March and May Decrees,
widely identified in the popular mind with the *recensements* and
the *maximum* of the year II, some return of popular confidence in
a regime that, up till then, had appeared uniquely repressive and
heartless in its dealings with the common people. The laundry-
women of Caen were not the only ones to dance for joy when the
first garbled versions of the decrees began to seep through the
curtain of official secrecy. Prefects' reports state that, while well-
to-do circles regarded the Decrees with deep dismay as a return
to 'the deplorable system of eighteen years ago'—requisitioning,
billeting, and garrisoning, the employment of force against the
rural landowner[6]—the Emperor had never been so adulated by
the poor. It must have been very embarrassing for him. But by the
spring of 1812 it was possible to withdraw the Decrees and to
return to normal. It was typical of the regime that their withdrawal
should have been accompanied by the banishment of former *sans-
culotte* militants from Paris and from some other cities. The best
way to remove the unpleasant impression left with the *honnêtes
gens* by this brief return to the economy of the Terror was thus to
demonstrate that the Government was still as repressive as ever as
far as the *classes populacières* were concerned.

---

[1] A.N. F 11 718: Prefect to Minister, 8 September 1812: '. . . Dans la ville de
Rouen . . . il y a eu beaucoup plus de décès pendant les sept premiers mois de
1812 que pendant les mois correspondants de 1811. . . .'

[2] A.N. F 11 709: '. . . Car c'est une vérité, un grand nombre a péri surtout
dans la classe des vieillards et des enfants' (lettre du directeur de l'hospice de
Bourg-Achard, 22 décembre 1812).

[3] A.N. F 11 710 (Prefet du Gers au Ministre, 29 juillet 1812): '. . .
L'année dernière les décès ont surpassé les naissances de près de 2000. . . .'

[4] A.N. F 11 711 (Préfet de l'Ille-et-Vilaine au Ministre, 18 avril 1812).

[5] Ibid. (Préfet de l'Indre-et-Loire au Ministre, 1er juin 1812).

[6] One infuriated Norman gentleman was to complain to his Sub-Prefect:
'Monsieur, ma maison, mes basses-cours, tous mes bâtimens enfin ont été
visités, et la gendarmerie a fini par s'emparer de ma personne. Nous voilà donc
revenus en '93' (A.N. F 11 718).

PART TWO
THE POPULAR MOVEMENT IN DECLINE
(1795–1818) AND THE NATURE OF
SANS-CULOTTE MILITANCY

'Ils sont au plus 60 hommes et autant de femmes et à
cette petite minorité ils voudroient mener la Section qui
est de 8 à 9,000 hommes. Je n'accuse pas la totalité de
la société, mais bien 6 ou 8 particuliers.'
(*An inhabitant of the Section du Panthéon*)

7. 'A LA RECHERCHE DU SANS-CULOTTE'

IN the previous section we have attempted to give a brief account
of the forms and of the chronology of popular protest between the
fall of Robespierre and the collapse of the Empire. Our concern
has been to outline what happened to the 'popular movement'
during these years and even to question whether such a thing
could be said to have existed at all. In the present section, if we
except the brief period of popular militancy that has been described as 'direct democracy' or as *le mouvement sans-culotte*, the
scope of our subject is limited to the various more traditional
forms of popular agitation, the ways in which it might impinge on
higher authority, and the general course of 'popular movements'
in their cruder, more spontaneous forms between 1795 and 1815.
What happened after the short period of popular rule may help
to explain both why that rule was so short-lived and why popular
protest was, on the whole, so ineffective. For it is in the post-
Terror period, particularly in the year III, that a key to the proper
understanding of the *sans-culotte* movement of the year II may
best be sought. In other words, the movement itself should not be
studied in isolation in the purely year II context. There is as much
to be learnt from the long years of failure and disenchantment as
from the highly dramatic, and largely accidental, experiment in
popular democracy, itself soon tempered by revolutionary bureaucracy and centralization. The whole 'problem', if there be a

problem at all, can most effectively be ventilated by thus working back from 1795, from 1796, and from the next nineteen years, to the conditions of 1793 to 1794.

First of all, then, we have to deal with the *sans-culotte* as such—that is to say, with a person not as he was, let us say, in 1792, or as he would have become in 1795 or in 1796, but as he was for a brief period from 1793 to 1794. For the life and death of the *sans-culotte* can be circumscribed within a period running more or less from April 1793 to April 1794, allowing for a possible overlap up to Thermidor year II or even to Brumaire year III. It would certainly be stretching the species too far to describe, as a Norwegian historian has done,[1] the course of the popular movement during the year III as *la défaite des sans-culottes*, for, from the second month (Brumaire) at latest of that year, there was nothing left to be defeated; the *sans-culotte*, no doubt, was unaware of this at the time, just as he had previously been unaware that he was, first, being used by the Revolutionary Government, and was then being dismissed with scant thanks by the same government, once his services were no longer required. Having once exercised a little power, at least at the level of the *commune*, the *sans-culotte* could not easily acclimatize himself to a situation in which he was excluded from even the humblest office. And it was largely his enormous self-confidence and self-righteousness, his conviction so often and so unwisely expressed in cafés and public places that *le règne des sans-culottes reviendrait* and that then the *honnêtes gens* would have to look to it, that was to precipitate his political destruction and often his personal ruin in the course of the year III. What he so blandly hoped for, others feared more than anything else; and they were in a position to see that his ill-advisedly expressed hopes would not be realized, if necessary by killing the man himself, his physical being, after destroying what had been a political reality. Certainly, by a mixture of imprudent threats and boastfulness, by the frequent evocation of a Terror, bigger and better than ever—and his remarks, so easily seized upon by Thermidorian magistrates or *comités*, would generally be further inflated *en cours de route*—he directly contributed to his own destruction.

The *sans-culotte* is not an individual with an independent life of his own. It could not be said of him 'once a *sans-culotte*, always a

[1] Kåre Tønnesson, *La Défaite des sans-culottes* (Oslo, 1959).

sans-culotte'; for, apart from the difficulties of an exact definition of this status, discussed briefly in the previous section, he exists at all only as a unit within a collectivity, which itself exists only in virtue of certain specific, unusual, and temporary institutions: once the sectionary institutions have been destroyed, or tamed, the *sans-culotte* too disappears; in his place, there is what there had been before—a shoemaker, a hatter, a tailor, a tanner, a wine merchant, a clerk, a carpenter, a cabinet-maker, an engraver, a miniaturist, a fan-maker, a fencing-master, a teacher.[1] There is nothing left save perhaps the memory of militancy and a hankering after Brave Times, that appear all the braver when remembered under very hard ones. The *sans-culotte* then is not a social or economic being; he is a political accident. So are the institutions that gave the *sans-culottes* their brief opportunity for collective expression. We shall return to this accident of history when we consider, in more detail, the much-disputed question of the relationship between the *sans-culotte* movement and the Revolutionary Government, between *la sans-culotterie* and *la bourgeoisie jacobine*, or more simply, to invert the order (for how could anyone put him second?), between Robespierre and the popular movement.

Most historians are now familiar with Albert Soboul's rather formalized account of the relations between the classes—especially the urban classes—in the course of the revolutionary period, both from his *Précis*[2] and from his even shorter *Que-sais-je?*[3] A *pas de deux* or sometimes a *pas de trois*, that might be set to music as a historical ballet. Opening scene: bourgeoisie and people, hand in hand, dancing on the prone figure of Privilege. Scene Two: (the people having done their stuff) bourgeoisie and monarchy, hand in hand, dancing on the prone figure of the people. Scene Three: bourgeoisie and people, hand in hand, dancing on the prone body of monarchy. Scene Four: an intermezzo between bourgeoisie and people, only occasionally hand in hand, more often hands vainly extended, both playing hard to get.[4] Scene Five: bourgeoisie dancing alone, on the prone bodies of people and monarchy. One knew it would turn out like this all along, for that is the rule of a

---

[1] See note E, p. 334.
[2] Albert Soboul, *Précis d'histoire de la Révolution française* (Paris, 1962).
[3] Albert Soboul, *La Révolution française* (*Que sais-je?*) (Paris, 1963).
[4] See note F, p. 334.

particularly rigorous choreography that will not allow a step to be taken out of place (and, if necessary, the *sans-culotte* may have to be nudged and reminded of his part: 'Get back into line, you are part of the Popular Movement'; the bourgeois, too, forgetting that he is either a Girondin, or Jacobin, or Montagnard, or Thermidorian, may have to be recalled rather roughly to realities, and not be allowed to wander off on his own to look at the shops or enjoy a walk in the country). It is admirably done, the actors know their parts, sink to the ground on the appropriate note, rise again when summoned. The prompter is very discreet and hardly at all in evidence.

Yet one has doubts; it all seems too well rehearsed. And the doubts are confirmed by the same author's definitive account of the *mouvement sectionnaire* in Paris and of its relations with the Revolutionary Government. For in this great work[1] the ballet steps are only briefly remembered, as a matter of form, at the opening and closing of chapters that in their massive middle disclose a much more confusing scene: uncertainties of contour, difficulties of definition, lack of clear objectives, shifting loyalties, internal contradictions, personal squabbles, the role of personalities and of militant minorities, preliminary committee work, the 'fixing' of an agenda, passion, confusion, credulity, myth, anarchy, noise. It is not even certain whether the two tentative partners are, at all times, aware of each other's existence, and there is much more groping and shuffling and searching and back-turning than anything like an ordered movement. This, in its always complicated, detailed narrative, looks much more like the real thing. Soboul's great merit is to have explored that narrative, recreated it, and put it end to end, so that, in the long-drawn-out and complicated process of gradual divorce between a very varied, highly decentralized *mouvement sectionnaire* and a Revolutionary Government that contains a wide range of revolutionary fervour, one is guided by a day-to-day chronology.

8. THE ROLE OF MILITANT MINORITIES

Albert Soboul is describing a mass movement that operated, for a limited period, through certain institutions. The movement did not create the institutions, but the institutions, which already

[1] Albert Soboul, *Les Sans-culottes parisiens et le mouvement sectionnaire* (Paris, 1958).

existed, created the movement and imposed upon it certain inbred structural weaknesses. These weaknesses necessitated forms of organization that were tentative and strongly federalist, and that in turn involved a great deal of preliminary negotiation. It is often stated that the popular movement during the French Revolution tended towards extreme forms of decentralization, and Soboul's Paris *sectionnaire* is taken as the obvious example. But the *sectionnaire* is federalist because the Section is; thus the institutions model the movement, and the Section forms the *sectionnaire*. The Section was an urban village, the Quarter, a world to itself. Of course, when confronted with threats from outside, the Sections would seek to work together, and to impose a common programme. But the peril had to be very great; and much time and energy were taken up by quarrels between different Sections and by personal bids for power within the Section itself. The movement, all forty-eight Sections lumped together as a *mouvement sans-culotte*, may reasonably be described as a mass one comprising some two hundred thousand Parisians; but within each Section, effective power is exercised by small minorities of revolutionary militants—twelve or twenty men at the most,[1] who, thanks to their skill, to the strength of their vocal organs, to their physique,[2] to the time they are prepared to devote to militancy, to their own prestige, to their own patronage (for a number were important employers of labour), are able to manipulate the proceedings of the larger assemblies *en petit comité* and push through their proposals well in advance. (Later their opponents made much of this, in their efforts to isolate the *dominateurs*, the *aboyeurs*, from the general mass of *sectionnaires*, and suggested that the experiment in 'direct democracy' disguised what was in fact the workings of a 'secret committee' manipulated by a handful of men. This is a constant theme in Thermidorian *enquêtes* and propaganda, and all the more convin-

---

[1] Mercereau, an *officier de paix* of the Section du Panthéon Français, comments on the manner in which the *société sectionnaire* was run: 'Je déclare que la société est le germe de toutes les haines, ils sont au plus 60 hommes et autant de femmes et à cette petite minorité ils voudroient mener la Section qui est de 8 à 9,000 hommes. Je n'accuse pas la totalité de la société, mais bien 6 ou 8 particuliers . . .' (A.N. F7 4774 d 3 (Mercereau)).

[2] One *meneur*, who is also an *inspecteur*, is accused, in the year III, of having terrorized his fellow *sectionnaires* by attending all the meetings of the *assemblée générale* and of the *société*, accompanied by an enormous and very fierce dog (Cobb and Rudé, 'Le Dernier Mouvement populaire de la Révolution à Paris', *Revue historique*, October–December 1955).

cing in that it corresponded to a certain degree with the reality, as recalled by people of many shades of opinion, a year later.)[1]

Soboul's own account shows that a great deal of preliminary work went into preparing Sectionary business, that there was often a lot of lobbying, that matters were seldom left to the chance of a free vote, and that the *sans-culotte* movement could hardly be described as spontaneous or even as particulary democratic unless we admit that there existed a degree of super-*sans-culottisme* which placed some *sectionnaires* over their fellow citizens, in a category apart, élitist and unassailable. For there existed, at least in the *bureaux*, an inner ring of self-taught militants who, though political amateurs, were soon learning how to manipulate an assembly and prepare business from within a *comité*. In time, they would have become professionals. Already, by the first months of the year III, when in *commune* after *commune* they were dislodged from their entrenched positions, generally by the outside intervention of a *Représentant en mission*—it would take nothing less to prise them out of their hold on a *comité* or a municipality—they had acquired a professional mentality, considering themselves indispensable to the forward march of the Revolution and to the particular interests of their own town or village. So much was this the case that, right up to the summer of 1795, their one thought was that they would soon get back, as their fellow citizens were bound to realize, sooner or later, that they could not do without their valuable services. But they were, of course, removable, even in the circumstances of the year II, and many of the bitter personal squabbles that take up so much space in Sectionary minutes—sometimes for weeks on end, to the exclusion of all else—arose out of attempts to dislodge the reigning clan that had, for one reason or another, made itself generally intolerable—and most of these *meneurs* were loud-mouthed, arrogant, intolerant, some of them were impossible little tyrants, constantly boasting of how they disposed of the power of life and death, gaily talking of the heads that would fall and taking an obvious enjoyment in sending shudders down the backs of those whom they were seeking to impress or to cow[2]—and to replace it by people who were popular in the assemblies or in the *sociétés*, areas in which the virtues of the proverbial 'good committee man' were likely to be less appreciated.

[1] See note G, p. 335.   [2] See note H, p. 335.

Even at this level, there were bound to be conflicts between the general mass of *sectionnaires*, for whom politics could only be very much of a part-time evening occupation, and the small groups of committed men, who claimed to do their thinking for them. Sectionary politics are full of clans, and so are those of provincial *sociétés*; for these were mostly people who knew each other well— that is to say, who knew much that was damaging about one another—and posts in the *bureaux*, especially those which raised their holders to a prominent position, above most of their fellows, on a *tribune* or in the president's high chair, were objects of as much envy and back-biting as an officer or non-commissioned rank in the *Garde nationale*. The butcher, the grocer, the shoemaker of the Quarter or of the *bourg* are bound to live in conceit. Their wives lived even more so and it was because of the corroding influence of feminine jealousies that some popular assemblies sought to exclude women, even as onlookers. The greatest glory was that which was visible to the whole street, to the whole village. The soldier decorated for gallantry and the scholarship boy will hurry home to exhibit themselves. And, though women did not vote in the assemblies, they did much to blow on the furnaces of neighbourly discord if they felt that their husbands or companions were not getting the recognition that they deserved for their patriotism and long service to the Revolution. If the *patriotes de 93* were in control, then the whole syndicate of the *patriotes de 89*—and the *sans-culottes* could generally muster a few of these—would be grumbling in the wings about newcomers, demagogues, and so on, in sulky deprivation. Revolutionary patriotism, they suggested, should be calculated in terms of length of service to the Cause.

To this the newcomers might reply that the first in the field had fallen by the wayside, having compromised themselves on one of the many occasions between July 1789 and May–June 1793 when it was possible to plump for the wrong side. There was much to be said, in the conditions of the year II, for having been out of public life till 1793. It might, in fact, more often be a conflict between the April men and the September men, for not a great many *sans-culottes* could show service much before 1792, and the great internal revolutions within the Sections occurred between the spring and the late summer of 1793. Many *meneurs* (*aboyeurs* as the Thermidorians were to call them) made themselves intolerable by their insolent bearing, and, at the beginning of the year III, there was a genuine and very widespread revulsion against the former *dominateurs*. They had at best been meddlesome, 'superior', and impatient of criticism, at worst tyrannical, heartless, brutal, and insufferable. Militancy is not likely to breed fraternal love; the militant had few friends and many toadies; and in the year III such people would have no friends at all, those whom they had once obliged or protected being the first to keep their distances. But already in the year II it is possible to distinguish between a minority of activists and the general mass of good, middling, or indifferent *sans-culottes*. As popular institutions everywhere declined, after Floréal, this distinction would already have become more marked, with a vast increase in this last category, so that the militants would become members of a tiny *cénacle*, devoted to keeping going a 'movement' that no longer existed—an act of revolutionary piety that was to be the principal concern of those who survived for the next twenty years.

Perhaps one of the greatest weaknesses of the popular movement of the year II was this reliance on very small groups of individuals, easily isolated and immediately identifiable, who through imprudence, conceit, or the foolish notion that their power would endure for ever, had made themselves and the movement with which they had become identified (and Thermidorian propaganda was devoted to 'personalizing' *la sans-culotterie* in a handful of names and character sketches) thoroughly disliked by a wide section of the community that included many people of their own condition. The hatred so often shown to them in the conditions of the year III cannot only have been the result of intelligent vilification; in some cases at least, particularly in Lyon and the Midi, they were hated because they had been hateful. Nothing very terrible happened to the former terrorists of the Upper Norman Departments. The most surprising thing about these zealous servitors of Terror and Repression was that they should have taken so many risks and offered themselves up so completely as hostages to the future. For few of their victims, real or potential, ever made the mistake of calculating that the Terror and the 'popular movement' would go on for ever, or that they could be anything other than temporary and accidental. Perhaps the enjoyment of power and genuine revolutionary patriotism were stronger inducements than common prudence. If one is to judge at all from Thermidorian reports— and these are, of course, heavily loaded—it is amazing how suicidal many of these militants had been, though more in speech than in action. Many of them were to pay with their lives for words uttered as boasts, to demonstrate that there was nothing that they could not, or would not, do.

In principle, Soboul is writing about a mass movement—this is his own approach—but in fact his celebrated thesis is mostly concerned with the role of élites and the methods employed by individual militants. He does name the militants, but he does not give any of them the benefit of a personality. The result is that we can see how they operated, but we gain virtually no impression of what they were like, whether they were sincere or were time-servers, whether they were out for publicity or for the fruits of office, whether they had sound sense or were crackpots. We just have to accept that they were militants and that something, whether ambition or sincerity, distinguished them from the general mass of their neighbours. He introduces us to *les sectionnaires*—that small core of six or seven hundred, sometimes even fewer, twenty or thirty in places like le Havre or Dieppe, ten or fifteen in small towns like Salon or Martigues—upon whom was to fall the weight of future successive proscriptions; but we do not meet *le sectionnaire*, the man himself, swimming in the history of the Revolution, fighting to keep his head above tormented and fast-flowing waters.

This is partly the author's own choice, for he is dealing with so large a team that, in a study of this kind, there could hardly be room for portraits of individuals. It might be objected too that recourse to personal 'case histories' puts too great a burden on the historian's imagination or on his powers of selection, that such a method is 'unscientific', and even borders on the anecdotal.[1] Even so, the impression remains that there is an element missing: Soboul has lived with his *sans-culottes*, but, perhaps, not very intimately— they are there to serve a purpose, and can then be dismissed. He gives only a cursory glance at their domestic arrangements and makes little attempt to track them down into non-political leisure; and, after 1795, they enter the night of time—unless they are lucky enough to have attracted the approving attention of Babeuf and his Revolutionary Selection Board.

[1] The present author has been criticized for having, in his *Armées*, allowed certain of his characters too long an audience, simply because they had a lot to say for themselves, or because they were attractive, or amusing, or curious. See the review article by Hr. Kåre Tønnesson, in *Past & Present*, No. 1, 1964.

This is a pity. The *sans-culottes*, particularly the more extravagant figures who, especially in small towns far from Paris, emerged at the head of them for a few months, were often intense individualists. They regarded the revolutionary movement as their own personal property and were unwilling to take orders from any man, however high placed and however covered in sash and ribbon. It is quite possible to add that further dimension by extending the time limit of research, as far as the Paris *sans-culottes* are concerned—hence the interest of following the 'popular movement' in Paris into the Slough of Despond from 1795 to 1816 or beyond, not so much to discover why the popular movement failed as to discover what happened to its leaders after the year III. The scope of research can also be extended by, for instance, investigating the 'pauperization' of the former *sans-culotte* cadres in the years IV and V, through petitions to the *Commission des Secours*, in order to justify indigence and so qualify for relief, at least in the form of free bread.[1]

Another method is to choose a smaller canvas and to study the *sans-culotte* milieu and certain dominant traits of the 'revolutionary temperament' in a provincial setting. For the real terrain of 'ultra-revolutionism'—a 'movement', if the term can be used for anything so individualistic and anarchical, far more extreme and less calculating than that of the Paris *sectionnaires*—was not in the capital, for the Parisians had the Revolutionary Government on their doorsteps and could not make a move without provoking threatening rumblings from the Committee of General Security. The opportunity for the 'ultra-revolutionary', a man who might be described, according to tastes, as *le révolutionnaire intégral*, as *un grand exaspéré*, or as *un grand naïf* and a fool of suicidal proportions, was in the Departments. There was a geography of 'ultracism' and revolutionary extremism. It extended in a vast half-moon, whose open end faced south, from Perpignan and Toulouse, via the valley of the Garonne (Moissac and Tonneins), to Libourne, thence to the Creuse and the Haute-Vienne. Parts of the Loiret and the Nièvre were at the top of the curve, which then sweeps down the valleys of the Loire and the Allier to include this last Department, thence via Mâcon to fan out into the present economic area of Rhône–Saône, from the Monts du Forez to the Swiss frontier, with Lyon as its

[1] See below, pp. 156, 160.

capital[1]—and finally down the valley of the Rhône to the Mediterranean.

These, and certain garrison towns elsewhere, are the places where the ultra-revolutionary may be encountered in his untrammelled splendour and where the full implications of the *mouvement sectionnaire*, often only hinted at in the constricting circumstances of Paris, are developed, although briefly, to a full flowering of anarchical freedom. This too was the terrain of revolutionary experimentalism in every direction—popular justice, popular fiscality, dechristianization and popular cults, popular armed forces.[2] In some instances this experimentalism was the work of locals; but more often those who carried out the experiments were strangers, sometimes Parisians, generally townsmen, with strong contingents of talent from such places as Moulins and Nevers, Mâcon, Toulouse, Valence, Vienne, Grenoble. Such men, for a time, had no one on their backs and were not restrained by the influences of family or community.[3] We do not need Kropotkin to remind us that 'communalism' could have a better run for its money in the *commune* of Crémieu,[4] in that of Heyrieu,[5] in that of Tonneins-la-Montagne,[6] than in the *commune* of Paris.

The Committees were themselves well aware that the Sectionary movement was much more dangerous in the Departments than in Paris. This is what they meant when they asserted that *hébertisme* was a provincial phenomenon (it was). When they spoke of *l'ébauche d'un nouveau fédéralisme populaire*, they had in mind what was happening in Valence, Avignon, Marseille, and Montpellier, rather than what was going under their noses in the capital. And, in the purges of the winter of 1793 and the spring of 1794, most of the arrests were in provincial towns, the nearest of which to the capital was Troyes; very few ultras were arrested in Paris itself, but a

[1] 'La Commission temporaire de commune affranchie', in *Terreur et subsistances*, pp. 55–94; *L'Armée révolutionnaire parisienne à Lyon et dans la région lyonnaise*.

[2] *Les Armées révolutionnaires*, ii. 425–63, 545–96, 618–33, 672–94, 707–40.

[3] Ibid., ii. 618–33.

[4] Contamin, the future *babouviste*, had been *agent national* of this small town in the Isère (see *L'Armée révolutionnaire à Lyon*, etc.).

[5] The *agent national* of the commune of Heyrieu, in the Isère, Dorzat, was guillotined in Paris in Messidor year II as an 'ultra-revolutionary'.

[6] Tonneins-la-Montagne was one of the few *communes* to have petitioned the Convention for the appointment of a *Grand Juge* and to have given active support to the *hébertiste* programme of more repression and of militarism (*Les Armées révolutionnaires*, ii. 814–15).

number of Parisians were arrested in Lyon, Bordeaux, Perpignan, Nice, Lille, and so on, along with their local helpers.[1] Again, as a result of the purges of the year III provincial ultras sought refuge in large numbers in Paris, which thus became, for the first time, the true capital of impenitent ultracism; their presence there did much to radicalize the surviving revolutionary movement, impelling it into channels never previously explored by the cautious, if vociferous, traditionalist, and generally backward-looking Paris *sectionnaires*. Ultra-revolutionism, like its antithesis, ultra-royalism, flourishes fastest and most furiously far, far from Paris. This may have been an accident of temperament or it may have had something to do with local traditions (dechristianization did); but it was certainly largely due to the fact that the further one was away from Paris, the more one could get away with. Like so many other aspects of the popular movement during the revolutionary period, ultra-revolutionism owed much to immediate, accidental causes: distance, a power vacuum, the urgent exigencies of repression (and repression, in the autumn of 1793, had to be regionalized), local peculiarities. It is for this reason that, like any other branch of French social history, it can only properly be studied at a local or regional level. We have in fact to adopt the angle of vision of the average ultra-revolutionist, whose horizon rarely extended very far beyond what he could see.

9. THE *SANS-CULOTTE* AND THE OUTSIDE WORLD

A problem that has much exercised present-day historians is why the popular movement in France went into a long decline from 1795, for twenty years or more, at the very time when, in England, the working-class movement was beginning to take shape—for Edward Thompson, 1795 is the year of England's 'abortive revolution'—and to tread, however timidly, the dangerous paths of sedition and armed revolt. If the course of the popular movement in England may have been influenced by what was happening in France, the contrary was certainly not the case, at least before the 1820s. The *sans-culottes* were supremely unaware of what was happening anywhere; for a long time they daily expected to hear that a mob had stormed St. James's and the Tower, that George III had been overthrown, and that a similar fate had overtaken

[1] Ibid., ii. 767–75.

Charles IV, the Emperor, the Empress, the Sultan, the King of Portugal, *le roi sarde*, *le tyran de Naples*, and so on (they were delighted to hear of the assassination of one of the club, Gustavus III). The *sans-culottes* of Lorient even deluded themselves into believing in the imminence of a mighty nationalist rising on the part of *le pauvre Hindou, doux et timide*[1] (a further illustration of just how wrong the *sans-culottes* could be)—a tempting belief, for it might have been the salvation of that decaying port. When none of these things happened, when foreign oppressed peoples failed to oblige, the *sans-culottes* hardened their hearts and developed a revolutionary chauvinism not very far removed from militarism and expansionism, while at the same time turning inwards, with the result that there was a revulsion at both popular and government levels in the early months of 1794 against the 'cosmopolitans' in Cloots's circus of professional, national-costumed refugees. By the summer of 1794 the surviving *sans-culottes* had become as wildly, madly xenophobic as Robespierre, Saint-Just, and Barère.

The *sans-culottes* could afford to be noisily bellicose and demonstratively patriotic. They were mostly beyond military age and in little danger, unless they belonged to skilled trades of use to national defence, of being sent away from home, much less to the frontiers. They certainly were patriotic and they wanted to win the war, but from a distance (the place to win it was Tonneins-la-Montagne). *Sans-culottisme* also had a vested interest in war. But unlike Jacobinism it was not outward-looking or exportable (after all, the frontiers of *sans-culottisme* were so often confined to a single *commune* and it was very difficult to link up the efforts of *sectionnaires* even in two neighbouring towns).[2] It is not surprising that it did not have an international audience. Indeed, Counter-Revolutionary Europe made no distinction between *sans-culottisme* and Jacobinism. Everyone, as far as Reeves or Playfair was concerned, was a 'Jacobin rascal', all were *banditti*. The *sans-culottes* might never have existed. No wonder they were to be kept out of the history books till 1958.

The popular movement during the Revolution was not only narrowly French but narrowly provincial. This is why, despite the occasional violence (and much of that violence was provincial also, the Revolt of Lyon in particular being both popular and anti-Parisian), it is reassuring. Later, no doubt, under the Directory,

---

[1] See note I, p. 336.   [2] See note J, p. 336.

with the popular movement narrowed down to a tiny group of irreconcilables, to a conspiratorial élite, well described in the contemporary word *exclusifs*, and with the influx of Italian refugees and conspirators, a change does come about. No Infernal Machine would have been complete without its accompanying Italian. And many former *sans-culottes* discovered the world not only beyond the hill, but beyond France, in the supply services of the French armies of occupation. But this was after *sans-culottisme* had disappeared, at a time when there was little or no hope at home and when the popular movement, hitherto open, public, and persuasive, had developed new, secret, conspiratorial forms that had nothing in common with *le mouvement sans-culotte*. We can then dispose without much difficulty of the fact that while something was happening in France, something very different was happening in England. There was no reason why it should have been otherwise; the English public too was hopelessly misinformed about the pace of events in revolutionary France and was always at least two chapters behind. By 1795 it had just about reached the Girondin phase; and although Austrian, Hungarian, Greek, or German democrats, after 1795, called themselves 'Jacobins', and were called 'Jacobins' by the repressive authorities of their respective countries or empires, they were in reality much more like Girondins.

10. CAUSES AND CONSEQUENCES OF THE FAILURE OF THE 'POPULAR MOVEMENT' FROM 1795 TO 1815

(i) *The White Terror*

Perhaps too much is made also of that other 'problem': the absence of an effective popular movement in France during the period 1795 to 1815 (or later). There is no great mystery about this as far as Paris and the other cities are concerned. Once the popular movement had been defeated, in Prairial year III, and the people disarmed, not only in Paris but in every town in France—even rural *communes* would have their dozen or so *désarmés*—then clearly the *sans-culottes* could no longer impinge on events by violence. An unarmed *sans-culotte* was politically a non-being. Two recent French historians have suggested that the attachment felt by the *sectionnaire* to his pike could be explained in sexual terms; certainly, once deprived of it, he lost his sense of citizenship along with the visible emblem of militancy. Just to make sure, the Thermidorian authorities did not stop at disarmament. More often than not it was the first qualification for arrest, and in every town more than half the *désarmés* were to spend anything up to six months in prison, the last of them being released at the time of the amnesty of Brumaire year IV. In Paris as many as five thousand people may thus have been arrested and deprived of their livelihood. The total number of arrests for the whole country has never been worked out. It must have amounted to more than eighty or ninety thousand, for even in a smallish town like le Havre, with a population of twenty thousand, between fifteen and twenty so-called *meneurs* were sent to prison,[1] and their absence from work would no doubt affect the existence of some fifty or sixty dependants. In Ingouville, with two thousand inhabitants, eight poor artisans were arrested as partisans of the former *maire*, Musquinet-Lapagne.[2] In both places, the arrests took place within a month of the fall of Robespierre. There do not appear to have been any arrests in Dieppe; but in the late spring and summer of 1795 about twenty former terrorists were expelled from the *Garde nationale*, were asked to be available to give an account of themselves at any moment, and were subjected to minor humiliations; in Dieppe and le Havre they had their windows broken in a series of week-end rowdinesses in the summer of 1795.[3] Many more such people left their towns of origin to escape arrest, taking refuge with friends in Paris, where a small colony of Havrais was established in the year III and the year IV, as the subscription lists to Babeuf's paper reveal.

Many Lyonnais attempted to hide out in the countryside of the Forez, where their appearance, their clothes, and their accents caused them to be rapidly detected.[4] A few of the more fortunate *mathevons* managed to reach Paris or Marseille, where they were immediate objects of suspicion, as the nuclei of groups of neo-terrorists. Mâconnais, inhabitants of a town that had given enthusiastic service to Terror and repression—partly, no doubt, out of

[1] *Terreur et subsistances*, pp. 221–55.

[2] A.N. F1b II Seine-Inférieure I (Membres de l'administration d'Ingouville, Graville, Sanvic, Lheure, Sainte-Adresse, Blesville, Saint-Jouin, destitués depuis le 10 thermidor, s.d. an III).

[3] Arch. Dieppe D 1 6 (municipalité, séances des 28 germinal, 4 et 23 floréal et 19 messidor an III). See also A.N. D III 269 d 48 (Comité de législation, Seine-Inférieure, Dieppe, commissaire national près le tribunal du district de Dieppe, au comité de législation, 1er pluviôse an III).

[4] See note K, p. 337.

hostility to Chalon, subjected to moderate influences—headed likewise for Paris, where they were at least physically safe; one, however, was ill inspired enough to show himself in Lyon in the year V. He was at once recognized, beaten to death, and thrown into the Saône.[1] Very few managed to escape attention altogether if they remained in France; the Thermidorian authorities at District and *commune* levels showed considerable zeal in tracking down each other's refugees and in sending them back to their places of origin, which in the south-east often meant sending them back to a messy, battered death by rural lynching or by massacre in an urban prison.[2]

The commonest opportunity for individual killing was when a former militant was escorted from the prison of the *chef-lieu* by a small posse of unenthusiastic *Gardes nationales* in order to be interrogated by the *juge-de-paix* of his former place of residence.[3] That thoughtful official would have taken care to announce the day and time of his arrival several days in advance, so that the villagers could look forward to a killing with much the same excitement as they might await a *corrida* or a gathering of *boulistes*. The progress of the prisoner would be announced by word of mouth, several kilometres ahead of him. He would enter the village as he might a bull-ring, between two lines of shrieking women and children, excited by the prospect of blood. Sometimes the *juge-de-paix* was even obliging enough to see that the prisoner's arrival coincided with meal time. In several cases the prisoner was dispatched there and then on the main square or even at the entry to the *commune*. In any case it was only a matter of waiting; for, in other instances, he was butchered in prison, at nightfall, in the rather naïve belief that darkness would make the murderers less easy to recognize. In the Loire, the favourite killing time was *à l'heure du souper*, between nine and ten, when men were sure to be at home—a few, however, under cover of darkness, were able to reach their attics and escape over the roofs.[4] In Lyon, in the favourable conditions of the years III and V, *on assassinait en plein jour*, a fact that the authorities take as a clear sign of the collective responsibility of the inhabitants. There are similar reports from the Loire and the Haute-Loire. Equally, urban terrorists would be

[1] See note L, p. 337.
[2] See note M, p. 338.　　　　　　　　　　　　[3] See note N, p. 339.
[4] For the murders in the Montbrison area, between Germinal and Thermidor year III, and in Germinal year V, see A.N. BB 18 690.

in constant danger from the moment they were transferred from the prison of their home town till they reached the town in which they were to be judged. Many never reached the courts at all. Here again the judges facilitated the work of potential murderers by informing their colleagues well in advance of the route to be taken by the prisoners. There is nothing mysterious about the geography of the White Terror and the many roadside and riverside murders of the years III, IV, V, and VII.[1] Any road leading to Lyon was dangerous and there were two or three hundred convenient sites for slaughter between Lyon and Grenoble, Mâcon and Lyon, Lyon and Moulins, Montbrison and Lyon, Montbrison and Feurs, Montbrison and Boën, Saint-Étienne and le Puy, Yssangeaux and le Puy (a road on which many soldiers and *gendarmes* were also killed, mostly in the year IV), between Saint-Anthème and le Puy, Langeac and le Puy, Pradelles and le Puy, Craponne and le Puy, between Mâcon and Bourg, between Avignon and Marseille, Nîmes and Aix, Toulon and Marseille, Sisteron and Aix, between Pamiers, Ax, Tarascon, and Saverdun.

For there is no denying the effectiveness of the White Terror as a deterrent to popular militancy in an area that represents about a third of the national territory, nor is there any doubt about its essentially anti-popular character, even if a number of victims were wealthy farmers or high-ranking officials and many of the killers men of the people. In crudest terms, the White Terror accounted for perhaps as many as two thousand popular militants in the area between the Swiss frontier and the Mediterranean, from Chalon-sur-Saône to Marseille and from the Monts du Forez and the Massif Central to the Alpilles. Bouvier, in the *Cinq-Cents*, reckoned that fifteen hundred had been murdered in the Vaucluse alone, in the killing grounds of the Haut-Comtat, between the year III and the year VII.[2] This may be something of a guess, and in Paris the extent of the White Terror was often deliberately exaggerated by authorities like Barras, Fréron, and Goupilleau de Montaigu, and by the press, in order to get repressive legislation introduced, while under the Directory, particularly in the year V, local garrison commanders, concerned to protect their own soldiers, no doubt tended

---

[1] See note O, p. 339.

[2] *Conseil des 500. Motion d'ordre faite par Bouvier* (séance du 26 fructidor an VII): '. . . Le nombre des brigans est de 1,000 à 1,200. Ils auroient commis 1.500 assassinats. Ces bandes sont composées principalement de réquisitionnaires. . . .'

to inflate the number of murders, so as to obtain full powers over the civil authorities with the introduction of a state of siege.[1] The figures quoted for Lyon in particular, for the period year III–year VII, varied wildly according to whether the informant was hostile or favourable to the capital of the south. But detailed examination of the judicial records of the Bouches-du-Rhône for the last five years of the century provides a definitive minimal figure. Eight hundred persons of both sexes were murdered between Brumaire year III (the date of the first murder of the White Terror proper, though already in October 1793 a *patriote* had been shot and left dead by the roadside at Saint-Ambroix, in the District d'Alès (Gard), and there had been previous murders in the Bouches-du-Rhône in 1792 and 1793)[2] and the end of Fructidor year VIII. Four hundred and twenty-eight of these were killed in the Bouches-du-Rhône; the remaining three hundred and seventy-two identified victims were killed in the Vaucluse,[3] the Gard (where there were about twenty victims in the year III alone),[4] the Lozère (with attacks on Protestant farmers), the Ardèche (the point of departure of many of the murder operations in the Haute-Loire in the year IV), the Drôme (a Department relatively immune),[5] the Basses-Alpes (where over fifty murders had been reported by the beginning of the year VI, most of them committed in the years IV and V),[6] the

---

[1] See note P, p. 340.

[2] A.N. F1b II Gard I (Département au Ministre de l'Intérieur, 1er octobre 1793). The victim, Servier-Labadier, had incurred the hatred of the municipal authorities of the *commune* of Saint-Jean-de-Valérsilse by showing an alarming zeal in rounding up deserters.

[3] Tissot and Blaze, in their address to the Convention, dated 14 Thermidor year III, mention a further twenty-five murders committed up to that date in the Vaucluse, principally in the communes of L'Isle-sur-Sorgue and Mondragon.

[4] Of these, nine were murdered in Nîmes. These included the former *maire*, Courbis, and two members of the former Revolutionary Tribunal. The other murders identified took place in Beaucaire and Pont-Saint-Esprit.

[5] 'Vous ignorez peut-être que le Département de la Drôme, entouré des Départements de Rhône, de Vaucluse, et de l'Ardèche, foyers de contre-révolution, où l'assassinat des républicains étoit à l'ordre du jour depuis le 9 thermidor, s'est conservé sain dans la corruption générale . . .' (A.N. F1b II Drôme I, commissaire du Directoire au Ministre, 18 frimaire an IV).

[6] A.N. F1b II Basses-Alpes I (les patriotes fugitifs des Basses-Alpes, actuellement à Paris, au Conseil des 500, 19 vendémiaire an VI). On 27 Frimaire, the Ministre de la Police wrote to his colleague of the Intérieur: '. . . Une longue continuité d'assassinats en a souillé depuis plus de deux ans le sol infortuné . . . il y a trois semaines qu'on assassinait encore aux portes de Digne, à Sisteron, à Manosque, à Oraison et dans quelques autres communes. . . . Les patriotes

Loire, with sixteen identified victims in the last four months of the year III,[1] the Haute-Loire, with thirty-two named victims, most of them killed in the spring of the year IV,[2] the Rhône, with a minimum of eighty-seven murders for the period year III–year XII (1795–1804) over and above the hundred and nine named victims of the three prison massacres of the year III (this too is a minimal figure).[3] Four or five people may have been killed in the Tarn in the year IV[4] and there were five victims of a single foray in

exilés depuis plus de trois ans n'y rentrent qu'en frémissant. . . .' A report later the same year states: 'Les assassinats se multiplient d'une manière effrayante dans le département des Basses-Alpes. . . . C'est contre les républicains, les acquéreurs des biens nationaux que sont dirigés ces actes de brigandage. . . .'

[1] A.N. BB 18 690. The known victims of the murders of Germinal–Thermidor year III are: Giron, *tisserand*; Bouarde; Clément, *greffier*; Perraud, *vigneron-jardinier*; Poche, *chapelier*; Paley, *officier de santé*; Bard, *maçon*; *l'abbé* Bouchet; Reprennant, a refugee from Lyon; Mari, *officier municipal* of Saint-Étienne; Magnien, *imprimeur*; Drouillet; two inhabitants of Saint-Étienne; Jay; Grison's brother. A further twenty-five inhabitants of Montbrison left the Loire in order to escape assassination, returning only in the early months of the year IV.

[2] A.N. F1b II Haute-Loire I. These included Samon, *négotiant*, of Yssangeaux; Géry, *cultivateur*, of Montgevin; Durand, *laboureur*, of la Gaillarde; Dusny, *tisserand*, of Tixe; Pamelier, *greffier*, of Yssangeaux; Bonfils, *aubergiste*, of Craponne; Pouviane, *cultivateur*, of Saint-Just; Charitat, *cultivateur et riche propriétaire*, *officier municipal de Négraval*; Fayolle, *lieutenant dans le 6me bataillon des côtes maritimes*, *de Retournac;* Sollilhac, *ex-gendarme de Beauzac;* Cartlet, de Vergues; and a score of *gendarmes* killed in operations against the *compagnies*.

[3] These include an *agent de police*, a refugee from Mâcon, two inhabitants of Saint-Genis, three terrorists from the Croix-Rousse, three former *officiers municipaux*, a refugee from Feurs, several soldiers, some of whom seem to have been killed in brawls with royalist-inclined hussars, others the victims of the Lyon *crocheteurs*; a refugee from Chasselay; two former *officiers municipaux* of Neuville, and several unidentified people whose bodies were found in the Rhône or the Saône (Arch. Rhône I L 208, 209, 382, 383, 393, Département, assassinats ans III–VII, and 2 L 53+. 93+. 96+, District de Lyon-Ville, an III). Other identified victims include a Lyon hatter, a Lyon jeweller, the wife of a stonemason, a prostitute, a night-watchman, a wine-merchant and his wife, all from Lyon, three children from la Guillotière, a wealthy landowner from Beaujeu, several *gendarmes* from Vaugneray, Thizy, and Tarare (A.N. BB 18, 685-6-7 -8, Ministère de la Justice, Rhône, ans III–XII) (Arch. Rhône 8d.1*, 18d. 10*–11*, 21d.1*–2*–3*–4*–5*, 12d.3*). Among those identified as Lyon *égorgeurs* and against whom legal proceedings were started were ten people in the drink trade—*aubergistes, marchands de vin*, etc.— 5 *crocheteurs*, 4 river-workers, 3 hairdressers, 2 butchers, 2 bakers, 2 *notaires*, 2 porters, 2 old-clothes merchants, 4 silk-workers (A.N. BB 18 690).

[4] A.N. F1b II Tarn I: '. . . Il y a eu 4 à 5 assassinats de patriotes, entr'autres à Semalens, à Teillet, à Saint-Gervais, &ca, et le commissaire n'a rien dit . . .' (*Journal des Hommes libres*, No. 97, 22 nivôse an V). The *commissaire*, Terral, admitted that a man had been murdered at Saint-Gervais, in Prairial year IV, but claimed that his murderers had been tried and condemned to death.

Clermont-Ferrand.¹ There appear to have been many murders in the Ariège (three victims are known by name); and we know of eight victims in the Ain, of three in the Var, and of one in the Gironde.² But this figure of eight hundred and forty-six is far from representing the total number of political assassinations—our calculations do not include private vendettas, family poisonings, murder with robbery, all common in the south-east during these years—in these Departments.

Many murders remained unreported and never reached the ears of the higher authorities.³ The *accusateur public* of the Gard had the greatest difficulty, on taking up his post in Brumaire year IV, in obtaining even the scantiest information about the murders committed in this unhappy Department during the previous year. An unknown number of those who had been severely wounded in pistol or sabre attacks died within a matter of weeks or months in the places of refuge to which their relatives had moved them (in the Ariège, one victim lingered on for three months). The figures extant for the Var are quite unrepresentative of the scale of the White Terror there both in the year III (following the Toulon rising) and in the year IV. And there were pockets of murder in the Isère,⁴ frequent murders in the Ain,⁵ and isolated affairs in the Mont-Blanc, the Jura, and the Saône-et-Loire.⁶ In the Rhône, as many as three hundred and fifty people may have been killed, though a number of these were soldiers and other strangers to the city; several were killed in duels between rival corps, a few may have

---

¹ A.N. F1b Puy-de-Dôme I. This was a particularly cold-blooded massacre. On Sunday, 21 Messidor year V, the members of a *cercle constitutionnel* organized a picnic in the Bois-du-Cros, outside Clermont-Ferrand. Their meeting was authorized by the authorities; but, in the course of the afternoon, a company of the *Garde nationale* surrounded the wood and fired at random into the Sunday crowd. Five were killed instantly, thirty-three were severely wounded, several of whom died in the next few weeks. The massacre was carefully planned and was carried out with obvious enjoyment by the *Garde nationale* and their female supporters.   ² See note Q, p. 341.   ³ See note R, p. 341.
⁴ A.N. F1b II Isère I (Burdet, ex-juge-de-paix de Vienne, au Directoire, 30 fructidor an V).   ⁵ See note S, p. 342.
⁶ A.N. F1b II Saône-et-Loire I (extrait du procès-verbal de l'administration municipale de Mâcon, 9 prairial an V): '. . . A Pont-de-Vaux, la semaine dernière, trois hommes ont été assassinés, point de témoins, il m'a été dit que deux sont morts, au faubourg de la Barre la semaine dernière deux citoyens ont été assassinés, ils sont morts . . . j'ai des soupçons que les assassinats sont organisés, les soupçons viennent de ce qu'ils ont tous le même caractère. . . . Notre commune a été tranquille . . . pendant 15 mois, un seul homme avoit été assassiné et tué en messidor [an IV] par des chanteurs du *Réveil du peuple*. . . .'

floated down from localities upstream on the Rhône and on the Saône, while some were undoubtedly the victims of criminal gangs.[1] Individual murders were almost a daily occurrence in Lyon itself and in the *communes* of its periphery (in Messidor year V, when the Second City was put under a state of siege, this was extended to Vaise, la Croix-Rousse, and la Guillotière)[2] from Pluviôse year III to the end of the summer of the year V, and seven known murders can be listed for the period Pluviôse–Germinal year III, before the prison massacres of Floréal and Prairial of that year.

The big murder year was the year III, with a minimum of four hundred and twenty victims for the three Departments of the Bouches-du-Rhône, the Gard, and the Vaucluse. A hundred and fifty people were killed the same year in the Rhône and the Loire. There were forty-five known murders in the former area, and twenty in the Rhône and the Haute-Loire, in the year IV. In that year, killings may have actually increased, when many former terrorists returned to public office, as a result of the amnesty of Brumaire year IV (though, in the Lyon area at least, there was a drop in the number of victims, thanks no doubt to the presence in the Loire of Reverchon). Thus Saurel, whose son had been assassinated in Frimaire year IV, was appointed *commissaire du Directoire* for the canton of Malemort-du-Comtat, in the former District de Carpentras, in the following Pluviôse but was unable to take up the appointment, as he knew that if he returned to his village those who had killed his son would not hesitate to kill him too. (This is what they meant when they said they would give him *le pouvoir exécutif*.)[3]

---

[1] Arch. Rhône I L 283. On 24 Messidor year V, a group of dragoons, associated with a prostitute called *Suissesse*, who was also a thief and who had been the mistress of a bandit, condemned to death in the year III for murder and highway robbery, attacked a *gendarme* outside the Caserne des Augustins. In many other cases, the Lyon authorities attempt to argue that the murders reported to the Directory are the work of small groups of professional criminals, themselves strangers to the city. Certainly the dragoons appear to have been deeply involved in theft.

[2] See note T, p. 342.

[3] A.N. F1b II Vaucluse I (Notes de Saurel, sur les propos des habitants de Mallemort). On 6 Brumaire year IV, a large crowd gathered outside his house, shouting: 'Descend, coquin de Saurel Robespierre et nous te ferons ton compte . . . nous voulons avoir ta vie, boire ton sang et manger ton foie.' His son, a member of the *comité* of the year II, was murdered at six in the morning of 5 Frimaire year IV on the road to Pierre Blanche, by a baker nicknamed *le*

Thirty-three murders are recorded in the Gard, the Bouches-du-Rhône, and the Vaucluse, for the year V, when conditions were especially favourable to the *égorgeurs* in the Midi—it was perhaps their best year—thanks to the presence of General Willot in Marseille and the return of many royalists to Department or municipal office. (One of them, Vincent, a member of the municipal administration of Marseille, was a leader of a murder gang in that and the following year.) In the year V, too, there were at least seven murders in the Saône-et-Loire at the time of the *assemblées primaires*; the murders appear to have been connived at by the members of the Departmental administration, who, in Mâcon, gave orders for the military not to be called out at the request of the municipality, whose members still showed some concern to protect the lives of leading republicans in the town.[1] If this was the position in Mâcon, it is not surprising that the year V—especially the summer months —should have been an exceptionally good period for the activities of the *compagnies* in Lyon, which the military authorities rightly described, in Messidor and in Fructidor, as the *centre d'impulsion* of the White Terror in the South;[2] there were twenty-one murders in and around the city between Nivôse and Fructidor, resulting in the death of at least thirty-one persons (the military authorities were to put the figure as high as sixty-seven); and there were some dozen murders or attempted murders in the Loire—mostly in Montbrison, in Germinal, at the time of the *assemblées primaires*.[3] As in the year III, these murders appear to have been carried out on orders from Lyon.

There is sparse documentation for the nine murders—three in

capucin and Barthélemy Gras, *dit le coupeur*. Saurel took refuge in Carpentras, 7 Pluviôse following. A year previously, 9 Frimaire year III, another terrorist, Antoine Mus, had been assassinated by the same group; his body was left outside for two days.

[1] A.N. F1b II Saône-et-Loire I (Rubat, commissaire du Directoire à Mâcon, à Roberjot, le 9 prairial an V; Dutroncy à Reverchon, le 13 prairial; Genty le jeune à Reverchon, le 13 prairial; lettre de Genty le jeune, de Mâcon, le 15 prairial; Genty le jeune à Reubell, le 19 prairial; Genty le jeune à Reverchon, le 28 prairial).

[2] '. . . Nous avons encore demandé au Bureau Central s'il existe dans Lyon une compagnie d'assassins à gages, organisée sous des chefs, et à laquelle on donne le nom de compagnie de Jésus. . . . Le général Canuel . . . nous a assuré . . . que c'étoit à 11 brigands vivant dans Lyon et épargnés par la police qu'étaient dûs les meurtres . . .' (Arch. Rhône I L 283, rapport du Département du 27 messidor an V) (A.N. BB 18 685–6).

[3] A.N. BB 18 690.

the Bouches-du-Rhône, five in the Rhône, one in the Var[1]—committed in the year VI, and for the twenty-five of the year VII.[2] But, with the exception of the Bouches-du-Rhône and possibly the Loire, these figures for the whole period year III–year VII (two murders in the Rhône, a department in which nine people were killed in the year VIII, five in the year IX, one in the year X, two in the year XI, and seven in the year XII) certainly do not represent even a quarter of the incidence of the White Terror in these south-eastern and south central Departments; and to obtain anything like an over-all picture of this carefully planned and well-organized system of extermination,[3] it would be necessary to extend the investigation to the Hérault, to the Cantal (where murders are stated to have been frequent),[4] and to the Ardèche, all places in which the *compagnies* controlled considerable areas, especially in inaccessible mountain fastnesses, the paradise of bandit and deserter. For the Haute-Loire we have figures only up to the end of the year IV. It is established too that there were isolated murders, at least in the year V, in Dijon.[5] It would certainly not be unreasonable to suggest that as many persons were murdered in the south-east and the west[6] between 1795 and 1803 as perished during the Terror of the year II. If only in terms of numbers, the White Terror was brutally effective.

It was even more so in the quality of its victims; for the movement was neither blind, nor anarchical, nor spontaneous. In this respect, it differed significantly from the ultra-revolutionary movements that had flourished in much the same areas in the autumn of 1793. Witnesses report that groups of *égorgeurs* wore identifiable uniforms—blue jackets with red woollen épaulettes. Their leaders were generally widely known—often local squires, back from abroad;[7] north of Lyon, the *gens à cadenettes* and the *oreilles de chien* are identified by name, as local royalists, either from Lyon itself, or from Chalon, and their victims were chosen with discrimination. They represented the *fine fleur* of *sans-culotte* militancy in places like Lyon, Marseille, Aix, Arles, Salon, Martigues, Tarascon, Beaucaire, Nîmes, Bagnols, Pont-Saint-Esprit, Bourg, Lons, Mâcon, Pont-de-Vaux, Privas, Montbrison, Feurs, Boën, Cha-

---

[1] Arch. Rhône I L 283 and A.N. F1b II Var I. The murder in the latter Department took place at Hyères on 12 Nivôse, New Year's Day.

[2] See note U, p. 342. [3] See note V, p. 344.

[4] A.N. F1b II Saône-et-Loire I (Dutroncy le jeune à Reverchon, 17 prairial an V). [6] See note W, p. 345. [7] See note X, p. 345.

zelles, Givors, Saint-Genis-Laval, Neuville, Oullins, Condrieu,
Yssangeaux, le Puy, Langeac; in rural *communes* and *bourgs*—Auriol,
Aubagne, Noves, Lambesc, Sénas, Orgon, Graveson, Mallemort,
and the equally sanguinary Mallemort in the Vaucluse, Saint-
Chamas, Istres, Eyragues, Barbentane, Pélissanne, Gémenos, L'Isle,
Mondragon, Morières, Hyères, Saint-Maximin-la-Sainte-Baume,
Rians, Porrières, Tourves, Saint-Just-en-Bas, Chalmazel, Pralong,
Champdieu, Magneux-Haute-Rive, Moingt, Vaugneray, Mornant,
Allègre, Saint-Paulien, Félines, Jullianges, Retournac, Craponne,
Beauzac—they were the artisans and the *journaliers* who, in the
year II, had established contacts with the urban *sectionnaires* and
had sacked the local churches.[1] Members of *comités de surveillance*
and of *comités sectionnaires*, of regional *tribunaux révolutionnaires*
and *commissions révolutionnaires*, are picked up for massacre first.
Several former *maires*—including those of Nîmes, Martigues, and
Port-Chamas—and *commandants de la garde nationale*, as well as
leading *sociétaires*, are killed. Three *agents nationaux de district* of
the year II, including that of Marseille, were murdered in this
area, for the White Terror of the year III was as much directed
against former Jacobins as against *sans-culotte* militants.

In social terms, however, the *sans-culotte* composition of the
égorgés is so strikingly apparent—much more than that of many of
the popular institutions of the previous year—that one might well
ask whether the White Terror was not as much directed against a
class, for being what it was, as against groups of officials, for being
what they had been,[2] though most of the murderers were people of
similar origin. In a number of instances, the widows or daughters
se déclarent réduites à l'indigence la plus extrême as the result of the
murder of the bread-winner. In one case, in Lambesc, all the male
members of the family, a father and his two sons, were killed and
the surviving womenfolk had to sell the family land.[3] Many of the
victims had large families of young children, who would grow up,
with vengeance in their hearts, among their parents' murderers

---

[1] On 7 Ventôse year III, the *comité* of Salon wrote to the municipality of
Mallemort: '. . . Nous avons reçu l'extrait des différentes déclarations . . . faites
relativement à la dévastation de l'église de votre commune et nous avons partagé
votre indignation. . . .' The same day they wrote to the *agent national* of Martigues: '. . . Il est venu à notre connaissance que les églises de ta commune
avoient été dévastées sous l'infernal régime de Robespierre par les sans-culottes
de ton pays. . . .' In both *communes*, those who were murdered later in the year III
or in the year IV had been denounced as the *dévastateurs des églises*.

[2] See note Y, p. 346.   [3] See note Z, p. 346.

and would sometimes themselves be struck down twenty years later, as people with an inconvenient memory. The White Terror was socially and economically effective as an instrument of the anti-popular offensive that began in earnest in the spring of the year III.[1]

But it also struck higher up. At least ten *commissaires du Directoire*—most of them former militants—were assassinated. More than forty claim to have been shot at in the street, in a café, or while sitting at their windows. A *commissaire* in Aix complains in the year VI that the *sabreurs* are in the habit of leaving the corpses of their victims on his front doorstep. In the Marseille area, Lyon, and the Haute-Loire, army officers and *volontaires* from urban battalions are frequently done to death, generally by stabbing or shooting, when caught out alone or in pairs. (The *sabreurs*, many of them deserters, rightly regarded the army as the most effective surviving citadel of neo-terrorism.) A number of unfortunate *gendarmes* were likewise slaughtered on their country rounds; but in the Saône-et-Loire it is claimed by republican sympathizers that the local *gendarmerie* is hand in glove with the *oreilles de chien* based on Chalon and on Lyon. In the Bouches-du-Rhône, the Gard, the Vaucluse, and the Lozère, the victims of some of the most appalling massacres are wealthy farmers (Protestants in the Lozère), killed at night, along with their families and servants, in their *bastides*; their bodies are hung from cypress trees at the entry to their farms. They were all *acquéreurs de biens nationaux*. We hear of similar victims in the Basses-Alpes. Other victims include a *receveur*, a chief inspector of police, an official concerned with recruitment, a tax collector. Near Mâcon, a *compagnie*, sent to kill a *commissaire* on his country estate, finding him absent, murders his *vigneron* instead.[2] Those who directed the White Terror were not content to kill off the survivors of the popular movement or to frighten its remaining potential leaders out of the area (there are references to a whole colony of Mâconnais in Paris, in the year V, headed by

---

[1] See note 2A, p. 347.

[2] A.N. F1b II Saône-et-Loire I (Tableau actuel du département de Saône-et-Loire, s.d. prairial an V): '... On croit votre commissaire près le Département (Rubat) à sa campagne à une demie-lieue de Mâcon, une compagnie d'égorgeurs s'y rend dans la nuit et après (avoir) examiné partout chez son vigneron et ne trouvant pas Rubat, ils assassinent ce malheureux vigneron et sa fille, ces scélérats n'étoient pas des voleurs, mais des égorgeurs qui en vouloient au commissaire Rubat. . . .'

Roberjot and Reverchon; in their letters to these high-ranking refugees, the local *patriotes* urge them on no account to return).[1] They also sought to make the republican government unworkable and to demonstrate its incapacity to protect life or property.[2]

The calendar of the White Terror reflects, though often in caricature, the general course of the political reaction in Thermidorian and Directorial France. There are only a few isolated murders in the winter months of 1794–5 (one in Brumaire, one in Frimaire, two in Nivôse year III). The killing season opens, but still spasmodically, in Pluviôse (three murders). By Ventôse, the *sabreurs* are beginning to exact a regular toll—on the 16th, in the Lyon *comité*, 'un membre a dit: des assassinats se commettent journellement'.[3] The anti-terrorist legislation of that month gave direct encouragement to the White Terror by placing its potential victims within easy reach of local gangs.[4] There are more murders in Germinal than in Ventôse, more still, including some of the big prison massacres, in Floréal. But the movement does not acquire its full intensity until Prairial, when it was spurred on by news from Paris, by the intensification of anti-terrorist legislation, and, above all, by the report of the neo-Jacobin rising in Toulon.[5] All over the south-east there was a genuine fear that, following the example of Toulon, the terrorists were everywhere about to return to power and to active terrorizing. In Marseille there were murders on the 1st, 2nd, 3rd, 10th, 13th, 14th, 17th, and 27th, some of them committed by *Gardes nationales* on their return from Toulon. Other killings took place in Tarascon on the 6th; in Pont-Saint-Esprit on the 8th, 10th, and 13th, when groups of prisoners, in transit from the Vaucluse to the Gard, were crossing the very long bridge over the Rhône (a monument as important in the geography of the White Terror as the celebrated bridge at Avignon or the bridge between the Saône-et-Loire and the Ain at Mâcon); in Pélissanne on the 12th; in Salon on the 16th; in Sénas on the 27th;

---

[1] See note 2B, p. 347.
[2] Arch. Bouches-du-Rhône L 174* (lettre du Département au Ministre de la Police, 3 germinal an IV): '. . . Cette impunité (des sabreurs) atterre les Républicains. Le peuple, qui ne juge des choses que par les effets, croit que les assassins eurent raison d'égorger les républicains. . . . On lui fait croire que tel est le sort réservé aux imprudens qui se mêlent des révolutions; que le triomphe du républicanisme n'est qu'éphémère . . . le Peuple le croira, et aura raison de le croire, tant que les assassins resteront impunis. . . .'
[3] See note 2C, p. 347.   [4] See note 2D, p. 348.
[5] See note 2E, p. 348.

and in Nîmes on the 28th. Prairial year III was the first really good month for the *sabreurs*. The momentum was maintained throughout the rest of the summer—murders in Tarascon, Entraigues, Salon, and Morières on 3 Messidor (a Sunday), in Saumane-de-Vaucluse on the 7th; in Avignon on the 8th; in Aubagne on the 9th; in Beaucaire on the 17th; and in Eyragues on the 21st; eight murders for Thermidor and Fructidor.[1] The pattern is similar for the year IV: fourteen murders for the winter months (Vendémiaire to Nivôse), seventeen *sorties* for the summer.[2] In the year V and the year VII, Messidor, Thermidor, and Fructidor top the list; but in the Saône-et-Loire the murder month in the year V is, as in the year III in so many other places, Prairial. The total score gives twenty-seven massacres or murders for Prairial (mostly in the special circumstances of the year III), sixteen for Messidor (nine in the year III), ten each for Thermidor, Fructidor, and Floréal—that is, in all, seventy-two massacres or murders between 20 April and 21 September, twenty-six for other seasons.[3] While killing in this part of the world went on all the year round, it reached its maximum intensity in summer violence, mid June to mid September being the height of the season, as it was that of the epidemics that, in the north of France, swept off the urban and rural poor in the years III and IV.

The course of the White Terror also reflects, with remarkable fidelity, the habits of rural and urban riot and turbulence. Predictably, then, Sunday heads the list, with twenty-nine murders or massacres; there are fourteen for Monday, twelve for Saturday, and eleven for Friday.[4] Fifty-six, out of a total of ninety-four *sorties*,

---

[1] There are murders in Montbrison on 1er Prairial, and again on the 4th (Ascension Day), in Geneva on the 7th (a pan-French affair), in Lyon on the 8th, in Montbrison on the 13th (a Monday), in Lyon and in Montbrison on the 25th (a Saturday); in Montbrison on 6 Messidor (the eve of the Saint-Jean), and on the 11th (Monday, the eve of the Saint-Pierre); in Pamiers on the 26th (Sunday). There are murders in Saverdun (Ariège) on 29 and 30 Thermidor (Saturday and Sunday).

[2] The year IV is the principal murder year in the Haute-Loire, whereas in the Lyon area the *sabreurs* seem to have gone underground. Murders in the Haute-Loire on 4 Brumaire (Monday), 3–4 Nivôse (Christmas Day), 6 Nivôse (Sunday), 15 Nivôse, 2–3 Pluviôse, 11 Germinal, 21 and 22 Germinal (Sunday and Monday). There are only three murders in the Lyon region for this year: 28 Nivôse (Givors), 26 Ventôse (Charney), 4 Prairial (Lyon).

[3] See note 2F, p. 349.

[4] In the Lyon area, the score is: Sunday 16, Saturday 13, Monday 17, Wednesday 17, Friday 14, Tuesday 9, Thursday 11: in other words, 42 for the week-end, 51 mid-week, including Friday.

are week-end affairs; thirty-nine take place mid week, most on Tuesday and Thursday, favourite days for markets and court proceedings. There are three murders on successive Christmas Days (after midnight Mass), two on successive New Year's Days, four on successive 9 Thermidor.[1] 28 Thermidor (15 August in the years III, IV, and V), Ascension Day, Palm Sunday, Whitsun Eve, Midsummer Night, and Saint-Bartholomew's Day are other favourites.[2]

Forty-two of the affairs summarized take place in Lyon and its satellite *communes*, eighteen in Marseille, fourteen in or near Montbrison, five in Arles, five in Tarascon, four in Noves, four in Aix, eight in the small town of Graveson, three in Nîmes, three in Pont-Saint-Esprit, five in Avignon, five in Mâcon, four in Lambesc, with scattered murders in twenty or thirty other places in the Bouches-du-Rhône, the Gard, the Vaucluse, the Rhône, the Loire, and the Haute-Loire. Three areas particularly notorious for violence and for gang rule were the countryside round Bagnols on the Rhône opposite to the Vaucluse, the canton of Saint-Paul-Trois-Châteaux, in the south of the Drôme, again bordering the Vaucluse, and mountain areas of the Haute-Loire bordering the Loire and the Ardèche (the inhabitants of the Haute-Loire had the reputation with their neighbours of being particularly uncouth and ferocious). The persistence of violence in such places as Noves, Barbentane (where murders had been going on ever since 1792), Graveson, and Montbrison is indicative of the organization[3] and impunity of the local gangs—some of them really popular, their exploits the affectionate pride of whole communities. It also shows the bitterness of personal, political, and religious feuds in small towns and villages. (Many of the victims of the White Terror in the Lozère and the Ariège were well-to-do Protestant farmers or city artisans,[4] and some in the Carpentras area were Jews.) Like the Terror of the year II, the White Terror of 1795–9 reached its ugliest proportions in small communities, *entre gens de connaissance*. Most of the murderers were well known to their victims—some, a few hours before dying of their wounds, identified them: 'C'est le fils

---

[1] See note 2G, p. 350.

[2] In the Lyon area, Christmas scores two murders, 1 January two murders; Ascension Day, 9 Thermidor, Palm Sunday, Whitsun eve, Carnival, the eve of St. John, the eve of St. Peter, and, suitably, Saint-Bartholomew's Day, one each.

[3] See note 2H, p. 350.

[4] See note 2I, p. 350.

Fabre', 'Ce sont *les Gros Yeux* et son frère *l'Effrayant'*.[1] Sometimes the customers of one inn go to the inn on the other side of
the square and proceed to kill all those who are drinking there. And
just as *on assassinait en famille*, whole families were assassinated.
Many women were killed—generally, republican reports would have
it, while clutching babies to their breasts. A number of children were
also bayoneted to death;[2] while, in Salon, Saint-Chamas, Noves,
Eyragues, children are reported at the head of the *égorgeurs*. Even
in Marseille the murderers insult their victims by name before
finishing them off; in Nîmes and Pont-Saint-Esprit, the victims
were public figures, well known to the whole population. Finally,
both in rural and urban incidents, women are revealed as particularly ferocious. They provide the incitement: 'Sabrez, sabrez, mes
amis, n'en laissons aucun, aucune, si vous êtes des hommes, tuez-
les tous, jusqu'aux femmes et aux enfants, et toi, petite Montagnarde, tu le regrettes bien, ton maximum' is the litany of *la femme
Colon*, an Arlésienne, as she attempts to enlist a group of *sabreurs*
against some *sans-culotte* neighbours (she also wanted to push a
mother and daughter into the *Vieux Port*).[3] Not only do they revel
in a cannibalistic vocabulary, but they actually take part in murder.
They dismember the bodies of victims—in Eyragues women drag
a body along by the hair, and tip it over the ramparts—and they
boast about their ability to kill (*c'est moi qui . . .*).[4] It was not
always mere boasts: in Lyon, Roux, a member of the municipality
of the year II, was recognized in the street, 29 Germinal year III
(a Saturday), by a group of women, who stoned him to death and
tore the body to pieces, scattering the bits into the Saône.[5]

[1] See note 2J, p. 351.   [2] See note 2K, p. 351.   [3] See note 2L, p. 351.

[4] '*Voici le beau Durand, le sansculotte*, la femme Tourette a dit à une voisine:
Je lui en ai bien foutu, j'ai de son sang au bout de mon bâton.' A witness adds the
detail: 'Sur les remparts, plusieurs enfans attroupés jetoient des pierres contre
led. cadavre . . .' (Assassinat de Claude Durand, ex-commandant de la garde
nationale d'Eyragues, à Eyragues, 21 messidor an III) (Arch. Bouches-du-
Rhône L 3072).

[5] Arch. Rhône 31 L 164* (29 germinal an III). We hear too of a group of
Avignonnaises, 'les nommées Thérèse, veuve de Baignet . . . porteur de chaise,
et la femme du nommé Bergin, devuideuse, et la fille de ladite Baignet', who,
after a former terrorist has been assassinated in the street, pick up the body:
'*Prenez avec la Bergin chacune par un pied chacune et moi qui suis plus forte je le
prendrai par la tête*, ce qu'elles firent . . . et le transportèrent en le laissant aller
avec rudesse, au milieu de la ruelle, en outre la Bergin se saisit d'une grosse
pierre. la lança sur ledit Fanton . . .' (Arch. Bouches-du-Rhône L 3082, par
devant le juge de paix du 1er arrondissement du canton d'Avignon, 9 thermidor
an V).

Most of the victims of the White Terror—especially in the countryside—are poor people who cannot afford the luxury of exile in a distant town and are tied to their work by debt, by family, or by easy credit. Some, it is true, took refuge with relatives in villages a few miles away, in a neighbouring Department or District; but this did not put them out of reach of the gangs, who came to get them in the course of a day's outing. The result was that a number of rural or semi-rural terrorists from the Bouches-du-Rhône were murdered just over the border of the Vaucluse, in some instances just on the far bank of the Durance, like that carpenter's wife from Châteaurenard whose headless body, half-eaten by wolves, was discovered at the riverside.[1] There was also a considerable amount of exchange of information between judicial and local authorities as well as between the gangs themselves, who appear to have kept in close touch between one Department and another, at least in the whole area from Lyon to the sea, and from Chalon and Montbrison to Lyon. (It was not unreasonable to see in Lyon the headquarters of a vast movement that covered the whole of the Rhône–Saône valley and the Monts du Forez; Lyonnais killers are reported in Mâcon, Bourg, Montbrison, Lons, Oullins, Neuville, Saint-Genis, and Yssangeaux, as well as in Marseille and Avignon, while killers from Montbrison boast of how they have lent a hand to the Lyon killers in the prison massacres.)[2]

The judges and the *juges-de-paix* were the most effective auxiliaries of the *sabreurs*, who would soon have been rendered harmless had the judiciary made the smallest attempt to carry out government instructions. They saw to it that their potential victims should be made conveniently available, and that the murderers should have nothing to fear from the law.[3] Persecuted *sans-culottes*, on the other hand, were unable to have their complaints registered with the *juges-de-paix*, who also failed to notify the higher authorities—*agents nationaux*, *commissaires du Directoire*—of the murders and acts of violence committed within the areas of their jurisdiction.[4] This is one reason why it is difficult to obtain an

---

[1] See note 2M, p. 352.

[2] The Thermidorian *comité* of Salon writes, on various occasions, in Nivôse, Pluviôse, and Ventôse, to the *comités* of Apt, Auriol, Marseille, Toulon, Sénas, Istres, and Martigues, in an effort to trace down the *terroristes salonnais* who had taken refuge in these *communes* and requesting that, if found, they should be returned forthwith to Salon (Arch. Bouches-du-Rhône L 1858, comité de Salon, an III).   [3] See note 2N, p. 353.   [4] See note 2O, p. 353.

over-all picture; indeed, in some rural areas, the families of victims were afraid to declare their dead to the *état-civil*. If really pressed, the *juges-de-paix* and the judges of the *tribunaux criminels* —in the year V, royalist almost without exception in the south-east —would warn *sabreurs*, some of whom were their close relatives, well in advance that a warrant was on the way. It was hardly surprising that most of the known murderers were declared in flight when their trials came up; a number of them are stated to be absent in Lyon *pour leurs affaires*.

In the south-east, distance offered no guarantee of security, and a *mathevon* was no safer in the Bouches-du-Rhône, the Gard, or the Vaucluse, than he would have been if he had sought refuge in the countryside of the Rhône and the Loire; Lyonnais perished in the prison massacres of Aix, Marseille, and Nîmes, Foréziens and Bressois in those of Lyon; a Mâconnais and a Forézien were lynched in Lyon in the year V, and *assommeurs* went out from Lyon to kill their own people in the Loire, the Haute-Loire, the Jura, the Isère, the Saône-et-Loire, and the Drôme.[1] Only the Puy-de-Dôme seems to have offered a comparatively safe refuge to the artisan from Lyon or from Montbrison during the dangerous months of Germinal year III to Brumaire year IV.[2] Despite strong local ties, the gangs appear to have had some sort of centralized command: in the Haute-Loire, their activities seem to have been directed from the Ardèche and the Gard, and there is talk there, in Floréal year III, of a concerted military action involving the *compagnies* from Marseille, Montpellier, Pont-Saint-Esprit, and Montbrison.[3] White terrorists were certainly far more successful at co-operation between neighbouring Departments, towns, or villages than the much more locally orientated *sans-culottes* had been. They also possessed a far more efficient network of escape and refuge. A carpenter from Lyon might hope to receive help from those in his trade in Marseille; but it was easy to look for him among other carpenters. The *sabreurs*, like the *chauffeurs* at the other end of the country, enjoyed the support of a chain of innkeepers, so that, their operations completed in the Bouches-du-Rhône, they could lie low for a time in Nîmes or in Montpellier.[4] The high road from Lyon to Montbrison and that from Lyon to

---

[1] See note 2P, p. 353.   [2] See note 2Q, p. 354.
[3] A.N. F1b II Haute-Loire I (rapports de germinal an IV).
[4] See note 2R, p. 354.

le Puy contained more welcoming *étapes* at the disposal of the *sabreurs* than they did official ones for troops on the march.[1] After the year III, save in a few Departments like the Nièvre where they continued to enjoy massive support at least from the urban poor, the former terrorists were above all the victims of their isolation within the communities in which they had to live. The *sabreurs*, on the other hand, could count on the complicity of virtually the whole rural population.

Murder was the most effective and dramatic weapon of anti-terrorism. Even in the north, individual terrorists were murdered by highwaymen or were driven in fear to live in the woods, 'comme les bêtes sauvages, hommes chassés, signalés et incarcérés', comments, with delectation, the *agent national* of the District d'Avignon, in his report for 21–30 Germinal year III. 'Voilà le sort de ceux de ces scélérats qui ont l'effronterie de paraître encore parmi nous. Les autres demeurent cachés, errans et vagabonds dans les bois avec les bêtes féroces, mais encore moins féroces qu'eux. . . .'[2] Reduced thus to animal status, they could be hunted down, like the wolves and the hyenas and the *tigres d'Afrique* they are so often called in standard Thermidorian vocabulary. Near Lambesc the three Martins, father and two sons, are hunted across half a dozen fields, by a group of *sabreurs* armed with shot-guns, before being finally shot down. Afterwards the huntsmen return to the *auberge* to celebrate their outing and display their kill.[3] In the Ardennes, the coldest Department in the country, in the middle of the fearful winter of the year III, the wife of a hatter from Sedan, after being driven out of her house in the night, gave birth to a child, which at once died, in the mighty forest of the frontier region.

---

[1] The Lyon *sabreurs* appear to have had convenient stopping-places in such convenient localities as Chazelles, Mâcon, Yssangeaux, Craponne; and one of the leading *assommeurs* of Montbrison is an innkeeper (A.N. BB 18 690 and F1b II Haute-Loire I).

[2] See note 2S, p. 355.

[3] We have already mentioned the nut repast of the Haute-Loire murderers. The culinary theme is repeated in a remark attributed to the young murderers from Montbrison: 'Il y a encore de ces coquins de mathevons à Montbrison, *il faut que nous ayons leurs foies*.' These operations, carried out mostly in Floréal and Prairial, prove to be thirsty; Magnien asks for a drink, his captors tell him he will get one on arrival, and then kill him at the roadside. They then go to an inn and ask for meat and wine; the landlord can only oblige with milk and eggs. And with this spartan meal they slake their thirst and appetite, while boasting of their exploit. After the Bois-de-Cros massacre, the murderers finish off the wine and food left by the dead or fleeing picnickers.

Two reports to the authorities in Dieppe, both for Frimaire year IV, tell much the same story: in the *canton* of Longueville 'on tue et on brûle . . . Les crimes restent impunis', while the *juge-de-paix* of Envermeu writes 'que ce canton commençoit à être inquiété des brigans et que récemment un homme avoit été tué d'un coup de feu dans la forêt d'Arques et dépouillé de tout ce qu'il avoit sur le corps'.[1] This, perhaps, was the main difference between the White Terror of the south and the banditry of elsewhere. In the south, people were killed deliberately, for political reasons, because they were known, had occupied certain offices. But their corpses were not rifled and they were left with their clothes;[2] in the north, people might be killed because they happened to be passing along a path in the forest, and their bodies were left naked.

(ii) *Moral and economic boycott*

Murder was the extreme form of anti-terrorism. There were other less dramatic but equally effective methods of dealing with the former militants. First of all, there was the 'climate' of the year III, the terrible moral and even physical isolation of the militant minorities of the previous year. '*Guerre à mort à ces monstres* est le cri général de tous nos administrés,' notes, with his usual satis-faction, the Thermidorian *agent national* of the District d'Avignon, 1–9 Floréal year III, 'et le seul qui plane avec prépondérance sur l'horizon de ce district. L'isolement dans lequel se sont placés les restes impurs des partisans sanguinaires de cet affreux système, le mépris qui les couvre, l'horreur qui les environne, le désespoir qui les tourmente . . . tous ces motifs ne servent pas peu à maintenir la tranquillité. . . .'[3] No wonder that, in the cities of the south, the surviving cadres of terrorism were in the habit of seeking out each other's company, huddling together in cafés and inns kept by their partisans where, in a hostile environment, they were a sitting target for a murderous mob as well as a constant source of inform-ation for the police.

But there were more practical ways of expressing this sense of moral banishment. The first time that Jacques Chérest, the head of the Chérest family, returned to the small town of Tonnerre, the

---

[1] Arch. Dieppe, Grand Registre de la municipalité, Frimaire an IV.
[2] See note 2T, p. 355.
[3] Arch. Vaucluse 3 L 48* (rapports décadaires de l'agent national du district d'Avignon, 1–10 floréal an III).

scene of his domination during the period of revolutionary government ('depuis près de deux mois ses adhérans annonçoient son
arrivée, et devenoient plus insolens, plus audacieux, à mesure
qu'ils la croyoient plus prochaine . . .'), on 10 Floréal year III, the
situation rapidly got out of hand. On the 11th, the municipality sent
a courier to Auxerre to ask for troops. The *procureur syndic* suggested
that in the mean time the *Garde nationale* take up positions in his
house, in order to protect him and his family from an increasingly
ugly mob, 'mais la garde nationale a déclaré nettement qu'elle se
croiroit deshonorée d'être mise en faction chez un scélérat, un
terroriste, un buveur de sang . . .'. In the evening, according to
Chérest's own account,

au moment où il se mettoit à table avec sa femme, ses deux enfants et
une ouvrière, sont entrés chez lui environ vingt citoyens tous armés qui
lui ont dit de les suivre sur le champ . . . plusieurs l'ont pris au collet,
l'un d'eux par le milieu du corps, et l'ont conduit jusques sur la porte
de la rue . . . ils l'ont laissé libre au milieu d'eux . . . il étoit injurié et
menacé par les uns . . . les autres engageoient au silence . . . ajoute que
sa femme a été aussi maltraitée chez lui. . . .

Hearing of his plight, the municipality sent an escort of *gendarmes*
to bring him to the prison, where he was shut up for the night.
Early next morning, the Chérests, who were well-to-do people,
took the hint and left for Saint-Florentin. They returned, however,
a year later, as a result of the amnesty of Brumaire year IV. This
time, on three successive nights (23–25 Prairial, Saturday, Sunday,
and Monday), two of their barns and most of their crops went up
in flames. The head of the family went to the *juge-de-paix*; the
case, on eventually coming up before the local court, was dismissed.
Chérest was told that he could seek redress before the *tribunal de
police correctionnelle*, 'pour fait de simple police'. A month later
their windows were broken, and some of their livestock were
poisoned. The Chérests, however, saw out the storm; they were
big employers of labour and time was on their side.[1]

It was much the same with the leading terrorists of Moulins and
Nevers; on 5 Fructidor year III (a Saturday) Delan, the former
mayor of Moulins and a well known doctor, Verd, Perrotin, and

[1] A.N. F1b II Yonne (1) (procureur syndic du district de Tonnerre, au comité
de legislation, 13 floréal an III) and ibid. (commissaire du Directoire dans l'Yonne,
au Ministre, 8 vendémiaire an V): '. . . A Tonnerre on proscrit, on désigne à la
fureur de quelques scélérats la famille Chérest, trois fois on attente à leurs
jours. . . .'

Agar were taken out of prison, for transfer to Grenoble; a threatening crowd at once collected and they were only saved from lynching by the prompt action of the *agent national* in having them reincarcerated. An imperative order from the Committee of General Security forbade their transfer to the Isère; they would quite certainly have been assassinated on their way through Lyon. (This had indeed been the intention of the Moulins judicial authorities, who had ordered the *gendarmerie* to route them through the Second City.) By the middle of the year IV, after varying terms of imprisonment, they were all back in office in the Departmental or municipal administration.[1] But, like the Chérests, these were fairly comfortable people—even *Marat* Chaix, the ultra-revolutionist of Corbigny, was a *propriétaire* and some of his devoted supporters were his employees.[2]

If such people could escape lynching or prison massacre, they could expect eventually to resume their ordinary activities and even public office. Others were less fortunate; the wives and families of rural *sans-culottes—tonneliers, bourreliers, galochiers, sabotiers,* blacksmiths—were subjected to an economic boycott, being unable to obtain bread or dairy produce in their own villages; when their wives or daughters went to the fountain or the *lavoir,* the village women drew together, pushed over their pails, trod on their washing; and on the way back home dirt and stones were thrown at them.[3] Their children had to be taken away from school. Their families walked in the village with *propos* and looks constantly in their backs. The local authorities refused to pay relief to the wives of soldiers—and a husband or a son in the army was an additional sign of guilt—but, of course, turned a blind eye to deserters, living comfortably at home.

Nastiness could be the most effective in a small community;[4] and rural nastiness was the worst of all, the most persistent and the

---

[1] A.N. F1b II Nièvre I (Discours de Rouyer, du 15 brumaire an IV) and F1b Allier I (Rouyer, au Directoire, 5 germinal).

[2] Ibid. (Chaix, de Lormes, au Directoire) (19 frimaire an IV). Also *Les Armées révolutionnaires,* ii. 619–22.

[3] In Montbrison, wives or widows of terrorists have their skirts pulled up and are then beaten by young men belonging to the murder gangs. Others are made to kneel in the street and ask to be forgiven for their past errors. A witness 'vit près de chez lui quantité d'individus qui tenoient la femme du C. Frioux, que pendant que les uns levoient ses jupes . . . Legrand dit *le Bourru* lui donnoit des coups sur les cuisses toutes nues avec des cravaches . . .' (A.N. BB 18 690).

[4] See note 2U, p. 356.

most chiselling. The *comité* of Aix, in a letter to Maignet dated 9 Ventôse year II, has some comments that might well be generalized:

Tu nous demandes, citoyen représentant, des renseignemens sur les principaux agitateurs de la commune de Berre; les divisions de ce pays ne nous sont point parfaitement connues, mais elles ne nous sont point tellement étrangères que nous ne puissions te communiquer quelques réfléxions, non seulement sur cette commune, mais sur la généralité des petites communes de notre Département. Dans ce pays les citoyens se trouvent depuis longtems divisés par des motifs absolument étrangers à la cause que nous défendons. La Révolution les a trouvés dans cet état d'opposition & sous le prétexte de la servir, les chefs des différens partis en ont abusé pour venger leur ressentiment & alimenter les haines particulières.[1]

Even as near Paris as Suresnes, the former militant was not safe from rural persecution; early in Ventôse year III, Dessirier, a former cook who had been a member of the *Commission Temporaire* in Lyon during the previous year, was out walking in the main street of the village with his wife and children when all at once they were pursued by a crowd of sixty or seventy screaming inhabitants —mostly women and children—including the school mates of the younger Dessirier, shouting for the death of the *buveur de sang*, the *buveuse de sang*, and of the *petits buveurs de sang*. The family managed to reach their cottage without more damage than having their clothes torn; but, for the next three days, they were barricaded in their home by a mob that kept up an incessant vigil and prevented the children from sleeping by maintaining a hubbub throughout the night. If the municipality did nothing to encourage this cruel sport, they did nothing to put an end to it, denying to the *sans-culotte* family the protection of the *Garde nationale*. Eventually some friends of the former militant among the village artisans were able to contact the Committee of General Security in Paris, informing it of the family's plight; they returned with a *commissaire* of the Committee, and an *arrêté* dated 4 Ventôse: 'instruit que des citoyens de Suresnes, égarés sans doute, ont employé la violence contre la famille du C. Dessirier [le Comité] charge la municipalité de Suresnes de prendre toutes les précautions nécessaires pour maintenir le calme. . . .'[2]

---

[1] Arch. Bouches-du-Rhône L 1707* (comité de surveillance d'Aix, an III).
[2] A.N. F7 4675 d 1 (Dessirier).

Dessirier was fortunate in living near enough to Paris to be able to attract the attention of a Committee that was to save many former militants from the effects of persecution. *Sans-culottes* even as near as the Yonne could not easily invoke such an august protector. In Sens, for instance, the local militants were subjected, throughout the year IV, to nightly concerts, organized by the *jeunesse dorée*, with rattles, French horns, drums, and trumpets, the firing of crackers, and the repeated singing of the *Réveil du peuple* until three or four in the morning.[1] The wives of former *meneurs* were refused the assistance of midwives. Doctors, on the other hand, so many of whom had occupied positions of power during the Terror, were better placed than anyone else to ride such storms of rural and small-town nastiness. For even the most convinced royalists might need their services; and they held one of the most effective means of escape from military service. It was not the same for the artisan. No wonder Paris—or the nearest big city—seemed to the harassed *sans-culotte* a golden land, in which it was possible to live in peace, protected by anonymity and indifference. In the year IV, four hatters from the Forez, with one suit of clothes between them, were to explain that they preferred thus to live in one room—with a single bed and one blanket—than to remain subjected to the constant nagging hatred of their neighbours. No wonder some of these unfortunates walked to Paris, from as far away as the Ardennes or the Puy-de-Dôme or Mâcon.

(iii) *The cost of militancy*

The Thermidorian Government added to the distress of the former *sans-culottes* by legislation directed both against their collective means of self-expression and their private livelihood. A law of 25 Vendémiaire year III prohibited all efforts at collective action on the part of *sociétés populaires*—the Thermidorians were only completing what the Jacobins had begun in the Law of 14 Frimaire—at the same time making the publication of membership lists compulsory. (This was later to be the most valuable source for the organization of collective purges.) A particularly mean law —dated 13 Frimaire year III—required former members of *comités de surveillance* and *comités révolutionnaires* to reimburse the *Trésor* for the sums that they had received as salary in 1793-4. As most of these officials had been in office for at least a year, this might

---

[1] See note 2V, p. 356.

amount to a lot of money, which small tradesmen and artisans who had abandoned their shops or trades to take up full-time employment under the Terror would hardly be in a position to pay back in the year III, when they were attempting to recover what was left of a family business, compromised by long absence. The former *commissaires* of Dieppe stated flatly that they were unable to pay the State back what the State had given them for devoting all their time and energy to the service of the Republic and to the pursuit of English agents. 'Sa composition'—they stated of the *comité*, when it first came under fire in the last days of the year II—'fut de tous citoyens laborieux, la plupart sans fortune et chargés de nombreuse famille . . . leurs commerces respectifs ont été totalement abandonnés . . . la plupart ont été obligés de contracter des dettes. . . .'[1] In this instance, that was the end of it. But the Dieppois showed little inclination to make life impossible for their former terrorists—the ex-*commissaires* were merely disarmed and excluded from the *Garde nationale*, while disparaging references were made, every now and then, to their mean background—and, as in other Upper Norman towns, both the Terror and the Reaction were remarkably mild, at least from the political point of view. It is not known how the law was applied elsewhere; but there can be no doubt that those who drew it up intended further to penalize the *sans-culottes* by economic sanctions just when they were least able to face up to them. (Only a month later, the *maximum* was abolished.) Militancy henceforth was indeed a luxury that former *sans-culottes* could ill afford. This is, in fact, the gist of an imaginary conversation between two *exclusifs*, reported for Ventôse year IV:

'S. Est-il vrai que D*** a donné sa démission et que vous n'êtes plus que deux de cette Section?

'C. Cela est vrai, D*** a refusé, étant obligé de donner tous ses momens au rétablissement de son commerce qu'il avoit négligé depuis trois ans pour servir la chose publique, comme vous savez; de sorte qu'étant seul avec sa femme, il ne pourroit pas donner le tems nécessaire aux fonctions qu'il avoit à remplir. . . .'[2]

---

[1] Arch. Seine-Maritime L 5329 (comité de Dieppe, les anciens membres des comités sectionnaires à l'agent national du district, 9 ventôse an III) (Dumès à l'agent national, 11 ventôse an III) (Guillaume Selle, tailleur d'habits, ex-membre du comité de la section Marat, à l'agent national, 12 ventôse an III) (Desmarquet à l'agent national, 16 ventôse an III).

[2] A.N. F7 3054 (rapport de police du 5 ventôse an IV, dialogue entre deux 'exclusifs') (rapporté par Charvin, officier municipal du 3ème arrondissement).

By the year IV, the majority of former militants would find themselves in the position of the imaginary D***; and those erstwhile terrorists who returned to public office after Vendémiaire year IV, especially in Departments like the Nièvre and the Allier, where they were to monopolize the Departmental and municipal administrations, were people well able to afford public office. Most of the former members of the *Commission Temporaire* from these two Departments were wealthy men of law, property-holders, or journalists. In such conditions, one would need to be an Antonelle or a Félix Lepeletier to be able to accept public office or to indulge in the luxury of conspiratorial militancy.

(iv) *Pauperization*

Equally effective deterrents to the survival of the *sans-culotte* political class were the long periods of detention which, combined with the famine of the year III and the collapse of the *assignat* and a winter without fuel (which meant unemployment for a great many artisans, unable to light their stoves or furnaces), spelt economic ruin for *sans-culottes* dependent on their work to keep themselves and their families alive. Many were thus reduced to the status of paupers; 's'il lui falloit acheter du pain', writes a father of seven, in Germinal year IV, 'ses forces & son courage ne pourroient y suffire et la misère auroit bientôt détruit sa famille malheureuse. . . .'[1] 'Il y a neuf mois', reports another, at the same period, 'j'étois garçon perruquier, mon état a tombé par la révolution . . . j'ai vendu ma montre . . . avec les boucles d'oreille de ma femme et d'autres effets pour louer une petite boutique pour vendre de la friperie, mais malheureusement je n'ai pas fait mes affaires. . . .'[2] A year earlier, of a former *commissaire*, Section de Brutus, it is reported: 'Il est pauvre. . . . Pour faire honneur à ses créanciers, il a été obligé de louer sa boutique [de pâtissier] et de vendre tous les ustensiles concernant son état.'[3] The wife of an artisan from Mouzon gives a dramatic account of the plight of the former *sans-culotte* milieu, in a petition to the Commission des Secours dated Prairial year III: '. . . Nous sommes regalés à sept personnes que nous sommes avec cette livre de pain [de la ration]

[1] A.N. F II 1812 (Pierre Hudelle à la Commission des Secours, 5 germinal an IV).
[2] A.N. F II 1814 (pétition à la Commission, s.d. germinal an IV).
[3] A.N. F7 4775 25 d 4 (Jacques Tavet).

. . . ma pauvre famille qui, remplie de talens, meurt de besoins, n'ayant pas un point d'ouvrage, vu la grande misère, car tout le pays est affamé, il n'y a que les impériaux qui ne manquent de rien, car ils ont notre pain . . .', and she goes on to refer to 'les spectres de Mouzon, ces anatomies vivantes', complaining that 'la munici-palité . . . les gens aisés voient toutes ces misères du plus grand sang-froid . . .'.[1] A former *frère de l'École chrétienne*, in a letter from Sens in Messidor year III, when the crisis was at its height, offers an even more apocalyptic picture of prevailing conditions, in a language suggestive of a clerical background: 'On laisse le malheureux dans ses fers et au milieu des épines tandis que l'on sème des fleurs sur le passage des riches', adding philosophically a judgement on the end of hope and on the general mood of apathy:

> Les aristocrates nous diront sûrement que l'histoire des révolutions, des empires, nous apprend que toutes les républiques n'ont eu qu'un temps de prospérité et qu'elles ont fini par se dissoudre. . . . A ceci je dis qu'il est malheureux pour les français que les cœurs se partagent. . . . La France devient aujourd'hui le théâtre de victoires au-dehors et des fléaux les plus violens au-dedans. . . . C'est un martyre bien doulou-reux d'avoir faim et de ne pas avoir du pain pour de l'argent . . . tous les jours l'on est obligé de vendre ses effets pour avoir du pain . . . les français sont fous, il n'y a plus de raison en France. . . .[2]

A former *sans-culotte* who in these conditions petitioned the Commission for entry into a workhouse or asked to be considered for the receipt of the bread of the *douzième secteur*, reserved for the totally destitute (even *indigence* seems to have been a privilege hard to come by officially in those hard times: 'il faut apparemment être au rang des gens dans le besoin, être dans la crasse, couvert de haillons, hurlant et jurant dans les rues', complains an inhabitant of Compiègne, an unsuccessful petitioner, in a letter dated 25 Messi-dor year III)[3] and distributed free, was not likely to give the Government any trouble. He would become, in effect, a pensioner of the Government, dependent on official favour to obtain the daily loaf; his position would be no more independent than that of a former militant, described in a police report of Germinal year IV:

[1] A.N. F15 2820 (Jeanne-Catherine Hervez, femme Christophe, de Mouzon, à la Commission des Secours, 1er prairial an III).

[2] Ibid. ('Le modeste Pierre Doyen, tenant ci-devant les petites écoles chrétiennes [à Sens] . . . ancien maître serrurier, entrepreneur en bâtiment à la Convention, 26 messidor an III).

[3] Ibid.

'. . . Potemont et Moreaux sont de mauvais citoyens; je ne parle pas de Diochet, depuis que la police le fait vivre, il n'est plus à lui, il est *vendu*. . . .'[1] And many other poor *sans-culottes* were reduced to a state similar to that of Diochet.

(v) *The diseases of the poor*

What was not achieved by political proscription, detention, persecution, exile, murder, extreme hardship, withdrawal from France, was often completed by disease, the companion of dearth, pauperization, hopelessness, and apathy; in many towns of the north of France—Rouen, Dieppe, le Havre, and in their suburbs, in the overpopulated countryside round Amiens, in Valenciennes, Fumay, in the Vosges, in a number of villages in the Orne and the Sarthe—the poorer sort of *sans-culottes* and their families were wiped out in a series of sweeping epidemics that struck, two summers running, in September (Fructidor) 1795 and 1796, following two intensely cold winters and two droughts that, while sparing the well-to-do, decimated the population of the poorer quarters and the *faubourgs*. In fact, there could hardly have been a greater concentration of misfortunes to have fallen on the heads of the urban and rural poor.[2]

(vi) *Suicide*

It was altogether too much for some of these underprivileged, including a few former militants. There are reports of frequent suicides, both from Paris (where, according to Duval, whole families disappeared in the waters of the Seine) and Saint-Denis, particularly among the women of the people, throughout the year III. There are thirteen such reports, for three Paris Sections, between the middle of Brumaire year III and the first month of the year IV.[3] A carpenter of the Faubourg, who had been a leading militant of the Section de Popincourt and a member of the *comité révolutionnaire*, threatened just after the Prairial Days with further imprisonment, decided that life had become completely intolerable for people of his condition and with his past. (His neighbours, who were very much afraid of him, describing him as a man given to violence and his household as one frequently punctuated by screams and blows, said he was a *septembriseur*; he had boasted

---

[1] A.N. F7 3054 (rapport de police du 5 germinal an VI).
[2] Section III, pp. 220–2.   [3] See note 2W, p. 356.

about it and displayed his sabre in several cafés. He had been arrested a first time on 9 Thermidor year II, on the orders of the *robespierriste comité*, with whose members he had had a series of violent quarrels, and had been released on 12 Frimaire year III. After the Prairial Days, he had good reason to believe that he would once more be proscribed; he had also been told by a friend, an inn-keeper, and like any good *sans-culotte* he was ready to credit any-thing that came from such an impeccable source, that the authorities were about to place the Duke of York on the throne of France: *vu l'horreur*, he comments, *qu'il avoit du nom d'un Roy*, this was too much for him.) He first of all attempted to poison himself, his wife, and three daughters, with an omelette containing verdigris; when this failed, he tried to gas his family with the fumes of the stove, but was no more successful. He then fetched an axe from his tool set, and slaughtered his wife and two of the girls, aged three and four, while they slept, during the night of 9–10 Prairial, after having taken the eldest to be cared for by a neighbour. Finally he had attempted once more to gas himself. He was eventually traced to the Hôtel-Dieu, after a week, when his landlord discovered the holocaust. On his recovery, he was interrogated in Messidor. The Committee of General Security was interested in his role in the Germinal Days and in those of Prairial. His defence was that, after falling out with the committee of his Section in the year II, 'convaincu qu'il n'étoit pas propre à se mêler des affaires politiques, il ne s'en est occupé en aucune manière . . .'. He was tried and condemned to death by the Seine criminal court, on 2 Thermidor year III, and was executed on the same day, just a year after the fall of Robespierre. He was clearly a very stupid, very naïve, very violent man, the prototype of many poor *sans-culottes* both of his condition and of his Section—a victim of his past and of circumstances that were beyond his control and that he did not fully understand. He did understand, though, that in the conditions of the year III, people like himself would lose, whatever they did, whether they kept out of politics altogether, or whether they once more took up arms, as he had been accused of doing, as in Germinal and Prairial. His utter desperation was symptomatic of the state of mind of a whole section of the *petit peuple*, in the terrible circumstances of Prairial year III, after the Faubourg had been disarmed and reduced to a funereal silence.[1]

[1] See note 2X, p. 357.

It is not known whether Denis Denelle had many imitators. There were a number of brutal murders in Paris, in the three Sections with which we have been mainly concerned, in the following months.[1] Already in the previous autumn the municipality of Saint-Denis, 'instruite des assassinats qui se réitèrent depuis quelque tems sur les routes de Paris et de Gonesse', had decided to increase the number and size of night patrols along the high road to the Pays de France.[2] None of these murders appears to have had any political significance, except in so far as they represented the increasing violence of a cruel period in which the law-abiding poor had little prospect, other than a lingering death from cold and starvation.

(vii) *The year IV*

It is not at all difficult to understand why, after the appalling experience of *Nonante-cinq*, the common people of Paris and of the other cities of the north had had enough of militancy and lay low and kept very quiet. In Rouen that year there were a number of disturbances, provoked by hungry women, but this time they were unable to shame their men into action.[3] In Paris former militants were often reduced to begging for bourgeois charity in dramatic petitions to the *Commission des Secours*, while others in desperation left the city in the hope of finding survival conditions in the Departments.[4] *Nonante-six* was rather worse, with even higher mortality rates in the cities, even less bread, less food and less prospect of employment; there was much murmuring, but more apathy.[5] The prediction made by a counter-revolutionary in

[1] A.P.P. A/A 95–8 and A/A 187–8. In the Section du Muséum there were two murders of *filles de confiance* of goldsmiths, on 30 Brumaire and 8 Pluviôse year III. In the Section de la Butte des Moulins there were three murders, one on 20 Vendémiaire, two on 21 and 22 Messidor, the same year. All three victims were women. The third murder was a matter of vengeance, the woman having been killed by an ex-lover.

[2] Arch. Saint-Denis I D 1 6 (séance du 12 nivôse an III de la municipalité de Franciade).

[3] *Terreur et subsistances*, pp. 307–42.   [4] See Section III, p. 230.

[5] 'En vérité, le peuple, la classe ouvrière, des citoyens, meurent de faim au sein de l'abondance', write the authorities of Lapalisse, in Brumaire. In Prairial of the same year, a former lawyer petitions the Commission: 'Je voudrois bien ne pas imiter ce juge du tribunal civil du Palais, mort, il y a 12 jours, d'inanition chez lui. . . . Comme cet exemple trop fréquent de mourir de faim n'est pas bon à suivre pour un ci-devant Procureur du feu Roi et qui ne peut mendier, je me recommande à vous . . .' (A.N. F1b II Allier I, and F II 1182, subsistances an IV).

March 1793 in a letter addressed to London and intercepted by the Dieppe committee, had at last come true.[1] In the year IV many women of the people returned to the old remedies of religion; others, according to Duval, used the Seine, in numbers even greater than in the previous year.[2]

(viii) *Exile*

The great mass of the former *sans-culottes* thus suffered at home. They were murdered, they died, they committed suicide, or just succeeded in keeping above water during the two terrible years of crisis until good harvests and high wages improved their economic position if not their political status. Those better placed economically took refuge in Paris, or at least left the scene of their former activities. The wisest of all did not wait for the anti-terrorist legislation of Ventôse, Germinal and Prairial, Messidor and Thermidor of the same year, to draw their own conclusions. Some took refuge in the reassuring anonymity of military bureaucracy—army transport, military hospitals, supplies—which kept them on the move, in France, always one or two steps ahead of the arrest warrant and just out of reach of the *accusateur public* of their home Department or of that in which they had been active in the service of the Terror.

In the year III, the French armies themselves were on the move, pouring into Sardinia, Catalonia, the Austrian Netherlands, and the Rhineland, and a number of ex-terrorists followed in their wake in similar employment. The *armée d'Italie*—and more particularly the entourage of the *adjudant-général* Brune—was said to have been a favourite refuge for people with a revolutionary past. Most of these were to occupy, for the next twelve or fifteen years, comfortable and even profitable jobs in or on the fringes of military government in distant parts of Europe. From popular militants and revolutionary bureaucrats, they were thus often easily transformed into repressors.

It was not so much a matter of inclination as of circumstance,

---

[1] 'Ce qu'il y a de triste, c'est que ce malheureux peuple ne reconnoît pas assez la main de dieu qui s'appesantit sur nous et il lui faudroit une famine pour crier miséricorde' (Arch. Seine-Maritime L 5328, comité de Dieppe).

[2] Duval, op. cit.: 'Cet état de choses poussa au désespoir une foule de malheureux, qui aimèrent mieux se donner la mort que de mourir dans les angoisses de la faim. Des familles entières prirent ce parti extrême, et les flots de la Seine en ont su quelque chose. . . .'

though the *sans-culotte* leaders had always tended to authoritarianism and had at all times been impatient of opposition, which, like Robespierre, they regarded as wicked and, therefore, counter-revolutionary. In many parts of Europe, especially in the Flemish areas of Belgium, the old town versus country conflict of the year II was translated, in much more dangerous terms, into one between French occupiers and foreign resistants. Former *apôtres civiques*, one-time *commissaires civils*, former commanders of people's armies now found themselves once more lording it over the peasantry, levying requisitions, carrying out house searches, applying price controls, billeting troops, blaspheming from Italian or Flemish pulpits.

This time, however, it was not a matter of Parisians or Bourbonnais making themselves felt at the expense of Briards, Lyonnais, Foréziens, or Dauphinois, but of Frenchmen making life hell for Flemings, Piedmontese, Catalans, and Rhinelanders. Thus some of these erstwhile *sans-culottes*—already in the year II displaying a marked class hostility to cosmopolitanism—closed in even more on themselves, ignorant of the language, complaining of the food, contemptuous of the dirt and of the 'superstition' of their *administrés*, acquiring a colonialist mentality, and themselves actively contributing to the repression of popular revolt. It is true that they could persuade themselves that such popular revolt as they encountered was clerically inspired, counter-revolutionary, and 'fanatical'. They were none the less carrying out the functions of police and were contributing to the solidity of a military regime in which they held the important stake of their own posts and their own salaries. No doubt they often had their families with them too, and these would increase the mental gulf between them and the locals.

Much has been made, it is true, of the revolutionary role of these semi-civilians in northern Italy. But these *commissaires des guerres* would have been former Jacobins and a cut above the ex-*sans-culotte préposé à l'habillement militaire*. There were few Stendhals at this level. Commanding a Spanish prisoner-of-war camp in Holland—the task that fell to one of the more active political officers of the old Paris Revolutionary Army—was not the best school for militancy; and the man cursed his luck when he had to give up his camp and return to France in 1813. For every Lefranc, so resilient in deportation and exile as to become the medical adviser and architect of the Sultan of Zanzibar and the protégé of a French *émigré* family in Batavia, there would be nine former *sans-culottes* confirmed in their instinctive *poujadisme* and *esprit de quartier*, as a result of contact with the Balkans, Egypt, or Poland. The comforts of occupation made them lazy as well as repressive, corrupt as well as unfraternal. By the time they were forced back to France in 1813 or 1814 there would not be much militancy left in them. They were of course bitterly disappointed because they had lost their jobs, blamed the new regime for the faults of the previous one, and grumbled as much as the *demi-soldes* they so much resembled. But long absence and a totally unfamiliar way of life had cut them off from the *petit peuple*. They came back as strangers and were thought of as such by their remaining relatives; and a number of them were so unhappy that, rather than remain in Paris, or wherever they had previously lived, they set up in trade with their savings in some unfamiliar place, in partnership with a fellow ex-bureaucrat of Occupation, and tried to prolong into civilian life the comradeship of a semi-military society. After selling up his affairs in Paris, the former commandant of the prisoner-of-war camp went off to Bordeaux, settling there as an oculist. They were by then completely lost as *sans-culottes* and more or less as civilians.

No one has attempted to assess the size of the French Occupation bureaucracy. It had already been very large when the armies were still at home in the year II and had formed the cement that had held together, for as long as the patronage lasted, the so-called *hébertiste* party. It gave that group representatives in every garrison town and provided it with an interested rank-and-file of eight or nine thousand *commissaires*. Nor has an attempt been made to analyse its composition, other than to follow up a few score *meneurs* to their deaths from the plague, from typhus, from cholera, in Egypt, Dalmatia, and Poland, or to their murder in a brawl in Geneva. But the transformation of many of them into allies of repression must have had some effect on the collapse of popular militancy, for the army took some of the best of the old Sectionary leaders and some of the most enthusiastic of the provincial ultra-revolutionists. By the time the survivors came back, at best they might make good *bonapartistes*. A few of course retained their convictions, evangelizing Poles and Illyrians. But a Lyonnais militant in Illyria was a militant lost to Lyon.

The actual number of people thus lost to popular protest in France may have been trifling; but their quality often made up for this. Many of them had sought posts in the army in 1795 because they could not bear the spectacle of political reaction and of the persecution of the *patriotes* in Thermidorian France. These were not the sort of people who could move with the times, taking refuge in the obscurity of their *arrière-boutique* and divesting themselves hastily of the compromising emblems of popular sovereignty, throwing themselves at the feet of Thermidorian charity, as so many poor *sans-culottes* with large families were forced to do. Lefranc, Eude, Paris, Gourgonnier, and their kind—to name a few of these exiles—were bachelors, men with few ties, of the roving sort (some of them had been members of the famous *commissions ambulantes* of the year II), the sort of servants of Terror that have been described so felicitously by Professor Godechot as the *hommes de liaison*, the very stuff in fact of militancy and ultra-revolutionism.[1]

Exiles of this calibre represented then a net loss to France in terms of militancy and of experience in repression, terror, anti-rural economics, anti-religious and egalitarian evangelizing. Many others of the rank and file of popular protest were lost before they even started. As militarism made increasing inroads into the younger *classes*, during the Directory and Empire (how many Brutuses, how many Émiles, how many Gracchuses, born to militant parents in 1793 and the year II, disappeared in the snows of Russia in 1812!), a great many potential rioters were swallowed up in the army itself. They might of course desert, but they deserted outside France, and preyed upon German farmers, not French ones. The army was a great centre of lawlessness and banditry, but at least till 1812–13 these were primarily at the expense of foreigners. The principal concern of the *gendarmerie* and of the *prévôté* was to prevent deserters from getting back into France and a watch was kept for them along the old frontiers.

But these various categories were in any case taken out of the main stream of popular history. One can only guess at the possible effects of their removal from France, of their conversion from individualistic militancy to colonialistic administration. And to use war as a means of removing *mauvaises têtes* from the scene of

[1] Most of the material for this section has been derived from *Les Armées révolutionnaires*, ii, *Epilogue*, pp. 877–93.

danger—that is, home—is an ancient device of repressive regimes, just as they have, again and again, provoked war in order to keep the people down. In France, it is true, war was at first the *sans-culottes'* opportunity; but in the long run, it was also their undoing, the means of their enslavement. The Thermidorians were the first to discover the army as a weapon of anti-popular repression, and military commissions as a discreet and expeditious form of anti-popular justice. The Directory and the Empire did not need to carve out an African empire in order to create their *Biribi*. Occupied Europe would do. All these, however, are purely negative factors.

(ix) *Repression*

What is much more important is the positive achievement at home. The Directory saw an enormous improvement in the police powers of government, at least within the urban context, and as far as the northern *sans-culottes* were concerned (the southern ones did not matter all that much). Under the Jacobin dictatorship, there had existed in Paris a dozen rival police organizations— each Committee had one of its own, the Commune had one, the Minister of the Interior had one, the Department had one, the Sections had one, the *Mairie* had one—mainly devoted to denouncing one another and sending their employers the sort of information that they wished to hear. The Thermidorians, too, had to contend with a similar *embarras de polices*, of the most varied political affiliations—the *inspecteurs*, oddly enough, tended to be neo-terrorists and to display most of their energy in the pursuit of royalists. Now, however, the police had a Ministry, a centralized direction, a *Légion*, regular pay, an increasing army of informers (with fewer and fewer people to inform on). It was getting better at its job, and it found allies in popular apathy, hopelessness, and humiliation.

A section at least of the popular movement, the one previously dominated by women, now turned in despair to the age-old remedies of loyalism, deference, and religion. Already in the hunger riots of the spring of 1795, if in Paris the slogan had been *du pain et la Constitution de 1793*, in Rouen in a similar riot, on the day the news of the Paris rising had reached the Norman capital with the postal coach, it had been *du pain et vive Louis XVII*. A great many women of the people came to prefer the rule of *notre bon Roy*, whoever he might be, to that of the Thermidorian Rump.

What had much helped the task of the police already in the year III was the revulsion very widely felt among the mass of *sans-culottes* for the former *dominateurs*, no longer feared, their excesses denounced in hundreds of reports and in all the papers, now distrusted as having used popular grievances to further their own ambitions, considered too, by their professional colleagues, as 'bad for trade'. So many shoemakers had been denounced up and down the country in 1795 as archetypal terrorists that the corporation must have cursed those compromising fellows who gave the whole trade a bad name. Repression carries its own lesson; there must have been something wrong with these people for them to have been so direly and so frequently punished. Repression, when intelligently directed, isolates, especially when combined with leniency towards the mass of the common people. The history of the period 1795-9 suggests above all that repression can be effective if applied intelligently and discreetly against a limited number of people, always the same. The Directory had the good sense to avoid political trials; unlike the Jacobin dictatorship, it did not need to persuade or to convince, for it did not rely on popular support, but on popular apathy.

The only affair that the new regime deliberately sought to publicize was that of the *babouvistes*, and for this it had every reason. It had caught the lot—it was the sort of inept conspiracy that any regime, authoritarian or weak, must dream of. The publicity would amply demonstrate the intelligence and vigilance of the authorities, frighten property-holders, and illustrate the isolation of the *babouvistes* from the common people. Finally the conspirators had obligingly left lists of some three thousand names, the *fine fleur* of revolutionary militancy all over France, ten to twenty for each Department, several hundred for Paris. Thus the Directory had a weapon with which to threaten the hard core of *meneurs* for the rest of their days. The lists were used repeatedly, both for arrests and for deportations. Never perhaps in history have conspirators rendered such a magnificent service to the police—and to historians. Not that most of these unfortunate men were even *babouvistes*; most of them were people whom, because of their past record, Germain and Buonarroti thought they could use. How these people must have cursed the honour thus rendered them by the idiotic *Égaux*.

Deportations, unlike the guillotine, did not make martyrs,

though the effect was much the same. Few ever returned from the Seychelles or Cayenne. Only three out of seventy-nine deported under the *Sénatus-Consulte* of Nivôse year IX ever got back to France, and these were at once hustled away from Paris to be confined to hot and sleepy little towns in the Aude and the Hérault.

(x) *Résidence surveillée*

The time-honoured French system of *résidence surveillée*, much favoured by the Ministry of Police of the Directory and by the Prefects of the Empire, was likewise an effective and unobtrusive method of isolating militant minorities, a condition being, of course, that it was to a place of confinement at a considerable distance from the previous area of militancy. It would have been silly to send Parisians to Pontoise or to Chartres (though Chartres is still the main centre for *interdits de séjour*). It was much more effective to send them, as Lefranc and Sormois were sent, to Lunel, or like Carlo Levi, who was from Turin, to Eboli. It was important, too, not to send all the militants to the same place, the surest way of creating a new *foyer de sédition* and of forming a University of Exile. To be effective *résidence surveillée* required a police numerous and efficient enough to prevent the *consignés* from returning secretly to their old stamping-grounds with the additional prestige of semi-outlawry. Nor would it do to confine former militants to places well known as disaffected and as centres of neo-terrorism and neo-Jacobinism, such as Lorient, Auxerre, Moulins, Nevers, Toulouse, Grenoble, Lons-le-Saulnier, Dijon, or Montbéliard. In the big 1813 round-up, the Napoleonic police took care to choose towns reputedly harmless, like Sens or Niort, small enough for the *consignés* to be at all times prominent and visible, yet not homogeneous enough for them to capture a following in a predominant trade or profession. Industrial centres and towns with a single, specialized craft (the Avignon *taffetassiers*, the Moulins hatters, the Cholet weavers, the Lyon silk-workers, etc.) were thus unsuited for this purpose. If it had not been so near the frontiers, Alsace would have been ideal; the interior of the Breton Departments was also well suited to isolate the lonely militant in unfamiliar, even hostile surroundings. In this respect, as in most others, the imperial police showed a very fine scale of discretion—not to say a humour of a cruel sort—in its allocation of *consignés*, condemning Parisians to places like Niort, Issoudun, or le Puy. The Fourth Republic did even worse and confined Joanovici to Mende and the King of Morocco to Corsica.

(xi) *The age of militancy*

Finally, there is the matter of the generations. The average age of militancy for revolutionary leaders at assembly level was between 30 and 40—a great many were born, like Robespierre, in the 1750s —and that of the humbler *sans-culotte* militants, less well fed and much worse housed, was somewhat higher: 38 to 45.[1] Country militants tend to be older than the urban *frères et amis*. The average age of the Dijon committee of the year II is 46.[2] On these figures, by 1815 most of the former popular leaders would be dying out or too old, too isolated, too lonely, too out of touch, too incapacitated, for effective militancy. A half-blind watchmaker like Eude is no longer much good for any movement; and *conciliabules nocturnes—* something that, like *signes de ralliement*, haunts the suspicious vigilance of successive French police organizations—are hardly dangerous when only attended by a handful of old decrepit men, come together to evoke the memory of better times. Many too, as we have seen, as a result of police persecution or economic boycott or unpleasantness from neighbours, or a combination of all these things, decided in 1795 or in the two following years to leave the towns in which they had played a revolutionary role, and set up in places where they might hope not to attract attention. The militants of the south and of Lyon came in large numbers to Paris; those of Paris, a great many of whom had not been Parisians very long, returned to their places of origin and lived out the Directory and Empire in Rouen, Amiens, Beauvais, Roye, Abbeville, le Havre, Alençon, Nogent-le-Rotrou, Sens, Auxerre, Melun, Pontoise, Orléans, Montargis, Gien, Pithiviers, Évreux, or in the neighbouring countryside, if they still had relatives there. In either

---

[1] These calculations are based on the ages of members of *comités*, though these may be slightly higher, owing to the popular respect for age and the belief that vigilance could best be entrusted to those with considerable experience of life, than those of less privileged *sans-culottes*. With this reservation, out of 98 members of Paris committees whose ages are given, the average age emerges as 46. In Dieppe, the average age of the *commissaires* is 38, exceptionally low; for in the neighbouring *commune*s it is 44 for Bacqueville, 46 for Eu. In the neighbourhood of le Havre, the average is: Ingouville, 40; Lheure, 49; Sanvic, 49; Sainte-Adresse, 48; Blesville, 42; and Saint-Jouin, a more rural community, 51 (A.N. Série Alphabétique F7, Arch. Seine-Maritime L 5329, and A.N. F1b II Seine-Maritime I).   [2] Arch. Côte-d'Or L 2658*.

case this voluntary exile was an admission of defeat and powerlessness; if there had been any hope at all they would have stayed on
and prepared for the next round of *journées*.

(xii) *The second generation*

In a few exceptional cases, however, death, exile, martyrdom,
persecution helped rather than impeded the survival of militancy,
by developing the conditions favourable to the creation of a family
cult. Widows of *guillotinés*, *fusillés*, and *déportés* were, by the nature
of things, the most eager thus to carry on the flame and to transmit
it to the next generation; it was a role almost forced upon them,
for what other claim could they make on people's interest and
sympathy? They would be the last to admit that their husbands,
or companions, had died in vain. The sensible ones—Anne
Levêque, the widow of Ronsin—did get remarried, and, in her
case, married even better. (Her new husband was a proper General,
and was sent under the Empire as Ambassador to the United
States.)[1] The irreconcilables nourished the coming generation on
a mixed diet of reverence, revenge, romantic republicanism, and
the purifying beauties of violence. They were, in fact, these professional widows, draped night and day in their weeds—the first
to contribute to that long and disastrous tradition of historicism
that, for over a hundred and fifty years, has been the bane of
French popular movements. *La veuve* Sijas,[2] *la veuve* Loÿs,[3] *la
veuve* Babeuf, *la veuve* Le Bas,[4] saw to it that their sons never
forgot: Émile, Babeuf's son, later known as Robert, and his

---

[1] *Les Armées révolutionnaires*, pp. 98–102. She married Turreau, who had
fought in the Vendée.

[2] '... La femme de Sijas court, s'agite, intrigue, prêche les ouvriers, et veut
absolument venger la mort de son mari' (rapport de police du 5 nivôse an V,
A.N. F7 3054).

[3] '... Notre commune renferme actuellement ... quelques anarchistes, vieux
partisans de Robespierre ... agens et amis secrets de Babeuf. ... Nous avons vu
paroître dans notre commune le C. Vial, membre du club de l'hôtel de Noailles,
les nommés Olivier et Poicelot, anciens membres du comité révolutionnaire de
la section du Bonnet-rouge. ... Nous savons qu'ils s'assemblent dans la maison
de la veuve d'un nommé Loys, de Loys qui étoit secrétaire des jacobins le 9
thermidor et qui, arrêté à Marseille, s'est pendu dans sa prison ...' (administration municipale de Fontainebleau au Ministre, le 6 messidor an IV, A.N. F1b
II Seine-et-Marne I).

[4] *La veuve* Le Bas, along with Buonarroti, might be described as the origin-
ator of the Robespierriste myth and the founder of the cult of Saint-Maximilien.
Worse still, she spoke of the coldly sanguinary Saint-Just as if he had been a
saint.

daughter-in-law were early schooled as Avengers.[1] If there were no sons, daughters would do. They were often even worse, more passionate, more single-minded, devoted, intransigent priestesses at revolutionary shrines; a number of them, logically enough, retained of Jacobinism its militaristic chauvinism, and ended up as convinced Bonapartists. At a lower level, there was a strong group of faithful—the wives of *sans-culotte* leaders who had been deported to Cayenne and the Seychelles and who, in the former Section du Panthéon and among the hutments of the Gros Caillou, in the former Section des Invalides, an area closely watched by the police from the year IV to 1818 and considered especially dangerous, because it contained in close proximity the very rich and the very poor, attempted to keep people together, with meetings, always known to the police, in cellars and cafés.[2] Women like *la femme* Marcellin, a laundress, seem to have shamed a few men back into momentary activity; there are references to them at the time of the 'discovery' of the Infernal Machine of the rue des Blancs Manteaux, and again with reference to the *affaire* Aréna.[3] Their activities were pitifully unsuccessful, but they gave the police something to report on.

Militancy was thus transmitted via widows or sons or daughters into the next generation, well into the nineteenth century. In 1830, 1848, and 1871 the militant would be acting the same old play over and over again, publishing the same old newspapers, taking over the same old titles, and many of the *insurgés* of the *Trois Glorieuses* had a second go in the June Days, many of the women of the Commune were the wives or the widows of the *proscrits de juin*.[4] It therefore becomes important to follow individual careers, to trace the family descent of terrorism and to describe the survival of a mentality feeding on violence and on a romantic desire to compete with the past, to be 'worthy of the past'. The worst thing about the popular movement of the year II was that it gave three generations of revolutionists something to live up to, to merit, to imitate, to re-enact, in conditions that were not remotely connected

---

[1] '*Babœuf-Robert*, libraire, prévenu d'avoir vendu le *Nain Tricolore*' (rapport de police du 26 février 1818); '*Finet, femme Babœuf* (Catherine), libraire, prévenue de complicité dans la vente du *Nain Tricolore*' (rapport de police du 1er mars 1818) (A.N. F7 3029). It is characteristic that the younger Babeuf should have been engaged in promoting Bonapartist propaganda.

[2] See note 2Y, p. 357.   [3] *Les Armées révolutionnaires*, ii. 892.

[4] Edith Thomas, *Les Pétroleuses* (Paris, 1964).

with those of 1793–4 and when the repressive powers of governments and armies had been vastly improved. It was a tradition
that drove several generations of popular protest into empty, hopeless violence, into building barricades easily toppled by colonial
generals back from Algeria, into provocations that gave narrowly
bourgeois governments the pretext that they were seeking for
solving the problem of poverty by the extermination of the urban
working class. It was a tradition that drove a section of the revolutionary movement into the pathless politics of hate and massacre,
producing, at each generation, a new Hébert—a Vallès,[1] a Rochefort,
a Darien,[2] a Baudelaire—*exaspérés* whose policies began and ended
with the evocation of a gigantic Red Dawn in the course of which
the *petit peuple* and the factory workers would settle accounts with
the French bourgeoisie. It was a tradition which also resulted in
polonomania and *Marchons sur Varsovie*, belgophobia, anglo-
phobia, neo-Jacobin war-mongering, the belief in the purifying
effects of an international blood-bath, the assumption that an
international war was the likeliest opportunity for revolution at
home, and many other similar ineptitudes that were to dog the
French Left throughout the nineteenth century and even through
part of the twentieth. It was a tradition rich in a constantly reno-
vated martyrology, evocative of *fusillades* and *murs*, barricades and
mutinies. One thing at least that the popular movement of the
year II was to ensure for France was a plentiful supply of revolutionary dead, a regiment of tombs in the Père Lachaise and the
Cimetière du Montparnasse, multiple occasions for bringing out
the red banners and looking steadfastly backwards into an ana-
chronistic *sans-culotte* past. The *sans-culottes* hardly deserved this,
for at least they had used violence, or more often the threat of
violence, to some purpose, and for a time with some success.
Another heritage was the Babeuf Plot, which has never ceased to
plague and bore historians right up to the present day.

[1] *T.L.S.* 4 (1965). (*Courc*, article on Vallès.)
[2] *A Second Identity* (O.U.P., 1969), pp. 342–55.

PART THREE

THE POPULAR MOVEMENT IN ITS PRIME: THE *SANS-CULOTTES* THE YEAR II

'L'oppression et la tyrannie les avoit tirés de leur
nullité sociale. La justice et l'humanité les y a replongés,
sans doute à jamais. . . .'
(*A Thermidorian judge on the Dieppois terrorists*)

II. THERMIDORIAN LANGUAGE AND ASSUMPTIONS

THERMIDOR was widely depicted by its early apologists as a
return to normal. People were told that with the *retour au règne des
lois* there would be an end to fear and judicial violence and that
things would settle down. This was partly wishful thinking on the
part of the new rulers; for the regime, as we have seen, especially
in the south-east, very soon lapsed into violence and anarchy,
with the active encouragement of such eminent Thermidorians as
Cadroy, Isnard, and Boisset, the heralds of the White Terror, even
if other equally representative *éminences* of a divided governing
class, such as Barras, Fréron, and Goupilleau de Montaigu, did
their best to keep the reaction within legal bounds and to re-establish the authority of Paris by putting an end to killing and violence.
At first, at least, there was something in the claim, for it was an
achievement in itself to have brought to an end a self-perpetuating
bureaucracy of Repression, purged the revolutionary tribunal, and
protected the population from the implications of the tentacular
and hideous law of 22 Prairial. Immediately after Thermidor, the
bourgeois and the *notables* were not the only people to begin to
sleep soundly at night, without fear of a nocturnal house search;
the relief was felt quite as strongly among the *petit peuple*, equally
threatened by the spread of a bureaucratic Terror tied to the
realization of the concept of unanimity, if necessary by the extermination of the whole male population over the age of thirty. It was
not only Thermidorian pamphleteers who were to confine *l'Ombre
de Robespierre* so joyfully *aux enfers*; there was at first plenty of

popular literature on the same theme. The end of Terror seemed a positive gain to the nation as a whole; and it took several months and the experience of famine to convert what Mercier and Duval call the *classes populacières* back to terror and to repression.

Of course, these hopes rapidly proved unfounded and the universal feeling of relief soon gave way to dismay and alarm as, even in the first weeks of the regime, demands for vengeance became increasingly vocal and the political reaction proceeded at a speed more and more difficult to control. Certainly in the year III there would be no end to fear, but rather a beginning of it, as far as a great many humble people and a number of *Montagnard* leaders were concerned. But what the Thermidorians also meant by a return to normal was that France should henceforth be ruled by the *honnêtes gens* and that the common people should be sent back —maybe with a grudging reference, when it could be proved that they had been 'misled', but with no reference at all when they had played a leading part in the affairs of the year II—to their proper place in society, one in which they could not meddle in politics or play at revolution. The time had come to end such nonsense. The Thermidorian view of the natural order of society—what contemporaries describe, in the language of the year III, as *une saine harmonie sociale*[1]—and of the family, is expressed baldly in a number of reports, pamphlets, and printed denunciations concerning the *dominateurs* of the previous year.

It is a view clearly stated by a judge, that eminent stand-by of Thermidorian 'order' (the judicature had, after all, been fully reinstated, and was henceforth guaranteed against competition from 'people's courts' and similar horrors), the *commissaire national près le tribunal criminel* of Dieppe, in a report on the members of the former *comité*, dated 1st Prairial year III, when the anti-terrorist tide was at its height: 'L'oppression et la tyrannie', he observes, on the subject of the eleven former *commissaires* (the twelfth[2] had defied the Reaction by dying in Pluviôse of the same year) 'les avoit tirés de leur *nullité sociale*. La justice et l'humanité les y a replongés, sans doute à jamais. . . .'[3] One could not hope for a clearer announcement of the Thermidorian programme for the

---

[1] Certainly not the same *Harmonie Sociale* as that suggested by a *société sectionnaire* of the same name in the year II!

[2] Michel Godeby, who had died on 12 Pluviôse.

[3] A.N. D III 269 d 48 (Comité de législation, Seine-Inférieure, Dieppe, commissaire national au comité).

future of the common people. For who were these people so properly confined once more to their *nullité sociale*? Apart from the usual shoemakers and innkeepers, and urban artisans, there was a brewer, described as *vivant de son bien*, an *officier de santé*, and finally a doctor.[1] It was in fact the archetypal composition of a *comité* in a town, even to the doctor, so often the butt of Thermidorian denunciation for having betrayed his class and abused his influence with the poor by allowing himself to be carried to positions of power. (It was easier to explain away the presence of *officiers de santé* in committees, for these were merely an inferior sort of doctor, constantly snubbed by the old *Académies*, and easily written off as *aigris*. The Thermidorians, like Anouilh, were much given to *Bitos*-like theses on the subject of revolutionary militancy.)

Equally revealing is the comment on some of the leading terrorists of the Allier, accused in a document of Pluviôse year IV of having preached 'le mépris des autorités constituées, en consultant les valets d'écurie et le cuisinier d'une auberge sur ceux des fonctionnaires qu'il falloit destituer . . .'.[2] Of a member of the *comité* of Gannat in the same Department, it was claimed in Vendémiaire of the same year that he had 'contraint les domestiques dudit Reclesne [a wealthy landowner of Gannat] à se mettre à table avec lui, leur disant de profiter du moment, que c'étoit la dernière fois qu'ils y mangeroient, leur défendant de servir davantage à table, qu'ils étoient autant que leur maître, qui n'étoit plus rien . . .'.[3] Marcillat too, a former priest and another well-known terrorist from the Bourbonnais—he had been a member of the *Commission Temporaire* of Lyon[4]—had similarly disgusting eating companions: 'Il mangeoit familièrement avec l'exécuteur de la justice, dont il prenoit des leçons. . . .'[5] The Thermidorians were particularly sensitive to what had so often been a deliberate effort on the part of the roving *commissaire* to illustrate, in as dramatic and enjoyable a manner as possible, the new *sans-culotte* order of things. The *commissaires* would get their victims to cook them copious meals, which they then had to serve standing up, while the

[1] See note 2Z, p. 358.
[2] A.N. F1b II Allier I (rapport du 1er pluviôse an IV sur les terroristes de l'Allier).
[3] Ibid. (tribunal correctionnel de Gannat, 12 vendémiaire an IV).
[4] *Terreur et subsistances*, p. 68.
[5] See note 3A, p. 358.

commissaires themselves sat down with the local *gendarmes* and the artisan members of the local *comité*—a Passion Play in food egalitarianism that was performed over and over again in the areas subjected to ultra-revolutionism.[1]

On Laporte, a *commissaire* from Moulins, there is the comment: 'son état d'aubergiste n'a pu lui procurer aucune des connoissances nécessaires pour la place importante qu'il remplit dans une commune de 15,000 âmes. . . .'[2] (He had been a member of the highly popular municipality of the year II.) *Bias* Parent, a former priest, and later *agent national* of the very revolutionary District de Clamecy, is stated to have 'démoralisé le peuple' in giving them false illusions about their political and social importance.[3] Nor was this all; not only had they preached and practised the subversion of the social order, they had also—it is still the same group of Bourbonnais—encouraged 'la dépravation des mœurs en traitant de despotisme la sollicitude d'un père pour ses enfants, de jalousie, le tendre intérêt d'un mari pour la réputation de son épouse, en disant à la tribune de la société populaire qu'une fille à 21 ans, une femme mariée, n'étoient plus soumises à aucune autorité . . .'.[4] (It is characteristic of Thermidorian views of society that the very liberal laws of the revolutionary period in favour of bastard children and younger sons and daughters should have been withdrawn, in the course of the year III, in favour of legislation re-establishing *l'autorité paternelle* and the legal rights of the eldest male child as established in some local *coutumes*.)

In the various accusations directed against the terrorists of the Allier and the Nièvre—probably the most advanced people of the ultra-revolutionary period—while there are few references to their cruelty and brutality, there is a constant harping on the company that they kept, on their own origins, on their stated views on society. To have eaten with an executioner, when one was an educated man, a former priest, and a *propriétaire*, that was what was scandalous, that was what represented a state of affairs which could not be allowed to continue a moment longer and that must never

---

[1] See Section III, p. 250.

[2] A.N. F1b II Allier I (la députation de l'Allier au Directoire, 25 floréal an IV).

[3] A.N. F1b II Nièvre I (tableau des fonctionnaires amnistiés de la Nièvre, 20 frimaire an V).

[4] A.N. F1b II Allier I (Mangenest, de Montluçon, au Directoire, 1er pluviôse an IV).

occur again. (The Thermidorians were confident that they could see to that.) People who behaved in this way were accused by them of having *démoralisé le peuple*. What they meant by this was that they had not kept them in their place, had given them dangerous and false ideas of grandeur, and had encouraged them in habits of laziness.[1]

In this sense at least, Thermidor did represent a return to normal conditions, for what was most abnormal, as well as most intolerable, was that a 'popular movement' should ever have existed at all, in its own right, should have developed its own institutions and forms of political expression, and should have been politically effective—in combination, it is true, with other forces—for so long, especially in a country so devoid of representative institutions as eighteenth-century France where, up to the Revolution, the only form of popular protest had been the traditional market riot or bursts of wild and hopeless violence. In the words of Professor Reinhard, 'ce fut la guerre qui révolutionna la Révolution'; and it was war that gave the *sans-culottes* their opportunity. It was understandable, with the example of 1793 behind them, that so many nineteenth-century neo-Jacobin and neo-*sans-culotte* leaders should have looked to war as the best means of achieving Vallès's longed-for *la Sociale*.[2]

12. WAR AND TERROR (1793–1794)

The Thermidorians were right to affect such amazement, even if their indignation was somewhat self-interested. For the development of the *sans-culotte* movement during 1793 was entirely accidental and arose from the convenient pretext of total mobilization and emergency. The *sans-culotte* movement was as much a product of the war as the *maximum*, the *réquisitions*, the law on hoarding, the economic controls, and 'dechristianization'. Six months before the Thermidorians, the *dantonistes* had drawn the right conclusions: to dismiss the Terror, to put an end to repression, to send the people's judges back to the obscurity of their shops and basements, to rule in the absence of meddlesome *sans-culottes*, and to deprive the revolutionary dictatorship of its alibi, it was necessary to put an end to the war. But they had come six months too early: the war had yet to be won, the government still needed popular

---

[1] See note 3B, p. 359.   [2] *La République Sociale*.

support, *sans-culotte* bellicosity was still something to be reckoned with, while the *dantonistes* put their heads in the noose by attempting to conduct an independent foreign policy in time of war, so that they could readily be branded as traitors. The Thermidorians, some of whom represented *la queue de Danton*, could keep the war and dismiss the popular movement, because the bulk of the armies was outside France, because victories gave the promise of a pillage economy, and because 'dechristianization' provided them with a treasure-chest of furniture and pictures that could be exchanged for grain through Swiss or other neutral intermediaries.

Until the outbreak of war, successive revolutionary authorities had proved themselves quite capable of keeping the people down both in town and in the countryside: indeed, the bourgeois *Garde nationale* was much better at it, more ruthless, and also more interested, than the old royal troops had been. If rural disorder was persistent and widespread throughout 1790 and 1791, it was also remarkably unsuccessful, bringing on brutal and effective class repression. It did not matter to Lafayette and Bailly, as long as the country was at peace, that the *habits bleus* were loathed by the common people of Paris. They had done what was expected of them at the Champ de Mars, and, outside Paris, in Étampes, Angers, Nîmes, and elsewhere; and they were to do it again and again, firing on rioters, who were often just petitioners, and showing none of the hesitation in the use of force and musketry characteristic of the old royal authorities.

The first opportunity for the emergence of *sans-culotte* militancy came with the opening in July 1792 of the *Garde nationale* to the *citoyens passifs*, though it took them more than a year to displace the previous officers and to gain control of the all-important artillery companies (*canonniers*), the object of bitter conflicts between moderate and plebeian Sections in June–July 1793.[1] The opportunity was created by mobilization and invasion; but it followed that the *sans-culotterie* as an effective force could last only as long as the emergency lasted, and that, like Terror and repression, its influence could only be transient. Indeed, it was not to last even as long as the emergency; for by the spring of 1794 the government had discovered that it could not only run the Terror without popular support, but also use it against the popular militants. So that war, once the people's opportunity, could also

[1] *Les Armées révolutionnaires*, i. 40–8.

be a pretext, when centralization had been firmly established, in the period December 1793–March 1794, for dealing with the so-called 'ultra-revolutionaries', creators and commanders of people's armies, who were inconvenient and expendable because they stood in the way of an increasingly invasive revolutionary government. At the same time, the war was used even more directly as a means of removing from Paris—and from other cities—the *sans-culotte*-controlled artillery companies, by sending them to the frontiers or to the west, where they were painlessly incorporated into the ranks of the army proper.

This process was not a straight conflict in class terms between a predominantly middle-class Jacobin dictatorship and a socially distinctive 'popular movement' drawing its support primarily from that alliance of small shopkeepers and artisans known as *la sans-culotterie*. There may have been elements of such a conflict. Many of the popular militants, however, were themselves people of middle-class origin, some of them *notables*, and quite a number of the 'ultra-revolutionaries' were professional men or ex-soldiers. It was much more a conflict over the exercise of power. The *sans-culottes*—or whatever we choose to call them—claimed to exercise sovereign power in the name of 'direct democracy': the deputies were merely their mandatories, and answerable to them as such. This claim they proceeded to substantiate by actually exercising power and 'legislating' through institutions of their own creation that were not responsible to the central government or to the subordinate authorities. Thus police powers and the control of armed forces fell to *sociétés populaires*, that is to the militant minorities that controlled these completely unrepresentative bodies, dominated, in most instances, by very small groups of *meneurs*, allied as much by friendship or common hatreds as by ties of trade or craft. For, as in the case of the Paris Sections, it would be difficult to identify the provincial *sociétés* with any particular class or social group. Their composition varied enormously and was never quite the same from one town to the next; if, generally speaking, they represented a good cross-section of professional and trade life in any given town, in many places they allowed little place to the lower ranks of urban society. Thus, in le Havre, membership ranged from sea captains, merchants, tradesmen, artisans, schoolmasters, to former priests and clerks; the *Grand Quai* was absent—many of its inhabitants were in prison in the year II—but so were the shipyard workers, the fishermen, and ordinary sailors.[1] In Lyon, the hard core, both in May 1793 and again in Floréal year II, consisted of a selection of the more skilled trades—printers, compositors, goldsmiths, and so on—municipal officials, including the director of the post office, and the middle ranks of the silk industry: *négotiants* and *fabricants en soie*, rather than *ouvriers en soie*.[2] It was perhaps not surprising that in the crisis of 29 May 1793 the club should have backed the Jacobin municipality, while the Sections went over bag and baggage to federalism; there was no doubt on which side the common people of Lyon stood. The membership of the *société révolutionnaire* of Lille is even more surprising, for it included some of the richest cotton manufacturers in the place, together with wealthy property-holders and investors in national lands, along with the usual rank and file of tradesmen and textile workers, most of the latter *fabricants* in their own right.[3] Membership of a *société* might have a plebeian look about it, and certainly some *sociétés* fell into the hands of genuinely artisan and shopkeeper elements, but very often—just how often it would be the object of further local research to prove—it was a convenient disguise under cover of which the old *notables* of 1790 or of 1792 continued to exercise their influence. Of course, they were prepared to make concessions, as long as they were able to retain positions of power; and some of them were in the forefront of *sans-culotte* revolutionizing. In 1793 the *société* was more important than the municipality. It was a sort of revolutionary *syndicat d'initiative*, devoted above all to the promotion of local interests; and, on this platform, there would be a wide consensus of agreements. Its first aim, then, was to attempt to control municipal government. This was easy, for the *société* held the decisive weapon of the delivery of *certificats de civisme*; in other words, it could control appointments and remove even elected officials who met with its disapproval.

From the vantage point of municipal government, the *sociétés* then proceeded to establish alliances, private treaties, exchange of information, and 'federations' with their neighbours in other cities. This resulted in endless fractionalization of authority and the establishment, especially in the south of France, of hundreds

---

[1] *Terreur et subsistances*, pp. 99–105 ('La société havraise').
[2] *L'Armée révolutionnaire à Lyon*, p. 50.
[3] *Terreur et subsistances*, pp. 151–78.

of 'municipalist' republics, within which the more dramatic forms of revolutionary action could be pursued without let or hindrance, while at the same time the particular interests of a given area were promoted. 'Communalism' has been described as one of the most characteristic traits of the popular movement and, if it can be taken to mean a tendency to anarchism, this is certainly true. But it could be put to other, more disguised, uses, and very often 'communalism' is simply the rebirth of regionalism or municipalism, in a more respectable, apparently revolutionary, form. It might serve the interests of a *République du Midi*, but it is questionable whether it would have done those of the One and Indivisible. The 'federations' of September–November 1793 were in fact the revolutionary equivalent of the duc d'Angoulême's Kingdom of the South of the summer of 1815; they even covered very much the same areas of the south-east and south-centre.

There were several of these 'federations' in existence—one grouping seventy-seven *sociétés* of the Midi, with permanent headquarters in Marseille; another in Alsace; a third in Upper Normandy—when the Jacobin dictatorship intervened, in the winter of 1793, no doubt to avert what might have been the next stage in the organization of a sort of counter-government, or at least of a parallel government (and there had been plenty of foolish talk to the effect that 'les sociétés populaires sont souveraines, elles sont donc au-dessus de la loi', in the course of the autumn) on a national level. The Revolutionary Government chose to think so, as an excuse for intervention against a process that it described as 'l'ébauche d'un nouveau fédéralisme populaire'. It is, however, unlikely that anything of the sort would ever have happened; it is hard to imagine Paris *sectionnaires*, Lyonnais or Marseillais *sociétaires* being prepared to co-operate with anyone else, other than in terms of the total subjection of their partners to the municipal interests of their own cities. (This, as we shall see in another chapter, was particularly true of the role of the *sociétés* as instruments of enforced provisioning in the normal supply areas around their cities.) There was much more danger of anarchy—especially when the 'federations' had started to raise their own armed forces, composed exclusively of *sociétaires*—than of the formation of a national rival to the Revolutionary Government.

13. 'COMMUNALISM' AND THE POPULAR MOVEMENT (AUTUMN AND WINTER OF 1793)

In the Departments this movement was largely spontaneous, in so far as it represented the traditional desire of each city, each town, each village to be left alone and not to be interfered with by strangers from Paris. It was truly a form of 'popular federalism', but it would bring in many other elements as well. For, being so anarchical and undisciplined, it also attracted men of a certain type, instead of men of a certain social condition: it attracted revolutionary optimists, zealots, and wild men, the 'perfectionists' of the revolutionary period, who believed in taking on everything and everybody at once and who, in the government's view, 'did not know where to stop'. It also, of course, drew patent demagogues, adventurers out for a good time or an opportunity to make up for a compromising past by some singular extravagance, all manner of crackpots, and a few men of blood who were out for pillage and vengeance and who equated revolutionary action with beating up.

All these categories were easy to compromise; some had pasts that would not look good when trotted out by government prosecutors, always prone to judge what people were by what they had been—a tactic used persistently by Robespierre and Fouquier-Tinville against poor Jacques Roux. All of them, by their intransigence and single-mindedness, were sure to have ranged against themselves a maximum of powerful and respectable enemies. Their verbal extravagance and impudence made them open to every sort of misinterpretation. Their conceit, their posturing, their arrogance, and their constant self-dramatization rendered them ideal subjects for official indictments as counter-revolutionaries, *exagérés*, *anarchistes*, and other bad things. They had done, and above all had said, so many silly and so many violent things, that their words and actions could be put to almost any interpretation. Nor were they the sort of people *qui pensaient au lendemain*. The government men, on the other hand, did, seeing to it that many of these imprudent enthusiasts were denied one altogether.

On this provincial level at least, it was much more a conflict of temperaments than of class or even of policies. For how to force an *exagéré*, a revolutionary individualist, into a class categorization? And the conflict was quite inevitable, both in human and in political terms. The government men had time on their side, and knew it; it was only a matter of waiting for the wild men to hang themselves in the coils of their exaggerated promises and threats and to make themselves so intolerable to so many people for their downfall to become a matter of urgent necessity. The *exagérés*, it is true, enjoyed a certain amount of popular support, and each one, in his own 'parish', possessed his select band of devoted partisans. But the support for them was too personal to be effective when it was decided they had had a good run for their money and it was time to bring them in. There was no wide movement of protest in their favour; in any case most of their supporters were too humble to matter. (What could *Marat* Chaix do with his little band of rural *galochiers*, *savetiers*, and so on, when the word went out against him from the people in Nevers?) Unlike the Paris *sectionnaires*, who could mobilize a considerable army of solid mastercraftsmen and shopkeepers, the provincial ultra-revolutionists could count ultimately only on poor village artisans and on the lower ranks of urban wage-earners. Many of their supporters were not even *domiciliés*, being drawn from the itinerant trades, from the rural poor, and from those who lived in lodging-houses.

Most of these provincial militants were incapable of seeing beyond the limits of their own town or District. They were anxious to exercise power, but once they had conquered it at the municipal level, by placing their adherents in the *mairie*, in the *société*, and in the *comité* (almost always the higher authority of the District escaped them and it was generally from the District that their eventual undoing would come), they felt that they had achieved their main objectives; it was then only a matter of holding on and laying the foundations of the social republic within their own parish. Neither they nor their supporters were prepared to think in national terms. So when it came to a contest for power with the 'government men', they were at an enormous disadvantage; they were not even prepared to consider a conflict on such terms. They were not interested in what might happen or was happening in Paris or who exercised power there, so long as they themselves were not interfered with. This put them in an impossible situation; for they would in any case have the District against them, and the District would have access to the *députation*. Their only hope would have been for them also to have someone in Paris to whom they could appeal for support and succour: the Cordeliers, a deputy, a Sectionary committee, the *Commission des Subsistances*. But they were generally too ignorant of Parisian affairs and of the various hierarchies of revolutionary power in the capital and too wrapped up in parish-pump revolutionism to think of looking for outside support; at best they might attempt to call in one of the regional commissions of summary justice. It was only in the District de Gonesse, and in other areas on the periphery of the capital, that such local ultra-revolutionaries were able to enlist support from a deputy, from a Section, or from one of the Ministries. Here they had the advantage of access to the many rival centres of power. Most of the wild men were much further away from the centre of political life than that; their very distance from the capital had often been their opportunity. So they were removed without much difficulty by *Représentants en mission*, backed by armed force, and by *commissaires* bearing arrest warrants.

Indeed one can hardly speak of a conflict at all, at least in political terms, for the local militants never at any time thought of power in national spheres. Nor, for that matter, did the far more politically sophisticated Paris *sans-culottes*. These at least possessed the force and the institutions which could have made the conquest of power quite possible. Yet they only used their force to persuade the Convention, never to drive it out and replace it. Ultimately, they did not question the sovereignty of the Convention, even if they did challenge the legitimacy of the Revolutionary Government.

14. *HÉBERTISME*

So much for popular militancy in its most spontaneous and decentralized form. There existed, however, a more serious political challenge to the Revolutionary Government from a group of Paris politicians who, while claiming to represent the popular movement and while imitating most effectively the popular language, were seeking power for themselves. Here the conflict was even more one of persons than of principles, the principal objection of the so-called *hébertistes* to the Revolutionary Government being that they were not in it. They were 'outs' who sought to use the popular movement in order to become 'ins'; their programme did not amount to much more than the fulfilment of rather limited personal ambitions. It is not even certain whether they were out to seize power, if necessary by force, since the Revolutionary Government did not give them a chance to show what their intentions might have been; but they could probably have been bought off cheaply enough: Hébert with the Ministry of the Interior, Vincent with that of War, Ronsin with the *Marine*, a strange choice for a former sergeant-major. Or they might have even been contented with the *Contributions Directes* or the *Postes*. The government would not bargain on that basis and, as the *hébertistes* too were committed to war, the great provider for their numerous protégés, and yet publicly called for the end of a wartime emergency government, they became tied up in the fatal contradiction of all wartime oppositions and were easily disposed of, so far as the public were concerned, on a charge of treason. They had no alternative programme to propose, but only an alternative government. They did not even intend to end the revolutionary dictatorship, but merely to exercise it on their own account.

15. *SANS-CULOTTES* AND JACOBINS

The conflict between the Jacobin dictatorship and the popular movement, the parting of the ways between the *robespierristes* and the *sans-culottes*, was much more straightforward than has often been suggested. Programme played little part in this divorce, nor can any 'inevitability' of conflict be discovered in terms of class. The two sides represented forms of government (un-government might be a better term to describe the communalism of the popular militants) that could not co-exist for more than a few months. It took the central government some time to realize what was going on in the Departments—it was uninformed or misinformed—and a good deal longer to make its will felt and to put an end to the administrative anarchy that had resulted from the various experiments in popular government. No government can tolerate anarchy indefinitely, and that of the year II had both the will and the means of putting an end to it and of subjecting France to a single central impulsion.

The destruction of the popular movement was carried out long before Thermidor; the first steps were taken in September 1793, the chains of centralization were forged in December, the first purge of 'ultras' occurred in January 1794, and the destruction of the popular institutions and the arrest of the militants followed in March–April. By May, though the common people remained armed, they no longer had any weapon save arms, or any way of putting pressure on the Revolutionary Government, or of making their opinion felt, than by force. There was no longer such a thing as popular opinion to be reckoned with, and all that was left to the *sans-culotte* was either armed revolt or a sulky apathy.

In other words, one has seen the last of *la sans-culotterie*, of *le sans-culottisme*, if not of individual *sans-culottes*, and one is back with the crowd; and even that failed to materialize and come to the rescue of the Revolutionary Government on 9–10 Thermidor. Popular protest was henceforth reduced to its purely physical expression: the *journée*, the riot, the leaderless uprising. After the fall of Robespierre, some popular institutions revived briefly, soon to be decisively checked. The revolts of Germinal and Prairial were hopeless, unprepared, almost leaderless, and without any clear programme; on both occasions the rioters had the Convention and the Thermidorian Government in their power, but they could not make up their minds what to do next, and eventually marched back to their quarters. They had lost the habit of political discussion and they were without the militant minorities of the previous year. But although these had not taken part in the uprising, being mostly not the sort of people to come out into the street at any time, they were dealt with later by the Thermidorian Government which then set about systematically destroying them economically.

In short, anything sufficiently organized to merit the description 'the popular movement' was only of very short duration and politically effective for only a few months, in the whole five years of the revolutionary crisis: March–April 1793 to March–April 1794, with September, October, November, and December representing the height of unrestrained 'communalism' in certain Departments. 'Communalism' was for a time possible, because nothing was done to check it. It had, too, its regional strongholds, inaccessible to rapid centralization, far from Paris, and drawing on village or regional loyalties that had little to do with the Revolution. Ultra-revolutionism not only had a regionalist appeal; it appealed to certain types of persons. Just as 'municipalist' republics could in the last resort be no match for the Committee of Public Safety, so these *naïfs* were no match for the 'government men' who were thinking more in terms of France and Europe than of Crémieu and the rural poor. The temporary importance of the popular movement was an accident that was rapidly put right. The government bought off some of the best militants, 'bureaucratized' some of the most effective popular institutions—there was no doubt an agreeable irony in getting the militants to do the government's dirty work and in transforming former *tribuns* into policemen. Militancy was, in the long run, a luxury that an artisan or an innkeeper could ill afford; but, once the militant accepted a salary, he became a government official. A few temporary concessions were made to popular demands, most of them spectacular but harmless. The irreconcilables were arrested and a number destroyed in the spring of 1794. Their fate was enough to discourage their disciples.

The Revolutionary Government had decided to govern; as soon as it did that, there was an end to the 'popular movement'. It is true that the Jacobin dictatorship itself suffered in the process, becoming anaemic for lack of popular support and increasing isolation; but that is another matter. We are concerned here to explain why the popular movement collapsed in the spring of 1794, and why, despite various attempts to revive it and to give it a new purpose, it henceforth never achieved anything other than blind revolt that provided the pretext for ruthless and effective repression, not to explain why *robespierrisme* failed.

Albert Soboul is right to emphasize that, in the long run, the *sans-culotte* movement could not possibly succeed; but he puts too much stress on its inner conflicts in terms of class and social content, on the class barriers that divided it from Jacobinism. Many of these are *vues d'esprit* of a historian aware of the course taken by European movements of popular protest in the nineteenth century. In year II terms, it was a choice between anarchy on a truly magnificent scale and rigorous, ordered government. As the country was at war, there is nothing surprising about the fact that after a period of vacillation and governmental indecision, after a few rounds of rather inconsequential scuffling, during which neither side seems to have been very clear about its objectives (indeed the popular movement was at no time clear about these, except that it wanted to act as a sort of permanent, luxurious, irresponsible opposition at ground level), the government should have won.

Perhaps the word 'conflict' is itself misleading for a situation that was never clear-cut in terms of programme or even of power. The popular movement was never totally opposed to the Revolutionary Government. The *sectionnaires* were content to criticize certain aspects of it; but, in a number of important ways, they were prepared enthusiastically to second its efforts and to act, in fact, as an unofficial government agency. Both wanted to win the war and defeat counter-revolution at home, though they might differ as to how these objectives might best be achieved. The militants, for instance, thought that the war could never be won till the army, the navy, the Ministries, the Commissions, and the police had been completely purged of all their more professional elements, suspect because they had served the previous regime. They believed, like the Jacksonians, that a sound heart, patriotism, revolutionary conviction, and unpretentiousness could in all circumstances replace professional skill and that there was no job that *un bon patriote révolutionnaire* could not undertake with confidence. They thought, in fact, that patriotic amateurs could always do better than uncommitted professionals, and their ideal general was the goldsmith's apprentice, Jean Rossignol, or the *suisse* from Saint-Eustache, Sépher, even though each in his sector had made a fearful hash of his campaign. They encouraged the election of officers by the lower deck in the navy. They succeeded in obtaining the head of the *général-comte* Custine, because he was a Count and had been insolent to his Minister of War, and despite the fact that he was an able commander. And they made sure that the *commissaires de police* were elected by the Sections (with the result that this was probably the only time in French history when the police were popular).

Yet, while they called for the employment at every level of amateurs, they also wanted endlessly to extend the sphere of governmental interference and make it embrace every productive or commercial activity. Food commissioners and *réquisitionnaires*— amateurs too—should be let loose on the farmers, should tell them what they could and what they could not cultivate; and *apôtres civiques*, some of whom were, in a sense, professionals, for, as former priests, they had learnt to preach before the Revolution, should be sent into the countryside to eradicate religion as a necessary preliminary to winning the war. (What would be the point of winning if one were still left with 'superstition' and 'old druids'?) The Committees had other priorities. They believed in employing talent where it existed, and strongly opposed hard-and-fast rules that would have minimized the freedom of choice they considered to be the prerogative of any government. They had no intention of letting such high appointments be dictated to them by ignorant artisans and semi-literate shopkeepers. They did not think that the war could best be won by raising against the Republic the maximum number of enemies both at home and abroad, by outraging Catholic opinion in the countryside, and by alienating the few remaining neutral powers. And in the thirst for information which they shared with the previous regime, they preferred professionals— informers, members of the old police, innkeepers, procurers, prostitutes—to amateur zealots. They listened more closely to the reports of *agents nationaux*, who were government appointees, than to those of *sociétaires*, the self-appointed Arguses of revolutionary orthodoxy. They were even prepared to do a bit of spying, to plant informers in prisons, to encourage the long tongues of portresses and *concierges*, to accumulate secret *dossiers* that might come in useful one day, as a means of combating the enemy within, rather than rely on denunciations made in open assembly. (The *sans-culottes*, it is true, went in for a great deal of delation, but they wanted to hold a monopoly of the trade.) They were quite ready to muffle the revolutionary war trumpet for Swiss, Dutch, Danish, or American ears, and they did not believe that every foreign refugee was a patriot by nature and right of birth and the ideal counsellor on foreign affairs.

The quarrel was about means, not about fundamentals. The militants were revolutionary perfectionists, and the members of the Committees were 'possibilists'. Both were right according to their own lights. The real dilemma was that neither side could get along without the other. The government needed the help of the *sans-culottes* to carry out its policies of food procurement and, since there was no single monolithic party, the Committees had to rely on the *sociétés populaires* to publicize official news and diffuse government instructions. In the absence of a centrally operated, political, secret police (not even its embryo existed in the year II), the Committee of General Security had to entrust the actual running of Terror and repression, surveillance, vigilance, denunciation, the control of lodging-houses, and the checking of passports to local men: printers, shoemakers, tailors, tinkers, gunsmiths, innkeepers, and clerks—with local prejudices and local axes to grind. The Terror itself had thus to be delegated and run at several removes. (There is an endless multiplication of *délégations* in the Departments during the year II, with an almost limitless laying on of hands to produce such sieved end-products of popular sovereignty as a *délégué d'un délégué d'un délégué d'un Représentant du peuple*, to such an extent that the government had to intervene, in December 1793, to put an official limit to the *délégation des pouvoirs*.) This was not a matter of choice: there were not enough professionals to go round, especially in the Departments. In this respect, the government was much more prisoner of the *sans-culottes* than the latter, even when they became its salaried officials, were the prisoners of the Committee of General Security. The local men knew what was going on, and they told the Committees as much, or as little, as suited their own purposes. The Terror was administered on a national putting-out basis, and the local men generally had the last word.

The popular militants were patriotic before they were revolutionary. And they were quick to suspect sinister motives when the Committees sought to moderate their ardour. If the Committees condemned the collective denunciation of all foreigners, the local zealots at once smelt an attempt to make a deal with the Allies and to sell out their Revolution for a compromise peace. If the Committees condemned, on grounds of political expediency, root and branch dechristianization, local 'ultras' became convinced that a deal with the Pope was in the offing. The *sans-culottes* were patriots; they were super-patriots, their patriotism was of the jealous, suspicious, and exclusive kind; they were the only patriots; and they alone, by their constant vigilance and civic devotion, were frustrating Pitt's plans to set fire to Châteauroux, to burn down the mills of Corbeil, to destroy the crops of the Pays de Caux, to deliver up Narbonne to the King of Spain, to subvert the *société populaire* of Bonnet-la-Montagne (Saint-Bonnet-le-Château), and to destroy, by calumny, *les bons bougres révolutionnaires* of Crémieu.

Everywhere the finger in the hole in the dyke that held back the flood waters of counter-revolution was that of a local *sans-culotte*. Each member of the *comité* of a small town in the south-west was well aware that Pitt had sent his hired assassins across France to remove his arch-enemy in Moissac or Tonneins. All the talk about dying at one's desk, of springing into the breach, of holding the bridge pierced by a thousand lances, of drinking the hemlock, and a lot else besides, was not just talk. They really believed in dangers that could not but flatter their self-importance. This was a patriotism so farouche as to be difficult to work with. There was no lack of patriotic response, on the part of the common people of the towns, to government appeals for co-operation. The trouble arose because the *sans-culottes* wanted that co-operation to be on their own terms. At the local level—that of enforcement—the Committees had little protection against côteries, family feuds, regional antagonisms, and local bully-boys. It was always possible, of course, for a *Représentant*, or a delegate of one of the Committees, to remove authorities that had clearly become obnoxious and intolerable; but this might bring in another gang and release the flood-tide of vengeance. And purges carried out at too frequent intervals would make administration impossible and might produce an administrative strike. Public office under the Terror could be dangerous and it was always compromising. Indeed, it is surprising how readily people accepted it, and how eagerly they clung to it once they had obtained it. There were compensations. Some of them were material and *patriotes* used the Terror to have a very good time: such an opportunity was unlikely ever to recur again in a single lifetime. But most of the compensations were in terms of pride and conceit; for the sort of people the Revolutionary Government had to work with, humour, encourage, and praise, were mostly not people who had ever previously been in a position of power. In short, there had to be some sort of pact between the government and the minorities of local militants, if the government was to be at all effective outside Paris. In this respect the Committees had to reckon, if not with the 'popular movement', at least with militant élites.

The government had, of course, advantages too, in its relations with these local minorities. It had prestige: the voice of Barère was heard afar, the name 'Robespierre' might produce the hush of respect—or of dotty fervour—in small towns in the Gers or the Tarn. It inspired awe: the roving *Représentant* arrived in a clatter of majesty, with the dust of an escort and to the sound of trumpets, that left the villager gaping and made the urban tailor anxious to be seen at the table of the great man. The *satrape* kept people waiting and ate his meals in public, while reports and petitions were read to him. He agreed condescendingly to spare a few precious moments to visit the local *société* and give them the Good Word and the honour of setting eyes on a portion of national sovereignty. The government had a monopoly of official news and could always count on the twin pillars of popular credulity and popular orthodoxy. Local *patriotes* believed what they were told about events in Paris; a former Friend of the People was an Agent of Pitt, if the *Représentant* or the *Bulletin* said so.

This readiness to accept the official version was also an indication of a considerable degree of local indifference about what was happening in the capital. Up to the spring of 1794, it is true, there were other sources of information—including half a dozen *Pères Duchesne* in various provincial towns. The news they gave was Cordelier-orientated, while Cordelier groups managed to obtain a hold over *sociétés* in garrison towns, thanks to the presence of *commissaires du Pouvoir Exécutif*; but only for a time. Once the *Représentant* had spoken, orthodoxy was re-established. But the *Représentants* themselves spoke with many voices, and quarrels among rival teams of *proconsuls*, sent to the same areas, often gave local minorities the opportunity to stay in power or to topple their rivals. The *Représentants* had prestige, but they differed violently about appointments to local offices, so that the system of sending them up into the Departments, far from increasing centralization and putting a premium on orthodoxy, often exacerbated local quarrels and multiplied local clienteles.

Orthodoxy then might speak with many different voices. The inhabitants of the District de Gonesse, visited by three rival groups in rapid succession, and sometimes together, learnt to distinguish between them and soon found out which group would favour which interest. It was in this manner that the political rivalries of the capital reached down into *bourg* and village. Ultimately, people were not enormously interested in what happened in Paris. Their chief concern was how to put distant events in the capital to local use: to renew a *comité*, to score off a political rival. So everyone would discover his or her own *hébertiste* or *dantoniste* at the right moment.

Finally, the government had money, the power of appointment and dismissal, of arrest, disgrace, imprisonment, and execution. A number of local 'ultras' were guillotined, in the summer of 1794, because they had been too impudent, too enthusiastic, too independent, too drunken, and too lecherous. Others were killed because they had had the wrong protectors; this is why there was a certain mortality among the agents of the *Pouvoir Exécutif*. Several people were arrested at this time because they had been seen talking to one of the roving *commissaires* who had turned out to be a *complice d'Hébert*. Thus many paid heavily for their pride in high company, or for the manner in which they had originally been appointed.

Nevertheless, in the conditions of the year II, the government was dependent to a considerable extent on the goodwill of *sans-culotte* minorities, on the patriotism and enthusiasm of the urban *petit peuple*. It could do without both and still govern, rather more effectively, since it no longer had popular opinion to consider, in a bureaucratic vacuum, with a stream of orders pouring down and a stream of echoes pouring up. This was what happened to the government in the summer of 1794. It gave a great impression of monolithic orthodoxy and of almost religious unanimity. In fact, both barely covered apathy and indifference, the deadliest of diseases for an embattled revolutionary regime—what Albert Soboul describes as 'l'usure morale du petit peuple'—disillusionment and boredom. Having destroyed their institutions, prohibited the free expression of popular opinion on such key issues as rationing and provisioning, religion and *épuration*, the government then turned to the emasculated militant and appealed to him: 'do not go away, we still need you', 'do not ease up', 'do not absent yourself from the club, the fight is still on'. It might well be, but the heart of the *sans-culotte* was no longer in it, he did not feel needed. People did not care any more; they had had enough of militancy and, if the government no longer had any use for the 'popular movement', the militants of the 'popular movement' felt it was time to return to private life, to the shop, to the family, and to billiards.

The government itself set about destroying the most effective popular institutions (*sociétés sectionnaires*, etc.), though these had served the dictatorship well. The others collapsed under the weight of indifference, from want of attendance, during the summer of 1794, the Summer of Disenchantment. The 'popular movement', having served its purpose, was dismissed. But it did not do the government any good. Administration had never been so efficient, but, as Saint-Just lamented, *la République s'est glacée*. However difficult the relations between the Jacobin dictatorship and the militants had been, the experience of Ventôse–Thermidor year II proved that the two were inter-dependent. The power struggle had at last been solved, at the expense of the popular militants. The amateurs had been replaced by the professionals—or at least by ex-amateurs who had been bought into bureaucracy as a result of full-time employment. Robespierre and his friends disappeared, leaving an endless trail of historical bubbles to mark the spot and to plague us ever since. They were soon followed by the whole paraphernalia of Revolutionary Government, which collapsed in bits, from the top downwards.

The people for a time rejoiced, so completely divorced had they become from a government with which they no longer felt personally associated and the rigour of which, victory having come, they could no longer justify. Why should there have been more Terror, more repression, more government, and more bureaucrats once the emergency was past and the danger over? The *sans-culotte* militants had been terrorists; and at one time they had actually been demanding more Terror, more repression, as a solution to every problem, and they had suspected the Revolutionary Government of moderation, of wishing to protect the rich and the greedy, when their demands had not been met. But, after Floréal, even the *sans-culottes* lost their faith in Terror and were converted away from repression—both of which they had envisaged only as a form of popular justice and as an exercise of popular vengeance. For one thing, both weapons were now being used against their own kind. But, above all, they could not see the purpose of a Terror that had become anonymous, bureaucratic, secretive, that no longer attempted to explain and to persuade—and a great deal of the people's Terror had been verbal exaggeration, blustering, bluff, and blood-and-thunder talk—and that struck out, with apparent blindness, at all sorts and conditions.

The degree to which the *sans-culottes* had become alienated from the government can best be gauged by the fact that, like the future Thermidorians, like Babeuf, they rejoiced at the end of fear, at the cessation of the *système de la dépopulation*, and pursued, in the wake of the Thermidorian hack writers, Maximilien Robespierre into an imaginary hell, there to torment him with his authoritarian tendencies. For had he not aimed at dictatorship, using the broad back of the common people as steps to the throne? The *sans-culottes*, like the *honnêtes gens*, were prepared to believe this, at least in the early weeks of the new regime. (When they later changed their minds, their judgement had become impaired by historical hindsight and nostalgia, and Robespierre and the much-evoked 'popular movement' had entered the realm of myth.)

The committees of government disappeared. Most *Représentants* were recalled. The *sans-culottes* were driven out of the *comités de surveillance*, one of the few places in which they had been allowed to remain, as servants of a government Terror, after Floréal. They were replaced by men of wealth, when the *comités* were not suppressed altogether. (They were maintained only in largish towns, a sure indication that what was left of the Terror was to be directed against the urban *petit peuple*, and that the country population could breathe again, sure of total impunity.) But many of the *agents nationaux* remained, and what survived of the Jacobin dictatorship was what had caused it to dry up and had isolated it: an invasive, self-interested, self-perpetuating bureaucracy, concerned only to continue.

If the Thermidorian regime eventually became almost as centralized as its predecessor, it was under pressure from a bureaucracy that it was unable to remove. But the Thermidorians were under pressure from many other lobbies as well. Far from acting with efficiency in a political vacuum once most potential sources of opposition had been removed or silenced, they had to satisfy a motley collection of contending interests—none of them popular: *députations*, now all-powerful both in Paris and in their fiefs; a reinstated judiciary, impatient to punish those impudent *sans-culottes* who had presumed to take the administration of justice out of the hands of the professionals (judges, magistrates, and *juges-de-paix* were the most ardent exponents of the anti-popular Terror of the year III, and without their help, encouragement, and complicity the White terrorists would have been unable to administer their own rougher, parallel Terror); a gilded youth of *embusqués*, anxious to revenge themselves for the frequent jeers and occasional blows that they had received from *sans-culottes*, by attacking anyone who was not dressed like themselves, and in revolt against the austerity of the previous regime; speculators and contractors who dictated to the government; the amoral, the licentious, and the pleasure-loving; officers avid for promotion and fame (any battlefield would do, especially the streets of Paris, where laurels could be won against hastily-erected barricades and where the *repos du guerrier*—the victor over the poor and the hungry—could be assured the same night); ladies of the new court, with their *salons* and their young protégés to promote. The Thermidorian Government was indeed so much a regime of lobbies that it was often difficult to distinguish the regime from its solicitants and to see where lobbies ended and government began. What was worst in the Jacobin dictatorship remained, soon to be joined by many elements worse still. The one thing that was effectively silenced was vox populi.

18. CONCLUSION

The expression 'popular movement' is a thesis in itself. When used by historians and examiners (and it is a great favourite with both) it implies a considerable degree of organization, leadership, the existence of a minimum agreed programme, and above all the realization by those who take part in it that they are taking part in it, and their awareness of a collective identity, both in relation to their 'brothers', and against certain other groups in society and politics. For the period of a little over twenty years that has been the object of this study, a 'popular movement' might be allowed some claim to existence for at most a single year (from April 1793 to April 1794). It might also be argued that the White Terror in the south-east, which enjoyed very wide popular support and employed *sabreurs* of popular origin, might be likewise described as a primitive 'popular movement'; the argument against this would be that the White Terror was not autonomous and that it was being used and manipulated by others, from outside, for political aims that had nothing to do with the popular cause. The other forms of popular protest are either too individualistic (suicide, murder, the cult of the dead, vengeance) or too transient (market riots, *bandes* of vagrants) to qualify as a 'movement', though desertion on a sufficiently large scale might so qualify, in a very negative sense. *Babouvisme* was a 'movement', no doubt, but with the people left out, and only a hypothetical following, in the form of a list of a few thousand names, left obligingly for the information of the police. There was nothing 'popular' about it, though Babeuf and his fellow *clubistes* were graciously prepared to use the people as cannon fodder in order to win, in a bloody coup, a revolutionary dictatorship which would have kept the People informed of what was best for it.

So we have used 'popular movement' with extreme caution and with reference only to *le mouvement sans-culotte*, or rather *les mouvements sans-culotte*; for each town, each *commune*, was to produce its own brand of *sans-culottisme*. It is doubtful, too, whether the *sans-culottes* ever had a clear idea of themselves as an entity, save

to distinguish themselves from those whom they disliked: bourgeois, farmers, wholesalers, entrepreneurs, *hommes de loi* and *hommes
d'esprit*, painters, and artists. (Common dislikes, it is true, are an
effective binding force, as long as the common hate-figures are
much in evidence.) And it is only in the year III, with the memory
of lost militancy, and in an effort to revive flagging hopes and rouse
failing spirits, that we hear the slogan *Vive les sans-culottes*, although already it was shouted along with *Vive la Montagne, Vive
les jacobins*. As the *sans-culottes* were so uncertain what they were,
what their 'movement' was, whether they were in it or not, it is
not surprising that historians should have some hesitation in
allowing them a distinctive identity and in asserting the exact
nature of their movement.

By concentrating first on popular militancy in decline, we have
attempted at the outset to illustrate the generally disorganized,
transient, and ultimately hopeless character of protest in a period
during which Authority could, with each succeeding year, meet
force with yet more force, uncontrolled violence with swift, effective, and, at the same time, discreet, unobtrusive violence, and
when the repressive powers of government were constantly improving. During the twenty years between 1795 and 1815, such
purely negative factors as disease, hardship, old age, exile, apathy,
hopelessness, are even more important perhaps than the positive
achievements of repression. It is the combination of the two that
makes the position of the common people so desperate.

Our second purpose in thus putting last first is to explore, from
the vantage point of 1795 (and beyond), the built-in weaknesses of
the so-called *sans-culotte* movement even in its prime, during the
year II. It is impossible to appreciate the true nature of the Terror
of 1793–4 without taking into account the Counter-Terror of the
year III (and, unlike 'movement', Counter-Terror is not a word
invented by historians and then foisted on their helpless forebears,
but an expression used most aptly to describe at the time something
that was exactly that) which was a sort of collective reprisal for the
excesses, threats, brutalities, humiliations, and enthusiasms of the
previous year. In the same way, one would obtain quite a false
impression of the energy and autonomy of *le mouvement sans-
culotte*, examined in isolation in the year II context, if one did not
move on to discover how rapidly and completely that movement
collapsed in the very different circumstances of the year III. It is

a matter of placing the two years back to back, in order to bring out both the basic contrasts, the prevailing consideration of vengeance (and vengeance is necessarily backward-looking; the ferocity of vengeance in the years III and IV is due to the fact that it did not have to look back very far), and also the comparative continuity of government policy (for the Jacobins finished off the 'popular movement'; the Thermidorians merely had to mop up individual militants, crush spontaneous protest, and disarm the people, and were in a much stronger position to do this than their predecessors). The year III is not just an epilogue to the year II, not just the year One After Robespierre (though some historians would suggest that this was its most important feature). It should be seen rather as the explanation of the year II.

The year 1795, from every point of view, is the decisive year of the whole revolutionary period, for it was basically the Thermidorian Settlement that survived into the *Restauration*. The one problem that the Thermidorians did not solve was that of government, but this was because they were themselves deeply divided. They did succeed in rendering the common people politically ineffective for the next thirty-five years, even if they left to the Directory a country in a state of advanced anarchy, profitable only to the royalist, the White Terrorist, and the bandit. Their successors merely had to clear up the pieces, using the printed lists drawn up by the Thermidorians, and every year, from 1796 at least to 1810, made the government stronger and the people weaker. The most formidable shackles and leg-irons to be applied to individual men of the people, the most ferocious legislation affecting the gathering together of more than two persons, were manufactured in the early years of that oppressive regime, between 1805 and 1808. In 1812 there was a timid renewal of popular protest, at once repressed with extreme ferocity. It is doubtful if the common people had much to do with the collapse of the Empire and the dispersal of the gangster dynasty.

One should not make too much of the contrast between the year II and the year III. Even if it sounds foolish, it is as well to remember that the year III came after the year II, and that the Thermidorians inherited from the Revolutionary Government most of the pre-conditions of the famine crisis of 1795–6, as well as a redoubtable legacy of hatred, envy, and the thirst for vengeance. To recall this is not to lessen the responsibilities of the Thermidorian governing class, nor to blacken their predecessors. It is only after six months or so of Thermidorian rule that the common people reacquired at least a negative self-awareness, out of hatred for the new ruling class, and began to idealize in contrast a dead Robespierre and Jacobin rule. The fact that they then began to look back on the year II as a lost Golden Age did not make the year II into a real Golden Age; the *sans-culotte* of the year II was a better judge of Robespierre than the same man a year later. It was just that in 1795 things were so much worse, so that, in retrospect, even former *sans-culottes* might begin to make the mistake of identifying the Jacobin dictatorship with a people's government. Things being worse still in the year IV, this tendency to myth-make about 1793–4 increased still more.

From whatever angle one wishes to approach French popular history during this period, 1795 is the ideal vantage point for looking back. There had been no disaster on this scale for eighty-five years, that is within living memory; and, as far as the common people were concerned, there would never be anything like it later. June 1848 and May 1871 were man-made blood-baths, and they affected only the urban working class; 1795 was both man-made and a disaster of nature. Apart from this, the Thermidorians, as we have seen, are the first, the most systematic, and the best informed, if not the most unprejudiced, historians of the previous 'popular movement', not only in Paris, but in every town and *bourg* in France. We should mistrust their evidence, but we certainly cannot do without it. It is also a much less 'orthodox' period than that of the Revolutionary Dictatorship. In the summer of 1794 we are so deafened by *les cris unanimes* (or rather by *le cri unanime*, for only one voice was needed) that we cannot hear any individual voice at all, at any level. Throughout the Thermidorian period, on the contrary, there is a veritable hubbub of confused shouting, vituperation, denunciation, and screams for vengeance, self-justification, and abuse. Nothing could be less *unanime* than Thermidorian France and, whatever faults may be attributed to the regime, it cannot be accused of having prevented the statement of unorthodox opinions. (It did not, in any case, have the force or the will to do so.) The neo-terrorists, furious at the turn of events, enraged by deprivation of office, stung by persecution, hit back in kind. They are not afraid to wake up towns with shouts of 'Vive la Terreur, vive les sans-culottes, la guillotine en permanence', and so on. At least up to

Prairial they are almost suicidal in their outspokenness,[1] and with the amnesty of Brumaire year IV to encourage them their militants rush once more into print and into speech. Nor, as we have seen, did the *sabreur* go about his work quietly; he talked before, during, and after a killing. And if witnesses speak of the 'silence of the grave' with reference to the Faubourg, it was a silence that only lasted a few weeks, under the stunned impact of defeat and disarmament, at the time when Denelle, feeling that there was nothing more to be done or said, took up his tools and killed his family. We have to wait for the year IV to see vox populi reduced to a pitiful whining for bread or for a place in a *hospice*. La Montagne, despite its name, does not command anything like the view offered from the level of the Thermidorian Plain.

If one thus makes a stand on the year III, and attempts, like the police, to see individuals *dans la durée*, rather than merely in the dramatic, hieratical attitudes of Soboul's *Ballet de l'An II*, then the perspectives become radically different from those offered by a day-to-day account of the courtship, honeymoon, rows, and divorce of naïve Popular Movement and cunning, calculating Revolutionary Government. And the former, instead of being a person in her own right, is revealed as an accident of a chance encounter, a hasty, shameful, furtive affair, *entre deux rames de métro*, that was never meant to happen. In this perspective the questions usually put by historians both of French and of comparative popular movements seem largely irrelevant or, at least, clumsy and slightly off the target: 'Why did the Revolutionary Government turn on the Popular Movement?'; 'Why did the Popular Movement decline in France at the very moment it was gathering force in England?'; 'What did the Popular Movement owe to *rousseauisme*?' (a poor question, as it can be answered in one word); 'What was the influence of Babeuf on the survival of the Popular Movement?' (same comment); and so on. The real question—and it is one that puzzled, astonished, and shocked the Thermidorians —to be asked would be: 'How did a popular movement ever come

---

[1] Jean Lafond, *vigneron*, is reported to have stated, in a café in Montbrison, on the eve of the Feast of Saint-John (16 Floréal year III), 'que c'étoit une horreur de voir les massacres qui se commettoient journellement dans Montbrison, mais que cela ne dureroit pas, et qu'on risquoit fort de voir une seconde fois la Montagne, que le nommé Tillon père, de Saint-Galmier . . . lui dit *tu es un scélérat de parler de la sorte et tu en mériterois autant que ceux qu'on a assommés . . .*' (A.N. BB 18 690, déposition de Jean Lafond, 10 nivôse an VI).

into being in the first place?' and not so much why it failed, but by what miracle it ever succeeded at all, however partially and however briefly. There is no doubt about the causes of its decline; but any assessment of the *sans-culotte* movement even at its height, in the autumn and winter of 1793, must bring out its accidental character, its fragility, its incoherence, and its endless fractionalization. How could the *sans-culotte*, himself a freak of nature, more a state of mind than a social, political, or economic entity, with his parish-pump outlook, ever have been the slightest threat to government? Certainly, he never thought of competing with it, much less of taking it over. (This was the fatal miscalculation of the *hébertistes*.)

The expression *le mouvement sans-culotte* is itself misleading, in another way, when applied to a series of attitudes that have in common only extreme individualism, regionalism, and a strong dose of anarchy. Before the Revolutionary Government took over, the Republic was in the process of disappearing in a welter of popular 'communalism'. And, just as *le mouvement sans-culotte* is a historical abstraction, the conflict between it and the Revolutionary Government has been greatly over-stated and over-simplified, whether in terms of class, of political methods, or of programme. The *sans-culotte* himself, an individualist, aware only of sharing a certain number of basic attitudes with people of his own kind and Quarter, did not know that he was engaged in such a conflict; hence his genuine surprise and indignation when, early in 1794 or later in the spring of that year, he found himself subjected to official persecution as an ultra-revolutionary and as an embarrassing enthusiast whose initiatives on many fronts at once had, by comparison, made the government appear unenthusiastic, moderate, and timid. He was only trying to be helpful.

This may seem to reduce the *sans-culotte* movement to such derisory proportions that, like the *peau de chagrin*, it eventually disappears altogether. But the argument is not that there was no such movement; rather that the movement was not nearly so coherent and single-minded as has often been suggested, and that there were movements very varied both in composition and in aims, rather than a single movement. In Lyon, for instance, the movement, almost by accident—and accident is our dominant theme throughout this section—became identified with 'federalism'; or, rather, the Parisian authorities, both *sans-culotte* and

Jacobin (it would take Lyon to make them agree), said that it had. But the Lyonnais did not think of themselves as 'federalists', 'royalists', 'counter-revolutionaries', and so on. In their own view, they represented the very essence of *sans-culottisme*. For they were defending Sectionary autonomy against the incursion of an arrogant and dominating Jacobin municipality, and were upholding the position of their own city as Capital of the South, a position that was being challenged, as usual, from Paris. It was equally natural for the inhabitants of Vienne-la-Patriote to feel that they were acting as true *sans-culottes* when, in response to the traditional anti-Lyon sentiments of the inhabitants of the former metropolitan see, they resisted the Lyon 'federalists', and co-operated with the armies. In Marseille the *sans-culottes* could not make head or tail of the situation but, so long as their Sections assured them that the best way of defending the Republic was to follow the example of the 'federalist' municipality and central committee, they did what the Sectionary leaders told them; for the Section could never be wrong, being the quintessence of *sans-culottisme*.

Sans-culotte was a new word, but it covered a clutter of ancient attitudes, traditional loyalties, and prejudices. What was new was the word itself, the institutions with which it was associated (and the institutions existed before the word), and, above all, the opportunity of the spring and summer of 1793. And the *sans-culottes* are uniquely important, in the history of the French Revolution, because they at once seized this opportunity and carried out, at least at municipal level, and intermittently in certain areas of the countryside, the first experiment in people's government. It was an experience so extraordinary, so unique, that it was never forgotten, either by the *sans-culottes*, who had enjoyed every minute of it, or by those who were briefly subjected to popular rule. In immediate terms, *sans-culotte* co-operation made Terror and Repression more or less effective, in proportion to the relative zeal or lack of zeal of the local militants, and ensured the success of the more important economic controls; but it was even more important as an example to the future.

It was not, however, an experiment carried out in a vacuum. There were few occasions and few places, even at the level of the commune, where *sans-culotte* militants could enjoy undisputed power. There was nearly always somebody else to be reckoned with: a municipality, an *agent national*, a District, a roving *pro-*

consul, a government spy, the Committee of General Security, which had eyes in so many places and a much clearer view of what was happening in the Departments than the more august Committee of Public Safety. The *sans-culottes* could not exist politically on their own; had they been given an opportunity to do so, France would have fallen apart. They were partners on a tandem; they did much of the footwork, but they did not steer and could not see where they were going. So one is obliged to describe once more the relations between *sans-culottes* and Jacobins, and to run through the rather sad history of the divorce between the 'popular movement' and the Revolutionary Government.

Our purpose has been to reassess the *sans-culotte* movement and to render it in its contemporary proportions. One way of doing this has been to emphasize the role of militant minorities. It was not a *mouvement de masse*, the masses did not respond, they were not even invited. It was much more a matter of clans and coteries—in some towns in the Landes it was little more than a family concern. The *sans-culottes*, who liked to keep their club small, *entre gens de connaissance*, did not attempt to bring in the population of the *garnis*, or the general mass of wage-earners—this possibly is one reason why wages figure so little in *sans-culotte* demands—for whom their programme would have little appeal.

At the same time, they would have been clueless and incoherent without their militants, their *dominateurs* (for they 'dominated' the *sans-culottes* as well as the bourgeois). Perhaps some of these may have emerged here in colours too black. We have not attempted to idealize them, and it is difficult to escape the impression that they were generally intolerable and occasionally brutal and cruel. But they were also enthusiastic, moderately disinterested, and undoubtedly patriotic. As we have compared Terror and Counter-Terror, the popular movement and the Revolutionary Government, so we should compare their servitors; and the *sans-culottes* were certainly preferable to the steely bureaucrats of *robespierriste* unanimity, or to the vindictive judges and heartless bourgeois of the Thermidorian regime. They were individualists sometimes to the point of eccentricity and anarchy; this was to be their undoing. They did not stand a chance in any case, and may even have been dimly aware of this; for, in their bluster, their precipitation, and their noise, there is a hint of desperation, as though they were engaged in a race against time. Equally they may have been blind to the dangers threatening them from the very first moment of militancy, for they were so self-satisfied, so convinced of their own indispensability for 'la marche en avant de la Révolution', that they could hardly believe that the Republic could be 'saved' without their vigilance and devotion. Even at the height of the Thermidorian Reaction they were looking forward to a return to power and revolutionizing—or talked as if they were; this may merely have been to keep up morale, or their talk may have been inflated by Thermidorian eavesdroppers to frighten middle-class opinion with the bogy of 'le retour au règne de la Terreur'.

They were probably not very intelligent, at least in their political methods. For they attempted to maintain their hold on an assembly or a *commune* more by bludgeoning opinion than by persuading it, though a great many people would not be open to their persuasion. They were deliberately rude and unnecessarily vulgar, as though they had taken a leaf out of the *Père Duchesne*—being polite was unrevolutionary—and they probably made many more enemies, both for themselves and for the *sans-culotte* Republic, than they need have done. But they were administering a medicine unpleasant to most, and it was difficult to be an effective terrorist and, at the same time, to be loved by many, for, in one form or another, the Terror was likely to indispose most people. It was both brave and disinterested of them to have taken on such a job in the first place, since it brought few profits, save in terms of pride, and many dangers. They were remarkably patient with those less educated than themselves, spending much time and energy explaining the meaning of words and commenting on events. (This concern was, of course, also another means of racing against *la force des choses* and of prolonging their own power.) Most, too, were quick to spot the revolutionary fraud, the demagogue, and to censure selfishness and personal misconduct. For people with no previous experience of administration and of authority of any kind they did not do so badly. The minutes of popular assemblies and committees, if erratic in spelling, are reasonably well kept and clear. They were both efficient and effective (which the Thermidorians found hard to forgive). Whatever their virtues or failings, the system of the Terror, as well as the so-called 'popular movement', had to go along with them.

Hence the importance of individual behaviour, of temperament; hence, too, the prime necessity of approaching the year II in terms of the *histoire des mentalités*. It is an approach that, unlike the statistical analysis of collectivities: crowds, assemblies, armies—which has its own rather frozen and, for a 'movement' dominated by minorities, largely irrelevant, rewards—must leave many vital questions unanswered. We did not meet these people after all, have either their own word for themselves, or that of their enemies, and we must place a considerable premium on imagination, selection, and surmise. Any attempt to reconstruct *l'homme révolutionnaire*, rediscover *la mentalité sans-culotte*, must in fact owe as much to the historian as to the evidence derived from his documentation. He is engaged on a work of invention, and it is up to him to persuade the reader that his selection has been representative, and not influenced by presupposition. Certainly it would be impossible to reconstruct a complete robot-revolutionary, a prototype of the local terrorist, to witness for the whole kind. All the historian can do is to indicate, from a wide selection of case histories and from long habit of these people, certain common traits, and at the same time constantly to reiterate the endless variety of the species. Just as the Terror in, let us say, the Seine-Inférieure, bore no resemblance to the Terror in the Gard, the Bouches-du-Rhône, or in the Département de Vaucluse, so the terrorist might in one place be a mild *attentiste*, anxious primarily to keep in with everybody, making a display of zeal for the benefit of his superiors and at the same time taking the sting out of terrorist legislation in order to spare his *administrés* hardship and persecution, and, in another, might be a man of blood, the personification of the Thermidorian *buveur de sang*, enjoying bloodshed and violence and the fear in which he was held, cultivating the image of his own ferocity. (Much would depend on the latitude.) No account of the Terror would be complete without the presence of a few people of this last kind; for, if most ultra-revolutionaries were wild merely in word and in gesture, some *dominateurs* appear to have used the Terror to murder or to have murdered their enemies and rape their daughters. Such people were more numerous on the other side, among the White terrorists, but the White Terror came after that of the year II, and some at least of the *sabreurs* had victims to avenge.[1] Whether these had been killed *révolutionnairement*, that is to say by judgement of some commission of summary justice, or had been simply murdered in the street or hanged from a tree,

[1] See note 3C, p. 359.

would not make much difference to their relatives or friends. The important fact was that they had been killed with violence. To many Moulinois in upper circles, the revolutionary authorities of that town who had sent thirty-two *notables* before the *Commission des Sept* in Lyon, which had condemned them all to death, were not revolutionary *patriotes*, but murderers; and so it seemed permissible to murder them (there were several attempts to do so) if the opportunity arose.

Any discussion on this period of the Revolution will begin and end with violence. Some may find excuses for the terrorists of the year II because they put violence to the service of a beleaguered Republic and of a state of emergency; and this is how the terrorists themselves were to argue when under attack, adding rather oddly that they had not been influenced by personal considerations and that they bore their victims no ill will. But, in the south at least, where there was a long tradition of vendettas, violence in the service of family vengeance would appear equally legitimate and unavoidable. And if one were to kill to preserve *la République une et indivisible*, why not kill for *Christ et Roi* (even if the former would not have approved and the latter, who was a child, dead or dying, had not been consulted)? 'Il faut du sang à la Révolution' was the one point of agreement between terrorist and *sabreur*. Many *sansculottes* believed that blood would even solve the problem of dearth, while, in the year III, the urban *petit peuple*, faced with famine, were to argue: 'du tems de la Terreur, quand fonctionnoit la guillotine, le pain étoit en abondance; maintenant qu'il n'y a point de guillotine, le pain manque, pour avoir du pain, il faut la guillotine en permanence, pour ne pas mourir de faim, il faut du sang.' And they were right, in the sense that the *maximum* without the guillotine behind it would have been a flop. The southern royalists used blood to assert their authority, and to demonstrate the powerlessness of a Republic unable to protect even its own officials and wealthy property-owners. At both ends of the political spectrum, particularly at popular level, there was a wide consensus of opinion that the Revolution could survive only on blood, that the comte d'Antraigue's 'Kingdom of the South' could be constructed only on blood. (His own stated ambition was that 'he would like to be the Marat of the Counter-Revolution'.) The historian does not have to decide between the two programmes; the best he can do is to put in the dock the men of blood from both sides and let them argue it out in their own abrupt way. What he cannot do is to leave blood out when dealing with popular movements and popular protest.

It will be objected that our account does omit something called 'Popular Thought' and that we have not made obeisance to Rousseau and to *rousseauisme*, to the Man and the Message. We have discovered attitudes, prejudices, hopes, mentalities, violence, credulity, and orthodoxy, but of 'Popular Thought' not a trace. An attachment to 'municipalism', the much-repeated statement that 'les sociétés populaires sont souveraines', demands for an upper limit on property, on income, do indicate a basic political programme; the passionate insistence on equality in everything, including such visible things as food and clothing, does reflect moral attitudes, but it is hard to see what they owe to a system of thought. Rousseau, it is true, is frequently and reverently evoked, along with Robespierre, Marat, Brutus, William Tell, and Algernon Sydney, in the proceedings of popular assemblies; but this is merely a formal statement of orthodoxy, a *sans-culotte* 'For what we are about to receive', to be got through before proceeding to serious business (food problems, the defence of local interests, denunciations, *scrutins épuratoires*). The *sans-culottes* were rough-and-ready people, engaged in a struggle to gain control of local administration, they possessed neither a national nor a world vision, and they were not political theorists. They voted with a show of hands or *par acclamation* not in homage to some abstract concept of unanimity, but in order to cow possible opponents. Rousseau is as irrelevant to an understanding of the *sans-culotte* movement as Babeuf.

What, it may be further objected, do murder, suicide, disease, mortality, desertion, the White Terror, prostitution, vagrancy, *chauffage*, pauperization, epidemics, have to do with the development or the decline of popular movements and popular protest? Are we not merely stringing together themes that are related only because we put them on end, one after the other? Will not the historian always find what he is looking for? In order to illustrate the dramatic, apocalyptic character of the crisis of the year III and the year IV, it is of course easy to levy an army of suicides, count up the murders, collect the corpses, and produce scattered reports of epidemics, up and down the country. But do not these phenomena always exist? Were there no suicides in the year II? Did not people die in the year I? Were there no murders during the Revolutionary Dictatorship? Are there not always deserters in time of war? Were there no serious epidemics between 1789 and the summer of 1794? The answer is: of course they do, of course there were, of course they did. It is a matter of scale, of extent, as well as of content and repetition.

For Paris, we have used the papers of the *commissaires de police* for 1793 and the year II; we were looking, it is true, for the Paris Revolutionary Army, and not for *suicidés*, assassins, and fallen girls; but we noted these too, *en passant*. Suicides were rare, and they were not women of the people, but generally elderly *ci-devants*, abandoned by their children, who had emigrated. Suicide, in the year II, witnesses to quite a different form of distress from that of the years III and IV. Murders, private murders, were rare during the Jacobin dictatorship, at least in the towns of the north. (They were no doubt numerous in the south.) Prostitution, relentlessly harried by zealous *sans-culottes*, was on the decline. The poor are always with us, but in the year IV they are poorer than ever, and there are many 'new poor' as well; whereas in the year II many of the latter had managed to keep their heads above water and to maintain their families in bread and themselves in employment, even if it were only as *gardes-scellés*. Desertion became a national problem in the year III, and it was closely connected with White terrorism, which recruited extensively among *réquisitionnaires*, and, right up to the year IX, it represented a conscious political protest, a vote of no confidence in the republican regime. Mortality rates began to rise in the last two months of the Jacobin dictatorship, as a sort of mute accompaniment to Robespierre's fearful *journées* of Prairial and Messidor, as though disease was attempting to keep up with the quickening pace of Terror. But, in the year III and the year IV, they were double or treble the average in towns like Dieppe, le Havre, and Rouen.

Who died? Primarily, the women and the small children of the urban *petit peuple*, of the *faubouriens*, and of village artisans, weavers, and shipwrights. Many urban artisans and elderly *indigents* also died; the rich did not die. And, unlike the cholera of 1832, the epidemics of the years III and IV (and those of 1812) were respecters of class. No leading Thermidorian died; indeed, Benjamin Constant and Madame de Staël returned eagerly to Paris, to see the fuming remains of Revolution, once it was all over and the danger was past, and to throw themselves avidly into the social round, in the middle of a famine of which they were no doubt unaware.

There were epidemics at the end of every summer, year in year out, but in comparative terms the revolutionary years had been healthy ones. The Revolution opened in 1789 and closed in the summer of the year II and the two following summers with waves of epidemics on a scale that was at once noted by the health authorities and that necessitated the sending of army doctors to the stricken areas. The second wave, from 1794 to 1796, the health authorities attribute to malnutrition, despair, and moral fatigue. There is no doubt in their mind about the connection between this sudden offensive of diseases of the poor and the contemporary political situation. They may, of course, have been wrong; but even if they were, these epidemics killed off a number of former *sans-culottes*, and increased the economic ruin of a great many more, as a result of long periods of unemployment and absence from work.

Prostitution, too, vastly increased in the year III,[1] not so much because vice had come back to its own, with Madame Tallien on her sofa and Madame Récamier in her draperies, but because its recruiting agent was hunger, its recruits girls of the people. *Chauffage*, too, was a form of protest, as well as a source of revenue, directed against the *sans-culottes'* principal enemy, the big farmer. Some *chauffeurs* came from trades and occupations similar to those of the *sans-culottes*. Denelle's crime was a political one, and has a direct bearing on the events of Prairial in the Faubourg. And the increase of banditry and highway robbery is both a product of famine conditions and an indication of the alienation of a section of the common people from a bourgeois Republic that had nothing to offer them; one seldom hears of either in the year II. The suicide of poor *Bourguignon* is a political gesture, as he makes clear in the letter pinned to his clothes.

Finally, the White Terror is even more directly relevant, for not only did it spring out of the previous Terror, it also killed off large numbers of very carefully selected militants (in this respect, more effective than epidemics that made no distinction between leaders and led) and drove many more to seek safety out of their Departments and away from the places where they enjoyed political in-

---

[1] On the subject of prostitution in Paris in the years II and III, see Section III, p. 234–9.

fluence. The White terrorists were in origins and temperament the same sort of people as the ultra-revolutionaries and terrorists of the year II.[1] Sometimes—we have at least two instances—they were the same people. In 1793-4 they had killed for the Republic; in the year III and later they hired themselves out to other masters. They had, after all, only one speciality. Not that such instances can be taken as characteristic; but it is interesting that such a transference should have been possible at all. White Terror and 'ultra-revolutionism' are opposite ends of the same phenomenon, and they occupy very much the same terrain.

All these phenomena, especially when taken together, had a direct, if often negative, bearing on the popular movement and its decline. Momentarily, it is true, under the impact of persecution and disaster, there may have been more unity among a common people reduced to a general bottom level of famine and impoverishment than had existed in the year II, when relative well-being, or at least sufficiency, isolated the politically, and often economically, privileged *sans-culottes* from the mass of wage-earners and *habitants de garnis*. In the year III, they were all engulfed together in the same catastrophe, but it was a unity in despair and in death, not one that would lend any strength to popular indignation. Of course, our figures are not complete, they do not include all the murders, all the suicides, or even a small proportion of the prostitutes; and our mortality rates are derived from half a dozen towns only, and the figures for entries to *hospices*, for about the same number. This is not a definitive study of the total impact of the crisis of years III and IV, any more than it is a definitive study of the *sans-culottes*. Such a study would in any case be impossible on a national scale, and it will be a long time before we have exhaustive studies of them even in a dozen towns. We are merely suggesting certain hypotheses, certain possible lines of research, and laying out a number of road signs: 'Work in Progress'—but, scrappy and scattered, they are indicative of the proportions of a crisis that, as a deterrent to popular militancy, was even more effective than the White Terror and years of repression. Vagrancy and armed begging and the formation of *bandes* constitute alternative forms of protest, when

[1] A.N. BB 18 689, for the Lyon assassins. Those accused of having taken part in the Marseille prison massacres include five *perruquiers*, two *boulangers*, a *chapelier*, a *chapelier*, a *cultivateur*, a *maçon*, a *portefaix*, an *emballeur*, a *tabletier*, a *fabricant de savon*, a *maître-ès-arts* (an interesting use of a University education), a *chapelier*, a *commis*, and an *armurier* (A.N. BB 18 174).

more sophisticated types of political protest are denied the common people. Protest is driven into these increasingly primitive and ultimately hopeless forms, as a result of the destruction of the popular movement and the disappearance of *la sans-culotterie* as a collectivity capable of political expression.

The common people were back where they had started; they were in fact much worse off, for they were now faced with a much more efficient and ruthless apparatus of repression than that of the *ancien régime*, and they had, besides, to carry the additional burden of failure and lost hopes; they had been in the High Seats—or at least they had seemed high to them—and they had been driven out of them, oppressed, insulted, humiliated. All they had gained was a strange religio-revolutionary mish-mash, the Cult of Robespierre, and a lot of good that would do them. It is a sad story; just how sad we shall attempt to illustrate in the next section. This section has been concerned with the political fortunes and misfortunes of the common people as a collectivity, and with the transcendent role of individual militants in a period when, owing to a most extraordinary combination of circumstances, a section of the *petit peuple*, though not a very representative one, was able to exercise some influence on the course of events, even, very briefly, at government level. Our next task is to confront the common people with its most ancient and most insistent enemy, hunger, and to study popular attitudes to the problems of food supply, food distribution, shortage, and rationing, all subjects that exercised the imagination of the common people to the full and offered the most favourable terrain to the development of every type of myth and exaggeration. Dearth, more than any other single problem, has the advantage, in historical terms, of illustrating the full illogicality of popular attitudes and of revealing the most hidden and intimate springs of the popular mentality.

Here then is the *sans-culotte*, as a political animal dead and buried. But, and some may regret it, that is not quite the end of him. It has often been pointed out that the Revolution left no permanent monuments in brick, stone, and marble—unless perhaps the strange *monument Sec*, in Aix-en-Provence—but only constructed in cardboard and papier-mâché. The *sans-culotte*, however, left a monument of another kind which survived at least right through the nineteenth century, leaving, to each successive generation, the example of the Revolutionary Passion Play. People remarkably like *sans-culottes* emerged during the *Trois Glorieuses*, their names are on the *colonne de Juillet*; and there are only eighteen years from the July Days to the June ones. During the Commune, there were pseudo-Héberts, pseudo-Chaumettes, pseudo-Robespierres, the *communards* had discovered *hébertisme*, they had not rediscovered *sans-culottisme*; but, among the *fédérés*, there were many who preached the old *sans-culotte* remedies on the subject of dearth and hoarding, and believed too in the same myths. In the spring and summer of 1848 and in the spring of 1871 'direct democracy' flourished noisily and at great verbal length, clubs multiplied in former churches. In Paray-le-Monial, in April 1848, the *clubistes* dug out of the *mairie* the minute book of the old *société* of the year II, and used it to note down the sessions of the year LVI of the Republic. All through the period popular protest recruited, too, its quota of crackpots, of men with empty, violent minds, of people dreaming only of blood, of bored intellectuals, the nineteenth-century equivalent of Jean-Luc Godard and his admirers, who awaited the coming of a great and bloody Revolution *pour se désennuyer*. The most permanent memorial to the poor *sans-culottes* was the evocation and the habit of violence. It was as if future generations had taken them literally, when they had spoken with threats and bluster. Yet there had been much more to them than that, more than a lot of windy, bilious violence *à la Vallès*, of avid appetite for decomposition and carnage *à la Baudelaire*. They deserved better of history. But they had to wait till 1958 for their definitive Paris Pantheon, and even in that they might feel rather ill at ease; they would have preferred something more modest, less grandiose, more in the spirit of the Quarter.

III

DEARTH, FAMINE, AND THE COMMON
PEOPLE 1793–1818

'Il ne faut jamais perdre de vue que le bled est donné
par la nature, que c'est le bien de tous.'
(*From a petition of the year IV to the Commission des Secours*)

III

DEARTH, FAMINE, AND THE COMMON PEOPLE 1793-1815

PART ONE

TOWN AND COUNTRY

'Les subsistances et les monnoyes sont deux objets sur
lesquels la plus légère erreur peut amener des conséquences dangereuses.'

(Prefect of the Ourthe, 22 July 1812)

I. INTRODUCTION

DEARTH was a recurrent phenomenon in eighteenth- and early
nineteenth-century France—it still had sufficient *droit de cité* to
earn its place, under ALARME, in a *Dictionnaire de police moderne*
published in 1823,[1] and it was still being written about as a major
threat to public order as late as 1828.[2] Though partial, regional
harvest failures tended to become milder in the course of the
century, the fear of dearth was permanent, especially at the lower
levels of society, and it took very little at any time for this fear
to become hysterical and to develop into the proportions of panic.
If dearth had been a national phenomenon, a national solution
might have been possible. Certainly there was no lack of proposals
for solutions by the egregious *agronomes* of the last years of the
ancien régime. But it was never in fact bad enough to afflict the
whole nation. There was always likely to be plenty somewhere and
this would be known or at least believed to be the case, so that it
was because of this regional, piecemeal character that the problem
could become so explosive, intensified by a sense of inequality and
contributing to regional feelings of deprivation and unfairness.

With the knowledge that the crisis was in fact partial, the natural
reaction of each locality was to save itself from becoming the victim
of its spread by holding on to the supplies it had. The same could

---

[1] Alletz, *Dictionnaire de police moderne pour toute la France* (Paris, 1823, 4
vols.), i. 22: 'ALARME: Il est défendu de répandre l'alarme parmi le peuple, par
de faux bruits ou de fausses nouvelles qui peuvent l'inquiéter ou l'effrayer tels
que la crainte de la disette, l'enlèvement des enfants, etc, et même en annonçant
des faits vrais, mais qui ne doivent être dénoncés qu'au magistrat de police
seul. . . .'

[2] B. A. Lenoir, *De la probabilité d'une disette prochaine* (Paris, 1828).

be said, at a particular stage of the Revolution, of dechristianization: if every church had been forcibly and effectively closed,
dechristianization would not have become a problem of public
order and the flashpoint of riot. It was the fact that some churches
were closed, while others, often only a mile or two away, remained
open, that led to so much trouble. For just as dearth could send
people scurrying towards markets that they did not normally frequent, in the hope of laying in extra stocks, so the uneven distribution of enforced, military dechristianization would send a deprived
congregation over long distances, to result, in some woodland
village well away from the high-road, in a vast concourse of the
faithful that would at once take on the proportions of a pilgrimage
and that very soon might take on those of a riot or of a rising.
Dearth, therefore, like most other problems of eighteenth-century
French popular history, can only be studied, in all its complicated,
overlapping intricacy and endless inter-penetration, in terms of a
traditional provisioning area. (And even that of Paris, enormous
though it is, embraces only about one-fifth of the national territory.)
Save for the quite exceptional crisis of 1795 and 1796, the study of
dearth will not lend itself to the type of over-all definitions and
apocalyptic descriptions that might have done for the great crises
of the sixteenth and seventeenth centuries.

Dearth also conditioned the attitudes of the common people to
authority; for, although they expected little of a government that
was generally present and visible only in its most repressive forms,
they looked to it for help in the matter of provisioning. As a result,
public authorities at all levels—and those at the lowest, being the
nearest, were, of course, the most exposed to public scrutiny and
to eventual popular wrath—had to move carefully as soon as dearth,
and its more dangerous outriders, rumour and credulity, were
announced once again in a province. It would be unwise to take
large-scale action immediately, for this might indicate alarm on the
part of those who knew the true state of affairs and would confirm
the people in their worst fears;[1] a panic would ensue, and would
make matters much worse.

[1] An example of how careful authority had to be, even in the most simple
matters, is given in a report by the Prefect of the Deux-Sèvres, in August 1812,
on the development of the crisis in Niort: '. . . Dans le premier mois de ces
décrets [the Decrees of 4 and 8 May establishing a maximum price for grain and
ordering requisitions for the city markets], la mairie de Niort étoit gérée par le
Sr. Moriceau, premier adjoint, homme zélé mais un peu disposé aux mesures

On the other hand, if the government waited upon events, the channels of distribution might freeze up, hoarding would follow, and prices would be driven up by the food commissioners of neighbouring towns in the attempt to outbid one another and sweep the board in the same provisioning areas (and the Paris commissioners could always be relied upon to outbid everyone else). The authorities would then have to bear the blame for a full-scale crisis. It was a matter of very fine calculation on the part of the public authorities as to how to, when to, and where to intervene, if indeed they were to intervene at all rather than let matters take their course. As it was also a problem of public order, food supply was the most constant preoccupation both of the old royal and of the revolutionary authorities and the subject formed the principal theme of correspondence between the Departments and the Paris government. Public order might sometimes be preserved by a display of reassurance, especially by the actual exhibition in public places of large quantities of government reserves of grain; this sometimes sufficed to calm popular fears and to deflate rumour. But, equally, the sight of so much wealth might tempt the hungry to pillage and enforced sale, and then the use of force would be necessary. It would also become necessary if the government decided to take a strong line with the farmers and to send out troops into the countryside. Force might make matters much worse; it would infuriate the rural population as a whole, and might convince the urban *petit peuple* that the government itself was in a panic.

Dearth was also a great divider. It set one region against another, one town against another, every town against Paris. It set the urban population—in so far as one can speak of such a thing in a country in which the line of division between townsman and countryman is still not at all clearly marked—against that of the countryside, urban consumer against rural producer (but there were rural consumers also), grain-producing areas against those rich only in forest, in mountains, in chestnuts, in lake and marsh, or in vineyards. If the dearth became extreme, these divisions would dominate all others, running even across the usual lines of trade or class, accentuating every form of regionalism, particularism, and separatism. It gave a spur to selfishness and brought out what

rigoureuses, parce qu'il est lui-même trop accessible à la peur; il ne paroissoit au marché que le sabre au côté et avec une garde. Ces formes sévères augmentoient l'inquiétude . . .' (A.N. F11 718).

was worst in those who had no cause to worry, and what was most irrational, hysterical, and violent—and very often, ultimately self-defeating—in those who did. It did no one any good to burn down a granary, set fire to a large farmer's crops, or destroy the mill of a miller suspected of watering his flour or of being in league with hoarders and monopolists, for, in such times, every mill needed to be pressed into service for the city. *Arrêts* and *taxation*, the commonest form of popular intervention in time of suspected dearth, might bring immediate and visible profit in the grain thus made available, at a reasonable price, to the consumer on the spot. But in the long run they would only lead to various forms of economic boycott on the part of the producers, repression on the part of the higher authorities, and the avoidance of towns and villages that had on previous occasions proved dangerous to traverse. There was always likely to be an alternative route, unless, of course, the *arrêts* had taken place on one of the great river ports that were so often the scene of such disorders.

2. THE HIERARCHY OF NEED

France might, then, be reduced into two camps: those who produced their own bread or could at least provide the baker with the flour to bake it, and those who depended on the baker for their own needs and those of their families. The former would be at most 40 per cent of the population.[1] They would include smallholders and subsistence farmers, and a great many farm hands and agricultural labourers, so long as they were in employment. Most of these latter would be in work during the dangerous summer months, whatever might become of them in winter. They were thus bought out of riot for at least the period when riot was most likely. (In the Pays de Caux, however, during the summer of 1795, the large farmers of the Dieppe region refused to supply the rural

---

[1] A.N. F11 1185 (Subsistances an IV), Braban, Plancher, Buquet et Devidal, rue d'Anjou, 9, au Directoire, 1er prairial an IV: '. . . Par un terme moyen, l'on porte la consommation de chaque individu à 2 septiers et demi de bled par an, le calcul le plus haut fait monter le nombre des français à 24 millions . . . d'après cette donnée, la totalité de la consommation annuelle seroit de 60 millions de septiers ou 120 millions de quintaux, poids de marc. La population de 24 millions de consommateurs ne doit guère donner que 16 millions d'acheteurs; ce nombre va même encore diminuer, parce que beaucoup de propriétaires qui louaient à prix d'argent ne loueront plus à l'avenir qu'en réserves, en grains, ou exploitant eux-mêmes. . . .'

labourers with grain, as they had refused to supply them with seed during the spring, so that the rural poor were driven on to the Dieppe markets.)[1]

Those who depended on the baker would include most urban artisans, tradesmen, and shopkeepers (except those who traded in colonial products that were in short supply in the countryside and who thus had something to exchange for bread or flour); wage-earners, except domestics, who were normally fed by their masters; transport workers, who generally got the worst of both worlds; *faubouriens* ('un faubourg ne commence à grouiller que lorsque le pain augmente'[2]); and most of the inhabitants of villages and small towns in wooded or river areas, in marshland and mountain and in wine-growing regions. In the dearth context, large cities were relatively better off, as they represented a higher priority in government calculations than the *bourgs* or villages in non-productive areas. Those most exposed to extreme dearth and even famine would be the wretched peasants of the wooded areas of the Aube, the mountaineers of the Puy-de-Dôme, the woodsmen and charcoal burners of the Ardennes,[3] village artisans of the Seine valley in the Seine-et-Oise, the Eure, and the Seine-Inférieure,[4] the

---

[1] Arch. Seine-Maritime L 5240 (comité de Dieppe, agent national de Tocqueville-en-Caux au comité, le 21 brumaire an III) and A.N. F10 242 (Commission d'Agriculture, Malôtain à la Commission, 15 frimaire an IV).

[2] *Le Tableau de Paris*, i. 352. Also *Le Nouveau Paris*, iv. 20: '... Les voilà, ces immenses faubourgs; plus grandes que des villes ordinaires, qui ont vomi des armées dans les grandes époques de la révolution; car les faubouriens sont travaillés dès qu'il se prépare un mouvement....' See also *Terreur et subsistances*, pp. 297–305.

[3] R. C. Cobb, 'La Disette dans le canton de Fumay au printemps de 1794' (*Présence ardennaise*, July 1954) and 'Trafic des denrées entre les Ardennes et les provinces belges après la conquête' (ibid., July 1958) and A.N. F15 230 (Secours) (officiers municipaux de Fumay, 10 December 1787): '... Il règne ici depuis plus de six mois une fièvre maligne qui a emporté 120 personnes au moins ... il seroit difficile d'exprimer la misère qui y règne, le peuple se trouvant sans linge, presque sans subsistances et couché immédiatement sur la paille ... dans ce moment surtout la disette se fait sentir d'une manière plus sensible ... sans le secours de nos voisins, la plupart pourroit périr de faim....'

[4] R. C. Cobb, 'Les Disettes de l'an II et de l'an III dans le district de Mantes et la vallée de la Basse Seine', art. cit., and A.N. F11 1476B (Subsistances an II) (2 messidor an II) (Boursier à la Commission des Subsistances): '... les districts de Vernon, Évreux et Louviers sont dans la plus grande détresse de pain ... les mères abandonnent leurs enfans à la mamelle pour chercher leur nourriture....' See also ibid. (canton de Fumay, à la Commission, 22 germinal an II): '... On diroit qu'on veut les nourrir d'espérance et de *pain en peinture* ... toutes les villes ... couperont toujours les vivres au canton de Fumay, placé ... sur l'extrême frontière dans les bois et les montagnes....'

poorer inhabitants of the Alençon region,[1] those of the uplands of the Ardèche, the Cantal, the Lozère, the Aveyron, the Puy-de-Dôme, and the Haute-Loire,[2] and, of course, everywhere, the inhabitants of the under-privileged *communes* on the edge of cities. All these people, in the sweeping epidemics that so regularly followed a dearth crisis as inevitably as the seasons and reached their height at the end of the summer,[2] were in the localities where mortality rates were highest. In the late summer of 1795 and at the same period of 1796, there was a relatively higher proportion of deaths among the inhabitants of Canteleu and Darnétal than in Rouen itself (where a number of those who died in hospital in these two years were inhabitants of the surrounding *communes*[4]); in Dieppe, many of those who died in the two hospitals during the years III and IV, when the death-rate was nearly three times the yearly average,[5] came from le Pollet; and, in the same town, of a hundred and forty-seven young men unfit for military service in the year III, a hundred and twenty-four were from the rural *communes* of the District, and only twenty-three were Dieppois.[6] Referring to an epidemic that had been raging in Bacqueville for the last eighteen months, a Dieppe doctor insisted on the natural proneness of these poor peasants to every imaginable disease.[7] People took refuge in the *commune* of la Guillotière to escape the attentions of the Lyon police, but the price of freedom was likely to be death, for this ancient centre of crime was also a well-known plague-spot.

[1] A.N. F11 715 (Préfet de l'Orne au Ministre, 16 juin 1812): '. . . C'était toujours des départements voisins et notamment celui d'Eure-et-Loir que nos marchés et nos boulangers tiraient leurs approvisionnements extérieurs. . . .'
[2] A.N. F11 706 (Crise de 1812, Aveyron), 708 (ibid.) (Cantal), 712 (Haute-Loire), 716 (Puy-de-Dôme).
[3] '. . . L'épidémie . . . a commencé dans la commune de Canteleu sur la fin de fructidor de l'an II . . .' (A.N. F8 78, rapport sur l'épidémie de Canteleu, an IV). See also *Terreur et subsistances*, p. 316 (30). The municipality of Ervy asks for relief 'à raison des maladies qui surviennent ordinairement au tems de la récolte . . .' (F15 249, hospices, Aube). In *Tableau de Paris*, v. 226, Mercier writes: '. . . La quantité de rats qui sont dans Paris surpasse l'imagination. Cachés pendant l'hiver le long des quais dans des piles de bois, ils descendent en été au bord de la rivière; là ils sont d'une grosseur démesurée. . . .'
[4] *Terreur et subsistances*, p. 327.
[5] Arch. Dieppe État-Civil, 1793–1818: 1793—427 deaths; year II—720; year III—968; year IV—1,071; year V—621; year VI—520; year VII—513; year VIII—420; year IX—621; year X—661; year XI—567; year XII—559; year XIII—455.   [6] Arch. Seine-Maritime L 5329 (comité de Dieppe).
[7] A.N. F8 78 (épidémies, Seine-Inférieure) (an IV).

During the three successive summers of 1794, 1795, and 1796, epidemics lapped the capital, but there was no dramatic outbreak in Paris itself, even in such unhealthy Sections as the Temple and the Panthéon Français, the one close to the rubbish heaps of Monfaucon, the other containing most of the Schools of Anatomy. Heavy death-rates are noted in Meudon and Versailles after a bread disease that killed off many of the poor.[1] In Saint-Germain and Meulan, where the poor had been eating the carcasses of diseased war-horses, the death-roll was heavy, as it was in Gonesse itself, the capital of Paris bread-making, where farm labourers had been eating unripe grain and vegetables and where mortality was further precipitated by an overcrowded cemetery in the middle of the bourg. So the recent dead of the revolutionary years, buried in shallow graves, called in the living. (The village had lost its second cemetery as a result of the Civil Constitution, which suppressed one of the two parishes.) In Saint-Denis also there were many deaths and again a cemetery was spilling over with the recent dead. Saint-Denis also had the highest crime rate in the Paris area.[2]

Again, in 1810–12, there were persistent epidemics in Pantin, Bondy, Vincennes, Villiers-le-Sec, Noisy, Fontenay-sous-Bois, while the Parisians were spared. This general phenomenon can be explained in terms of sheer poverty, ignorance, apathy, housing conditions, and dirt. In most of these communes housing and sanitation were even more primitive, if that were possible, than in the cities. According to a medical report of 1795, the wine-growers and artisans of Meudon lived in windowless hovels with a hole in the roof to let the smoke out, and slept on the mud floor.[3] We hear

[1] Arch. Versailles I D I 78–9 (procès-verbaux de délibérations du Conseil général, an III) and A.N. D III 282 (Comité de législation, Seine-et-Oise, Versailles). It was rumoured that so many had died that the commis à l'état-civil had developed writer's cramp. The maire, Gravois, blamed for not having taken proper precautions to examine the sacking in which the grain had been contained, committed suicide on 28 Frimaire year III.

[2] A.N. F8 77 (Hygiène, Seine) (Préfet de Police au Ministre, 5 mars 1805): '. . . Les maladies endémiques qui se sont manifestées à différentes époques dans la ville de Saint-Denis appellent toute la sollicitude de V. E. . . . Les débordements de la Seine et les inondations . . . peuvent être regardés comme l'origine première de ces maladies. . . . Le . . . cimetière . . . manque d'étendue, le sol en est entièrement saturé et les cadavres qu'on y dépose sont tellement à découvert que la municipalité à cru devoir défendre aux habitans d'y séjourner . . . pour étendre du linge. . . .' See also Arch. Saint-Denis I D I 4 (séance de la municipalité du 24 brumaire an III).

[3] A.N. F8 79 (rapport du médecin Lavergne, vendémiaire an III).

of similar conditions in the epidemics that raged in a number of villages of the Seine-et-Marne in 1814 and 1815.[1] There was considerable overcrowding, in Pantin and Canteleu from seven to ten persons to a room,[2] whereas the largest number of beds ever mentioned in a Paris *garni*, after a suicide, an accidental death, or a murder, is six. The local water supply was often a source of infection,[3] the inhabitants tended to be extremely poor and, in periods of dearth, were reduced to eating what would normally be rejected as unfit for human consumption.[4] After five years of anxiety as a result of the Revolution, they had been subjected to a further two years of semi-starvation (and in 1812, too, they had behind them eighteen years of war, and two of shortage). They seldom knew where the food of the morrow would come from; often they were engaged, when they did have work, in very unhealthy occupations and, like the peasantry, they were very dirty, much dirtier than the inhabitants of towns.[5] Soap was obtainable, at a price, in the cities, even in the year III, but the city authorities would not allow the inhabitants of neighbouring *communes* to take it out with them. There were also few doctors in such places, and the disinherited of these semi-rural *communes* in any case put their faith in quacks, of whom there were many: aged women, with their ancient concoctions, itinerant *guérisseurs* and sellers of patent medicines, and wandering holy men, who preached and killed to cure.[6]

Underlying this descending hierarchy of want and woe were insufficient and bad food, years of malnutrition, poor clothing, terrible housing, anxiety, hopelessness and apathy, a credulity even greater, if that were possible, than that of the urban *sans-culottes*, and consequently an even readier propensity to panic, ignorance, superstition, and resignation to death. If that were not enough, the poor *vignerons* of the hills overlooking Paris drank heavily of their own execrable wine and were among the first victims of a concoction that also caused havoc among the Paris poor. There was never any shortage of bad wine. Probably as many people died from drinking too much adulterated wine as from malnutrition. Wine

[1] A.N. F8 78 (rapport de Lagrange, 9 pluviôse an IV). See p. 112.
[2] A.N. F8 79 (see Section II, p. 112).
[3] Ibid. (épidémie de Meudon).
[4] Ibid. (rapport sur les épidémies de Meulan et de Saint-Germain, pluviôse–ventôse an IV).
[1] See note A, p. 360. [6] See note B, p. 360.

was the great consoler of the poor; and in periods of anxiety or dearth, they would drink more and eat less. There was more drunkenness in the year III than in the year II and consequently much more popular violence. Dearth should never be considered as a phenomenon apart; its partner was always excessive drinking.

3. THE COUNTRY IN THE TOWN

One should not make too much of the division of the population into two camps, although contemporaries were very much aware of it and may even have exaggerated it, and although it did correspond to the simple facts of life and death in conditions of extreme shortage, such as those of 1795 and 1796. The urban population was still very country-minded. Part even of the permanent population of Paris, if not countrymen, were engaged in country pursuits and were themselves involved in food production as market gardeners and rabbit-breeders. If *Marius* and *Olive* are to be believed, cows and goats were to be found living in sixth-floor apartments in the *Vieux Port* during the Occupation; and in revolutionary Paris chickens were as much at home as canaries in the upper floors, flower-pots are frequently reported to the *commissaire* as falling from attics, and the streets themselves teemed with animalia led by rustic types.

There were plenty of green spaces behind tall lodging-houses. A police report, describing the Section furthest to the north of the city and within easy walking distance of the grainlands of the Pays de France, states: 'La Section de Bondy est composée en grande partie de jardiniers, cultivateurs et maraîchers', one of whom had his whole potato crop stolen in the winter of the year III. And among members of the Paris revolutionary committees there are to be found such rural craftsmen as market gardeners, vegetable gardeners, and basket-makers. Many *traiteurs* grow their own vegetables; and, in the year II, members of village committees, in the disputatious District de Gonesse—an area of bitter class conflicts between local *notables* and well-to-do farmers, and a teeming population of day labourers and rural artisans—walk to Paris, call on the *commissaires* of the Faubourg du Nord to ask their help against the local tyrants. There is a constant interchange between Paris militants and rural revolutionaries of the Pays de France and the Brie[1] and some the of strongest Cordelier outposts are among the *vignerons* of Vaugirard, Issy, and Clamart.[2] Paris *sectionnaires* were well informed of what was happening in rural places along the city's supply routes, because local revolutionaries came and told them. Equally, when people are stopped at the *barrières*, attempting to remove bread, soap, candles, coffee, and sugar from the city, or are arrested for illegally trading in meat or butter from a handcart, on interrogation they state that they are from such places as Sucy-en-Brie, Crécy, Tournan, Arpajon, Saint-Cloud, Sèvres, Bougival, and Chaville, and, even further afield, from Gisors, Aumale, Liancourt, and Dreux.[3]

4. DIVIDED FAMILIES

Innumerable ties of family criss-cross between the capital and the Departments of the north-east, the east, the north-west, and the countryside around Paris. Very occasionally these are revealed by a chance remark to a *commissaire de police* during an interrogation or a *constat*. Thus, in making a *déclaration de grossesse* to the *commissaire* of the Section du Muséum, on 22 Pluviôse year III, Marguerite Barrois states 'qu'elle est arrivée à Paris le 9 thermidor dernier, qu'étant descendu chez son frère, le lendemain elle fut voir le C. Duhaud, marchand fripier, quai de l'École, son cousin . . .'. Having found a bed for herself for her second night in Paris, with the help of her cousin, she eventually succumbs to the persistent attentions of a *garçon de boutique* who sleeps in a cupboard at the end of the corridor. His clinching argument—and its success is visible for the girl is eight and a half months pregnant—

---

[1] *Les Armées révolutionnaires*, ii. 606–33.

[2] *Terreur et subsistances*, pp. 143–9.

[3] A.P.P. A/A 187 (commissaire de police de la Section du Muséum, procès-verbal du 15 fructidor an II), A/A 95 (de la Section des Buttes des Moulins, 21 nivôse an III).

[4] A.P.P. A/A 187 (procès-verbal du commissaire de police de la Section du Muséum, déclaration de grossesse de Marguerite Barrois, 22 pluviôse an III). The song could also go to a slightly different tune. Louise André, *fille de confiance*, who has a sister in Paris, Agnès André, 'femme de limonadier', tells the same *commissaire* that her seducer, Jean Jérôme Gaillard, *imprimeur*, 'lui a dit qu'elle soit tranquille, qu'il auroit soin d'elle et de l'enfant, qu'elle le mette en nourrice près de Paris afin qu'il ait le plaisir de le voir souvent, et que le tems étoit trop dur à présent pour qu'il mariât [sic] ensemble, que sitôt que le tems seroit un peu meilleur, il se marieroit avec sa sœur . . .' (ibid., procès-verbal du 5 vendémiaire an III).

is 'qu'il n'y avoit pas de danger, qu'étant du même pays, dans peu il devoit retourner au pays et (ils) se marieroient ensemble'.[4] A girl of fourteen from Argenteuil, sent to Paris by her parents to learn to read and write, is looked after on arrival by a cousin who finds her employment with a seamstress. In this instance, the girl is anxious to break the bonds of family and to enjoy the freedom of the capital, clearing out of her room at night, to set up *en chambre garnie* in the dangerous neighbourhood of the Palais-Royal.[1]

Then there is the Cauche family, two sisters and a young brother, all from Montreuil-sur-Mer, in the Pas-de-Calais. The girls steal linen and clothing from their mistress, and sell it to a *brocanteur*, also from Montreuil. The brother, a *garçon perruquier*, apprenticed to a hairdresser, likewise from Montreuil, has been in Paris for only six months; he has a room with a *logeuse*, herself from Montreuil. The sisters' excuse is that they needed the money to return home and go back to their parents.[2] We can glimpse in this episode a whole network of relationships and mutual help between Pas-de-Calaisiens camped in the capital, relationships that subsisted even after they had been established there for a number of years. Equally, in Pluviôse year III—all our examples are from that year —the body of a building worker from the Creuse, who had fallen from some scaffolding on the Samaritaine, is at once identified at the *commissariat* by the poor man's uncle and by his first cousin, both from the same Department.[3] In Messidor, a *fabricant de soie* from Lyon, established in the Section de la Butte-des-Moulins, denounces to the *commissaire* one of his compatriots, also a *fabricant*, as a terrorist and a partisan of Collot-d'Herbois; the other man says that he is the victim of a private vendetta 'et qu'il croit que cette haine vient depuis Lyon, où ils étoient ensemble . . .'.[4] So it was not always a matter of mutual aid between fellow provincials; the Lyonnais could carry on their own bitter political feuds against

---

[1] Ibid. (procès-verbal du 25 fructidor an II).

[2] Ibid. (procès-verbal du 28 nivôse an III). See also Restif, *Les Nuits*, ix. 1987 (L'auberge à 6 sous, faubourg Saint-Germain): '. . . Je vis une grosse femme . . . assise pour recevoir l'argent. Deux Jeunes Filles assez jolies, dont une surtout que j'entendis appeler Julie étoit également bien faite . . . portaient les plats, à mesure qu'ils étoient garnis par le Découpeur, frère de Julie. C'étaient le Neveu et la Nièce de la grosse Femme; Térèse était leur Cousine. . . .'

[3] A.P.P. A/A 98 (commissaire de la Section des Buttes des Moulins, procès-verbal du 17 messidor an III).

[4] A.P.P. A/A 187 (commissaire de la Section du Muséum, procès-verbal du 7 pluviôse an III).

a Paris background. We hear too of a conversation between a prostitute of twenty-five, a native of Dammartin, and 'une de ses payses qui l'engageoit à ne pas faire l'état'.[1]

The move to Paris was clearly no escape from the ties of provincial origin. Indeed it would seem that few sought to escape them; as soon as they had disembarked from the *coche*, their first thought was to seek out relatives or those from their home town to whom they had letters of introduction or to whom they could introduce themselves verbally. The fate of those who had neither family connections nor provincial ties is illustrated by those unfortunates —runaway children, fleeing parental brutality, and adolescents, drawn to the capital, like Dick Whittington, whom the police round up every night sleeping in alleyways, under arcades, or in porches. When questioned, they state that they are orphans, or that they have no relatives in Paris. The children are sent back to heavy-handed fathers and mothers in Saint-Germain, Versailles, or Marly.[2] Just as, in more recent times, *Milo l'Andouille*, dressed in Auvergnat smock and wide-brimmed hat, and *Dédé les Bretelles*, in Limousin outfit, competed, boulevard du Montparnasse, for the crown of salesman eloquence, the title of *le roi du baratin*, the provinces spread deep into eighteenth-century Paris and the rustic-sounding inn signs (*Au panier fleuri*, *Au bon laboureur*, *Au bouquet fourni*, *A la rose rouge*, *Au filet de cochon*, *Au pied de porc*, *A la vache enragée*) were not the only reminders that in the capital itself there persisted *l'odeur de la campagne*.[3] It was a fact that most of the inhabitants must have found reassuring, for only a minority had been born in the city, and many would have identified themselves with the titles of those two well-known papers, still appearing, *L'Auvergnat à Paris* and *La Bretagne à Paris*. Mercier has a page on the cheap restaurants of the rue des Boucheries in which 'vous avez l'avantage . . . de connoître, en deux ou trois jours, l'accent des différentes provinces de la France, gascons, provençaux, limousins, francs-comtois, normands, picards, &ca.'.[4] To Mercier, a real *bourgeois de Paris*, this diversity and lack of roots—or rather, this persistence of old ones—appeared sinister and rather alarming: 'La canaille d'une grande

---

[1] A.P.P. A/A 96 (commissaire de la Section des Buttes des Moulins, 16 ventôse an III).

[2] A.P.P. A/A 98 (ibid., procès-verbaux des 10 thermidor, 13 fructidor an III et 18 brumaire an IV).

[3] See note C, p. 360.   [4] *Le Tableau de Paris*, xi. 152.

ville, *qui n'y est point née*, et qui abonde de toutes parts, est une canaille sans nom. . . .'[1] He wrote of the rue des Boucheries in 1788; but this last phrase was written in 1797, with the experience of the Revolution behind him.

The urban population, then, was still very much rural-orien-tated, with families divided; the eldest son staying in the village to cultivate the diminutive holding, the second or third son coming to the city, where he might eventually marry and settle. *Edmond* and *Ursule* came to Paris—with consequences suitably disastrous for themselves. (Restif, who was something of a Physiocrate, pointed to the clear moral that they should have stayed in Noyers.)[6] But their nine brothers and sisters remained at home, 'chez notre Bon-Père'. *Edmond* and *Ursule*, as they majored in corruption and went up in the social scale of metropolitan vice, increasingly neglected their filial duties and sent back news only rarely, much of it mendacious. But in general the correspondence between the divided ends of a family remained intense and was further helped by the regular dispatch from the country of clean shirts and under-wear, bonnets and shawls, parcels of butter and eggs, brought by villagers who came to the capital. All the time her son was in Paris, the mother of Ducroquet, the unfortunate *commissaire aux ac-caparements* of the Section Marat, sent her son regular news—generally very gloomy, for she was desperately poor—about their relatives and neighbours in Amiens. The last letter she posted and a parcel of clothes reached Paris after he had been guillotined, and ended up, with many other such pathetic objects and mail, in the papers of Fouquier-Tinville. The poor woman had read in a local paper that one of the 'conspirators' was called Ducroquet

---

[1] *Le Nouveau Paris*, I, xx. Mercier is prepared to attribute most of the evils of the revolutionary period to these newcomers: '. . . C'étoit à Paris que se rendoient tous ces personnages alléchés par les aubaines que procure une révolu-tion (ibid. 5, ccxi). Restif is a little more generous: '. . . Du fond de leurs pro-vinces, de jeunes gens accourent à la capitale, attirés par l'ambition, ou conduits par le devoir . . .' (*Le Pornographe*, p. 13). But he is equally convinced that it is only the unhealthiest elements of the rural population that have come to the capital: '. . . Jette un coup d'œil sur cette multitude de figures presque hideuses, qui inondent nos villes; vois la laideur et les tailles petites ou défectueuses . . .' (ibid. 21).

[2] *Les Nuits*, ix. 2044: '. . . Multipliez les petits propriétaires: interdisez aux Riches l'excessive consommation, qui, outre qu'elle épuise tout pour le Pauvre, est de mauvais-exemple pour le Demi-Riche. . . . Surtout ne protégez pas le luxe! . . . il ne produit rien de solide, et cependant il occupe des bras qui feraient double labeur, cultiveraient les champs, ou la vigne, tisseraient la toile. . . .'

but, as she wrote to her son, knowing his ardent patriotism, she was sure that she had no cause for worry. *Edmond* and *Ursule* were in one respect untypical; for their father, an inexorable moralist, was also a fairly well-to-do farmer, with half a dozen *valets* and farm-girls. There were certainly many more people in Paris who could not count on the family food parcel, or on anything much other than curses, or warnings about the dangers of city life.

5. PROVINCIAL MONOPOLIES

Whatever the situation of the family, and the relation to it of its absent members, the connection was seldom entirely broken off; and certain urban trades were still monopolized—some of these monopolies appear to have been very ancient—by people from a given village or a certain province. Once such a monopoly had been established, it was likely to be self-perpetuating, as there would always be many eager recruits from where the first in the city had come from. Much of the recruiting was on a family basis. Thus the Paris water-carriers nearly all came from one District of the Aveyron. The horse-dealers, like the horses, were Normans. Building labourers were Limousins—'on a spéculé sur les terrains, on a appelé des régimens de Limousins', writes Mercier in 1786—or from the Creuse. Stonemasons were Normans; *crocheteurs* and *porteurs de chaise* were from Lyon; the Savoyards specialized in the filthier trades—*décrotteurs, frotteurs, dégraisseurs*, chimney sweeps. We find Foréziens as hatters and sweeps (a seasonal job). Doormen were Swiss ('Portiers et Suisses sont devenus synonymes en France'), the market porters were generally Picards, often to be found too as domestic servants. The best women cooks were supposed to be Picardes and the best-paid chefs were from Languedoc. Hired servants, the plague of foreigners, travellers, and temporary residents, were Gascons, with, claimed Mercier, a Gascon sharpness of wit; they also had a second line of business as police informers. Mounted smugglers, Vidocq stated, were Picards too—perhaps the phenomenon that so many Picards left their homes might account for the fact, remarked upon by many contemporaries, that in the region of Abbeville there were three girls to every man. *Marchands de salade* and *marchands de fil* were from Normandy. *Marchands de peaux de lapin* and coal-heavers were from the Auvergne, and so were the poorer sort of *logeurs*. (*Edmond*, during his period of slumming, Faubourg Saint-Marceau, has one as a landlord, 'un gros auvergnat, assez bon diable, s'il n'étoit pas plus intéressé qu'Harpagon'.) There were many Jews from Alsace among the *fripiers*, especially those who plied their trade on the *marché du Temple*. Most *blanchisseuses* working in Paris came from Vaugirard and Grenelle. *Flotteurs* were from the Morvan or from Vermenton, or Voutenay, in the Yonne: drawn to Paris by the rivers—Cure, Yonne, Seine—they often became workers on the wood ports, while some graduated to the more advantageous position of *cocher de fiacre* and police informer (the two trades were complementary). Other *flotteurs* enlisted in the *Gardes-Françaises*.[1] Retired soldiers and fencing-masters tended to be from Alsace. There were many *ébénistes* of Bohemian or Prussian origin; and Italian music teachers and *maîtres de langue* were much in demand in the *Noble Faubourg*. *Scieurs de long* were from the Haute-Loire, *dentellières* from Caen or Beauvais. There was even a considerable English colony, made up of governesses and *dames de compagnie*. *Nourrices* came mostly from the villages of the Beauce and were supposed to be particularly healthy.[2]

---

[1] On the connection between the *flotteurs* of the valley of the Cure and of the Lac des Settons, the wood trade and the riverside Sections of Paris, see Claude Hohl, *Un agent du Comité de sûreté générale: Nicolas Guénot* (Paris, Bibliothèque nationale, 1968). Guénot had first come to Paris with the *trains de bois*, and then become a *cocher de fiacre*, a position which enabled him to acquire a secondary employment as a police informer. During the Terror, he devoted much of his revolutionary activity to denouncing well-to-do wood merchants from his own village who had set up in trade on the Paris wood port. See also Restif, *M. Nicolas*, ii. 1018: '. . . Je trouvois mes deux cousins Mairat . . . qui arrivoient de Paris, où ils avoient travaillé tout l'automne, à fossoyer, après avoir conduit des trains de bois-flotté. Ils étoient proprement arrangés en hommes-de-rivière. . . .' See ibid. iii. 1605: '. . . Mes deux cousins, par leur mérite personnel, s'étoient élevés à l'emploi de facteurs . . . leurs voyages étoient payés comme pour un trayeur, à chacun des 10 trains descendans à Paris, qui étoient sous leur inspection, et ils faisoient bien leurs affaires. . . .' On the link between Auxerre and Paris via the Yonne and the Seine, see ibid. iv. 1808: '. . . Elle sourit, comme pour se moquer de mon adieu éternel, en allant à Paris, à 45 lieues, et dont, au moyen de la rivière, notre Ville n'est qu'un Fauxbourg: il n'en coûte que 6 francs pour s'y rendre par eau. . . .'
    See also on the subject of monopolies and frequentations, *M. Nicolas*, ii. 982: '. . . Plusieurs ouvriers logeoient dans une auberge [d'Auxerre] . . . tenue par un Italien. . . . Cet original logeoit par goût, par similitude, par convenance, tous les charlatans, tous les opérateurs, tous les jongleurs, tous les escrocs, tous les mauvais sujets, tous les coureurs qui passoient par la ville. . . .'

[2] See note D, p. 361.

In times of shortage, many such townsmen, with one foot still in the countryside, could expect to be able to exchange such urban goods as coffee, soap, candles, and sugar for grain. Under the threat of dearth, townsmen of all conditions were likely to rediscover their provincial or rural origins—some of these rather recently acquired by *bourgeois* who had bought country estates and farms. Thus the shipowners of *le Grand Quai*, in le Havre, came through the famine of 1794–6 unscathed, thanks to the produce of their tenant farmers in the District de Montivilliers,[1] and landowners could always insist that their rents be paid in kind rather than in money.[2] Townsmen might also recall the providential existence of a country cousin.

6. DEARTH AND *LE RETOUR AU PAYS*

In periods of shortage, too, for seasonal labourers (many of them harvesters from the region of Sézanne), who came to the Pays de France for the harvest and sought winter work in Paris, the solution might appear simple—return to their villages where they were sure to be provided for.[3] In the lower ranks of urban society, among the *commissionnaires*, the *perruquiers*, the *garçons brocanteurs* (very much a temporary occupation at the best of times)[4]—the porters and all those who worked with their muscles, the thought of home was always a goal ahead to be attained when they had saved enough. Even in normal times they lived five or six to a room, especially in the quarters behind the Hôtel de Ville, even borrowing each other's clothes to go out in the evening (in the year IV we hear of three *garçons chapeliers*, refugees from the Forez, with one blanket, one bed, and one complete suit of clothes between them),[5] just above the starvation level and in conditions of extraordinary

[1] Robert Richard, 'Le Grand Quai', *La Porte Océane* (1950).

[2] A.N. F11 1185 (Subsistances, an IV) (1er prairial an IV).

[3] They might also be sent back by the police. Alletz, op. cit., ii (717), s.v. 'MOISSON. Les moissonneurs qui viennent des départements pour travailler aux moissons, et qui mendient dans Paris, doivent être arrêtés et conduits à la préfecture de police, pour être renvoyés dans leurs pays.'

[4] In Fructidor year II, the *commissaire de police* of the Section du Muséum cross-examines Denis Minet, aged 43, a native of Ferrières, near Meaux, asking him how long he has been a *brocanteur*: 'répond qu'il le fait depuis trois semaines . . . à lui demandé ce qu'il faisoit avant d'être brocanteur, répond qu'il faisoit toutes sortes de métiers . . .' (A.P.P. A/A 187, commissaire de police de la Section du Muséum, procès-verbal du 28 fructidor an II).

[5] A.N. F11 1182 (Subsistances an IV).

discomfort. When it was a matter of seducing a girl—one of the rare free pleasures available to such people—they would seek out a *payse* among their employer's female servants, and promise her marriage and return to the village, in order to obtain her favours free. Once these were obtained, in fact, it became impossible for the girl, eight months pregnant, to return home at all. Certainly most people at this sort of level—including the majority of the population of the *garnis*—had no intention of remaining in the city permanently. They resembled the Aveyronnais who in the eighteenth century tended to go to Spain as itinerant pedlars, tinsmiths, or farm labourers, for periods of from six to ten years and return at regular intervals with their savings to buy small parcels of land in their native villages. The eventual, though problematical, benefit from the wretchedness they endured was to set themselves up at home, where they could display to advantage their city lore. Of the Swiss, particularly the *portiers* whom he so much dislikes, Mercier observes: 'Quand ils ont gagné quelqu'argent, ces valets reviennent chez eux faire les républicains.'

The appeal of the *retour au pays* would become more insistent in times of economic distress, extreme cold, or extreme shortage. In 1795 and the following year, a great many wage-earners, especially women, ruined by emigration, the partial collapse of the luxury trades, the closing of religious establishments, the bankruptcy of hospitals and *hospices*, the withdrawal from Paris to their country estates of many well-to-do householders, and the decimation of the *Enfants Trouvés*, applied to the *comités de bienfaisance* or to the *Commission des Secours* for passports and financial assistance in order to return to their native towns or villages *pour avoir du pain*:[1] an admission of defeat particularly humiliating for girls who had set out for Paris only a few years earlier, full of hope, and had sent back, in the interval, via Jeannot or Pierrot, reports of success. As a number of them, on their own admission, had fled from home to escape parental tyranny, their home-coming cannot have been particularly enjoyable. Nor did it often satisfy their most urgent needs; for those who had left Paris during the winter of the year III were quick to discover that what might only be a dearth in the capital looked much more like a famine in the village. Having fled from shortage, unemployment, loneliness, cold, and the *garni*, they

[1] See note E, p. 361.

were now to encounter starvation, hostility, and closed doors from a community that rejected them as 'strangers'. Many of them were back in Paris by the spring of 1796 and began once more to petition the *Commission des Secours*:[1] their plight was now even worse. Unable to establish a year's residence, they no longer qualified for a free bread ration under a *douzième secteur* reserved for residents. (One of those who benefited from this charity was that arch-protagonist of the *retour au pays*, Restif de la Bretonne.)[2] Women who had worked in Paris for as much as five or ten years thus had to pay dear for a momentary flight. If they could not have themselves recognized once more as residents, they were liable to starve, and they were in danger of being expelled as non-resident *indigentes*.

They might have saved themselves the journey in the first place, had they been aware of a movement in the opposite direction which had been going on since early in the year III. This brought large numbers of inhabitants of the rural *communes* round Paris into the Sections nearest to their villages. From Franciade, Bagnolet, La Chapelle, Belleville, Émile, Clichy, Bezons, Argenteuil, Montreuil, people went to the Sections of Bondy, Faubourg du Nord, Faubourg Montmartre, Bonne-Nouvelle; from Versailles, Auteuil, Passy, Sèvres, Saint-Cloud, Chaville, Bougival, Chatou, they went to the Champs-Élysées, Lepeletier; from Vincennes, Alfort, Fontenay-sous-Bois, to the three Sections of the Faubourg Saint-Antoine;[3] from Auffargis, Antony, Sceaux, Versailles, to the Sections des Invalides, Panthéon Français, Luxembourg; from Choisy and Vitry, to the Section du Finistère.[4]

At the height of the crisis of the year IV, there was also a temporary movement away from the towns, and the wives and daughters of artisans, fishermen, and sailors began to wander in small

---

[1] See A.N. F11 1178, 1181-3, 1185-6, 1221, 1236, 1241, 1242 (Commission des Secours, an IV). [2] See note F, p. 361.

[3] A report on the *indigents* of the Section de Montreuil, dated 20 Pluviôse year IV, gives a clear indication of this movement: '. . . Cette classe s'y augmente chaque jour', writes the *comité de bienfaisance*, 'tant par le ralentissement des travaux, que par le grand nombre de journaliers des communes voisines qui y viennent fixer leur domicile pour procurer du pain à leur nombreuse famille . . .' (A.N. F11 1183, Administrateurs des Secours au Ministre, 20 pluviôse an IV). See also the report of the Commission Administrative des Secours for 3 Frimaire year IV: '. . . Les non-cultivateurs qui habitoient les campagnes [de la banlieue] ont été obligés de déserter, faute de subsistances. On sait que dans les environs de Paris c'est cette classe de citoyens qui est la plus nombreuse . . .' (A.N. F7 3054).

[4] A.N. F11 1184-5.

groups through the surrounding countryside, begging for bread. On 27 Ventôse, Marie Jeanne Pacon reports to the Dieppe *comité de bienfaisance*

que Jacques Blondel, journalier, son gendre, et Jeanne Charbonnel, sa fille, femme dudit Blondel, demeurant à Dieppe, rue du Cœur ... sont partis de cette commune et ont amené avec eux Marie-Rose Blondel, leur fille, le 15 de ce mois, pour aller mendier le pain leur manquant à Dieppe, qu'ils ont été arrêtés à Neufchâtel. ...

The next day, Constance Thuillier, femme Thuillier, *revendeuse*, 'qui est partie de Dieppe vers le 16, ... pour aller chercher du pain dont les habitans de Dieppe manquent malheureusement ...' is likewise arrested by the *gendarmerie* of Neufchâtel. There are similar reports concerning two *dentellières* and a *journalier* who had left Dieppe around the middle of the month.[1]

Throughout the spring of the years III and IV there is a steady stream of people from Dieppe who leave for the Pays de Caux, generally in small family units, and who are brought in by the rural police a few days later, on the orders of village municipalities. But, as in Paris, there was a movement the other way. Mâlotain, a Dieppe watchmaker, and one of the acutest observers of the famine crisis of the years III and IV, reports to the Commission d'Agriculture: 'Une chose que je n'ai jamais pu apprécier, c'est d'avoir vu des malheureux journaliers être obligés d'emprunter un cheval, ou un âne, pour venir à la ville acheter un boisseau de grain ou deux pour leur subsistance, tandis qu'ils avoient à leur porte des laboureurs qui en apportoient à la halle ...'.[2]

There is a further reference to the plight of these village labourers in a letter from the *agent national* of Tocqueville-en-Caux, in the District de Dieppe, dated 21 Brumaire year III. He informed the Dieppe *comité*:

... Les cultivateurs de notre commune laissent souffrir les consommateurs, faute de ne pas vouloir leur fournir leur nécessaire, il existe au

---

[1] Arch. Dieppe Registre 1 (comité de bienfaisance, 25, 26, 27 ventôse an IV). This was the season for vagrancy of this kind. Two years earlier, on 29 Ventôse year II, some soldiers bring to the *comité* of the Section Marat 'les nommés Jean-Baptiste d'Épinay, sa femme et quatre de leurs enfans arrêtés par une patrouille, en mendiant dans la commune des *****(?) chez le nommé Gamolin, où ils étoient couchés dans une étable à vaches ... se disant de la commune de Sainte-Foy ...' (Arch. Seine-Maritime L 5230, comité de la Section Marat, séance du 29 ventôse an II).

[2] A.N. F10 242 (report dated 15 frimaire an IV).

moins 40 vaches dans notre commune et les individus qui n'en ont pas sont réduits à faire de la soupe sans y mettre du beurre par l'égoïsme des cultivateurs qui ne veulent pas leur en délivrer. . . .[1]

A month later, in a report dated 3 Nivôse, we hear of a large farmer from Anneville, in the same District, 'qui a refusé de délivrer au C. Étienne Gervais, manouvrier . . . un quintal de bled pour alimenter sa famille. . . . Il est d'observer que dans cette commune les manouvriers et autres n'ayant point de récolte, sont approvisionnés par les cultivateurs. . . .'[2] In the Fécamp riots of 25–8 Prairial year III, the port was invaded by the *manouvriers* of the rural *communes* inland, who unloaded and distributed among themselves the cargo of the Danish grain ship, the *Anna-Caterina*.[3] Under the impact of extreme shortage, rural solidarity soon proved a myth. The big farmers of the Pays de Caux displayed as much indifference to the needs of their own labourers, during their winter unemployment, as to the appeals of starving people from Dieppe.

7. PROSTITUTION AND THE PARIS FEMALE POPULATION

Other women, who had fallen from such humble estates as seamstress, *revendeuse*, *brocheuse*, after their third or fourth appearance before the *commissaire* as prostitutes, or on being discharged from hospital (where, according to Mercier, there would be at any time a constantly changing population of from five to six hundred girls), were forcibly sent back to their places of origin by the police authorities—especially alarmed by the enormous increase in the trade during the year III—or elected to throw themselves on a somewhat uncertain parental mercy, until times were better. Most of these girls declare that they have been reduced to prostitution pour avoir du pain', 'pour pouvoir vivre', 'pour nourrir un enfant', 'pour payer une nourrice', and so on. Few of them, if they can be believed, have been in the business for more than a few months or a year.

Much is to be learnt from their case histories about the composition of the Paris female labour force in general, how long it had been in the city, its local origins, and what were the conditions of

[1] A.D. S.M. L 5240 (comité de Dieppe, correspondance).
[2] Ibid.
[3] A.N. D III 270 (Comité de Législation, Fécamp, rapport du maire sur les événements des 25, 26, 27 et 28 prairial an III).

female employment as a result of the crisis of the year III. Prostitution represents perhaps the largest single form of feminine
employment, although normally combined with other occupations,
if only those of *marchandes ambulantes*,[1] *crieuses à la Grève*, or
occasional thieves. It is also the one on which the police were the
most informed and about which the historian can, in consequence,
obtain something like an over-all picture. Thus prostitution can
witness admirably not only for all the lower ranks of feminine
employment,[2] but also for problems of pauperization and for the
commonest provincial origins of much of the floating population.
Restif comments, in *Le Palais Royal*: 'Madame *Janus* (there is no
need to explain her occupation) a plus de quarante Jeunes-Filles
de cet âge (17 ans), prises dans les fauxbourgs et les provinces. . . .'[3]
Mercier, too, refers to a similar lady, *la Mère*, 'qui a décrassé ce
troupeau de province et des campagnes . . .'.[4] Paris-born prostitutes were in fact the exception, not because the Filles-de-Paris
were more virtuous, though they were more intelligent and better
able to look after their marketable value, but because women and
girls born in the provinces were easier to recruit and were less
protected. (They were also much more exposed both to seduction
and to unemployment, the one often following the other.)

In the cases recorded for the year III, except for a minority of
native-born Parisiennes, most of the girls interrogated had been
in Paris for a maximum of two years, two for just over a year, one
for eighteen months, one for five months, two for three months,
one for a fortnight. Three were picked up two days after their
arrival, one from Brussels, two from Versailles.[5] There is one

---

[1] Restif, *Les Nuits*, viii. 1806: '. . . Je sentis en moi-même que c'était un mal
que les Femmes de la populace fussent uniquement employées à colporter vaine-
ment des choses inutiles, comme les fleurs. . . . Je sentis en outre qu'il serait
sage, utile, de supprimer insensiblement toutes les Colporteuses de fruits, qui
ne sont que des Fainéantes, des inutiles . . . que tous les membres des cris
de Paris sont de mauvais-sujets, dont les Enfans ne sont que des Espions, des
Voleurs, et des Prostituées. . . .'

[2] Prostitution itself offered a tremendous range. Restif, in *Le Pornographe* and
in his *Parisiennes*, divided it into twelve classes, descending from the *femme
entretenue*, to the poor *raccrocheuse*, operating in *garnis*, and to the wretched
barboteuse, living in the faubourgs, and plying for the favour of unmarried
water-carriers and poor artisans, in unfrequented streets.

[3] *Le Palais Royal*.

[4] *Le Tableau de Paris*.

[5] See also Restif, *Les Nuits*, ix. 2096: '. . . Depuis quand est-elle ici? Mais . . .
depuis trois jours! — C'est une Provinciale? — On le dit — Mais bien singulière. . . .'

example of a prostitute in her late thirties, a native of Besançon, who had been in the capital for twelve years. Her case is altogether exceptional.

Of ninety-six avowed prostitutes, some claim to have taken up the trade only recently as a result of unemployment. A few attempt to argue that they earn enough as *revendeuses* or shop assistants to keep themselves in food and clothing and to pay for their *garnis*; but when pressed by the *commissaires*, they admit that most of their earnings come from men. These girls were interrogated in 1793, 1794, and 1795 by the *commissaires* of the three Sections of the Arcis, Montagne, and Muséum. Only twenty-eight are Paris-born, sixty-five are provincials, three are foreigners. Of the provincial group nineteen have recently arrived from the Eastern Departments,[1] Alsatians and Lorrainers to the fore.[2] A further eighteen come predictably from the countryside around Paris, and five from Versailles, a great provider of every form of female immigration, as a result of the disappearance of the Court, unemployment, and general misery.[3] Eight girls come from Burgundy and the Bourbonnais,[4] and eight from the north and north-east,[5] the principal source of masculine labour in the capital. There are only five girls from the west,[6] in striking contrast to the origins of nineteenth- and twentieth-century prostitutes. There are only five *Normandes*.[7]

---

[1] Three from Metz, two from Verdun, one each from Colmar, Longwy, Huningue, Sarrelouis, Vesoul, Commercy, Remiremont, Besançon, Bar-sur-Aube, Clermont-en-Bassigny, Nogent-sur-Seine, Pont-à-Mousson, Gray, Château-Thierry. This predominance of girls from the East of France is confirmed by Louis-Pierre Manuel, in his *La Police de Paris dévoilée* (Paris, 1791, t. ii). Of the girls mentioned, eleven are from the East (Vaucouleurs, Strasbourg, Metz, Rumigny, Serre, Vesoul, Gray, Sedan). He comments on the subject of one of them: 'Encore une Lorraine! encore une élève de marchand de modes . . .!' There are four girls from Normandy in his list.

[2] '. . . Nous avons là-dedans une petite Alsacienne de 13 ans; jolie, c'est une miniature! Maman la réserve pour les vieillards . . .' (*Le Paysan Perverti*, p. 84). See also *Monsieur Nicolas*, iv. 2358: '. . . Tu sais bien, la petite Débutante dont je t'ai parlé, qui me remplacait pour les Pratiques difficiles, & surtout les Vieillards? C'est une Alsacienne charmante. . . .'

[3] The others are from La Villette, Saint-Denis, Marly, Vaucresson, Longjumeau, Corbeil, Argenteuil, Saint-Vérin, Choisy-sur-Étiole, Dammartin and Fontainebleau.

[4] Dijon, Auxerre, Sens, Viteaux, La Charité, Bourbon-l'Archambault—two sisters from this town; the younger had arrived first and had then sent for her elder.

[5] Amiens, Arras, Soissons, Montdidier, Méry, Sourdun, Clermont-sur-Oise.

[6] Chartres, Angers, Rennes, Orléans.

[7] Rouen, Alençon, Gagny, Sainte-Cécile.

Two girls are *Lyonnaises*[1] and one is surprised to find even that number; there is a single *Auvergnate*, from the Haute-Loire. Finally, there are three Belgians.[2]

It may, of course, be objected that these figures, drawn from only three out of forty-eight Sections, are inadequate and unrepresentative. The Section de la Montagne, however, was the very microcosm of Paris prostitution, containing, as it did, among the *dames du Palais-Royal*, the top, bottom, and middle of the profession, and most of these figures are drawn from there. The girls interrogated mostly lived outside the Section, some of them on the Left Bank, if 'live' is the right word for people who state 'qu'elles couchent tantôt par çi, tantôt par là' and they operate there only in their real, or stated, profession, prostitute or shop-assistant.[3] Furthermore, these figures confirm very much what we already know of the composition of the male population of Paris during the revolutionary period. Alsace sent its soldiers and its girls to the city and, more generally, there was considerable recruitment from the east.

Only a very few of these girls had come to Paris with the intention of becoming prostitutes. Nearly all had been in service, or had worked as laundresses or *revendeuses*. Their places of origin are, then, indicative of the composition of the female 'floating population' of the capital, and, perhaps, even of the female population as a whole. A final observation is that the majority were not country girls, but had been born in towns.

Of a hundred who were questioned by the three *commissaires* and whose ages are given, the average age is twenty-two.[4] Two are

---

[1] *Monsieur Nicolas*, v. 2440, on the road from Auxerre to Paris, passing through Joigny, on the subject of two Lyonnaises walking to the capital: '. . . Pardieu! j'aurai la Nièce! disait le Voyageur. Je n'aurais pas payé le Souper pour un Vieux cuir-tannée, rebut de la Place-Bellecour à Lyon. . . .' The niece prudently decides to return to Lyon, while her so-called aunt continues the journey to Paris.

[2] Brussels, Mons, and Louvain. See also *Les Nuits*, ix. 206: '. . . La première des Ouvrières (d'une boutique de modes) se nomme *Raimonde*. C'est une jeune Bruxelloise, blanche comme lis. . . .'

[3] See the cross-examination by the *commissaire* of the Section de la Montagne of Julie Chevalier, 26, native of La Charité: '. . . à elle observé qu'il n'y a cependant pas beaucoup de marchandises dans sa boutique pour exciter les passants à acheter chez elle du tabac qu'elle vend, a répondu que lorsqu'on n'étoit pas riche, on ne pouvoit pas bien garnir sa boutique . . . interpellée quel étoit son état avant d'avoir sa boutique, a répondu couturière en robes et qu'elle occupoit ladite boutique depuis environ quatre mois . . .' (A.P.P. A/A 96, 15 ventôse an III).

[4] Restif divides his *Parthénion* into six age-groups: 30 to 36; 25 to 30; 20 to 25; 18 to 20; 16 to 18; 14 to 16 (*Le Pornographe*, 67). See also *Les Nuits*, iv. 817:

fourteen years old, two fifteen, four sixteen, four seventeen, nine eighteen. At the other end of the scale, there is a veteran of forty-four, one of forty, and one of thirty-eight. Most, then, had left their homes at nineteen or twenty. On their expulsion or voluntary with-drawal[1] from the Promised Land, they could still look forward to a long life of provincial unhappiness, dirt, brutishness, and child-bearing. They were among the saddest victims of the famine of 1795, and their fates illustrate how tenuous remained the roots of the *petit peuple* in the intractable, inhospitable *pavé de Paris*. In this respect, prostitution witnesses for the feminine population as a whole, emphasizing its fluidity, its insecurity, the enormous risks encoun-tered by the provincial girl: from *déclaration de grossesse* to unem-ployment; from that to part-time prostitution and occasional pilfering (*vol de mouchoir* is the item that recurs the most insistently in the reports);[2] from that to full-time prostitution[3] and cohabita-

'. . . Je vis entrer deux Jeunes-personnes, l'Une de 16 à 17 ans, fort-jolie mais très-effrontée, et l'Autre de 11 à 12 ans. . . . Nous y employons les Filles Faites, mais nous ne les fesons pas. . . .'

[1] 'Souvent une fille publique, lasse de la Capitale, ou craignant la vengeance de ceux à qui elle a communiqué le poison qui circule dans ses veines, va ré-pandre ailleurs la contagion . . .' (*Le Pornographe*). Mercier, in 1788, draws attention to a new form of *prostitution ambulante* that 'environne les auberges des grands chemins, marche avec la poste, et répand les maux vénériens des villes de province jusque dans les bourgs et hameaux . . .' (*Le Tableau de Paris*, xi. 7).

[2] See note G, p. 361.

[3] '. . . Que sommes-nous? La plupart des Infortunées sans principes, sans éducation; des servantes, des femmes-de-chambre tout au plus. Qui nous dé-bauche? Nos Maîtres; des Hommes qui ont un état, une éducation. Quelques-unes d'entre nous, sorties de la plus basse condition, sont portées au mal par des Soldats, ou même des Officiers, corrupteurs-nés de notre sexe . . .' (*Les Nuits*, iv. 827). '. . . Il n'est personne au monde de si dangereux pour les Filles d'un certain ordre, que les Étudiants en médecine; on se défie des Militaires, des Abbés . . .' (ibid. vi. 1206). The military in particular had a well-estab-lished reputation both for libertinage and for extreme brutality. Restif writes of the pupils of military schools: '. . . Ils ne voient dans l'habit d'Officier que le grade; ils ne songent qu'aux privilèges de libertinage qu'un long usage accorde aux militaires . . .' (*Tableaux de la Vie ou les Mœurs du XVIIIᵉ siècle . . .*). Nothing, he comments in *Monsieur Nicolas*, could be more deplorable than the fate of a prostitute whose protector is a soldier in the *Gardes-Françaises*. Not only will she be at the disposal of the whole regiment, she will also be subjected to the brutality of a corps notorious for its cruelty and violence (see also Claude Hohl, op. cit.). Far more fortunate were those who had protectors among police informers. Of one of his companion apprentices in Auxerre, Restif states: 'Ce Tourangeau avoit été tartare, valet d'armée . . . le tartare tourangeau avoit aidé son maître à violer, à piller en Flandres, il nous racontoit froidement comme son maître . . . lui remettoit quelquefois des filles de ferme dont il s'étoit rassasié . . .' (*Monsieur Nicolas*, ii. 702).

tion with a procurer, who might also be a receiver; and expulsion or the hospital at the end of the line. Historically, prostitution is important if only because the police took a minute interest in the trade,[1] so that we have a wealth of information that reflects on other female occupations, previously or concurrently exercised by so many *filles de joie: revendeuse, ravaudeuse, repasseuse, crieuse de fruits, marchande de falourdes, bouquetière, fille de confiance, fille de salle, ouvrière en boutique,* and so on.[2]

These girls in their teens or early twenties were imitated in the years III and IV by an even more pathetic army of elderly people: church organists, those who ran boarding establishments for middle-class children, fencing masters, governesses, spinsters, and widows (often of soldiers), *rentiers* and pensioners, *gargotiers,* chemists, music teachers, instrument makers, retired lawyers. All these were driven back to provinces they had left twenty or thirty years before and now sought a family charity hardly likely to be forthcoming from relatives who had long abandoned them for dead. Either way it was a matter of life or death for such people: if they stayed in Paris they were likely to die of cold or of starvation —these are the sort of people who are found dead in attic rooms forced open by locksmiths during the winters of 1794 and 1795, and of whom the *officiers de santé,* called by the *commissaire,* observe: *Vus son grand âge et la grande misère du tems, est mort de mort naturelle.*[3] The decision whether to stay in Paris or to throw oneself on the uncertainties of family charity was usually a choice between places to die.[4]

[1] A.N. F7 4774 35 d 3 (Marino). Jean-Jacques Marino, inspecteur des garnis, is denounced by the comité of Bonne-Nouvelle, 12 germinal an II: '. . . Nous avons su que Marino étoit en fonctions pour arrêter les femmes publiques, ne faisant arrêter que celles qui étoient indigentes, tandis que celles qui étoient plus à leur aise n'étoient point arrêtés au moyen de ce qu'elles régaloient Marino. . . .' See also *Monsieur Nicolas,* iv. 2014: '. . . Maman m'a répondu qu'il valait mieux un Espion, afin d'être plus sûrement averties, en cas d'enlèvemens; que c'était un moyen de se faire bien venir de la Police, qui nous donne à certains espions, comme on donne à d'autres l'escroquage de certains billards. . . . Elle a répété que la Police *aimait* que nous eussions des Espions . . . souteneurs ordinaires des Filles un peu au-dessus de celles abandonnées aux Gardes-Françaises. . . .' Ibid. iv. 2221: '. . . La Police (dit Nannette) a sans doute ses raisons pour nous rendre la vie la plus dure qu'elle peut. . . . Le pis, c'est le fait-chanter des Espions. Aussi plusieurs s'abonnent-elles à l'Inspecteur, pour n'en point avoir. . . .'

[2] See note H, p. 362.

[3] A.P.P. A/A 61, 62, 95–8, 187–8, 199, 202, 219, 221.

[4] A.N. F11 1178, 1181, 1182, 1183, 1185, 1186, 1221, 1236, 1239, 1241, 1242 (Subsistances an IV, Commission des Secours).

8. RURAL MIGRATIONS

This movement away from the town—partly spontaneous, always encouraged, and in some cases enforced by the urban authorities, to relieve pressure on food supplies and charity—would happen at the very time when many poor villagers began to invade the towns, in search of food or admission to urban *hospices*.[1] Dearth was always likely to set people on the roads, in one direction or another, and the increased pressure on the normal urban or village markets could only aggravate a situation that *ab initio* might not have been disastrous. During the great famines of the seventeenth century many landless peasants, vagrants, and even smallholders had died on the roads, before reaching the hoped-for urban market. In eighteenth-century conditions nothing so dramatic occurred, but, just as it was the instinctive reaction of every community to hold on to its grain and to prevent it from moving, so one of the principal concerns of the authorities was to persuade or force people to stay put. Charity and relief could only effectively be organized on a local basis, at a level where people would be personally known to the bakers and the municipal or royal authorities. (This was why the Prefects of 1812 were so anxious to see that the roving armies of vagrants were rapidly broken up and their components sent back to their own towns or villages.)[2]

Furthermore, in times of dearth, travellers were given short shrift and were made most unwelcome. It was suggested that no one could be travelling for avowable purposes, they were the object of even more suspicion than usual, and no one was prepared to help them, other than to speed them foodless on their way, as in each recurrent crisis the unfortunate transport workers found to their cost.[3] Also large numbers of people on the roads—especially whole families, with their wretched carts, their shapeless bundles, their hordes of half-naked children and their faces of desperation—increased the danger of disorder and panic. As in the *Exode* of 1940, rumour and fear walked with the traveller, engulfing each locality as it was traversed by an ever-increasing army of want.

[1] *Terreur et subsistances*, pp. 307–42: 'Disette et mortalité: la crise de l'an III et de l'an IV à Rouen.'

[2] See the previous section, pp. 104–9.

[3] R. C. Cobb, 'Le Mouvement revendicatif parmi les bateliers de l'Oise et de la Marne au cours de l'hiver 1793–94', in *Revue d'Histoire économique et sociale*, xxxii, 1954.

Why were they on the roads? Because they had left behind them starvation and pestilence, because they had heard that ahead of them there was abundance, that beyond the next chain of hills dearth was something unknown. Travellers coming the other way had told them so. During the 1812 crisis, the Prefects became alarmed at the number of delegations that came to Paris to depict to the Minister of the Interior the plight of their *administrés* and to plead for relief in money or in kind; and, on 9 June, Fouché wrote to the Minister: '. . . Vous êtes instruit que plusieurs municipalités de quelques-uns des Départemens qui, relativement aux subsistances, se trouvent dans une position plus difficile, ont pris le parti d'envoyer à Paris des députations chargées de présenter aux Ministres de S.M. des pétitions plus ou moins indiscrètes, et toutes portant l'empreinte de la plus dangereuse exagération. Ces députations répandent sur leur route, dans les auberges, et sèment dans la capitale, les bruits les plus alarmans. . . .'[1] The main purpose of the whole system of *livrets*, *patentes*, and internal passports was to cut down on any untoward immigration towards the cities. The authorities, however, themselves contributed to such migrations; in their anxiety to remove from Paris, not only the usual 'floating population'—assessed by a recent historian as normally reaching the hundred thousand mark[2]—but also those residents who had fallen below the subsistence level, they rounded up and drove out beggars and seasonal labourers, as well as hordes of children—girls and boys whose ages ranged from five to fourteen[3]—delivering passports to anyone who claimed a family prepared to feed them.

The ideal solution was to prevent such people from getting into the city in the first place and to ensure at the same time that as many as possible of those who were engaged in non-productive work or had no work at all got out. At the same time, stringent measures were introduced to prevent those who lived just outside the city boundaries from taking bread or any other article of primary necessity through the barriers. These measures were in fact particularly productive of riot, as they increased the resentment of the normally under-privileged *faubourien*, driving him into

[1] A.N. F11 704 (crise de 1812, Paris).
[2] Jacques Godechot, *La Chute de la Bastille* (Paris, 1965). These figures are confirmed by a report of 15 Floréal year IV which refers to 'plus de 100,000 malheureux' who are dependent on the free distribution of bread (A.N. F11 1183). [3] A.P.P. A/A 61-2 (Arcis) and 95-8 (Montagne).

alliance with the law-breaker and forcing him to the head of sedition. They were also likely to be self-defeating. As the inhabitants of Vincennes, most of them extremely poor, could not go into Paris and bring bread out with them, the obvious solution was to go and live in Paris until the crisis was over. This would account for the newcomers in the three Sections of the *faubourg*. A *jardinier* who, after living in Paris for twenty years, had moved out to Belleville to be nearer his place of work, stated, in the year IV, that he had returned to Paris with his family as a result of the crisis to be sure of obtaining a regular supply of bread.[1] More generally, it was unwise thus to antagonize people who were in the habit of regularly supplying the Paris markets with fresh fruit and vegetables from the market gardens of the suburbs. 'Plusieurs rapports de la surveillance générale et nombre de procès-verbaux', wrote the *Commission administrative* to the *commissaires*, on 27 Germinal year III,

indiquent que . . . des citoyens amenant à Paris des denrées de première nécessité sont exposés à chaque instant à être pillés par une multitude d'individus qui se croient autorisés par les circonstances à ne rien respecter. . . . Nous croyons devoir t'inviter . . . à exposer aux citoyens qu'il est de leur intérêt de ne point souffrir qu'il soit fait de violence aux habitans des campagnes . . . qui apporteroient des denrées à Paris, que les citoyens, ne pouvant pas compter sur la protection des loix . . . ne voudroient plus rien apporter et n'apporteroient plus rien effectivement dans cette grande cité, où il est si important d'entretenir des relations avec les communes voisines surtout pour les subsistances. . . .[2]

As far as public transport was concerned (*coches* and *diligences*), the numerous paper checks imposed by royal, revolutionary, and municipal authorities might meet with some success. During the Terror many suspects were thus caught, in the dangerous stage of seeking safety in a place where they were strangers; in the year III also, *mathevons* and other similar refugees were often similarly caught on the road. But there was no real remedy to the steady flow of orphan children (perhaps as many were set on the roads by their parents) prepared for any form of mischief and proficient in most forms of theft, nor to that of poor peasant families who walked by night and slept in barns or woods by day, carrying their possessions

[1] A.N. F11 1812 (Pierre Hudelle, Section du Temple, à la Commission des Secours, 5 germinal an IV). He is the father of seven children, the eldest aged nine.

[2] A.P.P. A/A 96 (commission administrative au commissaire de la Section des Buttes des Moulins, 27 germinal an III).

on their backs, and who, by ruse or as a result of complicity, would sooner or later find an opportunity of getting through the barriers. France had a population that, in its vast majority, walked; and there is no one more difficult to control than the pedestrian.

9. DEARTH AND SOCIAL DISUNITY

So the lines of division between the two camps are not always easy to distinguish, and dearth, by increasing mobility along with vagrancy ('Les professions qui donnent le plus de vagabonds sont les tailleurs, les cordonniers, les perruquiers & les cuisiniers . . .',[1] all trades badly hit by the year III crisis), added further to the varied and elaborate hierarchy of need. The Parisian artisan would think of himself as on the edge of famine or ruin (especially when the daily loaf, if obtainable, took up 70 per cent of his budget), but there were plenty of others much worse off. At the bottom of the scale were the forester or shepherd in a mountain area or the fisherman of a Channel port to whom even fish was denied, because wartime regulations forbade the operations of the fishing fleets in areas of English naval activity. In between came the *faubourien*, neglected by all the established authorities, but well placed to divert the sources of urban food supply, and enjoying the freedom of a community long organized for law-breaking.

Dearth introduced new, unaccustomed hierarchies. The prisoner (in the Versailles prison, during the year III, he was fed on cats),[2] the debtor, even the *galérien*, were *privilégiés* of a kind—at least when compared with the urban artisan—for their daily bread, of a sort, was ensured to them by the Republic. One had to enjoy some measure of freedom in order to die of hunger. Even the wretched soldier of the year III was fed—or fed himself. He had the advantage of belonging either to an army of occupation, in which case food and drink were for the taking, or of serving in France, in which case he would be keeping the people down, and no regime is going to allow its forces of repression to go short. No one in the food or drink trade was likely to go desperately short either, as he would always have something to exchange for bread; while *revendeuses* branched into undreamt-of markets, by setting up in the

[1] *Le Tableau de Paris*, xi. 7.
[2] A.C. Versailles 1 D 1 79 (registre de la municipalité, séance du 15 thermidor an III).

illegal sale on the street of stale or adulterated bread, the scrapings of the bakeries.[1] Again, no young girl was obliged to starve; and many told the *commissaires*, in the course of the year III, that they had become temporary prostitutes *pour avoir du pain*.[2]

Nothing more forcibly illustrated the basic social and economic disunity of *la sans-culotterie* than one of these great cyclical crises. Bakers, who were *sans-culottes*, though hedged in by the strictest regulations, might make enormous profits. They worked by night, and though, in periods of shortage, they were forbidden to make pastries and could only bake one type of bread, there was little to stop them from doing just what they pleased. In the years III and IV, while the poor had to make do with a bread that was scarcely eatable—and, at times, actually poisonous—the well-to-do could generally find a baker who would keep them supplied with the pure wheaten loaf. The police did their best, multiplying visits to bakers' ovens, but there were so many bakeries to watch, and the skilled craftsman could always find a place to hide his illegal manufacture.

Dearth, such an appalling tragedy for the urban poor, would also be the opportunity for the ingenious few, not only among the producers and speculators, but in certain fringe occupations of the *petit peuple*. A developing black market (*forêt noire*) would bring a temporary return of occupation to the old-time smuggler and to an army of intermediaries, drawn mostly from the transport trades and from the *faubouriens*, while anyone who had easy access to stolen wood, peat, and coal had no need to fear for his daily bread. As the public prosecutor of Le Havre was to observe at the height of the crisis of the year III, it was not only the farmers' wives who displayed unaccustomed jewellery; the wives of horse-dealers, the prostitutes of Sanvic and Graville, were going about wearing two or three striking watches, while widows of army officers parted with their jewellery, their furniture, and their best clothes.[3] Never, at any time, did *la brocante* come so much into its own, and one effect of dearth was to increase enormously the number of temporary *brocanteurs* and *fripiers*. Dearth was a challenge to the sharp and the cunning, who put it to good effect, not only to remove themselves from the level of want, but also temporarily to improve their economic situation.

[1] See note I, p. 362.
[2] A.P.P. A/A 95 to 98 (commissaire de police de la Section de la Butte-des-Moulins, ans III et IV).   [3] *Terreur et subsistances*, p. 246.

Vidocq has much to say about the activities of what he calls *l'armée sans troupe* or *l'armée roulante* in Lille and along the no man's land of the old frontier, in the lush years of 1795 and 1796.[1] Those who had only the force of their arm to recommend them did not need to walk in want; they could kill and rob the travelling *notable*; they could murder the *filles de confiance* of Paris jewellers and then clear out the contents of their workshops.[2] Beggary, charity, or slow starvation were by no means the only alternatives, and if we have spoken of 'two camps' it is primarily because contemporaries—especially in the conditions of 1795—saw themselves and the others in that light. In the south, the Thermidorian *société* of Marseille, referring to the divisive politics of this unhappy region, describes France as divided into *deux tribus diamétralement opposées*, and what it called for was what Marseille was to get for the next five years: a tribal war. (No wonder contemporary pamphleteers and polemicists were always talking about 'Iroquois' and 'Hottentots', 'hyènes' and 'tigres d'Afrique'.)[3] In the north, a poor clerk employed, one would have thought rather strategically, with the Paris *Commission des Approvisionnements* divides the nation more suitably for this area into the fat and the thin, making it quite clear that while he would have liked to have belonged to the former, he did in fact belong to the latter.[4] More than anything else, it was this sense of grievance on the one side, of callous indifference on the other,[5] that gave to dearth its bitter social content.

[1] *Les Chauffeurs du Nord*, iii. 8: '. . . Les fripons . . . comprirent que le moyen le plus simple de gagner du premier coup la confiance . . . consistait à revêtir l'habit respecté de l'officier républicain, et peu à peu les épaulettes s'accrurent en nombre et en or. . . .'

[2] A.P.P. A/A 187–8 (commissaire de police de la Section du Muséum for three unsolved murders of this kind in the course of the spring of 1795).

[3] See the section on the White Terror. See also Restif, *Les Tableaux*. (Le Vicomte dit) '. . . Je passois tout à l'heure par la petite rue Sainte-Anastase; j'ai vu un mari et une femme enceinte qui se battoient! le sujet de leur querelle étoit une fille de 10 ans que la mère avoit corrigée & qui étoit allée se plaindre à son père, maître tonnelier. Cet homme est venu furieux se jeter sur sa femme . . . j'ai compris que c'étoit un homme brutal, fort violent, qui n'avait pas le cœur mauvais, & auquel l'éducation seule avoit manqué. . . . Je frémis, dit la Marquise, et l'on nous parle des Hottentots, continue le Marquis! dans la même ville, au sein d'une capitale policée, nous avons des Hottentots à notre porte. . . .'

[4] A.N. F11 1182: '. . . Les autres sont devenus si gros et si gras qu'à peine ils peuvent se remuer, et moi devenu si maigre qu'à peine je puis marcher. . . .'

[5] A.N. F15 252 (8 germinal an III): 'La Tyrannie a desseché tous les canaux de la bienfaisance, et s'il est encore des riches, ce sont des riches *modernes* pour qui la bienfaisance est une déité à qui ils n'ont pas encore offert des vœux. . . .'

PART TWO

POPULAR ATTITUDES AND THE POLITICS
OF DEARTH

'Nous subissons les supplices de Tantale, car nous
sommes en train de mourir au sein de l'abondance.'
(*Any petition of the year II or the year III*)

10. DEARTH AND VERBAL EXAGGERATION

'DEARTH' and 'famine' are dangerous words. Used by the common people, they immediately evoke horrors as well remembered
as cholera or the plague. They are words productive of panic, fear,
and disaster. As popular language tends to exaggeration and is
notoriously inaccurate especially where figures are concerned (a
riot or an epidemic will always result in *hundreds*, even *thousands*,
of deaths, never in ten or fewer, and *une vingtaine* would appear to
be the lowest numerical unit in the popular vocabulary of dearth
and terror), both dearth and famine are likely to be difficult to
define in eighteenth-century terms, if we go to the people for our
evidence. Popular reports, magnified by pedlars, by travellers,
always pleased to obtain a briefly respectful and attentive audience
as the prophets of doom, statistically magnified, are as wildly inaccurate with respect to events: an entire town burnt to the ground,
its gutters running with blood; rivers obstructed by corpses, or
changing colour with blood; the poor falling down dead in the
street from hunger—there is always someone who has a friend who
has just witnessed such a thing; mothers screaming to be killed
and for their babies to be killed rather than left to die on their
feet of hunger—and somehow it is much worse thus to be
exposed to death standing up; the poor people roaming the
countryside and reduced to the condition of wild beasts, eating
bark and roots, acorns and berries, and the food of pigs; women
struck down by the sabres of repression while suckling a baby
—or two babies (why not?) at each breast; hundreds of corpses
removed from the hospitals; thousands of corpses taken from

the morgue and furtively disposed of by night, in quicklime; whole families throwing themselves into the wild waters—they are always wild—of the Seine or the Rhône;[1] tens of thousands of bushels of grain sent abroad through underground passages, to the enemies of France; three hundred people falling ill and dying, after eating rice; five hundred people struck down by *le pain maudit*—a further tribute to the paramount importance of bread. This is the language of fear and of dearth, the language too of women, which can be so easily transformed into the language of screaming hate and of incitement to murder.[2] And as the problem of dearth is so strongly conditioned by popular assumptions and exists, in fact, as much in the mind as as an agricultural or economic reality, it is necessary to reckon with this verbal exaggeration. Only thus can one interpret it—and it would be unwise to interpret it literally—and one must always bear in mind the effects of such verbal intemperance in worsening a situation already precarious.

In the popular vocabulary, even pride can be expressed in terms of food. The narrow—and, for that reason, all the more important—margin that separates bare subsistence from want is commonly expressed in the phrase: 'Nous avons du pain à la maison.' Anyone who gives this answer, generally with a touch of indignation, when questioned by the *commissaire* on his means of existence, implies that he is not a pauper; 'avoir du pain à la maison' is the ultimate and simplest formulation of the *sans-culotte*'s much cherished economic independence.[3]

The national authorities were well aware of the power of words and were extremely reluctant to use the expression 'dearth' at all, much less 'famine', banished from the administrative vocabulary, at least at national level, since 1709. At District or municipal level, on the other hand, there is no such reticence, and 'famine' is bandied about in reports from below upwards by *agents nationaux* or *maires*, in 1793, 1794, and 1795, to describe local conditions and try to obtain relief in kind or in money from the Commission des Subsistances, or from its Thermidorian successor, the Commission du Commerce et des Approvisionnements. This is the one subject on which local authorities can be relied upon to be strenuously over-pessimistic and at the same time to depict conditions in the neighbouring District or town in deliriously over-optimistic terms. 'Famine here, abundance just over the border'—this is the tune to

[1] See note J, p. 362.   [2] See note K, p. 363.   [3] See note L, p. 364.

which it goes, in hundreds of *rapports décadaires*, from the spring of 1793 to the first months of the Directory.[1] It is a fearful tribute to the gravity of the crisis of the year III that at the beginning of the year IV the Commission d'Agriculture sent out to every *administration cantonale* a printed circular, *Question No. 170* of which asks: 'La cherté des subsistances n'en a-t-elle pas fait périr un grand nombre de vos administrés les moins aisés ?'[2] But the Commission is careful to refer to the high cost of food and not to mention shortage.

It would be easy to accuse the authorities of callousness and hypocrisy, or to suggest that they were refusing to look facts in the face, just as the Indian Federal Government has often been criticized for calling a famine a 'drought';[3] but 'famine' is not a word readily to be employed, or very easy to define. Can one speak of a famine when people are reported to be dying of hunger in garrets or falling down in the streets from malnutrition? If so, eighteenth-century France was almost always in a state of famine, for every day someone would die from an epidemic to the effects of which years of malnutrition had made him more vulnerable. Can one speak of famine when a particular geographical area, poor, over-populated, marshy, with few grainlands and no grain reserves, is feeling the effects of acute shortage? If so, according to the local authorities, famine was endemic in certain areas of the Ardennes, in the hamlets of the forest of Ervy, in the Aube, and in many other places. To proclaim famine conditions is to give them official recognition and thus, at least in the initial stages, to aggravate them. The reluctance of successive Indian Governments to re-introduce the old Famine Code is as much the result of common sense as a refusal to face ugly facts. Even in eighteenth-century France, where local authorities were so prone to plead famine on the slightest hint of shortage, some provincial administrators

---

[1] *Terreur et subsistances*, pp. 211–19.

[2] A.N. F10 240 (Commission d'Agriculture).

[3] A.N. F11 1185 (Subsistances an IV): '. . . Il faut manger pour vivre. . . . Que font les Peuples pendant ces longues calamités ? Ils souffrent, ils meurent. Ils voyent souvent renaître ces longues années de famine qui ont rendu si célèbres les années 1709, 1725, 1741. Le gouvernement s'excuse aux yeux du peuple . . . en disant froidement: *C'est l'intempérie des saisons.* . . . Il est certain que des fléaux passagers ont nui quelquefois à l'abondance des moissons . . .' (Braban & Plancher, au Directoire, 1er prairial an IV). There is a similar reluctance to employ the word 'famine' in Alletz, ii (262), 'FAMINE. Voir *Disette*'. Under DISETTE', one reads: 'Ce terme s'applique spécialement aux grains.'

protest at the word as reflecting on their own competence and as in some way derogatory to the reputation of the province.

The description most generally accepted for a region habitually dependent on imports of grain was the adjective *disetteux*—'liable to shortage'. This was altogether a safer word, since it did not imply neglect on the part of the local administrators. A region normally well supplied was described as *fromenteux*. This reticence was not only based on caution; it also contained an element of shame. 'Famine' was not a word that rightly belonged to *notre âge éclairé*: its proper place was in the sanguinary reign of the tyrant Louis XIV. The most favoured expression for the various problems of production, grain circulation, supply, and provisioning was the over-all phrase *le problème des subsistances*. This covered food problems in general, but more especially those of marketing and distribution (more exactly described as *les arrivages*) which was the weakest, most delicate link in the chain that brought the grain from the fields to the baker's oven in town or village.[1]

II. POPULAR ATTITUDES TO FOOD

The common people took little interest in these technicalities, which were not their concern. Even in normal times, they ate badly, at least in the north of France,[2] and often had to make do for meat with the left-overs and offal that could be obtained from the *triperies*.[3] But this did not mean that they did not want to eat well. One of the baits offered by intelligent recruiting sergeants to induce young Paris apprentices to sign up with the old Royal Army was the description of an ordinary day's menu enjoyed by those who wore the King's colours: 'Mes amis, la soupe, l'entrée, le rôti, voilà l'ordinaire du régiment; mais je ne vous trompe pas, le pâté et le vin d'Arbois, voilà l'extraordinaire; je ne vous trompe pas, vous n'aurez ni vin d'Arbois, ni pâté, mais l'ordinaire: la soupe, l'entrée, le rôti, la salade que j'oubliois. . . .'[4] According to Mercier,

[1] *Terreur et subsistances*, pp. 211–19.

[2] '. . . Aussi n'y a-t-il de pays où la nourriture soit plus mauvaise pour le petit peuple. Dans les pensions, dans les séminaires, les jeunes gens crient la faim toute l'année . . .' (*Le Tableau de Paris*, xi. 154).

[3] '. . . Elles sont à l'extrémité des fauxbourgs. . . . Les pauvres gens achètent ces menus après leur cuisson, & les coins des rues les offrent dans des paniers restaurateurs . . . objets peu agréables à la vue; mais la faim en haillons n'est point délicate . . .' (Ibid. x. 245).

[4] Ibid. xi. 198.

the promise of so much splendour was enough to get thirty apprentices of twenty-one signed up there and then; the *racoleurs* knew
their business. The *petit peuple* may have had to put up with the
sort of Sunday fare described by Restif[1] but there is no reason to
believe that they were content with this.

In the favourable circumstances of the year II local *commissaires*,
searching the houses and the farms of the well-to-do, saw to it that
they were well looked after by their involuntary hosts. To sit down
at a well-stocked table, and eat and drink to ribald remarks at the
expense of the wives and daughters of *ci-devants* or of *gros bourgeois*,
was not only an object lesson in equality—rather like the liberties
so joyfully expressed during the *Bal des Quat' Z'Arts*, when the
dancers ate out of other people's plates in the most expensive restaurants in Paris;[2] it was also a pleasure and a recompense for
political virtue. Perhaps nothing in the whole Terror shocked the
Thermidorians more than these *agapes*, and their complaints were
based on the feeling that the common people had no right to eat
well and that good food was wasted on them.[3]

When, by 1797, higher wages and the return of good harvests
improved his condition, the urban artisan set his sights higher,
leaving 'le chou au lard de côté pour la poularde en cresson . . . la
pinte d'étain . . . pour la bouteille cachetée'.[4] If the *sans-culotte*
expressed his political pride through his pike, the visible emblem
of his citizenhood, his pride as an independent artisan who owed
nothing to any man, would take the form of a well-stocked larder,

---

[1] '. . . Boire d'un vin détestable, & manger d'un ragoût de cheval équarissé . . .'
(*Le Paysan*).

[2] '. . . Dans les quartiers à populace, les dîners civiques furent de véritables
orgies où les convives finissaient les uns par rouler sous la table, les autres par en
sortir un peu moins ivres, mais encore assez pour se répandre dans les quartiers
tranquilles, se placer sans façon aux tables qu'ils trouvaient mieux servies que les
leurs, s'y faisant servir d'autorité du vin, des liqueurs, embrassant les femmes de
force en leur tenant les propos les plus obscènes . . .' (Duval, *Souvenirs Thermidoriens*).

[3] Guyot, a member of the comité of Gannat, is accused, in Vendémiaire
year IV, 'd'en avoir fait excès à son repas, d'en avoir ainsi consommé plus de
100 bouteilles, d'avoir fait main basse et mangé toute la volaille, même de vieux
pigeons . . . de s'être fait faire des repas recherchés, donnant à cet effet im-
périeusement des ordres pour que l'homme d'affaires lui fît faire bonne chère,
consommant les comestibles qui étoient dans la . . . maison, d'avoir reproché à
l'homme d'affaires . . . qu'il ne le régaloit pas suffisamment . . . attendu qu'il
avoit été accoutumé de bien vivre . . . d'y avoir passé presque tout son temps à
table à boire et à manger . . .' (A.N. F1b II Allier I, 12 vendémiaire an IV).

[4] *Le Nouveau Paris*.

a full plate, and a full bread-bin. For food was the most apparent sign of *une honnête suffisance*. These were not people who enjoyed eating like brutes; popular prejudice against the potato, still strong in the year II, was based on the feeling that it was a food fit only for pigs or for the *hospices*. (It was food that distinguished the *sans-culotte* from the pauper and the domestic servant, sub-citizens in the popular view because they were unable to feed themselves.) In the year III, on top of genuine hardship, there was the humiliation of being reduced to eating roots, berries, nettles, dandelion leaves, and the scourings of the forest 'que l'on se dispute aux bêtes'.[1] To be shown on all fours, eating the grass off the ground—one of the recurrent images of the year III—was too much altogether for popular self-esteem. As soon as matters improved, the wage-earner would spend more money on food than on anything else; the traditional Paris working man has always been a big eater.

In normal conditions, then, *les subsistances* meant good, varied, and plentiful food—anything that was within reach of the working class or artisan's budget. In times of dearth, it would indicate much more basic things: how to keep alive, how to find the money to feed a large family, how to discover food when it was being hidden by wicked and pitiless men, how to find time to leave the city and wander from farm to farm in search of bread and dairy produce, how to find something to exchange that the farmer might accept. It implied, in the last resort, the right to live, *le droit à la subsistance*. This is how the *sans-culottes* envisaged the problem and in September 1793 they took it one stage further, proclaiming that 'les produits du sol appartiennent à la Nation'.[2] The same concept dominated their opposition to agricultural individualism, to the landowners' dream of *la liberté de la culture*.

No expression recurs more frequently than *les subsistances* in official correspondence from below upwards, and, on the printed questionnaires sent from above downwards, in 1793 and in the years II to IV, the word figures under the more general rubric of *esprit public*. Clearly, the only sort of 'public opinion' to which the

---

[1] A petition from Rocroi refers to 'des aliments dérobés aux bestiaux . . .'. From the Creuse comes the cry: '. . . Il nous est impossible de continuer de manger des glands. . . .' In a village in the Nièvre, the inhabitants live 'de fruits verds, d'oseille sauvage, d'horties . . .'. In Rouen, the poor are fed on 'orties et herbes'. The population of Fécamp is 'réduits à ne manger que du son et des herbes . . .' (A.N. F11 1776B and D III 270 d 13). All these reports are from the year III. [2] See note M, p. 364.

Revolutionary Government was especially sensitive was precisely that concerned with food procurement and distribution. Nothing else, apart from *émigrés rentrés* and *prêtres réfractaires*, appeared dangerous enough to be given the permanent honours of an official form. The word *subsistances* in fact takes up almost as much space as that of *police*.

12. *SANS-CULOTTE* INSTITUTIONS AND THE *PROBLÈME DES SUBSISTANCES*

It is the same in the minutes of popular institutions: *sociétés populaires, sociétés sectionnaires,* even *comités de surveillance,* both during the period of *sans-culotte* rule and during the Thermidorian Reaction. The subject was in fact one in which the local authorities of both periods displayed a common interest, though their solutions were often radically different. The Thermidorian committees, which were generally composed like the *comités de bienfaisance* of well-to-do *notables* and lawyers,[1] naturally did not look with favour on *sans-culotte* remedies for the problems of provisioning and at first tended to favour the farmers; but under the impact of a rapidly worsening situation even the committees of the year III began to revert to force, denouncing the egoism of the big farmers and the extension of the *forêt noire,* the contemporary expression for the black market in foodstuffs. By the spring of 1795, the Dieppe Committee was calling before it recalcitrant farmers from the District who had failed to carry out requisitions for the local market, upbraiding them for their indifference to the fate of their urban 'brothers', and sending them to prison for periods of two to three days.[2]

In Orléans too there was a similar evolution,[3] while the *comités* of Dijon, Beaune, Arnay, and Lons-le-Saunier devoted much o their time, in the winter and early spring, to discussing how best to overcome rural unwillingness to keep the urban markets provided.[4] Indeed, it would be no exaggeration to suggest that there was a partial resumption of the economic Terror in Ventôse year

---

[1] See the composition of the Thermidorian *comité* of le Havre, *Terreur et subsistances,* pp. 221–52.   [2] See note N, p. 365.

[3] Georges Lefebvre, *Études orléanaises,* ii. 000.

[4] Arch. Côte-d'Or L 2602*, 2604* (comité de Beaune), 2658*, 2660* (comité de Dijon), 2582* (comité d'Arnay), Arch. Jura (Grand registre de dénonciations du comité de Lons).

III, at the very time when the *comités* were going out of existence;[1] and measures of force were in operation in the countryside of many Districts under the aegis of urban *agents nationaux*, till Fructidor of the same year.

Left to themselves, *sociétaires*, once they were through the rigmarole of the *Bulletin des Lois* and reading or drawing up congratulatory addresses, settled down to discuss the market situation. It was a subject that was considered so important as to merit discussion at least once a week. In Dieppe, for instance, when the *comités sectionnaires* first decided to form a *comité central*,[2] a rough agenda for its week's work was drawn up, to guide the newly appointed members: *Monday*—business outstanding; *Tuesday*—'que l'objet des subsistances, ainsi que les denrées, soit l'ordre du jour le mardi . . .'; *Wednesday*—arrests (and a majority of these, in this District, were of farmers who had refused to supply the market) and petitions for release; *Thursday*—general meeting with the *comités sectionnaires*; *Friday*—discussion of the decisions made at the general meeting; *Saturday*—minutes.[3] It was soon apparent, however, at least in this port, that one day a week was not enough, and throughout the winter *les subsistances* creep in on time set aside for other matters. Equally, when the central committee supplies lists of those imprisoned in the *maison d'arrêt*, in the ten-day returns for the year II and the year III, after the names of those arrested for failure to discharge their obligations to the local market on time or for having taken part in the riots of Floréal and Prairial, year III, there is the single, explanatory abbreviation '*subs.*' to explain the cause of their detention.[4] When a word becomes an abbreviation, especially in a revolutionary regime, it can really be said that it has acquired *droit de cité*.

Discussions that could be classified under this broad heading took up even more time than personal denunciations; and they could be approached from the most unexpected angles, as almost

---

[1] The *comité* of Arnay met for the last time on 20 Ventôse; those of Lons on the 25th, Beaune and Dieppe on the 29th, Dijon on the 30th.

[2] The decision to form *comités sectionnaires* was taken at an *assemblée générale* of the Première Section on 22 September 1793. On the 27th the *comités* voted to form a *comité central* which, it was stated, 'employera tous les moyens qui seront en son pouvoir pour faire renaître l'abondance dans la halle de Dieppe . . .' (Arch. Seine-Maritime L 5328).

[3] Ibid. (Projet de règlement).

[4] Arch. Seine-Maritime L 5216 (comité de Dieppe, an III) and L 5329 (ibid., correspondance).

any topic—even *déchristianisation*—could be envisaged *sous le rapport des subsistances*. If there were complaints about the state of the roads or the waterways, it was because grain did not reach the local market quickly enough and the local engineer must be harried into activity; or, if there were no convenient road, then the District must be induced to supply the money and labour for its construction. The frequent denunciations of municipal authorities were based on the accusation that they were not showing sufficient vigour in applying the *maximum* or in using force against the surrounding countryside; the *maires* of both Dieppe and Gannat were denounced, under this count, in the year II, with fatal consequences for the latter, guillotined in Moulins.[1]

The even more frequent attacks on the local authorities of surrounding villages derived from the belief—more than a belief, a certainty—*qu'elles mettoient des entraves aux arrivages*.[2] The demand that *apôtres civiques* should be sent into the villages of the hinterland was given greater urgency by the need that they should appeal to the countryman to come to the help *des frères de la ville*.[3] Refractory priests were accused above all of attempting to persuade large farmers to delay carrying out the *réquisitions* imposed on them by the District authorities. With the advent of the Terror, far less attention was devoted to the pursuit of the politically dangerous than to punishing recalcitrant farmers; an ingenious terrorist from Lons-le-Saunier had his own solution in this respect: 'pour expédier la besogne plus vite, il falloit établir une guillotine à eau, qu'il en connoissoit l'emplacement qui étoit auprès du pont neuf au bout de la rue neuve avec un puits de six pieds de profondeur pour recevoir le sang. . . .'[4] The only *mauvais propos* likely to attract immediate and vengeful attention were those relating to food problems and economic controls: a very common cause of arrest is 'd'avoir mal parlé du maximum'—in *sans-culotte* ears a form of blasphemy.[5] Most of the activities of the *armées révolutionnaires* and of similar bodies were directed to improving the supply of urban markets by a mixture of force and threats.[6] Local attitudes, not only towards the villages of the surrounding countryside, which

---

[1] See note O, p. 365.

[2] Arch. Seine-Maritime L 5216 (comité de Dieppe, séances des 25 frimaire, 9 frimaire, 16 nivôse, 3 pluviôse an III) *A.C.* Dieppe D I 6 (registre de la municipalité, séances des 18 germinal, 24 germinal, 23 floréal, 2 prairial, 16 prairial III).   [3] *Les Armées révolutionnaires*, ii. 451–63.   [4] See note P, p. 365.

[5] *Les Armées révolutionnaires*, p. 419.   [6] Ibid., pp. 451–62.

were reminded that the best way for them to express their revolutionary patriotism was to carry out the requisitions on the dot and show an appropriate zeal in the supply of the local urban market, but also towards neighbouring towns, generally seen as possible rivals in the procurement of food (there is an excellent example of this in the prolonged strife between the rival and successive *chefs-lieux* of a District of the Haute-Garonne, Beaumont, and Grenade, and one could find similar examples of inter-urban 'food wars' in any Department in the years II and III),[1] were dominated by this concern with provisioning.

The committees, too, showed so much zeal in keeping a strict watch on local inns and lodging-houses, not because, as they were supposed to be, they were greatly concerned about the comings and goings of strangers and foreigners, but because every traveller represented an extra mouth to feed; they were less interested in the travellers than in what they ate, and they were quick to believe gossip about the copious menus that unpatriotic *aubergistes* were said to be putting before more prosperous-looking customers. Even a *représentant du peuple*, in his full travelling kit and surrounded by a small court of secretaries, *commissaires*, *délégués*, and patriotic girls, was not entirely safe from scrutiny of this kind. Vigilant members of the local *comité* watched each mouthful into the portion of the sovereign people and reported in detail to their colleagues on the composition of the great man's meal. It was important, in terms of local prestige, to be seen at the *proconsul*'s table, but it was a duty to note what he ate.[2] They subjected the local prison to a similarly exacting scrutiny; it seemed a pity to waste good food on unpatriotic stomachs. *Les subsistances* were no doubt a right, but they had to be deserved.

After Thermidor and the rapid worsening of the food situation throughout the autumn and winter of 1794 and the spring and summer of 1795, the problem takes up even more space if possible in the deliberations of bodies now purged of their *sans-culotte* elements.[3] The matter is discussed by the municipality of Dieppe

---

[1] Ibid., pp. 436, 551, 561, 574, 591–2.

[2] See note Q, p. 366.

[3] The new *comité* of Dieppe set up by Sautereau on 25 Vendémiaire year III is composed of 3 *hommes de loi*, 4 *cultivateurs propriétaires*, 2 *commerçants*, a *rentier*, a *cafetier*, and a shipowner (Arch. Seine-Maritime L 5216). The new municipality, formed the same day, contains no less than 16 *commerçants*, 2 *rentiers*, 2 *cabaretiers*, 2 *cordonniers*, a butcher, a joiner, a watchmaker, a manu-

in its sessions for 1 and 15 Fructidor year II; 19 and 28 Pluviôse; 17, 28 Ventôse; 4, 24, and 28 Germinal; 23 Floréal; 2 and 14 Prairial; and 12, 19 Messidor year III; by the committee on 25, 26, 27, 28, and 29 Frimaire, 16 Nivôse, and 3 Pluviôse year III.[1] With the deterioration increasingly visible on the local market, attention is directed towards outside help, and in the Midi and the Channel ports the movement of foreign shipping is closely noted, after the end of winter, almost every day. There are reports of a grain ship having left Tunis, help is on the way from Genoa, a merchant writes from Copenhagen that two shiploads of grain have been dispatched.

In their daily preoccupation with this relentless problem, the minutes of these narrowly parochial bodies extend beyond the familiar ring of villages which normally supply the market to include the Barbary powers, Genoa, Berne, Copenhagen, Hamburg, Altona, Wismar, Salonika, Lubeck, Charleston, and they reflect the immense hopes raised by the occupation of the Belgian Provinces and of Holland. In Dieppe, the talk is now not only of Bacqueville-en-Caux, but of Denmark, and in Le Havre the *notables* have one eye on the garrisons in the District de Montivilliers, another on their purchasing commissioners in Wismar.[2] Already at the time of Fleurus the immediate reaction of local *sans-culottes* in Lille, Douai, Cambrai, Béthune, Maubeuge, Valenciennes, in Charleville, Givet, Fumay, Rocroi, had been to rejoice in advance at the thought that the supposedly 'immense resources' of the *Provinces Belgiques* would soon be available for local consumption and that it was only a matter of a few weeks before their troubles were over. The *représentants* in the Nord and the Ardennes—those in Brussels were more reticent—had said as much, enjoining the local population to be patient and to await the arrival of the grain barges from Tournai and Courtrai and by the Meuse. Even victory was translated, immediately, into terms of food.[3] No won-

---

facturer, a chemist, a grocer, a *cordier*, a *compassier*, a *parfumeur*, a *peintre* and a *plafonnier* (Arch. Dieppe D I 5, registre de la municipalité). The new *comité* set up in Beaune on 27 Frimaire year III consists of 4 rural *propriétaires*, a *négotiant*, a *huissier*, a *charpentier* and a *perruquier* (Arch. Côte-d'Or L 2604*, registre du comité de Beaune).

[1] Arch. Seine-Maritime L 5228–9 (comité de Dieppe) and A.C. Dieppe D I 5, 6, and 7 (municipalité).   [2] *Terreur et subsistances*, pp. 221–55.

[3] '... Le général Dugommier est détenu sur son lit à la suite d'une blessure, sans cela il auroit déjà mis la récolte de la Catalogne à votre disposition', writes Roussillon, in Messidor year II, to the Committee of Public Safety (A.N. F11 1476B). See also *Terreur et subsistances*, pp. 243–381.

der culinary metaphors figure so large in the revolutionary vocabulary and in the language of the common people.[1] If the *sans-culotte*
had believed in a god, it would have been in a *dieu nourricier*; the
papier-mâché statue of the Supreme Being was made to hold an
ear of corn, even if the accompanying sphinx gave out only water;
and when *sans-culottes* talked of the wicked men *qui arrachoient le
pain à la bouche de leurs enfants*, they meant it quite literally, as if
they could see it happening.

13. DEARTH AS A TECHNICAL PROBLEM: PRODUCTIVITY AND SHORTAGE

B. A. Lenoir, writing in 1828, calculated that between 1776 and
that year, France had experienced five major dearths, three of which
had in certain areas reached the proportions of a full-scale famine.
In other words, a dearth occurred on an average every ten years,
with its usual accompaniments—hoarding, double or triple purchase, market riots, *arrêts*, and pillaging along the channels of
distribution, the consequent interruption of circulation, the use
of force against the grain rioter and the recalcitrant farmer, popular
fears for the future, appeals to the past (back to the prices of 1775
or September 1793), malnutrition, disease and epidemics, popular
credulity, feminine provocation and violence.[2] Even as he wrote,
Lenoir was convinced that France was due for a sixth experience
of this kind.

The dearths that attained something like national proportions
occurred in 1788–9, 1794–6, 1801–2, and 1816–17. In certain areas
of the north and north-east and in Upper Normandy,[3] a true
famine situation had prevailed in the winter of 1788 and the spring
and summer of 1789,[4] and, over a two-year cycle, from August
1794 to September 1796, famine conditions spread throughout
most of the country, with the exception of the Mediterranean belt

---

[1] See note R, p. 366.

[2] B. A. Lenoir, *De la probabilité d'une disette prochaine* (Paris, 1828).

[3] According to a letter written by Louis Niel, an *officier municipal*, on 26
Nivôse year II, Dieppe had undergone famine conditions in the first seven
months of 1789 (Arch. Seine-Maritime L 5240, comité de Dieppe, correspondance).

[4] There had been a severe famine, accompanied by a murderous epidemic, in
Fumay and its neighbourhood, from August 1788 to July 1789 (A.N. F8 18,
Hygiène, Ardennes).

and the Valley of the Garonne,[1] with results comparable in severity to the great catastrophe of 1709. The years III and IV represented, in fact, the last great famine in French history. Dearths had recurred regularly, before these dates, throughout the previous period of 1710 to 1774; four Parisian writers recall particularly those of 1725 and 1741.[2] They were caused by partial grain failures and the improvidence of the government, which, however, could never calculate the total yield of any harvest, given the sources of information then available, before November, so that the winter would be well on before it could set about measures of relief and seek alternative supplies. Other causes were population pressure, poor agriculture, poor or slow communications, and popular fears. The dearths were probably worst when they coincided with, or immediately followed, periods of war, as in 1762, 1775, 1795, 1801, and, above all, 1812. They tended to be most acute in the north, north-east, and north-west, especially in those cities and surrounding areas whose normal provisioning areas would be invaded by food commissioners and private purchasers from Paris.

In other words, dearth was most likely in those areas where agricultural techniques were most advanced, or, perhaps, even more, in areas which, not highly productive, were within easy reach of grainlands with a normal surplus to export—the District de Rouen is a good case in point. In any period of scarcity, there would also be great suffering among the population of some of the wilder and more backward regions of the *Massif central*. Save for the rich plain of the Lauragais and the *Plaine d'Arles*, which were also served by an excellent system of transport (the *canal du Midi*, Marseille, and the Rhône), agriculture in the *Midi* was backward, with a low yield in wheat. But, for reasons that have little to do with agriculture, this area seldom experienced a dearth. Even in normal years it drew largely, through Marseille and Sète, on the great

---

[1] F11 1436B (Roussillon to the Committee of Public Safety, messidor an II): 'Comme je n'ai cessé de le dire, ce sont les départements de l'Aude et de la Haute-Garonne qui vous offriront toujours les plus grandes ressources. . . .' The Prefect of the Aude reported in 1812: 'Le département n'a pas manqué de subsistances. . . . Les arrondissements de Castelnaudary et de Narbonne ont peu souffert. . . . La ville de Castelnaudary est située dans la contrée la plus fertile du département, sur le bord du canal du Midi. Son marché est l'entrepot naturel des grains des départements de l'Ariège, de la Haute-Garonne & du Tarn. . . . Ce qui doit encore augmenter la sécurité, c'est la culture du maïs, dont se nourrit une grande partie de la population. . .' (A.N. F11 706, crise de 1812, Aude).

[2] A.N. F11 1185 (Subsistances, an IV).

grain market of the Mediterranean, from Thrace to the Maghreb. The very fact that it normally had a low production in grain was thus a protection. Also, in the south-west at least, there had been considerable progress, in the years following the year III, in the cultivation of maize. The inhabitants of the Aude, of the Tarn, and of parts of the Haute-Garonne were thus no longer reliant on a single crop. Such reliance was the principal cause of hardship, and even of famine, in other areas and constituted the basic weakness of the French eighteenth-century food economy. But some, if not similar, progress had been made between 1795 and 1812 in the production of other alternatives, especially the potato, in a number of normally poor areas in the *Massif central*, the east, the centre, and the west. The Prefects of 1812 refer specifically, in this respect, to the Puy-de-Dôme and the Cantal, the Doubs, parts of the Nièvre where the inhabitants had long been accustomed to do without bread, the Ain, the Indre, and the Sarthe.[1]

In this respect at least the experience of 1795 had been ultimately beneficial. It brought home not only to local authorities but also to the poorer inhabitants that it was unwise to rely on a single crop, that potatoes were a reliable and cheap stand-by, and that it was possible to do without bread and still keep alive. It took a catastrophe of the proportions of 1795 to break down something of the food conservatism of the French consumer, who even in 1812 displayed a rooted distrust of rice. The spread of the potato was one of several factors that were to make the difference between the disaster of 1795 and the temporary hardship of 1812. This was another reason why areas considered habitually *disetteux* were ultimately better protected, being forewarned, than those which, while having themselves a low production, were within easy reach of the great grainlands. Certainly the misfortune of a place like Rouen was to have almost on its doorstep the *fromenteux* areas of the Vexin, the Beauvaisis, and the Soissonnais. For, save in time of war, the poorer inhabitants of Dieppe or Le Havre could normally expect to fall back on fish, while, year in year out, the poor of the Lozère and the Ardèche would look to the chestnut for their principal source of sustenance. There were some advantages in being habitually underprivileged.

In any given year (except for the disasters of 1788-9 and 1794-5 and such localized accidents as the terrible winter of 1785, evoked

[1] See note S, p. 367.

ten years later by the Versailles authorities, that stopped all circulation for two months) France probably produced enough grain *in toto* to meet the needs of a rising population, about five million of which was, by 1789, concentrated in towns and *bourgs*, varying in size from twenty thousand, thirty, forty, fifty thousand, seventy thousand, to five towns of from eighty to one hundred and twenty thousand, and finally to the six or seven hundred and fifty thousand occupants of the capital. In small towns under the twenty-thousand mark, closely linked to the countryside, there would normally be no great problem, though those situated in woodland or in mountainous areas were probably harder hit than anywhere in the crisis of 1795. In periods of dearth, the main problem was to ensure the supply of the two million or so inhabitants of the more important cities and the satellite villages that were dependent on their markets. The 'danger list' would always include Paris and its periphery, Rouen and its populous District, Lille and its satellites, Amiens[1] and its hinterland, Abbeville, Le Havre and its fringe, Honfleur, Lisieux, Pont-l'Évêque, Dieppe, Fécamp,[2] Saint-Valéry,[3] Caen, Alençon, Calais,[4] Elbeuf, Évreux, Troyes, Bar-sur-Seine, Bar-sur-Aube, Givet, Rocroi, Fumay, Charleville, Valenciennes, Lyon and its periphery (an area fully exposed to the 1795 famine, but, thanks to purchases in South Germany, largely exempt from the full effects of the dearth of 1812), Mantes, Vernon, Meulan, Saint-Germain, with the valley of the Lower Seine and the Channel coast. The area from the Cotentin to the border of the Austrian Netherlands was very high on the list both for scarcity and in potential disorder. No one can, in fact, calculate what was the average national yield or whether, in times of partial failure, there was enough grain to go round. The question is academic, for

[1] See note T, p. 368.

[2] '. . . L'état de famine dans lequel se trouve la commune . . . a occasionné des incursions chez les citoyens aisés . . . qui ont été forcés de partager le peu d'approvisionnement qu'ils avoient . . .' (A.N. D III 270 d 13, 23 prairial an III).

[3] '. . . Quel espoir nous reste donc? La douleur de voir une quantité prodigieuse de familles livrées aux horreurs de la famine . . .' (A.N. D III 274 18, 27 messidor an III).

[4] '. . . Eh! qui n'a pas vérifié qu'en effet la misère dans les villes a quelques degrés de plus encore que dans nos campagnes? . . . Comparons nos pêcheurs avec quelques autres qui se trouvent sur l'une des communes du canton de Saint-Pierre; les nôtres n'ont que leurs bras, et, s'ils périssent, leurs enfans tombent à la charge de leurs concitoyens; ceux de Marck, au contraire, ont tous une habitation à eux, un jardin, et même des terres . . .' (s.d. an V, Mémoire des administrateurs municipaux de Calais, A.N. F15 293).

it was widely believed that at the best of times the situation would be 'tight'; that, with the slightest shortage, there would not be enough to go round; and that, if not today, then tomorrow, next week, or next month[1] the markets would be empty and those who bought their bread from bakers would starve. It is academic too because, after a good harvest, the countryman would himself consume more wheat and less barley and rye, and so there probably would not be any considerable variation between the total amount of wheat available for urban consumption from the one period to the other.

A similar situation could be artificially induced if, in a period of scarcity or war, the government imposed a maximum price on grain and on meat. In the year II, for instance, in many of the richest grainlands (the Brie, the Soissonnais, the Pays de France, the Santerre, the Vermandois, the Bassigny), farmers fed their surplus grain to their livestock, rather than supply it to the towns. Consumption of pork and veal likewise enormously increased in the countryside and remained exceptionally high throughout the crisis of 1794–6.

To envisage the problem primarily from the point of view of total yield, or even from that of imports, is in any case misleading and to some extent irrelevant. Ultimately, in eighteenth-century France, the problem was not so much one of production—and, therefore, improvement—as of marketing, pricing, and distribution. It was a matter of getting grain from one province, and, in the revolutionary period, from one District, to another. The breakdown was always most likely to occur at certain fixed points, where the *arrêts* took place again and again throughout the century, along the supply routes to the cities. As grain travelled in bulk mostly by water, and more especially along the valleys of the Upper and Lower Seine, the Oise, the Aisne, the Yonne, the Ourcq, the two Morins, the Loire, the Saône, the Rhône and the Garonne, and the *canal du Midi*, it was not difficult to predict where breakdowns would occur. The *carte des arrivages* was almost as changeless as the *carte des troubles*, and everything pointed to places like Pontoise, Beaumont, Conflans, and Pont-Saint-

---

[1] In all reports, the *problème des subsistances* is declined in the future tense, and Lenoir makes the admirable point that the most acute, and most dangerous, of popular fears are those that are for the morrow and that it was not 'this day's daily bread' that mattered, but the next day's.

Maxence, Mantes and Vernon, Château-Thierry, Bray, Gray, Villefranche, Moissac, and Castelnaudary as the likeliest places for *arrêts*, because more grain would be passing through them than through any other towns.

Lenoir, like other writers on dearth before him, is well aware of this problem. Writing of the enormous importance of the Seine, the Loire, and the Rhône to grain supply, he makes the obvious but useful point that it was, in terms of distribution, easier to export than to import; exports went with the current, imports had to be pulled against it. No wonder that even as late as 1828, when the French government made heavy purchases of Baltic grain, *les grains du Nord* arrived only in the late summer, after the harvest and often in a condition of rot.

This, and the mentality that conditioned the *problème des arrivages*, was the major weakness. France, unlike eighteenth-century England, could not supply her main centres of population through an active and inexpensive coastal trade.[1] It took anything from three weeks to a month to tow grain up from le Havre to Paris. A further weakness already referred to was that, at least until after the crisis of the year III, the great majority of the population was dependent on a single crop for its sustenance. The common people ate bread and little else; there was no second-line article of general consumption to fall back on.[2] Potatoes came in on a national scale only after 1795, and even as late as 1812 there was still considerable popular prejudice against rice as a foodstuff.[3] Maize was confined to a couple of departments of the south-west. Food riots were nearly always bread riots, only rarely riots about *les denrées de seconde zone* (meat, eggs, butter, milk, groceries, fuel, candles, etc.); people might grumble about the price or the shortage of these but they were rarely the cause of a major turbulence. Indeed, a grocery riot was something of a luxury, an indication at least that people were not in fear of starvation. In 1794, there were

---

[1] Much of the trade in grain between Marseille and Genoa went, however, by coaster, especially in 1794 and 1795, when the English blockade made the use of larger vessels dangerous.

[2] Unlike some Italian departments. In 1812, the Prefect of the Po was to report: '. . . Les trois quarts [de mes administrés] se nourrissent presqu'entière-ment de *Polenta* faite avec de la farine de maïs, aussi quoique la récolte du froment ait été médiocre en 1811, il en restoit cependant encore assez pour la consommation du Département jusqu'à la fin de cette année au moment de la moisson . . .' (A.N. F11 716, Préfet du Pô au Ministre, 13 août 1812).

[3] See note U, p. 368.

complaints about the favouritism shown by butchers towards their wealthier customers and much jealousy was aroused by the rich fare ordered by the aristocratic inmates of the Paris prisons. The readiness to believe the 'prison plot' and the popularity of the prison massacre should be seen in this context, the former justifying the latter, and the latter removing many 'useless mouths'. In the year II, the *sans-culottes* were unable to get their way in this respect and the Revolutionary Government organized its own 'prison massacres' in the vast trials of Messidor and Thermidor. In the year III, the prison massacres had the additional appeal of offering a slight alleviation to a food situation which was to be particularly acute in Floréal and Prairial, when the first big massacres occurred. In order to destroy the *hébertistes*, the government attempted to blow up the temporary shortage of dairy produce on the Halles in the spring of 1794 into a full-scale 'food plot', without getting much popular support. All this shows that in the year II the common people did not have to worry about bread. They did not realize at the time how lucky they were, but they did a year later. In the year III view, Robespierre's Year meant Bread Year.

The shortage of bread was always a matter for panic; the more so, as one of the 1812 prefects pointed out, because the working man could never predict just how much bread was likely to be available on his usual market:[1] the shortage of other foodstuffs was more in the nature of an irritant. It was bakers, and millers, and corn-factors who were murdered, mills and granaries that were burnt. No butcher and no grocer was done to death during the revolutionary period, however much he might be harried by zealous *sans-culottes*, for hoarding and infringements of the *maximum*.

14. THE CALENDAR OF DEARTH

Dearth was not only a cyclical, but also a seasonal phenomenon. Most eighteenth-century dearths extended over two harvests, that of 1812 was the climax of three successive partial failures. For purposes of research, the effects of dearth should be calculated over

---

[1] '. . . Les subsistances d'une partie du peuple sont chez l'autre, celles de l'habitant des villes sont chez l'habitant des campagnes, celles du consommateur sont chez son boulanger, ce qui fait qu'il [le peuple] ne sait jamais assez au juste s'il y a assez ou pas assez pour le faire vivre . . .' (Préfet du Bas-Rhin au Ministre, 27 juillet 1812, A.N. F11 716, crise de 1812, Bas-Rhin).

the harvest year (from September to August), not over the calendar year. Within each year, there was a potentially dangerous period, for it would produce some shortage, at least on the urban markets, even in normal conditions. This was from May[1] to the middle of August (in the *Midi* to the end of July) as the likeliest riot months, and March and April, when the rivers had unfrozen, as the most probable months for *arrêts* and other disturbances of circulation. The municipal authorities of Dieppe were to state, in Pluviôse year III, that in normal years the harvest began to be brought in in Thermidor; but, owing to the excessive cold of the winter of 1794–5, they did not expect that of the year III to be in before the beginning of Fructidor, with the result that in that terrible year extreme distress was likely to be stretched over an exceptionally long *période de la soudure*, from Ventôse to Fructidor, a period of over six months.[2] At the same time, they observed,[3] 'le laboureur craintif se désaisira plus facilement au mois d'avril qu'au mois de juin . . .'. Their calculations in this respect seem to have been accurate, for, in the following year, the effects of the harvest, a good one at last, were only beginning to be felt by the middle of the month of Fructidor, when the municipality was able to double the bread ration of the children of the needy.[4] *La peur du lendemain* would thus mount steadily throughout this long period of six or seven months, when the winter grain had been entirely consumed and the yield of the next harvest was still uncertain, to reach its climax at the very moment when grain prices were highest, on the eve of the harvest. Curiously enough, so dominant was the fear of the future that there were few riots after the harvest, even when this turned out disastrously poor—but this could not be generally known for two or three months.

The calendar might have been deliberately calculated to cause the maximum distress to the urban poor. Shortage of bread and

---

[1] '. . . C'est depuis le 15 mai jusqu'à la fin de juin que la disette s'est fait sentir le plus généralement et le plus fortement . . .' (Prefect of the Seine-Inférieure, to the Minister, 8 September 1812, A.N. F11 718). '. . . Suivant les rapports que j'ai recueillis, la misère s'était fait sentir d'une manière particulière dans beaucoup de campagnes pendant le mois de mai . . .' (Prefect of the Doubs, 18 July 1812, A.N. F11 709).

[2] Arch. Dieppe D I 6 (séance de la municipalité du 19 pluviôse an III).

[3] Ibid. (séance de la municipalité du 24 germinal an III).

[4] Arch. Dieppe D I 8 (séance de la municipalité du 14 fructidor an IV): '. . . L'abondance reparaissant aux halles semble promettre aux indigens d'y trouver dorénavant leurs besoins à doux prix. . . .'

other essentials due to the spring *arrêts* would coincide with the April quarterly *terme*. (In the year III, the *terme* nearly coincided with the *journées de germinal*. The riots occurred in Paris on the 12th, in Rouen, Amiens, Le Havre, on the 14th,[1] rent being due on the 18th.) The urban consumer would be hit by the highest grain prices at the very moment—again almost to the day, since there is only a week between 7 July and 14 July—when he was faced with the problem of having to pay the third quarter. In the year II, and even more in the years III and IV, the crisis, like the sweeping epidemics it provoked, attained a maximum virulence during the second decade of Messidor. For, as far as the urban *petit peuple* were concerned, each *terme* represented a major domestic crisis. The poor man's year jerked from the January peak to the peak of April, from April to July, and from July to October, with periods of comparative quiet in between, and, always, on the eve of the *terme*, the baker, the grocer, the butcher would be likely to suspend credit, only to resume it once the dreaded 7th of the month had been safely passed, thanks to some miracle of borrowing or pawning.

It has been calculated that in the Paris *faubourgs* from three to four thousand households would decamp, *à la cloche de bois*, on the eve of each *terme*, or would make the move legally, shedding sticks of furniture, in lieu of payment, on each occasion, until they were left with little more than a single blanket and the sort of bed that could be carried away on one's shoulders.[2] Even these poor wretches were perhaps not so badly off in this respect as the unfortunate *habitants de garnis*, who would be faced with at least twelve such crises each year; but it was much easier for these to decamp, taking the *logeur*'s sheets and blankets with them, and reports of such thefts are part of the regular stock-in-trade of the *commissaires de police*.[3] Girls were particularly proficient at such gymnastic descents from a fourth- or fifth-floor window. Tradiionally, it is true, *Les Rois* is thought of as the grimmest date in the calendar of the poor, the *terme de janvier* coinciding with extreme

---

[1] *Terreur et subsistances*, pp. 257–95.

[2] *Le Tableau de Paris*, x. 352: '. . . Grandes rumeurs ces jours-là dans toutes les maisons. . . . Mais grande joie dans le galetas quand le terme est payé, parce que le crédit . . . se renouvelle après le passage critique. . . .'

[3] A.P.P. 61–2, 95–8, 187–8, 199, 202, 219, 221 (Arcis, Montagne, Muséum, Observatoire, Panthéon, Popincourt, Quinze-Vingts, *commissaires de police*, ans III and IV).

cold and unemployment for building workers and for most others who normally worked outside; and its grimness was further accentuated by contrast with the previous rejoicings of Christmas and the New Year, on which the poor were likely proportionally to spend more and to entertain more generously than the prudent *bourgeois* ('Le petit peuple', writes Mercier, 'est plus pauvre le 8 janvier, que dans tout autre tems de l'année et c'est à cette époque que les hôpitaux se remplissent . . .').[1] But Nivôse is not a riot month; it was probably too cold for an *attroupement*, and bread prices would still be low. As for *le terme d'octobre*, it was certainly the least intolerable: grain prices would be at their lowest and seasonal workers would still have some savings from the harvest work. The *garnis* filled up at this time of the year, when men on the run sought out their winter quarters, and all manner of criminals returned to town.[2] That the criminal's year rarely coincided with that of riot the police were well aware, and October was the favourable season for one of the great annual sweeps of the furnished rooms. With autumn, the repressive authorities would turn from riot and assembly to the *filou* who, like a homing pigeon, headed for the *garni*, the *mauvais lieu*, and the *bal musette*, as soon as the leaves began to fall.[3]

Finally, there were riot days. The old royal authorities, the revolutionary *agents nationaux*, and the Imperial and Restoration Prefects all refer to *ces lundis inquiétants*. There is, perhaps, no need to elaborate why Mondays should have been so dangerous.[4] Owing to the prevalent habit of taking Tuesday off as well, riot would often spread to that day. Sunday too, with its idle crowds, could be provocative of riot in time of dearth. Of the Fécamp riot of 23 Prairial year III, the *maire* was to note that the crowd collected rapidly 'et cela d'autant plus facilement que c'étoit jour de fête'.[5] Many of the rioters had come a long way, from the villages of the Pays de Caux four or five miles inland.

Also, during the revolutionary period, once the new calendar

---

[1] *Le Tableau de Paris*, viii.

[2] A.P.P. A/A 98 (Commission administrative au commissaire de police de la Section de la Butte des Moulins, messidor an III).

[3] *Le Tableau de Paris*, xi. 198. See Section 1, pp. 20–1.

[4] Georges Lefebvre, 'Foules révolutionnaires'; *Le Tableau de Paris*, x. 345: '. . . Les ouvriers font ce qu'ils appellent le *lundi* et même le *mardi*. Voilà deux jours de la semaine pour la fainéantise et la boisson. . . .'

[5] A.N. D III 270 d 13 (Comité de législation, interrogatoire du procureur de la commune de Fécamp, le 5 messidor an III).

was in use in the cities the authorities showed an almost obsessive nervousness with regard to the *décadis*. It was as if, just as dearth turned up every ten years, people would only riot on the tenth day. This fear extended from the food riot to every sort of predicted *coup*: military plot, prison plot, and so on. *Le grand coup de chien, ce sera pour le prochain décadi!* How often do we hear this prediction, both in popular speech and in informers' reports. (The *petit peuple*, just as they thought of dearth for the morrow, liked to keep their threats for the end of the *décade*—it was one way of frightening the *bons bourgeois* and of alarming the police. It was also a means of keeping up morale, especially on the aftermath of an unsuccessful *journée*.)

When the Faubourg was disarmed, after the Prairial Days, it was rumoured that there would be a final settlement of accounts on 30 Prairial—others said the 25th, for the *quintidi* would do just as well. These rumours circulated not only in Paris, but in the surrounding *communes* of Vincennes and Saint-Denis.¹ Nothing in fact happened, but the Thermidorian authorities called out the garrison and doubled the guard.² The *décadi* not only had a magical ring about it; it was also a holiday. The persistence of this belief, long after the popular movement had been decisively defeated, is a dramatic indication of the extent to which the new calendar had gained popular acceptance. The historian of dearth and of popular protest needs to have constantly to hand his *Table de Concordance*.³

Lastly, of course, bread riots occur on market days. As Lenoir remarked,⁴ what made *la disette* so particularly dangerous was that it brought large numbers of people together on one day and in one place—*qui assemble le peuple, l'émeut*, as a Napoleonic Prefect

---

¹ Arch. Saint-Denis I D I 4 (séances de la municipalité des 2, 3, 5, 6, et 9 prairial an III); Arch. Vincennes I D 3 (séance de la municipalité du 7 prairial an III). Similar rumours circulated in Mantes. On 14 Pluviôse year III, the comité of Dijon orders the arrest of a citizen, Baudier puîné, 'prévenu d'avoir tenu des propos tendant à répandre l'alarme *le jour de la décade* 10 pluviôse'. He was one of several persons 'affectant de semer l'alarme . . . en disant qu'il n'y a pas suffisamment de bleds . . .'. There were further rumours of an impending dearth on the following *quintidi*, 15 pluviôse (Arch. Côte-d'Or, L 2658*, comité de Dijon, an III).

² Arch. Vincennes I D 3 (ibid., 25 prairial). A hundred soldiers had been sent from Paris to Saint-Denis on the 9th.

³ *Concordance des Calendriers Grégorien et Républicain* (Paris, Clavreuil, 1963).

⁴ Op. cit., p. 51.

noted.[1] They could see both high prices and shortage: a remedy much favoured by *sub-délégués* and revolutionary authorities was to display, as prominently as possible, an imposing number of sacks of flour, the same sacks doing duty again and again, as they were taken from one place to another.[2] They would stoke up one another's indignation to furnace heat. A large market, by bringing together the inhabitants of a number of villages, was likewise a magnet to riot, as it would give rise to disputes between different villagers, who would then claim support from their own group, in the name of village solidarity.[3] By a similar reasoning, the eve of a market day could be equally dangerous or even more so. The man arrested on the Pont-Neuf in Germinal year III was accused of having shouted: 'Il n'y aura pas de pain demain sur le marché de la Section.'[4]

The bread riot, like the week-end murders of the White Terror, had its own strict time-table, just as it followed a pattern governed by strict rules and based on the memory of the past. In the years III and IV, at every such gathering, there is a constant harking back to *le pain à trois sols la livre*; and, in the Deux-Sèvres, we even hear of such a demand in the crisis of 1812.[5] In one place, during that crisis, there was an attempt to go back to the *tarif* of 1775.[6] Anyone concerned with the economy of the grain market is bound to be historically minded; in all inter-urban disputes, localities that have lost their markets as a result of the Revolution will appeal back, sometimes to edicts of the sixteenth century, in order to regain their markets.[6] Both the Prefects of 1812 and those who write about dearth in the year IV are prepared to quote

[1] The Prefect of the Bas-Rhin, in 1812. See section II.

[2] Lenoir, op. cit., p. 51: '. . . En voyant les piles de sacs, on se dirait *nous mangerons demain* . . . que la population puisse, à chaque instant, évaluer, avec son exagération ordinaire l'étendue des approvisionnements qu'on lui réserve, et elle supportera avec patience les plus dures privations. . . .' See also the author's article, 'Problèmes de subsistances en l'an II et l'an III: l'exemple d'un petit port normand: Honfleur' (Congrès des Sociétés Savantes de Rouen, 1958).

[3] See note V, p. 368.

[4] A.P.P. A/A 187 (commissaire de police de la Section du Muséum, séance du 11 germinal an II) (procès-verbal).

[5] A.N. F11 718 (Préfet des Deux Sèvres au Ministre, 25 juillet 1812): '. . . L'effet des décrets sur l'esprit public a été bon et mauvais. . . . Je ne sais quel bruit précurseur s'étoit répandu dans le peuple; il ne s'entretenoit que d'une prétendue promesse qu'on supposoit avoir été faite par S.M. de mettre partout le pain à 3 sols la livre. . . .'

[6] A.N. F11 707 (Préfet du Calvados au Ministre, 24 mars 1812).

[7] *Les Armées révolutionnaires*, p. 379.

chapter and verse on the subject of the proper organization of markets, from Philippe le Bel, Louis XI, and François Ier.[1] With an empty market before its eyes, in the winter of 1794–5 the municipal authorities of Vincennes think at once of the conditions ten years before, during the bitter winter of 1784.[2] Markets were potentially dangerous in so many ways, then, that some public authorities suggested suppressing them altogether and having the distribution of bread organized through private commercial channels.[3]

15. GOVERNMENT AND THE PROBLEM OF DEARTH: 'PHYSIOCRATES' AND 'TRADITIONALISTS'

Before returning in detail to popular attitudes to dearth and the question of how these attitudes affected the problem and before discussing popular remedies, a short digression is necessary on government policies, both in their own right and in connection with popular assumptions. The *problème des subsistances*, as we have seen, had become something of a French institution, ensconced even in the calendar—no better recognition could be expected—and with its ancient *lettres de noblesse*. In eighteenth-century conditions, it had become above all a political problem, as perhaps it had always been, demanding political solutions and involving the reputation of the public authorities up to the highest level. The government had only itself to blame, since the organization of the grain trade had been the subject of endless polemics between 'physiocrates' and 'traditionalists', total free-traders and restrictionists, partisans of *greniers d'abondance* and upholders of unlimited exports, intendants and parlements, ministers and estates, *contrôleurs* and clergy, each of whom blamed the other for having, wilfully or through negligence, by a show of panic, by interfering or by doing nothing, provoked a shortage. It was

[1] See note W, p. 369.
[2] Arch. Vincennes I D I 3 (séance du 13 frimaire an III): '. . . Nous sommes sans pain, que deviendrons-nous si par malheur un hiver tel que celui de 1784 interrompoit tous les charrois . . .?'
[3] '. . . Qui assemble le peuple, l'émeut, l'émeut bien davantage qui l'assemble quand il a faim, et c'est alors surtout que bien loin de le rassembler, on doit tout employer pour dissoudre ces rassemblemens. L'assembler affamé sur une place de marché, comme dans une arène, pour se disputer quelques sacs qui seront le prix des vainqueurs, qu'est-ce autre chose que de le provoquer à l'émeute . . .?' (Préfet du Bas-Rhin au Ministre, 27 juillet 1812, A.N. F11 716).

government, as the acute de Tocqueville reminds us, that invented the *pacte de famine*, and it was authority that first gave credence to the *disette factice*, by denying that shortage could ever be explained in natural terms, those of productivity, drought, or other disasters. As shortage was thus 'artificial', the implication was that it had been contrived for political reasons. It followed that plenty would return, once the 'guilty' had been punished. The State and its opponents dug their own grave in thus laying the foundations for what was to be the most persistent and most strenuously held of popular attitudes.

In the second half of the century, dearth and the more general problems of the grain trade were dragged into the middle both of court and of provincial politics. Turgot used shortage to discredit Maupeou and Terray; and, after May 1775, he himself became widely discredited as an *affameur*, which served him right for having made unjust accusations against the higher clergy and the rural *curés*.[1] The *physiocrates* did the most damage in this respect as in most others. They talked and read each other papers on agriculture and husbandry, about which they had only the most theoretical notions (they were too grand ever to have put their hands to such practical matters); and, like most *salonnard* intellectuals, they knew what was best for the People, while completely leaving out of account both popular attitudes and popular remedies, of which they were probably unaware and which they would have dismissed in any case as based on ignorance or fear. So they reckoned without popular habit, turning their backs on several centuries of French popular history. In a country with a rapidly increasing urban population—as Lenoir insists, it was the urban population, particularly that of the twenty or so larger cities, that conditioned the eventual gravity of the problem[2]—they preached against the evils of cities. Their remedy, no doubt, would have been to send back the more recent arrivals to an over-

---

[1] George Rudé, *The Crowd in History* (New York, 1965).

[2] It was not only a technical problem: towns were also more rumour-prone, and thus more subject to riot and fear. 'Dans les villes ou gros bourgs, les hommes sont plus rapprochés, plus en communication les uns avec les autres, plus hardis, plus entreprenans. Il seroit à craindre que, forcés de vivre au jour le jour, et manquant d'occupations productives, ils ne se portassent ou ne se laissassent plus facilement entraîner à des excès préjudiciables à l'ordre. . . . J'ai cru, par ce motif, que, dans cette circonstance, les villes méritoient de ma part une sollicitude particulière . . .' (A.N. F11 715, Préfet d'Alençon au Ministre, 13 novembre 1812).

crowded countryside, from which they had but recently been driven by need. As they detested Paris and its population, they were hardly likely to be aware of the many difficulties, both practical and psychological, involved in keeping its markets properly supplied. For all they cared, if they ever gave the matter a thought, Paris could starve. It would have done if their policies had been adopted in time of dearth or concurrently with a sudden increase in the fear of shortage.

They were also fanatical believers in freedom of the grain trade within the kingdom, and they even defended the unlimited export of grain. Only if there were no restrictions, no interference, would the channels of supply flow freely and grain find its economic price. In time of dearth, especially in the late summer, this would certainly have meant starvation for the urban artisan—a solution, of a kind, to the urban problem, but one that it is unlikely that even the *physiocrates*, so deaf to popular demands, would have advocated, had they realized its inevitability. Mercier was right to refer to their system as one 'qui a affamé le peuple'; and he quotes a *lieutenant criminel*, an impeccable witness, who attributed the sharp rise in urban crime in the second half of the 1760s to massive exports of grain and the resulting hardship to the urban consumer.[1] Certainly such a connection might well have existed: for the 'physiocratic' crisis of the year III brought the formation of the *chauffeurs* as well as a series of brutal murders with robbery as a motive, just as the dearth of 1788 had been accompanied in Marseille by an unprecedented outbreak of burglaries.[2] Mercier realized above all that physiocratic policies, in time of shortage, represented a direct and brutal attack on the subsistence of the urban poor, that the poor would at once so interpret them, and that the consequences would soon be felt in the sphere of public order and grain circulation. The famous publicist was no lover of the

[1] *Le Tableau de Paris*, viii: 'Venez, économistes, qui, comme des étourdis, avez prêché en 1767 l'exportation illimitée du blé et avez donné à la cupidité la plus effrénée le signal d'affamer le royaume.' Mercier, who wrote this in 1786, proved himself a singularly poor prophet when he went on to write: 'Plus de ces années désastreuses où l'on a vu l'homme couché sur le ventre, brouter l'herbe à l'exemple des animaux', which was, very exactly, the position so often adopted by the poor in 1795.

[2] A.N. F1b II Bouches-du-Rhône I: 'Policarpe Constans, commissaire du Directoire Exécutif à ... Rabaut le jeune, membre du Conseil des Anciens ...' (à Aix, an VI). '... Je me rappelle que l'hiver de 1788 fut fertile en vols; plus de 300 magasins furent enfoncés et pillés à Marseille. ...'

people, but at least, unlike the *économistes*, he could put himself in their place and knew how much they would put up with, how far they could be pushed. He would have made a good *lieutenant*, whereas any *physiocrate* would have been disastrous in that office.

For they had no suggestion to offer how to maintain circulation in the face of widespread provincial and popular interference. Their solution no doubt would have been to call in the forces of repression and to enlist the Suisses, the Gardes-Françaises, and the *maréchaussée*—those well-known specialists in food problems—in order to re-establish freedom of movement (and demonstrate the practicality of physiocratic theory). They would have had to go to war with the whole people of France, with most magistrates, *curés*, and local officials. At the same time, they poured scorn and venom on those who, unlike themselves, had had practical experience, in public office, of grain-supply problems, and who had, in times of dearth, reintroduced the habitual restrictions on exports abroad, on the time and place of the sale of grain, had ordered a maximum price and had recourse to estimates and requisitions backed, when necessary, by force. Force would be necessary for either policy; requisitions could not be carried out without using it against the rural producer; and free trade could not be enforced, in time of dearth, without using large numbers of soldiers against urban and rural consumers, to maintain the flow of grain from the corn areas to the urban markets. In a choice between two evils, the second policy would necessitate more force against more people; but they were people less well placed to dictate to the government than the farmers who, when faced with force, might simply fail to cultivate their land, with disastrous long-term effects for French agriculture.

In other words, where agriculture was concerned, force might bring immediate results in terms of provisioning, but would jeopardize the future, as the year II was to show. On the other hand, phsyiocratic policy, applied during a dearth, would be certain to produce widespread disorder; and, in terms of repression, it was more economical to be tough with a few large farmers than to take on the whole consumer population, of whose interests the *physiocrates* proved callously unaware. (Their argument was based on the belief that, for agriculture to be improved, the interest of the producer must come first, whatever the consequences to the mass of consumers.)[1] Finally, the *physiocrates* accused the 'traditionalists' of encouraging panic by revealing the fears of the higher authorities through their various interventions. No better way, they argued, of creating a shortage could be imagined than a series of public ordinances designed to prevent one.

Like the *philosophes*, whose only successful dream-child was to be the King of Sweden, the *économistes* were unfortunate in their choice of country. Their policies might well have suited the very different conditions of Arthur Young's England, where the whole system of circulation and distribution hardly constituted a problem save in times of acute shortage, like the 1795 crisis in England and Wales.[2] In French terms, their policies had much to recommend them in, say, nine years out of ten, when the total yield, together with limited imports for the south, could meet the needs of a growing population; but in the tenth year they could only lead to starvation and a rapid spread of riot, which would end by freezing the channels of supply. And no government could allow a situation which exposed to starvation the population of Paris, or of any town on the supply-lines of the capital—that is, almost any town in the north, north-east, and north-west. They were preaching an English solution in an Indian setting.

The 'traditionalists' included most of those who had had to contend at any level with a dearth situation or with the threat of dearth, while in a position of authority. They were as attached as the *économistes* to the principle of free trade in grain, at least within the kingdom. Unlike them, however, they were aware of what could and what could not be done once a dearth appeared likely, and they took into account popular assumptions and the natural 'immobilism' of local authorities. They recognized also that food procurement was a State responsibility which, for moral reasons and in the interest of public order, could not wait while large sections of the urban—and even rural—population were exposed to starvation. In times of dearth, they not only forbade all export of grain, but also recognized that there were limits to the rights of property where the *denrées de première nécessité* were concerned and that prices must be kept down and the markets

---

[1] See note X, p. 369.
[2] On the English dearth of 1795, see E. P. Thompson, *The Making of the English Working Class* (London, 1964).

supplied by government intervention, backed by force if necessary, as it almost always would be.[1] Their solutions were far from original, representing as they did some three hundred years of ordinances concerning the *police des marchés* and the *police du pain*: a fixed price; enforced sale at a specified time and place where individual consumers would be supplied first; the strict control of mills and bakeries; the prohibition of the pure wheaten loaf; requisitioning and house searches by food commissioners; and the arrest and punishment of recalcitrant farmers.

The only matter about which the 'traditionalists' were not entirely in agreement among themselves was the important, and delicate, question of publicity. Some argued that the *problème des subsistances* should be viewed as a State secret and treated as such.[2] In wartime, in particular, an open statement of the country's needs would reveal France's most dangerous weakness to her enemies, who would thus be tempted to aggravate the situation by sending in agents to drive up grain prices.[3] Again, if the government were to discuss the situation openly, private individuals would feel impelled to do the same and, once the subject had become a matter for public debate, the situation would rapidly worsen. The government should, then, act in secret, imposing restrictions piecemeal from one locality to another,[4] and with extreme caution.

The opponents of secrecy argued that it would only lead to the wildest rumours, that many of the measures called for could never really be kept secret and that secrecy would lose the government the gratitude of the common people for introducing measures that were no less popular for being expected. The debate continued during and after the Revolution. The Committee of Public Safety favoured secrecy and branded as *malveillant* anyone, especially a poor artisan, presumptuous enough to raise the problem of provisioning in a public place. Napoleon's Prefects were for the most part of the same opinion. The matter, they argued, was much

---

[1] See note Y, p. 369.

[2] '. . . Il est reconnu que, s'il faut s'occuper beaucoup de subsistances, il faut, officiellement, n'en parler jamais, ou en parler le moins possible . . .' (A.N. F11 712, Préfet du Puy au Ministre, 12 octobre 1812). '. . . Il est certain . . . qu'en voyant ce Gouvernement le plus secret qui fût jamais publier le secret des subsistances, secret qu'on avoit regardé jusqu'à lui comme de tous les secrets d'État le plus essentiel à garder, chacun crut que le mal fût extrême pour qu'on en vînt à cette extrémité . . .' (A.N. F11 716, Préfet de Strasbourg au Ministre).

[3] See note Z, p. 370.　　　　　　　　　　　[4] See note 2A, p. 370.

too complex to be thrown open to an ignorant, hysterical, and vengeful 'populace'. It could be dealt with only on the level of high statecraft. The police authorities of the Restoration, like all their predecessors, subscribed to the thesis of *malveillance*, and thought that the matter should be dealt with only behind a curtain of silence.[1]

If the true disciples of the *physiocrates* were first the *monarchiens* and then the Girondins, the policy of the 'traditionalists' was given its most effective elaboration by the Revolutionary Government, under strong popular pressure and very unwillingly. For Robespierre, Lindet, and the other Montagnard leaders were in theory as much attached to total free trade as the Girondins. There was no serious disagreement between them in this respect, but rather a difference of priorities, and the Montagnards, under the pressure of circumstances, were prepared to water down their theories and put them away 'for the duration'. In the autumn of 1793, then, the Revolutionary Government imposed a general *maximum*, ordered vast requisitions for the armies and cities, appointed food and hoarding commissioners, and resorted to a widespread use of force against the farmer and the hoarder.[2] Napoleon too, in 1812, revived much of the economic terror of the year II in the interests of Paris.

The 'traditionalists' did not really have a theory at all, but regarded restrictions as necessary, if temporary, palliatives, to tide the population over a temporary, but passing crisis. Whatever their theoretical shortcomings, however, their policies were undoubtedly successful in a dearth crisis for they saved the urban population from starvation and secured the supply of the larger units: Paris, Rouen, Le Havre, Lille, the armies, and they enforced the circulation of grain from the *pays fromenteux* to the *pays disetteux*. Such policies had the further advantage of being widely popular and thus securing the enthusiastic and sometimes troublesome co-operation of the *petit peuple*. A policy that ensured the support of the common people had much to recommend it, especially in war.

The physiocratic policy, on the other hand, was likely to prove unworkable in wartime conditions. The Paris *sans-culottes* were easily convinced that the Girondins were hostile to the capital. Had

[1] A.N. F7 3028–9.
[2] *Les Armées révolutionnaires*, ii. 369–463.

they not preached against Paris, were they not also *affameurs*?
When, in June, Jacques Roux told the Montagnards that they, too,
were *affameurs* and that they had done nothing to fill the empty
bellies of his parishioners, there was a roar of protest from all
directions, including the *Père Duchesne*. It was clear that anyone
who talked this way would have to be got rid of; and, from that day
till the following February, the troublesome priest was hustled to
his suicide. Even so, Montagnard policies were to meet immediate
needs, though at the expense of considerable damage to French
agriculture. This was the price that had to be paid for a policy of
force, serviced in the interest of the urban consumer, the armies,
and the Republic.

There was already in the late eighteenth century a third school
which favoured even more drastic intervention by the State in the
problems of supply. The intervention envisaged was to be permanent and would take no account of the variations between years
of plenty and years of scarcity. It sought a long-term, rather than
a temporary, solution to dearth in a country with a rising population. Its adherents advocated the formation of State granaries to
combat hoarding and speculation, and the socialization, at least
at municipal level, of the bakers' shops. There was, in fact, no
quarrel between the 'traditionalists' and these interventionists.
Both took into account popular reactions and were consequently
able to reckon with them. They had a good idea of what the
common people expected; they knew almost to an inch how far
the people could be pushed without being driven into riot; and
they knew how to circumscribe such riots with the minimum of
fuss, if they did break out. The only quarrel that the 'traditionalists' might have with the enthusiastic and pamphlet-prone
champions of the *greniers d'abondance* was on the wisdom of
establishing State granaries at all. In times of shortage, these might
well become sitting targets for pillage, because of the considerable
supplies that they contained or, more important, were believed to
contain. It would be even worse, of course, if they were revealed
as not containing what they had been believed to contain; and, if
they were empty, then the people would turn with savagery on the
government's officials. In the years II and III the frequent attacks
on the *magasins de la République* situated in the Channel ports and
along the Lower Seine showed that the danger existed.[1] The solu-

[1] 'Les disettes de l'an II et de l'an III dans le district de Mantes', loc. cit.

tion was to set them up in peacetime and in periods of plenty. This is what Lenoir was arguing when he claimed that, by establishing State grain reserves, Napoleon had saved Paris from famine and riot,[1] and when he called for the formation of a permanent government grain reserve large enough to meet any situation. This, he argued, would eliminate the danger of pillage; for the government, with vast reserves always to hand, could at any time nip in the bud a threatened dearth and lower prices by putting government grain massively on the market.

Throughout the eighteenth century, the old government had followed a zigzag course, enforcing internal free trade in grain, but reverting to restriction as soon as dearth was feared. Free trade was imposed, often with disastrous consequences, during the early years of the Revolution. Under the impetus of mobilization, and as a temporary concession to popular pressure, however, the Revolutionary Government adopted a more thorough system of enforced food procurement than any previously attempted. Even so, once the requisitions had been carried out, over an initial six months, for the armies, Paris, and half a dozen large cities, it showed a precipitate eagerness to revert to a policy less harmful to agricultural interests; and for the last four months of *robespierriste* rule there was a general slackening of the economic Terror. At the same time, the government made the *problème des subsistances* a forbidden subject for public discussion.

The Thermidorians waited till the winter crisis was at its worst, the cold the most acute, and the hardship of the urban and rural poor and the elderly the most pressing, in Nivôse year III, to abolish the *maximum* and proclaim the principle of the total freedom of the grain trade (though a certain number of restrictions were maintained).[2] But a famine situation developed soon afterwards: farmers were being arrested in the District de Dieppe that very month and the *comité* adopted a threatening language reminiscent of the strongest denunciations of rural egoism the previous year. They were soon obliged to revert to measures of force that

---

[1] Lenoir, op. cit., p. 24: '. . . La sagacité de l'empereur Napoléon lui avait fait sentir que la consommation d'une ville comme Paris, où quelques 100.000 individus vivent à peu près au jour le jour, devait être rendue indépendante des variations dans les récoltes. Il ordonna la construction d'un grenier d'abondance. . . .'

[2] On the extremely complicated legislation of this period, see Georges Lefebvre, *Études orléanaises, II, Maximum et subsistances*.

reached full effectiveness in the spring and summer of 1795. Most of these were retained till the harvest of 1796.

Finally, by the Decrees of 4 and 8 May 1812, the Napoleonic regime established what were in fact a *maximum*, requisitions and estimates—with the usual house searches, denunciations, and economic Terror, though they took care not to use these evocative words. But farmers and property-holders were quick to draw the parallel with the system of eighteen years previously, while the common people looked eagerly forward to *le pain à 3 sols la livre* and the discomfiture of large farmers, hoarders, and grain speculators.[1]

16. DEARTH AND POPULAR CREDULITY

In short, whether it intervened or stood aside and let things take their course, the government recognized some degree of responsibility for the problem of provisioning, which thus inevitably became politicized.[2] Hence the combination 'Dearth and Terror' and the channelling of much popular violence, verbal and physical, towards simple, over-all solutions of a single problem. No better banner for violence could have possibly been provided, for this one offered the general mass of urban, *faubourien*, or rural consumers identifiable hate figures: the miller, the corn-factor, the hoarder, the monopolist, the speculator, the exporter, and, long before the Revolution, the Queen of France. Attitudes to the problem fed too on a host of popular beliefs: the belief in hidden exports abroad ('the grain is going out of the country, to feed our enemies, so that we shall all be starved out and reduced to subjection');[3] the belief in the existence of vast and preferably underground supplies at home;[4] and the belief in the deliberate and calculated malevolence of stated persons holding public offices and who were intent on creating an artificial shortage, for exactly what purpose it was not very clear. (The government had only itself to blame by so

---

[1] See note 2B, p. 370.

[2] '... Le peuple se montre beaucoup plus exigeant que par le passé. Il voit que les Préfets et Sous-Préfets sont chargés d'approvisionner les marchés et il sera difficile à contenir si les marchés ne sont point garnis . ..' (A.N. F11 716, Préfet de Niort au Ministre, 23 mai 1812).

[3] 'Les disettes de l'an II et de l'an III dans le district de Mantes et la vallée de la Basse Seine', loc. cit.

[4] A.N. BB 73 (comité de surveillance du département de Paris, juillet 1793) and 'Les disettes', p. 240.

sedulously promoting the *malveillance* thesis.)[1] So every *disette* is a *disette factice*, and there can be no such thing as a *disette réelle*. The authorities did much to accredit this belief by constantly insisting that everything would turn out all right, that there was no real shortage, that there would be enough to go round as long as people kept their heads, obeyed instructions, allowed the grain convoys to flow freely, bought and sold their grain at the official markets, and did not spread rumours about something which they did not understand and which was so intricate, so complicated that it was best left to the secret of High Government. When, despite these assurances, things did not in fact turn out all right, and there was not in fact enough to go round, then, not unnaturally, people took the authorities at their word, and started looking for 'guilty men', who had contrived shortage, for whatever obscure purpose.

So any shortage was bound to have immediate political results. In May 1775 Terray and Maupeou and possibly Terray's friends in the priesthood used it to discredit Turgot; it did in fact finish him off politically. In 1789 there is the *pacte de famine*, with the Queen and the Comte d'Artois—it would be hard to find a more ill-assorted pair—in fell alliance to keep the people down through hunger. Later the same year, there is the murder of the baker François and martial law. In 1795 we can choose between *Du pain et la Constitution de 93*, and *Du pain et vive Louis XVII*. In 1802 in some places in the north, there is the cry *Du pain et vivent les Anglais*. In 1812, in Caen, it is *Du pain et de l'ouvrage*, or *Du pain et à bas les machines*, and it is rumoured that the Emperor has died in Moscow. People were prepared to believe anything, even Malet and his Proclamation, in that year of dearth and disaster. In 1816 the dearth goes to the tune of *Du pain et vive l'Empereur*, while shortage is enlisted in the service of the *Nain jaune*.[2] The police yet again blame the English, and officers on half pay are stated to have deliberately worked on popular fears.[3] So no doubt it went

[1] See below, p. 288–90, on 'Food plots'.

[2] *Le Nain jaune* (p. 257) enlisted in its cause the dead, with the suggestion that the increase in mortality in Paris in 1816 could be attributed to famine: '. . . Sans compter les protestans massacrés à Nîmes et dans tout le Midi, les individus amnistiés par les commissions militaires . . . les malheureux empoisonnés par la putridité des cachots . . . le relevé des registres de décès des 12 municipalités de Paris donne, sur 21,549 décès, 385 suicides . . .' (June 1816).

[3] A.N. F7 3028 (note de police des 25–6 avril 1816): '. . . Darlincourt, ex-colonel-général de la garde de Murat, et autres individus, signalés comme accaparant le blé dans des intentions criminelles'. See also *note de police* for

in a variety of combinations until the Second Empire, when railways brought an end to the problem.

Shortage, then, on the government's own admission, was explainable in political terms. It was deliberately induced, artificial. How then to end it and to re-establish plenty? The solutions too must be political. One can see how easy a step it was to argue that, by stringing up a few farmers and corn-factors (and even an unfortunate *prévôt des marchands*, to keep them company), it would be possible to produce grain from its hiding-places, see it spring up from the ground, and see the grain convoys heading once more towards the authorized markets. Hébert's solution to the most insistent problem of eighteenth-century French life had all the merits of simplicity; and it was in an ancient tradition of popular justice and popular self-help. It was hard to prove wrong: if it did not bring immediate remedies, it could always be said that not enough farmers had been killed.

Indeed, like the Dreyfus Affair, it was largely in the mind. It was all very well for a nineteenth-century critic like Lenoir to proclaim that governments themselves provoked uneasiness and panic by being secretive about the actual state of resources and that all they had to do to reassure opinion was to come clean and publish a balance-sheet of the harvest intake. Lenoir was writing in 1828, under a highly statistical regime, when governments could actually come by information of this kind. Eighteenth-century governments could not. They were often as much in the dark as their *administrés* and they could never calculate a yield on a national level. They did not even know, at least before 1800, how many mouths there were to be fed. (The estimate of the Paris population in 1795 varies wildly from six hundred thousand to three quarters of a million.) They could only guess at the number of people who were not dependent on the baker to keep themselves in bread or flour, *recensements* were very much hit-and-miss affairs, based on what the central authorities had been told by local officials; and, in time of expected shortage, no local official was likely to reveal that his area actually possessed a surplus.[1] On some occasions during the Revolution, certain regions—though far fewer than those that complained—really were cleared right out by successive requisitions far in excess of their actual resources.

17 October 1817: 'Individus qui tiennent des propos alarmans sur les subsistances. On les fait surveiller.'   [1] See note 2C, p. 371.

All an eighteenth-century government could do would be to go on precedent and work out a normal scale of comparative resources. Thus it was reasonable to assume that, even in a year of dearth, the Brie, the Pays de France, the Soissonnais, the Bassigny, the two Vexin, the Lauragais, the Santerre, the Vermandois would have a surplus of some sort or at least that they would not all be deficient at the same time. It was reasonable to assume that the District d'Alençon would always need help from outside. Clearly, eighteenth-century and revolutionary food commissioners could form a pretty good idea who was lying, which authorities were underplaying their resources and which were really in urgent need. But they could never gain anything approaching an accurate, over-all impression of the total output of a harvest, much less of variations in output from one region to another; so they too had to grope their way in a dark conducive to the worst fears, and, like their poorer *administrés*, they tended to think that things were worse than they were.[1] *De la peur de la disette naît la disette*; in such matters, it is not the reality of the situation that is important, but what people think about it. The *problème des subsistances* is situated in a dark forest of myth, supposition, and alarm. Eighteenth-century governments tended to be secretive about this important aspect of public administration. But they did not in fact have much to be secretive about, unless it was their own uneasiness.

In a country so agriculturally varied as eighteenth-century France, it would have been incredible if there had been failures everywhere—or even in a majority of grain-producing regions.[2] We hear much of the drought of the summer of 1789, the hailstorms of May 1789, the sudden, monsoon-like downpours of the late summer of 1794, the excessive heat of the summer of 1795, the bitter cold of the winters of 1784–5, 1788–9, 1794–5, 1795–6, which followed and preceded exceptionally hot summers; yet, on closer inspection, the drought is revealed as confined to half a dozen provinces, the hailstorms to a few villages in Burgundy, the downpours to certain localities of the Ain. Only the cold, the excessive, terrible cold of *Nonante-cinq*, seems to have been

---

[1] 'A cette époque des bruits sinistres de disette se répandaient. On débita que les subsistances manquoient dans la Capitale; que le Gouvernement faisoit des achats considérables pour les armées d'Espagne . . . la crainte provoqua des précautions et la crédulité vit la famine à sa porte . . .' (A.N. F11 716, Préfet de Mâcon au Ministre, 23 juillet 1812).   [2] See note 2D, p. 371.

universal, killing the poor in streets and garrets in Rouen, Dieppe, le Havre, Lisieux, and Paris, burying poor men in search of bread in great snowdrifts in the steppes of the Brie and the Beauce, killing off the olive trees in Provence, ruining the silk harvest of the Gard and the Ardèche, freezing the rivers and estuaries of the Channel coast, seizing in its grip Avignon and Marseille, isolating the mountain villages of the Puy-de-Dôme, sending the old and the poor into the woods (whence they emerged, bent under faggots), driving the wolves before it—and wolves, it is said, of a 'new race', never previously seen in France—to the outskirts of Paris and Lyon, to the markets of Saint-Germain and Versailles, Sceaux and Vaise. It was because *l'année du Grand Froid* was so utterly exceptional that it was so widely remembered and so often compared with 1709, a year that had lingered over three generations in the chronicles of popular horror. The important point is that at the best of times the system was so delicately balanced that even a localized failure, especially in the provisioning area of Paris, could set the whole edifice toppling, with food commissioners from rival towns and, in wartime, from rival armies, rushing to outbid one another and with the whole *carte des approvisionnements* being pushed beyond its normal frontiers, northwards or westwards, or southwards or eastwards, or all at once, to crush other, well-marked marketing areas.[1]

The worst possible combination would be partial dearth at the same time as foreign and civil war. Mobilization on the scale of the year II would place on the government the responsibility of supplying bread to over a million men—and most of these from that part of the population which would normally supply itself. In the year II, the armies of the west had to be supplied from the Beauce and the Orléanais. What they were able to reserve for themselves was at the expense of some neighbouring Districts and even of Paris, and much of the wealth of the Lauragais was savagely disputed between the two armies at each end of the Pyrenees. Elsewhere wealthy areas were subjected to double or triple requisitions in

---

[1] This type of confusion would become even more marked once a general *taxe* had been imposed. The Prefect of the Puy-de-Dôme was to describe a similar situation, following the May Decrees, in his own and in neighbouring Departments: 'Toutes les relations de département à département se trouvaient soudainement modifiées, altérées. . . . Peu s'en est fallu que le département de l'Allier n'affamât celui du Puy-de-Dôme, et il ne falloit dans le Puy-de-Dôme qu'une fausse mesure pour affamer la Haute-Loire et le Cantal...' (A.N. F11 716).

favour of Paris, of Rouen, of an army. Occasionally they might be bled white; more often, they took advantage of the resulting administrative confusion not to deliver to any of these, while informing the commissioners of each that they had just delivered—only the week before—to one of the others. Rival food commissioners, because they were rivals, were unlikely to compare notes or to consult one another.

Equally, there were few insuperable natural barriers to distribution. France, after 1770, had excellent high roads, a network of canals and waterways. Grain could travel, thanks to the *sapines*, in even a foot of water. Every tiny stream—many of them now half-remembered names: the Essonne, the Bièvre, the Morins, the Ourcq, the Loing—carried its quota of grain and *bois flotté*, until they dried up altogether in the dangerous summer months. Only a few mountain areas might have difficulty in getting supplies in the winter, but such places normally built up their reserves in September to tide them over. Help, especially in winter, might be long in coming but it would come eventually, once the ice broke up, in March or April. The obstacles to distribution were much more human than natural.

17. DEARTH AND INEQUALITY

The *problème des subsistances* had a particular and inexhaustible appeal to the simple man—we have seen how much time he was prepared to devote to discussing it—for it aroused in him the resentment derived from a sense of privilege and inequality. The *sans-culotte* might have been prepared to live for a time at least with shortage, had he believed that everyone was going short, that it was a necessary, if temporary, concomitant of war and emergency. But he was convinced that this was not so, that in fact *il était en train de mourir au sein de l'abondance*, that there was plenty of food going to the tables of the rich, that the butchers were reserving their best pieces for their well-to-do customers and that, in the semi-rural inns on the edge of the city, the rulers of the day —*Conventionnels*, republican generals, even members of the Committees of Government—were 'living it up', banqueting hilariously and enormously in fashionable feminine company (probably wives of *émigrés*, thick on the periphery of Paris after the decree of 14 Germinal)—as indeed they often were.[1] Even Robespierre had

[1] '. . . Dès le mois d'avril (1793) nos séjours à la campagne devinrent plus fréquens et plus prolongés. Nos dîners étoient nombreux; des femmes entre-

friends in Choisy, who received him under an arch of roses. The *hébertistes* went in for semi-rural dinner-parties under the creeping vine at de Kock's place in Passy. Danton had a house in Ivry and the *dantonistes* ate in an inn with a garden, *tonnelles*, and a maze at Belleville.

It was a problem that had the irresistible appeal of the basest, most primitive form of envy; and envy was perhaps the most effective recruiter for Terror and for the terrorist, just as the White terrorist was to march behind the banner of vengeance. Women, in particular, who are most at home in forms of violence inspired by shortage, are the likeliest agents of that ugly sentiment. What really finished Hébert off politically was the story of the hoarded lard in his cellar—a brilliant propaganda stroke, whether true or untrue. The Cordeliers were likewise disposed of by the sordid affair of *le rhum de Robert*, a phrase which came well off the tongue. Fouquier could have made an excellent historian of the popular mentality. One of the worst things he produced against the Girondins was that they were given to meeting over dinner-parties; and, at the *hébertiste* trial, someone was produced who reported what Vincent had said at another dinner—remarks so wild that it could only be concluded that he had been doing himself very well indeed. ('Tandis que le pauvre sans-culotte arrose de ses larmes un morceau de pain moisi disputé aux chiens'—for that is how the popular formula *en usage* goes: stale bread and tears.)

Gluttony was the characteristic vice—or virtue—of the Thermidorian ruling class, but then it no longer mattered very much, as the Thermidorians did not need to reckon with the popular mentality. The people, in any case, were by then past envy and were really starving.

18. REGIONAL ANTAGONISMS

The same sense of grievance and injustice would raise the population of one town against another and add further bitterness, if that were possible, to regional antipathies.[1] The Rouennais were

tenues, des actrices, y étoient souvent invitées. Nos réunions, autrefois si paisibles, dégénéroient en orgies . . .' (*Souvenirs de ma vie depuis 1774 jusqu'en 1814*, par M. de J***** (Jullian), Paris, 1815, p. 143). These dinner-parties took place at Bas-Meudon.

[1] Among the causes of the outbreak of the revolutionary crisis in the summer of 1789, Sénac de Meilhan refers to 'la vente forcée des bleds expédiés à Remiremont, faite en vertu des ordres du Comité de Mirecourt; l'opposition constante de celui de Carantan au versement des bleds du Cotentin dans le Bessin;

easily convinced—and they did not take much convincing—that, if they went short, it was because Paris got the first pick and weighed the most heavily in government preoccupations; and the Havrais were equally quick to point out that they were being stripped for the benefit of Rouen. So it went on down the scale, until once again one reaches rock bottom: the bitter envy of the *faubourien* for the city-dweller. Rouen accused Paris, le Havre, Rouen. Musquinet-Lapagne led his shipwrights, sailors, and fishermen down from the village of Ingouville into Le Havre, whose authorities, he claimed, were selling their grain to the English.[1] It was particularly easy to rouse any community in the north of France against Paris, by references to the avid appetite of its inhabitants and the privileged position of its *Halles*. Was it not generally known that the Parisians got more and cheaper bread than anyone else? (This was no legend, for, generally, they did.)

One of the most effective arguments of the federalist authorities in the summer of 1793 was thus to draw attention to the 'food imperialism' of Paris, just as one of their most dangerous weapons was the threat to cut off the capital's sources of meat supply in the Pays d'Auge.[2] When federalism collapsed and the movement of livestock from the Pays d'Auge to Poissy was resumed, it soon became evident that beasts were showing a curious reluctance to go beyond the town of Mantes, a place notoriously ill-disposed towards the capital, and in which a number of cows and bulls regularly elected to die; the meat thus made available was sold on the local market. The villages of the Isère, the Ain, the Saône-et-Loire, the Haute-Saône, and the Côte-d'Or that normally had to supply the Lyon markets with grain, fish, and meat (Lyon had important stores and regular purchasers at the grain ports of Saint-Jean-de-Losne and Gray, obtained fish from the Dombes, meat from the Charolais, and considerable supplies of grain from the Isère, as well as from Marseille and the *Plaine d'Arles*)[3] were delighted to find a similar excuse to cut off supplies to the city

les excès où vient de se porter celui de Toulon; ceux qu'a commis celui de Bordeaux . . .' (*Éclaircissemens historiques et impartiaux sur les causes secrettes et les effets publics de la Révolution de 1789*, 1790).

[1] *Terreur et subsistances*, pp. 97, 105, 226, 231 (28).

[2] A. Goodwin, 'The Federalist Movement in Caen in the Summer of 1793' (*Bulletin of the John Rylands Library*, 1960).

[3] R. C. Cobb, *L'Armée révolutionnaire parisienne à Lyon et dans la région lyonnaise* (Lyon, 1952), pp. 43–5.

when, on 29 May 1793, Lyon went federalist. During the siege, very little came through, so that there was more for Vienne, Grenoble, Valence, Villefranche, Mâcon, Chalon. These places could not only offer themselves the luxury of being *patriotes* in contrast to Lyon's villainy, their patriotism was rewarding and they could actually eat better out of it, with the added satisfaction that what they got, the Lyonnais would not. *Autant de pris aux Prussiens.*

Indeed, it might well be argued that many of these towns remained faithful to the Republic, which they thus served by preventing the revolts of Lyon and Marseille from joining up or from spreading up the valley of the Saône or towards Geneva, because of their hatred of Lyon, a hatred derived in part from the knowledge that they had always had to take second place in the hour of need, when Lyon got the first helping. It was exceedingly lucky for them that Lyon had plumped for the wrong side. Once the city had been recovered, the surrounding countryside continued to refuse to supply it, making much of their recent virtue, and stating that they could not let food go to traitors. In order to rescue the population from famine, the *Représentants du Peuple envoyés à Commune-Affranchie* had to disguise requisitions for Lyon as requisitions for the *Armée des Alpes*, to which they were also accredited. Both in 1794 and in the year III, the conditions for a similar conflict existed in the Bouches-du-Rhône, between Marseille and Aix, as well as between Marseille and the semi-rural *communes* of its own District.

Even provincial *sans-culottes*, always ready to come to the rescue of the sacred *bercail de la liberté* when it came under fire from well-to-do *notables*, were less enthusiastic when called upon to make sacrifices of food and fuel for the capital. The Parisians were not the only patriots. It was a clever, if unscrupulous, move on the part of the Revolutionary Government to place among the accused at the *hébertiste* trial a Parisian food commissioner, Antoine Descombes, who had made his weight felt, in the interests of Parisian needs, in the grainlands around Provins. Paris might be indestructible, its food commissioners were not. Descombes was guillotined. But in all the departments subjected to requisitions for Paris, under pressure from the local authorities the Committee recalled the more energetic emissaries of the *Commission des Subsistances*. Some of them were accused by the local authorities of *hébertiste* leanings and of having promoted enforced *déchristianisation.* Of these they may or may not have been guilty, but their real crime was to have relentlessly harried the districts and to have seen to it that the great requisitions were carried out without too much delay. By the spring of 1794 they were expendable; the first round of requisitions had been fully discharged and Paris had some reserves with which to look ahead. It was an excellent time to make some concession to the hard-pressed authorities of the grain Districts of the Seine-et-Oise, the Oise, the Seine-et-Marne, the Eure, the Eure-et-Loir, and the Aisne, on which the weight of Parisian needs had fallen the most heavily. So the *commissaires* were sacrificed to rural vindictiveness.

As a short-term measure the operation was wholly successful. The districts were finally rid of their more embarrassing *surveillants*, the *administrateurs* could at last sit back and luxuriate in their natural torpor, and the *agents nationaux*, henceforth complete masters in their own areas, could feel reassured that they would no longer have to contend with interference from outside. Rural opinion was informed that it no longer need fear root and branch *déchristianisation* and was won over, to some extent, to support of the Revolutionary Government. (The other victim of this pause was the *maximum*.) But, in the long run, such a policy was dangerous. Sooner or later the authorities in Paris would once more need to resort to force and recruit men who were strong and determined, in order to ensure Paris its supplies. The ingratitude shown by the Committees on this occasion to its food commissioners was not likely to encourage others, when the time came, to emulate the single-mindedness of Descombes and his more fortunate colleagues.

However, for the moment, the Committees had successfully disposed of their more dangerous Left-wing opponents and had furthermore persuaded rural opinion in the Paris provisioning zone of the existence of a 'food plot'. It was quite a clever way of exploiting, in Pontoise, Provins, Melun, Brie-Comte-Robert, Lagny, Pont-Saint-Maxence, Compiègne, Clermont, Beauvais, Dourdan, Soissons, Laon, les Andelys, and so on, the unpopularity of Paris; and, in order to emphasize that this was not just an empty gesture, along with the recall of the *commissaires aux subsistances* came the abolition of the *armée révolutionnaire parisienne*, the most hated, because the most effective, instrument of Paris food imperialism.

19. 'FOOD PLOTS' FOR POPULAR CONSUMPTION

So much for rural opinion in the area surrounding the capital. The Committees had something too for Parisian opinion; for there were two sides to the *complot pour affamer Paris* and, while Descombes was sacrificed to the farmers and grain merchants of the Brie, the pathetic Ducroquet was guillotined in an effort to reassure wholesalers (the *hébertistes* were accused of having *voulu tuer le commerce*) while the office of *commissaire aux accaparements* was abolished. The *sans-culottes* were fobbed off with the *complot des arrivages*; there was Hébert's lard, there was Robert's rum. The so-called *hébertistes* of the rural *communes* of the Département de Paris and of the Seine-et-Oise—places always the object of almost paranoiac suspicion on the part of the Paris *sectionnaires*—were at the same time accused of having taken part in a 'plot' by holding up and appropriating for their own people supplies on the way to Paris. There were *hébertiste* plots, it was said, in Meudon, Vaugirard, Passy, Auteuil, Boulogne, Suresnes, Belleville, Vincennes, Saint-Cloud, Lagny, Fontenay-aux-Roses, Joinville, Étampes, Arpajon, Étréchy, Sceaux, Montrouge, and, of course, Versailles. These places sounded convincing, as they were constantly being denounced by the Parisians as centres of *arrêts*, *pillages*, and *taxations*. Just to drive the point home, the government had the *agent national* of Belleville guillotined, the *maires* of Étampes, Arpajon, and Étréchy arrested, the former *curé* of Vaugirard guillotined, an official from Lagny imprisoned, and there were numerous arrests in Versailles, Passy, Boulogne, Auteuil, Vincennes, Choisy, and Franciade (Saint-Denis).

No effort was spared to give substance to this half of the 'plot'; already, almost a week before the arrest of the *hébertiste* leaders in Paris (Mazuel was arrested in Versailles on 27 Ventôse), Fouquier had sent *commissions rogatoires* to a score of *communes* on the principal supply routes to Paris to gather material about efforts on the part of local authorities to interfere with the normal flow of *arrivages*. As usual, the *accusateur public* made a thorough job of it; in Fouquier's indictment there was something for everybody. For the Parisian *sans-culotte*, alarmed at the usual seasonal worsening of the food situation in the spring (Ventôse was, in this respect, an excellent month to choose), *la crise de ventôse* had a convincing ring about it. Of course, the choice may have originally been made, not by the Committees, but by Ronsin, Vincent, and Mazuel, in the belief that the seasonal crisis was the best moment to launch a vast popular insurrection. If that is so, the 'conspirators' did the Committees' work for them—one way or another, for six weeks or more previously, it had been widely rumoured that *le coup est pour la seconde décade de ventôse*, and when the 20th came and went without anything happening, it was predicted for the 30th. There was something too for the farmers of the Brie, ground down by continuous requisitions, and for the wholesaler and the *accapareur*, stung to fury by the zeal of the *commissaires aux accaparements*.

The Revolutionary Government at the same time put the *problème des subsistances* on the already long list of subjects not to be talked about. Anyone who did talk about it must, therefore, be a counter-revolutionary and in the middle of Germinal fifteen poor artisans, water-carriers, *gagne-deniers*, carpenters' apprentices, were arrested for having dared raise the question of meat rationing in the *assemblée générale* of the Section des Lombards. The government was quite prepared to use the subject to discredit a political adversary. It was a dangerous game to play. For one thing, even after the execution of the 'food plotters' the situation did not improve, so that *sans-culotte* opinion might either call their 'guilt' in question, or conclude that they had been only the advance guard of a whole army of similar conspirators. They might then call for a massive repression of farmers and hoarders at the very time the Committees were attempting to moderate the course of the economic Terror and replace it by purely political victims. Again, as the situation still did not improve and although people obediently refrained from discussing it, some might think that the Committee of Public Safety was itself to blame. (Lindet had been called by some *l'organisateur de la famine*, an expression many Thermidorians were to reserve for Boissy d'Anglas.)[1] Finally, the Committees and Fouquier had blown up their 'food plot' to such vast proportions that they had killed it in the process as a subject for indictment; it could hardly be served up again, even when the

---

[1] Mercier, too, offers a political interpretation three years later: 'L'idée d'organiser une famine n'étoit pas neuve; la cour en avoit quelquefois usé; durant l'été de l'an III, Boissy-d'Anglas mentit comme un Barère'—no one could have lied like Barère—'et favorisa, comme un des agens les plus actifs de la faction des Anglomanes, cette disette désespérante au moyen de laquelle on comptoit conduire un peuple affamé à demander un roi . . .' (*Le Nouveau Paris*, pp. iv, 43).

situation obviously got worse. Fouquier had to wait till Messidor before using it in one of his *pots-pourris*, this time at the trial of Madame Dubarry, who, he argued, had attempted to starve the people out by putting her estates under clover. It was always a mistake to overplay a single article of indictment. Death labels are not inexhaustible, even in revolutionary periods, and it does not look good to have three or four identical plots in a row. Fouquier and his masters had flogged a magnificent, all-purpose subject almost to death.[1]

20. THE *SANS-CULOTTE* VIEW OF THE COUNTRYMAN

Dearth not only put teeth into regional or inter-urban antagonisms, it polarized in the sharpest terms the conflict between town and country, urban consumer and rural producer to which we have already referred and the effects of which were somewhat lessened by the hybrid nature of a population often semi-urban and semi-rural. One should be careful not to overplay this conflict in a society where so many townsmen were still countrymen at heart, but there is no doubt about its acuteness in the economic Terror of the year II and in the famine of the year III. Contemporary language leaves no doubt about what the *sans-culottes* thought of the rural population as a whole. The official slogan *guerre aux châteaux, paix aux chaumières* was singularly empty and spurious, and the *révolutionnaire* of urban armies, let loose on the countryside, was as hostile to the cottager as to the *châtelain*.[2] The wife or daughter of any peasant whatever was good for ribald language and pinching, any peasant at all was good for a drink and a slap-up meal, any countryman was *ignorant, grossier,* and *fanatique,* and, in *sans-culotte* proceedings, it is as impossible to find the words *gros laboureur* unaccompanied by the adjectives *avide et égoïste* (with variants on *au cœur de bronze, d'airain, de pierre,* according to choice), as to find Pitt without his Siamese twin of Cobourg.

---

[1] For the preceding section, see *Terreur et subsistances,* pp. 121, 149; *Les Armées révolutionnaires,* ii. 807–76; and 'Jaubert et le procès des hébertistes', AHRF, no. 147.

[2] The members of the Paris Revolutionary Army, and no doubt many other *sans-culottes* from the capital, were further imbued with that spirit of Paris imperialism to which Restif refers: '. . . Je parlais à des Parisiens, à des Gens qui ne se doutaient pas qu'il dût y avoir de la réciprocité dans le monde, et pour lesquels, après eux, leur Famille et leur Côterie, tout le reste de l'Univers n'était que des Marionnettes . . . ' (*Les Nuits,* ix. 2056).

The *sans-culottes* made few distinctions between the various components of the rural population. The *valet de ferme*, the *journalier*, the *vacher*, and the *vachère* were seen as the allies of the farmer—as, indeed, to some extent they were, since they were generally fed by him and so did not see the *problème des subsistances* from the same side of the barricade as the *sans-culottes*—and as potential recruits to the armies of 'superstition'. With the experience of the Vendée and of peasant revolts in the Brie, very near Paris,[1] before their minds, the *sectionnaires* were inclined to lump all countrymen together as religious fanatics, inspired by an undying hatred of a town-made Revolution and for the *bercail de la liberté*. They should therefore be made to feel the full weight of a town-made Terror, directed by townsmen. If the *sans-culottes* showed such a predilection for *ambulances* and wanted wheeled guillotines to accompany them, or for water ones worked by local power, if the most popular of all *sans-culotte* institutions was the *armée révolutionnaire*, especially the provincial variety, it was because they wanted the Terror to reach right out into the depths of the countryside and believed that the Revolution, their own well-being, and that of their families depended on making the countryman feel the whip of *sans-culotte* summary justice.[2] *Le père Duchesne* fulminated almost as much against the *rustauds*, millers, corn-factors, and farmers as against Marie-Antoinette or lawyers; and, in Paris, those *qui avoient l'air d'être de la campagne* —women with baskets of eggs, *marchands de salade*, market-gardeners from Montreuil—are frequently the centre of angry verbal exchanges which end up in blows.

The only countrymen who found any favour were the rural equivalents of their own condition: village artisans, blacksmiths, *galochiers*, innkeepers, *tonneliers*, and so on. For one thing, the rural Terror would have been inoperative without the help of such people. The townsmen, on their own in a village, were innocents abroad, ready to listen to the first innkeeper—*la mère Duchesne*[3] and others of her hospitable kind—who gave them a drink. They could not distinguish between village personalities and were incapable of recognizing in such and such a ragged peasant the richest man in the place. For another thing, if one wanted to know about farmers, how much they had put away in their barns, where

---

[1] *Les Armées révolutionnaires*, ii. 669.
[2] Ibid., ii. 394–7.   [3] Ibid., ii. 508, 520, 513–14.

they had hidden their treasure (and the *révolutionnaires*, great believers in *magots*, spent much of their time in the country pulling down communicating walls, pulling up floorboards, searching behind chimneys for treasure), how far behind they were with the requisitions, the man to ask was the blacksmith. He was a source of information as indispensable to the urban terrorist as, two years later, to the *chauffeur du Nord*, to whom he suggested suitable operations.[1]

For our purposes, these people could hardly be described as countrymen at all. They did not produce their own bread, they worked for the passing traveller or for the urban innkeeper as much as for the local community, and they drew their tools and materials from the city. These were the people who in the year II called in the townsmen to help them topple a municipality dominated by big farmers and lawyers; it was they who formed the *comités de surveillance* of *bourg* and village, and very often they were the local iconoclasts and *déchristianisateurs*.[2] In the year II, they were hated and feared by the rural population as a whole, as traitors and 'foreigners'. They were to be the first, most accessible, victims of the White Terror.[3] Finally, *sans-culotte* anti-feminism drew fresh vigour from the experience of rural riots provoked by peasant women when church bells were removed or a *prêtre réfractaire* was being arrested. The Terror of the year II was so popular largely because it was so anti-rural.

It was natural, too, for the urban artisan, when faced with the threat of shortage, to want to *aller chercher les subsistances là où elles se trouvent*: and one of the most persistent of *sans-culotte* beliefs was that, while the patriotic townsman drew in his belt, did his guard duties, attended his Section, and saw his sons go off to the frontiers, the countryman sat down every afternoon to a five-course meal (his eyes glinting at the thought of what the townsman would not get), fed his grain to his pigs, slaughtered and ate his livestock, and harboured his sons who were deserters, while his wife and daughters attended the semi-clandestine mass of non-juror priests. The countryside, it was said, even a few leagues from Paris, *nageoit dans l'abondance*—a view that, after September 1793, was soon confirmed by many *sans-culottes* (members of urban battalions) with their own eyes, in letters addressed from a despon-

---

[1] Vidocq, iv. 184. [2] *Terreur et subsistances*, p. 300.
[3] See above, pp. 131–50.

dent and infuriatingly inactive rural exile to the *frères et amis* of their Sections.[1] In some instances, especially where the grainlands around Paris were concerned—the Brie, the Vexin, the Santerre— these reports were no doubt true and there was no shortage on the long farm-house table, at least of food. But the *sans-culotte* tended to overlook the horrors of rural poverty, the wretched housing and the constant prevalence of disease that made the life of the poor peasant of certain areas of marshland much shorter than that of the townsman in a city like Paris or Bordeaux.[2] The townsman might be underprivileged as to provisioning and have much greater difficulty in keeping his family regularly supplied with bread, but he had a far wider choice of employment and was better housed and better paid. His view of the countryman was conditioned entirely by his own attitude to the *problème des subsistances* and by his belief that the Revolution (his Revolution) was not loved among ling and fern, chestnut and marsh. His prejudices are quite understandable, if not justifiable. The important thing is that he thought the way he did and that this conditioned his belief in Terror as a magic formula for plenty, as well as his own activities and behaviour, if he were ever let loose in the *plat pays*.

21. THE COUNTRYMAN'S VIEW OF THE TOWNSMAN

Of course, there was something to be said for the countryman too, and the author has rightly been chided for allowing the *sans-culottes* to dictate to him their own views of the *cultivateur avide et égoïste*.[3] The sense of deprivation, so strongly felt by the *sans-culotte*, on the subject of the crying inequalities of *les subsistances* in time of dearth, could be felt just as acutely by the countryman fresh to the town, even in normal conditions. In one of his first letters home, *Edmond* complains: 'Si tu voyois comme on est sensuel et glouton à la table du Maître, en comparaison de chez nous! chaque personne y consomme autant de viande que trois de nos gens; on diroit qu'à la ville on ne vit que pour manger. . . .'[4] The Parisian, particularly the Parisian of recent origin, took an impudent delight in demonstrating his new status by snubbing the poor countryman who had probably arrived only a few months or

---

[1] *Les Armées révolutionnaires*, pp. 398–405.   [2] See note 2E, p. 372.
[3] Norman Hampson, in his review of *Terreur et subsistances*, *E.H.R.*, July 1966.
[4] *Le Paysan*, i. 13.

a few weeks later. Country girls in service were good enough to be seduced; but they were mocked for their simplicity and the ease with which they had been taken in by urban blandishments. *Edmond*, still in his first few days in the city, waxes indignant on the subject, in another letter to *Pierrot*:

> Si tu voyois les libertés qu'on y prend avec ces pauvres filles qui ont abandonné leurs bons parens et leurs villages... pour venir à la ville.... Il semble que ces pauvres filles (et nous tous tant que nous sommes gens de village) soient au-dessous de l'humanité, et qu'il n'y ait plus de pudeur à garder avec elles qu'avec les animaux. . . .[1]

Most of the *déclarations de grossesses* made before the *commissaires* concern country girls fresh to the capital. Poor Marguerite Barrois, it will be recalled, was seduced on her second night in the city, on 10 Thermidor year II, a date as memorable for her no doubt as for history. There was a certain class of men that hung around the post-houses, for the arrival of the *diligences*, or at the landing-stage of the *coche*, lying in wait for the gullible peasant girl. We have already referred to the way the Parisian authorities and the inhabitants in general treated the peasants and peasant women who arrived in the city after walking through the night, to bring dairy produce or fresh vegetables to the morning markets.[2]

Edmond, it is true, soon lost his sense of indignation and took care to divest himself of his rustic manners. It was not long before he had adopted *le ton de la ville*, while *Ursule* took even less time to adapt herself to city ways. But the visiting peasant did not feel the need of such a conversion. He was not at all ashamed of his calling, or of his appearance, but was, on the contrary, well aware that the townsman could not get along without him, and for the impudent Parisian, at each successive visit, he merely felt more contempt and more resentment. He, at least, did an honest day's work, while so many of the insolent fellows who made fun of his *gaucherie*, of his clothes and of his manner of speech, were nothing

---

[1] *Le Paysan*, i. 14.
[2] '. . . Et puis si tu voyois encore comme on fait ici aux paysans qui viennent chaque semaine apporter les denrées nécessaires! Ils y sont traités avec un mépris que je ne conçois pas, et qui me paroît marquer de la bêtise dans les gens de la ville, car ces pauvres villageois les détestent, et se vengent de leurs mauvaises façons, en vendant le plus cher qu'ils peuvent, et en trompant de toutes manières ceux qui les méprisent . . .' (ibid. i. 15).

better than lackeys, proud of their livery, the sign of their slavery;[1]
so many of the overdressed girls who laughed at his grammar
were ladies' maids, who had caught the conceit and the snobbery
of their mistresses. For these were the sort of people who took the
most ostentatious pride in being Parisians *à part entière*, and what
better way of doing that than emphasizing the chasm that separated these gorgeous, liveried souls, from the poor farmer, *tout
crotté*, clinging nervously to his hat? *Pierrot*'s opinion would be
that of many farmers: 'quand une fille a servi dans les villes, vois-
tu mon cher Edmond, ça lui donne un mauvais chapeau; mon père
et ma mère nous l'ont dit cent et cent fois. . . . Une servante à la
ville, un laquais à livrée, . . . ça répugne . . . parce que les gens de
cœur ne se ravalent jamais jusqu'à ça. . . .'[2] Restif himself reflects
the rural good sense he so much admires, and perhaps idealizes,
in this disparaging excuse for the manservant: 'Le Valet, ravalé
au-dessous de la qualité d'homme . . . endure le mépris, quelquefois les coups, toujours l'impertinence . . . voue son existence au
faste. . . . Bien des gens sacrifient tout à leur parure. . . .'[3] For the
countryman would judge the people of the town by this most
impudent and, to him, ridiculous, representative of the urban
population: the servant who had adopted something of his master's
tone and who, once away from his quarter, hastily buckled on a
sword; the parlourmaid who, when going out, walked in her lady's
discarded silk dresses; the *garçon perruquier*, swollen-headed,

---

[1] '. . . Je sortis, réfléchissant sur nos mœurs actuelles, sur notre grossièreté
brutale, effet de l'aisance de nos Jeunes-Seigneurs, mal imités par tous les
Faquins, qui l'ont entée [*sic*] sur la rusticité auvergnate ou limousine . . .' (*Les
Nuits*, ix. 2057).

[2] *Le Paysan*, i. 31. See also *Monsieur Nicolas*, ii. 822: '. . . Mon cœur, révolté
de sa chaîne, s'élançait vers cette aimable fille — Mais elle était Servante! & mes
parents m'avaient inspiré une sorte d'horreur pour la servitude de la ville, surtout
pour celle des filles: aimer une servante me paraissait déroger à l'honnêteté
naturelle. . . .' Ibid. iv. 1886: '. . . J'ai été femme de chambre & je sais ce que
c'est: si la Maîtresse elle-même ne taponne pas une jolie fille comme ça, le
Maître, l'Intendant, le Maître d'hôtel, le Valet de chambre, & jusqu'aux Laquais
vous attaquent, vous tripotent, & quelquefois, une pauvre fille est violée . . .'

[3] *Le Paysan*, i. 162. See also *Le Tableau de Paris*, vi. 75: '. . . Ce vol d'individus,
fait aux campagnes, à l'agriculture n'a pas même été frappé d'un impôt propre
à cet égoïsme révoltant. Et tandis que le galon d'or et d'argent entre dans la
livrée de la servitude, le sarron de toile couvre à peine le laboureur et le vigneron....' Sénac de Meilhan expresses an opposite point of view: '... Ce peuple
des campagnes, en voyant ainsi réduire les moyens de pourvoir à sa subsistance
dans ses villages, a éprouvé de même la plus sensible diminution dans les
ressources que les villes lui procuroient, soit pour être domestiques, soit pour
y trouver quelque autre genre de travail . . .' (*Éclaircissemens* . . ., p. 164).

loquacious, and unsettled, who squandered his earnings *au billard*. Who were these people to judge a man who produced their food and who arduously tilled the soil?[1]

It was unwise to humiliate useful people in this way, for the time came, every ten years or so, when the goodwill of the countryman would be a matter of life or death for the city-dweller. Long before the Revolution, the peasant who was in contact with the city, particularly with Paris, though he might profit outrageously from the trade of the urban food markets,[2] had suffered years of social affront and bureaucratic insolence. The whole history of the Revolution reminds us that public humiliation and outraged pride affect the choice of political commitment more fundamentally than the search for material gain. As the Revolution in the conditions of 1793 and the year II became increasingly a townsman's affair, operated by and for townsmen—and the *sans-culottes* made no bones about saying so: it was their Revolution—it is not surprising that many countrymen turned against a revolution from the benefits of which they were apparently to be excluded.

The events of the Revolution constantly accentuated the economic, religious, and political gulf between town and country, especially after the outbreak of war. Dechristianization was a direct assault on the countryman's faith, the implementation of the Civil Constitution was an attack on the countryman's priest, the father of his flock. The *sans-culotte* wanted cheap and abundant bread from the countryman, but denied him the right to take anything out of the city in return. Some *coquetières* and other rural provisioners were subjected to such vexations by the *commissaires aux accaparements* and the revolutionary committees—their *acquits à caution*, a form stating the place of sale of their goods—had not been properly filled in, and so on—that they decided not to bring

---

[1] A.N. F10 210 (Commission d'Agriculture) (société populaire de la commune de Pact, district de Vienne (Isère), à la Convention, s.d. fructidor an II): '. . . Nous avons encore pensé pour ce qui regarde l'agriculture que rien n'impliqueroit de faire sortir des villes tous ces individus sans occupation qui ne passent leur tems qu'à crier contre la pénurie qu'ils occasionnent des comestibles et qui insultent par leur oisiveté les cultivateurs qui s'énervent pour leur conduire leurs denrées et de n'y laisser que ceux qui sont occupés aux manufactures, à l'administration et au commerce. . . .'

[2] '. . . Les grandes villes ne dévorent point les campagnes, elles ne les rendent que plus florissantes par les moyens de reproduction et de consommation. L'agriculture n'est jamais plus brillante qu'autour des villes populeuses . . .' (*Le Tableau de Paris*, x. 1).

their goods to the town any more, but preferred to sell them to the ever-obliging innkeepers of the *faubourgs*, or to eat them at home. Seen from the level of the rural producer who might be as much the smallholder, the subsistence farmer, the *métayer*, as the big farmer, since even the smallest farmer would reserve his wheat for sale on the urban market—the economic policies of 1793 and the year II could only be interpreted as collective brigandage, a policy of violence, exercised with the help of armed force on the part of the towns, over the neighbouring countryside. This was reasonable enough when the requisitions were carried out by soldiers, sent from the towns, billeted on the farmers, and behaving just as if they were in enemy territory; indeed, many of these urban soldiers said that they were in enemy territory.

Since *la politique du maximum* was, in fact, a weapon of war against the country population as a whole[1] and only the village artisan was likely to gain from it, the peasant naturally failed to appreciate that he was behaving like a counter-revolutionary when he attempted to meet force with force and, with a charge of buck-shot, tried to hold off the urban food commissioners and their escorts, for these officials were the most detested of all and gave rise to endless complaints about their 'despotism' and their constant interference in every side of village life. Perhaps the most surprising fact about the Terror of the year II is that the armed opposition to the urban busy-bodies was not greater, but the countryman relied more on the old rural weapons of dissimulation, inertia, and patience, than on open defiance. For dearth, dreaded and so often misrepresented by the urban artisan, was a longed-for opportunity for the peasant who had even inferior grain to sell.

Of course, the big farmer, like the corn-factor, could expect to do best out of the lean years. He could afford to hold his stocks till the last possible moment, even at the risk of a sudden fall in price, if he waited too long, a risk that the smallholder and the subsistence farmer could ill afford. He might, too, make additional profits by loans at usurious rates to smallholders in financial difficulties. But even the subsistence farmer would probably reserve a tiny surplus for sale and keep for family consumption only the inferior grain (oats or millet), putting on the market the wheat which his minute strip produced to meet cash needs. He stood to gain from a period of shortage, even if he could not hold

[1] See note 2F, p. 372.

on till the last moment. In 1812, it is true, the smallholder seems to have been denied the opportunities so eagerly seized by farmers with estates of a hundred acres or more. According to one report from the Eure, the smallholders were the first victims of the low yield of the 1811 harvest, and in the Doubs they borrowed from millers and bakers and were reduced to buying their own bread. They were no doubt similarly hit by the partial failure of the years II and III. Even so, 1788–9, 1795–6 should in the normal course of events have been good years for the rural producer, large and small, and 1801–2 and 1811–12 certainly were, at least for the large. (The small producer, having less to hide, would find it more difficult to conceal his resources, in the event of a *taxe* or requisitions.) The years 1793–4 should have been good ones too, but owing to the intervention of the government and the fact that this was about the only occasion the urban *petit peuple* were ever able to impose most of their own favourite remedies for the problems of high prices and shortage, the small farmer was not only deprived of his opportunity, but forced to yield patiently accumulated stocks at prices that could hardly even meet production costs and that might result in his becoming so indebted as to be driven into the lower ranks of the agricultural proletariat.[1] If anything were likely to re-establish rural solidarity—and the smallholder normally had no special love for the *laboureur* and the grain merchant—it would be the *maximum*.

At the same time, the burden of war and mobilization fell more heavily on the farmer than on any other section of the community; as he had more to give, so more would be taken from him. Conscription deprived him of many of his best workmen, most of his horses and carts went to army transport (generally never to return), and many of his implements, if made of iron or steel, went the same way. He was subjected to all manner of vexations from urban commissioners billeted on him and whom, along with their soldiers, he had to keep in food and drink and even pay for having come at all (*frais de course*). He and his family were woken up in the night or early morning by groups of impudent townsmen who ransacked cupboard and cellar, and subjected his wife and daughters to a mixture of threats and ribaldry. It was all great fun for the *révolutionnaire*, who much enjoyed this type of outing, but the farmer was outraged, indignant, and no doubt frightened. The

[1] See note 2G, p. 373.

Terror of the year II was still being evoked with horror in the countryside fifty or sixty years later; and in villages like Villeblevin or Heyrieu, where in the 1950s one could still meet the surnames of 1793–4, the period of *sans-culotte* rule was remembered even as late as this.[1] When, in August 1944, the *F.F.I.* from Paris came into the Bessin with authority to requisition butter and dairy produce, the local peasants at once talked of the men of the year II.[2]

It was this sense of outrage, this sense of having been cheated of a legitimate and traditional profit, which lent such ferocity to the countryman's vengeance in the favourable conditions of the year III. The economic Terror of the year II had been directed primarily at the farmer's pocket, but with the politics of revenge in the year III many of those who had been enthusiastic in the service of *sans-culotte* economics were done to death. This was the penalty for having pulled down the rural altars, for having laid a sacrilegious hand on church plate, and for having denied the countryman his expected profit. The year 1795 saw at last the unqualified prosperity of the farmer; it also offered him a much-savoured revenge for eighteen months of humiliation and harassment. Now at last he was in a position to dictate his iron laws to the townsman and to town government.

Les fermiers ne donnent plus leurs grains pour des assignats, ils ne veulent plus de meubles, leurs maisons sont montées, ils ne veulent plus de bijoux, leurs femmes et leurs filles en sont garnies de toutes espèces, on voit des demoiselles fermières avec des montres d'or à répétition, avec des chaînes d'or au côté; ce ne sont plus de ces filles qui, avec de grosses galoches ferrées, avec de gros cotillons de toile qui rouloient dans leurs cours et dans les rues de leurs villages parmi la boue et la fange, tout cela est bien changé; on ne voit plus de ces bons fermiers assis au coin de leur feu mangeant leur soupe dans une jatte de terre sur leurs genoux, ou une trempette de cidre avec du pain bis émietté dedans, c'est

---

[1] The Lorillon family, so deeply divided in the Terror, still plays an important part in the political and economic life of Villeblevin; in the 1950s the *secrétaire de la mairie* was married to one of the Lorillon brothers. In Heyrieu, to the east of Lyon, Dorzat, the *agent national* of the year II, who was guillotined in the summer of 1794 as an 'ultra-revolutionary', was the principal villain of a play written by the local schoolmaster under the Second Empire. He is still spoken of with extreme loathing by the wealthier inhabitants. (I am indebted to M. Fernand Rude, Sous-Préfet of Vienne, for the latter information.)

[2] This was my own experience, whilst in H.Q., L. of C., in and around Bayeux, from July to September 1944. See 'Un soldat britannique dans le Calvados', in *La Renaissance du Bessin* for August 1944.

aujourd'hui des tables bien servies, la serviette à la boutonnière, recevant
ceux qui viennent demander du bled avec un ton d'Altesse sérénissime,
tandis qu'à leurs portes de malheureux journaliers meurent de faim. Il
y a huit ou dix jours on trouvoit encore un boisseau de bled pour 9 l. en
argent, aujourd'hui ils n'en ont plus pas même assez pour eux, mais si
on leur montre trois écus de 6 l., on dit *nous allons voir si cela se peut*, et
on finit en vous obligeant, de vous donner un boisseau de bled, on vous
fait dîner parce que vous avez apporté du beau poisson dont vous avez
commencé par leur faire présent en arrivant, voilà l'histoire du jour,
aussi plusieurs d'entr'eux ont-ils bien dit qu'il faudroit des dents
d'argent pour manger du pain. J'aurois huit jours à vous écrire si j'entre-
prenois de vous faire un tableau sur le caractère en général des habitans
de la campagne et sur l'antipathie qu'ils ont toujours eue de tous les tems
pour les habitans de villes, mais que demander à des gens sans mœurs,
qui n'ont jamais connu que leur cupidité, et si on n'y met pas des bornes,
on verra les habitans des villes périr de misère. . . .[1]

These farmers of the Pays de Caux were typical of most of their
kind in the conditions of the years III and IV. At least Mâlotain
succeeded in coming away with a bushel; in many other places,
the townsmen were sent away empty-handed, after having had to
listen to a lecture on the theme that the Revolution of the year II
had been operated by the town and for the town, and that now it
was the countrymen's turn and they were going to take it. They
certainly did. All over the north in these years we hear a litany of
complaints about their pitiless rapacity, their insulting arrogance,
and their total lack of compassion. There are numerous descriptions
of the inappropriate objects with which they filled their farm-
houses: pictures in gilded frames, busts of celebrities whose names
they did not know, Turkey carpets piled one on top of another,
clavichords, pianos, and harps, gold and silver plate, shelves of
bound volumes that they could not read, clothes in the height of the
fashion of five or six years before, a profusion of clocks, Bohemian
glass, Venetian mirrors, and chandeliers, even with candles to
light them and to contribute to this blaze of wealth, and, of course,
a roaring fire in the hearth and well-fed dogs and cats stretched
out towards it.[2] Whatever they had lost in the year II the farmers

---

[1] A.N. F10 242 (Commission d'Agriculture, Mâlotain, horloger de Dieppe,
à la Commission, 15 frimaire an IV).

[2] '. . . L'aisance se répandit dans les campagnes, les fermiers eurent des
rideaux de soie, des sofas, de toile de Perse, et se dorlotèrent dans des lits
d'acajou . . .' (Duval, op. cit.). '. . . Les granges des fermiers des campagnes
furent transformées en magasins de tapissiers. . . . Leurs femmes ont acheté

won back tenfold in the unheard-of conditions of the year III. The farms of the Pays de Caux, the Brie, the Beauce, the Soissonnais, of Flanders, the Orléanais, and the Gâtinais were like well-stocked furniture stores and salerooms, crammed with the pillage of cities. After what he had been through in the year II the farmer no doubt had some excuse; but his rapacity knew no measure. At least the *sans-culotte* economic restrictions of 1793–4 had contributed as much to the *magasins de la République* as to the poor man's ill-stocked larder (and each got only the necessary minimum); whereas there was something insultingly indecent about the rural profiteering of the years III and IV. This was more than revenge; it was downright cupidity.[1] The farmer would no doubt argue that he had to make the most of a situation that could be only temporary; and it is true that after this golden period grain prices fell and that for the next seven years the condition of the farmer was hardly enviable. It was not till the year X that something like prosperity returned.

In such a manner were the conditions created for the spectacular activities of the great bands of *chauffeurs* of the year IV onwards. There is one item missing in Vidocq's reassuringly moral tale: his *chauffeurs* are monstrously cruel, some from childhood upwards; their leaders are villainous, desperate, and fiendishly cunning; and their victims have all the rural virtues of hard work, a vigorous frugality, kindliness for their employees, a generous table for travellers, a simple, happy family life honoured by frequent visits from a revered, white-haired *curé*. But nowhere does Vidocq state how they came by their considerable, and to their contemporaries no doubt scandalous, wealth. This was in fact the last stage in the politics of revenge, fought out, ever since 1793, between town and country. Not that the *chauffeurs* were concerned with the victory of either side. They did not strictly belong to either camp, but they had their roots in both, and this accounted for their strength and for the considerable impunity with which they were often able to operate over months or years. They were drawn indistinctly from the rural and semi-rural crafts: blacksmiths, wheelwrights, horse-dealers, pedlars, *journaliers*, and farm-hands, as well as former soldiers, smugglers, urban and rural

toutes les nippes des bourgeoises; elles mangent sur des assiettes d'argent, elles ont la migraine . . .' (*Le Nouveau Paris*, v).

[1] See note 2H, p. 373.

innkeepers,[1] urban artisans, and a few exceptional elements such as gipsies. The policies at least that they carried out with such ferocity represented a much simplified version of the *sans-culotte* programme of the year II, though the profit was much more direct. After the experience of the year III, it is perhaps not surprising that a certain number of former *sans-culotte* militants, who had never been lacking in violence, even if in 1793–4 their violence had been to the advantage of the Republic, should adopt this desperate method of turning the tables on the *gros laboureurs* and enlisted, this time, in the ranks of the *bandes*.[2]

22. DEARTH AND TERROR

Even in the context of the year II, and faced with the whole panoply of the economic Terror, the farmer would be likely to have the last word. It is true that a great many farmers were arrested, on the orders of urban food commissioners and of members of city committees, in the autumn and winter of 1793. There was a last desperate wave of arrests for economic offences in the countryside just before the *hébertiste* crisis in Ventôse year II, the last occasion when the *sans-culottes* got their way with their food policy of repression.[3] But no farmer was executed for infractions of the *maximum* or for any other sin against the food economy of the year II. Those put to death were condemned for purely counter-revolutionary crimes. Even arrests were a weapon that was likely eventually to harm the interests of the urban consumer. For since labour was so scarce in the year II, a farmer in prison might mean a couple of fields going to waste, and when nineteen big farmers from one village in the District de Sens were arrested on the eve of the spring sowings in Ventôse year II, it was pointed

---

[1] A characteristic progression towards crime is that of Étienne Lhuya, 52, 'dauphinois, revendeur d'eau-de-vie et de tabac, puis aubergiste cabartier', described as leader of the murder gang that operated, from the year III to the year V, in and around the commune of Eyragues, in the Bouches-du-Rhône (Arch. Bouches-du-Rhône, L 3072 (assassinats, an III) (Acte d'accusation devant le tribunal de Tarascon, 15 frimaire an IX)).

[2] See note 2I, p. 374.

[3] On 24 Ventôse year II the Dieppe prison contained ninety-five inmates, twenty of whom had been arrested since the 1st of that month. There is a similar rise in the prison population of Versailles and Orléans in the second decade of Ventôse (Arch. Seine-Maritime L 5329), *Études Orléanaises, Terreur et subsistances*, p. 141 (61).

out that the economic life of the whole community would be brought to a halt and they were all released within a few weeks.[1] So it was with most farmers who had for one reason or another fallen foul of the revolutionary authorities in the cities. Arrest could not make the corn grow any quicker or any higher, but rather the contrary.

Farmers had plenty of other ways, too, of hitting back if urban zealots made life intolerable. In most areas they do not seem to have been particularly impressed by the Terror, despite all the noise and fury of *sans-culotte* preachings in village churches and the threatening language of the Committees of Government. The *sans-culottes* made the mistake of thinking that the farmers were fools as well as knaves. They were in fact much wiser men than most of the ultra-revolutionary optimists who marched into the countryside at the head of their small band of dishevelled, often drunken, and sometimes frightened, civilians pretending to be soldiers, swollen with pride, convinced that they could terrorize the country bumpkin into trembling submission by their tongues, and that they could convert, in a matter of hours, Coulanges-la-Vineuse into *Égalité-sur-Vertu*. Coulanges, and many other places, were made to change their names, but that was about as far as the change would go. Country opinion was irritated, or infuriated, rather than frightened, by the posturing of townsmen come to lay down the law and preach the new gospel.

As for the gospel itself, it seemed to country opinion just a lot of nonsense. The threats of food commissioners and *agents nationaux* were more serious; at least something had to be done about them, at least part of the amount demanded for a requisition would have to be supplied. The main thing was to hold on as long as possible without provoking a massive display of force by the urban authorities, and to gain time. The *sans-culottes* might believe that a Republic, social, egalitarian, fraternal, was in the process of creation, but rural opinion was convinced that the Terror would not last, that an undisturbed Sunday would once more measure out the course of the week, as it always had done, and that the urban commissioners were people who had to be put up with for the time being and even humoured and that sooner or later they would go and would never be seen again. The farmers, judging their visitors more correctly than the visitors gauged them, thought them

[1] *Les Armées révolutionnaires*, ii. 514–28.

knaves as well as fools. There was no doubt about the knavery. Had they not kept the whole village awake till eleven or midnight with their bellowing at the *auberge*? Had they not removed the gold crosses from the necks of the farmers' wives? And what did they know about agriculture? What did they mean by sticking their noses into dung, in search of seeds of grain? Who were they to decree what a farmer was to cultivate on the land of his forebears, what he was to sow, how quickly he was to thresh?

Rural dilatoriness and immobilism had an arsenal of weapons, most of them invisible to the passing commissioners. But they were visible to the local artisan, the village blacksmith or wheel-wright. This was why the minority of rural *sans-culottes* were so much detested. They had revealed to the townsman carefully kept village secrets—how much a farmer would normally produce, what were the hidden channels of clandestine sales, where he hid the stocks he was holding back from the markets, how much profit the illegal sale of grain was bringing to the *gros laboureur*.

In areas of extensive agriculture and large farms, it might be possible to obtain a rough over-all idea of the importance of the annual yield simply by counting the haystacks immediately after harvest, but it was much more difficult to estimate resources at all in *pays de petite culture*.[1] *Sans-culotte maires* were rare in villages—and those, like the shoemaker *maire* of Villeblevin, who were, found themselves subject to incessant harassment from the District, so often dominated by large farmers and lawyers[2]—and most rural *maires* were themselves producers or owners of grain. Was it likely that such people would show enthusiasm for the strict application of the *maximum* and the execution of requisitions for the urban markets? Even in the far more autocratic and repressive atmosphere of the Empire, the Imperial authorities were powerless in the face of rural inertia and covering up. A village *maire* was a match any day for a Prefect or Sub-Prefect, as the latter soon

[1] '. . . dans les pays de grande culture, où ce qui reste de la moisson précédente peut être facilement constaté par le nombre de meules, par les quantités engran-gées qu'on ne bat qu'au fur et à mesure de la consommation, je crois que l'ad-ministration peut calculer ses ressources avec quelque certitude; mais dans ce département, où les propriétés sont très divisées, où les grains battus immé-diatement après la récolte échappent à tous les regards, il est impossible de constater exactement la quotité des ressources . . .' (A.N. F11 711, Préfet de Rennes au Ministre, 24 juillet 1812).

[2] *Les Armées révolutionnaires*, ii. 514–28.

discovered in the 1812 crisis after the May Decrees.[1] Every peasant was a master in the art of disguising his resources; and few urban officials could penetrate the rags to the hidden wealth the rags disguised. 'Sur quoi compter', complains the Prefect of the Calvados in July of that year, 'avec une population dont le sentiment habituel et prédominant est la méfiance et dont les premiers mots sont toujours négatifs?'[2]

Eighteen years before, commissioners from Caen or from le Havre had had to contend with the limitless guile and *peut-être bien que oui, peut-être bien que non* attitudes of the Haut- and Bas-Normand peasant, a very old hand at the game. It was always easy to delay threshing, especially in wartime conditions such as those of 1794 and 1795 or of 1812, on the plea that threshers were unobtainable in the neighbourhood. Even if urban food commissioners answered by supplying the threshers from elsewhere, the farmer and his hands would make life so unpleasant that they would ask to be taken away.[3] An even simpler method was not to sow; and there is plenty of evidence that, harassed by government requirements and *sans-culotte* vexations, the farmers would retaliate with a production strike. If, eventually, the yield of the 1794 harvest turned out in some areas to be only two-thirds of the normal output,[4] particularly in the great grain-producing areas— always the worst offenders—this was not due only to the drought of Robespierre's Red Summer and a sudden outbreak of hailstorms in May.[5] There is no doubt that a great many farmers had decided to suspend cultivation, or put their land under pasture, a decision for which the shortage of labour and horses provided plenty of

---

[1] '... Les décrets n'ont été que partiellement et faiblement exécutés... comme on devait surtout l'attendre des maires qui, manquant la plupart de zèle et de capacité ... sont plus généralement trop foibles pour remplir à la rigueur des devoirs qui les exposent à la malveillance ...' (A.N. F11 705, Préfet de Bourg au Ministre, 28 août 1812). 'Elle [l'exécution du décret du 8 mai] a été éludée sans doute dans les campagnes isolées, où la force des magistrats est faible et la puissance de l'inertie presque invincible ...' (A.N. F11 712, Préfet de Nantes au Ministre, 22 août 1812).

[2] A.N. F11 707 (Préfet de Caen au Ministre, 24 juillet 1812).

[3] 'L'Armée révolutionnaire dans le district de Pontoise', A.H.R.F., no. 119, July–September 1950. [4] See note 2J, p. 374.

[5] A.N. F10 242: '. . . Le 13 mai 1794 il tomba une neige accompagnée de pluie qui geloit à mesure qu'elle tomboit et s'attachoit aux arbres, au froment, seigle et autres ... les seigles qui étoient en fleurs, froment et autres furent couchés ... sur terre comme si on eût roulé par-dessus un cylindre ... ce qui occasionna une disette considérable . . .' (report from the Ain, 28 Frimaire year IV).

plausible excuses. According to many Prefects of 1812, corn-production was the most onerous and expensive type of cultivation even in normal conditions, whereas pasture required much less initial expense. The imposition of a *maximum* (which did not include livestock, though it did include butcher's meat) was an open invitation to abandon wheat-production. In certain areas of Normandy, 1794 saw an impressive switch-over from cereals to stock-breeding.[1]

In the same way, in order to evade the provisions of the *maximum* on butcher's meat, many farmers slaughtered their calves and livestock. Force could not control the eating habits of the rural population. Nor could it be everywhere at once. And to have had any durable effect, even in the short term, it would have had to be. But the Committees, for political reasons, were not prepared to use it on the massive, ruthless scale that *sans-culotte* opinion so persistently demanded right up to the last moment in Ventôse year II. Once the Paris Revolutionary Army was disbanded in Germinal, it became clear that force would not be used any more at all, at least by that particular regime—a year later, in Ventôse year III, there were more troops billeted on the countryside than there had been under the Jacobins and *sans-culottes*. No wonder the *commissaires observateurs* reported broad smiles on the wide red faces of the fatstock merchants from Sceaux and Poissy and of the corn-factors from the Brie during the weeks following the execution of the *hébertistes*.

The *sans-culotte* solution to the problems of provisioning had not been proved either right or wrong. In the hands of a cautious Revolutionary Government it had scarcely been given a trial at all. Very little force had been used and, when it was used, it was generally under local authorities rather than Parisian commission-ers, and these latter were seldom entirely free agents. If popular remedies really had been adopted, they would have meant an urban militia of at least a hundred thousand, or even three hundred thousand, to be raised among married men with children—a further guarantee of anti-rural zeal—aged between thirty and fifty (the age limits of popular militancy). Wheeled guillotines and courts of summary justice would have had to be sent to the villages and *bourgs* of the grainlands and the *loi sur l'accaparement* would have had to be applied with relentless rigour. For failure to

[1] See note 2K, p. 374.

carry out requisitions there would have had to be really long terms of imprisonment and heavy fines, instead of warnings and gentle chidings ('Don't do it again', 'Remember your brothers in the city') and release after a few days in prison. Again, *agents nationaux* would have had to be placed under the direct control of urban *sociétés*, and a very few big farmers would have had to be guillotined on the place d'armes *pour encourager les autres*, and so on. In short, the rural Terror, instead of consisting of threats, chiding, persuasion, appeals to patriotism (not a tune that the farmer would be likely to pick up), muddle, contradictory orders, half-measures, would have had to become a reality.

If this programme had really been carried out, there is no telling what might have happened.[1] Probably the countrymen, who had numbers on their side, would have met force with force. Most of them were armed and well trained in violence, many of them being ex-soldiers. There would have been a civil war all over the north, hundreds of Vendées in the Pays de France and the Brie, the Vexin, and the Soissonnais. On the other hand it is just possible that the popular panacea might have worked for the time being. After all, even a modest display of force had ensured that the population of Paris and most cities were supplied with eatable bread at *trois sols la livre* during the Jacobin dictatorship. What is certain is that in the short run it would have killed French agriculture and in the years to come caused unheard-of distress in both town and country. (It could of course be argued that a famine from which all suffer is preferable to one like that of 1795 from which some, in this instance all the urban and rural poor, suffer.)

Even the limited and rather timid experiment of the year II left French agriculture in a pitiable condition, its livestock reduced by two-thirds, the grain yield by a third, the countryside left horseless, cartless, very short of labour, and in a state of sullen resentment. The Thermidorians may themselves have further contributed to the development of a famine situation, but their predecessors had not made their task any easier. When Robespierre fell the harvest was already in, there had been three months of extreme drought, mortality rates in cities were already showing a sharp rise,[2] and, if the first big wave of epidemics did not sweep the north till Fructidor year II, it had already been prepared by conditions of malnutrition, dirt, anxiety,[3] and fear. It is very easy and very usual to

[1] See note 2L, p. 375.   [2] See note 2M, p. 375.   [3] See note 2N, p. 376.

put all the blame on the Thermidorians, an unattractive lot at the best of times and devoid of glamour. Some historians have even gone so far as to subscribe to the *sans-culotte* view of things and suggest that Boissy d'Anglas and his colleagues deliberately set about contriving famine in order to finish off the 'popular move-ment' or bring the Princes back, or for whatever fell purpose. It is at least true that their rather heartless class policy (but, in view of their support, their electorates, what else were they to do?) contributed directly to worsening the plight of the urban poor. But, like the *sans-culotte* solution to dearth, to finish off the 'popular movement' by famine was a *remède de cheval*. (The Thermidorian regime was one of lawyers and landowners, not of veterinaries, as was the Third Republic in its prime.) And no one has so far suggested that the Thermidorians organized *le Grand Froid* and the epidemics as well. In fact they inherited from the Revolutionary Government a food situation already seriously if not irredeemably compromised.

23. POPULAR FOOD MORALITY

No one can blame the *sans-culottes* for putting their own inter-ests first. If not a matter of life or death to them (things were not as bad as that in the year II) it did at least make the difference between a pretty Spartan existence and economic ruin, of a kind they were to experience in the year III. Nor can they be blamed for advocating solutions both crude and likely to be self-defeating. They were not trained economists. They merely went by what they saw; and what they saw was that most people went very short while a few had plenty of everything and that the townsman drew in his belt, confined himself to the single *plat républicain*—a one-course meal, bread and perhaps a little cheese or fruit—while the farmer sat down to a groaning board. Their attitude as in so many other matters was a moral one. It was not right in a republican regime that a few should do so well, and many do so badly.

When they turned to the related problem of disease, their indignation could find a further source in what historians have called *l'inégalité devant la mort*. In periods of extreme shortage, the urban and rural poor would eat not only less than the farmer or the rich man, but worse. Even in the year III the urban well-to-do, like Duval's employers,[1] were able to obtain the pure wheaten loaf, but the bread that the poor man 'moistened with his tears' was very bad indeed, so bad that the poor contracted and died of bread diseases.[2] Medical reports of 1795 and 1796 attribute most of the epidemics that killed off the poor but spared the rich in towns like Dieppe, le Havre, Rouen, Amiens, Versailles, Saint-Germain, Meulan, and in *bourgs* like Bacqueville-en-Caux to eating food unfit for human consumption: unripe fruit, unripe corn, rotten fish, putrid meat, impure flour.[3] But by the time the urban poor—less fatalistic than the wretched *journalier*, who apparently awaited an early and inevitable death with complete resignation[4]—became fully aware of this inequality, it was already too late.

What the *sans-culottes* of the year II were searching for, rather gropingly, was a rationing system that would reduce everyone to a common wartime austerity, which would be just and which, one suspects, would also be 'good for one'. When they rail against the magnificent meals that well-to-do prisoners can obtain from *traiteurs* (and even the *robespierristes* awaiting execution, except for Robespierre himself, who was in no fit state to eat, sat down to a meal that included four bottles of wine, soup, chicken, an *entrée*, and cheese),[5] it is not because they themselves want such splendid fare, but because they do not want anyone at all to have it. One may even question whether they really believed that small, stated groups of people were creating a shortage by indulging themselves, by eating too much, or by hoarding. What they found intolerable was that anyone should have been able to over-indulge, eat too much, or have anything to hoard. So they constantly insist on their

---

[1] '. . . M. Chavet . . . acheta un sac de fine fleur de farine avec un four de campagne, et, au moyen de l'un et de l'autre, un pain d'une blancheur éclatante, un pain qui faisait plaisir à voir, était chaque jour confectionné dans sa cuisine et servi sur sa table. Malheureusement, il n'était réservé qu'à lui, à sa femme, et à ses deux filles d'y mettre les dents. Pour moi, je dus me contenter . . . de ma bouillie de pommes de terre cuites à l'eau, et de supposer que je croquais du pain . . .' (*Souvenirs Thermidoriens*, ii. 92).

[2] A.N. F8 18 (Ardennes), 21 (Bouches-du-Rhône), 46 (Eure), 59 (Manche), 67 (Mont-blanc), 69 (Nord), 70 (Orne), 75 (Rhône) 77 (Seine), 78 (Seine-Inférieure), 79 (Seine-et-Marne), 80 (Somme) (Hygiène et épidémies, 1788–1815).

[3] See p. 2O, p. 376.

[4] A.N. F8 78 (rapport de Lucas sur l'épidémie de Bacqueville, 9 nivôse an IV, A.N. F8 78, Seine-Inférieure).

[5] A.N. F7 4438 (papiers trouvés chez Robespierre, etc.).

own patriotism and on the lack of patriotism, selfishness, and indifference of others: countrymen, the wealthy, even the rulers of the day who so much forgot the times as to organize dinner-parties.

Yet they were applying a double standard. Food was a moral issue but not shoes if they were shoemakers, nor clothes if they were tailors. If they were *vignerons* (and *vignerons*, for our purpose, may be reckoned honorary *sans-culottes*) or innkeepers, wine was not, and if they were wage-earners, wages were not. The *sans-culottes*, so prompt to drape themselves in their rather exclusive patriotism when it was a question of obtaining cheap bread for themselves and their families, were quite prepared to take collective action in order to profit from the labour shortage and force another increase in their *journées*. Many *révolutionnaires* who, while in the country-side, complained of the neglect of the *loi sainte du maximum*, dis-covered that the *maximum* lost much of its holiness once applied to wages. A *sans-culotte* shoemaker who denounced a countryman for refusing to thresh his grain or for eating his livestock, rather than produce shoes to be sold for the *maximum* sought employment as an *inspecteur des souliers* in an army store. A great many tradesmen and shopkeepers, faced with the *maximum*, threw up their busi-nesses altogether and found jobs 'under the Revolution', in the bureaucracy of Terror and repression.[1] (No wonder they called so insistently for more of both, especially against the countryman, who represented most of the population.) Yet they would have been shocked if it had been suggested that they were displaying a lack of patriotism. In fact they were merely luckier than the countryman, in that they enjoyed a much wider range of choice. If the countryman could not make a living out of food he produced, what else was he to do? The *sans-culottes*, like most people, were moralists when it suited them and forgot their morals when it did not. For them morals began and ended with food—and, more particularly, with bread and wine (or cider for a Norman and beer for a Picard) because bread took up most of their budget and wine (or beer or cider) supplied them with much of their pleasure as well as with much of their enthusiasm and patriotism. So anyone who speculated in food, anyone who held out on food, was not only selfish but wicked, an enemy of the people, *qui méritoit mille morts*.

---

[1] *Terreur et subsistances*, pp. 151–79.

Like everyone else, they could offer only political and moral solutions to what was primarily a technical problem. Indeed, in their attitudes to agriculture, they supported a backward-looking programme which, if widely adopted, would have transformed situations of potential dearth into real famines. One solution would have been to encourage the cultivation of potatoes, maize, or rice, so as to relieve the burden placed on a single article of nourishment; but the *sans-culottes* shared with most of the urban *petit peuple* an instinctive food conservatism that rejected the potato as fit only for paupers; and of rice, as we have seen, the common people were deeply suspicious. Yet it was rice that finally saved the towns of the Seine Valley and the Channel ports from the full effects of famine at the end of the year III. The *sans-culotte* solution was always to grow more wheat, on more land, everywhere, even in the most unsuitable conditions. So they eagerly supported the policies of revolutionary governments in their drives for clearing and draining swampland. But they were bitterly opposed to the *liberté de la culture*, looking to the Revolutionary Government to force landowners to grow only cereals, and convert pasture to arable. Agricultural improvements like the *prairies artificielles* seemed to them attempts to organize famine in the interests of greed. For similar reasons, they were enemies of stock-breeding; meat, in any case, seldom came their way.

Finally, they were fanatically opposed to the existence of large farms and called once more on the State to legislate against *la réunion des fermes*.[1] Their ideal was best expressed in the petition of the Section des Sans-culottes of September 1793 which asked the Convention to decree that no man should be allowed to possess more land than he personally could cultivate with a single plough.[2] Here, too, they were groping their way towards a moral solution: a Republic of smallholders, in which each citizen would be given just enough land to ensure his own subsistence and that of his family. In short, they not only supported all the most backward features of French agriculture, but sought to have them extended. In their food policies, they left no profit margin to the farmer, and their agricultural programme was bound to prevent the increase of grain-production since it could come only from improved

[1] Georges Lefebvre, *Questions agraires au temps de la Terreur* (new edition, Paris, 1950).
[2] Markov and Soboul, op. cit., p. 136.

techniques and an industrialized form of cultivation possible only on very large farms provided with a considerable labour force. For the *sans-culotte*, the *gros laboureur* was as wicked as the wholesaler and the entrepreneur. They were obsessed with the need to grow more food; but they wanted it grown in the most onerous, wasteful, and unproductive conditions. A mass of fifteen or sixteen million smallholders was hardly likely to succeed in feeding the seven hundred thousand inhabitants of Paris. They ought to have been well aware that the *gros laboureurs* held no monopoly of rapacity in periods of dearth since the smallholder would be all the more concerned to sell his tiny surplus at a maximum profit. They wanted to increase total grain-production, but they also wanted to prevent the only way by which it could be achieved.

24. 'COMMUNALISM' AND THE FOOD PROBLEM

With the benefit of hindsight it is easy to point out the weaknesses and the illogicality of *sans-culotte* solutions. The decisive solution that was to remove all the traditional checks on distribution and offer the conditions for a greater specialization than had been possible in the eighteenth century was something neither the *sans-culottes* nor any of their contemporaries could have foreseen: this was the construction of the railways. Demands for improved forms of conventional transport were already a step in the right direction. The Dieppois of all political hues called insistently, from 1789 to 1815, for the construction of a canal from Dieppe to the Oise, via Forges-les-Eaux, so as to accelerate the arrival of the *chasse-marée* on the Paris fish-market and make the grainlands of the Vexin and the Pays de Caux more accessible to the port.[1] The Honfleurois wanted a canal that would open up the markets of the Eure to them via Quillebeuf.[2] Every *société populaire* had its pet project for a canal or a new road or a change in the routeing of an existing road. In each case the guiding principle was local advantage. The governing idea, in all such projects, was to get more food, more quickly, to one's own market; and this generally meant

[1] A.N. F14 723 (Travaux publics) (Lapeyre, ingénieur du port, à la Commission des travaux publics, 25 prairial an II). Arch. Dieppe D I 5, 6 et 7, D 31 (registres de délibérations de la municipalité).

[2] 'Problèmes de subsistances en l'an II et en l'an III: l'exemple d'un petit port normand, Honfleur' (Mémoires du Congrès des Sociétés Savantes de Rouen, Paris, Imprimerie Nationale, 1958).

diverting the flow of grain to one's own advantage from some other centre. Many *sociétés* made no bones about it: the rival town, they would insist, did not deserve a market or a new road; its population was composed of *ci-devants* and their *intendants, hommes de loi*, and *fanatiques*. Patriotic towns should be given top priority in the programme of the *Commission des Travaux Publics*.

Just as in their political aims and methods, the *sans-culottes* were incapable of seeing beyond the horizons of their own physical environment in this matter of provisioning. For the Parisians, only the supply of Paris was a matter of urgency; they did not see that if the Rouennais were to be penalized for the benefit of Paris, the capital, too, would eventually feel the pinch; and in his attitude to dearth, each individual militant was a Rouennais, a Havrais, a Dieppois, a Moulinois, an Auxerrois, a Lyonnais first, and a *sans-culotte* only second. Only the Committees and the technical Commissions were capable of thinking in terms of national need. The militants of the year II even opposed imports, as likely to enrich the Baltic traders of le Havre, Rouen, Honfleur, and other ports—people who counted high among their class enemies. In 1793–4, most of the inhabitants of the *Grand Quai* were in prison; and, after the recapture of the city, repression fell most heavily on the big ship-owning families of Marseille. In the year II, *sans-culotte* busybodies, from positions on local committees, made life so intolerable for neutral captains and crews who put in to the Channel ports with cargoes of northern grain that many of them decided to give these ports a miss so long as *sans-culotte* rule lasted in places like le Havre, Honfleur, Fécamp, and Dieppe. One of Fouquier's indictments against the alleged 'accomplices' of Ronsin and Vincent was that they had alienated the few neutral powers by ill-treating the crew of a Danish brig.[1] In the spring and summer of the year III, the arrival of a Danish or an American ship in a northern port was repeatedly the occasion for a massive riot; the municipal authorities were passive onlookers and the cargoes of grain, bought for Paris by the Commission, were unloaded and sold at the quayside to individual bidders among the *petit peuple*. All this could have been avoided, the local authorities would argue, in their embarrassed reports to the government, if the Commission and the Committees had paid more attention to their pleas for immediate succour.[2]

---

[1] *Terreur et subsistances*, pp. 121–49. [2] Ibid., pp. 244, 246.

They were right: only events of this kind, directly harmful to Paris, would induce the Commission and the Thermidorian Committees (in any case much more susceptible than those of the previous year to local pressure groups) to do something about the plight of the inhabitants of the Channel ports. The 'blackmail of riot' would work only after a riot.[1] In the year III, some ports even sent their pilots out to meet neutral shipping and entice them into harbour. In this way, Dunkirk pirated on Saint-Valéry-sur-Somme, Saint-Valéry on Dieppe, Dieppe on Fécamp, Fécamp on le Havre, le Havre on Rouen, and so on right down the coast or down the valley of the Lower Seine. Paris might always come first in government preoccupations, but it stood at the end of the line and there were scores of opportunities for *arrêts* between the sea and the *port de la Grenouillère*. This was exactly the direction in which popular food policies led. They were the policies of a siege mentality. (It was not surprising that so many of their beliefs and phobias reappeared in Paris in 1870–1.)[2] The *petit peuple* believed in what it could see and the solution was to lay hands on as much food as possible, wherever it came from and wherever it was supposed to be going (and popular suspicion was inclined to treat most certificates of destination, most cargo certificates (*connaissements*), as false and designed to facilitate illegal exports). In this sense, *arrêts* were a patriotic duty, since the people were only intervening to prevent grain from falling into the wrong hands. Large farmers were fair game, being bound to have big stocks, as were millers. Nothing could equal the fury of the common people breaking into a barn or a mill only to find nothing. They had been cheated of their purpose, *ils ont été devancés*, and the miller or the farmer was either hiding his stock or had sold it to 'strangers'. Deception of this kind would be followed by arson.

Such an attitude was the negation of planning and greatly added to the difficulties of distribution. But the *sans-culottes* were scarcely aware of these. Their concern was to see the grain on the market of their home town, the bread in the baker's shop. The problem began and ended there and they were not to be fobbed off by promises of relief next week or next month. They must have bread tomorrow at the latest. As Lenoir pointed out, it all came from a phobia about future shortage—but a very immediate future. Nor were they to be fobbed off with reminders of the needs of *nos frères de Paris, nos frères de Rouen, nos frères de Dieppe*, and so on. Fraternity went down the drain when people lived in fear for the morrow and they were not likely to listen to explanations that outlined the problem in national terms. Their reaction, however illogical, was perfectly understandable: they must have bread for their families, the government in Paris was not interested in their plight, the municipality was incapable or feeble, or in league with the farmers and the hoarders.

Municipal government was extremely uncomfortable in the year III, so uncomfortable that when early in the year IV municipalities were abolished to make way for the *administrations cantonales*, and thus decrease the force of 'communalism' by drowning it in a larger unit, the members of the new administration refused to take office and supported their refusal with a variety of medical certificates—hernia, heart, lungs, rheumatism, 'tremors'. Never perhaps in French history did the *notables* enjoy such poor health. The result was that in many localities in the north the unfortunate members of the municipalities of the year III were still forcibly confined to the *Maison Commune* throughout a second year of famine. Thus they underwent further physical ill-treatment at the hands of infuriated women, who held them responsible for the starving condition of their half-naked children.[1]

In short, if the people wanted bread, they would have to help themselves. Where better than from a *magasin de la République*? For were they not republicans too? This was the logic of the *arrêts* of the year II and the grain-riots of the year III. Both brought some immediate local relief, but repression, retribution, and a worsening of the situation would follow until, after the next riot, or the one after that, the government decided that relief might be cheaper than repression. Thus the rural *communes* surrounding le Havre

---

[1] A.N. F1b II Seine-Inférieure 12 (Dieppe). On 14 Pluviôse the members of the Conseil général of the year III announced their intention of resigning en bloc. But they were still chained to office in Floréal of that year. On 18 Brumaire, the Department wrote to the Minister: '. . . Outre la commune de Dieppe où personne ne veut être dans l'administration municipale, la majeure partie des grandes communes, telles qu'Elbeuf, Darnétal, Fécamp, nous présentent les mêmes dispositions. . . . L'extrême répugnance qu'éprouvent même les meilleurs citoyens pour occuper aucunes places administratives prend incontestablement sa source dans l'état de pénurie où se trouve tout notre département du côté des subsistances.'

finally obtained government rice in the year III, after making themselves repeatedly intolerable.[1] The grain-riot of the year III only took one stage further the *sans-culotte* attitude of the year II: hold on to what you have got, and grab as much more as you can. The *sans-culottes* of the year II and the women rioters of the year III were not subscribing to any grand plan of food procurement, but were thinking of their plates which, if not empty, might soon be. They had a right to eat; and, if they were not actually hungry at the moment, they feared that they very soon might be. The only way to reassure them was to see that each family received its 2-lb. loaf; and this, not by virtue of *sans-culotte* methods, but by measures of force worthy, in their drastic brutality, of the government of Louis XIV, the Revolutionary Government succeeded in doing.

The *sans-culottes* were not at all grateful at the time—the government was only providing them with what was their due. On the contrary, they grumbled at not getting a lot else besides. The *problème des subsistances* indeed is like a Ukrainian doll and there is always something else inside. If people get bread, they will complain about the price, shortage, and inferior quality of wine. If they get wine as well, there will be complaints about meat. If they get bread, wine, meat, and vegetables (almost the menu of Mercier's *racoleurs*), they will turn to groceries, candles, and fuel. There is almost limitless scope for that ever-observant sense of envy, admirably analysed by Restif, always on the alert, always eager to point the finger of popular vindictiveness at those who are fatter, better lit, warmer, better housed (oddly enough, there are few complaints about the immense inequalities of housing conditions in the petitions of 1793–6),[2] better clothed. They will point to those who *roulent carrosse*,[3] those who have a healthier appearance, who live longer, who have a better education,[4] who have a wider outlook, who have been abroad, who have prettier wives or mistresses (probably foreign ones). This is a nudging, carping jealousy which is far removed from the fraternity and generous optimism of much of the *sans-culotte* movement, and

---

[1] *Terreur et subsistances*, pp. 245–6.

[2] See note 2P, p. 377.

[3] Transport, as in India today, was one of the most visible signs of class. A street accident, as in New Delhi today, was likely to provoke a riot, especially in the event of a child being killed.

[4] *Terreur et subsistances*, pp. 3–53.

which reached its coarsest,[1] most bitter expression in the mouths of women and in the more appalling atrocities of the revolutionary period. In this respect at least, the *problème des subsistances* was not a matter of most having enough, but of some having more; and for that the Revolution could offer no solution, though the *sans-culottes*, in vain and rather gropingly, proposed some.[2]

25. CONCLUSION

The problem was an ancient one, arousing ancient fears and imposing ancient remedies. Though no word occurs more often than that of *subsistances* in the minutes of popular institutions— *sociétés, comités, assemblées générales*—it would be hard to describe the topic as revolutionary, or the solutions proposed as revolutionary. In some ways it was just the opposite. Such an obsession with possible shortage canalized popular militancy away from other potentially more dangerous subjects: wages and *coalitions*, collective bargaining, the demand for a system of national education, annual parliaments, 'direct democracy', the legitimacy of the 'revolutionary dictatorship' and the relation between it and the popular movement, the right of insurrection, the subjection of women, the rights of property. For, ultimately, popular insistence on this obsessive problem was not necessarily dangerous to government; once supplies arrived, and were displayed, there was an end to it. Here was a 'movement' that could easily be bought off; and the grain-riots of the year III, far from endangering the Thermidorian settlement, actually consolidated it by tying closer together all those who had something to lose and who had reason to fear popular violence and by creating a complicity between repressive magistrates and repressive army. In most cases they were put down without difficulty. They even provided the government with a pretext to shut up, shoot, or deport the more dangerous of its popular or Montagnard critics.

The persistence of the problem, then, well into the nineteenth century, is striking testimony to the survival of traditional attitudes and a traditional economy and to the primitive nature of a popular movement constantly forced by fear of shortage into a regionalist

---

[1] A drunken chestnut saleswoman, arrested in Vendémiaire year III, Section des Arcis, greets the *commissaire*: '*Mets ton nez à mon cul* . . . et pour toute réponse nous ayant dit: . . . *qu'elle nous avoit dans le cul et nous chioit demain, nous traitant de grédin, de puant* . . .' (A.P.P. A/A 187, Arcis).

[2] See note 2Q, p. 378.

or narrowly 'communalist' framework. The common people of France lived with these ancient fears. Indeed two recent French historians have attributed the *penchant* shown both by popular militants and White terrorists for the cannibalistic metaphor, to the ever-present memory of famine, to centuries of past hunger and, no doubt, past habits of eating one another: an interpretation as attractive yet as far-fetched as that which relates Terror to the experience of the plague—*Peste et Terreur*—when applied to a people that had not experienced famine since 1709, and plague since 1720.[1,2] As long as these fears persisted there could be no chance of a popular movement developing on a national level, with a specific programme, a permanent organization, and a trained personnel. Everything about the *problème des subsistances* and the attitudes it provoked among various sections of the common people was divisive, impermanent, sporadic, and unplanned. Far from uniting the urban and rural *petit peuple* in a single movement of popular protest, it accentuated the divisions between town and country—divisions that were to a large extent unreal and that without this great divider would have tended to disappear. It did not even unite the *sans-culottes* decisively, since all of them did not feel the pinch with the same sharpness, and those who enjoyed private sources of provisioning felt out of sympathy with those at a stage lower than themselves who faced the facts of hunger. Few former popular militants took part in the hunger-riots of 1795.

It was not a permanent problem that would keep the people permanently mobilized *sur pied de guerre*, since it recurred only at increasingly wide intervals, and the attitudes it inspired could only be temporary. This form of popular protest would disappear with the return of plenty or, alternatively, would collapse in the rare extremity of famine. It was only a very marginal situation, this side of famine or extreme want, but with fear for the immediate future persistently nagging the popular mind that would for a time produce a movement with a specific programme. That, too, was an ancient, and largely irrelevant, one. For where would the aged idea of 'popular justice' lead, save to massacre? It could hardly be suggested that a repetition of the September Massacres—

[1] *Terreur et subsistances*, p. 31 (49) (René Baehrel, 'Épidémie et Terreur', A.H.R.F., April–June 1951).

[2] François Furet and Denis Richet, *La Révolution*, vol. i (Paris, Hachette, 1965).

the longed-for Red Dawn of Hébert and many *sans-culottes*—
would have caused the popular movement to advance half an inch,
and what Georges Lefebvre has so daintily called *la volonté punitive
du peuple* could be translated in English as empty, primitive, blood-
lust. There was enough senseless and purposeless violence without
the addition of all these traditional hate-figures, trundled out
at each successive crisis. The murder of the baker François did
not make bread any more plentiful; nor did any other heads on
the ends of pikes. In this respect, the only point in killing people
would have been to eat them. The *sans-culotte*, like the White
terrorist, talked a lot of doing just this—particularly when it was
a matter of eating suitably cooked and appropriately seasoned
heads; but it was all talk and no action. They no more sat down
to a counter-revolutionary or a terrorist head than they played
bowls with them or drank blood out of skulls.

A movement so closely tied to the seasons, the passage of
months, even of days, was hardly likely to change the face of
France, nor would it take the repressive authorities unawares.
Nothing in fact was more easily predictable than what the common
people would think, and how they would act, when spurred on by
the fear of shortage; they would say and do what they had said and
done a score of times before, generally in the same places as before.
It was a popular cause, too, that played into the hands of authority,
for authority would always see to it that Paris at least would not
starve, so that any serious outburst would take place without the
capital, a sure guarantee of rapid failure. Finally, such an obsession
was to drive a substantial section of the common people into the
fairyland of myth and legend, where it was safe from the realities
of political analysis. It was an easy step from attacks on mills, from
indignation over the inequalities of distribution, to sheer banditry;
the activities of the *chauffeurs* were the logical last stage of this
sense of deprivation. The *chauffeurs* were undoubtedly very
popular among important sections of the urban *petit peuple*, who
looked on them as heroes and as social avengers, but it is difficult
to see how their *faits d'armes* improved the conditions of the poor.

Yet it is easy for historians to mock panic fears and to underline
the backwardness of attitudes that repeatedly sought their terms
of reference in a remote past. Those who exercised themselves
over the *problème des subsistances* did not have their eyes fixed on
future generations of historians and political theorists. They were

not attempting obligingly to unroll the red carpet of socialist thought—*loi agraire*, collectivization or what not—on which Babeuf and Buonarroti and a clatter of political theorists and politicians in their wake might walk up to the altar of whatever vintage of Marxism they fancied (and there are many mansions in that house). They had no Holy Writ to go to before rioting, only popular memory. Their ambitions were, in fact, more modest and more concrete—they knew there was grain or bread to be obtained somewhere, and they were determined to obtain it somehow, so that their families should be *à l'abri du besoin*. It was a modest aim, but not an unworthy one; nor were they always unsuccessful. Even the Thermidorian authorities, after the Germinal and Prairial days, set about organizing relief at least in Paris and the Channel ports. Even the Directory, in its first year in office, established a *douzième secteur* for the free distribution of bread to those in absolute need. Both the *Directeurs* and Napoleon understood that the most effective way to deal with this type of popular agitation was to drown it in charity; not charity on a lavish scale, but enough to separate the really poor from what had once constituted *la sans-culotterie*. The poor got their bread but had to work for it, and the Imperial authorities generally took care to distribute very little charity in kind and to tie it to a programme of public works.

Historians, few of whom have ever experienced hunger, have no business blaming poor people for accepting, even gratefully, the product of bourgeois charity; and it would be indecent to upbraid the *affamés* of the past for allowing themselves to be bought out of what historians have decreed were 'forward-looking' movements by the grant of relief. Perhaps no twentieth-century western historian can appreciate the problem and the attitudes that it provoked at all, so far is it from his experience. Yet two great wars might remind him that food problems can arouse maximum popular suspicion and anger against those in authority, or against those believed to be getting more than their dues. In both the great wars, rationing was a constant stimulus to the expression of popular envy; both wars might remind him, too, that in such circumstances Town versus Country is a conflict not yet confined to historical museums. Moreover famine can be seen, if not experienced; it is sufficient to go to Calcutta. In India the myths, legends, beliefs, and neuroses of shortage, far from being the relics of a submerged, archaic, popular mentality, multiply and flourish, even to the extent of causing government to tread cautiously and use dangerous words with the utmost care, while grain travels slowly and visibly in ancient boats, dragged along by the Bengali counterparts of the *tireurs à la corde* towards the grain ports of the Hooghly River. Popular remedies—arson, attacks on trains and mills and government stores and attacks on landowners, price-fixing, pillage, *arrêts*, and unloading—are likewise daily occurrences, in the dangerous period that precedes the monsoon.

Finally, one can hardly assert that the *sans-culottes* and their even less coherent brothers among the *habitants des garnis* were being absurd and panicky in expressing their fears and prejudices in the year II. After all, in the year III they were subjected to the realities of a full-scale famine. The year 1795 was the best testimonial—a hideously cruel one—to the fact that neither their fears nor their attitudes were out of date. It was, it is true, the last time in French history that a disaster on quite such a scale occurred, but, as it turned out, the *sans-culotte* had every reason to look in fear to the immediate future and to tremble for the morrow. The morrow, when it became today, was far more fearful than anything he could possibly have imagined—so fearful that to find a comparable disaster one had to go back to the first decade of the century. There may have been a few ninety-year-olds still alive in 1795, much revered for their sheer staying power, who could recall 1709 for their fellow villagers and make the comparison with *Nonante-cinq*. Most people had to fall back on local village lore and family tradition.

The crisis of the years III and IV gave the problem a new lease of life. In the 1780s and during the Revolution there had been publicists who spoke of famine as a thing of the past, a skeleton in the national cupboard, best forgotten along with *ces siècles gothiques et barbares*, along with the Valois, the wars of religion, and Louis XIV. They were not to tempt providence again in such a way until the 1830s. As for the common people, let no one tell them that famine was a thing of the past. Seventeen years later all eyes are turned in fear to the recent past. The memory of the year III and the year IV made the 1812 crisis much more bitter than it need have been. For this time there were any number of people who had experienced both. In 1870–1 we encounter the reflexes of the year II and the year III; and from 1940 to 1946 the urban worker, and even the bourgeois, found himself in the position of the Dieppois described by Mâlotain, going cap in hand, his purse filled with gold coins, his pockets filled with jewellery, to His Highness the Farmer, to solicit butter, eggs, or a sack of potatoes, perilously balanced on a bicycle pushed through the murk and the cold. Once more the winter nights were full of shadowy figures, with voluminous bundles on their backs, or dragging enormous fibre suitcases through frozen streets;[1] once more the farms filled up with grand pianos and *lessiveuses*, while in the cities *la brocante* prospered, the *Puces* enjoyed unheard-of activity and a new race of intermediaries, the *B.O.F.* (the *Beurre Œufs Fromage*), grew rich and fat on general misery. Joanovici made his fortune then out of rags and scrap-iron. Many more of his kind dined copiously and no doubt enjoyed the thought of what they were getting and no one else could, *chez Félix*, or in a score of similar establishments whose lights blazed merrily behind the black-out curtains.

Then also rumour found ready credence even in the highest places: the B.B.C. informed its listeners in 1944, a few months before the invasion, that French children in the Nord had been so reduced by famine that, if they had the slightest fall, they broke a limb. Cats and dogs disappeared, even rats became nervous, mysterious bread diseases revived, and townsmen invaded the fields at night, digging up unripe potatoes and beetroot. Parties of schoolchildren scoured the forests for bark, roots, and vipers, and many ancient recipes came back into their own. Park benches vanished, the Bois de Boulogne and the Bois de Vincennes were denuded, and crouching figures with faggots on their backs were once more part of the walking landscape. After Liberation, bands of Parisians, armed and in motley uniform, roamed the countryside, had themselves billeted on Norman farmers, and delivered requisition orders in the name of shadowy, uncertain authorities. The coal barges on the canal de Roubaix, caught hard in the iron grip of ice during the bitter winter of 1944–5, were plundered by the inhabitants of Wasquehal, who might be seen at dusk pushing away prams full of coal. (They were luckier than most in having a captive barge to hand. They were more experienced, too, in the economy of dearth, many of them having lived through 1917 and

---

[1] The historian should see the film of Aymé's novel, *La Traversée de Paris*, the most eloquent record of shortage.

1918 and starved alongside their occupiers.)[1] Smuggling along the
old border, in the *chauffeurs'* territory, took on a new lease of life
and drew in, along with the usual professionals (who included the
brother-in-law of the novelist Van der Meersch), the drivers and
passengers of British army lorries, rapidly familiar with the thirty-
odd frontier posts between Roubaix and Tournai, between Tour-
coing and Courtrai. There were thousands of people on the road
in search of food; British soldiers were greeted everywhere in the
Nord by hordes of famished children, sent out to beg by their
parents, and the Transit Camp at Valenciennes resembled a vast
encampment of vagrants. Marcel Aymé's story about the *carte du
temps* was not so fanciful after all; and that old favourite of revolutionary records, illegal slaughtering (*l'abbatage clandestin*), flourished once more in cellars and even on upper floors in carefully
muffled rooms.[2] Long after the hunger years were over, marked
perhaps only by physical deformity and the persistence of food
slang (the *B.O.F.*, *Au Bon Beurre*, the admirable Brussels word
for a Brussels profession, the *smokeleer*, the equally evocative
tonnenklinker), an ancient horse-drawn hearse was out most days
for two months in the small town of Pont-Saint-Esprit, carrying
off the dead, who had consumed *le pain maudit* during a summer
of the 1950s. Some scores died, many more were rumoured to be
dead, the word *ergot* came back into usage in the papers and the
origin of the outbreak was traced to rotten sacking issued by a
miller from the Loiret.

Hunger employs its own outriders. Those who have already
experienced it can see it announced, not only in the sky, but in the
fields, scrutinized each year with increasing anxiety week by week
during the hot summer months, by thirty million anxious eyes; in
the figures for grain prices on the markets; in the amount of
movement on rivers and roads; in the traffic of the *barrières*; in the
conversation of visiting countrymen, the letters of country relatives or the discreet decrees of government; in the unspectacular
efforts of municipalities to extend the limits of their cemeteries;
in the number of times two men carrying a covered object emerge
from a hospital by night; in unusually massive orders of quicklime;
in the dispatch of a food commissioner to Genoa, to Geneva, to

---

[1] Maxence van der Meersch, *Invasion 14*. The author died in 1947, before
completing a similar account of civilian life in Roubaix-Tourcoing during the
Second Occupation.   [2] *La Traversée de Paris*, in *Le Vin de Paris*.

Hamburg, to Berne, to Tunis, to Copenhagen; in the prayers of the pious or the secret sermons of barn priests; in the cards of *diseuses de bonne aventure* (for whom famine was a better customer than marriage, violent death, war, or success in money or in love); in the anxious faces of women, or in the pallor of those who have eaten dead warhorses; in the sword worn by an imprudent *maire*; in the shadow, thrown at a certain hour of the day, seen from a certain angle, of a certain statue, in a certain town. It is something that comes by stealth, without fanfare, yet preceded by a thousand imperceptible signs that the eighteenth-century 'marginal' could pick out, just as those who were in the know—the *maire*, the borough engineer, and the members of the rat-killer's department —knew that *Gaston*, with his broad brown and black back, the size of a largish mastiff, displayed behind drawn curtains in his cardboard box, was just *one* of a race of invaders, a new race of giant rats already in possession of the city and waiting only for the signal to come up from the sewers and take over.[1]

[1] Pierre Gascar, *Les Bêtes* (Paris, 1958).

NOTES

SECTION I

(A) Bretons are said to be drunken and prone to use their fists or broken glasses or bottles; Lyonnais are so accustomed to violence, by the year IV, that they call the big sticks that they carry *juges-de-paix*. Men from the Mediterranean will stab, using knives or stilettos, and a *marchand de cannes* from Bordeaux, having moved in the favourable circumstances of the year IV, with an arsenal of sticks and sword-sticks in their thousands, to Marseille, where there was much demand for any weapon of death, makes a fortune. In the Vaucluse, the weapon of death is derisively known, in the early years of the Directory, as *le pouvoir exécutif*, and, in all this area, the method of killing is frequently evoked in such expressions as *je t'ouvrirai les tripes, je t'ouvrirai le ventre, je te mangerai le foie*. Picard servants are often depicted, in eighteenth-century novels, as beating up their masters' rivals in love; and one Picard is quoted as saying that he would whip somebody with a leather strap, 'comme j'arrangerais une femme d'Abbeville'. No self-respecting Garde-Française would feel that he had absorbed the spirit of his regiment if he had not killed at least one man in defence of its honour. Restif, in *Les Nuits de Paris*, describes a young officer, well connected—he has a relative in high rank—who kills a poor girl—a *veilleuse*—with his sword, because she had refused to come with him. His conduct is the subject of almost universal reprobation; even his colleagues tell him off: 'Quelle folie! quelle barbarie! tuer une Fille, parce qu'elle ne veut pas te suivre? Te croyais-tu dans le camp de Closter-Seven avec ces Hanovriennes, que nous fesions aller et venir à notre caprice?' But he walks off the scene of the crime without hindrance. He is an officer, and this is said to have taken place in 1778, on the Boulevard du Temple.

In his *Tableaux* and on several occasions in *Monsieur Nicolas* the author returns, with fascinated repulsion, to the violence of the military, and more especially of the officer corps, a violence that found its most characteristic expression in libertinage and in the ill treatment of women of humble condition: servants, farm girls, foreign girls, the spoils of war—an attitude that they were able to communicate to the other ranks—in some cases, if we are able to believe the boastful and cruel *Tartare*, who had been an officer's servant in Flanders during the Seven Years War, passing them on their victims, for their own use. Of boys entering the military academies, he observes: '. . . Ils ne voient dans l'habit d'Officier que le grade; ils ne songent qu'aux privilèges de libertinage qu'un long usage accorde aux militaires. . . .' Elsewhere, he refers to an officer 'brave, violent, et un peu fou, trois qualités essentielles pour appeler quelqu'un en duel . . .'. The sense of personal honour, such an obsession with the French officer of the late eighteenth century ('rien de si *avantageux* qu'un petit officier franaçis'), clearly did not extend to the lower ranks of the feminine population, even of France; there was nothing dishonourable in an officer deflowering a servant girl; he might, of course, offer her some form of compensation. Honour was reserved only for ladies of high rank. But, as Restif, always a good observer of the *guerre des sexes*, did not fail to observe, women themselves did much to stimulate the sexual aggressivity and the bloodthirstiness of officers: 'Je n'ai jamais pu supporter que dans les tems de chevalerie, des Belles excitassent aux combats sanglans; ni que du nôtre, elles encouragent les guerriers et les chasseurs.' The latter, it will be recalled, only earned their place—and hardly one *à part entière*—in the bed of *la Marquise*—*after* the hunt. If the ancient military theme of *le Repos du Guerrier* was so generally accepted in French honourable society, it must have been because women of high birth subscribed to the same crude conventions as the men. Restif wrote as a civilian, who had himself, when first in Paris in the 1750s, been the victim of the unprovoked violence of *les Grands*—in this instance members of the Orleans family and their retainers, so it is without surprise that we find him insisting on the unparalleled brutality of the Princes of the blood as displayed during a night out with girls from the Palais-Royal: 'Tout cela n'est rien auprès de nos Princes. Quand ils arrivent dans un endroit, tout tremble, tout fuit. Mais la porte est gardée. Ils font aussi mettre nues les Filles. . . . Ils fouttent les Filles nues à grands coups, ou les font fouailler par leurs Coureurs. . . . Ils donnent presque toujours une jolie collation' (once the damage had been done).

Such an example was not lost on others. There is an account in *Monsieur Nicolas* of what happened to a young Auxerroise, the sister of a locksmith, on her way home on a winter's night: '. . . Un soir qu'il faisoit très sombre . . . entre la Cathédrale et la Cité, Médérique-Maufront, guettée, y passa . . . ils environnèrent Médérique, la saisirent, la troussèrent, la fouttèrent, tandis que d'autres . . . arrachoient de sanglans trophées, que quelques-uns portoient une main libertine et profane sur d'autres appâts . . . ils avoient goudronné ses blonds cheveux, ses sourcils et tout ce qui étoit ombragé de poil sur ce beau corps . . . il lui falloit raser la tête, ainsi que les sourcils et le reste. . . .' This was the evening out of a group of carters and transport workers, well known for their extreme brutality towards women. The reaction of the girl's brother, and of the whole corporation of locksmiths, saddlemakers, tanners, and so on, was equally violent. They went into the streets, armed with clubs, to seek out the aggressors. It is doubtful if they were much concerned with what had happened to the unfortunate Médérique, who might thus witness for the prevalent brutality of a masculine-dominated society; but her brother had been insulted in his honour—and even a locksmith had honour—and it was his duty to avenge this insult to his family. There is nothing more revealing of the attitudes of a society, still in a state of savagery even at the highest levels, than this apparently general acceptance of a state of affairs that left the women of the people largely unprotected against the casual or joyful violence of the male. Restif is an unusually good witness in this respect. It was not surprising that, in some of the more favourable circumstances of the revolutionary period, there should have emerged a sort of tribal war between the sexes, with women taking a sanguinary revenge on the former seducers of their own kind. Herein lay the principal seam of violence in eighteenth-century France. There were others of a more professional and specialized kind.

The *commis des fermes*, for instance, are given to punching people in the stomach with their thumbs opened out. The *crocheteur* carries a heavy stick, to help him with his burden, but also to use on those who get in his way; and in the reports of the Lyon *Bureau Central* for the years V, VI, and VII, when murders were frequent in the Second City, the *crocheteurs* of the port Saint-Vincent are depicted as the principal allies of thieves and prostitutes, in attacks on *gendarmes* and republican soldiers, and as the strong-arm men (*les forts à bras*) of the *Compagnie* (Arch. Rhône 1 L 382–3, assassinats, ans V–VII). The *flotteurs*, like anyone connected with the river, are also described as particularly violent and brutal, though apparently they do not fight among themselves. The *faubouriens*— or the *suburbains* as Mercier sometimes calls them—in their sheer ignorance —are described as ready recruits to any form of violence; and, in the year VI, the inhabitants of Vaise, la Croix-Rousse, and la Guillotière are the object of redoubled attention on the part of the Directorial authorities and the police. Horse-dealers are stated to be naturally brutal; and Restif depicts one—a Rouennais—as being quite unable to contain himself when his anger is aroused; he kills one man with a blow, another with a stick, and is eventually broken on the wheel. Most contemporaries—*ancien régime* or revolutionary—have much to say about the savagery of women. According to Restif, young de Belsunce, the victim of a July 1789 riot in Caen, was lynched by a woman. Others are depicted, in the rue Saint-Martin, screaming 'Pendez, pendez!' as the unfortunate Berthier de Sauvigny is brought in. Many authorities refer to the natural violence of mountain villagers and sailors. All are puzzled, and horrified, by the violence, cruelty, and lawlessness of the inhabitants of the south-east. Louis Chevalier draws attention to the combination of violence, sexuality, and joviality that still characterizes the muscular inhabitants of les Halles, 'cette puissante et joviale animalité' (*Les Parisiens*).

(B) The police would subscribe to the 'salutary maxim' proposed by the *comité* of Domfront, in a letter to that of Dieppe, in Fructidor year II: 'Nous ne pouvons que trop rappeller cette maxime salutaire qu'une sage méfiance doit nous tenir en garde contre les inconnus.' The Dieppe *comité* is further informed, in an anonymous letter, 'que dans la commune de Vencestainville il y a un nommé Nicolas Levasseur qui est suspect . . . il est laboureur, il se dit marchand aussi, personne ne connaît son commerce, aussi est toujours à cheval, il est des huit jours parti de chez lui, il va souvent à Rouen et à Dieppe et à la ville d'Eu . . . au Havre et à Abbeville et autre part . . .' (Arch. Seine-Maritime L 5329). Police assumptions on the subject of strangers are further confirmed by Restif, when he writes: '. . . les Soldats employés hors de leur ville sont féroces . . .' (*Les Nuits*, iv. 843). The complaints of the inhabitants of Domfront were directed against the soldiers of a Paris battalion who had previously formed part of the Dieppe garrison.

(C) 'Poignards, stilets, tromblons, couteaux en forme de poignard, pistolets de poche . . .', Alletz, ARMES. The Directory, faced with hitherto unparalleled violence, particularly in the south-east, displayed a similar concern. In a circular dated 19 Germinal year IV, Mangeret, commissaire du Directoire in the Gironde, writes: '. . . J'ai reçu du Directoire . . . un arrêté par lequel, prenant en considération les prétendues fabrications de poignards et de cannes à lance qui ont lieu à Bordeaux, il ordonnoit l'arrestation des nommés Huguet et Abeille, prévenus de ces fabrications. . . . Chez Abeille on a trouvé 450 fers de lances . . . Lescuyer a déclaré qu'il avoit promis de livrer à un marchand de Lyon 600 fers de lances, il y a six mois . . .' (A.N. Fɪb II Gironde I).

Earlier in the year, the *administrateurs* of the Puy-de-Dôme acknowledged, on 23 Brumaire, receipt of 'l'arrêté du Comité de sûreté générale du 11 de ce mois, qui défend de vendre et de porter des cannes à sabres, épées & batons ferrés ou plombés . . .' (A.N. Fɪb II Puy-de-Dôme I).

(D) There is a reference, in a report from the *gendarmerie* of Saint-Paulien, in the Haute-Loire, dated 14 Germinal year IV, to a group of *assommeurs* engaged in the activities of the White Terror: '. . . 14 Lyonnois vêtus à la mode du pays sont venus courir nos montagnes et encourager les brigands . . .' (A.N. Fɪb II Haute-Loire I). See also *Les Parisiens*, p. 100: '. . . Aux causes professionnelles s'ajoutent des causes ethniques. Savoyards, Limousins, Auvergnats, Creusois—ainsi baptisés de noms qui évoquent aussi bien le métier que l'origine provinciale—sont vêtus à peu près de la même manière dans l'imagerie de l'Ancien Régime que dans celle du XIXe siècle parce que le costume du métier est celui de la province. . . .' Thus, *crocheteurs* were not only *habillés en lyonnois*, their professional uniform becomes identified with that of Lyon. Even in the Paris of the 1930s, *bougnats* (*Vins Charbons*) still tended to use the Auvergnat loose smock, while oyster salesmen sported the costume of the Dieppe fishermen and *mareyeurs*.

Louis Chevalier is admirably perceptive on the whole subject of clothes, on the proud semi-nudity of the nineteenth-century working man, in contrast to the *bourgeois emmitouflé*, and on the influence of Revolution and violence in accentuating such contrasts. 'Enfin viendra Billancourt: veste de cuir et bleu de chauffe sont l'uniforme obligatoire des héros de Carné et des manifestations du Front populaire. . . .' In the 1930s, the Paris working class was still distinguishable by its clothing, and the bourgeois expression of *salopards en casquette* corresponded to a physical reality.

(E) Mercier has his own explanation for the revolutionary vocation of certain trades: 'Dans les écoles de charité (on puisoit les leçons) de l'ingratitude, de la paresse, du mensonge et de la brutalité. . . . Voilà pourquoi, dans les assemblées sectionnaires, les projets les plus atroces . . . ont été proposés et exécutés . . . par le plus grand nombre de cordonniers, de tailleurs, des menuisiers . . . des perruquiers. L'insolence des nobles et des riches qui ne les payoient pas avoit exalté leur haine. Mais on ne trouvera ni assommeurs, ni révolutionnaires parmi les bons charbonniers, les bouchers, les forts de la Halle, les commissionnaires, les savoyards, parce que, plus dépendans des habitans à cause de leurs besoins domestiques, ils n'éprouvèrent pas comme d'autres le manque d'argent; et que, d'ailleurs, par leur caractère pacifique, ils étoient moins accessibles à la corruption . . .' (*Le Nouveau Paris*).

(F) The Thermidorian *comité* of Lyon comments, in Brumaire year III: 'Les étrangers qui ont été ici la véritable cause de l'égarement de cette commune, quelque costume qu'ils prennent, quelqu'idiome qu'ils affectent . . . n'échapperont pas à la surveillance. . . .' And a few days later, 'un membre a dit que la grande affluence d'étrangers dans cette commune exigeoit la plus grande surveillance . . .'. A month later, another member returns to the same subject: 'Les étrangers affluent dans Lyon, il seroit urgent de prendre des mesures pour s'assurer qu'il n'existe parmi eux que des gens probes . . .' (Arch. Rhône 31 L 164, comité de surveillance de Lyon, an III).

The District expresses a similar point of view in a report dated 24 Pluviôse year III: '. . . Les malveillans affluent dans la commune, les étrangers y sont peu surveillés . . .' (Arch. Rhône 2 L 2 L 19*, District de Lyon-Ville).

In a long and angry reply to the 500 on the subject of the murders committed in the city in the years III and IV, the authorities of the Rhône state: ' . . . Encore moins dissimulerons-nous les désordres particuliers auxquels le relâchement des mœurs, une population nombreuse, le mélange des étrangers et le défaut d'action de la police peuvent donner lieu. Pourquoi ces désordres, communs à toutes les grandes cités, ne sont-ils donc imputés qu'à Lyon . . .?' (Arch. Rhône 1 L 382, s.d. an IV).

A chief inspector of police reports, in Pluviôse year VI: '. . . Je ne peux vous dissimuler . . . que Lyon a dans son sein plus de 4,000 individus dont on ne connoît point l'existence et qui peuvent fournir de très mauvais sujets. . . . Ces hommes ont ici un comité de Brigans. . . . Tous les jours, il arrive des étrangers . . .' (Arch. Rhône 1 L 383).

The Directory itself allows some validity to these arguments, for in its *arrêté* dated 14 Pluviôse year VI, it refers to 'l'affluence des chefs des compagnies de Jésus et du Soleil, des assassins du Midi . . .' (ibid.).

It could, however, be argued that the Lyon police authorities proved remarkably hospitable to these numerous 'strangers', whose presence they either ignored or connived at (see above, the White Terror, pp. 131–49).

The authorities of the Loire likewise refer frequently to the presence in Montbrison of killers from Lyon; those of the Haute-Loire favour both Lyonnais and Foréziens (see above, the White Terror, pp. 131–49).

(G) See, for instance, *Mémoire sur le Midi présenté au Directoire . . . par Jullian . . . et Méchin . . .* (an IV): '. . . Les départements du Midi sont . . .

hérissés de montagnes au milieu desquelles se sont établis un grand nombre de villages; ces habitations servent d'asile à tous les malfaiteurs; c'est toujours des Montagnes que se sont précipités dans la plaine les rassemblements armés qui ont porté dans les communes la désolation et le meurtre. On n'arrive à ces villages que par des sentiers étroits . . . ce sont autant de citadelles dans lesquelles se refugient les brigands. . . .' The author of a royalist pamphlet, *La Lanterne magique républicaine* (July 1799), refers to 'les *légifères* sans-culottes, descendus en sabots et en bonnets rouges de leur pays montueux et arides, pour régénérer les plaines fertiles et florissantes . . .'.

(H) Mercier writes, on this subject: '. . . Les lieux publics sont les pièges où les voleurs et les filoux viennent se prendre . . . car les filoux et les brigands ne volent que pour passer le reste des nuits entre les filles, les pots de vin et les cartes . . . ainsi que l'on traîne une charogne dans la campagne pour attirer les loups, de même la Police ouvre certains endroits pour que les mauvais garnemens y tombent' (*Le Tableau de Paris*, xi). Comminges, the *commissaire* of the Section de la Montagne, has more to say on the same subject: 'Cette Section . . . renferme dans son enceinte une infinité de maisons garnies, de cafés, tripots cachés, maisons de jeux et de celles qui recèlent des filles publiques chez lesquelles se retirent souvent les voleurs. . . . Les filous, les assassins se rassemblent plus particulièrement dans son arrondissement, parce qu'ils y trouvent un plus grand nombre de repaires. . . .' The Commission reminds him that 'les maisons garnies sont plus particulièrement, aux approches de l'hiver, le refuge des gens intéressés à se soustraire aux regards de la Police . . .' (A.P.P. A/A 95–8, commissaire de police, an III). In Lille there seems to have been a certain specialization in the localization of crime: 'le café Massé et le café de la Paix, situés sur la place d'Armes, étoient fréquentés par les escrocs . . . les voleurs de boutique se réunissoient au café de la Montagne. Une maison, rue de l'Hôpital ou des Jésuites, servoit de repaire aux assassins . . .' (Vidocq, *Les Chauffeurs du Nord*).

(I) 'Cette bande comprenait une quarantaine de membres actifs et initiés. Cette société, qui embrassait le peuple, le commerce, la bourgeoisie et l'Armée était une espèce de compagnie industrielle, ayant ses agens dans chaque ville. . . . Une nuée de colporteurs, de brocanteurs, de marchands ambulants . . . entretenaient les communications entre tous les associés. L'armée auxiliaire comprenant deux classes d'affiliés: les fripiers et les aubergistes, également repartis sur tous les points du territoire qu'exploitaient les Chauffeurs. Les premiers achetaient les effets qui provenaient des éxpeditions . . . tel Chauffeur arrivant dans la soirée avec de tels habits, en changeait complètement chez le fripier associé. . . . Quant aux cabaretiers, hôteliers ou aubergistes, outre qu'ils offraient un gîte aux Chauffeurs . . . les moindres mouvements des voyageurs étaient annotés avec soin extrême; mais toute cette prétendue exactitude servait à préparer des alibis en cas d'alerte. . . .' Another essential element is provided by Gallois, 'maréchal, au faubourg Notre-Dame à Lille . . . homme d'excellent

conseil quand il s'agissait d'un bon coup à faire, car il connaissait presque toutes les fermes . . .'. Who, indeed, better than a blacksmith, would know the inside of a score of farms in a given region? (Vidocq, op. cit.).

(J) A.N. F7 4775 21 d 4 (Antoine Souvier). It was normal too that a suspected assassin from Nîmes, who had served for fifteen years both in the navy and the army, should have spent the evening playing cards in a Marseille café with three sailors, a fencing master, a *gendarme*, and a *perruquier sur le port*, the night after he had probably stabbed a chief inspector (Arch. Bouches-du-Rhône L 3082). It was normal that a *scieur de long* from Mamers should have got drunk in the company of 'charrons et scieurs de long du faubourg antoine . . . et avec d'autres du faubourg denis . . .' (A.N. F7 4774 25, Lochet). It was normal for a horse-dealer from Saint-Valéry to have spent the night drinking and betting with three other horse-dealers from Bacqueville in a Dieppe inn (Arch. Seine-Maritime L 5329, comité de Dieppe, 21 Nivôse year IV). It was normal that *tanneurs* should not spurn the company of *décrotteurs, tondeurs de chiens*, and *vidangeurs*, for no one else would have been likely to seek them out. It was natural that deserters should seek out *fripiers*, that the *bourreau* should marry the daughter of a colleague, and that the business should have been in a couple of families for over two hundred years. There was nothing unusual either about the composition of a group of card players observed by Restif: '. . . Je trouvai une Assemblée composée de Gens-de-Rivière, d'Ouvriers de toutes les professions, et de quelques petits marchands . . .' (*Les Nuits*, ix. 2023).

SECTION II

(A) If we are to believe Thermidorian reports of the terrorist vocabulary of the preceding year, some leading militants appear to have envisaged the Revolution solely in terms of blood, murder, and massacre, and their language, in the reported speech memorized by witnesses—many of whom had been the recipients of such threats—is one long litany of blood. There is, in fact, no reason to believe that the terrorists were any less bloodthirsty in speech, and occasionally in action, than their successors of the years III to VII. An example, no doubt extreme but also very evocative, can be found in the *livre de dénonces* of the Thermidorian *comité* of Salon: a leading terrorist, who had been directly involved in three murders committed in this town, on 21 February and 10 March 1793, is reported to have said, immediately after these events: '. . . Nous en avons assassiné trois et nos opérations seront suivies pour assassiner Périnat père, Gujot, le médecin Roux, Condolet, Rousier, Bernard Rose, Vachier', adding 'Il faut que tous les bourgeois de Salon périssent, il faut du sang dans Salon, et je vous assure avec certitude que nous en aurons beaucoup. . . .' In December 1793 the *concierge* of the local prison is quoted as saying, to a woman prisoner: '. . . Les pères et mères seront guillotinés et assassinés et nous coucherons avec leurs filles et alors les femmes [ne] nous manque-

ront pas, nous sommes faits pour jouir de tous les plaisirs du monde. . . .'
After the murders of March 1793, one of the murderers, Jean Laugier—
who, like the previous two terrorists, was himself to be murdered in the
White Terror—meets a girl in the street: '. . . Je viens de foutre un coup
de sabre au père Roland, l'un des assassinés, et à présent je m'en vais boire
une tasse de café à la santé dudit Roland. . . .' The *sans-culotte maire* of
Saint-Chamas comes into an inn, saying: 'Peut-on faire l'omelette sans
casser d'œuf? Non, la révolution ne peut se faire si tranquillement, il faut
du sang.' And a few days later, he returns, saying to the cook: 'Carbonnel,
prépare-nous un bon déjeuner, nous ne voulons pas d'agneau, il nous faut
de volaille, quelque chose de bon, nous l'avons bien gagné . . . nous venons
d'assassiner Paul Lamanon . . . je lui ai foutu un grand coup de sabre, et
puis après nous l'avons enterré . . . donnez-nous du pain que nous trem-
perons dans le vin pour raffermir mon estomac, je préférerois de tremper
mon pain dans un verre de sang que du vin. . . .' Another member of the
company says to one of his comrades: 'Ton épée a l'odeur du sang'; the
latter agrees: 'Tu as raison, j'en ai tué plus d'un, si tu veux, ce sera bientôt
fait.' The usual verbal exaggeration? Possibly, but these terrorists had
actually been involved in three murders (Arch. Bouches-du-Rhône L
1862).

(B) Events in the provinces during the Revolution gave a further boost
to the power of words as a source of violence. There are frequent references in documents relating to the course of the White Terror to *les deux
partis, les deux tribus*, and so on. In the whole Lyon area, the word
mathevon is the most effective of death labels at any time from the year III
to the year VIII. In an address to the inhabitants issued on 27 Messidor
year V, the authorities of the Rhône appealed to them: '. . . Nous vous
exhortons surtout à vous abstenir des qualifications réciproques de *mus-
cadin*, de *mathevon*, et des autres noms de parti qui éternisent les haines.
Ne vivez pas comme ennemis avec ceux qui ne peuvent pas vivre avec
vous comme frères. Si le langage de l'inimitié pouvoit s'abolir, la vengeance s'éteindroit dans tous les cœurs . . .' (Arch. Rhône 1 L 283,
Département, assassinats). The appeal seems to have fallen on deaf ears,
for in Brumaire year VII we hear of a poster stuck up at night in a number
of prominent places in Saint-Genis-Laval: '*AVIS AU PUBLIC*. En passant,
je donne la liste de tous les *matons* [*sic*] de la commune de Saint-Genis-
Laval . . .' (Arch. Rhône 1 L 293. See above, the White Terror).

(C) In certain communes of the Bouches-du-Rhône, at least, it is impossible to make a clear distinction between public terror and private
vengeance; in Salon, Saint-Chamas, and Martigues, there were at least
eight political murders in the spring of 1793. In some instances they seem
to have been actually carried out by local terrorists; in others the authorities stood aside while the murderers did their work. In one instance the
corpse of one of the victims, a doctor, was displayed for three days. Not
only did these authorities participate in these crimes, or stand aside while
they were being committed; they also went about quoting names for the

next round of murders. Many people were so frightened by these reports that they left their homes to take refuge with relatives, preferably in Marseille or further still. One of them, who was staying in Marseille, accidentally encountered, on the *Cours*, a member of the *comité* of Salon, who greeted him: 'How nice to see you, do not worry, we have not forgotten you, your turn will come, if necessary, we will come and kill you here.' It is hardly surprising that in these *communes* the politics of the year III should have been dominated by considerations of vengeance. Elsewhere too, in Arles, in Avignon, in Tarascon, the period of popular rule had been marked by massacre and murder. We should not, then, automatically dismiss Thermidorian reports of the atrocities of the *buveurs de sang* as standard elements of anti-terrorist propaganda, though such incidents are, on the whole, uncommon. The *sans-culottes* made themselves much more objectionable elsewhere by their exactions, by their threats, by their impudence, than by actual acts of violence (Arch. Bouches-du-Rhône L 1856 bis, L 1857, L 1858, L 1862, comité de Salon, registres et correspondance, an III).

(D) There are a great many references both to the increase in crime and to the impunity of the criminal in the years IV, V, VI, VII, VIII, and IX. On 1 Frimaire year IV, the commander of the Bordeaux *Garde nationale* reports: '. . . A mesure que le service se néglige les malfaiteurs augmentent d'audace. Chaque nuit on vole dans plusieurs endroits de la commune, il s'en passe très peu où l'on n'arrête dans les rues, même de très bonne heure . . .' (A.N. F1b II Gironde I). Already, in Pluviôse year III, Tellier and Richaud report to the Convention from Lyon: '. . . Les vols se multiplient dans cette commune . . . les magasins séquestrés deviennent particulièrement la proie des brigands . . .' (Arch. Rhône 2 L 96*). In Frimaire year V the Minister of Police draws the attention of the Lyon authorities to the need to carry out repairs to the local prisons 'dont l'état de dégradation est encore une des causes de la multiplicité des assassinats. Les détenus échappés de leurs cachots rentrent plus redoutables dans la société, où ils apportent la destruction . . .' (Arch. Rhône 1 L 283). In Ventôse year IV, the *chauffeurs* are reported in the neighbourhood of Charnay, scene of several robberies and murders (Arch. Rhône 1 L 392). Following the murder of a peasant girl near Sainte-Catherine, in the former District de la Campagne, the authorities of the Rhône send out a printed appeal to the local inhabitants: '. . . Que l'horrible assassinat de Ste. Catherine, dans le canton de Mornant, soit un avertissement de nous serrer contre les malfaiteurs. . . . Il ne faut pas se le dissimuler: les vols et les assassinats ne se multiplient d'une manière si effrayante que par l'insouciance et l'égoïsme des citoyens . . .' (ibid., L'Administration Centrale à ses Concitoyens, le 6 nivôse an VII). The Lyon authorities of the year VIII frequently refer to the activities of engravers and other specialists in the manufacture of false *assignats* and other branches of the counterfeiter's trade. They seem to have had their headquarters in a series of semi-rural retreats, in Vaise, la Croix-Rousse, and further afield up the valley of the Saône as far as Belleville and Île-Barbe, the latter also a well-known robbers' hide-out. Vaise appears also to have been the principal headquarters, in the years VIII and IX, of the frequent attacks on the Lyon–Paris mail coach, that passed through the *commune*; the culprits are said to have met regularly in an inn kept by one of their accomplices. The police authorities of the year VIII further emphasize that Lyon represents the ideal hunting-ground for the criminally inclined, owing to a geographical situation that enabled the man on the run to escape, in a matter of minutes, into the Isère, over the pont de la Guillotière. During all these years, as a result of the Siege, there remained a large number of ruined buildings of easy access that served as depots for stolen goods; many houses had lost their protecting walls, while thousands of keys from destroyed buildings were openly on sale on the quays. The *assommeurs*, in their numerous attacks on the prisons, released many hardened criminals, who then joined their ranks, while killing the *mathevons*. Lyon was situated on the route between the *bagne* of Toulon and that of Rochefort; on the occasion of the twice-yearly transfer of convicts from the one to the other, between the year VII and the year XI many disappeared while passing through Lyon, apparently with the connivance of the local *gendarmerie*. In short, in Lyon at least, and no doubt in Marseille as well, the facts of geography, the results of the Siege, the politics of violence and the weakness of the repressive authorities all contributed to making the Second City into a paradise of crime. Furthermore, with the steep gradients of La Grande Côte and of Vaise, there were many accidents provoked by runaway carts; these accidents in turn provoked arguments between the carters and the passers-by that frequently resulted in blows and deaths (A.N. BB 18 685–92). On 29 Nivôse year IV, the deputation of the Bouches-du-Rhône writes to the Minister of Justice: 'depuis l'établissement de la Constitution divers assassinats ont été commis à Marseille.... Ces assassinats demeurent impoursuivis. . . . L'impunité enhardit les méchans . . .' (A.N. BB 18 174, Ministère de la Justice, Bouches-du-Rhône).

(E) One is reminded of Marcel Aymé's admirable fantasy, 'La Carte du temps', in *Le Vin de Paris*. The Préfecture, in 1942 or 1943, have decided to ration time; there are rumours of the impending measure well in advance, some people are forewarned—for who cannot claim at least a cousin or a school friend in that important place?—and there is soon a busy trade in the new ration books—genuine and false. While some are thus able to enjoy the experience of living through January 39th, of reading *Le Matin* or *Paris-Soir* dated February 83rd, of tearing off their calendar March 41st, having stocked up on coupons, obtained from poor men with large families, for those months, others, once their rations have been used up or sold, simply disappear—it might happen anywhere— leaving just a bundle of clothes, collar, shirt, and tie, on a dining-room chair, in the middle of a meal, or at work in a factory.

(F) The *sans-culottes* did not exist in their own right; it was the Jacobins who invited them to join the dance, and it was the Jacobins who told them that the dance was over and that the time had come for them to return home. If, for a very short period, the *sans-culottes*, taken together, represented a national force, it was because the Jacobins needed such a force for their own purposes. The true isolation of the *sans-culottes* is demonstrated in the conditions of the year III, when, far from enjoying the support of the governing class, they were actively persecuted by the Thermidorians. The *sans-culottes* were then revealed as completely powerless and also very unpopular. This isolation took its most dramatic form in the extent, the impunity, and the widespread complicities of the White Terror in the south-east.

(G) In an indictment drawn up in Vendémiaire year IV against the former members of the *comité* of Gannat, one member, Louis Ballet, is accused 'de s'être souvent retiré avec ledit Rouchaud fils et quelques autres membres dud. comité dans une chambre à côté de celle des séances et séparément des autres membres, d'être rentré ensuite en chambre des séances . . . et avoir fait adopter et signer . . . ce qu'il avoit arrêté . . .' (A.N. F1b II Allier I, extrait de la procédure criminelle au greffe du tribunal correctionnel de Gannat, 12 vendémiaire an IV). A leading terrorist of Salon, talking to the cook of the local inn about a dinner to be held, states: 'Tu le sais, je te l'ai dit cent fois, quand je parle d'un souper de 10 à 12 personnes, tu dois savoir qu'il y a toute la municipalité, moi et David . . . nous mangeons à la chambre rouge', 'en effet . . . quand il étoit question de ces repas, il se faisoit monter tout le repas en une seule fois sur la table . . .' (Arch. Bouches-du-Rhône L 1862, comité du Salon, dénonciation contre les terroristes de Port-Chamas, 22 ventôse an III).

(H) If there were many local terrorists who behaved as those of Salon and Martigues, or those of Gannat, are alleged to have behaved and, above all, talked, it is not surprising that there was a considerable revulsion of feeling against them, once they had been edged out of office and could no longer inspire fear. It is possible that they talked big, but their big talk was widely believed, and reported minutely in the exhaustive *enquêtes* of Ventôse year III, at a time when a return to the Terror was still very much feared by many people. It would not look good, in the year III, to see oneself quoted as having exclaimed, in 1793, on entering the local inn: 'Il faut bien avouer que la jeunesse de Salon, vous êtes des couillons avec votre pièce de 24 ou 30 sols que vous gagnez par jour, si vous voulez avoir bientôt de l'argent en abondance, faites comme la jeunesse de Tarascon, la jeunesse de Tarascon, ils vont à l'auberge, boire et manger, pour payer leur dépenses ils vont chez un riche et se font donner de l'argent avec le sabre et le pistolet sur l'estomac, et quand ce même riche n'a plus d'argent, il faut le pendre . . . voilà, foutus animaux, comment est-ce qu'il faut faire . . .' (Arch. Bouches-du-Rhône L 1862, comité de Salon, dénonciation faite contre Conrad Orty et Antoine Michel, juge de paix, 19 ventôse an III). No doubt many of the local *sans-culottes* would still have secretly subscribed to this hearty programme, particularly when faced with the realities of Thermidorian rule; but they would have taken very good care not to give it any public support; and, in any case, this type of evidence was not meant for the *sans-culottes*, it was designed to frighten the *honnêtes gens* and prepare an ambience favourable to the emergence of the White Terror. Perhaps the most important difference between two years so close in time and so different in political realities was that, in the year II, local leaders talked a great deal of killing, of blood, of hanging and shooting, while in the year III, at least in this area, local leaders—often of much the same condition—killed, hanged, and shot the talkers.

(I) *Terreur et subsistances*, pp. 43–4. The *société* of Martigues took a passing, and somewhat patronizing, interest in the affairs of Poland. On 5 Prairial, 'lecture . . . des papiers nouvelles renfermant les détails de la révolution qui commence à s'effectuer en Pologne et qui peut s'assimiler à celle de notre République, suivant les réfléxions du journaliste; le lecteur les a traduites en langue ordinaire du pays et les a commentées afin de les rendre à la portée de toute l'assemblée. . . .' But Poland is soon forgotten for matters much nearer home: '. . . Il a été souvent interrompu par différentes questions; il s'est toujours fait un devoir d'aider de ses lumières ses frères qui lui ayant demandé ce que c'étoit que les *modérés*, leur a démontré que les *Modérés* étoient des contre-révolutionnaires accomplis; alors un membre l'ayant interrompu . . . a démontré qu'il y avoit encore une autre secte de contre-révolutionnaires dont le lecteur ne parloit pas, que c'étoit, suivant la force du terme un ESCALAMBRA, c'est à dire ayant un pied d'un côté et l'autre de l'autre, que cette sorte de gens étoient les plus dangereux. . . .' By this time the discussion had become far removed from the banks of the Vistula (Arch. Bouches-du-Rhône L 2080, société de Martigues, séance du 5 prairial an II).

(J) *Sans-culottisme* did not even have a common language, and despite the efforts of *représentants en mission* to impose French as 'the language of liberty' and to discourage the public use of local dialects—for the Jacobins, the role of the local *société populaire* was to be, among other things, a language school, and the *Propagande*, sent to Strasbourg, was Jacobin-rather than *sans-culotte*-orientated—the *sociétaires*, when left to themselves, readily reverted to dialect. The matter was fully discussed at the *société* of Martigues: on 7 Pluviôse year II, 'sur la motion d'un membre qui étoit de faire la lecture des papiers nouvelles seulement en langue françoise, pour que les soldats de la compagnie puissent l'entendre, il s'est élevé de vives discussions; un membre observe qu'il s'étoit délibéré de lire tout en langue provençale et qu'il falloit passer à l'ordre du jour. A la fin un autre membre a observé . . . que . . . le lecteur pourroit lire un chapitre en françois et puis en patois. . . .' This was not the end of it, for the question came up again, 11 Floréal, on the subject of 'la lecture du *Moniteur* au sujet duquel s'est ouverte une discussion tendant à ce qu'il soit fait par le lecteur l'explication de quelques passages en le commentant en patois lors qu'il en sera requis par quelques membres . . .' (Arch. Bouches-du-Rhône L 2080, société de Martigues. See also *Terreur et subsistances*, p. 35).

(K) Arch. Rhône 2 L 93 (District de Lyon-Ville, an III): 'Nous commissaires envoyés en détachement pour donner la chasse aux brigands avons
. . . investi la maison du C. Marmouzet, commune de Grigny, pour y
prendre le nommé Louis Dubois, ci-devant officier municipal . . .
compris dans la loi du 5 ventôse. . . . Nous avons demandé à la citoyenne
Marmouzet si elle n'avoit pas Dubois caché chez elle, sur quoi elle nous
a répondu que non, et dans le même moment nous avons vu sortir en
courant un individu de son clos, lequel, après avoir traversé les terres,
sauté les buissons, n'a pu échapper à notre poursuite, cet individu s'est
trouvé ce même Dubois . . .' (Certificat d'arrestation, 24 germinal an III).
Questioned in Lyon on 28 Germinal, Dubois, *fabricant de soie*, aged 40,
a former member of the Department, stated that he had left Lyon for
Grigny 'pour se soustraire aux mauvais traitements qu'éprouvoient les ci-
devant fonctionnaires publics . . . il y a environ trois mois' (that is, at the
time of the first murders). On 6 Floréal, he was given a prison sentence
for having illegally left his place of residence. There is every likelihood,
therefore, that he was massacred ten days later. On 2 Floréal year III, the
agent national of Saint-Cyprien-sur-Anse (Loire) informed the committee
of la Croix-Rousse: '. . . le nommé Sigeaud, se disant de votre commune,
muni d'un passeport de la Croix-Rousse, daté du 11 ventôse, est ici chez
un de ses parens qui nous est prévenu mais que je sais qu'il n'a pas
coutume de visiter. . . . Il arriva le 30 germinal avec sa femme. Cette
dernière est repartie d'hier . . .' (ibid.). Sigeaud, *dessinateur*, was a
member of the former *comité* of la Croix-Rousse. Sigeaud and Dubois
made the mistake of not moving far enough away. In the neighbouring
Department, once the White Terror had begun to take its toll in and
around Montbrison, in Germinal year III, the surviving terrorists mostly
took care to move at least as far as the Puy-de-Dôme or the Saône-et-
Loire, many of them finding work in Clermont-Ferrand. Few returned
to their homes before Brumaire year IV, when Reverchon was sent to the
Loire. Chantelauze, a lawyer from Montbrison, fled in Floréal year III,
first to Feurs, then to Bellegarde, 'mais que ne pouvant y rester en sûreté,
parce que c'étoit sur la grande route de Lyon, il se rendit dans la commune
de Chalmazel . . . située à l'entrée des grands bois où il demeura caché
pendant environ un mois et demi . . . que deux jours après [il] se rendit à
Paris par la route d'Auvergne, d'où il n'est rentré que le 2 nivôse an IV . . .'
(A.N. BB 18 690, Loire, assassinats). Chantelauze survived; he could
afford to; another terrorist, from Feurs, Jacques Poche, *chapelier*, was less
fortunate. In Floréal year III, his wife induced him to leave Feurs; he
took refuge with relatives in Néronde, 'que cependant leurs affaires ne
leur permettant pas de demeurer longtems absents, ils réintégrèrent leur
domicile . . . à Feurs . . . que le lendemain de leur arrivée son mari
fut arrêté à peu de distance de la commune de Feurs . . .'. Transferred to
the prison of Montbrison, he was murdered there with Paley, a lawyer from
Saint-Galmier, in the prison massacre of 1 Prairial year III (BB 18 690).

(L) A.N. F1b II Saône-et-Loire II (Genty le jeune, de Mâcon, à ****
à Paris, 15 prairial an V): '. . . le jeune Revillon, celui qui travailloit au

bureau des domaines . . . avoit été à Lyon il y a une quinzaine de jours pour des affaires qu'il y avoit, il avoit écrit le 7 du courant à un de ses amis qu'il alloit partir pour revenir à Mâcon, il y a 4 jours qu'une femme est venue rapporter qu'elle l'avoit vu assommer sur le pont de pierre et jetter à l'eau. . . .' (See also Dutroncey le jeune à 'mon cher Représentant', same date: 'Encore un nouvel assassinat sur un jeune et vertueux républicain, Revillon fils, commis au Département, nouvellement exclu, a eu l'imprudence d'aller à Lyon, reconnu et dénoncé par un mâconnais comme mathevon, il a été poignardé et jeté à la Saône. . . . Dis bien à Reverchon de ne pas revenir. . . .') Jean Fricour, *chapelier*, aged 48, from Montbrison, only narrowly escaped a similar fate: 'dans le courant du mois de ventôse an III . . . il se trouva dans la commune de Lyon pour ses affaires et se trouvant dans un café quai de la Saône près du pont de pierre . . . entrèrent les nommés Dutaillon, de Montbrison, et Labrousse, de Saint-Maurice-en-Gourgeois, qu'ils le saisirent en lui disant *te voilà, bougre, tu n'échapperas pas à la guillotine* . . . chemin faisant, sur la place des Terreaux [ils] s'écrièrent *Voilà un scélérat de Montbrison*, et tout à coup il tomba sur lui une grêle de coups de batons et de pierres qui le renversèrent, lui firent perdre connoissance . . .' (Déclaration de Fricour, 6 nivôse an VI, A.N. BB 18 690).

For a similar instance, see BB 18 686 (assassinat de Bigot, tourneur de Roanne, et maquignon, rapport du 27 prairial an V): '. . . Bigot étoit natif de Roanne, marié depuis environ 8 ans, et domicilié à Feurs depuis sept ans, tourneur de profession et se mêlant de différentes affaires de commerce, et notamment de chevaux. Bigot partit le 7 du ct. avec le nommé Lapra, fripier, avec lequel il étoit associé pour cette partie de chevaux. Le même jour [ils] achetoient un cheval de réforme qui leur coûta 100 l. Le 8 ils se rendirent à Charabart, pour en acheter d'autres, se trouvant au cabaret avec son associé, et d'autres citoyens aussi marchands de chevaux de nos environs, étant à boire tous ensemble. . . .' Two other inhabitants of Feurs provoke them on the subject of the sale of a saddle, suggesting that they settle the dispute by leaving the inn in order to see a *notaire*. Once Bigot and his companion are out in the street—the rue Écorchebœuf—a predestined name—in Lyon, 'aussitôt on crie *au voleur, à l'assassin*, dans la foule Bigot reçoit deux coups de poignard, et les assommeurs l'achèvent à coups de massue, aussitôt l'on crie *c'est un juge du tribunal révolutionnaire de Feurs* . . .'. Another report states: 'Le malheureux Bigot n'eut jamais aucune place dans la Révolution, il étoit tourneur de profession, illettré et faisant alternativement le métier de maquignon . . .' (rapport du 14 thermidor an VI).

(M) Even a military escort of considerable size was no protection against a hostile population. 'Le 6 ventôse an III', a Nîmois judge reports, 'plusieurs prévenus étoient conduits de la maison d'arrêt à la Citadelle, deux brigades de gendarmerie et 400 hommes de la garde nationale les escortoient, le peuple força cette garde, sur 9 prisonniers, 4 furent massacrés. . . . Le 23 floréal an III, environ minuit, des hommes attroupés et armés forcèrent le poste de la Citadelle, la garde fut enfermée . . . le 28 prairial

... un attroupement d'hommes et de femmes força la garde de ce prison-nier. ...' The best that can be said is that, on these occasions, the *garde* put up remarkably little resistance. Many of these prisoners could have been saved had they been escorted by regular troops, rather than by a totally unreliable National Guard, itself deeply penetrated by royalists (A.N. F1b Gard I).

(N) A good example of this is the murder of Magnien, *imprimeur*, on the road from Boën to Montbrison, in Floréal year III. Magnien was being brought from the village in which he had taken refuge, to be cross-examined in Montbrison. A few miles short of the town he and his escort were intercepted by a group of a dozen young men on horseback. On seeing them, Magnien is reported to have said: *Voilà des jeunes gens de Montbrison qui viennent pour m'assassiner, je suis mort.* He was then shot, his head cut open with a sabre and squashed with a heavy stone; his body, clothed only in breeches, was left in a ditch (A.N. BB 8 690). His murder-ers then retired to a roadside inn, boasting to the landlord 'qu'ils venoient de se débarrasser d'un foutu coquin de mathevon ... et qu'ils venoient de lui faire son compte ...'.

(O) In the Loire, many of the murders take place in attics or on the roofs of houses; one man got as far as the middle of the river before being shot down. Several were dispatched outside their front doors, a number were killed on the roads, their bodies thrown into the ditch. In the Haute-Loire, victims were shot outside their farms, after being tortured, or in woods. Many were killed, in the year IV, on the road from Yssangeaux to le Puy and on that from Pradelles to the *chef-lieu*. All over the south there were multiple killings in vineyards. In Lyon, of sixteen murders the details of which are amply documented, one took place on the pont de la Feuillée, one on the *pont de pierre*, one on the pont de l'Arsenal, one on the pont Saint-Vincent, one on the pont de la Guillotière, two on the banks of the Saône, one on the river port of the Rhône, two on the road to Rive-de-Gier, one in the barracks of the Célestins, two in the street, near the Saône, one in a *traboule* off the rue Écorchebœuf, one near the fort Saint-Jean, one aux Pierres Plantées, two in la Croix-Rousse, two in Vaise. Other places mentioned as the sites of Lyon murders in the years V, VI, VII, VIII, and IX, are the pont de l'Arsenal, the pont Saint-Vincent, the pont de pierre, the pont la Feuillée, the port du Temple, where the *crocheteurs* worked, 'sur les quais', rue de la Juiverie, near the Saône, in a riverside inn in the suburb of la Mulatière, on the Rhône, in les Brotteaux, in an inn, rue Longue. Lyon was ideally placed for murder; the town was still largely in ruins, and it was sufficient to cross the Rhône to be out of each of the Rhône courts. Proximity to the river seems to have been the governing factor in the choice of a place of slaughter. The Bourg massacre took place just beyond the gates of the town. In the Haute-Loire, a number of the murder spots, la Chaise-Dieu, Craponne, Jullianges, Allègre, are within easy reach of the puy-de-Dôme; Saint-Victor, Retournac, Yssangeaux are easily accessible from the Loire. In the neighbourhood of Pradelles, the killers move out of the forest of Bauzon, in the Ardèche. Apart from the *Cours*, the Marseillais *sabreurs* chose, as a favourite murder spot, the various *portes* leading out of the city, especially that on the road to Aix. Septèmes is on the main road from Marseille to Aix, Aubagne on that from Marseille to Toulon—a route that was to be strewn with scattered corpses during the Second White Terror of 1815. Auriol and Saint-Zacharie are on the high road from Marseille to Brignoles. Lambesc, Sénas, and Orgon are all on the road from Aix to Avignon. Pélissanne is on the road from Salon to Aix; Eyragues and Châteaurenard are on the road from Saint-Rémy to Avignon. Mallemort and Morières are on the banks of the Durance and, at the same time, within easy reach of the Lubéran. Graveson is half-way between Avignon and Tarascon, while Barbentane is on the road from Avignon to Beaucaire. Very many murders are committed at the entry to a village. A town like Mâcon was almost ideally placed, in respect of the activities of the *égorgeurs*; many of the murders there, and nearly all the riots, took place on the quays by the Saône. From there, over the bridge, there was an easy escape route to Saint-Laurent-lès-Mâcon, a suburb situated, most conveniently for the murderers, in the neighbouring Department of the Ain, whence many of the *égorgeurs* came, and whither they could not be pursued by the local *gendarmerie* of Mâcon.

(P) The example of Lyon in the year V suggests how difficult it is to reach any accurate estimate of the number of murders. According to the Directory, informed by the *commandant de la place*, sixty-seven persons were killed in the city between Nivôse and Messidor year V—about three a *décade*. The Department, on the other hand, only admits to eight murders of a political character during this period. My calculations, based on the report of the *Bureau Central*, suggest a total of twenty-four victims. The military authorities certainly tended to exaggerate the numbers, in their desire to have Lyon placed in a state of siege, as it was in Messidor year V. But the Lyonnais authorities rather suggest that people who got themselves murdered in or near the city did so in a deliberate attempt to discredit the city with the Paris government! Not only is the White Terror political, the counting of its victims also involves taking a political stand. The *État-civil* is hardly any help in the matter, as people did not dare state the cause of death. For a further estimate, based on more recent research, see above, pp. 135–40.

But clearly, also, certain authorities had a vested interest in exaggerating the number of murders, in order to force the central authorities to intervene. Many affairs may thus be blown up into massacres, the cutting down of a tree of liberty may be depicted as a Counter-Revolution. There is a reference, for instance, to the murder of an old woman in a village in the Var in the year V; according to the Department, 'ce fait n'est pas exact. Ce prétendu assassinat est une coupure d'un doigt qui n'a pas deux lignes de profondeur . . .' (A.N. F1b II Var I, rapport du 1er fructidor an V). Equally, with reference to former terrorist officials, the royalist-inclined administration of the Lot observes 'ces administrateurs donnent à entendre à leurs amis que tous les patriotes vont être assassinés parce qu'une fille de service a attaché son bonnet de paille avec de fil blanc . . .' (A.N. F1b II Lot I, Département au Ministre, 16 thermidor an V).

(Q) Seven were killed in the Bourg massacre of 5 Floréal year III. There were further murders in the Ain in the year VI and the beginning of the year VII (Arch. Rhône 1 L 383 and 2 L 53*). In the Ariège, there were murders in Foix, Pamiers, Saverdun, Ax, Tarascon, and Mazères. 'Chaque Département est marqué par des usages particuliers; celui de la Haute-Garonne est remarquable dans ce moment par sa tranquillité; celui de la Landes par ses cloches et ses prêtres, et le nôtre, citoyen, se distingue par des assassinats . . .' (Labeaumelle, officier de génie, au Représentant Bordes, 20 frimaire an V, A.N. F1b II Ariège I). Several of the victims of the murders in Saverdun are stated to have been Protestants. In the Var, there were murders in Fayence, Hyères, and Saint-Maximin-la-Sainte-Baume, over and above the prison massacres in Toulon (F1b II Var I). One man was murdered in Blaye (Gironde) in Germinal year IV (F1b II Gironde I).

(R) A.N. BB 18 690 (déclaration de la veuve Clément au sujet de l'assassinat de son mari, 1er nivôse an VI): 'Ajoute qu'il ne fut dressé aucun procès-verbal . . . qu'elle est instruite que son décès n'a été couché sur les registres civils que 3 mois après, où on ne voulut pas lui laisser insérer le genre de mort de son mari. . . .' Clément had been murdered in Montbrison in Floréal year III. See also A.N. F1b II Haute-Loire I (rapport de la gendarmerie d'Yssangeaux du 15 nivôse an IV au sujet de l'assassinat près de Retournac d'un officier): '. . . Sortis du château, ils continuent de conduire le malheureux auquel chemin faisant ils écrasent la tête . . . le dépouillent et vont boire ensuite dans la commune de Retournac où tous les habitans les virent, il n'étoit que 3 heures de l'après-midi, sans qu'on puisse cependant obtenir aucune preuve . . . le plus grand nombre qui leur prête la main périroit plutôt que de les dénoncer . . . qu'il s'ensuit de à qu'aucun coupable, même de ceux pris les armes à la main n'a subi aucune peine, et qu'ils sont soutenus dans leur inconduite . . . d'ailleurs il est dans la nature que le père répugne à condamner le fils, et que chacun soutienne les siens. . . . Voilà nombre d'assassins de ce genre qui se passent sous nos yeux, de meurtres et de vols sans fin, sans qu'il se soit fait d'autre procédure que pour ce dernier. . . .' In Germinal of the same year, after several gendarmes had been killed on the road from Yssangeaux to le Puy, the commissaire du Directoire commented: '. . . Je suis persuadé que nulle poursuite [ne] se fera, c'est l'ordinaire des juges de paix de la campagne, les uns sont contenus par la crainte, et la majeure partie sont dirigés par la perfidie, aussi voit-on le crime se commettre avec hardiesse. . . . Les républicains agissent par crainte, les exemples fréquents de pillages et d'assassinats les découragent . . .' (commissaire du Directoire dans la Haute-Loire au Ministre de la Police générale, 21 germinal an IV).

On other occasions, the death was declared in the normal way, but without mention of its cause. Thus, having killed Bard, in his attic, in

Floréal year III, his murderers tell his widow: *Tu iras demain faire ta déclaration à la municipalité, tu diras que tu as un homme mort chez toi, mais si tu dis qui c'est, je t'en ferai autant* (déclaration de la veuve Bard, 3 nivôse an VI, A.N. BB 18 690).

(S) A.N. F1b II Ain I (Paté fils, de Bourg, à Gauthier de l'Ain, 28 brumaire an V): '. . . Furieux de n'avoir pu tromper le Directoire sur les principes de ses commissaires, dans cette commune, ils ont conçu l'atroce projet de les livrer à ces assassins, aussi depuis l'arrivée de celui qu'ils appellent leur digne représentant (Valentin Duplantier) on voit les assassins de germinal et prairial an III reprendre leur première audace et menacer publiquement les commissaires qui ne veulent pas condescendre à leur abominable conduite, déjà ces vampires disent tout haut que les terroristes sont encore très nombreux et qu'il faut s'en faire justice (ce propos a été tenu au spectacle dans les premiers jours de ce mois) . . . l'administration municipale . . . a refusé d'établir au spectacle une garde de police et de prohiber l'entrée dans la salle de gros bâtons et pistolets qui ne paroissent pas. . . .'
See also A.N. F1b II Saône-et-Loire I (Rubat, commissaire du Directoire à Mâcon, à ****, à Paris, 9 prairial an V): '. . . Les événements se multiplient ici, vous avez été instruit de l'assassinat de **** gens à Vinxelles. . . . Le jour de la foire . . . deux citoyens assassinés à la porte de la Barre sont morts, l'un sur place et l'autre à l'hospice, toujours point de témoins. . . . Je ne vous parle pas des assassinats commis dans le département de l'Ain à notre porte. . . .'

(T) Arch. Rhône 1 L 383. Lyon and its three *communes* were placed *en état de siège*, under the authority of General Kellermann, by the Directory, on 24 Messidor year V and again on 14 Pluviôse year VI. The local authorities, bitterly hostile to Canuel, the *commandant de place*, and to his troops, attempted to have the garrison removed and civil authority re-established, in the interest, so they said, of the city's trade. Their real objection to the presence of the troops was, no doubt, that it limited the activities of the murder gangs, the municipal officers being good friends of the *compagnie de Jésus*, and because the soldiers were Parisians or Dauphinois who hated the Lyonnais. It was for this reason that they consistently argued that the bodies seen floating in one of the two rivers must have been killed upstream, north of Lyon, and why they so persistently attempted to play down the constant repetition of political murders.

(U) The figures for the incidence of the White Terror have been based on the following sources: first of all, on the judicial records of the Bouches-du-Rhône (assassinats politiques, years III to VII) in Arch. Bouches-du-Rhône L 3072 (tribunal criminel du département, assassinats, an III), L 3077 (ibid. an IV), L 3082 (ibid. an V), L 3089 (ibid. an VI), L 3094 (ibid. an VII). These include murders committed in neighbouring Departments, many of the cases having been transferred from Nîmes or Avignon to Aix, in the belief—generally quite unfounded—that the Aix judges would be more likely to secure convictions. The dates are not those of the murders, but those of the trials, which in many instances took place three or four years after the events themselves. Secondly, we have used L 174* and L 175 (correspondance de l'administration centrale du Département avec le Ministre de la Police générale, pluviôse an IV–ventôse an VII). Thirdly, L 948*, L 949*, L 950*, and L 954* (district de Marseille, an III). Fourthly, L 1707* (comité de surveillance d'Aix, an III, correspondance); L 2031*–2* (société populaire d'Aix, an III); L 1856 bis, 1857, 1858, 1860 (comité de Salon, an III); L 2080 (société de Martigues, an III). Fifthly, A.N. F1b II Bouches-du-Rhône I (esprit public) and A.N. D III 29, 30, 31 (comité de législation). For the Vaucluse, Arch. Vaucluse 3 L 26*, 27, 28*, 34*, 36*, 48* (agent national du district d'Avignon, correspondance et rapports décadaires, an III) and A.N. F1b II Vaucluse I. For the Gard, we have used A.N. D III 86 d 17 (comité de législation, Nîmes) and F1b II Gard I. For a group of south-eastern Departments, we have used: F1b II Basses-Alpes I; F1b II Aveyron I; F1b II Ardèche I; F1b II Cantal I; F1b II Drôme I; F1b II Ain I; F1b II Isère I; F1b II Loire I; F1b II Saône-et-Loire I. For the Rhône, Arch. Rhône 31 L 164* (registre de délibérations du comité de surveillance de Lyon; an III); 33 L 78* (registre du comité de Villefranche, an III); and 2 L 39* (district de Lyon, correspondance, an III); 1 L 208, 209, 382, 383, 392 (Département, assassinats, ans III–VII). 8 L I* (administration cantonale de Belleville, an V); 12 L 3* (ibid. de Condrieu, ans V, VI et VII); 18 L 10 (ibid. de Neuville, an VIII); 21 L 1* (ibid. de Saint-Genis-Laval, ans IV à VII); A.N. BB 18 685–92 (Ministère de la Justice, Rhône). For the Jura, Arch. Jura, registre de dénonces du comité de Lons (an III). For the Loire, BB 18 690; for the Haute-Loire, F1b II Haute-Loire I; for the Ariège, F1b II Ariège I; for the Dordogne, F1b II Dordogne I; for the Puy-de-Dôme, F1b II Puy-de-Dôme I; for the Tarn, F1b II Tarn I; for the Gers, F1b II Gers I; for the Gironde, F1b II Gironde I; for the Lot, F1b II Lot I.

We have also used the following printed sources: Fréron, *Mémoires historiques sur la réaction royale et sur les massacres du Midi* (Paris, an VII, p. 299); Thibaudeau, *Mémoires;* Bouvier, *Conseil des 500. Motion d'ordre faite par Bouvier, sur le brigandage exercé dans le département de Vaucluse* (séance du 26 fructidor an VII); *Rapport du général de brigade Tisson . . . sur les événemens qui ont eu lieu à Avignon dans les journées des 24, 25, 26 et 27 du mois de pluviôse an 5me* (Paris, 12 prairial an V); *Au nom du département de Vaucluse et du district d'Avignon, Tissot, administrateur du département, et Blaze, administrateur du district, à la Convention nationale* (14 thermidor an III, p. 33); *Quelques éclaircissemens sur l'établissement du Robespierrisme dans le Midi . . . par J. E. B. Duprat, citoyen d'Avignon* (à Avignon, s.d.); *Pétition à la Convention nationale des citoyens de la commune victimes de la faction Robespierre, sur les atrocités commises . . .* (Avignon, 19 brumaire an III, p. 20); *Les Républicains Avignonnais traduits devant le tribunal criminel de la Drôme, au peuple français* (à Valence, le 24 floréal an IV); *Les Sans-culottes de Carpentras à leurs frères d'Avignon* (18 ventôse an II); *Rapport . . . par les représentants . . . Auguis et Serres sur leur mission dans les départements des Bouches-du-Rhône, du Var et de l'Ardèche* (ventôse an III); *Chambon . . . sur sa mission dans les départements des Bouches-du-Rhône, du Var et de Vaucluse . . .* (fructidor an III); *Mémoire sur le Midi présenté au Directoire exécutif par Louis Jullian et Alexandre Méchin, chargés par les anciens comités de gouvernement d'accompagner le C. Fréron dans les départements méridionaux* (Paris, chez Desenne, an IV, p. 72); *Histoire du terrorisme dans la commune d'Arles* (floréal an III); *Il est tems de parler ou Mémoire pour la commune d'Arles* (s.d.); *Les Patriotes monaidiers d'Arles à la Convention nationale* (23 thermidor an II); *Rapport . . . fait par Espert . . .* (ventôse an III); *Liste des condamnés à mort (à Nîmes) 1791–1884, par un ancien magistrat* (Nîmes, 1884); *Adresse des membres de l'administration municipale de la commune de Lons-le-Saunier, au Corps Législatif* (s.d. an VI).

Thus only the records for the Bouches-du-Rhône and the Rhône have been explored systematically. The impression of the incidence of the White Terror in the south can only be a fragmentary one until similar sources have been used for the Var, the Vaucluse, the Gard, etc. Further information could be obtained from an examination of the *État Civil* in the *archives communales* of the principal centres of White terrorism. Our purpose here has been merely to give the subject a preliminary ventilation.

(V) F1b II Saône-et-Loire I (notes s.d. prairial an V). '. . . Les provocations et les attaques éprouvés par les patriotes de Mâcon . . . coincident avec les provocations dirigées à Paris contre le C. Reverchon et autres patriotes. Elles sont l'explication bien formelle de cette atroce annonce du *Miroir*, dans son numéro du 8 prairial: "Les Compagnons de Jésus sont à Paris; ils se proposent de faire boire un coup de l'eau de la Seine aux Jacobins à qui l'on n'a pu faire boire de celle du Rhône ou de la Saône. . . ." '

There is plenty of similar evidence to indicate that in the south-east the movement was centrally organized, and with its headquarters and its leaders in Lyon. In Lyon itself, the *compagnie de Jésus* distributed small cards, bearing the royal emblem and a picture of Jesus Christ, to teen-age children (14 to 17) and toughs (everywhere the movement relied on young supporters, while their victims tended to be men in their late 30s or 40s, a further example of the revolt against the fairly mature terrorist age group). In the Haute-Loire, a *commissaire* described the *preux* as sitting at a round table—a conscious piece of neo-medievalism. Their armies are further stated to be 'bien armés, bien vêtus, . . . ils parlent bien le françois et ils sont bien commandés . . .'; '. . . Le nommé Lamothe étoit leur général et . . . il étoit parti pour l'Auvergne . . . ils vouloient aller jusqu'à Paris . . . ils avoient des appuis dans Lyon. . . .' In the same Department, there are references to a concerted plan for Floréal year V to capture le Puy, Saint-Étienne, and Alès and then to carry out the link-up between Marseille, Montpellier, and Lyon.

All over the south, the Directorial authorities are convinced of a link-up between local *assommeurs* and a secret headquarters in Lyon. In the Haute-Loire, there are references to men 'arrivés de Lyon et de Montbrison par la route de Craponne . . .' (3 pluviôse an IV) as well as to '14 Lyonnois vêtus à la mode du pays . . . venus courir nos montagnes et encourager les brigands . . .' (14 germinal an IV). In the Cantal, 'les ci-devant . . . se coalisent, correspondent avec Lyon' (14 thermidor an VII). One of the *assommeurs* of Montbrison, Chovot fils, *aubergiste*, a man with several murders to his credit, stops off at an inn at Chazelles, boasting: 'Je viens de Lyon, les mathevons ont passé entre nos mains, j'en ai tué 20 pour ma part . . .' (germinal an III).

In the Loire, the murderers worked off a printed list of *dénonciateurs* and *mathevons*, provided by an official of the District. In Brumaire year VII, we hear of a placard stuck up in Saint-Genis-Laval: '*Avis au public. En passant, je donne la liste de tous les matons [sic] de la commune . . .*' (a dozen names follow). Two bodies discovered, 19 Floréal year III, in Neuville, have notices pinned to their breeches: 'Pierre Cotton, officier municipal de Neuville, assassin des Lyonnois', 'François Gense, maire de Neuville, assassin des Lyonnois' (for references, see note U above).

(W) A.N. F10 210 (Commission d'agriculture, les administrateurs du district de Ségré (Maine-et-Loire) à la Commission, 12 vendémiaire an III): '. . . Nous vous dirons que des brigands sortis de la Vendée, soit produits de notre pays, tuent, pillent, brûlent sur tous les points du District, que depuis bientôt six mois, pas une route n'est libre, que les corps de garde seuls, où se refugie le peu de troupes que nous avons, sont au pouvoir de la république . . . plus de 300 patriotes ont été égorgés, 40 officiers municipaux ont subi le même sort, tous les patriotes sont en fuite, les campagnes sont désertes ou deviennent le tombeau de ceux qui les habitent, le deuil et la consternation couvrent le district, pas une commune qui ne soit teinte du sang de quelques républicains, chaque jour annonce de nouvelles scènes toutes plus sanglantes . . . les officiers municipaux qui ne sont pas égorgés sont refugiés. . . .'

(X) '[Ils] se rendirent au temple de la raison avec toute la kirielle fanatique composée en grande partie de leurs bordiers manouvriers illetrés . . . et encore de tous les ci-devant nobles de haut étage . . .' (Jean Sol, de Saverdun, à la Convention, 5 brumaire an IV, A.N. F1b II Ariège I). He adds that the leaders of the gang in this town were the wealthiest inhabitants, whereas most of their victims were members of the important Protestant community.

The leading assassins of Montbrison are: Granjon, *homme de loi*, Méjasson, *géomètre*, Chovot fils, *cabaretier*, Portailier père et fils, *boulangers*, Anselme, *hussard*, Coire, *marchand*, Lattard, *défenseur officieux*, Dutaillon fils, Verd fils, Chassagnon fils, Bouvier fils, Legrand, lyonnais, Feuillet, lyonnais, Turquois, Latourcy. Save in the case of the two Portailiers, all are young men, in their 20s. Among the Clermont-Ferrand *massacreurs*, there are four members of one family, Manard, his son and his daughters, Chausson, *entrepreneur*, Tixier, *tisserand*, two *cultivateurs*, a *traiteur*, a *confiseur*, a baker, Vazeilles cadet, *officier de la garde nationale*. In the

Haute Loire, the *bandes* are led by non-juror priests, peasants, and ex-soldiers. The main leader is stated to be Allier, the brother of the curé of Chambonas (Ardèche) (A.N. BB 18 390, F1b II Puy-de-Dôme I and Haute-Loire I). See also pp. 130–49 above, White Terror.

(Y) Of 93 victims identified by name and trade, mostly in the Bouches-du-Rhône, 15 are *cordonniers*, 7 *tailleurs*, 6 *maçons*, 6 *menuisiers*, 6 *perruquiers*, 5 *cafetiers-aubergistes*, 4 *boulangers*, 4 *tonneliers*, 3 *calfats*, 3 *porte-faix*, 3 *potiers*, 3 *chandeliers*; among other victims there are a *cribleur*, a *musicien*, a *gagne-denier*, a former *garde-scellés*, a *salpêtrier*, a *porteur de place*, a *batelier*, operating a ferry across the Durance, a miller, a *charretier*, a locksmith, an *employé aux charrois*, a *garde-magasin*, a *bourrelier*, an *emballeur*, a *maréchal ferrant*, a *commissionnaire*, a *fripier*, a *taillandier*, a *dégraisseur*, a *cuisinier*, an *instituteur*, a *vitrier*, an *ex-chanoine*, a *fabricant de savon*, a *marchand de coton*, an *accoucheuse*, a female servant, a *blanchisseuse*, a *couturière*, in short, as representative a selection of the *sans-culotte* spectrum, in social terms, as one could hope for.

In the Montbrison area, the victims include Girou, *tisserand*, Clément, *greffier*, Perraud, *vigneron*, Poche, *chapelier*, Paley, *officier de santé*, Bard, *maçon*, Magnien, *imprimeur*. And among those who took refuge outside the area to escape assassination: Fontlup, *teinturier*, Fricour, *chapelier*, Favier, *charpentier*, Richard, *cabaretier*, Ponsonnat, *marchand*, Nicolas and Perruchon, *jardiniers*, Arnaud and Reynaud, *journaliers*, Griot, *cordonnier*, Roche, *serrurier*, Drivon, *tisserand*, Girin, *vigneron*, Chantelauze, *homme de loi*. The victims in the Haute-Loire, on the contrary, tended to be well-to-do *acquéreurs de biens nationaux*.

(Z) Arch. Bouches-du-Rhône L 3094 (veuve d'Antoine Martin à l'accusateur public du tribunal criminel du département, 23 brumaire an VII). The three men were murdered on 30 fructidor year III by Jean-Pierre Tronc and his two sons. The father, after the murder, goes with his sons to the local inn, and, addressing a customer, asks: 'Tu ne me félicites point?... Sur quoi?... Est-ce que tu ne sais pas que nous venons de nous débarrasser de ces scélérats de Martin, à présent les honnêtes gens sont tranquilles....' The widow comments: '... Il est à connoissance de tous les amis de la République que les trois Martin furent la famille du canton de Lambesc la plus fortement attachée au gouvernement républicain....' See also A.N. BB 18 690 (assassinats, Loire): '... Girin, vigneron ... Marcilly ... pour se soustraire à la vengeance de ce monstre (Dutaillon) ... fut obligé de vendre tous ses bestiaux et d'abandonner le domaine quoiqu'il eût encore trois arrhes à tenir....' The wife of Portalier, a baker from Montbrison lucky enough to escape before his assassination, is told by her husband's would-be assassins: 'C'est un gueux et un scélérat qui ne mérite pas de vivre, tu n'en seras que plus heureuse lorsqu'il n'existera plus; à l'égard de tes enfans, on les mettra à la Charité, comme on vouloit mettre les nôtres....' In this case, the murderers were unable to carry out their threats, but there is no doubt as to their intention to penalize the family of a former *mathevon*, as well as to kill the man himself.

(2A) There are some clear indications that it was not only anti-popular but, in the particular context of the Département de Vaucluse, also anti-semitic. Among the signatories of a petition, 'Les patriotes de Carpentras au Ministre de l'Intérieur', dated Frimaire year IV, and protesting against the impunity enjoyed by the *sabreurs* in this District, one notes the names of Mossé Crémieux, Lange Crémieux, Élie Crémieux, Isaac Monteux, Mossé Monteux, Abraham Crémieux, David Crémieux, Mardoché Digne, Mossé Crémieux, Jacob David Lyon, Mossé Naque, Aaron Monteaux, Ruben Crémieux, Joseph Léon, François Lazare, Siffren Comtat, Siffren Valentin, Manuel de Baze, Daniel Baze, Joseph Mérieux, Issano, Mardoché Carcassonne, Ilissac Samuel. One of those they mention as having been murdered by the *sabreurs* is called le Citoyen *Carpentras* (A.N. F1b II Vaucluse I).

(2B) A.N. F1b II Saône-et-Loire I (Genty le jeune à ****, à Paris, le 15 prairial an V): '. . . Revel et Chaumet prennent mal leur tems pour revenir, pour moi je sais si j'étois à Paris, j'y resterois, et j'attendrois un moment plus favorable pour regagner mes foyers. Paris sera toujours l'endroit où l'on pourra exister en plus de sûreté que dans les Départe-ments. Sous les yeux du Gouvernement les Royalistes prennent plus de précautions pour ne pas l'effaroucher, ils font la contre-révolution dans les Départements, ils les couvrent de deuil. . . . Ainsi les Royalistes ne seront jamais assez maladroits pour couvrir Paris de meurtres, ils feroient ouvrir les yeux au Gouvernement qui certainement ne veut pas la Contre-Révo-lution. . . . Donc je conclus que Paris est la ville où les Républicains y puissent vivre en sûreté. . . .'

(2C) Arch. Rhône 31 L 164* (comité de surveillance de Lyon, séance du 16 ventôse an III). The steady build-up of fear, mutual suspicion, and mutual recrimination in the course of the winter, culminating in the detailed denunciations of Ventôse, when, no doubt directly encouraged by the *comités*, many tongues became untied to evoke both events and conversations of eighteen months or even two years back, is strikingly illustrated by the progression of events in Salon and in the neighbouring *communes* of Martigues and Port-Chamas. On 4 Brumaire, the *comité* expresses alarm at the increasing talk of vengeance; on the 8th, the first arrests take place in the bitter *commune* of Mallemort; on the 19th, there are rumours about a *rassemblement* of terrorists in a *bastide* near the same village; the same day, the first group of terrorists are arrested in Salon. On 5 Frimaire, further rumours of a *rassemblement*, this time in Concors. On 17 Frimaire, a hussar is accused of having stated at the *société* 'qu'il y avoit une loi qui ordonnoit que tous les coquins seroient conduits en rase campagne pour y être jugés par le peuple . . .'. The next day, the *comité* is informed of nightly meetings of former terrorists in the café de Dauphin, one of their number (he was later murdered). On 19 Nivôse, the *comité* reports: '. . . Il y a eu plusieurs disputes dans les rues qui ont eu lieu par le fait de haines particulières . . . il s'y tenoit des discours qui annonçoient des projets de vengeance, d'autre part les terroristes ne cessent pas de dire que leur tour reviendra. . . .' Threatening language on the part of an ex-terrorist on the 22nd. On the 23rd, a citizen is stopped at night by a soldier and is so frightened that he is unable to reply to his challenge; the town is crossed and recrossed by bands of armed men. . . . On 18 Pluviôse, further threats, against persons named, by a group of children, led by a drummer. On 20 Pluviôse, in Port-Chamas, a *farandoulle*, led by drummers, and shouts, through the night, of *Vive la montagne, Vivent les jacobins, La guillotine en permanence*. The whole of Ventôse is taken up by denunciations against former terrorists, with particular reference to the sanguinary remarks they were said to have made in the course of 1793. By then, hatred would have been whipped up to fever pitch, while all sorts of half-remembered grievances would have been given a maximum publicity. The former terrorists themselves contributed to their own undoing by a mixture of threats and over-confidence. The shadow of the White Terror extends in fact right back over the winter of 1794–5 (Arch. Bouches-du-Rhône L 1856 bis, 1857–8, 1862, Comité de Salon, an III).

(2D) Particularly the two laws of 3 and 5 Ventôse year III obliging former officials of the year II to return to their places of residence under the Terror and calling on municipalities to draw up lists of the refugees living in their area and to send them to the higher authorities. Both laws were an enormous stimulus to persecution and to murder, especially in small rural *communes*, where memories were more persistent and hatreds more bitter. The *agent national* of Avignon, in his report for the last *décade* of Germinal: '. . . C'est surtout dans les petites communes, où les réactions sont plus vives, plus fréquentes, les haines plus vives et les violations des loix plus marquées, soit par l'ignorance des membres composant les autorités, soit plutôt par méchanceté et par animosité privée qui fait taire l'amour du bien public. . . . Dans certaines communes on obligeoit tous les ci-devants fonctionnaires à se présenter à la Maison Commune une ou plusieurs fois par jour à une heure donnée, dans d'autres, on leur refusoit des permissions pour aller dans des communes voisines chercher des grains pour leurs subsistances et celle de leurs familles, d'autres on les mettoit en arrestation chez eux, partout enfin on n'a pas seulement exécuté ce décret exactement, mais très rigoureusement. . . . La ligne tracée par la loi est toujours outrepassée, les passions y sont mises à la place des décrets, la justice violée et les craintes exagérées' (Arch. Vaucluse 3 L 48*).

(2E) '. . . la fâcheuse nouvelle de la révolte des Toulonnais . . . a éveillé les espérances des terroristes, ils se plaisent à égarer l'opinion publique. . . . Ils ont dans cette commune l'audace du crime. . . . Le représentant Poujol a harangué le peuple qui a applaudi à son discours; mais il n'en a pas été de même en parcourant la Carreterie et les divers quartiers y adjacens, à peine disoit-il d'aller à Toulon que des vociférations se faisoient entendre, *à Lyon*, des cris de *vive la Montagne*, et *vivent les sans-culottes* ont montré à découvert les intentions criminelles des terroristes. Oui . . . malheureusement ils sont nombreux dans cette commune et le nombre s'en accroît tous les jours par les étrangers qui y abondent...' (Arch. Vaucluse 3 L 34*, agent national du district d'Avignon, à Goupilleau, 6 prairial an III). The next day he wrote to Cadroy: '... Toute la Jeunesse d'Avignon s'est présentée en masse... mais leur zèle n'a pas été secondé par les malveillans, qui sont très nombreux dans cette commune....' On the 13th, in a letter to the municipality accompanying the dispatch of thirty copies of Cadroy's declaration on the subject of the fall of Toulon, he insists: 'Nous vous invitons à la faire afficher tout de suite et surtout dans la Carreterie. Nous vous prévenons à ce sujet que les affiches des événemens du fauxbourg Saint-Antoine n'ont resté qu'un seul instant placardées....' On the 23rd, he writes to the garrison commander: 'Il se répand, citoyen, que des malveillans conçoivent l'affreux projet de se porter aux prisons....' And on the 26th he orders that prisoners should be held in barracks, rather than taken to the Castle. The political temperature had been mounting throughout the month.

See also Arch. Rhône 1 L 208 (Boisset à la Convention, 8 prairial an III): 'J'apprends en ce moment... que 3 personnes ont été tuées cette nuit dans les prisons; les événemens qui ont eu lieu à Paris et à Toulon ayant aigri les esprits et enhardi les partisans de la terreur, j'ai cru devoir pour rassurer les bons citoyens les faire arrêter....' Most of the latter were thus murdered on 25 Prairial.

The White Terror was slightly quicker off the mark in the Lyon area than in Marseille. There were twelve murders in Floréal, as opposed to seven in Prairial; but the figures may not be entirely accurate, as many of these murders took place in Montbrison, and relatives of survivors, questioned three years later, in the year VI, tend to confuse the two months, attributing to Floréal events that undoubtedly took place in Prairial. But Lyon definitely had a small lead on Marseille.

(2F) The score for the Lyon area (Rhône–Loire–Haute-Loire) is slightly different:

Floréal—14 murders,
Germinal—12,
Prairial—11,
Ventôse—10,
Nivôse—8,
Messidor—7,
Thermidor—5,
Frimaire—4,
Pluviôse—3,
Vendémiaire—1,
Brumaire—1.

Floréal year III tops the list, with 11 murders, followed by Prairial (7).

In this area, the killing season opens a little earlier than in the far south: 19 February to 20 May.

(2G) In the unhappy *commune* of Mallemort-du-Comtat (Vaucluse), the royalists and 'papalists' who represented the majority of the inhabitants—'dans notre pays nous ne sommes pas plus de 25 à 30 patriotes républicains' the *commissaire du Directoire* complained, nine months later—decided to make a day of it for the first anniversary of the fall of Robespierre: '... Puis le 9 thermidor [an III] la garde nationale, les déserteurs, environ au nombre d'une quarantaine firent un serment solennel, sous le noyer de Sylvestre, émigré, d'exterminer tous les patriotes républicains. . . . Ce même jour, la municipalité, le juge de paix, les assesseurs, le conseil général . . . firent faire un repas et s'assemblèrent tous pour manger un veau gras . . . après le repas fini [ils] . . . s'assemblèrent . . . pour faire . . . une farandoulle par tout le village où ils crioient à haute voix *vive le roi, vive le pape, merde pour les représentants . . . à bas les patriotes, à bas les Saurel, à bas les Joseph Roux . . .*' (Notes de Saurel, commissaire non-installé du directoire dans le canton de Mallemort, A.N. F1b II Vaucluse I, s.d. an IV).

(2H) The *patriotes* of Mâcon were convinced, as well they might be, when faced with sudden clusters of murders and attacks on individuals, on the same day, in a dozen localities, that the White Terror was centrally organized and that the central organization sent its emissaries to Mâcon to carry out its orders from its headquarters in the café Loup on the quays of the Saône. 'Tu sauras', writes Dutroncy le jeune to Reverchon, 15 Prairial, year V, 'qu'un mois avant l'assemblée électorale il existoit à Chalon un comité secret dont les chefs étoient les Changarnier, les Vaudelin, les Polissard, les Nardon, les Lavaure. . . . Mâcon seul les inquiétoit, aussi est-ce sur ce point qu'ils ont jeté leurs regards haineux, c'est sur ce point qu'existe une municipalité forte et courageuse qu'il faut abattre . . . il est plus que constant que l'assassinat est organisé à Mâcon . . . je ne te parlerai pas de l'assassinat des frères Gentil, des deux beaux-frères de Roberjot. . . .' In a letter to Reverchon, dated 28 Prairial, Genty has much the same to say: '. . . on tient pour certain que dans tous les chefs-lieux il y a des chefs et des directeurs des Compagnies d'égorgeurs . . . Lyon est le point central . . .' (A.N. F1b II Saône-et-Loire I).

(2I) On 27 Prairial year IV, General Châteauneuf-Randon, garrison commander at Privas, wrote to the Minister: '. . . Les assassinats individuels se multiplient dans le département de la Lozère d'une manière alarmante, et toujours . . . sur les patriotes, et des patriotes de 89, purs vertueux, et, surtout, protestans et aisés. Les fanatiques . . . veulent établir cette guerre antique du fanatisme dans les Cévennes. . . .' A week earlier, on the 20th, a wealthy Protestant farmer had been murdered in the neighbourhood of Florac (A.N. F1b II Lozère I, Châteauneuf-Randon to the Minister of the Interior, 27 Prairial year IV).

The same seems to have been true of the Ariège, at least as far as the small country town of Saverdun was concerned: 'Depuis le commencement de la Révolution, cette commune, comme bien d'autres, a été divisée en deux partis. La différence des cultes . . . n'y a pas peu contribué . . .' (commissaire du Directoire à Saverdun, au Ministre, 3 ventôse an IV).

'... La commune de Saverdun est mixte en fait de culte ci-devant protestant et catholique romain. Ces derniers, moins instruits en général des vrais principes du culte religieux ... ont été plus faciles à tromper. ... Des prêtres condamnés à la déportation ... ont porté leur scélératesse ... pour massacrer les soi-disants protestans duquel culte la grande majorité des individus de l'ancienne municipalité étoit composée, qu'ils appellent terroristes et buveurs de sang...'.' In the principal Catholic suburb of the town, the annual feast day was held on St. Bartholomew's Day, an occasion which, suitably, was celebrated, in the year III, by the murder of some Protestants and by attacks on many more (Jean Sol à la Convention, 5 brumaire an IV, A.N. F1b II Ariège I).

(2J) According to Saurel, the principal assassins of his eldest son were Jean Jean, *cordonnier, dit capucin*, Barthélemy Gras, *dit le coupeur*, and his brother, the brothers Cotton, etc. 'Le lendemain de notre affaire (du 9 au 10 prairial an V) l'on vit Chachua, le fils du directeur de jury, ayant un œil poché d'un coup, on assure qu'il étoit du nombre des assaillans ...' (A.N. F1b II Saône-et-Loire I, lettre de Genty le jeune du 13 prairial an V). '... la femme Perraud, en pleurant, disoit: "Messieurs Latourcy et Dutailloux, ne faites point de mal, je vous en prie, à mon mari, conduisez-le en prison, et s'il est coupable, faites-le juger. ..."' The two men then finished her husband off by smashing his head with a large stone (A.N. BB 18 390, déposition de la veuve Perraud, nivôse an V).

(2K) *Mémoire sur le Midi présenté au Directoire Exécutif par Louis Jullian et Alexandre Méchin* ... (chez Desenne, an IV): '... Le désarmement ordonné par la loi de prairial [an III] a jeté dans les familles des germes de haine et de vengeance qui ne s'éteindront qu'avec la génération. ...' 'Dans les campagnes de Rochegude, les barbares égorgent le père et étouffent l'enfant au berceau en lui pressant le crâne ... à Velleron ... le sein d'une femme qui allaite est déchiré par ces cannibales. .... Grand Dieu! où sommes-nous, où vivons-nous, quelle est notre patrie? L'histoire des crimes commis dans le XVIme siècle n'est plus qu'un jeu d'enfans en comparaison des forfaits dont nous sommes les victimes ou les témoins ...' (*Les Républicains avignonnais* ... *au peuple françois*, Valence, 24 floréal an V).

(2L) Arch. Bouches-du-Rhône L 3089 (par devant le juge de paix du 8me arrondissement du canton de Marseille, 10 ventôse, 2 et 14 germinal an VI, dépositions contre la femme Colon, d'Arles). This woman, the wife of a tailor, is reported, on seven different occasions, as having incited to violence, in the following phrases: 'Assassinons-les et les jetons à la mer', 'Arrête, la Montagnarde ... je me fais assez forte pour jeter la plus jeune dans la mer, que les autres y jettent l'autre', 'Petite montagnarde, tu te croyois donc encore avoir le dessus puisque tu me dansois devant ce matin', 'Il faut que nous ayons la tête de tous les montagnards', 'Il viendra un tems où nous jouerons aux boules avec les têtes des enfans de tous ces brigands', 'Coquine de montagnarde, il faut que le plus gros morceau de ton corps devienne comme l'oreille'; on this occasion, she adds: '"Je reviendrai demain avec une bande de bons bougres qui jetteront bientôt ta porte par terre", qu'en effet à la pointe du jour du lendemain elle vint à la tête de 8 sabreurs et entrèrent dans la maison . . . en disant auxdits sabreurs "Sabrez, sabrez, tant petits que grands et n'en laissez pas échapper un" . . . les sabreurs ayant toujours leurs sabres nuds à la main en disant "que ferons-nous . . . il faut avoir pitié de la mère qui est enceinte, autrement ils y passeroient tous" et s'en alloient, qu'alors ladite Colon . . . leur dit "qu'êtes-vous venus foutre ici en ce cas, ce sera à moi qu'ils auront à faire".' According to other witnesses, this woman had frequently been seen at the head of 'une horde d'égorgeurs, hommes, femmes, enfans, armés de sabres, bâtons, pistolets, poussant des hurlemens . . .'. Much of her violence was reserved for other women, including her next-door neighbour, a midwife whose son was to be killed in a prison massacre. *La femme Colon* had been arrested in 1793, after Carteaux had recaptured the city, but had been acquitted by the Commission Militaire (Commission Brutus). See also the accounts of the Clermont-Ferrand massacre of 21 Messidor year V: '. . . Les deux filles et la mère Manard montées sur la galerie [ne cessèrent de] crier à ceux de la garde "tuez-les! tuez-les! ces coquins-là" . . . elle entendit les deux filles Manard crier à ceux de la garde "Avancez, les coquins, les voleurs, les assassineurs du Bois de Cros se sauvent . . ."' On this occasion, the Manards operated as a family unit; while the two girls and their mother encouraged the *gardes* in their work of massacre, their father and brother were in the forefront of the killing. Another witness states 'qu'il a vu une femme appellée *La Calotte* (revendeuse) . . . donner un petit paquet d'épingles à un de ceux de la garde pour mettre dans son fusil', to fire on the picnickers (A.N. F1b II Puy-de-Dôme I, thermidor an V).

A woman witness of the murder of *Branche-d'Or*, shot down in the river at Montbrison during the Floréal year III massacres, 'entendit la citoyenne veuve Trézette qui étoit à sa fenêtre sur la rivière . . . leur demander [aux assassins] s'ils avoient fait bonne chasse, qu'ils lui répondirent que les moineaux étoient dénichés . . .' (A.N. BB 18 690, dépositions sur les assassinats commis à Montbrison, nivôse an VI).

(2M) Arch. Vaucluse 3 L 34* (agent national du district d'Avignon à la municipalité de Morières, 5 messidor an III). For similar 'invasions', see the reports of the *commissaire du Directoire* in the Var on the attack on Saint-Maximin-la-Sainte-Baume: '. . . Ce rassemblement étoit composé de citoyens de Rocquevaire, Auriol, Aubagne et Trest, communes des Bouches-du-Rhône. . . . La commune de Saint-Maximin étoit accusée d'avoir donné asile à tous ces hommes dangereux qui s'étoient faits un nom sous le règne de la Terreur et qui étoient expulsés du département des Bouches-du-Rhône . . .' (A.N. F1b II Var I, rapport du 4 fructidor an V). In a letter dated 1 Fructidor, the same official wrote: '. . . Portez toute votre attention . . . sur la commune de Trest et prenez les mesures les plus sévères pour dissiper des rassemblemens qui sont les précurseurs de la guerre civile entre deux départements limitrophes . . .' (ibid.).

(2N) A.N. F1b II Saône-et-Loire I (Dutroncy à Reverchon, 13 prairial an V): '. . . La procédure contre Gentil s'instruit vivement, ses assassins déposent dans cette affaire, le nombre des témoins pour lui est petit, cette place étant interdite aux républicains sous peine d'être jeté à la rivière, plusieurs ont vu et n'ont osé déposer, craignant la vengeance de ces Messieurs. . . .' The judges from Chalon appear to have gone on the principle that the guilty parties were those who had been attacked by the *sabreurs*, and had been lucky enough to survive. It was in order to combat the complicity of the local judicial authorities that, following the experience of the year III, the Minister of Justice, in a circular dated 21 Fructidor year IV, ordered that 'les individus détenus comme prévenus d'assassinats dans le département du Rhône et dans celui de la Loire doivent être renvoyés devant d'autres tribunaux que ceux de leurs départements respectifs, pour cause de suspicion légitime ou de sûreté publique . . .' (A.N. Rhône 1 L 392).

(2O) In a report drawn up on 7 Ventôse year IV by the *accusateur public* of the Gard, Pascal Blanc, there recurs the phrase, after the summary of each massacre: 'Aucun coupable ne fut reconnu. . . .' And of a murder committed on 11 Prairial year III, he comments: 'Les déclarations des témoins . . . ne sont parvenues à l'accusateur public que le 6 ventôse an IV.' On the subject of a murder committed in Beaucaire on 17 Messidor year III, he observes: 'Aucune information ne fut faite, l'accusateur public n'a été instruit que depuis peu de cet événement. . . .' He himself had come into office on 15 Brumaire year IV; his predecessor had done his best to conceal from him the murders that had been committed during the previous year. Blanc was an eccentric, for he actually attempted to bring some of the murderers before the Courts (A.N. F1b II Gard I).

(2P) '. . . Vous avez attribué aux habitans du Jura, à la population de Lons-le-Saunier l'assassinat des prisons; et il est notoire . . . que c'est du sein d'une commune trop connue par ses malheurs et par ses torts politiques qu'étoient vomis dans notre département ces égorgeurs salariés . . .' (*Adresse des membres de l'administration municipale de la commune de Lons-le-Saunier, au Corps législatif*, s.d. an VI). There are similar reports from the Isère. A former *juge-de-paix* of Vienne reports to the Directory, on 30 Fructidor year V: '. . . Chaque aurore éclairoit des placards sanguinaires. . . . Des gens inconnus . . ., venant surtout de Lyon, affluent chaque jour dans notre commune . . . ces mêmes hommes annonçoient hautement . . . que Lyon alloit être le siège de la monarchie françoise et que Vienne . . . en seroit le Versailles . . .' (A.N. F1b II Isère I). The authorities of the Drôme complain of the frequent incursions into their territory, especially the cantons of Donzère and Saint-Paul, of *bandes* from the Vaucluse; the murders committed in the three communes of Clansayes, Lagarde, and Montbrison are attributed to the presence of these 'invaders'. Later, in the year V, they inform the Minister: '. . . Vous n'ignorez pas non plus que Lyon est un foyer dangereux, qu'on y fasse des amas de poudre . . . qui empêcheroit les rebelles de cette commune de fondre sur

le département de la Drôme?...' Département au Ministre, 15 Pluviôse year V, A.N. Fıb II Drôme I). For the presence of Lyonnais *sabreurs* elsewhere, see A.N. BB 18 690 (Loire, assassinats), Fıb II Haute-Loire I, and Fıb II Cantal I.

(2Q) Most of the Montbrison terrorists who could afford it or who possessed relatives there took up refuge in Clermont-Ferrand, Thiers, Riom, and Ambert between Germinal year III and Brumaire year IV, when, after making discreet inquiries from relatives who had stayed in Montbrison, they returned to their homes—or what remained of them. A few, however, only moved to the immediate outskirts of Montbrison, in order to keep an eye on their property and to be well primed on the course of events. Several, established as close as Moingt, were about to return to their homes when cousins or sisters came out to their places of refuge to warn them that their houses were being watched by groups of *sabreurs*. Most had the sense to stay on till the arrival of Reverchon. A few went to the Saône-et-Loire, one or two to Paris. See, for example: Antoine Font-lupt, *teinturier*, 'déclare que dans le courant du mois de floréal an III ... instruit qu'on avoit assassiné dans la commune de Moingt le neveu du nommé Bouarde ... il prit le parti de quitter son domicile et de se mettre ses jours en sûreté dans le département du Puy-de-Dôme où il est resté jusqu'après l'arrivée du Représentant Reverchon ...'; Degalle, *tailleur de pierre*, 'alla travailler de son métier dans la commune de Saint-Maurice, département de Saône-et-Loire ... il s'étoit auparavant approché de Montbrison faisant venir à Prétieux ses parents pour savoir ce qui s'y passoit, ils lui ont dit que ses jours y étoient en danger, c'est alors qu'il est parti ...'; Griot, *cordonnier*, took refuge first of all in Salles; but he was so frightened by the reports of what was happening in Montbrison, that he went to Thiers; even there, 'craignant d'être arrêté, [il] se travestit en femme ...'. Another refugee, although over thirty kilometres from Montbrison, encountered a fellow terrorist hiding trembling behind a bush who told him that a group of armed horsemen had just ridden by on the high road. The Montbrison *assommeurs* were successful in creating an atmosphere of terror over a whole Department (A.N. BB 18 690).

(2R) Arch. Vaucluse 3 L 28* (agent national du district d'Avignon au juge de paix de Pujant, 29 nivôse an III, on the subject of the murder of seven persons on a country estate near Tavel): '... J'ai découvert que led. Olivier Payen restoit à Avignon en germinal an II ... et qu'il est actuellement à Montpellier avec sa femme. C'est un homme de 40 à 45 ans, il a un bras plus court l'un que l'autre, c'est une espèce de marchand du Piedmont ou du Dauphiné. ... Je te dirai encore qu'il y a une espèce de compagnie ou société de ces espèces de gens qui sous prétexte de commerce volent et assassinent tant qu'ils peuvent, il paroît qu'il est entré dans cette société des personnes de ces contrées. Je te dirai encore qu'à Nîmes il y a un nommé Barbien, aubergiste, qui a été longtems lié avec eux, et il pourroit bien se faire qu'il fût de la partie. ...' One of the members of the Compagnie du Soleil identified as having taken part in

the massacre of the Fort Saint-Jean is Delcurrou, native of Vicdessos, *liqueuriste*, in Marseille for two years only. His excuse is that, as the *sabreurs* were in the habit of frequenting his establishment, he had little choice but to appear at least to go along with them. Like so many in his profession, he was the hostage of the political convictions of his customers (Arch. Bouches-du-Rhône L 3077, déclaration devant le juge de paix du 8me arrondissement de Marseille, 19 pluviôse an IV). '... Dans la journée du 25 [pluviôse an IV], trois *parisiens* remarquables par le grotesque de leur costume, arrivés le matin à Avignon, parcouroient les rues.... Sur ces entrefaites encore, plusieurs scélérats arrivèrent de Montpellier. C'étoient de ces vagabonds qui n'ont d'autre patrie que les lieux où règnent l'anarchie et le crime; de parti, que celui qui leur permet le pillage et l'assassinat ...' (*Des Républicains avignonnais traduits devant le tribunal criminel de la Drôme, au peuple françois*, 24 floréal an IV).

(2S) Arch. Vaucluse 3 L 34* (correspondance décadaire de l'agent national du district d'Avignon, germinal an III). In the Lyon area, the murders were carried out with extreme brutality and with ferocious good humour. After the assassination of the printer, Magnien, on the road from Feurs to Montbrison, the killers retire to an inn, boasting to the customers: 'Voilà un beau jour pour faire la chasse aux moineaux!' A passer-by 'vit et s'approcha du cadavre dudit Magnien, qu'il vit sa tête écrasée, son ventre ouvert et son corps tout nud et criblé de coups ...'. One of the murderers of the priest, Bouchet, mocks the body with the words *Ecce homo!* and when the body suddenly begins to twitch, exclaims 'Ah! le bougre n'est pas encore mort!' taking up a stone with which he knocks out his brains. Displaying the corpse in the street, another of the killers mocks a woman, who is in tears: 'Souffle-lui au cul, et vous le ferez revenir!' While Decelle père, who had been an informer in the service of Javogues, is being beaten to death, one of his assailants tells him: 'En attendant, porte ça à Javogues!' Another of the murderers of Magnien comments on his exploit: 'Ce bougre avoit l'âme si dure qu'on ne pouvoit pas l'achever, qu'on lui tira 9 coups de pistolet, et qu'il se relevoit toujours, mais que, pour lui, il lui en avoit tiré un 10me qui l'avoit étendu....' On meeting an officer on a country road near Retournac, a group of killers questions him: 'As-tu servi? — J'ai servi trois ans la République — Tu n'as que trop servi', whereupon they cut him to pieces with their sabres, and, leaving the body, retire to a near-by castle, where the *châtelaine* offers them drink and nuts. After killing Clément, the *assommeurs* face his widow, 'que pour lui ils lui répondirent d'un air de risée: "Va, va, il n'est plus" '. In the Ariège, the murderers of Moncla 'exhalèrent encore leur rage en lui écrasant la tête comme un hâchis à coups de crosse de leurs fusils ...'. All eye-witnesses report, in the Loire, that the killers 'ont l'air effarouché et sont tout en sueur ...' (A.N. BB 18 690, F1b I Haute-Loire I and Ariège I).

(2T) This was not always the case, however, in the south-east and south-centre, where the activities of the *compagnies* sometimes appear to have been indistinguishable from banditry. In the Loire, the body of the printer Magnien was left naked in a ditch. Near Allègre, in the Haute-Loire, a gang, having broken into the farm of the *agent national* of the village of Neyraval, tortured the owner in an effort to discover his treasure. Having shot him outside his farm, they went off with six bulls and cows and a hundred and twenty-five sheep. The farmer, Charitat, was a very rich man. In a visit to a farm at Talhac, canton de Saint-Paulien, the murderers warn the farmer and his son: 'Vous avez encore du numéraire et des assignats, il nous les faut . . .' (A.N. BB 18 690 and F1b II Haute-Loire I).

(2U) '. . . Le C. Raymond Boy . . . a deux vignes qu'il a cultivées de ses bras; malgré la grande disette de vendanges cette année dans ce pays . . . les mauvais citoyens de cette commune . . . dès que les raisins commencèrent d'être bons, s'attroupoient . . . dans la nuit au clair de lune, alloient vendanger la vigne dudit Boy, emportant un plein tablier de raisins chacun chaque nuit (car ce sont tous charpentiers ou maçons) et repassant devant la porte dudit Boy ils l'insultoient . . . en lui jetant sur la figure des raisins qu'ils avoient à demi-rouges . . . dans l'instant même Boy prend la fuite, abandonne femme et biens et s'en va errer ses chagrins dans la commune de Toulouse où il se tient caché de crainte que quelqu'un de ses assassins ne l'y poursuive . . .' (Jean Sol, ex-juge de paix de Saverdun, à la Convention, 5 brumaire an IV, A.N. F1b II Ariège I).

(2V) A.N. Fb II Yonne I (des citoyens de Sens au comité de législation, 22 vendémiaire an IV, au sujet des événements arrivés à Sens le 12 vendémiaire précédent, et pétition des républicains de la commune de Sens, 29 vendémiaire an IV). See also for an example of a similar employment of a psychological terror F1b II Saône-et-Loire I (lettre de Genty le jeune, 13 prairial an V): '. . . Ce matin cinq étrangers de grande taille ont passé devant ma porte, on m'a rapporté que Bafreau, le chasseur qui les accompagnoit, la leur a montré en disant *c'est là*. Le commissaire de police Fournier, et Gondieux, mes voisins, l'ont entendu, et ont averti ma femme. . . .'

An even more dramatic example comes from Saverdun, in the Ariège: '. . . Leurs projets commencèrent d'éclater le 22 — jour auquel la municipalité fit un feu en réjouissance de la paix faite avec l'Espagne. Ce feu fut fait vers les 5 h. de l'après midi . . . vers 10 h. du soir, au moment où déjà la majeure partie étoit au lit, on entendit un bruit effrayant dans la rue d'une masse du peuple énorme, hurlant, criant à plein gosier, armée de bâtons, de sabres, de fusils, pistolets, tirant des coups de fusil, de pistolet, criant *à bas les Terroristes, les Buveurs de sang, il faut les égorger tous*, criant *Vive le Roy* . . . il y avoit parmi ces *séditieux* des MM à cadenettes et avec cravache, des principaux riches de la ville . . . courant dans toutes les rues . . . de là frappant aux portes de droite et de gauche . . .' (A.N. F1b II Ariège I, Jean Sol à la Convention, 5 brumaire an IV).

(2W) In the three Sections of the Montagne, the Muséum, and the Arcis, all of them in riverside quarters, the corpses of suicides are brought in on

14 Brumaire, 4 Nivôse, 22 Pluviôse, 4 Germinal, 22 Germinal, 26 Germinal, 2 Floréal, 3 Floréal, 9 Prairial, 13 Messidor, 21 Thermidor year III, and 1 and 8 Vendémiaire year IV. One of the victims, Tiédard, a thirty-five-year-old *cordonnier*, born in Dijon, living on the Section des Arcis, left a note pinned to his clothes by the Pont-Royal, which was found on the morning of 7 Germinal, a few days before the first of the great hunger risings of the year III: 'Mes chers concitoyens,' it read, 'je vous écris ces deux mots pour vous dire que je me suis écarté des bons principes et d'éducation que j'ai reçus sept ans de mes parents [ainsi] que de la femme que je viens de quitter, je ne serois pas où je suis, si je regrette quelqu'un dans le monde, c'est elle surtout, la laissant dans la position où elle se trouve aujourd'hui [the poor woman is nine months pregnant] — que c'est bien de ma faute et non de personne, c'est que j'ai les sentimens trop légers et trop foibles, c'est ce qui est la cause de mon malheur et de ma perdition, et puis d'ailleurs vous voyez que nous sommes tous prêts à être pris par la famine et une guerre civile qui ne tardera peut-être pas, aussi j'aime mieux prendre l'avance que d'attendre à être égorgé par des scélérats et des intrigans qui nous font la barbe, les laissant jouer leur rôle, je sais moi-même que je suis coupable de tout ce que j'ai, mais j'ai eu du repentir, mais je vois qu'il n'y a plus de ressource, c'étoit avant de commettre les crimes qu'il falloit réfléchir, après il n'est plus tems, mais je demande grâce à l'être suprême de ne l'avoir pas réservée pour mes protecteurs. Tout ce que je peux vous souhaiter [c'est] que les choses tournent bien, adieu tous mes parens et amis je n'y suis plus, Tiédard, dit *Bourguignon*.' Tiédard had lived in Paris for eighteen years (A.P.P. A/A 61, 62, 95-8, 187-8, *commissaires de police* des sections des Arcis, de la Montagne et du Muséum).

(2X) A.P.P. A/A 219 (commissaire de police de la section Popincourt, enquête sur les assassinats commis 35 rue de la Roquette, 16 et 28 prairial an III) and A.N. F7 4669 d 3 (Denelle). One witness claimed that, on the first day of the September Massacres, at 5 a.m., 'il a vu revenir ledit Denelle, lui étant à sa porte et lui a demandé d'où il venoit, led. Denelle répondit, en lui montrant son sabre, *tiens, vois-tu, j'en ai détaché*, et le sortant hors du foureau, il a aperçu du sang . . .'. Another claims that on 2 September, 'étant à boire chez lui de l'eau-de-vie, que la femme dud. Denelle en conversant avec lui sembloit louer son mari de ce qu'il avoit fait dans la nuit et lui montrant son sabre qui étoit encore teint de sang . . .'. Others claim, that, on the night of 9–10 Thermidor, he had been to the Commune, and had been heard to say, on his return, 'Oui, foutre, ça ira, il faut que ça pète.' On 16 Prairial, the *assemblée générale* had decided his arrest, as 'l'un des assassins du 2 septembre'; and it was in this way that the triple murder was discovered.

(2Y) See, for instance, a report for 30 Brumaire year IV: '. . . Aux *bains chinois*, les têtes sont exaltées si fort qu'ils disent qu'ils sont patriotes de 1789 . . . qu'ils ne veulent pas la constitution de 1795, mais bien celle de 1793. . . .' See also a report, dated 4 Germinal year VI, on the former

Section du faubourg Montmartre: '(L'assemblée) se tient maintenant chez un nommé Flamand, marchand de vin, rue de Bellefond . . . il y a chez lui un cercle constitutionnel. . . . Dans le nombre de ce rassemblement il s'y est trouvé Pépin-Desgrouhettes . . . homme très dangereux, Chrétien, du café en face les Italiens, Poste, peintre, rue Bleue . . . le nommé Guibert, jardinier . . . Duroure, anglais . . . ex-membre du comité révolutionnaire de la section Montmartre . . . j'observe que la plus grande partie des personnes qui se rassemblent chez ce Flamand sont du camp de Grenelle et quelques-unes de l'affaire de Vendôme . . .' (A.N. F7 3054). 'J'ai été informé', reports Dubois, on 13 November 1807, 'que certains exclusifs formoient des réunions . . . à Versailles. . . . Parmi ces particuliers se trouvoient François-Louis Fournerot, ouvrier rubannier, ancien membre de la Commune de Paris, . . . Didier, serrurier, . . . ancien juré au tribunal révolutionnaire, . . . Lécrivain, peintre en bâtimens, . . . ancien membre du comité de surveillance du département de la Seine [sic] . . . Edmé Planson, metteur en œuvre . . . ancien membre du comité révolutionnaire de la section des Gravilliers . . .' (A.N. F7 7011). The former terrorists of Dijon, as we have seen, met habitually in a café on the Place d'Armes kept by Lavergne (Arch. Côte d'Or, L 2658*, comité de Dijon, séances des 11, 12, 13 et 14 pluviôse an III).

(2Z) Arch. Dieppe (Registre I de la municipalité, séance du 15 ventôse an III). The members are: 1. René Pouteau, *cordonnier*, 2. Jos. Pierre, *cordonnier*, 3. Simon Gautier, *officier de santé*, 4. Auguste Belamy, *cabaretier*, 5. Louis Gourdain, *brasseur*, 6. Louis Breton, *tonnelier*, 7. Jean Langlois, *chandelier*, 8. Jean Loret, *marchand orfèvre*, 9. René Lucas, *médecin*, 10. Privat Mairier, *serrurier*, 11. Guillaume Selle, *tailleur*. Lucas, who was arrested and detained for a brief period in the year III, showed great devotion to his duties in the course of the famine crisis of 1794–6 in Dieppe. He seems to have been an army doctor, but with Riolle, *directeur* of the Hospice, he took on also the treatment of the sick, the organization of relief, and the petitioning of the *députation*, in an effort to draw the attention of the Paris authorities to the plight of the port and to the extraordinarily heavy rates of mortality among the poor. It is from his reports that one can obtain the most detailed and most harrowing picture of the effects of famine in an urban setting. See p. 220 (5).

(3A) A.N. F1b II Allier I (*Tableau des crimes du comité révolutionnaire de Moulins*, Imprimé, s.d. an IV). He is also accused—and this again is characteristic—of having said 'qu'il mettoit les femmes en réquisition pour ses menus plaisirs . . .'. This is a very common accusation in Thermidorian documents; the point, once more, is that the awful crime of these people was not to have commandeered just any girl—there would be no fuss about a *fille d'auberge*—but the daughters of *notables* and big farmers. In the denunciations made against the former *concierge* of the Salon prison, the girl Cadenet is above all scandalized that such a wretch should have had the impudence to suggest that he would like to kiss her and sleep with her, as she was pretty; on her own admission he did not succeed in doing either. But what effrontery! (Arch. Bouches-du-Rhône L 1862, dénonciation de la fille Cadenet, 17 ventôse an III). There is every probability that, just as they commandeered meals, many *commissaires* may thus have commandeered girls, especially the daughters of the well-to-do and of *ci-devants*. It was a matter of combining business with pleasure, and there could be no more dramatic way of expressing the new *sans-culotte* hierarchy. It was also one of the military aspects of Terror and Repression; and in any war or revolution the soldier might see himself as one of the eighty, 'Dans le lit de la Marquise'.

(3B) '. . . Une foule d'oisifs inondent le port [Marseille], le cours et les places publiques, il faut encore attribuer ces désordres au gouvernement révolutionnaire, qui, en élevant aux fonctions publiques, sans distinction de talens et de capacité, des citoyens que leurs occupations et leur peu d'instruction devoient en écarter, a démoralisé des hommes simples et honnêtes, et a jeté dans leur âme des semences d'une ridicule et dangereuse ambition. . . . C'est surtout dans le Midi qu'on trouve la preuve de cette vérité. Il est arrivé à l'un de nous un fait assez plaisant: un homme qui pouvoit avoir de bonnes intentions, mais qui ne savoit ni lire ni écrire, demandoit à être nommé ou chef d'un hôpital, ou président d'un tribunal criminel, ou enfin, par accommodement, administrateur du département. Nous avions beau lui démontrer qu'il falloit, pour remplir ces fonctions, des connoissances qu'il lui avoit été impossible d'avoir acquises, puisque, toute sa vie, il avoit été savetier, nous étions loin de le persuader; enfin . . . il nous répondit froidement, *belle f**** révolution! j'ai commencé savetier, et je finirai savetier!' (Mémoire sur le Midi,* an IV).

(3C) After the murder of Poche and Paley, in the prison of Montbrison, one of the killers gave back the keys of the cell to Verd, *concierge*, with the remark: *Tiens, je viens de venger la mort de mon père.* Another, on the same occasion, explained to the other prisoners: 'Mes amis, ne vous étonnez pas, nous vengeons le sang de nos pères, de nos mères, de nos frères, de nos sœurs.' Before killing him, Lattard, one of the assassins of Poche, comments: 'Tu as battu mon frère, tu le paieras' (A.N. BB 18 690, dépositions de nivôse an VI au sujet des massacres de Montbrison). In the Ariège, Astruc, from the village of Bonac, was 'poursuivi et tué par les amis et les parens de Marc aîné . . .' (A.N. F1b II Ariège I, frimaire an V). Boisset, in a letter dated 5 Floréal year III, on learning of the prison massacres in Lyon, comments: '. . . La garde nationale, composée d'une grande partie des victimes intéressées à la vengeance, est nulle. . . . Le *mathevon . . .* qui tombe sous le poignard vengeur a des fils qui voudront aussi punir les assassins de leurs pères, ils n'examineront pas s'ils furent vertueux, ils ne verront que leur mort . . .' (Arch. Rhône 1 L 208, Boisset à la Convention, 5 floréal an III). The Bureau Central, in a report for the year IV, makes the same point: '. . . Il a été un moment où l'impuissance des délations les plus atroces a appelé des vengeances cruelles dans une ville où le fils a pu si souvent rencontrer le bourreau de son père, et le père, celui de son fils . . .' (Arch. Rhône 1 L 382, Lyon, assassinats, an IV).

SECTION III

(A) In his report on the Pantin outbreak, dated 25 July 1811, Lherminier has this to say: '... On ne peut pas se figurer jusqu'à quel point la classe indigente de Pantin, réunie par 5 ou 6 ménages dans la même maison, est négligente sur cet objet essentiel. Les cours, les escaliers, les logemens sont encombrés de matières animales et végétales de toute espèce en décomposition. ...' In a report on the epidemic of the year XIV in the villages of the Seine-et-Marne, a Melun doctor informs the Prefect: '... A Machault et Villiers, comme dans tous les autres villages de l'arrondissement, les fumiers n'ont point d'égoût et couvrent le seuil de la porte, mais nulle part la malpropreté ne m'a paru plus insigne qu'à Villiers ...' (A.N. F8 77 and 79).

(B) A.N. F8 48 (épidémies, Doubs) (Barray, médecin à Besançon, au préfet du Doubs; 5 pluviôse an X): '... Si l'on compte 15 victimes dans la commune de Pelousey ... on le doit en grande partie aux poisons administrés par le visiteur d'urines, domicilié à Beurre. Cet assassin, plus redoutable que ceux qui chérissent pour retraite les forêts voisines des grandes routes, compte plus de victimes dans notre département que n'en pourrait faire l'épidémie la plus redoutable et la plus répandue. ...' See also F8 80 (Somme) (Sellier au Gouvernement, 12 floréal an IX): '... Il ne se trouve que de mauvais chirurgiens dans les campagnes et presque point de bons médecins.' On the subject of an outbreak at Thieux (Seine-et-Marne) in the first month of the year VII, the Department reports: '... La misère des habitans augmente la maladie ... par la nécessité à laquelle elle les réduit de se procurer, à peu de frais, des drogues nuisibles d'un charlatan qui abuse de leur crédulité ... 20 personnes ont péri par suite du traitement de ce charlatan et il n'en est mort qu'une seule depuis que les malades sont livrés aux soins des gens de l'art ...' (A.N. F8 79, registre du Département, 7 vendémiaire an VII). We hear more of this 'particulier ... sans talens, sans connoissances de la médecine et dont la profession est d'être charlatan vendant des drogues sur les places publiques, qui leur administre les remèdes les plus contraires' in a report from the municipality of Dammartin the same month.

(C) There is a charming passage in Le Tableau, vi. 26, on the subject of the ass: '... M. de Buffon dit qu'il est joli; mais l'a-t-il vu comme moi, lorsqu'il porte, mieux que des reliques, des paniers remplis de fleurs, lorsqu'il est conduit par une fraîche jardinière, se promenant avec lui aux premiers jours du printemps? L'attirail forme un groupe qui plaît à l'œil; le gentil animal passe auprès du cheval pressé par le fouet et mordant son frein. Il devance la pauvre haridelle écorchée et défigurée qui traîne le fiacre; il rencontre le chien crotté, le bœuf qui va se faire assommer; mais, pour lui, propre et svelte, sans crainte du boucher, averti par la baguette, et non frappé, il réjouit la vue et l'odorat. Leste comme sa conductrice, il a marché sur le pavé fangeux plus légèrement encore que le petit-maître en équilibre, aucun tache ne défigure son sabot. Il dépose aux portes les fleurs dont il est paré plutôt que chargé, et revole ensuite à la campagne. Le plus fortuné Parisien n'y va que le samedi soir; mais lui, il ne couche jamais à la ville; il part avec l'aurore qui l'égaie. Quand le soleil se couche, il a déjà pâturé abondamment autour de la cabane champêtre, et il s'endort, comme la jardinière aux joues de roses, sans trouble et sans souci, après avoir été flatté de sa belle main. . . .'

(D) In Restif's novel, *La Fille naturelle* (1769), there is a reference to a wet-nurse: 'Elle est de Palaiseau et se nomme la Martin. . . .' There are traces of similar specialization in the register of Dieppe *logeurs*; in Brumaire year II, 'chez le C. Michel Sauniez', there are six *fondeurs de marmites*, all from the district d'Aurillac, in the Cantal, and, 6 October, for he has staying four *terrassiers*, two from le Puy, one from Ambert; for 29 October, Crépin, *logeur*, declares three inhabitants from 'Bézy [*sic*] en Languedoc, tous ensemble faisant voir des mécaniques'. On 14 November, he puts down a merchant from Saint-Genest-en-Limousin. All the other travellers are *mareyeurs* or cattle-merchants from the Dieppe area (Arch. Seine-Maritime L 5238, comité de Dieppe, vendémiaire–frimaire an II).

(E) A.N. F15 2892 (Secours) (Pétition au Bureau Central, 6 germinal an V): 'Bauchot (Toinette) . . . vous expose qu'étant du métier de couturière et depuis 2 mois sans occupation . . . cette jeunesse de 22 ans désespérée et voulant toujours se conduire honnêtement, voudroit retourner à Dijon, son pays natal et ne point se trouver exposée où malheureusement les personnes de son sexe sont continuellement. . . .' See also A.N. F15 2820 (attestation du comité de bienfaisance de la Section des Arcis, du 22 thermidor an III): '. . . le présent certificat à la citoyenne Anne-Louise Droz, ex-religieuse, âgée de 32 ans env. et depuis 18 mois femme du C. Ch. Mollet, perruquier chambrelant . . . mais dont le chagrin causé tant par le défaut de pratiques que par la circonstance des tems difficiles a fortement porté led. C. Mollet à délaisser sa femme enceinte de 6 mois avec un enfant d'un an pour s'en aller courir le pays, après encore avoir vendu jusqu'aux cendres du feu. . . .'

(F) A.N. F11 1183 (arrêté du Directoire du 1er vendémiaire an V): 'Le Directoire exécutif arrête que le Ministre de l'Intérieur fournira au C. Restif-Labretonne les subsistances nécessaires et les autres secours de première nécessité dont il peut avoir besoin comme cela s'est pratiqué à l'égard du C. Raynal.' On the 22nd the *administrateurs des secours* write to the Minister: '. . . Nous avons donné ordre tant au directeur de l'école de boulangerie qu'au préposé à la distribution de la viande des maisons d'arrêt et autres de délivrer chaque jour au C. Restif Labretonne 5 l. de pain et une livre et demie de viande. Nous croyons que ces secours suffiront à cet auteur et à ceux de sa fille veuve et de ses petits fils, dont l'aîné n'a pas encore six ans, qui demeurent avec lui et sont à sa charge. . . .'

(G) See, for instance, A.P.P. A/A 187 (Muséum, procès-verbal du 20 germinal an III): '. . . Antoine Benoît Tardy . . . 17 ans . . . orfèvre, natif

de Clermont-Ferrand . . . répond que . . . se trouvant dans un extrême
besoin et n'ayant pas de l'argent pour souper il a . . . dérobé le mouchoir
dans la poche dud. C. et que son intention étoit de le vendre pour faire de
l'argent, (ses parents) sont établis épiciers à Clermont . . . combien il y a
de tems qu'il est à Paris? répond, environ six mois.' See also a case of a
theft of sheets, A.P.P. A/A 95 (Montagne, p.v. du 11 frimaire an III):
'. . . Marie Charpillon, veuve Cordier, âgée de 47 ans, native de Colmar
. . . faisant des ménages pour les particuliers lorsqu'elle en trouva l'occasion . . . à elle demandé quel est le motif qui l'a porté à soustraire des
effets qui ne lui appartenoient pas, a répondu qu'elle n'avoit point d'assignats pour subsister et que devant en toucher le 5 du mois prochain . . .
pour deux de ses fils qui sont aux frontières, elle espéroit retirer led. drap
(du Mont de Piété) et le remettre à son lit. . . .'

(H) A.P.P. A/A 61, 62, 95, 96, 97, 98, 187, 188. On 16 Thermidor year II,
the *commissaire* of the Section du Muséum interrogates a suspected prostitute, Nanette Lucotte, 21, *revendeuse à la halle*, native of Vitteaux: '. . . A
elle demandé si comme revendeuse elle a un livre de commerce . . . répond
que oui . . . qu'elle travaille à la journée . . . à elle observé qu'elle nous a
dit tout à l'heure qu'elle ne faisoit plus le commerce depuis un certain
tems, et qu'elle vivoit de l'argent qu'elle a reçu de son pays . . . à elle
demandé si elle fut toujours revendeuse, répond que non, qu'elle ne l'est
à peu près que depuis neuf mois et qu'avant elle étoit fille de cuisine, à elle
demandé si elle ne vit pas avec un homme, répond que précédemment elle
a vécu avec des hommes, mais qu'après elle n'en a pas, à elle demandé si
elle ne fut pas en prison, soit comme femme publique, soit comme sus-
pecte ou voleuse, répond qu'elle ne fut jamais incarcérée . . .' (A.P.P. A/A
187).

(I) A.P.P. A/A 202 (commissaire de police de la Section du Panthéon
français, an IV), 11 nivôse. In this case, a woman of 28, from Clermont-
Ferrand, had been selling stale bread on the Place Maubert. Normally a
couturière, she stated that she had been a *revendeuse de pain* for the previous
two months. The Republic itself seems to have gone into the trade in
adulterated bread. There is a report by Parmentier dated 10 pluviôse
year IV: 'Dans le dernier examen que nous avons fait des magasins de
subsistances de cette commune, nous avons trouvé des farines qui n'en
méritoient réellement pas le nom et que le garde-magasin des Théatins
avoit refusées. . . . C'est un mélange de son remoulu, de vesce, de pois, de
haricots, avec lequel on altère depuis longtems la nourriture des habitans
de Paris . . .' (A.N. F11 1178, subsistances an IV).

(J) The Rhône in particular seems to have exercised a peculiar fascination
both for the popular mind and for the Parisian journalist. On 27 Messidor
year III, the *agent national* of the District d'Avignon wrote to the editor
of the *Bulletin Républicain*, in Paris: '. . . Nous avons vu . . . avec la
plus grande surprise dans votre feuille du 20 courant que des lettres
d'Avignon annoncent que près de 300 citoyens ont été égorgés dans

leurs maisons. Rien n'est plus faux que cette nouvelle', the origin of which is characteristic: '... Une déclaration faite par une femme au sujet d'un cadavre qu'elle vit passer sur le Rhône, c'est là le fameux verbal dont ***? parle dans le *Bulletin Républicain* ... vous verrez qu'elle a dit dans cette déclaration qu'il passoit un plus grand nombre de corps sur le Grand Rhône d'où **? est **? d'induire que si de fait on a vu des cadavres dans le Rhône, ils venoient du côté de Lyon ou d'une partie qui nous est supérieure ...' (Arch. Vaucluse 3 L 34*, agent national à Blaze, 17 thermidor an III). The Rhône exercised a similar hold over the imagination of the White terrorists of the Loire, one of whom is quoted as saying, in the course of the murder month of Germinal year V: 'Nous aurions besoin que le Rhône passe ici pendant quinze jours pour nous débarrasser d'un tas de coquins qu'il y a par là ...' (A.N. BB 18 690, déclaration de Curtil, jardinier, au sujet des propos tenus par Guyot, de Saint-Maurice-en-Roannais, lors des assemblées primaires de germinal an V). As we have seen, there were incessant reports between the years III and VI, about bodies seen floating, *entre deux eaux*, in the Rhône, underneath the Lyon bridges. Once such reports reach Paris, a single corpse soon becomes an army of *égorgés*. Some witnesses even state that a given corpse is blind-folded with a spotted handkerchief and has its hands tied behind its back. (See above, Section II, on the White Terror.) For other examples of exag-geration, see *Les Armées révolutionnaires*, p. 550, and *Terreur et subsis-tances*, p. 15.

(K) A good example of feminine verbal provocation comes from Dieppe (A.C. Dieppe Registre 1er, séance de la municipalité du 15 floréal an III): '... est comparu le C. Vincent Mounier, marchand et notable ... lequel a déclaré qu'il a été assailli à différentes reprises par des femmes, lesquelles le menacent en lui disant qu'il avoit fait la motion de ne plus délivrer aux habitans de cette commune qu'un quarteron de pain, qu'à chaque instant il est insulté par des femmes passant par devant sa porte, notamment hier les deux filles du C. Louchet, gardien du fort Blanc, tinrent différents propos séditieux et propres à exciter la révolte en disant: "Va, sacré gueux, s'il y a une révolte, nous serons les premières à nous porter chez toi & à t'assassiner", que journellement les poissonières tiennent ces mêmes propos, en disant "Tiens, voilà le bougre au quarteron de pain." ...' A further example of feminine provocation comes from the report of the *com-missaire* of the Arcis for 25 Ventôse year III (A.P.P. A/A 61): '... Pierre Casimir Baillard, inspecteur de police ... nous a dit que passant sous la voûte du Châtelet ... Section de Bonconseil, il a vu dans un groupe une femme qui disoit qu'il y avoit plusieurs jours qu'elle ne mangeoit point faute d'ouvrage et que son mari depuis trois ans qu'il étoit aux frontières elle n'avoit pas encore reçu aucun secours accordé aux parens des défenseurs ... que le comparant lui ayant observé que quand on avoit bonne envie de travailler, on alloit chez ses connoissances pour s'en procurer, et que l'on ne venoit pas au coin d'une rue pour troubler les esprits et attrouper le peuple en tenant des propos sur les comités et disant qu'ils ne donnoient point de secours à ceux qui en avoient besoin et que ce n'étoit point le

Pérou, que le comparant, pour faire cesser ses propos et dissiper l'attroupe-ment, a invité la citoyenne à venir avec lui, et qu'il alloit lui acheter du pain . . . qu'elle le suivoit d'abord et ensuite a dit qu'elle ne vouloit pas être humiliée à ce point-là . . . est revenue sur ses pas au même endroit où elle étoit la première fois et où elle a fait rassembler une seconde fois un groupe en recommençant les mêmes propos . . . a dit se nommer Elisabeth Gourdin . . . culottière . . . qu'elle n'auroit pas bavardé comme elle l'a fait si elle n'avoit pas bu un petit coup. . . .' Another example of how sensitive food problems can become as a result of exaggeration or fear is the adven-ture attributed to a former terrorist of Beaune: '. . . La femme de Dubois, qui étoit pour lors sa gagée, fit un millet, qu'elle porta cuire au four. Dubois, grand amateur de ce mets, en mangea tant qu'il en eut une in-digestion, comme il ne connoissoit point cette maladie, croyant ses con-citoyens aussi scélérats que lui, il écrivit sur le champ à son confrère Monot [another terrorist from Beaune who was at the time on a mission to Paris] qu'il venoit d'être empoisonné par les aristocrates de Beaune; au reçu de la lettre, Monot se transporta aux Jacobins . . . annonça que le meilleur des patriotes venoit d'être empoisonné, il se transporta aussi dans plusieurs groupes de Paris où il raconta la même chose, mais . . . la diges-tion du millet se fit et Dubois n'eut pas besoin de contre-poison . . .' (Arch. Côte-d'Or L 2604*, comité de surveillance de Beaune, séance du 2 ven-tôse an II). Dubois was a former priest, who had been *vicaire* of Arnay-le-Duc till 1792, being elected *curé constitutionnel* of Beaune in the same year. He married his housekeeper in the year II.

(L) Arch. Bouches-du-Rhône L 3082 (interrogatoire de Bernard Maillan, tailleur, de Nîmes, par devant le juge de paix du 2me arrondissement de Marseille, le 27 fructidor an IV): '. . . Dit qu'à Nîmes il travaille de son état de tailleur, qu'il a toujours du pain dans sa maison.' Maillan was being prudent as well as proud; suspected of having been sent from Nîmes by a secret society and paid to murder a chief inspector of police, he was anxious to prove that he had money and did not need outside assistance. He did, however, have to pawn his sister's jewellery to pay his hotel ex-penses, pending the murder, which did not take place till nearly a month after his arrival in Marseille.

There is a similar expression of pride—or of shame—in a petition to the Commission des Secours of 2 Thermidor year III (A.N. F15 2820). 'Le C. Bertin, agé de 61 ans, maître d'écriture, demeurant rue des Juifs . . . se relevant d'une longue maladie, s'étant trouvé mal de besoin plusieurs fois, ne pouvant se procurer du pain à 16 francs la livre, ose . . . implorer votre humanité . . . pour obtenir de l'administration une livre de pain par jour, pour attendre de la moisson, il saura se taire là-dessus, et il ira chez le C. Cailly, son boulanger, à des heures où il n'y aura personne. . . .'

(M) Markov and Soboul, op. cit. See also A.N F10 210 (Simon, de Corbeil, à la Convention, 23 avril 1793): '. . . Le pain est cher, et depuis plusieurs années les récoltes sont abondantes. Pourquoi cette espèce de famine? Pourquoi? C'est que les fermiers sont devenus trop riches. . . .

Quoi! ils ont moins d'impôts à payer, et le quart de blé à semer, le double à recueillir et on les laisse maîtres du prix d'une subsistance commune à tous, *et dont ils ne sont que les dépositaires.* Qu'on fixe donc le prix de cette denrée, . . . qu'on divise les terres, qu'il ne soit pas permis à un seul homme d'en cultiver plus de 100 arpens. . . .' See also A.N. F11 1185 (Subsistances, an IV), 'Encore un mot sur les bleds, 1er prairial an IV': . . . 'Il ne faut jamais perdre de vue que le bled est donné par la nature, que c'est le bien de tous et que la loi doit en surveiller l'indispensable répartition. . . .'

(N) In the middle of the winter the *comité* was using a language full of threats and reminiscent of that of the previous year. On 14 Nivôse, it wrote to the *agent national*: '. . . Tu nous instruis de la conduite criminelle et contre-révolutionnaire que tiennent beaucoup de cultivateurs de la commune de Longueil. Oui, citoyen agent national, les mêmes principes instamment nous animoient d'avance: indulgence, bonté, vertus que nous chérissons, vous ne seroient plus de saison pour ces cultivateurs et rebelles. Vous allez, cultivateurs cruels, sentir toute la rigueur des loix, nous allons amollir vos cœurs de bronze au feu de notre zèle . . . les mandats d'amener, d'arrêt vont voler de tous côtés; sans être les partisans du terrorisme, nous allons par nos vigoureuses mesures jeter la terreur parmi ces cultivateurs meurtriers, et si dès demain ils ne comparoissent pas tous devant nous, ce ne sera que le petit nombre de gendarmes qui existent dans notre commune qui ralentira un peu notre activité, mais, un jour de plus, un jour de moins, ils n'échapperont point à la juste punition qui les attend . . .' (Arch. Seine-Maritime L 5329). On 3 Nivôse the *agent national* denounced to the *comité* Jacques Bailliet, 'batteur en grange [qui] s'est absenté depuis 8 à 9 jours et refuse de battre son grain . . .' (Arch. Seine-Maritime L 5340). On the 21st, the *comité* wrote: 'Nous t'avons fait part hier que les 6 cultivateurs de la commune de Gruchet Siméon [Gruchet-Saint-Siméon] . . . étoient entrés provisoirement en arrestation. Nous t'annoncions que notre intention étoit de les mettre sous peu en liberté. . . . Après leur avoir fait la réprimande que leur négligence méritoit nous les avons renvoyés chez eux avec injonction de verser dans le plus bref délai. . . .' After the disappearance of the *comité* at the end of Ventôse, measures of force were carried on by the municipality, the *agent national*, and Sautereau, the Thermidorian *Représentant en mission* in this area. On the receipt of a report from the *commune* of Saint-Sulpice against François Berches, 'un des principaux cultivateurs de la commune, au sujet du refus opiniâtre qu'il a montré à obéir aux réquisitions qui lui ont été données, refus qui approche de la mauvaise foi puisque, visite faite chez lui, on lui a trouvé et du bled en gerbes et du bled battu', Sautereau ordered his arrest on 13 Germinal; he was brought to Dieppe on the 14th (Arch. Seine-Maritime L 5329).

(O) The *maire* of Dieppe is denounced to the *comité* of the Section de la Montagne, 25 Vendémiaire year II, 'par des personnes qui ont dit avoir entendu que le maire de Dieppe avoit dit à un cultivateur de Neuville qu'il n'avoit pas besoin de s'inquiéter de ses semences, qu'il apporte jours du bled à la halle, que sous un mois nous serions tous tués . . .'. In this case, the denunciation was not treated seriously (Arch. Seine-Maritime L 5223, comité de la Section Égalité). Frénaye, the *maire* of Gannat, is accused, in Messidor year II, of having said to a member of the local *comité*, in the course of a discussion on the food problem: 'Ba, ba, votre Convention a beau faire et beau dire, les marchands de bled seront toujours les maîtres . . .' (Arch. Allier L 842, comité de Gannat, séance du 21 messidor an II).

(P) Arch. Jura, Grand Registre du comité de Lons, séance du 5 nivôse an III. Another local terrorist is accused of having said: 'S'il y avoit du bled au marché? On lui répondit que non, on a fait hier au club la motion de construire une guillotine . . . nous prendrons les canons et la guillotine pour aller chercher le bled chez ces cultivateurs égoïstes . . .' (ibid., séance du 18 ventôse an III). In the years III and IV, faced with an ever-worsening situation, popular opinion became more convinced than ever of the efficacy of Terror as a solution to dearth. '. . . Lanoux, officier invalide . . . disoit que l'on reverroit des comités de gouvernement, des Commissions, des Clubs et des sociétés populaires; que tout seroit à bon marché, que le peuple vivroit et que l'agioteur et le cultivateur n'auroient pas bon tems . . .' (A.N. F7 3054, rapport de police du 25 nivôse an IV). A terrorist from Beaune, Bauzon, *arpenteur*, is accused, in Pluviôse year III, 'avoir tenu des propos très dangereux, en disant à une citoyenne qui se plaignoit de la cherté des grains qu'elle les verroit encore augmenter; si on ne réincarceroit pas de nouveau les fonctionnaires publics destitués . . . les aristocrates de la commune de Beaune, le bled vaudroit bientôt 50l. la mesure . . .' (Arch. Côte-d'Or, L 2602*, comité de Beaune).

(Q) Typical is a letter from a Dieppe soldier, Dubois, dated 16 Brumaire year IV, about Casenave, *Représentant en mission*: '. . . Ce député a depuis six mois 12 à 20 couverts chaque jour à sa table, et sont-ce nous qui payons cela? On voit aller chez lui tous les matins des citoyens qui lui portent des barils de farine et des 40 à 50 plats de bonne chère tandis que le peuple est ici 11 jours sans pain. Il vient de mettre dans un cachot un père de famille qui a été seul, les larmes aux yeux, lui demander du pain, et lui reprocher sa vie luxurieuse. Ma foi, citoyens, si vous voulez que nous disions que l'égalité est à l'ordre du jour, il est tems de rappeller tous ces proconsuls qui insultent à la misère du peuple et qui, entourés de licteurs-gendarmes, semblent oser l'impunité . . .' (A.N. F1b II Seine-Inférieure I).

(R) In Thermidorian Dijon, the principal meeting-place of the former terrorists is the café Lavergne, on the Place d'Armes. On 9 Pluviôse year III, the evening is stated to have been noisy, on the receipt of a report that a Dijonnais, Gaillard, commandant du premier bataillon de la Côte d'Or, had just been murdered in Lyon. Two days later, Bellemel, *gendarme*, is reported as having shouted: 'Oui, je suis terroriste et je m'en fais honneur, Vive le Terrorisme, La Terreur finit trop tôt et les Patriotes

sont vexés par les aristocrates', then, referring to the *muscadins*, 'Je veux
éventrer 3 de ces mâtins-là aujourd'hui ... je veux leur tirer les tripes du
ventre, j'en veux éventrer 4 demain, 5 après-demain, 6 un autre jour ...'
(Arch. Côte-d'Or, L 2658*, comité de Dijon, séances des 9 et 11 pluviôse
an III).

(S) See, for instance, the letter of the Prefect of the Indre, dated 20 July
1812: '... La disette que nous venons d'éprouver aura, cependant, un
résultat dont la pensée peut adoucir le souvenir des malheurs qui l'ont
accompagné, c'est qu'elle a habitué le peuple à remplacer les grains dont
il faisoit sa nourriture ordinaire par des légumes de toutes espèces ...
aussi la culture de ces légumes a-t-elle considérablement augmenté cette
année...' (A.N. F11 711, crise de 1812, Indre). The Prefect of the Cantal
likewise notes: '... Les pommes de terre avoient complètement réussi et
comme cette culture ne s'est propagée que depuis peu de tems dans ces
montagnes, elle fournissoit une ressource nouvelle ...' (Prefect of the
Cantal to the Minister, 17 August 1812, A.N. F11 708, crise de 1812,
Cantal). The Prefect of the Nièvre reports, in November 1812: '...
L'arrondissement de Château-Chinon ... où l'avoine et le sarrazin ayant
beaucoup donné, la gêne a été peu sensible vu la manière de vivre des
habitans qui, dans les bonnes ou mauvaises années, font à peu près leur
unique nourriture, après la germination, de pommes de terre, de bouilli
d'avoine ou de bled noir...' (A.N. F11 715, crise de 1812, Nièvre). There
is a similar report from the Doubs, for 8 August 1812: '... Les consommateurs ont continué à se nourrir en partie des pommes de terre et légumes
dont ils s'étoient pourvus selon leur usage ...' (A.N. F11 709, Doubs).
The Prefect of the Ain writes on 28 August: '... Dans les communes qui
consistent principalement en bois ou en vignobles, beaucoup d'habitans
ont été plusieurs mois sans manger de pain, ils se nourrissoient exclusive-
ment de raves et de pommes de terre bouillies, de pâtes, de maïs, de sar-
rasin et de millet...' (A.N. F11 705, Ain). '... Dans la partie appellée
Limagne,' writes the Prefect of the Puy-de-Dôme, '... la majorité des
habitants n'a vécu qu'avec des pommes de terre et lorsque cette ressource
lui a manqué, elle n'a eu pour nourriture que les soupes économiques ...'
(A.N. F11 716, Puy-de-Dôme). In his August report, the Prefect of the
Sarthe states: '... La disette a été réellement grande dans mon département. ... Heureusement on avoit cultivé beaucoup de pommes de terre,
leur récolte surpassa l'espoir des cultivateurs. C'est à ce précieux légume
que nous avons dû d'être sauvés des horreurs de la famine. Pendant
plusieurs mois, non seulement les pauvres, mais la plupart des habitants,
même aisés de la campagne, n'ont pour ainsi dire pas eu d'autre nourriture ...' (A.N. F11 716, Sarthe).

The Prefect of the Aveyron reports in August: '... L'introduction de
la pomme de terre et du maïs a fait une révolution dont la science économique ne tient pas assez compte. Ces deux subsistances ont sauvé la
France deux fois en dix-huit ans, et il paroît démontré que la famine ne
peut plus exercer ses ravages en Europe aujourd'hui ...' (A.N. F11 706).

On 28 Frimaire year IV, the commune of Saint-Germain-de-Joux

(Ain) replied to the *Commission d'Agriculture*: 'Pommes de terre . . . il s'en sème en quantité dans ce canton, elles ont chassé la grande disette et famine qui se présentoient l'année dernière dans ces environs . . . sans les pommes de terre nous étions dans une grande famine . . .' (A.N. F10 242).

(T) On 13 Floréal year III, the municipality states: 'La commune d'Amiens est la proie à la famine, les 40,000 habitans sont sans pain depuis plusieurs jours . . . au mois de ventôse dernier, les habitans mouroient à cette époque comme aujourd'hui de besoin et d'inanition. . . .' Ten days later a *commissaire* from Amiens encounters in the village of Totonnes a dozen beggars 'dont on lui a dit que ce n'étoit rien et que s'il falloit être 300, ce nombre se rassembleroit dès demain . . . il sut par les autres que la misère les avoit tous forcés de se mendier. . . .' By Prairial there were 12,000 *indigents*, that is, a third of the population (Arch. Somme Lc 1435, district d'Amiens, an III). On 7 Prairial, the municipality reports: 'Chaque jour 5 à 6,000 personnes sortent des murs . . . et se répandent dans les campagnes pour y vivre en commun avec les cultivateurs . . .' (A.N. D § 1 9). On 30 Messidor, the municipality writes: '. . . la famine qui dévore nos contrées depuis si longtems donne . . . de justes raisons de craindre que nos moissons soient pillées et volées dans les champs mêmes; le peuple affamé les dévore d'avance, il n'attend que l'approche de la maturité pour s'en saisir' (A.N. D III 285, Comité de législation, Somme).

(U) On 24 June 1812 the Prefect of the Calvados reports: '. . . On est parvenu à faire croire à un grand nombre de malheureux que le riz se fabrique avec de l'alun, que tous ceux qui s'en nourrissent un mois périssent et on cite un nombre considérable de décès dans les hospices . . .' (A.N. F11 707, crise de 1812, Calvados). On 24 August the Prefect of the Aube writes: '. . . Les comités [charitables] ont eu beaucoup de peine à persuader aux indigens que le riz étoit bon, et qu'en le préparant avec soin ils trouveroient en lui une nourriture agréable et substantielle . . .' (F11 706, Aube). Similar reports and rumours are exceedingly common in the year III. In some Norman ports it was rumoured that the government distribution of American rice represented a 'plot' to kill off the poor wives of fishermen and other people inconvenient to the new ruling class (see *Terreur et subsistances*, p. 221).

(V) There is a good example of this type of inter-village market riot in the District de Dieppe, in the middle of the winter of 1794–5. On 26 Frimaire year III, the *comité* is informed by the *agent national* 'qu'une émeute avoit éclaté le 24 ct. dans la commune d'Anglesqueville dont le C. Nicolas Férêt, de la commune de Vaast du Val se seroit montré le principal auteur, en prétendant réclamer le grain qui étoit destiné à tout le canton, que ce grain appartenoit à sa commune, puisqu'il en sortoit, qu'il devoit y retourner, qu'il avoit appellé à lui tous les habitans de sa commune pour se saisir par serrement de ce grain, que le maire d'Anglesqueville (et) le gendarme de Tôtes auroient couru des risques . . .' (Arch. Seine-Maritime

L 5216, séance du comité du 27 frimaire an III). Férêt is stated to have called out, in the middle of the riot, *A moi Vaast du Val*. He was arrested, 'mais comme ce citoyen est pauvre et chargé de trois petits enfans, l'intention du comité est de le mettre demain midi en liberté . . .' (Arch. Seine-Maritime L 5329, séance du comité du 28 frimaire).

(W) The Prefect of the Aveyron in a long report dated 8 August 1812 compares the May decrees to edicts of 1254, 1482, 1531, 1535, 1539, 1544, 1565, 1567, 1573, 1574, 1577, 1587, 1723, 1794 (A.N. F11 706, crise de 1812, Aveyron). The Minister was not impressed by this massive display of historical erudition, writing in the margin in pencil: 'Il y a bien peu de jugement dans ce long verbiage. . . .' The Prefect of the Gironde, in his report for 24 August 1812, displays a similar learning, quoting largely from the *arrêtés* of the parlement de Bordeaux (A.N. F11 710). The four authors of 'Encore un mot sur les bleds', addressed to the Commission on 1er Prairial an IV, quote from legislation in the Austrian Netherlands, Switzerland, Savoy, England, Barbary, the Porte, Spain, Portugal, and the Two Sicilies, on the subject of market restrictions (A.N. F11 1185).

(X) This attitude is criticized with considerable skill by the four authors of 'Encore un mot sur les bleds': '. . . On ne manquera pas d'élever deux objections favorites qui ont toujours trouvé beaucoup de partisans: 1°. la libre circulation des grains doît être permise. 2°. il faut que le cultivateur soit *riche*. . . . Riche en bled, on tient la vie de 20 millions dans ses mains, et on les fait vivre ou mourir à son gré. . . . On a proféré un blasphème politique en disant: en enrichissant la classe agricole, d'une part, donne de l'autre de gros revenus pour payer, c'est une hérésie. Est-il bien vrai que l'aisance des consommateurs soit une suite nécessaire de l'opulence des cultivateurs? Il nous semble, au contraire, que le vendeur ne peut s'enrichir qu'aux dépens de l'acheteur; qu'ainsi le haut prix des grains . . . appauvrirait inévitablement la classe consommatrice et ruineroit par conséquent la population des villes et la richesse de l'État. . .' (A.N. F11 1185).

(Y) '. . . Les réquisitions furent les inévitables conséquences des recensemens. La voie des garnisons a été constamment employée pour faire porter quelques sacs dans les marchés. Sans elle, il ne s'y en seroit pas trouvé un seul. . . . L'arbitraire est inséparable des recensemens, des réquisitions, des déclarations, des visites domiciliaires. Ce cortège inhérent aux décrets a dû les accompagner partout. Ces mesures . . . font naître des haines et des divisions, qui vivront longtems après que le souvenir des maux soufferts sera effacé . . .' (A.N. F11 718, Préfet de Rouen, au Ministre, 31 juillet 1812).
'. . . Pour obtenir une connaissance précise . . . des quantités de bleds qui pouvoient exister dans les fermes et prévenir l'abus des ventes secrètes, il auroit fallu une force armée considérable, et l'employer très rigoureusement et presque simultanément sur tous les points . . .' (ibid., Préfet d'Amiens au Ministre, 8 août 1812).

'. . . On ne doit pas oublier que lors de la disette de 1709 pour faire exécuter de pareilles dispositions, on fut obligé d'envoyer dans les provinces plusieurs commissaires avec des troupes à leurs ordres . . .' (A.N. F11 710, Préfet de Bordeaux au Ministre, 15 août 1812).

(Z) '. . . L'influence de l'Angleterre n'a pu être douteuse, d'après les provocations à la révolte manifestées notamment à diverses reprises par les placards les plus atroces et les plus sanguinaires . . .' (A.N. F11 715, Préfet d'Alençon au Ministre, 24 juillet 1812). With reference to the crisis of 1801–2, the Prefect of the Somme, who was at the time Prefect of the Pas-de-Calais, was to write, on 8 August: 'un grand nombre d'agens du Gouvernement anglois, dont même j'ai fait arrêter quelques uns, parcouroient tous les Départements Septentrionaux et y achetoient des grains à tout prix' (A.N. F11 718). '. . . On a cherché à me donner lieu de penser que les suggestions de la malveillance irritoient encore et compliquoient les difficultés des circonstances, on a prétendu même que les Anglois avoient jetté sur la côte des émissaires qui devoient profiter habilement de l'occasion de la levée des cohortes et de la gêne des subsistances, pour souffler la discorde et opérer un mouvement . . .' (A.N. F11 710, Préfet de Quimper au Ministre, 12 juillet 1812).

(2A) '. . . Dans un régime aussi vaste, il est devenu . . . impossible et que la police des grains soit soumis à un régime uniforme et qu'elle soit suffisamment surveillée. Si perçant qu'il puisse être, le même œil ne peut voir de Hambourg à Raguse . . .' (A.N. F11 716, Préfet de Strasbourg au Ministre, 19 décembre 1812). This was not, however, the view of the Prefect of the Manche, who suggested to the Minister: 'Je pense . . . qu'il n'y a point de mesure particulière à adopter pour ce département, mais que peut-être une mesure générale pour toute la France en deça des Alpes et du Rhin sera peut-être nécessaire. . . . Cette mesure consisteroit dans un recensement aussi exact qu'il est possible . . . et dans la fixation d'un *maximum* pour le froment seul . . . ce maximum devrait être absolument le même pour toute la France, quel que soit l'état de la récolte dans ses différentes parties. . . .' His report is noted as 'système absurde . . . il y a des départements qui ne récoltent pas et où le blé est un tiers ou la moitié plus cher que dans le département de l'Eure-et-Loir, p.e.' (A.N. F11 713).

(2B) '. . . Les recensemens, les réquisitions, les mesures prises pour les faire exécuter ont été bien vus des pauvres, mais fort mal vus par les propriétaires . . . et généralement par toutes les personnes qui pensent. Elles voyoient avec beaucoup d'inquiétudes ces mesures exciter la jalousie haineuse des pauvres contre les riches, donner lieu aux délations et aux perfidies des valets, et ressusciter déjà fort sensiblement tous les élémens du système de terreur de 93 . . .' (A.N. F11 718, Préfet de Niort au Ministre, 25 juillet 1812). '. . . Les idées du vieux et fatal *maximum* et de ses hideux accessoires se sont réveillés. Les propriétaires, les négotiants ont été saisis d'effroi. Ceux qui n'ont rien que le besoin de manger ont paru se laisser tromper par l'apparence d'avoir du pain à meilleur marché . . .'

(A.N. F11 709, Préfet de Valence au Ministre, 21 juillet 1812). '... Certes, la Terreur, il y a 18 ans, ne rendoit pas les recensements plus exacts, les déclarations plus fidèles, les taxes plus inviolables, elle a seulement rendu les recensemens et les taxes plus odieux ...' (A.N. F11 716, Préfet de Clermont-Ferrand au Ministre, 3 août 1812). '... Cette législation [the Decree of 8 May 1812] ... a fait beaucoup de mal ... parce qu'elle a provoqué des délations et réveillé de vieilles haines; parce qu'elle a mis les subsistances aux enchères entre les préfets. ... La taxe surtout a prêté des armes à la malveillance, elle a fait faire des rapprochements fâcheux, parler de maximum, de réquisitions, de visites domiciliaires ...' (ibid., Préfet de Mâcon au Ministre, 23 juillet 1812).

(2C) (*Recensements*) 'J'ai ordonné un recensement général en prenant la précaution d'y faire procéder dans chaque commune par un maire voisin et étranger à la commune. ... Ces recensemens, malgré ces précautions, n'ont encore produit que des résultats fautifs, presque partout on a déguisé la vérité, du moins dans les arrondissements de Péronne et de Montdidier, les seuls qui pouvoient présenter des ressources. ... Pour obtenir une connoissance précise ... des quantités de bleds qui pouvoient exister dans les fermes et prévenir les ventes secrètes, il auroit fallu une force armée nombreuse. ... On prétend même que des grains ont été enterrés ...' (A.N. F11 718, Préfet d'Amiens au Ministre, 8 août 1812). On the same subject, the Prefect of the Saône-et-Loire writes, on 23 July of the same year: '... En effet, le cultivateur qui n'auroit pas fait la déclaration de ses 5 ou 6 hectolitres, craignant d'être pris en contravention, de voir enlever son bled ... et d'être lui-même traduit aux tribunaux, n'auroit pas eu à hésiter. Sur l'avis du recensement, il auroit jeté son bled dans la Saône; perte pour perte, il y gagnoit au moins de n'avoir pas un jugement à subir ...' (A.N. F11 716). '... Il faut se rappeller que les agents de l'administration se composent de maires qui, pour la plupart, sont propriétaires de grains ou cultivateurs. Ajoutez que dans les lieux où la disette étoit à craindre, chaque autorité gardoit à elle; et craignoit de faire connoître ses ressources à l'autorité supérieure ...' (A.N. F11 711, Préfet de l'Indre-et-Loire au Ministre, 25 juillet 1812). '... Toutes les ruses furent mises à contribution pour soustraire les bleds: cuviers à doubles fonds, faux plafonds, doubles cloisons; si j'eusse voulu étendre mes visites domiciliaires, j'aurois eu à punir presque tous les cultivateurs de mon département ...' (Préfet de Rouen au Ministre, 31 juillet, A.N. F11 718).

(2D) '... Les années de disette sont rares; et la liberté du commerce les rend très rares dans le Puy-de-Dôme, dont les productions sont l'objet habituel d'un commerce très étendu. On croit que ses récoltes suffisent ordinairement à ses besoins et les excèdent quelques fois; rien n'est moins prouvé ni plus difficile à prouver, car ce Département ne consomme point ses récoltes, elles passent en majeure partie dans les départements méridionaux, et les habitants du Puy-de-Dôme consomment les grains de l'Allier, de la Corrèze, de la Creuse. ... De ce mouvement continuel qui se propage de proche en proche, il résulte que la disette ne peut s'y faire sentir à moins que le fléau ne s'étende sur la totalité de l'Empire. Or la France manque bien rarement de grains quand les exportations à l'étranger seront réglées sur la mesure ou sur la possibilité des importations venant de l'étranger . . .' (A.N. F11 716, Préfet de Clermont-Ferrand au Ministre, 3 août 1812).

(2E) '. . . Dans ces tems malheureux où il ne se trouve que de mauvais chirurgiens dans les campagnes et presque point de bons médecins, où la misère publique accable presque tous les citoyens, devenus pauvres les paysans, voulant résister au mal qui les accable et ne point cesser de travailler, tombent presque tous morts subitement sans leur pouvoir porter remède . . .' (A.N. F8 80, Somme, Jacques Sellier, architecte d'Amiens, au Gouvernement, 12 floréal an X). '. . . Dans la cabane du pauvre, le mari, la femme et les enfans couchent presque toujours dans la même chambre, et quelquefois dans le même lit. . . . Il est difficile d'être plus superstitieux que ces paysans . . . aussi trouve-t-on chez eux des gens qui prétendent guérir par de simples attouchemens et à l'aide de mots mystérieux . . . sont-ils atteints de maladies chroniques, ils se persuadent qu'elles leur ont été données par leurs ennemis' (A.N. F8 79, rapport de Goupil, médecin de Nemours, sur les épidémies de Dormelles, 2 mai 1806). '. . . La crainte, les autres affections de l'âme y disposent d'autant plus les habitans qu'à peine alités, ils perdent tout espoir et se regardent comme victimes assurées de cette maladie . . .' (A.N. F8 78, rapport sur les épidémies de Bacqueville-en-Caux, 9 nivôse an IV).

(2F) For an eloquent expression of rural resentment, see A.N. F10 210 (Commission d'Agriculture, société populaire de Bagnols (Rhône), à la Convention, s.d. vendémiaire an III): 'Notre société n'est presque composée que d'agriculteurs, aussi . . . l'agriculture y est constamment à l'ordre du jour, et jusqu'à ce que les abus qui couvrent nos terres de ronces et d'épines soient entièrement stirpés (sic), nous ne cesserons de vous porter nos réclamations. . . . Jusqu'à présent tous les conspirateurs, tous les dominateurs ont dirigé leurs efforts contre l'agriculture, chaque faction s'étant efforcée de lui faire une plaie. Elle est aujourd'hui dans un état d'affoiblissement. . . . Le cultivateur se voit chaque jour enlever ce qui lui est indispensable pour la culture de ses terres; il manque absolument de tout, les bras, les bestiaux, les agrets aratoires, les fourrages, les grains, tout lui est enlevé . . . il est obligé d'abandonner les terres qui sont aujourd'hui ou incultes ou légèrement cultivées. La denrée la plus essentielle, le bled, est pour eux regardée comme la récolte la plus ingrate. . . . Il n'est malheureusement que trop vrai que la réquisition des mules et des chevaux a enlevé successivement jusqu'à 3 et 4 couples à des cultivateurs qui sont par là ruinés; et comment ne le seroit-il pas? Une de ses mules est requise, on la lui paye, et fort tard, au maximum; il va à une foire la remplacer, elle lui coûte le double, deux jours après cette dernière lui est encore requise. . . . Enfin la loi du maximum ne pèse que sur l'agriculteur, les grains et les denrées qu'il récolte ne peuvent être soustraits aux consommateurs, les recensements et les réquisitions les mettant continuellement en évidence. Il n'en est pas de même des autres objets nécessaires à l'agriculture, les huiles, le savon, les étoffes, les fers ... sont presque tous cachés par le marchand avide. ...'

(2G) The *taxe* of May 1812 provoked a similar and equally understandable sense of grievance among rural producers (who had had, it is true, ample time to make enormous profits in September 1811–April 1812). '... La taxe a péniblement affecté les propriétaires et les cultivateurs qui se relevoient du découragement causé par les pertes qu'ils ont éprouvées dans les années antérieures: "Lorsque les produits de notre industrie sont abondans", disaient-ils, "on les laisse sans valeur se détériorer dans nos greniers; et lorsque la pénurie de ces mêmes produits doit naturellement en élever le prix, il est fixé par l'autorité à un taux qui n'est point en rapport avec la quantité existante de la denrée, les frais que sa production a occasionnés, et la demande qui en est faite. Que l'on taxe donc aussi le fer, le bois, les étoffes, la main-d'œuvre, tous les objets nécessaires à l'agriculture et dont les prix toujours croissans ne lui laisseront bientôt plus d'avantage à cultiver la terre ..." ' (A.N. F11 710, Préfet du Finistère au Ministre, 12 juillet 1812). The Prefect of the Aveyron expresses a similar point of view: '... La taxe est une mesure désastreuse, injuste et impracticable. ... Elle est injuste en ce qu'elle impose aux bénéfices du cultivateur une borne qui n'est pas commune aux autres professions. ... Le premier résultat seroit l'oppression du cultivateur, son découragement et l'abandon des terres ...' (A.N. F11 706).

(2H) '... Le cours des grains que vous annoncez nous épouvante ... il est donc vrai que les habitans des campagnes veulent tyranniser ceux qui ont besoin de leurs denrées ... librement demander dix fois la valeur de ce qu'ils nous remettent, c'est le comble de l'égoïsme ...' (Arch. Rhône 2 L 39, district de Lyon aux commissaires pour les subsistances envoyés dans le district de Pont-de-Vaux, 19 nivôse an III). The Prefects of 1812 give similar reports of the rapacity of the large farmers. 'Il a fallu souvent menacer', writes that of the Aisne, 'et, à regret, punir, car, il est pénible de le dire, j'ai trouvé en général chez les propriétaires cultivateurs, et surtout chez les fermiers, peu de dévouement et de bonne foi ... les fausses déclarations ... toutes les ruses employées pour faire accepter le mauvais grain et pour soustraire le bon, pour en augmenter le poids et diminuer le volume de l'hectolitre ...' (A.N. F11 705). Girardin, the hard-pressed Prefect of Rouen, is even more severe: '... Les propriétaires des grains ont seuls montré une avidité et une dureté dignes de blâme; mais si, placés entre l'honneur et l'intérêt, ils ont pour la plupart écouté une basse et sordide avarice, on peut en partie rejeter l'odieux de cette conduite sur les circonstances qui ont si puissamment éveillé leur cupidité et sur le défaut d'éducation qui leur rend presqu'étrangers les sentiments nobles et généreux ...' (A.N. F11 718). '... Je ne parle point des petits cultivateurs,' writes a former landowner from the Eure, 'ceux-là ont souffert, ils avaient une mauvaise récolte et ont fini par acheter du pain. ... Mais le gros cultivateur ... compte sur les besoins du Gouvernement ...

son luxe augmente, il n'hésite pas à faire l'emplette de 3 ou 4 chevaux. . . .
Les cultivateurs ont en bourse peut-être 5 à 6 millions provenans de la
vente de leurs grains . . .' (A.N. F11 709).

(2I) Arch. Bouches-du-Rhône L 3072 (assassinats an III). In the *commune*
of Barbentane, a *bande* had been in existence from 1792 to the spring of
1795. It was composed of the local terrorists, including the commander
of the *Garde nationale* and members of the *comité de surveillance*, and it had
terrorized the villagers, first of all in the name of the Terror of the year II,
then in that of the Counter-Terror of the year III. Its members were Jean
Plumeau, dit *le dard*, Jacques Plumeau, dit *le vieux*, Antoine Fontaine,
dit *le marseillais*, André Linsolas, dit *le beau*, Claude Ardiguier, dit *l'effrayant*, Étienne Reynaud, dit *les gros yeux*, Pierre Versin, dit *le grelot*,
François Plumeau, dit *le janneton*, Joseph Chabaud, ci-devant curé (!) et
commandant de la garde nationale, Claude Raoult, charron, François
Raoul, maréchal ferrant, who, in the year IV, also shot a soldier on the
Cours in Marseilles. Their headquarters was *chez Jean Vinon, cafetier*.
Their first murders had been committed in September 1792, their last in
Pluviôse year III. The case of Barbentane is no doubt exceptional. But
in Marseille a member of another gang admits, in Brumaire year IV, to
having been a terrorist and to having been dismissed from the *gendarmerie*
as such shortly after 9 Thermidor (ibid., interrogatoire de Raoust,
maquignon, 3 brumaire an IV).

(2J) Arch. Vaucluse 3 L 48* (Subsistances, district d'Avignon). The
agent national is at first highly optimistic; in his report for 1–9 Messidor
year II, he writes: 'L'on avoit craint que la rareté des bras n'apportât de
grands retards à la récolte des grains. Ces craintes, qui n'étoient pas sans
fondement, se sont évanouies. . . . Tous les citoyens de ce district ont été
mis en réquisition pour ce travail. . . . La récolte paraît assez abondante,
elle l'eût été sans doute davantage sans les pluies et les vents qui ont régné
lors de la maturité des bleds. . . .' Ten days later, he is much less hopeful:
'. . . On n'a point encore acquis des renseignemens assez précis sur le
produit de la récolte actuelle pour pouvoir en donner en ce moment un
aperçu, mais à vue d'œil on peut assurer qu'il sera infiniment moindre
que celui de la récolte précédente.' On 10 Thermidor he writes: 'Il s'en
faut bien que la récolte soit en réalité ce qu'elle a paru en apparence;
elle (est) certainement peu considérable et rarement a-t-on vu au moment
de la coupe des grains une sorte de pénurie comme celle que nous éprou-
vons ici . . . .' For the month of Vendémiaire year III, he reports: 'Les ressources en grains diminuent chaque jour dans ce district et comme la
récolte a été moindre de la moitié de l'année dernière, plusieurs communes
commencent à refuser d'obtempérer aux réquisitions.'

(2K) A.N. F10 242 (report to the Commission d'Agriculture, frimaire
an IV). See also A.N. F10 210 (Watier, administrateur du district de
Brest, à la Convention, 2 nivôse an III): '. . . On ne parviendra jamais à
ranimer la culture de la terre qu'en portant les grains à un haut prix, comme

on l'a fait, et en fixant modérément celui des bestiaux, sinon l'agriculteur, ne consultant que son intérêt, laissera ses terres en friches parce qu'il est plus aisé d'élever des bestiaux que de cultiver des champs. . . . Notre excessive consommation de viande rendant les bestiaux assez rares, on tue des cochons de 6 mois et des veaux de 15 jours, des taurillons, des génisses, et peut-être des vaches pleines, n'est-ce-pas là le moyen de tout détruire en peu de tems? . . . Je pense qu'il faudroit aussi une loi qui ne permit l'usage de viande que pendant 5 jours de chaque décade. . . .'

Eighteen years later, the Prefect of the Indre-et-Loire expressed his conviction that corn-growing was on the decline in France. 'Tout me porte à croire', he writes on 25 July 1812, 'que la culture du bled diminue en France et cela parce que cette culture est une des plus chères et une des moins profitables depuis longtems. Le pain deviendra donc plus rare et plus cher. Mais, en revanche, on élève plus de bestiaux, on cultive du tabac, des betteraves, du pastel, on sème plus de bois . . . plus de vignes . . .' (A.N. F11 711).

(2L) For the *sans-culotte* programme to have been at all workable, not only enormous forces would have been needed, but also an extensive bureaucracy, such as even the Empire was not to possess. The point is made by the Prefect of the Aveyron, in a report dated 8 August 1812, on the subject of a *maximum général*: '. . . En effet cette mesure est impraticable, même quant aux grains pris isolément. Pour l'exécuter il faudroit lever une armée entière de commis et monter un service à peu près semblable à celui qui opère la perception des droits sur les boissons: inventaires, recollements, déclarations, congés, passavants, acquits à caution, portatifs, exercices, buralistes, commis, contrôleurs &ca, immense et redoutable appareil . . .' (A.N. F11 706). The *sans-culottes* were in any case great believers in such paper checks, which, in office, they applied with rigour and without imagination. It is also likely that they would have welcomed the formation of a bureaucratic machine of this type, as it would have offered them limitless opportunities of employment under the economic Terror.

(2M) Mortality was already abnormally high in le Havre for the year II (607 deaths), though not as high as in the next two years (*Terreur et subsistances*, p. 325). In Dieppe, too, it was somewhat above normal in the year II (721), though in the year III it was to attain 968 and in the year IV, 1,071, reverting, in the year V, to 621 (Arch. Dieppe, État Civil de Dieppe, 1793–1818). The 1812 crisis left no trace in the mortality of that and the following year in this port—a clear indication that the crisis was far from having the famine proportions of that of the years III and IV. Furthermore, in le Havre, mortality is already very acute right at the beginning of the year III, no doubt as a result of the drought and of the epidemics of the summer of the year II; there are 95 deaths for Vendémiaire year III, the highest figure for any month from the year II to the year VIII. It is much the same in Dieppe, with 90 deaths for Vendémiaire, 109 deaths— the highest figure in the whole crisis—in Pluviôse year III. In these two ports, the crisis had thus been prepared under the Revolutionary Government, though, in Rouen, it was to have a more specifically Thermidorian character. In Meudon, the epidemic breaks out in Thermidor year II, with 130 deaths by the beginning of the year III (A.N. F8 79, rapport de Lavergne, vendémiaire an III). In Canteleu, it begins in Fructidor year II (A.N. F8 78). A doctor from Valdajol (Vosges) reports, in Pluviôse year III, on an epidemic that has been raging for the previous six months, that is from Fructidor year II (A.N. F15 254). A report on the epidemic of Gonesse gives the same starting date (A.N. F8 79). A report from the District de Saint-Geniez (Aveyron) attributes the heavy mortality of the year III to 'la disette affreuse que nous avons éprouvée la DEUXIÈME année [qui] a réduit le peuple à vivre avec du pain fait avec la racine de fougère, les coquilles de noix, des cendres, ce qui a appauvri le sang, ruiné le tempérament et causé la destruction d'une infinité d'individus . . .' (A.N. F10 242). The authorities of the Creuse write, in Frimaire year III, of '5 années de disette' (A.N. F15 251).

(2N) A doctor from Annecy, enumerating the causes of an epidemic that had broken out in the commune of Gevrier, around 20 Thermidor year II, concludes: '. . . A toutes ces causes, joignez-y l'état moral dans lequel se sont trouvés ses habitans, par suite inévitable d'une révolution' (A.N. F8 67). The administrators of the Haute-Saône, in a report dated 24 Vendémiaire year IV, write: '. . . Les sentimens et les affections naturelles ayant été comprimés pendant longtems par la terreur, les mariages sont devenus plus rares, et, par une suite funeste à l'état et aux individus, le nombre des morts a excédé celui des naissances . . .' (A.N. F10 242). Those of the Aveyron report, the same month: '. . . Depuis 1790, le nombre des morts a excédé de beaucoup celui des naissances. La disette d'un côté, les chagrins domestiques de l'autre ont abrégé les jours d'une infinité de personnes . . .' (ibid.). Referring to the epidemic in Bacqueville-en-Caux, Lucas and Riolle report, 9 Nivôse year IV: '. . . Il nous a paru que l'épidémie attaquoit indifféremment tous les âges, mais qu'elle affectionnoit les femmes. . . . La crainte, les autres affections de l'âme y disposent . . .' (A.N. F8 78, Seine-Inférieure). The seasonal nature of most of these epidemics is further emphasized in a medical report for July 1811 on the subject of the outbreak in Pantin: '. . . Cette fièvre est évidemment l'effet de la saison et ne pourroit être, sans malveillance, attribuée comme les fièvres intermittentes, à la situation particulière de la commune de Pantin. Il est d'expérience que tous les ans dans les mois d'été les habitants des campagnes sont attaqués . . . de fièvres bileuses . . . de choléra morbus, de dissenterie &ca . . .' (A.N. F8 77).

(2O) '. . . Toutes les rues de la ville [d'Amiens] sont infestées de boucheries particulières . . . l'on vend de la viande de bêtes mortes et malades, de cheval, l'on met pour ainsi dire des viandes infectes et pourries, des ordures dans les viandes qui se vendent au public sous le nom de saucisses . . .' (A.N. F8 80, Somme, Sellier au Gouvernement, 12 floréal an IX). '. . . La qualité de la terre convenant mieux au seigle, ce bled fait la majeure partie de leur culture, malheureusement il est rempli d'ivraie et très sujet, en presque totalité, à la maladie qu'on nomme *ergot* en Sologne, *ebrun* en Bourgogne et *bled cornu* en Gâtinois. ... Je les engageai à cribler de suite soigneusement leur bled, ce qu'ils se gardaient bien de faire auparavant, par économie et disette de bon grain, qu'ils aimaient mieux vendre ...' (A.N. F8 76, rapport de Juchereau, médecin à la Flèche, sur une épidémie qui règne à Guionnières (Sarthe), 8 mars 1812). '. . . Une partie des malheureux habitans s'empressent à l'envie d'acheter à 20 sols la livre de ces charognes, dont ils se nourrissent en partie, sans souvent aucune autre espèce d'alimens; et on ne voit déjà que trop sur leurs figures livides les tristes effets d'une nourriture aussi malfaisante . . .' (A.N. F8 79, Bertrand, ancien officier de santé de Meulan, au Ministre, 24 pluviôse an IV). A report dated 13 Frimaire of the same year attributes the epidemic existing in Gonesse for the previous eighteen months to 'les privations multipliées, qu'un grand nombre de citoyens a éprouvées peu de tems avant la moisson, les légumes et fruits verds, le pain de grains récemment cueillis . . . l'intempérance qui a dû nécessairement succéder à une pénurie momentanément supportée . . .' (ibid.). '. . . La mauvaise nourriture que les habitans de ce district sont obligés de se servir, faute de grains, a causé dans la commune de Saint-Julien-sur-Sarthe un genre d'épidémie qui fait des ravages assez considérables puisque depuis un mois plus de 100 sont morts de ce genre de maladie, qui commence par un mal de gorge et finit par la pourpre . . .' (A.N. F8 70 (Orne), l'agent national du district de Mortagne, à la Commission des Secours, 21 pluviôse an III).

(2P) It is only as the result of a police report on sudden death or suicide that the contents of a room may be revealed. We hear of a Marseille *sabreur* 'qui couchoit dans une chambre à trois lits . . .'. There are six beds in a room, one of them occupied by the body of a *journalier* of 58, during the winter of the year III, *chez un logeur*, Section de la Montagne. There are four to a room, Section des Arcis: an *invalide*, three *couvreurs*; four to a room, Section du Panthéon, all of them chimney-sweeps from the Haute-Loire; three to one bed, Section de Popincourt, all three *chapeliers* from the Forez.

In a report on the Citoyenne Cossou, dated 14 Messidor year IV, the *comité de bienfaisance* of the Section du Temple reports: '... Nous l'avons trouvée sans meubles, n'ayant qu'un méchant grabat, une paillasse, un drap et une couverture, sur lequel ils couchent 5 ensemble ...' (A.N. F15 3336, Secours). During one of his rounds, Comminges, the *commissaire* of the Section de la Montagne, discovers five girls, sleeping with five men, in a room off the Palais Royal. Among the effects of a laundry-woman who has been sent to Charenton, having gone mad, Section des Arcis, are '3 fers à repasser, un fourneau et un poëllon de terre, une cruche de terre, une petite marmite et 2 petits pots de terre, 8 assiettes et une tasse de faïance, 3 gobelets de verre, un petit plat de faïance, une grande et une petite bouteille de verre, une cuillière de bois, un chandelier de fer, un couvert d'étain, une commode de bois de noyer à 2 grands et 2 petits tiroirs garni de mains . . . de cuivre en couleur et une seule clef, une petite cassette sans couvercle, une autre cassette avec son couvercle et sa serrure dans laquelle il ne s'est trouvé que des chiffons ne méritant aucune description, dans un coin de la chambre 2 chemises sales, 3 paires de bas, un fichu de mousseline, 4 torchons, 2 paires de mauvais bas, 2 mauvais jupons, 2 mouchoirs rouges à petits carreaux, 3 bonnets à 2 rangs, un bout de dentelle mauvais, une bande de mousseline festonnée, une petite table ployante, sur laquelle une petite couverture de laine blanche, et un tapis servant à repasser, une petite couchette à roulette, une paillasse de grosse toile, un mauvais matelas de crin et de laine, un traversin rempli de paille, un oreiller rempli de plumes, une taie d'oreiller aux mauvais draps, une très mauvaise couverture de laine blanche, un mauvais jupon bleu, un tablier rouge et un mauvais tas de chiffons . . . sous le lit un pot de faïance et un grand plat et un autre pot, le tout rempli d'urine, que l'on a été jeter, sur la table un petit portefeuille dans lequel s'est trouvé en assignats 3l. et 5s.; et 6s. en monnoye . . . sur le carré une fontaine de grez rouge dans sa chemise d'osier sur son pied et son robinet de potin. . . .' What a litany of *mauvais*! (A.P.P. A/A 61, Arcis, 16 vendémiaire an III; also A/A 62, 95–8, 202, 219).

(2Q) This sense of deprivation is frequently expressed in reports and petitions, especially at the height of the crisis of the year III. In his report for 1–10 Nivôse year III the *agent national* of the district d'Avignon complains: '. . . Le district d'Orange, qui regorgeoit de bled, qui de tous les districts du département s'en trouve le mieux pourvu, nageant dans l'abondance, insultoit à notre misère et à nos malheurs et voyoit froidement, que dis-je? peut-être même avec plaisir, s'organiser la guerre civile. . . . Mais si le district d'Orange, notre voisin, nous a traité comme des ogres, que d'actions de graces n'avons-nous pas à rendre à celui d'Arles qui, beaucoup plus humain, s'est privé de ses subsistances pour subvenir à nos pressants besoins . . .' (Arch. Vaucluse, 3 L 48*, rapports décadaires de l'agent national du district d'Avignon, an III). On 1 Vendémiaire year IV, the municipality of la Salle (Gard) petitions the Convention: '. . . Sa commune fait partie d'un pays appellé les basses Cevennes, dans lequel il ne se recueille presque point de blé, que par conséquent ses habitans sont obligés de tirer leur subsistance des pays voisins . . . elle auroit peut-être trouvé dans ses environs de quoi subsister, si les propriétaires des grains, qui sont presque tous fermiers, ne refusoient de vendre leurs denrées. . . . Il arrive . . . que dans un pays où l'on est dans la plus extrême misère et que dans l'autre l'on vit plus au large et avec beaucoup plus d'agrément qu'on eût jamais fait. Si ce désordre n'est pas incessamment réprimé, il en résultera deux maux inévitables, ou la famine pour certains pays, ou la guerre civile et l'établissement du brigandage . . .' (A.N. D III 86 d 17, comité de législation, Gard). A woman from Mouzon writes to the Commission des Secours, 1 Prairial year III: '. . . Tout le pays est affamé, *il n'y a que les impériaux qui ne manquent de rien*, car ils ont notre pain, car ils en sont fournis . . . car pour les pauvres, ils vivent comme des bêtes d'herbe, ah! si vos yeux voyoient les spectres de Mouzon, ces anatomies vivantes, les larmes couleroient des yeux les plus invulnérables, hé bien, la municipalité, les gens aisés voient toutes les misères du plus grand sang-froid . . .' (A.N. F15 2820, Commission des Secours). A petition from Lapalisse, of Brumaire year IV, tells a similar tale: '. . . En vérité le peuple, la classe ouvrière, des citoyens meurent de faim au sein de l'abondance . . . le riche voit périr de misère le malheureux avec une inhumanité, une barbarie, un sang-froid, une cupidité, une avarice dont il n'y a pas d'exemple chez les peuples barbares et sauvages . . .' (A.N. F1b II Allier I).

NAME INDEX

Alletz, author of *Traité de la police moderne*, 15 (1), 21 (1), 23 (3, 4, 5), 26 (1), 215 (1), 230 (3), 248 (3), 328 (C).

Allier, brother of the *ex-curé* of Chambonas (Ardèche), alleged leader of the White Terror in the Haute-Loire, 346.

André (Agnès and Louise, sisters), 224 (4).

Anselme, *hussard*, member of a Montbrison murder gang, 345 (X).

Antraigues (*le comte d'*), xv, 205.

Ardiguier (Claude), dit *l'effrayant*, member of the Barbentane murder gang, 374 (2I).

Astruc, from Bonac (Ariège), victim of the White Terror, 359 (C).

Auguis, Conventionnel, 32 (3), 343.

Aymé (Marcel), 49 (1), 322 (1), 323 (2), 334 (6).

Babeuf (Gracchus), 71, 72, 97, 171, 193, 206, 320.

Babeuf (Catherine), 170 (1).

Babeuf (Robert), 170 (1).

Babeuf (*la veuve*), 169.

Baehrel (René), 318 (1).

Barbanche, *marin*, executed after the Caen riot of 2 March 1812, 114.

Barbien, *aubergiste*, of Nîmes, alleged member of a murder gang, 354.

Bard, *mâcon*, victim of the White Terror in Montbrison, 341 (R), 346 (Y).

Barère, 50.

Barras, 134, 172.

Barray, *médecin*, Besançon, 360 (B).

Barrois (Marguerite), 224, 294.

Baudelaire, 171.

Bauchot (Toinette), *couturière*, 361 (E).

Bauzon, *arpenteur*, a former terrorist of Beaune, 366 (P).

Baze (Daniel), inhabitant of Carpentras, 347 (2A).

Baze (Manuel), inhabitant of Carpentras, 347 (2A).

Belamy (Auguste), *cabaretier*, member of the Dieppe *comité*, 358 (2Z).

Bellemel, *gendarme*, of Dijon, 366 (R).

Belsunce (*le comte de*), 327.

Béraud (Henri), 33 (3).

Berthier de Sauvigny, 327.

Bertin, *maître d'écriture*, rue aux Juifs, 364 (L).

Bigot, *tourneur et maquignon*, of Roanne, assassinated in Lyon, victim of the White Terror, 338.

Blanc (Pascal), *accusateur public du tribunal criminel du Gard* in the Year IV, 353 (O).

Blaze, *membre de l'administration du département de Vaucluse*, 135 (3), 343, 363.

Blette (Pierre-Jean), *fabricant de rubans*, former member of the *comité de la Section Bonne-Nouvelle*, 68 (2).

Boisset, Conventionnel, 172, 359 (3C).

Boissy-d'Anglas, 289, 308.

Bon, Lyonnais, alleged member of a Marseille murder gang, 31.

Bonfils, *aubergiste*, of Craponne, victim of the White Terror in the Haute-Loire, 136 (2).

Bordes, Conventionnel, 341.

Bouchet (*l'abbé*), victim of the White Terror in Montbrison, 136 (1), 355 (2S).

Bonnijoly, ex-terrorist of Nîmes, 65 (2).

Breton (Louis), *tonnelier*, member of the Dieppe *comité*, 358 (2Z).

Bouvier, *membre des 500*, 134, 343.

Boy (Raymond), *vigneron*, inhabitant of Saverdun, 356 (2U).

Cadenet (*la fille*), inhabitant of Salon, 358 (3A).

Cadroy, Conventionnel, 172, 349.

Canuel (*le général*), *commandant de la place de Lyon* under the Directory, 139 (2), 342 (T).

Carcassonne (Mardoché), inhabitant of Carpentras, 347 (2A).

Caron (Pierre), 81.

Cartlet, *cultivateur*, of Vergues, victim of the White Terror in the Haute-Loire, 136 (2).

Casenave, Conventionnel, 366 (Q).

Cauche (*la famille*), from Montreuil-sur-Mer, 225.

Chabaud (Joseph), *ex-curé*, member of the Barbentane murder gang, 374 (2I).

Chaix (*Marat*), inhabitant of Lormes (Nièvre), 152, 181.

Chambon, Conventionnel, 344.

Charitant, *cultivateur*, of Négraval (Haute-Loire), victim of the White Terror in the Haute-Loire, 136 (2), 356.

Charpillon (Marie), accused of theft, 362.

Chausson, *entrepreneur*, member of a Montbrison murder gang, 345 (X).

Châteauneuf-Randon (*le général*), garrison commander at Privas in the year IV, 350 (2L).

Chaumié (Jacqueline), xv.

Chérest (Jacques), inhabitant of Tonnerre, 150–1.

Chevalier (Louis), xv (1), 19 (3), 22 (4), 26 (1), 80, 81, 328 (D).

Chovot (*fils*), *aubergiste*, member of a Montbrison murder gang, 345.

Chrétien, owner of the *café Chrétien*, 358.

Clément, *greffier*, victim of the White Terror in Montbrison, 346 (Y), 355 (2S).

Coire, *marchand*, member of a Montbrison murder gang, 345 (X).

Colon (*la femme*), arlésienne, Marseille White terrorist, 351 (2L), 352.

Comminges, former printer, *commissaire de la police de la Section de la Montagne*, 14 (1), 330 (H), 377 (2P).

Comtat (Siffren), from Carpentras, 347 (2A).

Constans (Polycarpe), *commissaire du Directoire exécutif à Marseille*, 271 (2).

Constant (Benjamin), 207.

Contamin (Joseph), *serrurier*, former

agent national of Crémieu (Isère), 32, 34, 128 (4).

Cossou (*la femme*), 377 (P).

Cotton (Pierre), former *officier municipal* of Neuville (Rhône), victim of the White Terror, 345.

Courbis, former *maire* of Nîmes, victim of the White Terror, 135 (4).

Courtois, Conventionnel, 50.

Crémieu (Abraham), inhabitant of Carpentras, 347 (2A).

Crémieux (David), inhabitant of Carpentras, 347 (2A).

Crémieux (Élie), inhabitant of Carpentras, 347 (2A).

Crémieux (Lange), inhabitant of Carpentras, 347 (2A).

Crémieux (Mossé), inhabitant of Carpentras, 347 (2A).

Crémieux (Ruben), inhabitant of Carpentras, 347 (2A).

Custine (*le général-comte*), 187.

Damilot, *marchand de vin*, former member of the *comité révolutionnaire de la Section des Gardes-françaises*, 68 (2).

Danton, 6, 52, 54.

Darien (Georges), 8 (1), 11 (1), 171.

Darlincourt (*ex-colonel-général*), 279 (3).

Dauphin, *cafetier*, former terrorist of Salon, victim of the White Terror, 347 (2C).

Decelle (*père*), victim of the White Terror in Montbrison, 355 (2S).

Dedijer (Vladimir), 12 (1).

Degalle, *tailleur*, ex-terrorist from Montbrison, 354 (2Q).

Delan, *médecin*, former *maire* of Moulins, 151–2.

Delcurrou, *liqueriste*, alleged member of a Marseille murder gang, 355.

Denelle (Denis), *menuisier*, former member of the *comité de la Section Popincourt*, assassin of his wife and children, 158–60, 357 (2X).

Descombes (Antoine), *commissaire de la Commission des subsistances*, executed with Hébert, 288.

Dessirier, former cook, inhabitant of Suresnes, 153–4.

Devèze, *charpentier*, Section de la République, 68 (2).

Didier, *serrurier, ancien juré au tribunal révolutionnaire*, 358.

Digne (Mardoché), from Carpentras, 347 (2A).

Doinelle, *compagnon maçon*, Section du Contrat Social, 66 (1).

Dorzat, former *agent national* of Heyrieu (Isère), 299 (1).

Doyen (Pierre), former *frère des Écoles chrétiennes*, inhabitant of Sens, 157 (2).

Droz (Anne-Louise), *ex-religieuse*, 361 (E).

Dubois (Louis), ex-terrorist, refugee from Lyon, 337.

Dubois, *soldat*, from Dieppe, 366 (Q).

Dubois, *vicaire*, ex-terrorist from Beaune, 364.

Ducroquet, *commissaire aux accaparents*, Section Marat, 288.

Duplantier (Valentin), leader of the White Terror in the Ain, 342 (S).

Duprat (J. E. B.), inhabitant of Avignon, 343.

Durand (Claude), dit *le beau Durand*, former *commandant de la garde nationale*, of Eyragues, victim of the White Terror, 146 (4).

Durand, *laboureur*, of la Gaillarde, victim of the White Terror in the Haute-Loire, 136 (2).

Duroure (Scipion), ex-terrorist, 358.

Dusny, *tisserand*, of Tixe, victim of the White Terror in the Haute-Loire, 136 (2).

Dutaillon (or Dutailloux), member of a Montbrison murder gang, 338, 345, 346, 351.

Duval (Georges), author of *Souvenirs thermidoriens*, xix, 21 (3), 48, 73, 74 (1), 75, 101, 161, 173, 250 (2), 300 (2), 309 (2).

Espert, Conventionnel, 344.

Eudes (Jean-Louis), former officer in the *armée révolutionnaire parisienne*, 164.

Fayolle, *lieutenant dans le 6me bataillon des côtes maritimes*, victim of the White Terror in the Haute-Loire, 136 (2).

Féret (Nicolas), inhabitant of Saint-Vaast (Seine-Inférieure), 368–9.

Flamand, *marchand de vin*, Section du Faubourg-Montmartre, 358.

Fontaine (André), dit *le Marseillais*, member of the Barbentane murder gang, 374 (2I).

Fontlupt (Antoine), *teinturier*, refugee from the White Terror in the Loire, 354 (2Q).

Fornier-d'Albe (*le général*), 35 (2).

Fouché, 241.

Fouquier-Tinville (Antoine-Quentin), 6, 9, 10, 17, 50, 52, 53, 284, 288, 289, 290, 313.

Fournerot (François-Louis), *ouvrier rubannier, ancien membre de la Commune de Paris*, 358.

Frénaye, *maire* of Gannat, executed, 366.

Fréron, Conventionnel, 134, 172, 343.

Fricour (Jean), *chapelier*, inhabitant of Montbrison, 338, 346.

Fuoc (Renée), 34 (1).

Furet (François), 318 (2).

Garat, Minister of the Interior, 52.

Gascar (Pierre), 324.

Gautier (Simon), *officier de santé*, member of the Dieppe *comité*, 358 (2Z).

Gense (François), *maire* of Neuville (Rhône), victim of the White Terror, 345.

Genty le jeune, inhabitant of Mâcon, 139 (1).

Gervais (Étienne), *manouvrier*, from Anneville, 234.

Géry, *cultivateur*, Montsevin (Haute-Loire), 136 (2).

Girardin, Prefect of the Seine-Inférieure in 1812, 108, 116, 373.

Girin, *vigneron*, victim of the White Terror in the Loire, 346.

Giron, *tisserand*, victim of the White Terror in Montbrison, 346 (Y).

Gnafron, 33.

Godard (Jean-Luc), 211.

Godeby (Michel), member of the Dieppe *comité*, 173 (2).

Godechot (Jacques), 164, 241 (2).

Goodwin (Albert), 285 (2).

Goupil, *médecin*, of Nemours, 372 (2E).

Goupilleau de Montaigu, Convention-
nel, 101 (1), 134, 172, 349.
Gourdain (Louis), *brasseur*, member
of the Dieppe *comité*, 358 (2Z).
Gourdin (Élisabeth), 364.
Gourgonnier (*adjutant-général*), 164.
Granjon, *homme de loi*, member of
a Montbrison murder gang, 345
(X).
Gras (Barthélémy), dit *le coupeur*,
member of the Malemort murder
gang, 351 (2J).
Gravois, *maire* of Versailles, 221 (1).
Griot, *cordonnier*, from Montbrison,
refugee from the White Terror in
the Loire, 354 (2Q).
Guégon, *breton*, 46.
Guénot (Nicolas), *flotteur*, of Vou-
tenay, 229 (1).
Guérin (Daniel), 63.
Guibon, *tanneur*, Section des Sans-
culottes, 74 (1).
Guiral (Pierre), xiii, xxi.
Guyot, former member of the *Com-
mission Temporaire*, 250 (3).

Hampson (Norman), 293 (3).
Hébert, 13 (1), 52, 53, 184, 191.
Hervez (Jeanne), inhabitant of Mou-
zon, 157 (1).
Heurlant-Dumez, inhabitant of Issou-
dun, 115.
Hohl (Claude), *archiviste de l'Yonne*,
229 (1).
Hudelle (Pierre), *jardinier*, Section du
Temple, 242 (1).

Ilissac (Samuel), inhabitant of Carpentras, 347 (2A).
Isabel, *agent national* of the le Havre
tribunal, 39 (2).
Isnard, Conventionnel, 172.

Javogues (Claude), 355 (2S).
Jaubert (Charles), 9.
Jean-Jean, dit *capucin*, *cordonnier*,
member of the Malemort murder
gang, 351 (2J).
Jullian, author of *Souvenirs de ma vie
depuis 1774 jusqu'en 1814*, 283 (1).
Jullian (Louis), 344, 351 (2K).

Kellerman (*le général*), 342 (T).

Kruber, member of the *comité de
l'Homme armé*, 46-7.

Laclos, 40 (1).
Lafond (Jean), *vigneron*, inhabitant of
Montbrison, 199 (1).
Lamenon (Paul), inhabitant of Saint-
Chamas, 332.
Lamothe, alleged leader of the White
Terror in the Ardèche and the
Haute-Loire, 344 (V).
Langlois (Jean), *chaudronnier*, member
of the Dieppe *comité*, 358 (2Z).
Laporte, *aubergiste*, member of the
Commission Temporaire, 175.
Latourcy, member of a Montbrison
murder gang, 345, 351.
Lattard, *défenseur officieux*, member of
a Montbrison murder gang, 345 (X),
359 (3C).
Laugier (Jean), terrorist from Saint-
Chamas, 332.
Lazare (François), of Carpentras,
347 (2A).
Le Bas (*la veuve*), 169.
Lebrasse, *gendarme*, 13 (1).
Lécrivain, *peintre en bâtiment*, former
member of the *comité de surveillance
du Département de Paris*, 358.
Lefebvre (Georges), 54, 253 (3), 266
(4), 277 (2), 302 (3), 311 (1), 319.
Lefranc (Jean-Baptiste-Antoine), 34
(4), 164, 167.
Legrand, lyonnais, member of a Mont-
brison murder gang, 345 (X).
Lenoir (B. A.), 215 (1), 257 (2), 261
(1), 267, 268 (2), 277 (1).
Léon (Jacob), inhabitant of Carpen-
tras, 347 (2A).
Lestapis (Arnaud de), 94 (1).
Lévêque (Anne), veuve Ronsin, 169.
Lhuya (Étienne), *aubergiste*, leader of
the Eyragues murder gang, 302 (1).
Linsolas (Antoine), dit *le beau*, mem-
ber of the Barbentane murder gang,
374 (21).
Loret (Jean), *marchand orfèvre*, mem-
ber of the Dieppe *comité*, 358 (2Z).
Lorillon, 101, 299 (1).
Louchet (*les filles*), inhabitants of
Dieppe, 363 (K).
Loys, 169 (3).
Löys (*la veuve*), 169.

Lucas (Colin), 64 (1).
Lucas (René), *médecin*, member of the Dieppe *comité*, 358 (2Z), 376 (2N).
Lucotte (Nanette), *revendeuse*, 362 (H).
Lyon (Jacob), inhabitant of Carpentras, 347 (2A).

Magnien, *imprimeur*, victim of the White Terror, inhabitant of Montbrison, 136 (1), 149 (3), 339 (N), 346 (Y), 355 (2S), 356.
Maignet, Conventionnel, 153.
Maillau (Bertrand), *tailleur*, nîmois, suspected member of a Marseille murder gang, 364 (L).
Mairier (Privat), *serrurier*, member of the Dieppe *comité*, 358 (2Z).
Malet (*le général*), 35.
Malôtain, *horloger*, from Dieppe, 219 (1), 233, 300 (1), 322.
Manard (*la famille*), of Clermont-Ferrand, 345 (X), 352.
Mandrou (Robert), xv.
Marat, 53, 205, 206.
Marcellin (*la femme*), Section des Invalides, 170.
Marcillat, *ex-prêtre*, former member of the *Commission Temporaire*, 174.
Marino (Jean-Baptiste), *inspecteur des garnis*, 239 (1).
Martin (*la famille*), inhabitants of Lambesc, victims of the White Terror, 149, 346 (Z).
Maupeou, 270, 279.
Méchin (Alexandre), 344, 351 (2K).
Méjason, *géomètre*, member of a Montbrison murder gang, 345 (X).
Mercereau, *officier de paix*, Section du Panthéon français, 122 (1).
Mercier (Louis-Sébastien), xix, 21 (4, 5, 6, 7), 40, 43, 44, 65 (1), 78 (1), 87, 88, 173, 219, 220 (3), 226, 227, 231, 234, 235, 243 (1), 249 (2, 3, 4), 265 (2), 266 (1, 3), 271, 289 (1), 296 (2), 300 (2), 328 (E), 330 (H), 360 (C).
Mérieux (Joseph), inhabitant of Carpentras, 347 (2A).
Michel (Antoine), former *juge-de-paix* of Salon, 335 (H).
Minet (Denis), *brocanteur*, 230 (4).
Moncla, victim of the White Terror in the Ariège, 355 (2S).

Monteux (Isaac), inhabitant of Carpentras, 347 (2A).
Monteux (Mossé), inhabitant of Carpentras, 347 (2A).
Musquinet-Lapagne, *maire* of Ingouville, 64, 132.

Namier (Lewis), 81.
Naque (Mossé), inhabitant of Carpentras, 347 (2A).
Olivier, member of the *comité* of the Section du Bonnet-Rouge, 169 (3).
Orty (Conrad), terrorist from Salon, 335 (H).
Paganel fils, 37 (1).
Paley, *officier de santé*, victim of the White Terror in Montbrison, 136 (1), 337, 346 (Y), 359 (3C).
Pamelier, *greffier*, of Yssangeaux, victim of the White Terror in the Haute-Loire, 136 (2).
Paré, Minister of the Interior, 52.
Parent (*Bias*), inhabitant of Clamecy, 175.
Paris, *commissaire des guerres* of the *armée révolutionnaire parisienne*, 164.
Payen (Olivier), assassin, 354 (2R).
Pépin-Desgrouhettes, 359.
Perraud (*la veuve*), widow of a victim of the White Terror in the Loire, 351 (2J).
Perrotin, former member of the *Commission Temporaire*, 151–2.
Pierre (Joseph), *cordonnier*, member of the Dieppe *comité*, 358, 358 (2Z).
Plumeau (François), dit *le jeanneton*, member of the Barbentane murder gang, 374 (2I).
Plumeau (Jacques), dit *le vieux*, member of the Barbentane murder gang, 374 (2I).
Plumeau (Jean), dit *le dard*, member of the Barbentane murder gang, 374 (2I).
Planson (Edmé), *metteur en œuvre*, member of the *comité* of the Section des Gravilliers, 358.
Playfair (William), 130.
Poche (Jacques), *chapelier*, victim of the White Terror in Montbrison, 136 (1), 337, 346 (Y), 359 (3C).

Poicelot, member of the *comité* of the Section de Bonnet-rouge, 169 (3).

Portailier (*père et fils*), *boulangers*, members of a Montbrison murder gang, 345 (X).

Poste, *peintre*, rue Bleue, 358.

Poujol, Conventionnel, 348.

Poulailler, celebrated eighteenth-century robber, 49.

Pouteau (René), *cordonnier*, member of the Dieppe *comité*, 358 (2Z).

Pouviane, *cultivateur*, victim of the White Terror in the Haute-Loire, 136 (2).

Raoul (François), *maréchal ferrant*, member of the Barbentane murder gang, 374 (2I).

Raoult (Claude), *charron*, member of the Barbentane murder gang, 374 (2I).

Raoust, *maquignon*, member of a Marseille murder gang, 374 (2I).

Reeves, 130.

Reinhard (Marcel), 176.

Restif de la Bretonne (Nicolas Edmé), xix, 16 (1), 19 (1, 2), 20 (1), 22 (1), 24 (1), 42 (2), 43 (1), 44, 80, 225 (2), 227 (1, 2), 229 (1), 235, 236 (2), 237 (1, 4), 238 (1, 3), 239 (1), 245 (3), 250 (1), 290 (2), 293 (4), 294 (1, 2), 295 (1, 2, 3), 325 (A), 326, 327, 331 (J), 361 (D, F).

Reverchon, Conventionnel, 139 (1), 140 (4), 337, 344 (V), 350 (2H), 353 (2N), 354 (2Q).

Revillon, inhabitant of Mâcon, assassinated in Lyon, 337–8.

Reynaud (Étienne), dit *les gros yeux*, member of the Barbentane murder gang, 374 (2I).

Richard (Robert), 230 (1).

Richet (Denis), 318 (2).

Riolle, *médecin*, of Dieppe, 376 (2N).

Roberjot, 139 (1), 350 (H).

Robespierre, xviii, 91, 130, 132, 162, 169 (4), 172, 181, 190, 193, 206, 275, 283, 307, 309.

Rochefort (Henri), 171.

Roland, 52.

Ronsin (Charles-Philippe), 6, 13 (1), 52, 54, 184, 313.

Rossignol (Jean), 187.

Rousseau, 206.

Roussillon (Henri), agent of the Committee of Public Safety in the Aude, 256 (3), 258 (1).

Roux (Jacques), 181.

Rouy, *magicien*, member of the *comité* of the Section des Lombards, 47.

Rouyer, *ex-avocat*, inhabitant of Moulins, 46 (5).

Rubat, *commissaire du Directoire à Mâcon*, 342 (S).

Rude (Fernand), *sous-Préfet de Vienne*, 299 (1).

Rudé (George), xv, 31 (1), 79, 92, 93, 98, 122 (1), 270 (1).

Saiffert, *médecin saxon*, 9.

Samon, *négotiant*, of Yssangeaux, 136 (2).

Samson, *excoriateur*, executed after the Caen riot, 114.

Saurel, *commissaire du Directoire* at Malemort-du-Comtat (Vaucluse), 138, 350 (2G), 351 (2J).

Sautereau, Conventionnel, 255 (3), 265.

Selle (Guillaume), *tailleur*, member of the Dieppe *comité*, 155 (1), 358 (2Z).

Sellier (Jacques), *architecte*, inhabitant of Amiens, 372 (E), 376 (2O).

Sénac de Meilhan, 284 (1), 295 (3).

Sépher (*le général*), 187.

Serres, Conventionnel, 32 (3), 343.

Servier-Labadier, victim of the White Terror in the Gard, 135 (2).

Sigeaud, inhabitant of la Croix-Rousse, refugee, 337.

Sijas (*la veuve*), 169.

Soboul (Albert), xv, 80, 81, 120–1, 123, 186, 311 (2), 364 (M).

Sol (Jean), *ex-juge-de-paix*, of Saverdun, 351, 356 (2V).

Solilhac, *ex-gendarme*, of Beauzac, 136 (2).

Staël (Madame de), 207.

Sue (Eugène), 21 (2).

Sydenham (M.), 87 (1).

Saint-Just, 50, 91, 130, 192.

Tabourin, member of the *comité de Guillaume-Tell*, 47 (6).

Taillefer (*l'adjutant-général*), 56 (1).

Tamponnet, member of the *comité des Droits-de-l'Homme*, 47 (6).

Tardy (Antoine), *orfèvre*, Section du Muséum, 361 (G).

Tavet (Jacques), Section de Brutus, 156 (3).

Tellier, Conventionnel, 333.

Terray, 270, 279.

Tiédard, dit *Bourguignon, cordonnier*, 357.

Tissot, *membre de l'administration du Département de Vaucluse*, 135 (3), 343.

Tixier, *tisserand, massacreur*, Clermont-Ferrand, 345 (X).

Thibaudeau, 343.

Thomas (Edith), 170 (4).

Thompson (E. P.), 273 (2).

Thuillier (Constance), inhabitant of Dieppe, 233.

Tønnesson (Kåre), xv, 119 (1), 126 (1).

Tronc (Jean-Pierre), of Lambesc, assassin of the Martin family, 346 (Z).

Turgot, 270, 279.

Turreau (*le général*), 169 (1).

Vallès (Jules), 171, 176.

van der Meersch (Maxence), 323.

Vazeilles, officer in the Clermont-Ferrand *garde nationale*, assassin, 345.

Ventujol, member of the *comité* of the Section de l'Observatoire, 47 (6).

Verd, former member of the *Commission Temporaire*, 151–2.

Versin (Pierre), dit *le grelot*, member of the Barbentane murder gang, 374 (2I).

Vidocq, 19, 33 (1), 38, 39 (1), 40, 41, 245, 292 (1), 301, 330 (H, I).

Vincent (François-Nicolas), Cordelier, *secrétaire-général de la Guerre*, 52, 54, 184, 284, 313.

Vincent, *officier municipal de Marseille*, 139.

Vinon (Jean), *cafetier*, member of the Barbentane murder gang, 374 (2I).

Vovelle (Michel), 92 (1), 98.

Watier, *administrateur du district de Brest*, 374 (2K).

Willot (*le général*), 139.

Young (Arthur), 273.

INDEX OF PLACE NAMES

Abbeville, 228, 260, 325 (A), 327 (B).
Achères-la-Forêt (Seine-et-Marne), 111.
Aix-en-Provence, 41, 60, 134, 140, 142, 145, 153, 210, 286, 342, 343.
Alençon, 168, 220, 236 (6), 270 (2), 281, 370 (Z).
Alfort, 232.
Allègre (Haute-Loire), 141, 339, 356.
Altona, 256.
Amiens, 56 (1), 99, 106, 110, 113, 115, 116, 158, 168, 227, 260, 265, 309, 368 (T), 369, 371 (2C), 372 (2E), 376 (2O).
Amponville (Seine-et-Marne), 111.
Andelys (les), 287.
Angers, 177, 236 (6).
Anglesqueville (Seine-Inférieure), 368 (V).
Anneville (Seine-Inférieure), 234.
Antony, 24, 232.
Arbois (vin d'), 249.
Argenteuil, 225, 236 (3).
Arles, 34, 140, 145, 333, 378 (2Q).
Arnay-le-Duc, 252, 364.
Arpajon, 224, 288.
Arras, 236 (5).
Auffargis, 232.
Aubagne (Bouches-du-Rhône), 141, 144, 340, 352.
Aubervilliers, 19 (3).
Aumale, 224.
Auriol (Bouches-du-Rhône), 141, 340, 352.
Auteuil, 232, 288.
Auxerre, 59, 62 (2), 151, 167, 168, 229 (1), 236 (4), 238 (3), 326 (A).
Avignon, 31, 32, 33, 47 (7), 100, 101, 128, 134, 143, 145, 146 (5), 147, 149, 150, 167, 282, 333, 340, 342, 343, 348 (2D, 2E), 355 (2S), 362 (J), 374 (2J), 378 (2Q).
Ax-les-Thermes, 134, 341.

Bacqueville-en-Caux, 168 (1), 220, 256, 309, 331 (J), 372 (2E), 376 (2N).

Bagnolet, 232.
Bagnols (Gard), 140, 145.
Bagnols (Rhône), 372 (2F).
Bar-sur-Aube, 236 (1), 260.
Bar-sur-Seine, 260.
Barbentane (Bouches-du-Rhône), 141, 145, 340, 374 (2I).
Beaucaire, 135 (3), 140, 353.
Beaujeu (Rhône), 136 (3).
Beaumont (Haute-Garonne), 255.
Beaumont (Oise), 261.
Beaune, 115, 252, 364, 366 (P).
Beauvais, 229, 287.
Beauzac (Haute-Loire), 136 (2), 141.
Belleville, 19 (3), 232, 242, 284, 288.
Belleville-sur-Saône (Rhône), 333 (D), 343.
Berne, 324.
Berre (Bouches-du-Rhône), 153.
Besançon, 236 (1).
Béthune, 256.
Bezons, 232.
Billancourt, 328.
Biville (Seine-Inférieure), 103.
Blaye (Gironde), 341.
Blesville (Seine-Inférieure), 168 (1).
Bobigny, 112.
Boën, 134, 140, 339.
Bondy, 112, 221.
Bonneuil, 112.
Bordeaux, 284 (1), 325 (A), 328 (C), 333 (D).
Bougival, 224, 232.
Boulogne-sur-Seine, 288.
Bourbon-l'Archambault, 102, 236 (4).
Bourg, 134, 147, 305 (1), 341.
Bourg-Achard (Eure), 117 (2).
Brest, 374 (2K).
Brie-Comte-Robert, 287.
Brotteaux (les), 339.
Brussels, 35, 235, 236 (2), 323.

Caen, 112–17, 229, 260, 279, 285 (2), 305, 327 (A).
Calais, 260.
Calcutta, xxi, 320.
Cambrai, 256.

Canteleu (Seine-Inférieure), 220, 222, 376.
Carantan, 284 (1).
Carpentras, 145, 347 (2A).
Castelnaudary, 258 (1).
Chaise-Dieu (la) (Haute-Loire), 339.
Chalmazel (Loire), 141.
Chalon-sur-Saône, 133, 134, 140, 142, 147, 286, 350 (2H).
Chambéry, 57.
Champdeuil (Seine-et-Marne), 111.
Champdieu (Loire), 141.
Chantelauze (Loire), 337 (K), 346.
Chapelle (la), 232.
Charenton, 28.
Charité-sur-Loire (la), 236 (4), 237 (3).
Charleston, 256.
Charleville, 260.
Charnay (Rhône), 333.
Chartres, 236 (6).
Chasselay (Rhône), 136 (3).
Château-Chinon, 367 (5).
Château-Landon, 111.
Châteaurenard (Bouches-du-Rhône), 147, 340.
Châteauroux, 189.
Château-Thierry, 236 (1).
Chatou, 232.
Chaumont (Oise), 106.
Chaville, 224, 232.
Chazelles (Loire), 149 (1), 345.
Choisy-sur-Seine, 232, 284.
Choisy-sur-Étiole, 236 (3).
Clamart, 224.
Clamecy, 175.
Clansayes (Drôme), 353.
Clermont-en-Bassigny, 236 (1).
Clermont-Ferrand, 137, 149 (3), 337 (K), 352 (L), 362, 371, 372.
Clermont-sur-Oise, 236 (5), 287.
Clichy, 232.
Cœuvres (Aisne), 102.
Colmar, 236 (1).
Commercy, 236 (1).
Compiègne, 157, 287.
Concors (Bouches-du-Rhône), 347.
Condrieu (Rhône), 141, 343.
Conflans, 261.
Copenhagen, 324.
Corbeil, 189, 236 (3).
Corbigny (Nièvre), 152.
Courtrai, 322.

Craponne (Haute-Loire), 134, 136 (2), 141, 149 (1), 339.
Crécy-en-Brie, 224.
Crémieu (Isère), 32, 128, 185, 189.
Créteil, 112.
Croix-Rousse (la), 28, 138, 327 (A), 333 (D), 334, 337 (K).
Dammartin-en-Goële, 226, 236 (3), 360 (B).
Darnétal (Seine-Inférieure), 220, 315 (1).
Dieppe, xi, xxi, 95, 101, 103, 105, 110, 126, 132, 150, 155, 158, 161, 168 (1), 173, 207, 218, 219, 220, 233, 234, 252, 253, 254, 255, 256, 257 (3), 260, 264, 277, 282, 300, 302 (3), 309, 312, 313, 314, 315 (1), 322, 327 (B), 331 (J), 358 (2Z), 361 (D), 363 (K), 365 (N), 366 (O), 366 (Q), 368 (V), 375 (2M).
Digne, 135 (6).
Dijon, xxi, 140, 167, 168, 236 (4), 267 (1), 358, 366 (R), 367.
Donzère (Vaucluse), 135 (3), 141, 353.
Dormelles (Seine-et-Marne), 111, 372 (2E).
Douai, 256.
Dourdan, 287.
Dreux, 224.
Dunkirk, 314.
Écuelles (Seine-et-Marne), 111.
Elbeuf, 115, 260, 315 (1).
Émile (see Montmorency), 232.
Entraigues (Vaucluse), 144.
Envermeu (Seine-Inférieure), 95, 150.
Ervy (Aube), 108, 220 (3), 248.
Étampes, 177, 288.
Étréchy, 288.
Eu, 168 (1), 327 (B).
Évreux, 260.
Eyragues (Bouches-du-Rhône), 141, 144, 146, 302 (1), 340.
Fayence (Var), 341.
Fécamp, 234, 251 (1), 260, 266, 313, 314, 315 (1).
Feurs, 134, 136 (3), 140, 354, 355.
Flèche (la), 377.
Florac, 350.
Foix, 341.
Fontainebleau, 236 (3).

Fontenay-aux-Roses, 288.
Fontenay-sous-Bois, 112, 221.
Forges-les-Eaux, 312.
Fougères, 115.
Franciade (see Saint-Denis), 232.
Fumay, 219 (3), 257 (4), 260.

Gagny, 236 (7).
Gannat, 102, 174, 250 (3), 335 (G), 366.
Gémenos (Bouches-du-Rhône), 141.
Geneva, 57, 144 (1), 163, 286, 323.
Genoa, 262 (1), 323.
Gentilly, 28.
Gevrier, 376 (2N).
Gien, 168.
Gisors, 224.
Givet, 256.
Goderville (Seine-Inférieure), 103.
Gonesse, 160, 183, 191, 221, 223, 377.
Graveson (Bouches-du-Rhône), 141, 145, 340.
Graville (Seine-Inférieure), 244.
Gray, 236 (1), 285.
Grenade (Haute-Garonne), 255.
Grenelle, 229.
Grenoble, 57, 128, 134, 152, 167, 286.
Guercheville (Seine-et-Marne), 111.
Guillotière (la), 28, 33, 136 (3), 138, 220, 327 (A), 334 (D).
Guionnières, 377.

Hamburg, 324.
Havre (le), 28, 34, 103, 105, 110, 126, 132, 158, 168 (1), 178, 207, 230, 244, 260, 265, 275, 282, 285, 305, 309, 313, 314, 327 (B), 375 (2M).
Heyrieu (Isère), 128, 299.
Honfleur, 115, 260, 312, 313.
Huningue, 236 (1).
Hyères, 141, 341.

Île-Barbe (l'), 333 (D).
Île-sur-Sorgue (l') (Vaucluse), 135 (3), 141.
Ingouville (Seine-Inférieure), 28, 168 (1).
Issoudun, 115, 167.
Issy, 224.
Istres, 141.
Ivry, 28, 284.

Jacqueville (Seine-et-Marne), 111.

Joinville, 288.
Jullianges (Haute-Loire), 339.

Lagarde (Drôme), 353.
Lagny, 287, 288.
Lambesc, 141, 145, 340.
Langeac (Haute-Loire), 134, 141.
Laon, 287.
Lapalisse, 160 (5), 379.
Lautrec, 96 (4).
Lheure (Seine-Inférieure), 168 (1).
Liancourt, 224.
Lille, 14 (1), 39, 47 (7), 110, 129, 179, 245, 275, 330 (H, I).
Lisieux, 115, 260, 282.
Longjumeau, 236 (3).
Longueil (Seine-Inférieure), 365.
Longueville (Seine-Inférieure), 96, 150.
Longwy, 236 (1).
Lons-le-Saunier, 140, 147, 252, 353 (2P), 366 (P).
Lorient, 130, 167.
Louvain, 237 (2).
Lubeck, 256.
Lunel, 167.
Lyon, 27, 28, 30, 31, 32, 33, 34, 36, 66, 70, 73, 94, 109, 113, 116, 125, 127, 128 (1), 129, 130, 132, 133, 134, 135, 136 (3), 137, 138, 139, 140, 144 (1), 144 (4), 145 (2), 146, 147, 148, 149 (1), 152, 153, 163, 168, 174, 179, 200, 201, 237, 260, 285, 286, 313, 325 (A), 328 (D), 329 (F), 332 (B), 333 (C), 334, 337 (K, L), 339 (O), 340 (P), 342 (T, U), 344 (V), 348 (2E), 349 (2F), 353 (2P), 355 (2S), 366, 373 (2H).

Mâcon, 127, 128, 132, 134, 136 (3), 137 (6), 139, 140, 142, 143, 145, 147, 149 (1), 154, 281 (1), 286, 337 (L), 340 (O), 344 (V), 350 (2H), 353 (2N), 371.
Maisons, 112.
Malemort-du-Comtat (Vaucluse), 138, 141, 350 (2G).
Mallemort (Bouches-du-Rhône), 141, 340.
Manchester, 113.
Manosque, 135 (6).
Mantes, 219 (4), 260, 267 (1), 276 (1), 278 (3), 285.

Marck, 260 (4).

Marly, 226, 236 (3).

Marseille, xxi, 32, 33, 41, 102, 128, 132, 134, 139, 140, 141, 142, 143, 146, 147 (2), 148, 169 (3), 180, 201, 209 (1), 223, 245, 258, 262 (1), 271 (2), 282, 285, 286, 313, 325 (A), 331 (J), 332 (C), 340, 343 (U), 346 (Y), 351 (2L), 355 (2R), 364 (L), 377 (2P).

Martigues, 126, 140, 141, 147 (2), 335 (H), 336 (I), 339 (N), 343, 347 (2C).

Maubeuge, 256.

Mazères (Ariège), 341.

Meaux, 230 (4).

Melun, 287.

Méry, 236 (5).

Metz, 236 (1).

Meudon, 221, 222 (3), 288, 376.

Meulan, 221, 222 (4), 260, 309, 377.

Mirecourt, 284 (1).

Moingt (Loire), 141, 354.

Moissac, 127, 189.

Moisy (Loir-et-Cher), 107.

Mondragon (Vaucluse), 135 (3), 141, 353.

Mons, 237.

Montbéliard, 167.

Montbrison, 133, 134, 136 (1), 139, 140, 144, 145, 147, 148, 149 (1, 3), 152 (3), 199 (1), 329 (F), 337 (K), 338, 341 (R), 345 (X), 346 (Y, Z), 352, 354 (Q), 355 (2S), 359 (3C).

Montbrison (Drôme), 353.

Montdidier, 236 (5), 371 (2C).

Montigny-sur-Loing, 111.

Montivilliers, 230, 256.

Montluçon, 102, 175 (4).

Montmorency, 232.

Montpellier, 128, 148.

Montreuil, 232, 291.

Montreuil-sur-Mer, 225.

Montrouge, 28, 42, 65 (2), 288.

Moret, 111.

Morières (Vaucluse), 141, 144, 340.

Mornant (Rhône), 141, 333 (D).

Moulins, 102, 128, 134, 151, 152, 167, 173, 205.

Mouzon, 156–7, 378.

Mulatière (la), 339.

Nantes, 305 (1).

Narbonne, 258 (1).

Négraval (Haute-Loire), 136 (2).

Néronde (Loire), 337.

Nevers, 182.

Neufchâtel, 233.

Nevers, 128, 182.

Neuville (Seine-Inférieure), 365.

Neuville-sur-Saône, 136 (3), 141, 147, 345.

Nîmes, 32, 33, 41, 60, 65 (2), 66, 73, 96 (3), 134, 135 (3), 140, 144, 145, 147, 148, 177, 279 (2), 331 (J), 338, 342, 353, 354 (2R), 364.

Niort, 167, 216 (1), 278 (2), 370 (2B).

Nogent-le-Rotrou, 107, 168.

Nogent-sur-Seine, 236 (1).

Noisy-le-Sec, 112, 221.

Noisy-sur-École (Seine-et-Marne), 111.

Nottingham, 113.

Noves (Bouches-du-Rhône), 145, 146.

Noyers, 227.

Oraison, 135 (6).

Orange, 378 (2Q).

Orgon (Bouches-du-Rhône), 141, 340.

Orléans, 8, 168, 236 (6), 302 (3).

Oullins (Rhône), 141, 147.

Ouzouer-le-Doyen (Loir-et-Cher), 107.

Pact (Isère), 296 (1).

Pamiers, 134, 144 (1), 341.

Pantin, 111, 221, 222, 360 (A), 376 (2N).

Paray-le-Monial, 211.

Paris: Arcis (Section des), 236, 317 (1), 357, 363 (K), 377 (2P); Bondy (Section de), 24, 223, 232; brocanteurs, 22, 74, 230; Champ-de-Mars, 62, 177; chiffonniers, 22; Cité (la), 21 (2); cris, 25; faubourg Saint-Germain, 229; gendarmes, 13 (1); Goutte-d'Or (la), 26 (1); Grève, 21; Gros-Caillou (le), 21, 35, 170; Gravilliers (Section des), 73, 358; Halles (les), 19 (3), 285, 327; Maubert-Mouffetard, 26 (1); Montagne (Section de la), 14, 22, 160, 225, 226, 235, 236, 244 (2), 330 (H), 357, 362, 377 (2P); Montmartre (Section du Faubourg), 358; Montreuil (Section de), 24, 232, 267; murder, 159, 160, 208, 357 (2X); Muséum (Section

Paris (*cont.*):
du), 224, 230, 236, 357, 362; *Nuits*
(*les*), 16 (1), 19 (2), 20 (1), 22 (1),
225 (2), 235 (1), 237 (2), 238 (3),
295 (1), 325 (A); Palais-Royal (le),
21, 25, 43, 235, 326; Panthéon (Section du), 122 (1), 362 (1); Pont-
Neuf (le), 21; Popincourt (Section
de), 159, 160, 357 (2X); port de la
Grenouillère, 314; *portiers*, 231;
prisons, 9, 10, 61; prostitution, 22,
208, 234–9; *quais*, 23 (1); Sans-
culottes (Section des), 311; Seine,
16, 25, 229; suicide, 158, 208, 357,
Saint-Marceau, 18, 19 (1), 21, 42;
Temple (Section du), 24; Thermi-
dor (le 9), 59; Vainqueurs de la
Bastille, 58.
Parthenay, 107, 116.
Passy, 232, 284, 288.
Pélissane (Bouches-du-Rhône), 141,
143, 340.
Péronne, 371.
Poissy, 285, 306.
Pithiviers, 168.
Pontoise, 167, 168, 287, 305 (3).
Pont-à-Mousson, 236 (1).
Pont-de-Vaux, 137 (6), 373 (2H).
Pont-l'Évêque, 115, 260.
Pont-Saint-Esprit, 135 (3), 140, 143,
146, 148, 323.
Pont-Saint-Maxence, 261.
Porrières, 141.
Pradelles (Haute-Loire), 134, 340.
Pralong (Loire), 141.
Privas, 140.
Provins, 287.
Puy (le), 134, 141, 149, 167, 344.

Quillebeuf, 312.
Quimper, 370.

Remiremont, 236 (1), 284 (1).
Rennes, 107, 115, 236 (6), 304 (1).
Retournac (Haute-Loire), 136 (2), 141,
339, 341.
Rians (Var), 141.
Roanne, 63, 338.
Rochegude (Vaucluse), 351.
Rocroi, 251 (1), 260.
Roubaix, 322–3.
Rouen, 28, 34, 103, 105, 108, 110, 158,
160, 165, 168, 207, 220, 236 (7), 240

(1), 260, 265, 275, 282, 283, 284,
285, 309, 313, 314, 327 (B), 369 (Y),
373 (2H), 376.
Roye, 168.
Rumigny, 236 (1).

Sainte-Adresse (Seine-Inférieure), 168
(1).
Saint-Ambroix (Gard), 135.
Saint-Bonnet-le-Château, 189.
Sainte-Cécile (Manche), 236 (7).
Saint-Chamas (Port-Chamas), 141,
146, 332 (A, C), 335 (G), 343, 347
(2C).
Saint-Cloud, 224, 232, 288.
Saint-Cyprien-sur-Anse (Loire), 337.
Saint-Denis (Franciade), 24, 112, 158,
160, 221, 232, 236 (3), 267, 288.
Saint-Étienne, 134, 136 (1), 344.
Saint-Florentin, 151.
Saint-Geniez (Aveyron), 376.
Saint-Genis-Laval, 136 (3), 141, 147,
332, 343, 345.
Saint-Germain-en-Joux (Ain), 368.
Saint-Germain-en-Laye, 221, 222 (4),
226, 282, 309.
Saint-Gervais (Tarn), 136 (4).
Saint-Jean-de-Losne, 285.
Saint-Jouin (Seine-Inférieure), 168
(1).
Saint-Julien-sur-Sarthe, 377.
Saint-Just-en-Bas (Loire), 141.
Saint-Laurent-lès-Mâcon (Ain), 340.
Saint-Maurice-en-Gourgeois, 338.
Saint-Maurice-en-Roannais, 363.
Saint-Maximin-la-Sainte-Baume(Var)
141, 341, 352.
Saint-Paul-Trois-Châteaux (Drôme),
145.
Saint-Paulien (Haute-Loire), 328 (D).
Saint-Vaast-d'Équiqueville (Seine-
Inférieure), 368 (V).
Saint-Valéry-en-Caux, 260.
Saint-Valéry-sur-Somme, 315.
Saint-Vérin, 236 (3).
Saint-Zacharie, 340.
Salle (la), 378.
Salon, 126, 140, 143, 144, 147 (2), 331
(A), 333, 335 (H), 343, 347 (2C).
Salonika, 256.
Sanvic (Seine-Inférieure), 168 (1), 244.
Sarrelouis, 236 (1).
Saumane (Vaucluse), 144.

Saverdun (Ariège), 134, 144 (1), 341, 345 (X), 350–1, 356.
Sceaux, 232, 282, 288, 306.
Sedan, 149, 236 (1).
Ségré, 345 (W).
Semalens (Tarn), 136 (4).
Semerville (Loir-et-Cher), 107.
Sénas (Bouches-du-Rhône), 141, 143, 340.
Sens, 154, 157, 167, 168, 236 (4), 356 (2V).
Septèmes (Bouches-du-Rhône), 340.
Serre, 236 (1).
Sèvres, 224, 232.
Sézanne, 230.
Sisteron, 134, 135 (6).
Soissons, 236 (5), 287.
Sotteville (Seine-Inférieure), 28.
Sourdun (Seine-et-Marne), 236 (5).
Strasbourg, 236 (1), 274 (2), 370 (2A).
Sucy-en-Brie, 224.
Suresnes, 153, 288.

Talhac (Haute-Loire), 356.
Tarare (Loire), 136 (3).
Tarascon, 140, 143, 144, 145, 333, 335 (H).
Tarascon (Ariège), 134, 341.
Tavel, 31, 47 (7), 354 (2R).
Teillet (Tarn), 136 (4).
Thieux (Seine-et-Marne), 360 (B).
Thizy (Loire), 136 (3).
Tixe (Haute-Loire), 136 (2).
Tocqueville-en-Caux, 233.
Tonneins, 127, 128, 130, 189.
Tonnerre, 150–2.
Tôtes (Seine-Inférieure), 368.
Totonnes (Somme), 368.
Toulon, 137, 143, 284 (1), 348 (2E).
Toulouse, 35, 36, 103, 127, 128, 167.
Tournai, 38, 323.
Tournan, 224.
Tourves, 141.
Trest (Bouches-du-Rhône), 352.

Troyes, 128, 260.

Ury (Seine-et-Marne), 111.

Vaise, 138, 282, 327 (A), 333 (D), 334 (D).
Valdajol (Vosges), 376.
Valence, 286, 371.
Valenciennes, 260.
Vaucelles, 112–14.
Vaucouleurs, 236 (1).
Vaucresson, 236 (3).
Vaudoy-en-Brie, 111.
Vaugirard, 224, 229, 288.
Vaugneray (Rhône), 136 (3), 141.
Velleron (Vaucluse), 351 (2K).
Verdun, 236 (1).
Vergues, 136 (2).
Vermenton, 229.
Vencestainville (Seine-Inférieure), 327 (B).
Vernon, 260.
Versailles, 8, 24, 221, 226, 232, 235, 236, 243, 282, 288, 302 (3), 309, 358.
Vesoul, 236 (1).
Vienne, 128, 137 (4), 201, 286, 353 (P).
Villeblevin, 107, 299, 304.
Villefranche-sur-Saône, 67, 68 (1), 286, 343.
Villeneuve-la-Guyard, 101.
Villette (la), 112.
Vincennes, 221, 232, 242, 267, 269, 288.
Viteaux, 236 (4).
Vire, 113.
Voutenay, 229.

Wasquehal, 322.
Wismar, 256.

Ygrande (Allier), 102.
Yssangeaux, 134, 136 (2), 141, 149 (1), 339, 340.

PRINTED IN GREAT BRITAIN
AT THE UNIVERSITY PRESS, OXFORD
BY VIVIAN RIDLER
PRINTER TO THE UNIVERSITY